SYMBOLIC ANTHROPOLOGY
A Reader in the Study of Symbols and Meanings

SYMBOLIC ANTHROPOLOGY

A Reader in the Study of Symbols and Meanings

Janet L. Dolgin, David S. Kemnitzer,
and David M. Schneider
EDITORS

New York ▪ Columbia University Press ▪ 1977

Library of Congress Cataloging in Publication Data
Main entry under title:

Symbolic anthropology.

Bibliography: p.
1. Ethnology—Addresses, essays, lectures.
2. Symbolism—Addresses, essays, lectures. I. Dolgin,
Janet L., 1947–   II. Kemnitzer, David S.,
1950–   III. Schneider, David Murray, 1918–
GN452.5.S95   301.2'1   77-3176
ISBN 0-231-04032-6
ISBN 0-231-04033-4 pbk.

New York   **Columbia University Press**   Guildford, Surrey
Copyright © 1977 Columbia University Press
All rights reserved
Printed in the United States of America

Contents

v

SYMBOLIC ANTHROPOLOGY
A Reader in the Study of Symbols and Meanings

ONE

Introduction

"As People Express Their Lives, So They Are . . ."

THE ANTHROPOLOGICAL STUDY OF culture, of systems of symbols and meanings, is the science of the basic terms with which we view ourselves as people and as members of society, and of how these basic terms are used by people to build for themselves a mode of life. Anthropology poses, and attempts to answer, questions like: "What is a human family?" or "Are we violent?" or "What is human nature?" And by so doing, anthropology implies the existence of ways of acting and being in the world which are alternatives to those habits and institutions which we have historically taken to be the most "natural": our own.

People everywhere act on the basis of knowledge and belief—about the world, about themselves, about action itself. Beliefs form, among every people, a *system:* this system can be seen as a group of *sets of propositions* about the world, which, on further examination, reveal themselves to be *ordered* in their relationships to one another. There are, for example, propositions of a very specific nature, about one or another aspect of the world, or of action, or of people; these form sets which are termed "domains." There are also, in every system of belief, propositions about the *distinctions between* domains, how the boundaries between them are drawn, and how the domains stand in relation to one another. This second sort of propositions constitutes what is called a "metalanguage," and it obtains in every belief system: it is a language about language.

Some beliefs are *shared* by all of the members of a group; others are specific to one or another subgroup or category of persons within a larger group; and others still are held by individuals only. Each of these constitutes systems at different levels: the system of beliefs shared (more or less) by all the members of a group is called a "culture" or "ideology"; an individual's system of beliefs—the totality of what a person shares with others and what is unique to that person—is an aspect of personality; the beliefs of a subgroup are often called a "subculture."

To say that culture is a system of beliefs may be a bit misleading, if only by implication. So too, the description of belief systems as sets of propositions and propositions about propositions may mislead. Because we know that *culture is not available to us in propositional form,* any more than personality

3

is, we cannot express our own culture, our own mode of life, our own beliefs, in such a way without stripping them of much of their richness, their ambiguity, their living power to direct our lives and give them meaning; and we cannot understand the fullness of the culture of another people by reducing their beliefs to a syllogism.

Of course, every culture—our own included—has a way to express itself in a simplified, propositional format, which is used principally to *explain* the culture, mainly to children, but also to strangers (including anthropologists). And, indeed, anthropological data gathering *is* a lot like the data gathering of a child. Both try to build a cognizable pattern of action out of the information they gather. Both use their own observations and their relationships with others to supplement the didactic culture they are consciously taught. The difference is that the engine of the child's effort is largely unself-conscious and natural, shaped by the developmental process and by the child's drives and needs as a whole person, while that of the anthropologist is a feature of the anthropologist's own culture: the need to understand belief and meaning, and the theory which guides that effort. Thus, while children *concretize* what they learn as their own orientations to action in the world, anthropologists *abstract* a general pattern from what they learn; they abstract a system which more or less comprehends the lives of foreign others, and thereby provides more grist for the comparative mill.

In this introduction we are concerned to situate "symbolic anthropology" within the broader discipline of social and cultural anthropology, to delineate differences in perspective toward the study of symbols and cultural systems, and to suggest implications in and for anthropology of a theory of *praxis*. Each of the articles included in this volume is concerned with meaning, with the elements (objects, persons, relations, acts) through which people understand, communicate about, and act within their worlds and with the constitution and interrelation of these elements. The authors, all contending with a set of related questions as to the modes through which people make sense in and of their worlds, represent methodological diversity in their approaches to these issues. By saying this, we do not, however, intend to imply "mere" technical differences. Rather, by methodology we mean something closer, as Theodor Adorno put it, to the "European sense of epistemology" than to the "American sense, in which methodology virtually signifies practical techniques for research" (in Fleming and Bailyn 1969:343).

Although we have tried to provide a sense of the historical roots and contemporary manifestations of symbolic studies in anthropology, we have not been able to be exhaustive in either endeavor. We have, neccessarily, excluded some materials and placed particular stress on others in order to articulate a point of view; in doing the same job, other anthropologists might well have made different decisions in this regard.

Anthropologists concerned with symbols and symbolic form begin with the premise that social action tends to be orderly, to be, in some degree, predictable or understandable by both participants and observers. Social life—made up of people, of gods and ghosts and ghouls, of beliefs about the possible and about the actual and about that which is right and that which is wrong as well as actions, things, relationships, and institutions—is constituted logically, attaining a coherence for those who live it out in its particularity. One person may, for instance, argue that ghosts exist, as another may argue that they do not, but among those who do believe in ghosts, they are *treated as* real. Our concern is not with whether or not the views a people hold are accurate in any "scientific" sense of the term—whether they hold up against the scrutiny of the rather particular domain of Western belief and knowledge called Science; in social action, that which is thought to be real is treated as real; and that treatment, by self and others, both contributes confirmation of "reality" and constitutes a decisive aspect of the meaning of the situation of action.

Anthropologists, in looking at symbols and meanings and their place in social action, have been influenced by investigations in psychology (especially psychoanalysis) and linguistics. (Below, we discuss, from a historical perspective, some less frequently noted, though fundamental, philosophical and intellectual roots of the study of meaning.)

From Freud's work comes an understanding of the importance of the unconscious aspect of beliefs, particularly in giving to knowledge significance and order *for the person*. In *The Interpretation of Dreams,* Freud described the processes through which symbols can take on multiple meanings, the process in which the mind *displaces* the content of experience onto a chain of reasoning, and the complementary process through which this chain of reasoning and memory is *condensed* during the process of displacement. Thus, *displacement* is the process through which one symbol (with negative implications for the person) is replaced with another (less threatening, more acceptable) symbol. The second (or third or fourth and so on), less anxiety-provoking, symbol is used to say, obliquely, what could not be said before, directly; simultaneously, various sets of meanings are displaced onto one symbol which becomes the condensation of many different meanings or chains of meaning. Freud thus explained, by tracing the interactive processes of condensation and displacement, how *conscious* thought becomes a *code for* the (repressed) unconscious. By unraveling this code, the structure of needs and understanding which motivate a person, the implicit pattern of significance which gives meaning to experience and to action for the person, could be discovered. Much of Freud's explication of the details of these processes—particularly his statements about the importance of instinct or of sexuality, or about the psychology of women—is now either dismissed or the subject of great debate; and much of this questioning has been the result of the comparative work of anthropologists such as Bronislaw Malinowski and Margaret Mead. But the basic skeleton of the workings of the mind and the dynamics of the relations between conscious and unconscious, of code and meaning—of the working, in fine, of *symbols* in human consciousness—is Freud's lasting contribution to the understanding of people.

(For the interested student, *The Interpretation of Dreams* is probably the most important of Freud's works;

Freud's *A General Introduction to Psychoanalysis* might be helpful to those who find the longer work more difficult. There are numerous studies of Freud which attempt to apply his insights to social phenomena: of these, the most comprehensive and interesting is Herbert Marcuse's *Eros and Civilization,* but see also Erik Erikson's *Childhood and Society,* Erich Fromm's *Escape from Freedom,* and Géza Róheim's *Psychoanalysis and Anthropology.* In recent years, there have been several attempts to relate Freud's findings to more general theories of symbolic action. Among these, Bateson's and Ruesch's *Communication: The Social Matrix of Psychiatry,* Jacques Lacan's *The Language of the Self,* and Paul Ricoeur's *Freud and Philosophy* are the most significant.)

Although linguistics has been rather faddishly overused and mechanistically applied in recent years (for example, by the ethnosemanticist school or many followers of French structuralism—see below), the study of language has given strong hints that what Freud said of the individual mind is true as well of the beliefs of groups: that groups have *symbolic codes,* or *systems of signs,* which give order to the beliefs held by their members, which shape the development of new knowledge in the group at the same time that they tend to insure that old observations will be repeated; and that these codes, like the conscious codes of individuals, represent a condensation of a complex set of motives, experiences, knowledge, and desire, which they help to shape and express at the same time that they keep so much of it unsaid and below the surface. Linguistics—like psychoanalysis, literary criticism, philosophy, and many other disciplines—has given us techniques with which to unravel these codes and thereby enables us to see belief, the elaboration of belief, and the development of belief, in action.

In the next section, we consider from a historical perspective, the developments and trends in Western society to which anthropology is heir. In doing this, we take a position which contrasts with the dominant view of the origins of anthropology; that view, as expressed, for example, by Marvin Harris in his *The Rise of Anthropological Theory* (1968), is that anthropology is a refinement of the impulse and the need to understand the many "strange" and "foreign" peoples with whom Europeans began to come into contact during and after the period of the Renaissance, that, specifically, anthropology derives from the Enlightenment attempt to find a rational basis for human diversity.

While Harris suggests that the impetus to anthropology lies in the brute facts of human diversity, we argue that the impetus to the anthropological enterprise is motivated by problems in our own society which gave significance to human diversity for our forebears. The conflict between Harris' view and the analysis we are about to offer stands as an example of the basic lesson of this book. In general, we feel that the influence of any kind of "external" facts on human actions is easily overemphasized; in particular, human groups have always and everywhere been aware of human differences and have developed ways to understand them and have acted on them in different ways. But no culture other than our own—for, indeed, anthropology is an inextricable artifact of Western European culture—has produced an inquiry of the scale or the nature of anthropology. And that is because *difference,* at a certain point in European history, took on a great deal of significance.

The Critical Roots of the Problem of Meaning

Up to the latter half of the eighteenth century, Western social thought was concerned with finding a *natural basis* for the social order which existed at any given time. Most of the social thinkers up to this period founded their descriptions of the social order either on assumptions about an immutable and universal human nature (akin to the medieval doctrine of Natural Law) or on some natural or divine, extra-human evolutionary scheme. At the end of the eighteenth century, with the rejuvenation of philosophical idealism and the development of radical philosophy on the Continent, this changed. Society began to be recognized, not as the product of immutable laws, but of the actions of people. This was directly due to a number of trends in European social development, philosophy, and culture, which coalesced to bring the direction of human aspirations and development decisively into doubt for the first time in Europe. A specter was indeed haunting Europe: the dissolution of European society as such. Anthropology, like a number of other related disciplines, grew out of people's attempts to understand and overcome what was perceived as a mortal threat to civilization itself.

This critical foundation of anthropology has not continued unabated, and the work of scholars like Harris, who argue for a natural, law-governed determination of social and cultural forms, repre-

sents an attempt to return to the old naturalistic form of explaining social facts. In Harris' case, it is particularly unfortunate because it is coupled with a truly principled social criticism; unfortunately, Harris' theory cannot integrate human freedom and human potential systematically into its discussion of how social forms come to be. His notion of anthropology loses the critical edge which an inquiry into belief, ideology, and freedom could have: but this is to be expected, since he does not recognize the critical role such an inquiry has played in the past; as Santayana has noted, "those who do not know history are condemned to repeat it."

Implicit here is the notion that anthropology itself is a social phenomenon— that the kind of criticism which it represents is a social fact which has had some effect on other social facts, as well as having been affected by them. We are here applying an analysis much like those that will be applied in these readings to kinship, religion, or other social forms, only here we are applying it to anthropology itself. One of the lessons to be drawn from this sort of analysis is that the boundaries which we draw around phenomena (like "the kinship system" or "religion"—see the essay by Schneider in this volume) are artificially limited and limiting, reflecting as much the analyst's theory as the state of affairs under analysis. Any particular social form is in fact a *conjuncture* of trends, forces, and structures which are each in turn aspects of a total social-cultural system, or totality; and an analysis of such a conjuncture is complex— it involves following a multiplicity of relations between various social forces and structures, incorporating a rigorous decomposition of *immediate* relations and correspondences as the analysis moves *away from* the event, as it were, through the manifold *mediations*, the different aspects or moments of the social-cultural totality, toward those characteristics which have *produced* the particular event or form. Elsewhere in this volume, this sort of method will be applied to an understanding of the role played by symbolic systems in a wide range of human activities. Here, we are using it to look at some of the influences which brought *meaning* to the forefront of intellectual concerns, which shaped the ways in which it is understood, and which tie the understanding of meaning ineluctably to the practice of social criticism.

Classical Greek philosophy defined the problem of meaning or belief in terms of *knowledge:* one either knew the Truth, the proper ways to do things and the proper goals of action, or one didn't. The problem of *motives* was conceived of as the study of the passions, which were thought to be the "baser" elements of the spirit, and this problem was considered to be separate from the more authentic and important problem of what the Truth *was:* one studied motives, passions, only to discover why people didn't know (or couldn't be convinced of) the Truth (see Gouldner 1965). Medieval social thought essentially followed the Greek example (a few writers, like William of Ockham, did not; but their influence, compared to that of St. Augustine, Aquinas, or St. Jerome, who did, was minimal). So, too, in this respect, did the philosophers of liberalism—the Utilitarians of Britain, and the Rationalists of the Continent.

What these philosophies have in common is the notion that, in some essential way, the Truth, or the Good, which is supposed to be the foundation of human cooperation and society, is a *discoverable* thing, it *exists* and can be *found*. This view stands in dramatic contrast to the contemporary truism that there exist a multiplicity of "truths" and "goods"; and that these are *made by* various peoples. Of course, the older views (which still have their adherents), did not hold that Truth, or the Good, was self-evident; on the contrary, those views required a community of inquiry, of the "best" men who, either because they were knowing in the ways of the world, or because they had been able to free themselves from the petty, transient interests which were the objects of the passions, were able in their virtue to develop their reason, if Truth and the Good were to be discovered and implemented. The philosophy is elitist to the core, and serves throughout history as a justification of one or another form of domination: with the dominant group or the would-be dominant group, of course, redefining the "best" men to include itself; when the liberal philosophers of the seventeenth and eighteenth centuries attacked the feudal equation of aristocratic privilege with honor, reason, and virtue, they were attempting to redefine "the best." And, in so doing, they redefined the Truth and the Good as well. But the liberal thinkers, from Descartes on the Continent and Hobbes in England to John Stuart Mill and Kant, retained a model of society founded on neoclassical conceptions of natural law and a metaphysical development of the social order toward an externally derived and predefined goal. Meaning became, in the liberal version, simply a question of the "scientific" discovery of that goal and the application of discipline to accelerate its (inevitable) development.

In the late eighteenth and early nineteenth centuries, however, the situation for philosophy and social thought changed, more or less as a direct result of crises which began to appear in liberal society itself. These crises took two general forms: a general social collapse and decades of turmoil on the Continent and a growing demand for social power on the part of the lower classes in Britain. Both of these crises—shaped as they were by the total social-cultural configurations in which they occurred—produced an awareness of the possibility of multiple social truths and, much more importantly, of the *opacity* of the social order: things were not as they seemed, and hadn't been for some time. But this awareness was far from unequivocal, and it certainly did not produce a single strategy, either for the understanding of the problems which confronted liberal society or for their remedy.

In Britain, social liberalism had combined with a Protestantism heavily influenced by the Puritan movement and with a highly developed, competitive industrial capitalism to produce a peculiar definition of the Good. Hobbes's horrific "state of Nature"—the "war of all against all" which he had held up to his contemporaries as the ultimate threat to mankind—had been stood on its head: Good was now to be found in the competitive marketplace, where individual striving for maximum personal gain and private accumulation of wealth would, through Adam Smith's "invisible hand of Commerce," bring the maximum good—defined in terms of material wealth and comfort—to the maximum number of people. What this view amounted to, however, was a charter for greed: a doctrine which granted as an inalienable right and as the highest achievement, unlimited private accumulation of wealth and power. But in such a system, of course, not everyone can accumulate infinitely: there must be some people without. And the nineteenth century saw the *rise* of those without: in the spread of trades' unions, the demands for reforms, the movement for an eight-hour working day, and the Chartists' demands for universal suffrage, especially. As these forces, and others, grew, and their (partial) victory became imminent, liberal thinkers turned to the doctrine—implicit in Utopian Puritanism and explicit in many of the philosophies of the Enlightenment—that the essence of humanity was not to become the maximal consumer of "utilities" but to use one's powers, talents, abilities, and energies to the maximum possible (see MacPherson 1962, 1973: Ch. 1). These ideas gave rise to both the *laissez-faire* social evolutionism of British conservatives during this period (for example, Sir Henry Maine and Lubbock)—since, if the social order allowed people to rise to the level of their own powers, then the distribution of wealth and power reflected the distribution of individual capabilities—and to welfare-state liberalism. In part, this confusion was a product of the continued silence of liberal thinkers as to what the individual powers might be (which would have raised the question of meaning significantly); in part, it was an aspect of the *practical* coexistence of the *laissez-faire* economy and welfare-state liberalism in Britain until the 1930's, a coexistence made possible by the steady expansion of the British colonial economy and a rare distaste on the part of the public for social disorder.

Curiously enough, but perhaps predictably, British social thought, until the postwar years, was dominated either by a conservatism which drew heavily on social evolutionism or a liberalism intimately tied to a sociological functionalism which simply *assumed* that consensus was at the root of social life. Not until the British social fabric itself began to weaken, during and after the 1930s, did the question of the nature and source of this consensus, how it was maintained and how it was developed—that is, the questions of meaning—begin to surface in the Anglo-American tradition (see Anderson 1968). And it began to surface significantly in American thought only in the post-World War II period (under the influence of Europeans fleeing the Nazi terror) and, especially after the early 1960s, when the American social order, too, began to exhaust itself. The only major figure in British intellectual life who brought these problems to the center of philosophy and of social thought was Ludwig Wittgenstein, an Austrian immigrant, whose concerns were shaped by Continental problems and traditions (see Toulmin and Janik 1973) and who, at any rate, did not begin to have real influence in Britain (save through logical atomist philosophers of science) until after World War II. The Pragmatist tradition in the United States—Charles Sanders Peirce, William James, John Dewey, and Josiah Royce—was something of an exception, but the Continental influences on all of these men were considerable; and the pragmatist project—closely related to problems of the development of technological science—

differs radically from the critical tradition, for all that their results often converge (see Bernstein 1972).

The concern with the nature, source, and role of meaning in human action— and especially such a concern which is not shaped by unacceptable Utilitarian or naïve empiricist assumptions—is largely a Continental contribution to social thought, and a contribution of the nineteenth century. On the Continent, the resistance of the *ancien régime* to political democracy was far stronger and more successful, the development of the various national economies toward capitalism more erratic; cultural differences, religious conservatism, and nationalist conflicts combined with these to make the social order in almost every European country increasingly unstable up to (and in many instances, for example, Germany, after) the First World War: they also rendered those conflicts which did arise increasingly complex and multi-dimensional, bloody, and unsettling. These factors—combined with the strong identification of philosophical and social speculation, not with the official Church as was the case in Britain, but with religious freethinking and the lack of a positivist tradition bred by capitalist progress—lent a decidedly skeptical, if not a downright pessimistic, air to social inquiry. This skepticism found the assumptions of Utilitarianism (that, especially, the foundation of the social order is rational, that the social good is self-evident, and that the extant system is ameliorable) and the simple-minded empiricism on which Utilitarianism is based untenable.

One of the key figures in both major Continental traditions—the French and the German—is the philosopher Immanuel Kant. Kant was the first philosopher in the European tradition who saw the various problems of philosophy—the nature and direction of the social order, the root and the possibilities of knowledge, and the nature of people—as being species of a single problem: the nature of symbolic form; and who realized the *irrational basis* of reason, whether in social or scientific thought.

Kant approached these problems in a manner which was, in many ways, defined by the Rationalists who, since Descartes, had insisted upon the autonomy of Reason in human affairs, on its rightful hegemony over the social life, and its exclusive capacity to recognize and implement the Good. The Rationalists, however, their arguments shaped by their polemic against feudal elitism, had left Reason completely *alone* and located it in the isolated, atomic individual. Kant was thus faced with a social universe which was not, in fact, a unity, a knowledge without continuity or necessity: an amorphous collection of individual atoms with no relations to one another. Kant saw this vision as a threat to public order and to the advancement of knowledge; more importantly, though, he saw it as a threat to human liberty and freedom: the absolutist state was too near to Kant for him to see the possibility of a social order based on reason, if that reason were weakened and scattered by the assumptions of atomism (see Goldmann 1971).

The extreme—almost nihilistic—individualism of the Rationalists was based on a theory of the workings of the human mind and on the presumption that the order of natural phenomena or the social world was external to the mind (that is, imposed on the world by God). Kant undertook to criticize this theory, which is a modernistic version of the Platonic doctrine of forms, and to go beyond it. He did so by seizing upon the natural science of his time—especially physics, chemistry, mathematics, and Copernican astronomy—as the archetype of mental activity and as a moral as well as an intellectual model of correct thinking. He criticized the English philosopher David Hume, who had attacked the notion of physical law by claiming that every event was completely unique, with no relations of cause between them; according to Hume, all that reason could construct out of observation and experience was a determination that events would be repeated with a certain regularity; any other conclusion was the result of "mental habits" which it was the business of rigorous thought to combat—as it was the business of rigorous thought to combat the superstition on which the society of his day was based. Kant countered by arguing that these "habits" were the basis of thought itself and, therefore, the key to its possibilities.

Out of Kant's analysis of scientific thought in the *Critique of Pure Reason* came a general theory of symbolic forms and their relation to thought which has been extraordinarily influential, especially in the social sciences and psychology. The great classical sociologists—Weber, Durkheim, Mauss, and their various followers—were self-consciously working on problems defined by Kant; so, too, were such major figures in nineteenth century psychology as Wundt, the founder of Gestalt psychology, and Freud. The major philosophers of language—de Saussure, Wittgenstein, and Peirce—were also concerned with problems defined, to a large extent, by Kant. Out of such a wide range of those he influenced, it is difficult to isolate just what it is they have in common. A few crucial features, though, can be isolated.

Kant argued that there were basic structures of thinking which were independent entirely of the content of thought. Thus, for example, the fact that human thought entails seeing objects as occupying time and space is independent of *what* objects are seen; similarly, according to Kant, the notion of "cause" neccessarily means that, if A causes B, then A occurs before B in time (we now know that there are systems of thought for which this is not the case, however: the notions of cause implicit in sympathetic magic, for example, or classical Chinese or Greek thought, and Hegelian dialectics—and note, also, some notions in modern theoretical biology, such as Waddington's notion of the chreod, or evolutionary "pathway" are causal without specifying temporal relations between cause and effect). All of Kant's followers, and those influenced, for example, in the questions they ask, concern themselves with the role that *form* plays in the processes of thought.

The works of both Weber and Freud, concerned with the operations of form, can be considered as representing a dynamic formalism (see below for a discussion of structuralism, which replicates Kant's strategy of investigation at a somewhat different level, and reproduces the radical distinction he drew between form and content). Weber, for example, isolated "ideal types" of mental activities, and showed how approximations of these types interacted in the development of various forms of political authority or, more generally, social action: a concrete phenomenon was not an *instance* of a given structure, but a product of the interaction of several.

Freud was concerned to show how certain basic structures and tendencies of the mind, which he conceptualized as instincts, interacted with aspects of the person's situation—especially in infancy—to bring about certain states of mind. For Weber and for Freud both, form is more dynamic than it is for the structuralists; but despite the fact that for Weber and Freud, form is dynamically integrated into the development of phenomena, as opposed to being merely *present in* them, form remains radically distinct from content.

The model of these form/content relations advanced by Durkheim has been the most influential in anthropology and other symbolic studies. Durkheim saw various social-cultural forms—religion, classificatory systems, sets of motives— as "collective representations" of the structure of society (or the structure of the "social mind"), in the same sense that Kant saw particular ideas about the world, such as scientific theories, as representations of mental faculties or innate tendencies of mind. For Kant, the senses and the data provided by them to the the intellect were a kind of *energy* which was shaped by the forms implicit in the mind and in thinking, and which in turn animated the forms and gave them direction. Society is likewise, for Durkheim, a *form:* a "system of constraints" which gives shape to the innate drives of people, which in their turn animate the social form and give it energy.*

This particular mode of the separation of form and content renders each a separate, independent reality, neither of

---

*Kant's argument is explicitly formulated in the section entitled "Refutation of Idealism" in the *Critique of Pure Reason;* Durkheim's *homo duplex* model is clearest in his arguments on "efflorescence" in *The Elementary Forms of the Religious Life.*

which can be explained or illuminated with reference to the other. This is shown clearly in what is perhaps Durkheim's most famous argument: his refutation of the Utilitarian doctrine of the social contract in his first book, *The Division of Labor in Society*. What Durkheim did here was to show that when two individuals make an agreement or a contract—whether the contract is a covenant to obey the rules of society (*qua* Hobbes or Rousseau) or a commercial contract—there are certain social forms implied in their agreement, which are *neccessary* to it: notions of what the agreement is, of what compliance or failure to comply entails, of what would constitute enforcement of the agreement, definitions of all matters touched upon by the agreement, etc. In other words, the social contract presupposes the existence of an *a priori* constitution of the nature of contracts. Now, Durkheim argued that this constitution was to be treated as if it were *sui generis:* which meant that the only significant characteristic of it was that it *existed* and that how or why it came to exist was not the proper object of study.

The *function* of this *a priori* form was the object of analysis. And in every case, for Durkheim, the function of the social form was to mold individual acts in the collective image, to render actions undertaken for reasons that were *not* part of the social reality, part of that social reality, compatible with other acts, interpretable by other actors, etc. The motives and drives which led people to do things were irrelevant to the study of the social forms themselves: thus, for example, Durkheim argued in his classic study of *Suicide* that the various reasons which people gave for killing themselves—financial ruin, disap-

pointment in love, loneliness, devotion to honor or an ideal—were irrelevant to the *social facts* of suicide, which were fluctuations in the suicide rate across space and time. These were to be explained, according to Durkheim, by reference to certain characteristics of social relations which essentially boil down to variations in the extent or the way in which a person is a part of social groups larger than himself or his immediate family. Different kinds of institutions—especially the Catholic as against the Protestant churches (since Durkheim seems to have operated under the assumption that the mode of transmission of the *ban* on suicide is the only, or the most, effective influencer of suicide rates)—were claimed to fulfill the same *function,* of creating and strengthening bonds between people, but to do so differently, in varying forms and to a greater or lesser degree.

For Durkheim and his contemporary followers, history is to be treated as an *accident,* or perhaps more properly a series of accidents: the nature of social forms is to be explained, not with reference to the events out of which the forms are sedimented, but with reference to an abstract structure which, it is argued, gives relevance and order to the events themselves and which, therefore, determines the course of history. For Durkheim, this structure was to be understood in terms of the way in which it fulfilled one basic function: the creation of patterns of solidarity between people and groups. The importance of this problem for Durkheim was a direct function of the various conflicts— between ethnic-religious groups, accentuated by the Dreyfus affair and the wave of anti-Semitism associated with it in France; between classes, accentuated by the Paris Commune and the growth of various left-wing movements—which seemed, to him, to be on the verge of fatally weakening French society at the time (see Lukes 1972). Durkheim turned to the study of societies other than his own France as a result of the investigations which led to the writing of *The Division of Labor in Society*. There he had found two ways in which people and groups are bound together: one, which he called "organic solidarity," was typified by larger, complex, industrial societies, in which groups were bound together by their differentiation and the mutual interdependence which this created. The second form, which Durkheim called "mechanical solidarity," was typified by societies without a sophisticated or extensive division of labor, composed of a series of like groups, bound together by their adherence to a system of beliefs, or their attachment to a single symbol (or set of symbols), such as their land. Durkheim argued, in *The Division of Labor* and later in his lectures on Socialism, that a society characterized by "organic solidarity" would be forever threatened by sectional and interest-group conflicts unless it were also bound together by a "mechanical" allegiance to beliefs or symbols. The remainder of his life's work was devoted to understanding the workings of these systems of belief.

Durkheim's work can be taken, in that sense, to be an inquiry into the roots and the basis of the *consensus* which, in his opinion, held society together. The critical edge of Durkheim's inquiry has been lost over the fifty years since his death, however: sociologists and anthropologists now *assume* the existence of a consensus which, for Durkheim, was something yet to be achieved by modern societies.

Anthropologists—who, as they have continued Durkheim's work, have found the basis of consensus in primitive societies, if there is such a thing, to lie at an increasingly abstract (or symbolic) level —have raised Durkheim's initial contrast to the level of an absolute dichotomy. Curiously enough, however, the followers of Durkheim—especially Lévi-Strauss, whose work can be characterized as an admixture of Durkheimian sociology and a model of thought and meaning derived from structural linguistics (see below)—have also shown that the so-called segmentary societies, which Durkheim claimed were held together by the "mechanical solidarity" of common beliefs, are also held together by the "organic solidarity" of internal differentiation and exchange; but created, in the instance of many primitive societies, not by the supposedly "real" (that is, privileged) relations of the division of labor, but by the symbolic distinctions which are attributed to groups, for example, in "totemic" systems of classification. But this line of inquiry has been neglected by anthropology (although see Schwimmer 1973, for a beginning approach): in part, because even the structuralism of Lévi-Strauss, which gives such importance to symbolic activity that it dismisses history and the lives of people altogether, considers the symbolic level to be in some sense a *secondary* reality, which merely reflects and copies some external, determining force (in Lévi-Strauss's case, the static force of biological necessity); in part, also, because the search for consensus which animated Durkheim's critical effort has been translated, over time, into the simple belief in the existence of consensus, a kind of wishful thinking which reflects both the increased passivity of social thought in the face of expanding mechanisms of social control, and the debilitation of reform movements in the face of the juggernaut which is the modern social world.

Weber's notion of the place of meaning in social action is much simpler than Durkheim's. It has also had less currency in anthropological studies until very recent times (when, through Parsons, it has become more influential); this is curious because Weber's is in many ways a more powerful model—although, because it is less schematic, it is also more difficult to use. In its simplest form, Weber was concerned with meaning in social action because and insofar as human action was *intentional,* that is, motivated by desires which included concepts of *what* was desirable and how it was to be achieved, etc.: in short, by a *plan.* Thus Weber, like Durkheim, held that a kind of consensus—in Weber's case a consensus of *values*—was at the base of the social order.

For Weber, this consensus had *both* a form and a content. Weber's thought was, as we have said, less schematic than Durkheim's, and he did not go out of his way to specify the complex relations between these two (this was also in part due to his less rationalistic approach: for Weber, the meaningful component of social action was more a sentimental than a logical order, as it was for Durkheim). Indeed, it might be taken to be the lesson of Weber's work that these two are not readily distinguishable: meaning—which is seen by Weber as having logical consequences in its form, and emotional/sentimental consequences in its content—is *in* social action, elaborated by it, and drawn out of it, in the complex ebb and flow of concrete events and real social actors. Weber explicitly objected to the

reification of form: to giving explanatory or deterministic power, in social inquiry, to the abstract characteristics which were considered significant by the analyst: he insisted on dealing with meaningful structures which had some psychological reality for social actors, and in so doing he objected to the procedures followed by Durkheim, his French contemporary. But Weber, by defining meaning in the way he did, also dissolves content into a functional consequence of form.

The major present-day objection to Weber's approach is twofold. First, it is argued, Weber's concentration on meaning as a system of values ignores the *cognitive* (or logical) dimensions of meaning, which were so important to Durkheim: the ways in which symbolic systems in essence *create* objects for the senses (and *thus* desire or need for them) by creating distinctions between them, by *classifying* them. A huge literature has been devoted to the analysis of these systems of classification, and to showing how even the most elementary classification systems, such as color-terms, are culturally created (this particular question is discussed by Sahlins in his article in this volume; another tradition is critiqued in Witherspoon's paper; Friedrich's paper in this volume is an example of one approach to cognitive analysis as well). Another objection to Weber's approach is its *individualism.* For Weber, meaning or intention was always a characteristic of action, and action was always undertaken by individuals; what made action "social" was the fact that it was oriented to, or inspired by, the actions of others. Weber's approach has a great deal in common, in this regard, with contemporary phenomenological approaches, typified by the ethnomethodological school of sociology (notably the work of Goffman, Garfinkel, and Sacks—see also the selections by Schutz and Geertz for continuations of Weber's approach which differ somewhat from the ethnomethodological school).

These two objections to Weber's mode of analysis are, in fact, closely linked. A major problem for analysis created by the individualistic tendency of Weber's theory is to describe and understand how it is that individual understandings or meanings become expressible in socially comprehensible codes and languages (this problem is defined in a clear and revealing way in Garfinkel and Sacks 1971), and the effect which such expression has on the content and implications of the original understanding (see the selections by Barnett, Kemnitzer, and Dolgin and Magdoff in this volume for approaches to the latter aspect of this problem, which is stated most clearly in Herbert Marcuse's *One-Dimensional Man,* 1964). With the modern knowledge—which neither Durkheim nor Weber had available to them—of the major role played by symbolic systems in shaping the individual understanding and, indeed, in shaping the very perception or cognition of the subject's world (see the papers by Friedrich, Hallowell, and Lee in this volume), this problem of Weberian theory becomes the problem of the relationship between individual (or group) interpretation of events in the light of a collective or encompassing symbolic code (see Attewell 1974): and the problem now goes to the heart of our understanding of belief and symbols: in a word, culture.

Weber's notion of system is weak in comparison to Durkheim's; but Weber's sense of the complexity of the *workings* of systems is far richer than Durkheim's. Weber's hostility to the analysis of structures—which he saw as reifications of the analyst's categories—is complemented by Durkheim's radical distinction between structures and the people who fill them, use them, or create them, and his assumption that it is the structures which determine the significant characteristics of action. What is needed in the study of meaning is an approach which *balances* these two perspectives.

A theory which would meet this need must have a few characteristics which are revealed by our criticisms of Durkheim and Weber. First, it must, like the ethnomethodological approach, refuse to give absolute primacy in symbolic action to either the formal structures of collective representations or the individual processes of understanding, interpretation, adjustment, and expression. It must, indeed, focus on the social processes in which these two sorts of force interact: the social relations of communication and interpretation, and those properties of the symbolic system itself, and of the social system of which the symbolic system is a part, which give coherence to communication: which either *stabilize* the symbolic order or which make change in it regular. The fact that such change *is* regular is proven by the fact that, even during periods of the most radical symbolic change, we have very little problem understanding each other (see Weinreich, Labov, and Herzog 1968): this fact also means that we cannot see the structural relations of symbols in a static, "elementary" way.

For Kant, and for both Weber and Durkheim, meaning was an alternative to *chaos*. The same is the case for their followers: for the structuralists, meaning is an alternative to *cognitive* disorientation, which it overcomes by defining the world (as a "natural" thing) through a process of discrimination and distinction between the objects in it; for the phenomenologists and the followers of Weber, meaning is an alternative to *existential* disorientation, which it overcomes by articulating a value-structure in which people can find a place for themselves.

The first thing we can note about the studies of symbolic activity which have been done since Durkheim and Weber is that they have shown us—whether or not their authors realized it, and by and large they have not—that this dichotomy is a false one. Symbolic structures—from the "elementary" forms to the more specific and specialized forms of ideology, ethos, and world-view—serve both functions equally. Moreover, cognitive orientation has affective or existential consequences (as is well shown, for example, in Lévi-Strauss's study, "The Effectiveness of Symbols," in *Structural Anthropology,* 1963); and one's sense of one's place in the world, or of one's values, has a profound effect on one's perception of the world as an object (see the selections by Marx, Melville, and Silverman in this volume, and the selection by Lefebvre for an overview).

The debate over these two forms of determinism lies at the root of many of the conflicts and differences in symbolic studies today. Moreover, it is extraordinarily rare to find a study which is not informed by one or the other position. But both of these miss the point altogether; and their co-dominance over the field of symbolic studies is the major obstacle to the development of the field and to the realization of its potential as a tool for the development of social-cultural criticism and our understanding of our own potential for development.

It must be remembered, however, that the basic position—that meaning is an alternative to chaos—is a nineteenth-century creature, an innovation, in effect, of the great crises that swept European society between the French Revolution and the First World War. Then, the alternatives to bourgeois society—and the dual tendencies of the collapse of the social order and the institution of absolutist regimes—were obscured by the nearness of the absolutist states, which were an oppressive memory for all of the social philosophy which was formed by or in response to the liberal tradition; and when these alternatives as well were obscured by the apparent impossibility of realizing any conceivable "utopian" alternatives, social turmoil *was* chaos—or, at the very least, the imminent threat of chaos. For Weber, totalitarianism, and for Durkheim, crippling alienation and social collapse, were animate, powerful possibilities which obscured any other. But one of the lessons of that century of turbulence, as well as of the anthropological encounter with extremely diverse forms of society, is that social order, as such, can survive turmoil; indeed, we have now come to realize that turmoil—more or less extreme, to be sure, but turmoil nonetheless—is the natural state of existence of societies, which we now know not to be a succession of forms, but of arenas in which the *process of formation* of the social order itself is perpetually taking place.

The threats of chaos shaped the social theories which hoped to help stave them off. Weber, in the Platonic tradition, looked with horror at the institutionalization of passion; Durkheim, the self-conscious follower of Kant, saw with equal horror the negative possibilities of the essential freedom of people, the destructive, centrifugal effect of what he felt was the essentially atomistic nature of human existence. Both saw belief and understanding—meaning—as the salvation of society, as the controller or translator of the destructive tendencies. This view neccessitated, curiously enough, that symbolic action be given a *secondary* position in the shaping of social action. Symbols and their meanings, to serve the role which Weber and Durkheim foresaw and earnestly hoped for, had to *refer to* a completely independent reality, *so that they could control it.*

There was, however, an alternative position to the mainstream created by Weber and Durkheim. This was the tradition created by Hegel and Marx. Its acceptance has been hampered by the apparent mysticism of the former and the uncompromising radicalism of the latter. But both Hegel and Marx saw that the alternative to meaning was not chaos: *it did not exist.* Meaning—as a cognitive framework for action and a constitution of the goals and desires of acting people—was an essential element of human existence, an aspect of the externalization of man in action and labor. And, with one of those ironic twists which the imagination can only approximate, Marx, the economic determinist, granted to the meaningful level of human action an independence and a primary determining force which Weber and Durkheim, the anti-materialists, did not. For Marx, as for Hegel, the meaningfulness of social action for actors is part and parcel of their *creation*—in thought *and* action —of a social world, of what Ludwig Wittgenstein called a "mode of life." In Marx's words, "As

people express their life, so they are . . ."

Contemporary Approaches and Problems in the Study of Meaning

Having situated the problematic of cultural anthropology in the history of Western social thought, we can now turn to *how* the anthropology of symbols and meanings carries out its project. We proceed by taking up two interrelated tasks: the delineation and methodological critique of current modes of symbolic analysis, considering phenomenological intuitionism, formal semantics, and other perspectives founded within a linguistic model of culture, including structuralism. Finally, we briefly suggest a direction of anthropological inquiry which consistently, though often implicitly, opposes itself to the sociological functionalism underlying each of the three perspectives just mentioned. Our consideration of the place of meaning in social action begins with a discussion of three inferences which have been drawn from the general statement that *shared,* or *culturally constituted, meaning entails symbols which stand for something in some respect;* as we find each of these inferences to be erroneous, though fundamental to the methodological perspective of one or more schools of contemporary cultural anthropology, the heart of the matter— the postulated relationship between meaning, experience, and reality—can be brought into clearer focus.

Meaning as Personal and as Social Phenomenon

The first inference to be drawn from the observation that social meaning entails symbolic expression informs studies from a phenomenological, intuitionist, or hermeneutical perspective (for example, Geertz 1973; Ricoeur 1967; Schutz 1932/67). This is the notion that meaning *is the act* of pointing or naming. As used, the notion implies the possibility of the independence of the experience of the actor and the real, objective nature of the world, and the possibility, moreover, of independence between the experience of the actor and some other, internal experience of the same actor. The implication, in short, is that meaning and naming on the one hand and experience on the other exist independently but may be related to each other by an actor who *assigns* meaning and *attributes a sign to* experience. At base, this methodological stance presumes experience to be unaffected by past experience; it also presumes that "bias" does not enter into the process of perception and that, therefore, objects are or can be perceived "as they are."

Questions as to the *distortion* of perception are not the only important matters raised by this view, however. At issue is the very nature of perception; and in this we are directly faced with a second inference as to the relation between meaning, experience, and reality which is, in our view, mistaken: the notion that meaning develops through the simple association of experiences with signs. From this view, either an experience is endowed with a sign and thus emerges into meaning, or a set of experiences is associated with each other and made meaningful, through the attribution of a sign.

Yet the phenomenologically-attuned students of meaning, whose own analyses imply the independence of experience and meaning, and the creation of meaning through the attribution of signs to experience, can hardly deny the importance of past experience to perception. The process of perception, it must be emphasized in refuting the idea that meaning and experience are or can be separate, is grounded in past experience, which is part of the constitution of a "set" in terms of which events are actually seen and experienced by real actors in real situations. Vital to this past experience are the learned meanings constituting the lens through which, and the context in terms of which, experience itself, *for the experiencer,* takes place (see the papers by Friedrich, Hallowell, Lee, and Witherspoon in this volume). Not only are people born and reared, thereby incorporating much from the outside world into their perceptual and experiential apparatus, but previous experiences occurred under the guidance of and in interaction with other people. The first people who guide children's interactions, and hence experiences and made of perceptions, are those who care for and socialize them. These people have told the child what to look for, how to look for it, what it is that is seen, how the child feels about it, should feel about it, and should react— what, in short, it *means*. They have said, "Don't cry now," or they have said, "You can cry now," by comforting instead of forbidding. They have said, "Don't touch that," or they have said "Feel it. Feel how nice it is." Of course, they have also told the child the names of things and discussed what these names mean and imply: they have discussed what will happen if, how the child feels when, what one should do because, and what to think when. The agents of socialization define the situation for children, who are not left free to experience each new situation entirely on their own. But even were they left alone, previous experience would color succeeding experiences, and so meanings would be built up. Thus, meaning is the product, not only of the association of "raw" experience with an already-reified "code" of names, but of the integration of successive past and present (and *future:* we experience our expectations, too) experiences into a coherent whole, a life-world, which each individual creates, but *also* internalizes (the creations of others becoming one's own experiences) and projects onto his or her interactions with others.

Meanings built up in such an individual fashion—like those built up in the context of social (familial) relationships—need not neccessarily accord with those of other members of society: thus, every child faces, to some degree, the problem raised by his or her uniqueness: the task of *making oneself intelligible* to others, a task which has as its extreme form, *making oneself respectable* to others.

From the point of view of the actor, this process is a *natural* one, taking place in the context of the meanings and signs of others, which are beyond the actor's control and which pre-existed the person's entrance into the situation. These are part of the wisdom and tradition, part of the culture of that society. Children do not create meanings on their own, nor do they react to the world *de novo;* socialization constitutes, among other things, the learning of the symbols and meanings of society and the rules which allow the generation of new, but intelligible, meanings, and these are incorporated into the perceptual and experiential set of the child. Thus culture is both the collectively shared, repetitious aspect (or moment) of experience and the *coming-to-be* of the shared, repetitious aspect of experience. Events, objects, the experiences of life, are embedded in a set of meanings enmeshed in a system of cultural symbols. "Reality" exists "out there," but not as "pure experience" or "pure event." In this regard, culture is the meaningful aspect of concrete or objective reality, and the *coming-to-be,* the appropriation to consciousness, of objective reality.

Sahlins' paper in this volume makes a similar argument, which is also suggested by an old baseball story. At a convention of umpires, the three most senior umpires stood alone in regal isolation from the crowd. As is their wont, they remained silent, surveying the scene. Since it was a social occassion, seeming to demand some sort of conversation, the most junior of the three ventured a remark. "Baseball," he said, "nuthin' but balls and strikes. I calls 'em as I sees 'em." After a pause, the umpire next in seniority announced, "Baseball. Nuthin' but balls and strikes. *I* calls 'em as they are." Finally, the oldest umpire said, "Baseball. Nuthin' but balls and strikes, and *they ain't nuthin'* til I calls 'em."

The central tasks of cultural anthropology, to provide a general theory of symbolic practice, stand behind the particular questions symbolic anthropologists ask: What are the conditions of existence? How is life defined? What kinds of units are specified and differentiated according to what assumptions or premises about the nature of the universe? How are these formulated, and how are they expressed? To take up Durkheim's word, how are they *represented?* Durkheim's "collective representations" are "collective" because shared by members of society, and "representations" by virtue of a correspondence to the structure of the reality in which human beings act, the situation of action, the state of affairs, the human condition, the way things are.

Orientations and motivations of the actor as a focus of study, however, must be distinguished from the cultural system as the focus of study. Each presents somewhat different problems, although they are ultimately related (as the cultural system is the range of choices within which people create and the instruments whereby people express a continually changing life). If we seek to account for any particular set of symbols or meanings we cannot do so on the basis of the experience of a particular actor, or even of the experience of groups of actors, precisely because the society and its system of meanings exist before the actor is born. This is not to deny the existence of certain common features of the human mind; people seem, for example, to be inherently capable of learning a language, but that does not mean that they invent only one language. It may mean that the range of possible linguistic forms is limited, although we do not know precisely what those limitations might be. Accepting the fact that the structure of the human mind is inherently capable of, and tends to produce, systems of symbols and meanings, does not answer the question: why *these* symbols and symbolic forms, and not others?

If we shift, however, to the orientation of the actor and consider individual motivations, we can see how a person looks to the existing system, as it were, drawing on it and using it: how the system is, or can be, is not, or cannot be, manipulated and fitted into a person's own motivations.

However, while we must insist on the difference between collective represen-

tations and the meaning-sets of individuals—and while we must grant, too, that analysis must proceed, at times, *as if* the line between the two were clear and definite, giving each dimension a certain measure of independence from the other—we must also realize that these two are in fact not "things" at all, any more than symbols are. Collective representations and individuals' meaning-sets are merely *aspects*—differentiated and selected out by analysts, not emerging from social action itself—of a single, complex whole. One aspect or moment may, of course, predominate at a certain time or in a certain way—which it is the task of analysis to discover—but in virtually any conceivable empirical example, counterexamples to any determinism can be found (and when they cannot, the *data* is incomplete). The point here is that symbolic structures and particular utterances stand in a genuinely *dialectical* relationship, in which both elements take on their actual character only as a product of their interrelationship: structure is, to use Barthes's phrase, "the sediment" of series upon series of particular acts, frozen with the analyst's glance or reified by actors attempting to control the future acts of others, and each act is in fact an actualization (and a simultaneous transcendance) of one or more structures. It is in *this* dialectic—mediated at times by necessity, and always by an entire complex of social relations and historical processes—that meaning is *continually* taking shape.

The third inference drawn from the notion that social meaning involves signs standing for something(s) in some way(s) is that "signs" and meanings can be distinguished and sorted, like two decks of cards, into separate piles. Such an inference is drawn with special ease when language is used as a model for cultural analysis and, specifically, the inference which we consider faulty has been accepted by some students who analyze culture from the point of view of formal semantics.

Analyses of language, however, show that although the *conventional* function of language is to provide a reservoir of objects to be used as signs along with a set of rules for their use, even language cannot be sorted so simply into those objects which are signs but not meanings, and those which are meanings but not signs. Language is also the metalanguage for the analysis and communication of meaning. A language-act can be seen—perhaps a bit mechanically, but with some accuracy nonetheless—as the *union* of a plane of expression and a plane of content, brought together by a rule or relationship. But these units, taken together, can themselves become the content or the expressive vehicle of *another* language-act, which is more complex than the simpler unit, since it comments upon it—the expression, and/or the content, and/or the relation between them. *Any* expression can be manipulated in this way, and in a number of ways and toward a number of ends; in our culture, satire and comedy provide clear examples. When a comic, say Lenny Bruce, takes an act or expression out of the context in which it normally occurs or "makes sense," he makes "someone else's" *act* into a *sign,* for example, of the silliness of some social rule. We do something very similar when we use words to define others words, or to build images, or to take social cues: indeed, it is very difficult to isolate a naturally occuring liguistic utterance *without* a metalinguistic aspect—such a purely nominalist utter-ance would, indeed, probably be incomprehensible (and would certainly sound artificial) to an audience. Rather than accomplishing simple reference ("this house", "14 July 1789") through such a pure object-language, we more commonly accomplish this function through the use of metalinguistic cues which progressively *limit* and *focus* the connotation or extension or implication of an utterance.

To hold that meaning and symbol are in themselves objects is to commit the fallacy of misplaced concreteness (a reification); at the systemic level, there is a constant interchangeability between meaning and symbol in terms of context or use. But meaning and symbol are not dependent as things on context: *they are relations,* not objects. Ignoring this point, seeing meaning and symbols as things, has allowed cultural analysts to erect a distinction between symbolic structures and concrete structures, to differentiate religion, ritual, myth, art—held to be "essentially" symbolic forms—from economics, politics, kinship, or everyday life—held to be "essentially" concrete structures, based on the "real" facts of goods, power, human reproduction, or ordinary living. This is a position we reject. "Concrete" structures are as much products of a way of life as are religion or art: no human act is without *style,* without the form which gives it meaning.

In considering what it means to say "'culture' is a system . . ." and noting the implications of the *active* or *creative* character we have just imputed to symbolic action, we begin by looking at the notion, which has been accepted by most students of culture, that symbols have many meanings, that is, that they are polysemic, multivocalic, or multivalent (a general exception to this notion is special, functionally specific languages, for example, mathematical notation). The polysemous character of symbols is significant for understanding the relations of symbolic structure to process: if a symbol has several meanings, then the *relationship between* its various meanings becomes important and often problematic.

The limiting case of polysemic relations is that where the meanings of a symbol are *unrelated*. A frequently embraced position is that polysemic relations tend to entail one primary meaning, with other meanings explained as derivations or extensions of the primary one. This general position may be accepted by theorists working from a variety of methodological perspectives, with the theoretical freight carried in the notion of primacy of meaning varying in its implications for the analyst.

Where a set of meanings is unrelated to what seems to be the same primary meaning, we have a case of homonymy, that is, two apparently identical symbols which are actually quite different because they have different sets of meanings. A simple example can be provided by the words "mail" and "male" in English. The words sound the same, and one can isolate the activities of the postal service from the sexual attributes of persons who are not female only in context (in this case, of course, the determination is simple). Or, to avoid the confusion introduced by two different symbols, we can take a word such as "mother." According to some, "mother" refers to the genetrix, but when used for the earth, a homonym occurs, since the earth cannot be regarded as a genetrix; however, if genetrix is defined broadly enough, "earth" can become

one of the meanings of "mother" by metaphorical extension. One of the connotations of the more general idea of generation is here related to one of the connotations of the generative capacities of the earth. We intend this example to suggest that it is, or can be, an important empirical question to establish whether two symbols are homonyms, as perhaps "male" and "mail," or related to each other in some additional way, which reveals the ideas and beliefs of their users.

In postulating a primary meaning and secondary meanings, the secondary meanings may, as noted, be related to the primary meaning systematically (as through metaphoric extension) or formally (for example, widening or narrowing of the criteria of significance). But more problematic than the specific modes of relationship is the notion of primacy in meaning itself; the problem here is similar to the distinction between denotative and connotative meaning.

The issue of primacy with symbolic systems has been dealt with through the notions of "key," "core," "master," and "central" symbols (either for whole cultures or for major parts of them): along with the concepts of "root metaphor" (Pepper 1942) and "configuration" (Kroeber 1944), these notions, not surprisingly, raise exactly the same problem as that of polysemy. Two basic relationships have been suggested as existing between central symbols and all the other major symbolic and meaningful elements in a culture (see Ortner 1973). Central symbols have been characterized as "elaborating" symbols, with other symbols and meanings seen as derivative, analyzed as "logical" extensions, metaphoric extensions, or even as temporally sequential elaborations of the "core." In contrast, central symbols may be seen as "epitomizing" in the sense that they express or evoke in a single or small set of symbols the array of otherwise apparently disparate symbols and meanings of a culture; the "epitomizing" symbol may state succinctly the common features of the different meanings and the special ways in which they resemble and relate to each other.

These two terms refer to functions, or uses to which any symbol may be put; although it is also often the case that a particular symbol, over time, becomes stripped of its elaborating uses and restricted to its epitomizing function: the American flag is an example. Even though the flag figures, for example, in a variety of ideological and political conflicts, meanings (interpretations) are not attached to or derived from it: rather, various groups try to appropriate the flag to themselves, to render themselves, in a sense, an instance or a token of the single—summarized and summarizing—meaning of the flag.

A cultural formation not entirely unrelated to that of epitomizing symbols entails an array of parallel sets of symbols and meanings, such that each "says the same thing" as the others, though in a somewhat different way and with different implications. A set of apparently different signs and meanings can be seen to have internal relations to one another through the discovery of some common element or elements of sign and/or meaning. Magical incantations, or more pointedly, proverbs, illustrate this sort of construction, as well as the dependence of this sort of form on contextual reference for the determination of options. We now mention (to discuss more fully below) the capacity of such a construction for supporting the repressive function of culture, through a process formally similar to that described by Freud, in which unconscious thoughts come to be expressed as the latent meanings of a conscious code (which masks the "real" meanings and symbols—Freud outlines these relations in a paper entitled "A Note on the Unconscious in Psychoanalysis," 1912, *Collected Papers,* Volume 4); this process is characterized by the analytically separate processes of condensation and displacement and is both dependent upon and a product of the existence of such parallel structures. Kirkpatrick's paper in this volume documents an instance of oscillation between two such structures, and the consequences thereof for domination, in Yap. At the cultural level, the consequence of this sort of oscillation is often opacity. Symbols (for example, proverbs) "a" through "x" appear, each substitutable for the other (though this substitutability is itself masked), with the plethora of substitutable forms working to disguise the *nonappearance* of meaning "y," the repressed ("real") meaning. The papers by Kemnitzer, Lefebvre, and Dolgin and Magdoff in this volume discuss and illustrate this phenomenon in more detail; Barnett's paper can also be read, in this light, as an inquiry into the conditions for such an opaque structure (as contrasted with the more transparent one discussed by Kirkpatrick).

Problems of Structure and Process: Linguistic Models and the Limits of Structuralism

There are two especially important relationships between meanings and/or between signs (meanings and signs being relations, disguised as unitary and therefore inseparable objects, only in use) which have emerged into anthropological analysis from linguistics: *marking,* and *analogy* (the latter comprehending *metaphor* and *metonymy*). The relationship of marking involves the possibility that a given sign may be used in two different ways in varying contexts. In one context, a sign may "mark" a special meaning, excluding others *for that context;* while in another type of situation, the same sign may be *unmarked,* including a number of meanings which are distinguished in the first context. The relation of marking obtains, for example, in the contrast between "man" and "woman" in our own culture. The word "woman" is marked and confined in its meaning to persons of the female sex. "Man," however, is considered unmarked in that it can be used to include people of both sexes (as a synonym for "mankind") or only persons of the male sex, depending on the context in which the term is used.

The concepts of metaphor and metonymy have also come into anthropology from linguistics, as well as from the study of literary texts, and have been of particular importance in the structuralism of Lévi-Strauss. As with "epitomizing" symbols, apparently subtle differences in the stating of the relations between metaphor and metonymy may have extremely divergent implications. Certain of the forms in which these relations have been conceptualized are untenable, albeit commonplace in anthropological work. We shall explain these terms and look at their analytic uses by quoting from Seitel's definitions of metaphor and metonymy and from Maranda's exposition of these concepts. Seitel defines the terms as follows: "Metaphor, in the most general sense, is

the relationship which obtains between entities of separate domains by virtue of the relationship each has with entities in its own domain." And "Metonymy, in the most general sense, is any relationship which obtains between entities by virtue of their mutual inclusion within the same domain" (1972:29 and 32).

Maranda employs a formula for characterizing the relation of analogy in explaining the meaning of metaphor and metonymy. That formula can be noted as "A/B = C/D" or as "A:B::C:D." "Analogy," Maranda writes, "is an operation of the mind. It rests on the recognition of relations between the terms: similarity and contiguity, in other words metaphor and metonymy." (1971:117). Each term, thus, is seen as being in a *metonymic* relation to the term on the *same* side of the equation as itself, and as being in a *metaphoric* relation to the corresponding term on the *opposite* side of the equation. In a similar treatment, Maranda looks at the notions of metaphor and metonymy through the notion of set. If A is the first set and a one of its elements, and B is the second set, with b one of its elements, then "the relations a/A and b/B are metonymic. The analogy $a/A = b/B$ underlies the equations, that is, the metaphors $a = b$ and A = B." (1971: 117). Maranda proceeds to supply the example: "the legs of the table." Here, the set A consists of people or animals and the element a is a leg; the set B consists of tables and the element x in the formula $a/A = x/B$ turns out to be "leg" (of the table). The large sets A and B are related in that they both consist of things which stand. From this perspective, these sets are in a metaphoric relation to each other, while the elements within each set are metonymically related.

While this exposition is didactically useful as a point of departure for the analysis of meaning in social action, it is crucial to note that Maranda's structural exposition is based on an understanding of relations which is essentially static. (And, as a result of this, we may note, it fails even to suggest the crucial question: how does the criterion which *produces* these relations—in this instance, the notion that "things which stand" have a significant characteristic in common—come to be a *signifying* element?)

As normally used in cultural analysis, and as Maranda outlines them, the terms metaphor and metonymy are formulated in such a way as to "operate" entirely without contextual specification. Metaphor, it is said, describes the fact that aspects of apparently different things are (considered to be) similar; Maranda stated that A may represent one set with a an element, and B represent a second set with b an element. Assumed is the absolute, *a priori*, difference between sets A and B; the context which differentiates them (that is, which produces the boundary between them, as both a structural relation and a substantive, content-filled one) is irrelevant to this formulation because it is assumed (1) to be static, and (2) to be the same in all cultures. It is, however, precisely this, the existence of context as a static "ground" rather than a structure in the process of becoming, which we find problematic in the use of the notion of metaphor, especially by structuralism. Similarly, this criticism can apply to uses of the point made above in considering the relationship between meanings of a given symbol, that is, that a sign has many meanings, meaning being the set of elements associated with that sign by the members of a society. To say the meanings of a sign X are (1, 2, 3, . . . n) implies the association of these meanings to be free from constraints of context, that when sign X occurs, all meanings 1,2,3, . . . n are equally applicable and equally implied, even if they are not explicit in the utterance. This is, of course, normally not the case: "cry," for instance, may mean to weep in one context, and to emit a loud noise in another; and note the difficulty many readers have with literature—for example, the later work of James Joyce—which *does* structure meaning in precisely this way.*

The summary statement of polysemy, that X has meanings (1,2,3, . . . n), omits the crucial information as to the context or specific rules of use for meanings. *The most significant aspect of meaning is neglected, if context (as rules of use) is not acknowledged.* Similarly, in the above explication of metaphor, there is no consideration of the possibility that a and b, posed as metaphorically related, may, from a particular perspective, given a particular context, be in the *same* set, and thus the relationship between a and b be metonymic, not metaphoric (Barnett's paper in this volume documents an instance of such alternation); the problem is compounded if it can be shown that a and b are from the same set while A and B, given certain contexts, remain in differ-

*In language meaning may be given by syntactical form irrespective of context as, for example, the formation of the English plural by the suffix /-s/; but for the large majority of linguistic usages as well, meaning is not given by syntactical forms alone, nor even by the "conventional" meaning of words themselves, for the obvious reason that any word has too many meanings, each only *somewhat* different from the other; those which are applicable in any utterance depend on the sociocultural context in which the utterance takes place, and on cues as to the relation between the utterance and its context which are supplied by the speaker *and* the audience.

ent sets. These problems inherent in the use of the concepts metaphor and metonymy are part and parcel of the difficulties about semantic domains which have long plagued the analysis of meaning.

The issue of semantic domains—of who defines and limits the domain and of how these domains are interrelated—may be settled by fiat. The analyst may decide the issue on what are thought to be logical or theoretical grounds. Since, of course, the line of argument goes, any sane person can discern that the domain of religion differs from that of kinship, the term "father" for genitor and the term "father" for priest are obviously metaphorically related. Indeed, there is some truth to this; any reasonable person can see that this is so—from a context and perspective in which genitor and priest are *treated as* metaphors; the natives—Americans and Western Europeans alike—*do* distinguish the institutions of family and kinship from religion, *in certain contexts*. However, and this is the crucial point, it has been argued that from a different perspective, that of the production of elements for each set, that is, in this instance *recruitment,* kinship and religion are *not* differentiated *by the same natives;* thus if the terms metaphor and metonymy are used here, the use of the term "father" for genitor and priest is, if anything, not metaphoric but *metonymic* (see Schneider in this volume).

The conceptual distinction demonstrated in linguistic analyses between metaphoric and metonymic relations does carry significance for the cultural analyst. However, these terms must, we feel, be employed in cultural analysis only *analogically*. Metaphor and metonymy, as descriptive of relations, do make sense but only on the condition that they are used in projecting *away from* relations between objects *toward* relations of *value* (that is, they cannot be used to represent forms of substitution of elements which appear legitimate or entailed in the analyst's view; they must represent substitutions which occur *in use*). The concept of value that we intend here is the sense of "valence"—that is, the static representation of dynamic relations (past or, in the form of latency, future).* Now, if metaphor and metonymy are used to characterize relations between relationships rather than relations between or within domains, the difficulties in analyses reliant on domains, and the conundrums about domain boundaries, intersection, or dependence, are avoided (see below for a further discussion of this point with regard to ideology). The difference here is that between a social science which relies on *a priori* definition of what *is,* reified as the categories of analysis, and a social science potentially able to study forms of action-in-process, such as *how* meanings become reified for and by the actors.

We are now able to return to the issue of primacy of meaning, viewing that issue through the formulations of metaphor and metonymy. To recall an example outlined above, it is only on the premise that the primary meaning of "father" is genitor in English that we can understand "fatherland" to be a metaphor, but not understand "father" as a metaphor for "fatherland." To see "fatherland" alone as metaphor here limits the possibility of analyzing ideo-

*"What", asks Marx, "is the value of a commodity? The objective form of the social labour expended in its production" (*Capital I:* 535). I.e., labour, *as it appears* as an object or *result*.

logical forms, since such an analysis appropriates native categories (and the stress placed on these categories in relation to each other) as the categories of analysis. Such a procedure also cuts analysis off from an important historical dimension—which is perhaps a different way of saying the same thing. To retain the same example, there is good evidence that, in the medieval period in Europe and England, the relations of dominance between the symbols of kinship (for example, "father") and those of political allegiance ("fatherland") were the *reverse* of those which obtain today (see Horkheimer 1972:97 ff.; Laslett 1965:chs. 5 and 6). These facts have yet to be the object of a detailed study, but their analysis may help us to understand the ways in which our own kinship system is an ideological adjunct to other aspects of the social system. Such an analysis should not be precluded artificially by theoretical formulations which prevent the introduction of a historical and critical perspective.* An excellent example of a powerful analysis which treats similar empirical and theoretical problems is provided by Barnett and Silverman, who suggest, in considering the equality presumed to exist between individuals in the West in contractual relations, that the corporation is the "perfect person." They suggest that it would be more precise—and more revealing— to "say that corporations are the metaphor for persons rather than the other way round" (n.d.: 41).

*Some of the ramifications of this empirical problem appear in the debate between Schneider and Scheffler, in Basso 1976; we might add, parenthetically, that Scheffler's position in this debate dramatically demonstrates the quietistic consequences of the artificial reification of historical results as *a priori* principles.

Even were one to say, to return to the "father"/"fatherland" example, that genitor and land belong to separate semantic domans, with neither domain able to claim primacy over the other, thus suspending the question of the primacy of meaning (for the understanding of the culture, viewed synchronically in the present), there would remain the question of how meanings *within* a domain are related. Indeed, formal semanticists, in the study of kinship terminology, have claimed that there is a primary meaning for each set of kinship terms, with other meanings being viewed as metaphorically derivative: thus, a kinship system is viewed as an extension of a few "elementary" relationships (for example, that between father and son), extended through the classification of various persons as similar to one of the partners in the "elementary" relationship. Scheffler and Lounsbury (1971) work through this position, constructing rules by which to describe how kinship terms are derived from the primary meanings of such primary terms as "mother" and "father."

Notions of primacy of meaning such as this have been widely applied in cultural analysis, the implication varying according to the methodological approach within which the analysts work. Thus, the typification of whole cultures as "Appollonian" or "Dionysian" by Ruth Benedict in her classic *Patterns of Culture* is like the hierarchical arrangement of a series of meanings of a given word (as "genitor" is the primary meaning of "father") or the distinction between denotation and connotation, in that each makes "primary meanings" into absolute qualities, attributes of *signs* rather than of the context of use of signs, giving them a privileged position which strongly affects or even determines all other meanings with which the primary meaning is associated—a position and a power which they have only in the analyst's imagination.

Yet, primacy of meaning need not carry that kind of theoretical baggage. If, instead of reifying and rigidifying domain boundaries and preconceived notions of the primacy of denotative as against connotative meanings, analysts study where a given symbol shows up and where it does not, establish the settings in which it appears, and carefully document the contexts in which it occurs, then primacy of meaning can be used to indicate an *outcome,* a *result* of people's use of symbols and meanings, rather than an abstract precondition of meaning *per se.** Thus when a sign occurs in a given, normatively defined context of action, its primary meaning may be one thing, but when it occurs in another context, then its primary meaning may be altogether different. All of those "things" may constitute the total corpus of meanings of a sign, but no one of them has any priority, except in the context of occurrence. All uses, insofar as each occurs in a normative context, are equally valid and equally part of the

shared meaning of the sign. What makes one meaning "primary" is the fact that it is the meaning which is normatively proper for that particular context; all other meanings associated with that sign, but in other contexts, become subordinate.

This too takes care of the problem of denotation *versus* connotation. Denotation is simply the proper meaning of the given sign under the normatively specified conditions of its occurrence. Our knowledge that the sign is also used in other contexts and with other meanings, which *can* be brought to bear on this situation as well as in those for which they are normatively entailed, thus become its connotations. But denotation and connotation cannot be established outside of context. The argument we are making, therefore, is that the structural-processual description of the cultural system *as a whole* (which is different from the whole thing, by the way: we refer here to those aspects of its structure which integrate it, provide the basic pattern for its existence) is neccessary to and part of understanding any one aspect of it, any one act or event.

This holistic form of analysis begins by using normative and social-structural data to discover the ways in which meaning is articulated in, by, and against the established order (as *context* and as situation or problematic). In so doing, it focusses on the way in which individual acts of signification (meaning-production) serve to *reproduce* the extant order, in new ways, perhaps, across new situations and for new actors. But as the analysis continues, it reveals as well how norms and social structure themselves come to be—are sedimented out of social action, as

*The reification of denotative meaning as primary to connotative meaning, it should be noted, is a product of the situation in which the anthropologist works; as we noted at the beginning of this Introduction, anthropologists, like children,elicit from their informants a *specialized mode of discourse:* the simplified (and often simplistic) explanation, in which the ambiguity and flexibility of principles so neccessary to real life are filtered out. The child, of course, enriches these formulae with an increasingly subtle and complex experience and consciousness; the principal point of this book might be taken to be that anthropologists must supplement *their* observation with a theory of daily life which is equally comprehensive and flexible.

meanings are used by social groups or actors differentiating themselves from others and establishing (or rejecting) relations of dominance: in this way, the *productive* or constitutive role of symbolic action becomes the object of analysis as well.

Neo-Kantian modes of analysis and perhaps especially those working from a linguistic model of culture tend to treat culture itself as a "text," as a *thing* which can be parcelled into units for analysis or which can be understood in general through the study of bounded textual material. Our notions of meaning, symbol, and context tend in another direction. We see context (itself only *arbitrarily* separable from meaning) as sets of symbols in relations to other symbols in structured systems at the widest level; the relevance of context derives from the fact that any one symbol can be situated within more than one structure, its meaning(s) being variable within those specific structures according to context. We must now make explicit our critique of the structuralist approach to culture, a critique which has been implicit in our earlier discussion, especially of the historical location and development of anthropological theories of meaning.

The structuralist approach—the major contemporary advocates of which are Claude Lévi-Strauss, Roland Barthes (a French literary critic), and Michel Foucault (a French psychologist and philosopher), as well as Durkheim, Mauss, de Saussure, and others—radically separates problems of the form of thought (and therefore its expression) from the problems of its content; in this, structuralism differs from a phenomenological perspective which attempts to transcend Kant's extreme differentia-

tion of form and content through the study of the *workings* of form. Kant's method was not deterministic in that it was not concerned with showing the cause of mental phenomena but only with demonstrating that all mental phenomena make use of basic mental structures. The structuralist program is the same: analysis is concerned with showing that the object—a text, or social form, or mode of action—exhibits some elementary structure.

Implicit in this approach, however—and the structuralists have been severely criticized for it—is the danger of *reductionism:* the lack of concern with all of the many forces which go into the occurrence of a social fact, or the production of a text or an act, *a lack of concern which is implicit in the attempt to isolate "elementary" structures*, militates for the altogether specious claim that the discovery of an elementary structure constitutes an explanation, or even a detailed interpretation, of the phenomenon itself. In point of fact, of course, it does not: in the process of the kind of abstraction this procedure entails, the phenomenon itself is *lost,* and ceases to be the object of inquiry, being replaced by the elusive "element." The distance between an "elementary" structure and the phenomenon or event which is supposed to "represent" it is too great, and as it is presented by the structuralists, the relationship is too direct, too much without mediation by and interaction with other aspects of mental, symbolic, or social practice, to say nothing of relations to other aspects of the human condition, to specify any event or phenomenon. Structuralism can be described as *static* formalism because of the passivity of both events and "elementary" structures in the vision of what thought is like that it produces.

Structuralists claim (see Lévi-Strauss 1966:116-17) that the program of research they use is provisional. A theory of culture, they claim, cannot specify mediations between elementary structures and actual events, because so many of these lie outside of culture. Culture, as one aspect or tendency in the determination of events, must, according to the structuralists, be studied on its own account before a reasonable description of its relation to other aspects can be undertaken. We think that the previous analysis of the problems associated with the separation of domains and the failure to consider context—which is at one level a social-structural feature of the speech act itself—as part of meaning relations like metaphor and metonymy, reveals the weakness of this sort of position. And, as also noted above, this position results in the altogether absurd proposition that there are aspects of the human condition, forms of action, or types of institutions, which are not symbolically constituted and which act divorced from the operations of meaning, interpretation, and signification. As we say, such a notion is simply absurd: human action without a meaningful component is inconceivable.

Meaning, Action, and the "Person"

What we have said so far is from the point of view of a system of symbols and meanings *as* a system, suspending the problem of its relation to the orientation of the actor to the situation of action. We now turn to a discussion of this problem, recalling that the structure of the situation of action is in large part there before any particular person, who does not and can not invent culture on the spot but learns in large part to play the roles and accept the meanings which society shares with this person. Yet, as has been remarked, an actor so conceived is a kind of social dummy, hardly a human being, someone filled with a quota of norms and roles, and who, if properly wired, may make it through life. For good or for ill, people are not social dummies. They are "wired" to some extent, in having learned their social roles and having learned what is meant when certain signs are given. But they can be something else as well: they can seize the situation, suffer acute states of purposiveness, feel joy and pain even when they are not socially supposed to, try to gain ends—many of which ends were learned as the "correct" ones to seek, but many of which, too, were not—and compete with each other for scarce ends. Intelligence and purposiveness make the actor more than the social dummy we have been examining so far.

With a little intelligence and some purpose more or less clearly in mind, the actor can take the set of meanings that are known to be variously associated with different norms for use and *create* a metaphor. No theory can adequately explain or predict this process—this creativity is the fundamental fact which makes social inquiry different from other sorts, and it is not reducible to or explainable in terms of anything else; but we can study the relationships between these creative acts and the social environment in which they occur. People may go along with an innovator or resist the whole attempt. But the human being, acting, can put new life into old meanings, can define a particular meaning as primary and demote all others to connotative status (with a variety of consequences), and if charismatic enough, or in a position of established leadership, or otherwise able to mobilize social forces (which only means if he or she can get away with it), then new meanings have emerged, new metaphors created, what was once metonym is now metaphor, what was once "proper context" may become old hat, passé, like "so's your old man" or "23 skiddoo." One must work with the materials at hand, otherwise it will not be understood that what has been composed is a powerful metaphor rather than a postprandial eructation—but what is at hand is *material* for the creative consciousness. And, while to some extent the outcome of this process is shaped by the symbolic code, which limits the range of possible meanings as well as providing the materials and tools (and to some extent at least the impetus) for creating new meanings, the process is also shaped, and its outcome determined by, the social-organizational processes which different groups or individuals mobilize in the process of the "circulation" of new meanings, the debate about them, the various practical actions which have, as one of their features, the negotiation of new or old meanings to situations (Silverman's paper in this volume is an excellent example of aspects of this process; see, also, for examples, Kirkpatrick in this volume, Oliver's discussion of big-man leadership in Siuai [1955: Chs. 10, 11, 13] or Barth's discussion of *Political Leadership among Swat Pathans* [1965]; for an excellent and too often ignored theoretical discussion, see Antonio Gramsci's *Prison Notebooks,* especially "The Study of Philosophy and of Historical Materialism," "The Modern Prince," and the "Programs" of *Ordine Nuovo*).

We would suggest, then, that metaphor and metonymy do not apply to the structure of systems of meanings taken apart from the intentions of actors. We suggest that primacy of meaning be reserved for that particular meaning, or subset of meaning, attached to a particular sign in its normatively defined context of use at a particular time, or a particular state of the development of norms. We suggest that the idea of domains needs further clarification and specification, especially in the light of a theory of *praxis,* before it can be of much use, if indeed it can be useful at all. And we suggest that, at the level of the culture, the *system* of symbols and meanings, the clusters and sets and subsets that may be found, the "foci" or "key" or "master" symbols, be regarded as merely associated; and that their interest, their importance lies precisely in their pattern, the form of their relations; but that these relations must be seen as instruments for the human creative capacity and not reified into "dominant" and "subordinate" symbols, such that the "key" or "master" symbols somehow whip the rest into line or exert some mystical influence on all of the others to do what is sometimes called "bring order to the set." It is *precisely* the active voice which is inappropriate and the passive voice which is appropriate to the study of the structure of symbols and meanings, the study of cultural systems. And it is the active voice which is proper to the definition of the ways in which actors structure and restructure their situations to the meanings they attach to signs and to the ways in which they relate those meanings to others in the light of their intentions and purposes. *A metaphor is made* by a poet or a speaker; it is not an inherent characteristic of the structure of a system of meaning, nor does it describe only relations between signs. At the level of culture as a system of symbols and meanings there are no metaphors, only symbols in structures of other symbols, associated with and differentiated from one another.

We have explored some specific ways in which meanings and symbols relate to one another, though we have scarcely exhausted this problem. Our purpose was to give examples of certain formulations of the relations between meanings, and to indicate some of the problems which each of them raise, while at the same time, where possible, suggesting alternate formulations.

Style, Communication, and the Constitution of Culture

It is now time to return to the place where this excursion began, that being the notion that human beings form societies, that the members of society share a system of symbols and meanings, technically called "culture," and that this system of symbols and meanings represents the reality of the world in which they live their lives. Whether this system of symbols and meanings is tightly and closely integrated (or even loosely integrated) is a question around which there is much disagreement. But there is little debate about the fact that it is a system to some degree—that it is more or less integrated and does not constitute a merely *ad hoc* collection of disparate items. This becomes self-evident when it is remembered that the group of people—be they two or three hundred or a few hundred million—have to act with respect to each other. Hence their roles must articulate in some degree; their definitions of what it is all about must be shared in some measure, even if not everyone agrees with every-

one else's definition. They must have at least *some* notion of what other people believe, they must be able to have a reasonable expectation of what their response to others, and others' response to them, will be, in order to interact with them and certainly to communicate with them. And communication is the *sine qua non* of any human society.

If the culture of a group of people constitutes, in some sense, an integrated whole, what is the *ground* for its integration? One mode of integration has to do with the roles people play to fulfill the functional prerequisites for the maintenance of any social system and, of course, the people within it. People must be fed. They must reproduce. And there must be some order to this; the integration of the cultural system provides common definitions of the state of affairs called life, some way to conceptualize all of those things which make physical and social life possible; and gives sense, too, to those that make it *worth* living; the style of life which is any people's uniqueness and identity, has been proven by people time and time again to be as valuable as eating. Culture is thus indispensable to the integration of the social system in two senses: it provides the constitution, as it were, of the individual roles and relations out of which the daily life is built; and it provides the unifying features—which might be seen as an aesthetic dimension—of these activities. Whatever the postulated relationship between culture and society, between thought and action—whether they can be seen as distinguishable in analysis (as argued by Kroeber and Parsons 1958), or as one embedded in the other, or as inseparable aspects of a single unity—life must have meaning, the things people do must be communicable—and this entails a system of signs or symbols in which this meaning is embedded and expressed.

Functionalist queries notwithstanding, we do not know enough about people's cultural life—in the narrow sense in which we use the term—to be able to spell out how, precisely, it is adaptive, and to what, and whether it can be accounted for on those grounds; or whether we need species specific grounds, which simply say "that's the nature of the human animal." Even here we know enough to know how little we know. We assume—we must assume—the capacity to learn language, to invent language, to use it as a form of communication; that it is no rude tool by any means. History may tell us that the people who live on the island of Yap speak Yapese now because they spoke it for some time, and that proto-Yapese is probably what they spoke before that. What, however, is the structure of Yapese, the rules which govern the way in which its signs and meanings are used? How does it vary from other languages? These, only comparative study can tell us. The same questions can be asked about human cultures. Even accepting that there are species-specific capacities for culture, the question as to what the parameters of these are, what the universals (if any) are, what the range of variants are and in what regard they occur, remain.

It is important, too, that we do not reify culture to the point that we no longer see it as an aspect of what people do. Every act that every person performs has its symbolic aspect, its meanings. That we abstract these meanings in order to understand a system of meanings is true, but we must remember that *we abstract them from the concrete actions of people*. As an abstraction,

culture cannot follow laws of its own; rather, what regularities it shows are those which inhere in the actions from which the symbolic and the meaningful are abstracted.

Fundamental to the study of symbolic anthropology is the concern with how people formulate their reality. We must, if we are to understand this and relate it to an understanding of their (and our own) action, examine *their culture,* not *our theories* (and if we study our theories, we must study them *as* "their culture"); study their systems of symbols, not our *ad hoc* presumptions about what it might or should be; what they actually do, not what we presume to be universal and therefore attribute to them—all too often only to discover that what we thought to be universal was not so universal after all. In other words, our task is not to study forms, but to study *praxis* (which makes use of, creates, and relates to forms)—self-consciousness and conscious action—and for that, we need a method, a theory, which does not dissolve it before we begin.

The Analysis of "Religious" Forms

Before turning to a consideration of *praxis,* we discuss several approaches to the study of religious forms which we think important for two related, though somewhat contrasting, reasons. First, the study of symbols and meanings within anthropology (now itself reified as "symbolic anthropology") began, in large part, with studies of religious behavior, ritual forms, magic, myth, and holiday. But, while this work was being done, and in large part undergirding it, the notion that the symbolic aspects of reality, though important, are essentially epiphenomenal and ultimately less than "real," was sustained. In this, as remarked above, it has not only been implied that religion, magic, ritual, and art have, with other "expressive" forms, a monopoly on symbolic functions, but concurrently, the crucial point that thought *is* action has been largely ignored or denied.

The proposition, in its extreme form, that religion (like art, music, and sorcery) exists to represent the realities of social life, developed as part of the wider view that certain types of action (sometimes called "institutions") are "based upon" (or are) socially recognized and ordered modes of dealing with the real, concrete facts of life: which facts are themselves, it is claimed, *outside* the social system. Thus economic institutions are seen to deal with production, distribution, and consumption of goods and services (but see the paper by Polanyi in this volume); kinship institutions are seen to be the social recognition of the real biological facts of sexual reproduction (but note that Sider's paper in this volume shows that the Trobriand kinship system is best understood in the light of the natives' *concepts*—which are erroneous—of those facts). Some people, it is held, have erroneous beliefs about, for example, aspects of the facts of reproduction, but those facts exist and must be dealt with; correspondingly, the function of culture or of the social system is posited as making the management of those problems orderly, predictable, and understandable, and in that adaptive sense giving sustenance to social life. So, such analyses continue, marriage and kinship, functioning to regulate sexual behavior, and economic norms, functioning to control acquisitive drives, ward off the chaos that would result if these were not channeled.

Van Gennep's conception of *rites de passage* provides an illuminating analytic example (see Van Gennep 1909/ 1960). These characteristic rites, tending to occur during the transition of a person from one status to another (for example, from youth to adulthood, from novice to initiate), have been understood as effective in easing the inherent difficulty of such transitions. There are, however, several trends within this general analytic frame. The patently functionalist variant assumes a dynamic effect of ritual upon its setting, regardless of the specific content of the ritual; ritual is thus seen as the poultice for social disjunction (Turner 1957, is an excellent example of this approach). A more symbolic approach understands ritual as a direct embodiment of social transitions and movements, this symbolic embodiment being credited as responsible for the dynamic effectiveness of ritual as a therapeutic agent (see Lévi-Strauss, "The Effectiveness of Symbols," 1963; Turner 1968). Within the symbolic perspective it has been suggested that rituals develop in reaction, and encapsulate a cultural retort, to socially menacing objects and events. Both of these somewhat different explanations of ritual assume the (logical or temporal) priority of a nonsymbolic social system which induces stress which is met in turn by ritual responses. So, while economics is seen to deal with fundamental reality in an outside world and kinship with fundamental realities of human biology, ritual is taken to deal with problems which social life creates for itself, problems which follow, by and large, from the *a priori* "givens" of social life itself.

Such analyses assume ritual and its kindred "expressive" activities to be analogous to a bandage for the social body; religion and art (including graphics, music, dance) are examined as symbolic statements of the trouble with life and are thought to have the same function. So religion, in general, like ritual, is seen to provide comforts, is seen as a form of self-expression projecting in representational form the joy or the hell of living.

However, there is no reason to assume that this Band-Aid theory is correct, or to assume the derivative character of ritual (Murray's paper, in this volume, provides a general theoretical background for a very different view). There is nothing more "down to earth" or "basic" about kinship, economics, or status changes than there is about rituals. All occur only in societies and are first and foremost socio-cultural activities. The assumption that social life is prior to culture has led to treatments of ritual, stressing either the ritual's special ("ritual") nature (as other than ordinary everyday life) or its symbolic aspects, while ignoring the entire social organization of the ritual itself (there are of course exceptions to this rule). By the same token, the symbolic and meaningful aspects of economics, kinship, and status transitions have been neglected.

When ritual and kinship are compared, we find that each entails a system of statuses, roles, and rules for how the roles should be played out, how the statuses relate to each other, and how persons move through these statuses. Each has its uses; each has its symbolic and meaningful aspects. Indeed, the belief that kinship orders *the* facts of biological reproduction is itself an interesting cultural statement. It is no longer enough to distinguish semantic domains which contrast, interact, or remain independent, and to associate meanings, symbols, or functions to these. Symbols exist in the context of other symbols, in ordered structures; the symbolic forms must be followed out through the structures if we are to do more than consider the problems we pose externally, if, that is, we are to explore the structures of meaning in use.

Toward Praxis

In the preceding sections, we have analyzed several problems which arise at the level of formal relations between symbols and symbolic structures; attempts to resolve these problems with formal analysis have been hampered by functionalist assumptions about the "representational," derivative, *status quo* maintaining nature of symbolic activity. Our analysis of *some* formal problems in practical interpretation has led us to two basic points about symbolic activity: (1) formal symbolic structures are structures *in use* (they are entities which are used *by* one person or group to refer to a different entity, *for* an audience); (2) the functional relations between symbolic structures and other aspects of social life must be understood, not as a superorganic operation which serves an *a priori* role in the relations of other superorganic operations, but as a structure of actors' intentions. Thus, for example, the distinction between symbols which impel and direct action and those by which the world is imagined, understood, and expressed is dissolved *at the formal (syntactic) level;* these are shown, instead, to be types of usage: any symbol can be used in either way, and, while that use is limited by the symbol's place in structures which pre-exist the particular situation, these structures are themselves recast as they are used. The process illustrated here is *praxis:* the complex unity of thought and action, meaning (as an *objective* aspect or consequence of action, as well as intentional meaning), and intention.

Action not only stems from within a people's cultural construction of the world, from within the sense of person and group, but is interpreted and interpretable by "natives" as well as anthropologists, in the light of such situatings. We must ask not only about how symbols are structured and made meaningful, not only about the processes through which symbolic forms create and are created in action, but also about *domination,* including those forms of oppression which are sustained, fostered, and produced in people's everyday lives. Each action or situation of action produces or becomes a result, and, as such, becomes a part of the environment of future events by virtue of its reification as a *token* of some (more general or abstract) value or object which is generally held to be good or desirable. Every action situation is the locus of such reification; and because such reification is the practical key and the ontological root of domination, every action situation is the site or negotiation for, or struggle against, domination.

Therefore, a sociology of reification, and especially its basis in the everyday life, is a central project for an anthropology of meaning which unifies in theory what is already a unity in fact: the symbolic processes with which people understand their world, themselves, and their actions, and the actions themselves, their objects and consequences. The process of reification is that through which people appropriate their created histories as "natural," through which cultural constructions are imbued with a sense of the inevitable. Within anthropology, the notion of objectification has been used (for example, by Munn 1973; Wagner 1975), although it is generally used in a way that dissociates it from the alienation (from self and products) implied by the term reification. Following Marx, reifications in general are distinguishable: there is, in the first place, that sort of reification which (close to Wagner's notion of objectification, for instance) entails an externalization and re-internalization of meaning through self-conscious action on the world, and the rediscovery of self in action which involves overcoming alienation at the moment of self-realization; and secondly those reifications which entail the alienation of people from their own externalizations (that is, the inability to see one's actions as truly one's own). It was Marx's contention that only with certain processes of production (capitalism)—which, it is to be remembered, is the same as saying "only with certain forms of self-externalization"—is objectification synonymous with alienation; and, it should be noted, while all cultures see themselves as "natural," only with alienation does culture actually *become* nature.

The point here is that when discussing the role of meaning in social action we are dealing with two sorts of process, whose relations are clearly shown in the notion of reification. On the one hand every human action entails the externalization in action or in an object (or in both) of a set of understandings, notions about the nature of things, actions, and people, which are given shape by the desires and intentions of the actor. Some of the actor's understanding is conscious and rational (in form, at least), constituting an assessment of the situation and a definition of context as well as a *plan;* some of this understanding is, at the same time, not conscious, but part of the actor's environment; similarly, an actor's intentions can be direct or mediated through his or her relations to others. On the other hand, actors recognize themselves and their meanings in their actions and their products. At times, this reappropriation is automatic and routine—which indicates only a correspondence between the structures in use for each of these moments; at other times, this reappropriation produces a reinterpretation of the action, or its object, consequence, or result; at most times, the process of externalization and reappropriation produces a gradual readjustment of the structures of meaning, a gradual process which has as its paradigm case "learning through experience" (Peirce/Buchler 1897/1955) or "normal science" (Kuhn 1962: chs. 2 and 3); at times, the process fails altogether, resulting in "loss" of meaning—of the equation of activity with the object it produces. But, while alienation is a feature of the failure of the process of objectification and reappropriation, it must be remembered that it is a failure which is a feature of the structure of the process itself, that is, a disparity between the objective consequences of action and the reasons for which it is undertaken: a function of a certain kind of reification (of the process) in a particular context (see the selection by Marx in this volume).

The process of reification in the broad sense is similar to what Roland Barthes identifies as the fundamental nature of myth, the "essential function" of which he identifies as "the naturalization of the concept" (1972: 131). Barthes is most concerned with contemporary bourgeois myth and thus sees myth as akin to those reifying processes which are embedded in and create situations of alienation, with myths which "freeze" nature and are, themselves, severed from history—from origins, from change, and from the human action which produces them. The subject of myth is the everyday life of the present; in being reified and fabulized, it is effectively separated from the past or future, and "the present" (itself a myth) becomes a substitute for both (that is, eternal). Certain kinds of myth, Barthes suggests, are "inessential" and "incidental" in that they are "poverty-stricken," their objects not being those of everyday life. Myth, externalizing the contingent and bestowing a sense of finality and (self-propelled) necessity on it, is most effective when reification becomes a dominant aspect of life, and especially of everyday life, when it affects a people's notions of marriage, cooking, the home, the theater, the law, morality, (147)—when these things cease, in a sense, to be recognized as *part* of life and become ends or objects in their own right. This notion evokes the image of the family in Ionesco's *The Bald Soprano:* at the beginning of the play, they sit, self-satisfied:

Mrs. SMITH: There, it's nine o'clock. We've drunk the soup, and eaten the fish and chips, and the English salad. The children have drunk English water. We've eaten well this evening. That's because we live in the suburbs of London and because our name is Smith.

Chaos erupts—or, rather, gradually emerges out of the banality of this existence. At the end of the play, however, it is reabsorbed by being *denied;* and it is denied in exactly the same words as those spoken at the beginning of the play. The significance of these people's lives lies in their "Englishness"—or, in the existence itself, which they will assert over everything else, reifying their lives *as* lives, that is, as totally abstract.

The process of reification (as alienation) occurs when relations between comparable relations become (or are made to appear) not merely similar, but contiguous; the abstract aspects of the meanings of these relations become dominant over their concrete, particular nature despite the impression of contiguity, of "realness." Formally, this is a crucial mode through which opacity occurs in ideology (see below). To put this somewhat differently, such ideological reification (as alienation) entails the subordination by actors of the intentional or analogic value of an event to an abstraction; analogic relations become necessarily implicative of other analogies. Ideology thus becomes, not specific beliefs or practices which are themselves restricted to certain "domains" of political life (as has been argued, for example, by Geertz, 1964); rather, ideology comes to be seen as the system of representation whereby everyday life is produced, and understandings of it represented as "natural" and about which, as it has been frequently remarked, those who believe in the ideology are not self-conscious exactly because ideology is obvious to those who are "inside" it, to those who believe in— and through—it (see Althusser 1971; Mannheim 1936). Further, in ideology that which is specific and historical is expressed as general and unconditional. Ideology entails reification and is itself altered or sustained in line with extant reifications. Ideology is not a reflection or simply a reproductive apparatus of predominant modes of production (as many orthodox Marxists have argued), although it does serve the function of the latter, but at the same time *it creates* modes of production of both "goods" and actions; ideology, forming and formed in action, is itself inseparable from action.

While ideology cannot be dissociated from action, it is equally the case that no ideology provides for a clear representation of its own relations with *praxis* (that is, with its own implications, consequences, and conditions), because of the dual character of ideologies: they are "general, speculative, abstract" but also they "are representative of determinate, limited, special interests" (Lefebvre in this volume); in ideology, "special interests" are generalized and represented as universal. Ideology "sees" real objects or tokens in the world *solely* as tokens of abstract concepts or categories; in other words, it ignores the process of externalization and reappropriation and sees only the *results* of this process (which it conceptualizes as process: in Marx's phrase, as "social relations between things").

At bottom, an ideology is predicated within a particular cultural constitution of the "person" (see Mauss 1938); correspondingly, the concept of the person varies with shifts in ideology. Western sociology (and anthropology), itself posited on and within the cultural notion of a unique, autonomous individual, has failed in large part to perceive alternative possibilities to this construct (see Dumont 1970a and in this volume; MacPherson 1962). Dumont advances two broad possibilities for the construction of the person: society may valorize (that is, stress "value," in the sense used above, to be at the level of) the individual or the structural (social-systemic) whole. While the individual as empirical agent exists in all contexts, the individual as *metaphor* for other individuals, for groups, and for society—the substantially defined and autonomous individual of Western thought—is not universal. In the situation of caste India, it is the whole, understood structurally through the opposition between purity and impurity, which represents value and provides both the model for order and the criteria for the placement of individuals, groups, and actions in that order (Dumont 1970a, 1970b). This model is not the action of an individual, but the transactional relation between *two or more collections* of people (although note that the general model of objectification and reappropriation—of reification—presented above applies here as well, only with groups and the totality as the frame of reference). But even within contexts which can be broadly distinguished as either holistic or individualistic, the forms through which the person is understood are various: for instance, the Balinese are portrayed by Geertz as submerging individual identity in the stress placed upon invariant "transhuman" categories which, however, differ from Indian caste (1973:387; see also, Dolgin and Magdoff, Kirkpatrick, Silverman, and Wagner in this volume, and contrast with the selection by Schneider).

Western individualism and caste holism occur, respectively, with (and themselves create the specific forms of) an egalitarian ideology in the first case and a hierarchical ideology in the second. Ideology tends to be pervasive within a general social context (Dumont 1970a). This is not, of course, to imply that ideologies never change. Indeed, Barnett (1973a and in this volume) has exactly demarcated a shift in India from a caste to a class basis for social action and from an ideology of hierarchy to one of equality, in pointing to the transformation of one upper, non-Brahman South Indian caste into an "ethnic group." This does not mean that "caste" has ceased to be an aspect of the decisions people make, or that decisions based on "caste" principles are somehow anachronistic or ineffectual: rather, the change has to do in large part with the altered consequences of action on "caste" principles: the point is not the impossibility of change in the structure of ideology, but rather *the possibility that change or difference will be (ideologically) perceived as similarity and that similarity will be ideologically perceived as change.* The substantialization of caste hierarchy—the shift from the transactional ideology of caste to the individualistic ideology of class—entails a move between ideological structures, as Barnett documents (in this volume). The substantialization of *groups* of individuals in the West, however (for example, the creation of ethnicity as an organizational principle, or of particular ethnic groups) occurs within and does not threaten the individualistic ideology.

The generalization—the extension of the range of objects against which ideology is applicable—of ideology in Western culture is concealed in the proliferation of items and events which are superficially or initially understood as *different,* although they are symbolically constructed so as to become *substitutable* (that is, essentially the same) *in practice*. This proliferation of indifferent differences takes a form made possible through an individualistic ideology wherein the individual is potentially (ideologically) substitutable for any other individual (see Lefebvre 1971). This generalization of ideology is shown in the similarity of structure between relations of what are conceived of by "natives" as the domains of kinship, nationality, and religion in the United States (as revealed by Schneider in this volume). The pervasiveness of such ideological forms is not necessarily, indeed is in the main *not,* perceived by people who identify as relative, citizen, or church member.

This process of substitution, on one level, or in one context, is the basis of symbolic action (at the level of enabling the proliferation of exchange value—see Kemnitzer, Lefebvre, Marx in this volume); at another level, it is a powerful form for the absorption of protest, the resistance of change, and the reproduction of the extant social order. Henri Lefebvre suggests that this process has become institutionalized in the contemporary West to the point that a terroristic universe has resulted—a universe devoid of style or significant differentiation, characterized by ultimately meaningless, but endless, substitutions of meaning and by "the significant absence of a general code" (1971:74), which is to say that this system of substitutable groups and objects and events cannot be anchored, by natives, to anything beyond itself.

In yet a more general sense the ideological character of a world based on substitutions is defined by relations of absorption (Marcuse 1964); formally, the absorption of protest or difference, the encompassment of separated groups (or concepts), is effected through the conceptual displacement of contradiction. The process of absorption, that is, occurs through alterations in the *level* at which particular symbols are (or can be) *invoked as* meaningful. Concretely, absorption occurs either through the creation of the conviction within people that that which is, is unavoidable, if not good, and that they are bound to participate in its production, or through the deflection of people's intentions so that, unaware, they cease to be potential sources of weakness or tension for the constituted system. The attempted representation of conditions and relations resulting from or part of colonial domination as "natural" illustrates the former possibility. In the colonial context, the possibility of rebellion or of noncolonial society is rendered unrealistic for people (*both* colonizer and colonized), not by denying the difference between colonizer and colonized, but by hypostatizing it and the dependence of the colonized on the "guidance" of the superior power which is the historical result of colonial domination, as a "natural" state of affairs, necessitated by the imputed inferiority (childishness, or—this ideology extends to the Left as well—the historical underdevelopment) of the victim (see Amin, 1973, 1975; Fanon, 1963, 1965, 1967, Memmi, 1965). Fanon, in a remarkable study of the significance of the veil and the importance of the radio in insurgent Algeria (1965), documents the reversal of that "natural" dependence, the transcendance of the colonial ideology within the self-consciousness of the colonized; relations of dependence were altered in the initial success of the Algerians in controlling the use of certain symbols, such as the veil, in explicit defiance of French power, thus deepening (and finally widening, as well) the Algerian self-consciousness as to the situation of colonization and the possibility of revolt.

Activist groups, and especially ethnic-activist groups, in the United States over the last decade or so exemplify the other pole of the dialectic of absorption. The substitutability of the forms through which particular ethnic identities are expressed and enacted work to render any identity merely a token of "ethnicity" *as such,* and the force of any specific protest can thereby be deflected and absorbed (Dolgin, 1977). While negations of the colonial situation are ideologically absorbed through the "naturalization" of dependence, the absorption of "ethnic" activism in the United States has occurred through an egalitarian ideology which swallows potential negations of the social order by fostering the generalization (and thus the attenuation) of the *forms* in which negation occurs. In both cases, however, the ideology is predominantly egalitarian (with stress in the understanding of social relations placed on individual substance rather than group structure—or on group substance rather than social structure). Absorption works through the manipulation of levels of symbolic *praxis;* although the specific form of the process of absorption described by Marcuse, in which contradictions are suppressed through symbolic displacement, may be restricted to the substantial universe established by class domination in Western society, the more general process of the encompassment and recruitment of people through the appropriation of their symbolic forms to an over-arching, encompassing struc-ture which is the property of a dominant group, is universal, and at the root of the stability of culture and its extension throughout a population (including the socialization of children and the healing of madmen).

Marx distinguished social orders on the basis of their transparency or opacity. Thus, relations of domination can be characterized as more or less opaque— or transparent. These two terms, basic to a theory of symbolic *praxis,* refer to relations between processes of social interaction and processes through which forms of consciousness of social life are produced; that is, they effectively characterize ideologies. Medieval Europe is often used to illustrate a situation of *relative* transparency (there is probably no such things as a truly or wholly transparent system)—see the selections by Lefebvre and Marx in this volume. Medieval social relations, enacted from within an ideology of personal dependence, did not "assume a form [in the ideology] different from their reality" (Marx). In contrast, in bourgeois society, existent dependence and inequality are not conceived as part of the natural order of things (as in Medieval Europe), nor as the outcome of the social order, but are disguised and denied in an ideology of individual performance, capability, and achievement. The contrast between caste hierarchy and racism presented by Dumont (in this volume) entails a similar difference. The holistic ideology of caste India is transparent, in that the concrete transactions between caste members are hierarchically based and are taken to be just that. Racism, on the contrary, entails inequality *as an exception* to an individualistic ideology which presumes equality. Lefebvre carries the argument as to the opacity of the social order in the modern, post-industrial world one step further in examining everyday life itself as the arena of greatest opacity. The individualistic ideology, he argues, spawns "values" (for example, technology, rationality, nature) which become "organized substitutes" for "institutions"—that is, abstractions which metonymically replace concrete action or forms of action—and in this way mask contradictions (by universalizing them). Even "equality" becomes a "value" in the individualistic world of modern society: it is a "value" which serves to reinforce (that is, legitimate) its own absence; hierarchy was not such a "value" in Medieval Europe—it was simply present, in concrete interaction and in the perceived nature of society. Opacity, in short, entails the reification of ideology (the reification, as it were, of reification); abstract "values" sustain false consciousness by hiding the actuality of social institutions behind a veil of asocial, ahistorical naturalness. "Thus," writes Lefebvre, "the ideal of every state bureaucracy is moral rectitude, and the more corrupt and corrupting it is, the more it will stress this ideal" (1971:71).

Whatever the form of ideology, however, the process of symbolization takes place within the structured relations of symbols to other symbols. This process involves *praxis* for it provides orientations toward kinds of action, action which can be reassimilated to the symbolic order immediately through objectification and its reification or transcendance. All symbolic structures grant meaning through reifications but the *separation* of people from their objectifications (alienation) is accomplished through specific sorts of symbolic operation, which are themselves aspects of

particular, historical developments of social form, especially the form taken by domination.

Conclusion

Basic categories of analysis are not (and do not refer to) things, *per se*, but relations—the relations between things, events, acts, people—conceived and enacted by people. In locating the "supreme mystification" of positivism to be denial of human ends in the present, Sartre suggests that while it was "legitimate" for the sciences to reject anthropomorphism

"it is perfectly absurd to assume by analogy the same scorn for anthropomorphism where anthropology is concerned. When one is studying man, what can be more exact or more rigorous than to *recognize human properties in him?*" (1968:157).

Symbolic action is part of a total mode of production and expression of creative human energy. The only *reference* of symbolic action is to the other aspects of the creative enterprise; symbolic action may determine, or be determined by, other aspects of social action, in any particular concrete empirical instance; but *in theory,* symbolic action always refers only to *itself:* to other symbolic action (because all action and all aspects of human action are symbolically constituted). Of course, for many Marxist writers, symbolic action is shaped by other forces, particularly economic structures; and indeed, on Marx's view, symbolic action *may* be secondary to other dimensions of action. This is not, however, a necessary condition of symbolization, according to Marx; the alternative to symbolic meaning is not, as Durkheim and Weber insisted, chaos. Such chaos *does not exist,* since for people, everything is symbolic, created (in part at least) by the mind.

This creation by the mind, moreover, is an *active* process, part and parcel of the human tendency to act on the world; if symbolic action is created by anything, it is by the predilection for action in a certain mode—which is to say, by previous action, previous meanings. What this view requires is a concentration on symbolic *processes,* instead of requiring that the analysis of meaning show only how a particular form represents a more elementary one; and it demands also that the process whereby people give meaning to their world and their action in it, be seen as a part of their lives and actions, a part of the general pattern of social relationship, instead of being artifically separated from it.

The choices offered in the papers in this book are not merely intellectual choices about how to study a foreign phenomenon. As we have tried to make clear above, theories of meaning are shared by the self-consciousness of people and their response to their own situa-tion. Our contemporaries who cling to the opposition between meaning and chaos do so largely out of a desire— perhaps not expressed or expressible, but nonetheless present and powerful— to escape the realities of freedom which the alternative view offers them and the responsibilities that reality carries with it. That responsibility is twofold: on the one hand, to combat the mystification to which we are subject as members of our own culture and, on the other, to struggle for the implementation of a world which sets the human spirit—and its apparently infinite potential to create new dimensions of meaningful existence—truly free.

People act on the basis of belief. To study belief in action—whether in New Guinea or New York—is to examine the possibilities of freedom, and the roots of oppression and alienation. But these can be studied only in the context of a *practical* commitment to freedom and a determination to overcome that which stands in its way. People made it, is the principal lesson of modern anthropology; people can remake it, must become the principal lesson of our work in the future.

TWO

Kinship and Social Organization

ONE

Kinship and Culture: Affinity and the Role of the Father in the Trobriands

KAREN I. BLU

When this paper was written, there was a great deal of controversy in the literature on the nature of the relationship between father and child in the matrilineal Trobriand Islands. One view was that the father was related to the child by bonds of filiation but not of descent. Another view affirmed that the father was merely the child's mother's husband and thus no more than an affine to the child. The nature of the controversy seemed to force an "either/or" position, and the protagonists of filiation denied affinity, while those of affinity denied the validity of the notion of filiation.

This controversy was but a special instance of the difference between alliance theory as developed by Lévi-Strauss (in his *Elementary Structures of Kinship,* 1949/69) and descent theory as practiced especially by Fortes (summarized in his *Kinship and the Social Order,* 1969), and as is common in such controversies, the issue became sharply polarized. (For a survey of the general debate on alliance and descent theory, see Schneider 1965a).

Sider, by using a cultural approach and asking what symbols marked affinity and what symbols marked filiation—if any—seems able to resolve the controversy simply and at the same time to throw new light on the whole Trobriand kinship system, thus once again demonstrating the power of a cultural or symbolic analysis.

To the best of our knowledge this paper has never been refuted or challenged in any of its major points, and it stands as a classic instance of this kind of analysis.

IT IS THE PURPOSE OF THIS PAPER TO consider matrilineal and affinal relationships in a "matrilineal society" from a cultural point of view.[1] The society under study is that of the Trobriand Islands as reported by Malinowski and Powell (see bibliography).

The interpretive problems addressed are concerned with matriliny and affinity and have been considered problematical by other analysts—the problem of the role of the father and that of the nature of *urigubu,* the annual harvest gift. By viewing these problems from a cultural perspective, beginning with how the Trobrianders themselves view the problems, I hope to clarify some of the issues involved and in so doing show the utility of a cultural analysis. In emphasizing the cultural perspective, the social structural aspects are not ignored but treated as complementary background.

Reprinted by permission from *Journal of Anthropological Research* (formerly *Southwestern Journal of Anthropology*), vol. 23, no. 1, pp. 90–109; copyright © 1967.

A brief sketch of Trobriand society is presented, followed by a discussion of the problems addressed and my own reanalysis of the Trobriand data in terms of these problems.

The Trobriands

The Trobriand Islands are a group of coral islands located in the Massim off the eastern coast of New Guinea. The islanders are horticulturalists who raise yams and taro as staples, which are supplemented by tropical fruits, coconuts, fish, and occasionally pork. Both men and women participate in gardening chores, and special interest and energy are invested in the yam gardens, as yams are ritually and politically a significant crop. The size, texture, and amount of yams raised may bestow prestige, status, and political influence upon the gardener; they are also necessary items of exchange in most rituals (Malinowski 1965:52–83).

Trobrianders live in villages, each of which is "owned" by one or more matrilineal subclans or *dala*. The subclans are members of matrilineal totemic clans *(kumila)*, whose member subclans are scattered. While the clans have certain ritual significance, it is the subclans which figure predominantly in Trobriand life, since they are the primary jural units. The "owning" subclans in a village are those with proprietary rights to certain sites and to surrounding garden land; all those resident in the village who are not members of owning subclans are legally "strangers" or "outsiders" *(tomakava)* and reside there using the owners' land by permission and grace (Powell 1956:1–86). The senior subclan (that is, the highest ranking) provides the "headman," who is akin to the Melanesian "big man"[2] in that his influence derives from personal qualities and manipulative abilities rather than from strictly hereditary office. While the headman must come from the senior owning subclan, Powell has stressed the fact that, within the subclan, actual genealogy has little to do with the choice of successors to the headman. Some villages are connected, by virtue of spatial location and political interaction, into clusters. Each village in the cluster has its own headman, but one headman is "chief" of the cluster of villages, higher ranking and more influential over a wider area than is the ordinary headman (Powell 1956:419,495).

The relations between villages are largely regulated by the interaction of their headmen and chiefs, depending upon their rank, their relations as cognates or affines, and the outcome of their competitions. Competing with one another through *kula* voyaging, *buriti-laulo* (garden challenges), and cricket (which has taken the place of warfare), the leaders are accorded relative prestige which contributes to a certain extent to their rank (Powell 1956:346–574; 1960). Rank is partially ascribed and to some extent achieved, a complication which accounts for some of the disagreements over rank reported by Malinowski (e.g., 1948:113). Ordinary villagers, then, try to join one or another big man's sphere of influence by relating to him through various kinds of kinship bonds. The most preferred bond is matrilineal, but if this cannot be traced, than an agnatic one is next best. Finally, even affinal ties can be utilized successfully.

Thus, although the ideal residence pattern for the Trobrianders is regulated by matrilineal principles, political and personal considerations often alter the pattern. Ideally, a man lives in his own subclan village, having moved there from his father's subclan's village either before or at marriage. The women live scattered in various villages, with their fathers if young and unmarried, and with husbands afterward. All men in the village should be owners, but in fact there are usually many non-owners, all residing in the village on account of cognatic[3] or affinal ties to owners. These ties are acceptable except in extreme cases of political rivalry when the owners can require the outsiders to leave.[4] Powell's data confirm this pattern of residence (1956: Tables 2 and 2a).

Some Problems in Interpretation

Two related problems to be dealt with in this paper are (1) the role of the father in matrilineal Trobriand culture and (2) the nature of the annual harvest gift of yams, *urigubu*. Both problems have so far been treated by other analysts as part of the relations of affinity among Trobrianders (with the exception of Robinson 1962), but they have not been satisfactorily resolved by such treatment. Malinowski and Powell are to be dealt with because they have both done intensive field work in the Trobriands, and Robinson because she has concentrated upon the jural aspects of the role of the father in her essay on patrifiliation (1962). Others who have also treated the problems will not be discussed here, either because it is felt that their interpretations are not relevant to the arguments in this paper (Leach 1958) or because this paper takes up where theirs left off (Lounsbury 1965). It should be noted that Leach (1961) has suggested an approach through the analysis of symbols of relationship similar to the approach taken here, and he has reached the conclusion that father is an affine. His interpretation, as will be seen, is different from mine. It is my view that the problems under consideration have not been better resolved largely because certain anthropological concepts such as "descent" and "affinity" are too often used without reference to the way in which the people under study talk about the relationships which are the referents of the concepts. It is my purpose to examine both Malinowski's and Powell's data in order to attempt to separate anthropological concepts from Trobriand concepts and to relate the two in a fruitful reexamination of some old problems.

The problem of the role of the father stems from the categorization of the father as *tomakava* = "stranger" or "outsider," as reported by Malinowski, and from the Trobrianders' apparent refusal to recognize physiological paternity. Malinowski consistently viewed "father" as "mother's husband," in addition to "outsider," and hence an affine rather than a cognate (1929b:6–7), because father appeared to be unnecessary to the jural identity of his children. Despite the fact that father was really an affine to his children, a warm and affectionate relationship existed between them, which at times appeared to result in special privileges for children when, by legal principle, these were the right of nephews and nieces. Malinowski interpreted the situation as the result of conflict between "mother-right" and "father-love" (1926:101). Fortes points out that for Malinowski father-love was the psychological reality opposed to and sometimes subvertive of the structural ideal of mother-right (1964:160, 169).

Powell also treats father as an affine, but his perspective is that of the matrilineal subclan or *dala* rather than that of the individual, which Malinowski used. From Powell's viewpoint, it is father's status as an affine to his son's subclan which is the important factor in the relationship (the formal relationship as opposed to the personal one). However, he carefully points out that the Trobrianders themselves make a distinction between persons as representatives of their subclans and persons as private individuals. It is this distinction which provides a clue to the ambiguities of father's position.

Robinson, unlike Powell or Malinowski, is explicitly concerned with demonstrating the presence of patrifiliation among the matrilineal Trobrianders.[5] Although she convincingly demonstrates the existence of "jural, economic and ritual roles, rights and responsibilities" pertaining to the father, it is still difficult to see why this should be so, given the Trobrianders' particular views of matriliny and paternity (Robinson 1962:155).

It will be the primary task of this paper to reinterpret the above positions, reconciling them with the Trobriand views of father, matriliny, and affinity.

The secondary problem is the nature of *urigubu*. *Urigubu* is the annual harvest gift consisting of a special variety of yams which are planted in a garden set aside for them and harvested with ritual care. The problem stems from the fact that various individuals present *urigubu* to a variety of kinsmen for a number of reasons, and these variables make it difficult to categorize the gift simply. Mali-

nowski has interpreted the gift as "really" given by brother to sister, even though it is formally presented to ZH by WB.

But in reality the *urigubu* is only handed over formally to the husband in order to finance the household of the wife. . . . It is because of her, for her and for her children's maintenance that the annual gift is given. (Malinowski 1965:190)

He emphasizes that this gift is the woman's due as a result of her absentee interest in her own subclan land.

We can . . . regard the *urigubu* as the annual return from the joint patrimony, the portion which is due to the woman from her brother; because the land which he husbands is partly his own, partly held in trust for the females of each generation. (Malinowski 1965:353)

For several reasons, Powell does not accept Malinowski's interpretation of who "really" receives the gift and for what reasons: (1) the amounts of *urigubu* are not governed by the size of the family receiving it; (2) statistically, the proportion of *urigubu* given by "own" brothers of the wife to ZH is relatively small (less than one-third of the cases examined. Powell 1956: Table 13); (3) the proportion of *urigubu* grown on "own" subclan land is even smaller; (4) *urigubu* is often given by sons to widowed fathers and mothers (Powell 1956:408). In view of these findings, Powell has interpreted *urigubu* as a presentation which symbolizes the renewal of the affinal contract and all the contingent rights and obligations (1956:410). Indeed, Malinowski himself notes:

the natives, in describing *urigubu*, would not naturally define it as the result of a woman's title to her land. But they are quite clear that it is due to her household, because she and her children are really part and parcel of her brother's kinship group. (1965:353)

The implication seems to be that it is subclan membership which gives a woman's household (which includes children and husband) a right to *urigubu*.

Finally, Robinson, in interpreting both Malinowski's and Powell's data, has suggested that *urigubu* represents interests held in a marriage, be it by the boy's and girl's subclans, their fathers, or whomever (1962:155).

It still remains to be explained, however, how other gifts come to be included by the Trobrianders in the category *urigubu*. Some of the other gifts have been recorded by Malinowski, who regarded them as "spurious" *urigubu*, although no such distinctions were made by the islanders themselves: (a) the chief receives *urigubu* from a subclan whose members are not properly affines, but who are co-residents in his village; (b) sons often present their fathers with *urigubu* even after the divorce or death of the mother; (c) a man may receive the gift from his own matrilineal kinsmen if he has not remarried; and (d) the chief may receive the gift from WF (Malinowski 1965:192–95).

The two problems outlined above have both been considered within the context of affinity by previous analysts. In order to evaluate this position and to suggest possible alternatives, it is necessary first to consider matriliny, since it is obviously an important conceptual as well as jural aspect of Trobriand life. Against this background, paternity and affinity can then be discussed with a view to clarifying the two problems outlined. It should be kept in mind throughout the following discussion that in referring to father and the role of father, I mean what the Trobrianders refer to as "own" or "true" (*mokwita*) father, not the kinship category *tama*, which includes own or true as well as classificatory father.

Matriliny

Symbolic Aspects

There are several symbolic links between members of the same subclan which stem from myths and a belief in common substance. Each subclan is associated with a myth which recounts the emergence from a special place of a mythical ancestress and her brother(s) (Malinowski 1948:112). The emergence generally establishes the rank of the subclan and the rights of the descendants to village sites and garden lands (Powell 1956:45). These myths provide the range of names by which a subclan may be called—the name of the emergent ancestors, the place of emergence, or the name of the village in which the subclan is an owner (Powell 1956:49).

Not only do subclan members share a myth of origin for the subclan as a unit, but they also share a belief that the birth of individual members of the subclan is caused by the entry of a "spirit child" (*waywaya*) into a woman's womb where blood has gathered. The spirit child is always the reincarnation of one of the woman's subclan ancestors. It is the activating force, the real cause of conception, although there are several necessary preconditions to conception which usually have to do with the role of the father—i.e., the "opening the way" and "stopping the blood" usually accomplished by intercourse—but which, since they are not thought to be sufficient causes, are mechanical processes which could be accomplished in other ways (Austen 1934–35; Malinowski 1929b:179–86). The *baloma* (spirit of the dead) who sometimes brings the child to the mother may apparently be either a matrilineal kinsman or a cognate (Malinowski 1948:216–17; 1929b:173–77). Powell was told that this account of conception was "men's talk," used in "formal" (i.e., jurally relevant) situations. Another account, "women's talk," which is equally "true" but "different," will be discussed below under "affinity and paternity" (Powell 1956:277–78).

In addition to being "caused" by reincarnated subclan spirits, subclan members are thought to share a common substance, blood, which is passed from mother to children. The mother feeds the child in the womb, and therefore, " 'The mother makes the child out of her blood'. . . . 'Brothers and sisters are of the same flesh, because they come of the same mother' " (Malinowski 1929b:4). Subclan members say, when children are born into the subclan, " 'The kinsmen rejoice, for their bodies have become stronger when one of their sisters or nieces has plenty of children' " (Malinowski 1929a:170, as quoted in Powell 1956:372). On the other hand, when a subclan member dies, it is " 'as if a limb were cut off, or a branch lopped from a tree' " (Malinowski 1929b:150). It may be noted that although subclan members and even clan kinsmen are thought to be related by "blood" (though the latter distantly), the relationship is not emphasized through the tracing of genealogy, either among subclan members (Malinowski 1965:345; Powell 1956:98–100) or among the founding ancestors of the various subclans of the same clan (Powell 1956:45–49).

Matrilineal kinsmen, whether subclan or clan members, are designated by the term *veyagwa* or in Malinowski's transcription *veyogu,* which is glossed by Powell as "my kinsfolk" (1956:191) and by Malinowski as "my kinsmen" (1929b:495, 501). Malinowski notes that this term "has an emotional colouring of cold duty and pride" (1926:115). The term may be further specified as *veyagwa mokwita* or "true" matrilineal kinsmen, referring to fellow subclan members, and *kakaveyagwa* or "pseudo" matrilineal kinsmen (Powell 1956:191; Malinowski 1929b:499, 513–14), referring to fellow clan members. It should also be understood that the term *mokwita* has been glossed "true" or "own" but suggests a special and close relationship. For example, a man who gardens for his classificatory sister and her husband tends to be regarded as "own" brother, in addition to non-classificatory brothers (Powell 1956:385). Furthermore, adopted parents and children are regarded as "true" or "own" kin, since the distinction "own" refers to children reared without regard to adoption (Powell 1956:374).[6] Thus, feeding a person tends to make him one's "own" kin.

The theme of common or shared substance is carried through rituals also. For example, at the death of a kinsman, those of similar substance (those matrilineally related) fall under a taboo which prohibits their touching the corpse or dealing with it in any way. This is a logical taboo, since it is believed that disease and death are caused by the *bwaulo,* a material exhalation like mist, invisible to all but sorcerers and witches, an element which issues from the corpse and which might harm others of the same substance (Malinowski 1929b:150).

Some of the implications of the symbols of matriliny are jural, stemming from the fact that loyalty to fellow sub-clan members is expected from those who share "blood," even if such support is detrimental to personal position. For example, in disputes in which subclan concerns are thought to be at stake (primarily those of a jural or ritual nature), support is expected from all members, both resident and non-resident, even if the latters' privilege of residing in another village is jeopardized (Powell 1956:108–09). Distinctions are made, however, between cases involving subclan interests and cases which are considered to involve private persons. In the latter cases, subclan members are free to express their solidarity through support or not as they choose, since it is not conceived to be a subclan matter. Such a case would be exemplified by the defense a man makes against sorcery accusations, unless the accusations were made by affines, in which case it would be a subclan matter (Powell 1956:110–11). The series of rights and obligations attendant upon affines, including the presentation of *urigubu,* the annual harvest gift, is conceived to be a responsibility of the subclan, which may then delegate responsibilities to members.

Common substance also symbolizes the privileges of subclan membership. To the extent that rank is ascribed in Trobriand society, it is determined by subclan membership, not clan membership (Malinowski 1929b:500). The right of land owning is also vested in subclan members, for only these may hold permanent title to land. The headmanships and chieftainships are also vested in the subclan and can be held only by certain subclans. How these rights and obligations are actually worked out is discussed in the following section.

Jural Aspects

As the Trobrianders themselves state, the subclan is the jurally and politically significant unit in their society:

As an informant put it, "A man's rank, his land, his wealth are those of his subclan; so are his renown *(butura)* and his power in the land." (Powell 1956:432)

That is, membership in a subclan determines to some extent a man's rank, his possibilities for becoming headman or chief, and excludes as marriage possibilities the women of his own subclan and clan. Since wealth, prestige, and power may all be increased by land ownership, obtaining land is a concern of diligent and ambitious young men, who, through making *pokala,* attempt to gain rights to land. *Pokala* is a system in which gifts and services are given to senior men, in or outside the subclan, with the intent of inducing them to give property or title to property, including land, to the one making *pokala* (Malinowski 1961:185–86; Powell 1956:416). Apparently it is usually only the industrious and enterprising who acquire land, for by no means all adult men own land. (Powell found that of 73 men in one village, 28 or 30 percent had no garden plots of their own. He further estimated that only about 10 percent of the total garden land belonging to a subclan was held by individuals other than the headman or chief, 1956:421–22.) Furthermore, land can be permanently transferred only to those within the subclan. Although a man can obtain the use of his father's land, this privilege is generally abrogated upon the father's death and certainly is terminated at the death of the son, at which point the original owning subclan reclaims it (Malinowski 1932:177). A man may also obtain land use privileges from his wife's subclan, in which case he may pass the lands to his sons by that wife (Powell 1956:418).

By demonstrating his abilities a man may eventually become a headman, but this is only possible if his subclan is the "senior" in its village. Otherwise there is no opportunity for him. Within the subclan there is often intense competition, particularly for chieftainships (Powell 1960).

Marriage as well as sexual relations are prohibited within the subclan by the *suvasova* taboo, which in theory applies to all matrilineal kinsmen, hence to clansmen as well as subclansmen. However, while close matrilineal kin are "dangerous," distant kin (i.e., clan kin) are less so; some marriages are reported among clan, but none among subclan, kin. Amorous intrigues between subclan kin are considered especially "piquant" (Powell 1956:152; Malinowski 1929b: 510). At a woman's marriage, her subclan as a unit takes on the responsibility of presenting *urigubu* (the annual harvest gift) to her husband, as a representative of his subclan.

each woman when married must be gardened for by at least one man of her subclan; preferably he should be of the same generation, and ideally he should be an own or personal brother . . . , but there is no rule that he must be. (Powell 1956:387)

This practice is put to political use by chiefs who take many wives and therefore receive more *urigubu* than ordinary men, and these gifts in turn may be used to further enhance their prestige and influence. The case of the chief makes it especially evident that it is the subclans which are the units involved in the exchange and in the marriage obligations rather than merely particular individuals. Furthermore, at the death of one of his wives, a chief will take another wife from her subclan in order to maintain the alliance between the subclans, which in his case is largely political. When a chief dies, his successor renews the alliances with the former chief's affines by marrying his wives or by marrying girls from their subclans (Malinowski 1929b:133–41; Powell 1956:288–89).

Affinity and Paternity

In the discussion of problems of interpretation, it was noted that the paternal relationship has been characterized as a relation of affinity. The validity of such a characterization may be determined by an examination of the symbolic aspects of both paternity and affinity. If the two are to be placed in the same category, it should be expected that the symbolic aspects accommodate each other, or at any rate are not incompatible. If this is not the case, alternative interpretations must be offered.

It is my hypothesis that the affinal relationship is treated by the Trobrianders as being one which links subclans rather than private individuals in a series of rights and obligations. Robinson has sought to show otherwise in her analysis of the gift exchanges which validate a marriage, by interpreting the roles of the fathers of the marriage partners as those of patrifiliation (Robinson 1962:127–37; Malinowski 1929b:89–94). However, the evidence upon which she bases her conclusions is ambiguous. Robinson has based her analysis of the gift exchanges upon a table given by Malinowski (1929b:89), but by comparing his comments in the text with the table, I have found that "father" becomes at times "girl's family" (1929b:91) and "girl's parents" (1929b:92), or in one case "he [the boy] and his family" (1929b:92). Nor is the term "family" defined. In short, it is difficult, if not impossible, to understand which persons are involved in the transactions, let alone their statuses. It seems to me that there are other possible interpretations of Malinowski's data. First, the fathers of the boy and girl might participate as affines of the mothers' subclans, since one of the major affinal duties is assistance in ceremonials (Malinowski 1929b:126–27; Powell 1956:411). Indeed, in two cases, in the redistribution of *pepe'i* and the *takwalela pepe'i* gifts, the boy's father's "own relatives" are involved; this suggests that his affinal status to the boy's subclan accounts for his participation (Malinowski 1929b:90–92). A second reason for father's participation might be his concern, as a private individual, not as a representative of his subclan, for his child's social welfare and prestige. Hence the anxiety on the part of two fathers, whose own prestige is also reflected by that of their sons and daughters, as to the worthiness and quality of the *vilakuria* gift and its return. Both fathers were of high rank (Malinowski 1929b:94).

The terminology used by Trobrianders may help to clarify their conception of the affinal relationship. The term designating affines, *da veivaisi,* is used to refer to all the affines of all the members of a subclan rather than to distinguish an individual's own affines from his subclan's affines (Powell 1956:192).

Marriage is a temporary alliance, undertaken and terminated at the will of the individuals involved (divorce) or at death, whereupon affinal ties are abrogated, except when another marriage links the same two subclans, in which case the affinal ties remain:

Should Ego's marriage end through the death of his wife, the formal affinal relationship between his and her subclans established by his marriage terminates also, and, after the transitional period of mourning during which he is termed *tovaleta* (formal mourner) by the members of her subclan, he and they become strangers (*tomakava*) to one another, unless there already exists another marriage between members of the two subclans. (Powell 1956:335–36)

Thus, the relationship between subclans takes precedence over the relationship between individuals at the termination of marriage. Divorce is generally easy and relatively frequent, particularly in the early years of marriage. The exceptions to this are marriages to chiefs, which are often maintained by subclan pressure encouraging women to stay married to the chief (Powell 1956:354–55; 362–65). The chief's system of alliances through polygyny was mentioned above.

Urigubu, the annual harvest gift, is one of the many obligations and duties which relate affinal subclans. Malinowski interpreted this annual harvest gift as having the primary or essential meaning of "a gift offered by real, i.e., matrilineal, kinsmen of the wife," and several secondary meanings to include various other kinsmen and non-kin, an interpretation which resulted in his categorization of *urigubu* into seven separate kinds of gift (1965:392). It is important here to note that while Malinowski counted seven kinds of *urigubu,* the Trobrianders themselves count only one. All the gifts given to "fill up the yam house" are termed *urigubu* (Malinowski 1965:188–96). *Urigubu* is also used by the Trobrianders to refer to the plot set aside for the growing of the gift yams over which special magic is spoken, the heaps of yams at harvest which are ceremonially displayed, and the gift itself. The gift yams are placed in the open ceremonial storehouses, to which the term *dodige bwayma,* "filling up the yam house," refers. Since it is a disgrace for a grown man to fill his own yam house, it must be filled by someone else, preferably an affine; but in cases where an affine is lacking, a matrilineal kinsman, a son, or even WF may do it. From the point of view of the individual Trobriander, *urigubu* is given for a variety of reasons. For example, a man who gardens for his parents, when asked why he does so, may answer either "because of my mother" or "mother's brother"; or "because of my father," by which he may mean in the first case that he gardens to fulfill his obligation to his mother or as an act of *pokala* (service rendered with a view to reward) to MB; and in the second case, he may mean that he gives *urigubu* either because of the personal relationship between him and his father or as a member of his subclan who gardens for an affine (Powell 1956:393). The answer depends upon the point of view of both the individual and his subclan. *Urigubu,* then, appears to be: (1) a gift which "fills up the yam house," (2) a gift preferably given by affines, but not necessarily, and (3) when given by affines, considered a subclan rather than a personal responsibility.

There are also other duties and obligations characteristic of affinity, such as assistance in building houses and canoes, in conducting fishing expeditions and ceremonies. In certain circumstances affines support each other in feuds, as they do in illness when they keep watch against sorcerers. The relationship is ideally one of helpfulness and assistance (Malinowski 1929b:126–27; Powell 1956:411): "Indeed one of the advantages of gardening for a sister is according to the native that by so doing a man obtains a 'friend' and 'helper' in her husband" (Powell 1956:369). Powell reports that, in fact, most commoner relationships are such; but rivalry tends to occur between affines of political importance, since each subclan leader attempts to maximize his position as a man of wealth and power at the expense of his affines (1956:369).

If the affinal relationship is defined by the Trobrianders in terms of relations between subclans, then the question may arise as to the symbolic character of the relationship. The symbolic aspects are suggested by ritual and linguistic evidence. First, the distinction between matrilineal kinsmen and affines is symbolized at funeral rites in terms of a kind of "natural" versus "artificial" contrast:

they [the affines] are not grieving for a loss which affects their own sub-clan *(dala)* and therefore their own persons. Their grief is not spontaneous like that of the *veyola* (maternal kinsmen), but a duty almost artificial, springing as it does from acquired obligations. Therefore, they must ostentatiously express their grief, display it, and bear witness to it by outward signs. (Malinowski 1929b:151)

The contrast appears to be at two levels—one, involving the loss of a person of "similar substance" as opposed to loss of a person with whom there is not such a fundamental natural bond; and the second, involving obligations and duties, the essence of subclan membership being the inherent responsibilities of members as opposed to the acquired obligations between affines. Subclan kinsmen, and indeed clan kinsmen, are not allowed to display formal ritual signs of mourning or to perform mortuary duties. But they must pay for having the duties performed. The affines perform the duties, bury the corpse, and display their grief by formal signs, since their grief is not "natural." For the same reasons, affines become the principal suspects in sorcery cases, while matrilineal kinsmen are excepted "naturally" by virtue of their relation to the deceased (Malinowski 1929b:151–61).

In the discussion of the marriage bond, the contingent character of affinity was suggested. This character is reaffirmed by linguistic usage. The Trobrianders use two forms of the possessive with kinship terms—unconditional and conditional. The unconditional form is used with most kinship terms and connotes an involuntary and non-contingent relationship between possessor and possessed. This form is also used with parts of the body. The conditional possessive indicates a voluntary and contingent relationship between possessor and possessed, based upon the will of one or both. This form is used only with the terms for husband and wife (which terms are applied only to a current spouse) and with the collective term for relatives-in-law, *da veivaisi,* which includes the spouse, (Powell 1956:260–61). The fact that the conditional is reserved for the general category of relatives-in-law but the unconditional for specific affinal kin types (as brother-in-law, sister-in-law, etc.) may be explained as follows: Marriage is contingent upon the will of husband and wife. The relationship between all affines except spouses is not contingent upon their relationship but upon the marriage which relates them. That is, the relationship between any particular in-laws (except husband and wife) is not directly contingent upon the relationship between these two in-laws (possessor and possessed) but upon the couple involved in the linking marriage. Given the marriage, the relation of in-laws to each other is not contingent, but involuntary and unconditional.

Relations of affinity, then, are ultimately symbolized by marriage, which is contingent upon the wills of those involved and which may also be ended by death: hence, the relationship is dissolvable. While it obtains, the relationship of affines is supposed to be one of helpfulness and "friendship," which directly contrasts with relationships between matrilineally related people:

But this word [*lubayla* = "his friend"] may only be applied to a man's friend from another clan, and it is not only incorrect, but even improper, to use it of a kinsman. Whenever I used the expression *lubaym* (thy friend) to denote a man's close companion from the same clan, I was rather sharply corrected. (Malinowski 1929b;501)

Affinity is associated with acquired, terminable obligations.

What then is the character of the paternal relation? Malinowski claims that the Trobrianders characterize father as "mother's husband," and that this is one indication of father's affinal status.

What does the word *tama* (father) express to the native? "Husband of my mother" would be the answer first given by an intelligent informant. He would go on to say that his *tama* is the man in whose loving and protecting company he has grown up. (Malinowski 1929b:6)

If this is an indication of how the question was asked of the informant, it is no wonder that the answer to "what does the word 'father' mean?" is "mother's husband." The answer should not imply the affinity of father and child, since many Americans give the same answer to the question. If the status of father as mother's husband were the significant one, one mother's husband should be as good as another, but such is not the case:

it is recognized that socially the best father for a child is the man who was married to the mother at the time of its birth, since he is likely to have a closer personal interest in the child than any other. (Powell 1956:359)

The fact that father is sometimes designated *tomakava* ("outsider" or "stranger") is taken to be an indicator of father's affinal status (Malinowski 1929b:5–7). The term *tomakava* on the one hand is used in discussions of the personal relationship between father and child:

The father, in all discussions about relationship, was pointedly described to me as *tomakava,* a "stranger," or, even more correctly, an "outsider." This expression would also frequently be used by natives in conversation when they were arguing some point of inheritance or trying to justify some line of behaviour, or again when the position of the father was to be belittled in some quarrel. (Malinowski 1929b:5)

On the other hand, it is used in discussions concerning subclan membership, which involves a relationship of affinity, as we have seen (see quotation from Powell 1956:335–36, above). The marriage existing between subclans makes all members of both subclans affines to one another, regardless of the status of particular individuals. Thus, a man is *veivaisi* ("member of a subclan linked affinally to one's own") to his wife's

(and hence his children's) subclan; when the marriage is terminated, he becomes *tomakava* ("member of a subclan not linked affinally to one's own") to them. However, a man may also be considered independently of his subclan, in private relationships. Hence, a man may be *tomakava* (in this sense, "non-member of my subclan or clan") to his son, but not his son's subclan if the man and the boy's mother are still married. *Tomakava* may also be used within the context of village residence, when it is used to distinguish "owners" from "non-owners" (Malinowski 1929b:7; Powell 1956:52, 44). In this instance the "outsiders" or "non-owners" may be clan kinsmen, affines, or cognates.[7] In all cases, *tomakava* seems to suggest a non-jural relationship—that is, in whatever context cited, whether inheritance, marriage bonds, or ownership of land, it seems to indicate someone with no jural rights in that particular situation. It should be noted that in disputes which involve only rights of private individuals, such as the ownership of palm trees, the relation between father and child is not that of "strangers:"

when listening to an argument over the ownership of a betel palm, the father [was] claiming a tree said to belong to his daughter, whose mother he had divorced. The people who were close by considered that the father "had no shame" in disputing the ownership of a tree which his daughter, whom he had helped to develop in the womb, was, rightly or wrongly, claiming as her own. (Austen 1934–35:112)

If the paternal relation, then, is not necessarily one of affinity, it must be asked what else it is. The bond between "own father" and child is symbolized by common appearance. Children look like their father:

Not only is it a household dogma, so to speak, that a child never resembles its mother, or any of its brothers and sisters, or any of its maternal kinsmen, but it is extremely bad form and a great offense to hint at any such similarity. *To resemble one's father, on the other hand, is the natural, right, and proper thing for a man or woman to do.* (Malinowski 1929b:204; emphasis mine)

This relationship is directly contrasted to relationships of "blood," since no matrilineal kinsman may be said to resemble another. Two brothers may not resemble one another, for they are matrilineal kin, but both resemble their father. The matrilineal tie takes symbolic precedence over the agnatic one, so that, in order to relate father's brother's children, the relationship must be traced, as one of appearance, through father's father. Father and his brother each resemble father's father, but not each other; father's brother's children resemble their respective fathers, who in turn resemble their father. Thus the line of shared appearance runs from FF to F to FCh and from FF to FB to FBCh. This is not to say that the Trobrianders in fact trace this line, but they do consider father's brother's children as "relatives" (Powell 1956: diagram 6).

The reasons given for paternal resemblance fall into two categories, one of which traces the relationship back to the personal relation between father and mother: "'Put some soft mash (*sesa*) on it [the palm of the hand], and it will mould like the hand. In the same manner, the husband remains with the woman and the child is moulded'" (Malinowski 1929b:207).[8] The second type of reason attributes the relationship to the

"nursing" (*kopo'i*) of the child by the father:

In fact, nursing the baby in the arms or holding it on the knees, which is described by the native word *kopo'i,* is the special role and duty of the father (*tama*). It is said of the children of unmarried women who, according to the native expression, are "without a *tama*" . . . , that they are "unfortunate" or "bad" because "there is no one to nurse and hug them (*gala taytala bikopo'i*)." Again, if anyone inquires why children should have duties towards their father, who is a "stranger" to them, the answer is invariably: "because of the nursing (*pela kopo'i*)," "because his hands have been soiled with the child's excrement and urine." (Malinowski 1929b:20–21)

It should also be noted that the story of conception, labelled "women's talk" by the Trobrianders who told it to Powell, gives the father a more intimate role in the creation of his children than does "men's talk." According to "women's talk" the semen acts as a coagulant of the menstrual blood to form a clot which is "quickened" or caused to grow by the entry of a spirit child. It is told by "fathers or their sisters" to "children as they became old enough to take more than a childish sexual interest in the opposite sex" (Powell 1956:278). Father may now be seen as a "co-contributor" to the "being" of his children without discussion of physiological knowledge (Scheffler 1965).[9] As co-contributor to his daughter's being, it is then understandable that the father should be considered a wrong sexual partner for his "own" daughter, even though he is not prohibited by the formal *suvasova* taboo on matrilineal kinsmen (Malinowski 1929b:529–36).[10]

The relationship between father and children is symbolized in ritual, where the special relation father-protector-fertility is brought out. At his daughter's pregnancy, her father goes to a sorceress known to possess black magic which could harm the girl and makes a payment to her to ward off any evil intent; the girl's subclan gives him the payment (Malinowski 1929b:224; Robinson 1962:143). The same father-protector-fertility relation applies to the fertility of the son's gardens. In magic spells, the father is called upon to insure the fertility of the garden, which is symbolized by a pregnant woman (Robinson 1962:148–49).

The affection of father and child for one another is also given as the reason for the performance of duties considered unpleasant by both fathers and sons. Fathers care for small children, removing their excrement, which is considered an unpleasant task (Malinowski 1929a:444). Sons "suck their father's bones," a repugnant duty, at their father's funeral (Malinowski 1948:50): "'it is right that a child should suck the father's ulna, for the father has held out his hand to its excrement and allowed it to make water on to his knee'" (Malinowski 1929b:156).

The symbol of the relation of paternity is shared appearance, a characteristic which is unalterable and which does not disappear upon the death of the father or divorce of parents (Malinowski 1929b:207). The symbolic character of paternity, then, is not compatible with that of affinity, which is a relationship of contingency and terminability. Rather, appearance is more like the symbol of matrilineal relation, "blood," in that it is not alterable or contingent and is transmitted from individual to individual. Father might better be characterized as a cognate than as an affine; and if this

were the case, it might be expected that: (1) the relationship between father's brother's children is formally similar to that between mother's sister's children, and (2) the children's relationship with father's kinsmen is maintained even after the death of the father. In fact, the kinship relation between FBCh and between MZCh is formally similar in that the same kinship terms are used for either—viz., "brother" and "sister" (*tuwa*/*bwada* = "elder and younger sibling of the same sex"; *luta* = "sibling of opposite sex" [from Powell 1956: diagram 6. Cf. Lounsbury 1965:161–62]). Furthermore, relations with father's kinsmen do not end with father's death:

after a man's death, his kinsmen and friends will come from time to time to visit his children in order to "see his face in theirs." They will give them presents, and sit looking at them and wailing. (Malinowski 1929b:207)

If father and son are cognates, as I have suggested, then how were they confused with affines to begin with? And are Malinowski and Powell both wrong? In the analysis above, it was seen that the Trobrianders themselves distinguish between situations in which a man is treated as a representative of his subclan and those in which he is a private person. Affinity was seen to be a relation in which subclan status is invoked. The question, "When is an affine not an affine?" must then be answered, "When his status is that of private individual." Paternity involves just such private individual status, which the Trobrianders themselves suggest by attributing to the relationship a highly personalistic character. Malinowski and Powell were not "wrong"; Malinowski simply did not distinguish between subclan and private person statuses systematically, and

Powell chose the perspective of that subclan while preserving the distinctions. I have tried to show that any given Trobriander may be at the same time (1) affine to his child's subclan and (2) father or cognate of his child.

Conclusions

The approach taken to the two problems addressed—the primary problem of the role of the father and the secondary one of the nature of *urigubu*—began by attempting to determine how the Trobrianders consider three basic kinds of relationship: matriliny, affinity, and paternity. Then, by examining the relevant symbols—the contrasts among them and the contexts in which they were used—it was found that an important collateral distinction which the Trobrianders make is that between the individual as a subclan representative and as a private person. This distinction was found to be analytically important, since status as subclan representative set the matrilineal and affinal relations apart from paternal ones, in which private individual status was invoked. Analysis of the content of the symbols of paternity and matriliny showed that the two might best be viewed as aspects of a cognatic dimension, to be opposed to affinity.

The symbols of matriliny and paternity are blood and appearance, both of which are unalterable, blood being associated with certain ascribed jural prerogatives and obligations, with loyalty and pride; and appearance with a highly personalistic relationship between father and child, which is characterized by love, protection, and nurturance, and moral rather than jural obligations. Since affinity is a contingent, conditional relationship associated with acquired obligations, it is not surprising that no symbols which are unalterable, "permanent" characteristics of individuals are reported connected with it, as there are with matriliny and paternity. It was suggested that the paternal relationship is better interpreted as that between cognates rather than affines. By considering the paternal relation as cognatic, the problem of the father's role in caring for his children and they for him (as in giving *urigubu* after the death of the mother), and the sexual prohibition between father and daughter become meaningful, whereas they do not if the father is considered an affine. *Urigubu* was seen as one of a series of obligations between affines, but it is not limited to presentations between affines.

The above analysis has tried to accomplish two things. First, it has, by examining the symbols of relationship for matriliny, affinity, and paternity, sought to clarify two problems in the Trobriand data, that of the father and that of *urigubu*. Second, it has, by using both Trobriand conceptions and anthropological distinctions, attempted to demonstrate the analytical utility of taking cultural factors into account.

Notes

1. The research for this paper was supported by a predoctoral fellowship (5-Fl-MH-24, 135-03) from the National Institute of Mental Health, United States Public Health Service. I am indebted to the following people for their valuable comments and criticisms: David M. Schneider, Gerald Sider, Fred Eggan, Paul Friedrich, F. G. Lounsbury, and Harold Scheffler.

2. Throughout Melanesia the constellation of political

authority and leadership centers around the institution of the "big man" (see Codrington 1891; Powell 1960; Sahlins 1962–63). Outstanding features of this institution are that leadership is largely achieved, to a greater or lesser degree independently of descent groups, and that big men tend to form nodes about which their cogniatic and affinal kin are interrelated both territorially and through networks of exchange and indebtedness. The role of the big man varies with his 'bigness"—that is, a man takes over additional functions as his prestige increases, but not all big men achieve the highest prestige level. This means that informal hierarchies may exist, with lesser big men deferring to greater, or allying with them for economic and political purposes.

3. I use the term "cognatic" to refer to a relationship traced either through males or females by persons who share "co-contributors." Mother and father are, in this case, to be thought of as "co-contributors" to their child's "being" rather than as "ancestors," in order to avoid connotations of "blood" kinship. The reasons for this become clear as the discussion progresses. The term "co-contributor" was suggested by Scheffler (1965).

4. One such incident cited by Malinowski involved a rivalry between the chief's son and his second eldest nephew who became involved in some litigation, resulting in the nephew's being sent to prison. The matrilineal kinsmen of the nephew, "owners" in the chief's village, required the son to leave (Malinowski 1926:102 ff.).

5. Robinson uses Fortes' definition of complementary filiation as "the essential link between a sibling group and the kin of the parent who does not determine descent" (Fortes 1953:33, as quoted in Robinson 1962:121).

6. Powell has suggested that possibly 50 percent of Trobriand children are adopted, principally by their own subclan kin, in which case the adopted parents and children become "own" kin (1956:128, 374). In cases of adoption the child apparently retains membership in the subclan of his birth (1956:383).

7. I am indebted to Harold Scheffler, who suggested an interpretation along these lines for the term involved (personal communication).

8. Austen (1934–35:112) reports similar reasons for the resemblance between father and child: "'When we two lie down together [a husband and wife] our breasts become hot. Because of the hot breasts of the man and the woman it is our child.'"

9. See also Schneider (1965a), who discusses the relationship between native beliefs about biology and kinship, and the scientific facts about it.

10. See Powell's account of a marriage between "distant" father and daughter (1956:117–18).

TWO

Kinship, Nationality, and Religion in American Culture: Toward a Definition of Kinship

David M. Schneider

Ideologies are based within culturally constituted notions of the "person." In *American Kinship* (1968), David Schneider demarcated the concept of the "person" as an object of analysis; there, Schneider characterized American kinship as a cultural system founded on the notions of ties of "substance" ("blood") and a shared "code for conduct." These concepts, respectively encompassed in American culture within the larger order of Nature and Law (or reason), define the links between people in terms of which kinship groups (the "family") are culturally constructed.

In this article, Schneider suggests that the native cultural domains of religion and nationality are structured similarly. Thus, three apparently separate areas of social life are seen to be undergirded— and produced by the natives through the use of—the same ideological form. In this paper Schneider provides a striking illustration of the ways concrete relations—here, relations of recruitment—result from the generalization of ideology. Ideological forms, in turn, are shown to be pervasive throughout the social order, rather than sharing the boundaries of specific institutions.

KINSHIP HAS TRADITIONALLY BEEN defined in anthropology in terms of certain concrete elements, relations of blood and marriage, or in terms of some set functional prerequisites to which those concrete elements are crucial. Thus Morgan deals with kinship in terms of relations of consanguinity and affinity, Malinowski in terms of how sexual relations are regulated and how the family is formed, that unit being defined as primarily concerned with the problems of reproduction, socialization, and social placement. Levy, in line with Malinowski, defines kinship with reference to the facts of biological relatedness and/or sexual relations, and his view is not very different from that of Gellner in this respect (Gellner 1957, 1960; Levy 1965; Malinowski 1930).

In these views the facts of biological relatedness and sexual relations are treated as scientifically demonstrable facts of life and the question that is asked centers on how the particular society organizes its cultural forms with respect to these facts of life. These facts

Reprinted by permission of the publisher from *Forms of Symbolic Action,* V. Turner, ed. (New Orleans, La.: American Ethnological Society, Tulane University, 1969), pp. 116–25.

are treated as having determinate or causal value, imposing certain sharp, clear limits on whatever forms may be posed with respect to them. Thus a tribe of Australian aborigines, the Trobriand or Yap islanders may deny the causal link between coitus and conception in their cultural forms, but if their beliefs call a complete halt to coitus it can be shown that they could hardly survive long as a society.

Whatever the legitimacy or productivity of this way of dealing with kinship, it seemed to me that there was another view which might be worth pursuing. This view is implicit in much anthropological thinking, but was made most explicitly to me by Parsons (1951). In this view culture is defined as a system of symbols and meanings. That is, any given culture is seen to consist in a system of units and their interrelations, and these contain the fundamental definitions of the nature of the world, of what life is like, of man's place in it. Instead of asking how a society is organized so as to assure its continuity over time, one asks instead of what units it is built, how these units are defined and differentiated, how they articulate one with another. And one asks what meanings such a state of affairs has and how those meanings may be spelled out into patterns for action.

Studying American kinship from this point of view yielded some results which proved to be rather different from those deriving from the traditional functional or the traditional "consanguinity and affinity" or "facts of biological relatedness and/or sexual relations" views. For indeed, the fundamental question was how kinship was defined in American culture, not the question of how those externally devised definitions partitioned the material of American culture.

The purpose of this paper is to ask whether the results of the study of American kinship from this point of view are of any value in helping us to understand the nature of kinship and to define it most usefully for analytic purposes.

Perhaps the most important point to be made about American kinship is that there is a fundamental distinction between the distinctive features of kinship on the one hand and the kinsman as a person on the other (Schneider 1968a). The former embodies those aspects which distinguish kinship from any other domain of American culture—the domain of kinship as distinct from commerce, politics, friendship, etc. Those features which distinguish kinship from other domains are necessarily present in any of its parts as these are further differentiated. Thus although mother, father, brother, and sister are all different kinds of kinsmen, each is a kinsman as against the storekeeper, the mayor, or the policeman, and as kinsmen all share the distinctive features of kinship.

The distinctive features of the domain of kinship in American culture can be abstracted from a consideration of the classification of the different kinds of relatives. There are two kinds of relatives in American culture: those related "by blood" and those related "by marriage."

"Blood" or blood-relationship is the outcome of a single act of sexual intercourse which brings together sperm and egg and creates a child. Mother and father are thus related to the child by the fact that they create it and that the child is created out of material substance which each contributes. "Blood" is thus a state of shared physical substance. This shared physical substance is an "objective fact of nature," a natural phenomenon, a concrete or substantive part of nature. And this "objective fact of nature" cannot be terminated for it endures. A blood relationship is a relationship of identity, and those who share a blood relationship share a common identity. The phrase "the same flesh and blood" is a statement of this.

Where "blood" is a substance, a material thing whose constitution is whatever it is that is really in nature, and a natural entity which endures and cannot be terminated, "marriage" is just the opposite. It is not a material thing or a substance in the same sense as biogenetic heredity is. It is not a "natural thing" in the sense of a material object found free in nature. As a state of affairs it is of course natural, but it is not in itself a natural object. And it is terminable by death or divorce. Where blood is a natural material, marriage is not; where blood endures, marriage is terminable; and since there is no such "thing" as blood of which marriage consists, and since there is no such material which exists free in nature, persons related by marriage are not related "in nature."

If relatives "by marriage" are not related "in nature" how are they related? They are related by "a relationship," that is, by the fact that they follow a particular code for conduct, a particular pattern for behavior. It is in this sense that a stepmother is not a "real" mother, not the genetrix, but she is in a mother-child relationship to her husband's child.

The distinctive feature which defines the order of blood relatives is blood, a natural substance and blood relatives are thus "related by nature." This, I suggest, is but a special instance within the larger class of *the natural order* of things as defined by American culture. That is, the natural order is the way things are in nature, and one special class of things in the natural order consists in blood relatives.

Correspondingly, the feature which alone distinguishes relatives "by marriage" or "in law" is their relationship, the pattern for their behavior, the code for their conduct. This, I suggest, is a special instance within the larger class of *the order of law,* which is opposed to *the order of nature*. The order of law is imposed by man and consists in rules and regulations, customs and traditions. It is law in its special sense, where a foster parent who fails to care properly for a child can be brought to court, and it is law in its most general sense of law and order, custom, the rule of law, the government of action by morality and the restraint of human reason.

The domain of kinship, then, consists of two major parts, and each of these parts is but a special case of the two major orders of which the world is composed, the order of nature and the order of law. And it is this, of course, which makes sense of the fact that those who are relatives "by marriage" are also called "in-laws," for they are related through the order of law, not through the order of nature.

In fact of course the complete typology of kinds of relatives distinguished by American culture is built out of these two elements; *relationship as natural substance* and *relationship as code for conduct.* These two elements combine to make three major categories as follows:

RELATIVES	NATURE	LAW
(1) In Nature: the natural child, the illegitimate child, the natural mother, etc.	+	−
(2) In Law: Husband, wife, step-in-law, etc.	−	+
(3) By Blood: father, mother, brother, sister, uncle, aunt, etc.	+	+

Blood is a matter of birth, birth a matter of procreation, and procreation a matter of sexual intercourse. Sexual intercourse as an act of procreation creates the blood relationship of parent and child and makes genitor and genetrix out of husband and wife. And sexual intercourse is an act in which and through which love is expressed; indeed, it is often called "making love," and love is an explicit cultural symbol in American kinship.

There are two kinds of love in American kinship. One can be called *conjugal love,* the other *cognatic love.* Conjugal love is erotic, having the sexual act as its concrete embodiment. Cognatic love, on the contrary is not an act but a state of affairs and marks the blood relationship, the identity of natural substance which obtains between parent and child. Cognatic love has nothing erotic about it. The conjugal love of husband and wife is the opposite of the cognatic love of parent, child, and sibling. One is the union of opposites, the other the unity which identities have, the sharing of bio-genetic substance.

It is the symbol of love which links conjugal and cognatic love together and relates them both to and through the symbol of sexual intercourse. Love in the sense of sexual intercourse is a natural act with natural consequences according to its cultural definition. And love in the sense of sexual intercourse at the same time stands for unity.

Finally, the contrast between home and work brings out aspects which complete the picture of the distinctive features of kinship in American culture. This can best be understood in terms of the contrast between love and money which stand for home and work. Indeed, what one does at home, it is said, one does for love, not for money, while what one does at work one does strictly for money, not for love. Money is material, it is power, it is impersonal and universalistic, unqualified by considerations of sentiment and morality. Relations of work and money are temporary, transient, contingent. Love on the other hand is highly personal and particularistic, and beset with considerations of sentiment and morality. Where love is spiritual, money is material. Where love is enduring and without qualification, money is transient and contingent. And finally, it is personal considerations which are paramount in love—who the person is, not how well he performs, while with work and money it does not matter who he is, but only how well he performs his task. Money is in this sense impersonal.

The facts of biological relatedness and sexual relations play a fundamental role in American kinship, for they are symbols, culturally formulated symbols in terms of which a system of social relationships is defined and differentiated. The beliefs about the facts of biological relatedness and sexual relations constitute a model in terms of which a series of conditions about the nature of kinship or about a domain of social relationships are stated. The statement of identity in terms of flesh and blood between mother and child, whatever significance the actual biological relations may have, is at the same time a symbolic statement of the kind of social relationship between them.

Once the symbolic significance of biological relatedness and sexual relations is perceived it becomes immediately apparent that an enormous number of other symbols might operate with almost equal effect for defining the domain of kinship and for providing for the internal differentiation of elements within that system.

And if it is indeed true that whatever it is that we are calling "kinship" might equally well be defined and differentiated in terms of any number of other symbols, we seem to have lost all hold on something we think of as "kinship in general," for if it could be anything how can it be something in particular?

But at this juncture there are some other important points to be made before we consider the question of definition. The problem that arises now is that of the boundary of the American kinship system. Where does kinship leave off and something else begin? Let us return to the problem with this question in mind.

The different symbols of American kinship seem to say one thing; they are all concerned with unity of some kind. The unity of those related by blood, of those joined in love, of the parent and child in the face of the child's growing up and going off to found a family of his own, of man and woman as husband and wife and so on. All of these different kinds of unity are expressed as the unity of substance or the unity required by a code for conduct.

Put somewhat differently, all of the symbols of American kinship seem to "say" one thing; they provide for relationships of diffuse, enduring solidarity. "Diffuse" because they are functionally diffuse rather than specific in Parsons' terms. That is, where the "job" is to get a specific thing "done" there is no such specific limitation on the aim or goal of any kinship relationship. Instead the goal is "solidarity," that is, the "good" or "well being" or "benefit" of ego with alter. Whatever it is that is "good for" the family, the spouse, the child, the relative, is the "right" thing to do. And "enduring" in the generalized sense symbolized by "blood"; there is no built-in termination point or termination date. Indeed, it "is" and cannot be terminated. But although a marital relationship can be terminated by death or divorce, it is, as the saying goes, "til death do us part;" it is supposed to endure and persevere and it is not to be regarded as transient or temporary or conditional.

The phrase "diffuse, enduring solidarity" is mine. The natives do not use it and although some of them understand it when I explain it to them, it falls like jargon on their ears. Which it should, of course, for that is just what it is.

Yet this generalization permits us to look at American culture and ask, Is this the only domain of diffuse, enduring solidarity? and see that the obvious answer is No! There are at least two others which obviously fit that description. One is called "nationality," the other "religion."

In American culture, one is "an American" either by birth or through a process which is called, appropriately enough, "naturalization." In precisely the same terms as kinship, there are the same two "kinds of citizens," those by birth and those by law. And indeed it would not be hard to show that the same three categories are derived from these two elements as three categories of kinsmen are derived from those elements. There is the person who is by birth an American but who has taken the citizenship of another country; there is the person who is American by naturalization but not by birth; and there is the person who by both birth and law is American.

What is the role of a national? To love his country, his father- or mother-land. Loyalty and support for his nation and all those who belong to it. Patriotism in the extreme of "My Country Right or Wrong" is one statement of it. But even where it does not take that particular form, loyalty to and love for one's country is the most generalized expression of diffuse, enduring solidarity.

I will not pursue this in any further detail. My point is not to demonstrate incontestably that kinship and nationality are structured in identical terms, but rather to make a plausible enough case for this so that we can consider its implications for the question of how to frame a useful definition of kinship.

One argument that might be presented against the view that kinship and nationality are structured in terms of the same set of symbols is that kinship contains things like family, uncle, in-laws, and so forth which do not have corresponding elements within the domain of nationality. States, counties, towns, and so forth do not seem at first glance like family, uncle, or in-laws, etc.

This argument brings us back to the opening statement in the description of American kinship; there is a fundamental difference between the distinctive features of kinship on the one hand and the relative as a person on the other.

As I have tried to show elsewhere (1968a:57–75), the structuring of the relative as a person is the outcome of the intersection of a series of different elements from different symbol systems of which kinship, age, sex, and class are but four among others, and only one of which is "kinship" in a "pure" sense. For example, not only is "father" a kinsman, but he is also male and the cultural definition of his maleness derives from the sex-identity symbol system; he is also older and those aspects of his definition as older derive from the age symbol system, and so forth.

What I am saying here is really quite simple but perhaps it appears to be somewhat radical. I am saying that what we have heretofore regarded as the single domain of kinship is really made up of two distinct domains. One is a "pure" domain of kinship *per se* which has as its defining element a single symbol, coitus (Schneider 1968a:30–54). The second is that domain which has traditionally been regarded as the domain of kinship, the system of person-based definitions. I believe that the importance of the difference between the "pure" domain of kinship and the "conglomerate" part has not been sufficiently appreciated.[1]

Now let us go back to the problem which is raised by comparing what seems at first glance to be the internal differentiation of the domains of kinship and nationality and finding them apparently quite disparate, the one being cast in apparently genealogical terms, the other in terms of states, cities, counties, and so on.

Once the distinction between the

"pure" and the "conglomerate" domains of kinship is appreciated, the same distinction can be applied to nationality. It is not nationality as it applies to what makes a person a resident of a county for purposes of meeting the relief requirements that is at issue. It is instead the comparison of the domains of kinship and nationality as "pure" domains, each defined in terms of a single symbol or a single set of closely interlocked symbols. At this level these are internally undifferentiated domains, and it is in these terms that their identity is being postulated.

Let us turn now to religion and consider the situation there. As a convenience, and purely for the purposes of this paper, I assume that "religion" means the Judeo-Christian tradition. I know that this hardly exhausts the many different beliefs that are to be found in America, not the least of which I call "devout atheism." But once again my aim is not to try to exhaust the material to show indisputably that kinship, nationality, and religion are all the same thing, but rather to build that case for what it may suggest with regard to the problem of defining kinship.

There is a special problem, too, in that there is a historical continuity to the relationship between the Jewish and Christian traditions. At the same time both co-exist in America and their co-existence as well as their historical relations pose special problems.

In the tradition of Judaism nation, state, and kinship group are one, and certainly the identity between kinship and nationality in Judaism is very clear. To be a Jew one's mother must be Jewish even if one's father is not and to be converted to Judaism is not an easy thing. Thus, the modern state of Israel has encountered a number of problems which arise from this special view that anyone who is by birth a Jew is also necessarily by nationality a Jew and correspondingly a Jew by religious definition.[2]

With Christianity, as is well known, the criterion for membership shifted from birth to volition. That is, in the most general sense, one is a Christian by an act of faith and not an act of birth, and correspondingly conversion to the Faith becomes a very different matter and a real possibility since it takes only an act of will to effect.

But this view leaves out two very important facts. Being a Jew is not simply being born a Jew. There is a code for conduct which is linked to the fact of birth. What is true is that it is the act of birth which has the quality of the defining feature, and so the other element tends to be easily overlooked. And it is here that the parallel between kinship and religion in Judaism is quite clear, for in both there are those two features, relationship as substance and relationship as code for conduct; the substance element is bio-genetic, the code for conduct is one of diffuse, enduring solidarity.

Although the shift from Judaism to Christianity seems to drop the condition of substance as the defining feature and rest it entirely on the commitment to the code for conduct, this is not really so. Certainly there is a shift away from the particularistic, biogenetic, criterion of substance as the defining features. But the shift entails a realignment so that commitment to the code for conduct becomes paramount as the defining feature, and the substantive element is redefined from a material to a spiritual form. It is the triumph of the spirit over matter that is at issue here. Closely linked to this is the prominent place given to love as a symbol, to the spiritual aspects of love, and to the spiritual aspects of creation as against its rather more narrowly material or biogenetic aspects in Judaism.

The prevalence of the symbol of "love" in Christianity, the prevalence of the use of kinship terms in Christianity, the importance of such concepts as "faith" and "trust" and "belief" all testify, to me at least, that the domain of religion may well be structured in the same terms as kinship and nationality, and the historical fact that Judaism is indeed so clearly defined as one nation, one religion, and one family suggests to me that there may be something in what I say.

Let me add one more point. If Judaism is the clearest and simplest case where kinship, religion, and nationality are all a single domain, then the transformation of Christianity centers on the separation of a natural and a supernatural element, so that kinship becomes differentiated as being based on relationship as natural substance, religion as relationship as supernatural (spiritual) substance. In other words, kinship and religion are more highly differentiated in Christianity than in Judaism, and this differentiation depends on a different form of the distinction between supernatural and natural.[3]

There is certainly no doubt in my mind that I am far out of my depth in this discussion. I am no theologian and have little command of this material. If I were pressed to spell this out in detail I would have to resign from the discussion. On the other hand, once again, I am merely trying to make a plausible enough case for the guess that religion (in the Judeo-Christian tradition) is defined in the same terms as kinship so that this can be taken into consideration in trying to reach a useful definition of kinship.

But once again we are faced with the problem of the double-domain, for at one level it is certainly indisputable that people tend to join the church of their parents and they are in this sense born to a church as they are born to a family, and this is hardly an act of volition at this level. And if one takes even a passing look at the bureaucratic organization of some churches or synagogues many of the highest ideals are systematically transformed into petty schismatic differences. The internal differentiation of any particular religious organization or set of beliefs is one thing; the domain of religion I would suggest quite another. There is the "pure" domain of religion which I am comparing to that of kinship and nationality and there is the internally differentiated "conglomerate" domain which I am not.

Let me summarize the argument briefly. From a close study of American kinship it seems clear that this particular system depends first on a distinction between the "pure" domain of kinship, defined in terms of the symbol of coitus and differentiated into two major aspects, relationship as natural substance and relationship as code for conduct, and a "conglomerate" domain of kinship, differentiated into "the family" on one hand and an articulated system of person-defined statuses (genealogical?) on the other.

If we consider only the "pure" domain of kinship and treat this as a system of diffuse, enduring solidarity, it seems possible that what is called "nationality" and "religion" are defined and structured in identical terms, namely, in terms of the dual aspects of relationship as natural substance and relationship as code for conduct, and that most if not all of the major diacritical marks which are found in kinship are also found in nationality and religion.

If this is true—and I repeat that I offer it only as a very tentative hypothesis—then it might well be that at the level of the "pure" domain, religion, nationality, and kinship are all the same thing (culturally), and that their differences arise through the kinds of combinations and permutations they enter into with other "pure" domains, and at the level of the "conglomerate" domain.

Thus far I speak only of American culture not from having carefully surveyed its precise boundaries, but precisely because I don't know what those boundaries are. Hence the next step is to generalize the view of American kinship, religion, and nationality and ask how widely applicable this view may or may not be to other cultures. At the moment, and from but a small grasp of world ethnography, I would hazard the guess that this generalized view will obtain fairly widely, but this remains an empirical question which can be answered only by concrete studies.

Finally, if all this proves true, the question arises of the utility of any definition of "kinship" until we have more fully explored the ways in which culture as a system of symbols and meanings is formed and its different parts articulated.

Notes

1. I have spoken here of two domains, one a "pure" and one a "conglomerate" domain. Perhaps it would be better to treat these as two parts of a single domain rather than as two different domains. But this is not my problem here, and so I will proceed simply as if the two domain mode of expression is adequate to the exposition here and leave to another time the question of one domain of two parts or two domains intimately linked.

2. This may be a convenient point to note that I have omitted from this paper considerations of race and racism, which cannot be omitted from any comprehensive or systematic review of this problem. I can refer the reader to Louis Dumont's brilliant discussions of this subject for its bearing on the questions before us and at the same time acknowledge the stimulus which his writings have provided for me, even when I have resisted his views. See his *Homo Hierarchicus* especially.

3. I think that I have absorbed this from Parsons somehow, but the closest form in which I have found the notion is in Parsons' article on Christianity (1968:427).

THREE

Caste, Racism, and "Stratification"
Reflections of a Social Anthropologist

LOUIS DUMONT

TO E. E. EVANS-PRITCHARD

Sociologists studying stratification have tended to lump all forms of inequality together. In this paper, Louis Dumont argues that because social theorists have viewed all societies from within the perspective of Western ideology, to which the notion of the autonomous individual is a central analytic concept, they have ignored variations in the valuation or understanding of inequality by social actors in different systems. As a consequence of this, in the study of Hindu caste, the ideological valuation of hierarchy in a holistic, rather than an individualistic, framework has been ignored: caste is thus seen, by a number of analysts, as an extreme form of racism.

Dumont here argues convincingly that it is not. Rather, when each form of inequality is viewed within the larger social formation in which it occurs, caste and racism can be seen as opposite modes of stratification: caste exists within and reaffirms a society which values hierarchy, while racism occurs as an exception in a society with an ideology based on individualistic egalitarianism. Thus, while inequality appears in both situations, it is ideologically stressed and transparent in caste society, but unstressed and opaque in class society, with radically different consequences for actors and for the system. Dumont's work, which takes cultural mediation seriously into account, constitutes an important step toward a truly critical anthropology—one which comprehends the analyst's own social order through the study of other forms of society and which uses the critical understanding of the analyst's society to inform the study of others. While there are several problems with his work in this area, Dumont has continued this critical enterprise with an interesting set of studies of Western individualism (Dumont 1965; 1970c).

IN A RECENT ARTICLE Professor Raymond Aron writes about sociology: "what there exists of a critical, comparative, pluralist theory is slight" (1960:29). This is indeed the feeling one has when, after studying the caste system in India, one turns to comparing it with other social systems and to seeing, in particular, how it has been accommodated within the theory of "social stratification" as developed in America. To

Reprinted by permission of the publishers from Louis Dumont, *Homo Hierarchus,* copyright © 1970, Chicago: University of Chicago Press, Appendix pp. 239–60; London: Weidenfeld and Nicholson, Appendix, pp. 239–58.

begin with, the problem can be put in very simple terms: is it permissible, or is it not, to speak of "castes" outside India? More particularly, may the term be applied to the division between Whites and Negroes in the southern states of the United States of America? To this question a positive answer has been given by some American sociologists[1]—in accordance with the common use of the word—while most anthropologists with Indian experience would probably answer it in the negative.[2] Ideally, this question might appear as a matter of mere terminological choice: either we accept the former alternative and adopt a very broad definition, and as a result we may have to distinguish subtypes, as some authors who have opposed the "racial caste" (U.S.A.) to the "cultural caste" (India); or we refuse any extension of the term and apply it exclusively to the Indian type precisely defined, and in this case other terms will be necessary to designate the other types. But in actual fact, a certain usage has been established, and perhaps it is only by criticizing its already manifest implications that a way can be opened to a better comparative view. I shall, therefore, begin by criticizing the usage which predominates in America in the hope of showing how social anthropology can assist sociology in this matter. Two aspects will particularly require attention: what idea the authors in question have formed of the Indian system, and which place they give to the concept of "caste" in relation to neighboring concepts such as "class" and to the broad heading of "social stratification" under which they often group such facts. Thereafter I shall tentatively outline the framework of a true comparison.

Caste As an Extreme Case of Class: Kroeber

A definition of caste given by Kroeber is rightly regarded as classical, for the whole sociological trend with which I am concerned here links up with it.

In his article on "Caste" in the *Encyclopaedia of Social Sciences* (III, 1930, 254b–57a), he enumerates the characteristics of caste (endogamy, heredity, relative rank) and goes on to say: "*Castes, therefore, are a special form of social classes,* which in tendency at least are present in every society. Castes differ from social classes, however, in that they have emerged into social consciousness to the point that custom and law attempt their rigid and permanent separation from one another. *Social classes are the generic soil from which caste systems have at various times and places independently grown up . . .*" [my italics].

By "caste systems" he means in what follows, apart from India, medieval Europe and medieval Japan. He implicitly admits, however, that the last two cases are imperfect: either the caste organization extends to only a part of the society, or, as in the Japanese "quasi-caste system," the division of labor and the integration with religion remain vague.

For us, the essential point here is that "caste" is considered as an extreme case of "class." Why? Probably in the first place because of the "universality of anthropology," as Lloyd Warner says while accepting Kroeber's definition.[3] In the second place, because "caste" is at once rigid and relatively rare, whereas "class" is more flexible, vaguer, and relatively very widespread. But the problem is only deferred, for in such a perspective it should be necessary to define "class," which is much more difficult than to define "caste." Never mind, "class," after all, is familiar to us, while "caste" is strange . . . We are landed at the core of the socio-centricity within which the whole school of authors under discussion develops. Actually, if one were prepared to make light of the relative frequency with which the supposed "class" occurs, and if one were solely concerned with conceptual clarity, the terms could just as well be reversed, and one could start from the Indian caste system, which offers in a clear and crystalline form what is elsewhere diluted and blurred in many ways. The definition quoted reduces a society's consciousness of itself to an epiphenomenon—although some importance is attached to it: "They have emerged into social consciousness." The case shows that to do this is to condemn oneself to obscurity.

Distinction between Caste, Estate, and Class

The oneness of the human species, however, does not demand the arbitrary reduction of diversity to unity, it only demands that it should be possible to pass from one particularity to another, and that no effort should be spared in order to elaborate a common language in which each particularity can adequately be described. The first step to that end consists in recognizing differences.

Before Kroeber gave his definition, Max Weber had made an absolute distinction between "class" and *Stand,* "status group," or "estate" in the sense of pre-revolutionary France—as between economy on the one hand and "honor" and "social intercourse" on the other.[4] His definition of class as an economic group has been criticized, but it has the merit of not being too vague. Allowing that social classes as commonly referred to in our societies have these two aspects, the analytical distinction is none the less indispensable from a comparative point of view, as we shall see. In Max Weber as in Kroeber, caste represents an extreme case; but this time it is the status group which becomes a caste when its separation is secured not only through convention and laws, but also ritually (impurity through contact). Is this transition from status group to caste conceived as genetic or only logical? One notes in passing that, in the passage of *Wirtschaft und Gesellschaft* which I have in view here, Weber thinks that individual castes develop some measure of distinct cults and gods—a mistake of Western common sense which believes that whatever can be distinguished must be different. Into the genesis of caste, Weber introduces a second component, namely a reputedly ethnic difference. From this point of view, castes would be closed communities *(Gemeinschaften),* endogamous and believing their members to be of the same blood, which would put themselves in society *(vergesellschaftet)* one with the other. On the whole, caste would be the outcome of a conjunction between status group and ethnic community. At this juncture a difficulty appears. For it seems that Weber maintains the difference between *Gesellschaft* and *Gemeinschaft:* on the one hand the *Vergesellschaftung* of a reputedly ethnic group, a "Paria people," tolerated only for the indispensable economic services it performs, like the Jews in medieval Europe, on the other the *Gemeinschaft* made up of status groups or, in the extreme case, of castes. If I am not mistaken, the difficulty emerges in the concluding sentence, which has to reconcile the two by means of an artificial transition from the one to the other: "Eine umgreifende *Vergesellschaftung* die ethnisch geschiedenen Gemeinschaften zu einem spezifischen, politischen *Gemeinschaftshandeln* zusammenschliesst" [my italics], or, freely translated, "the *societalization* of ethnically distinct communities embraces them to the point of uniting them, on the level of political action, in a *community* of a new kind." The particular group then acknowledges a hierarchy of honor and at the same time its ethnic difference becomes a difference of function (warriors, priests, etc.). However remarkable the conjunction here achieved among hierarchy, ethnic difference, and division of labor may be, one may wonder whether Weber's failure is not due to the fact that to a hierarchical view he added "ethnic" considerations through which he wanted to link up widespread ideas on the racial origin of the caste system with the exceptional situation of certain minority communities like Jews or Gypsies in Western societies.

What remains is the distinction, as analytical as one could wish, between economic group and status group. In the latter category, one can then distinguish more clearly as Sorokin did,[5] between "order" or "estate" and caste. As an instance, the clergy in pre-revolutionary France did not renew itself from within, it was an open "estate"

"Caste" in the U.S.A.

At first sight there is a paradox in the works of the two most notable authors who have applied the term "caste" to the separation between Whites and Negroes in the U.S.A. While their purpose is to oppose the "colour line" to class distinctions, they both accept the idea that caste is a particular and extreme form of class, not a distinct phenomenon. We have seen that Lloyd Warner accepts Kroeber's idea of continuity; however he immediately insists, as early as his article of 1936, that while Whites and Negroes make up two "castes," the two groups are stratified into classes according to a common principle, so that the Negroes of the upper class are superior from the point of view of class to the small Whites, while at the same time being inferior to them from the point of view of "caste" (Warner and Davis 1936:234–37). Gunnar Myrdal also states that "caste may thus in a sense be viewed as the extreme form of absolutely rigid class," in this sense "caste" constitutes "a harsh deviation from the ordinary American social structure and the American Creed."[6] The expression "*harsh* deviation" is necessary here to correct the idea of continuity posited in the preceding sentence. In other words, the supposed essential identity between class and caste appears to be rooted in the fact that, once equality is accepted as the norm, any form of inequality appears to be the same as any other because of their common deviation from the norm. We shall see presently that this is fully conscious, elaborately justified in Myrdal. But if, from the standpoint of comparative sociology, one purports to describe these forms of inequality in themselves and if, moreover, one finds that many societies have a norm of inequality, then the presumed unity between class on the one hand and the American form of discrimination on the other becomes meaningless, as our authors themselves sufficiently witness.

The use of the term "caste" for the American situation is justified by our two authors in very different ways. For Myrdal, the choice of a term is a purely practical matter. One should take a word of common usage—and not try to escape from the value judgments implicit in such a choice. Of the three available terms, "class" is not suitable, "race" would give an objective appearance to subjective justifications and prejudices, so there remains only "caste" which is already used in this sense, and which can be used, in a monographic manner, without any obligation to consider how far it means the same thing in India and in the U.S.A.[7] In point of fact, the pejorative coloration of the word by no means displeases Myrdal. While the word "race" embodies a false justification, the word "caste" carries a condemnation. This is in accordance with American values as defined by the author in the following pages. The American ideology is egalitarian to the extreme. The "American Creed" demands free competition, which from the point of view of social stratification represents a combination of two basic norms, equality and liberty, but accepts inequality as a result of competition.[8] From this one deduces the "meaning" of differences of social status in this particular country, one conceives classes as the "results of the restriction of free competition," while "caste," with its draconian limitations of free competition, directly negates the American Creed, creates a contradiction in the conscience of every White, survives only because of a whole system of prejudices, and should disappear altogether.

All this is fine, and the militant attitude in which Gunnar Myrdal sees the sole possibility of true objectivity could hardly be more solidly based. In particular, he has the merit of showing that it is in relation to values (a relation not expressed by Kroeber and Warner) that the assumed continuity of class and caste can be best understood. But was it really necessary in all this to use the word "caste" without scientific guarantee?[9] Would the argument have lost in efficacy if it had been expressed only in terms of "discrimination," "segregation," etc.? Even if it had, ought one to risk obscuring comparison in order to promote action? Gunnar Myrdal does not care for comparison. Further, does he not eschew comparative theory, in so far as he achieves his objectivity only when he can personally share the values of the society he is studying?

Unlike Myrdal, Lloyd Warner thinks that "caste" can be used of the southern U.S.A. in the same sense as it is used of India. This is seen from a "comparative study" by Warner and Allison Davis (Warner and Davis 1936), in which the results of their American study are summarized, "caste" defined, and two or three pages devoted to the Indian side. This Indian summary, though based on good authors, is not very convincing. The variability of the system in time and space is insisted upon to the point of stating that: "It is not correct to speak of an Indian caste system since there is a variety of systems there."

In general, caste here is conceived as a variety of class, differing from it in that it forbids mobility either up or down. The central argument runs as follows: in the Southern States, in addition to the disabilities imposed upon the Negroes and the impossibility for them to "pass," there is between Whites and Negroes neither marriage nor commensality; the same is true in India between different castes. It is the same kind of social phenomenon. "Therefore, for the comparative sociologist and social anthropoligist they are forms of behavior which must have the same term applied to them" (p. 233).

This formula has the virtue of stating the problem clearly, so that if we do not agree with Warner we can easily say why. A first reason, which might receive ready acceptance, is that under the label of "behavior pattern" or "social phenomena" Warner confuses two different things, namely a collection of particular features (endogamy, mobility and commensality prohibition, etc.) and a whole social system, "caste" in the case of India obviously meaning "the caste system." It is not asked whether the sum of the features under consideration is enough (to the exclusion of all the features left out of consideration) to define the social system: in fact there is no question of a system but only of a certain number of features of the Indian caste system which, according to the author, would be sufficient to define the system. There is really here a *choice* which there is no necessity to follow.[10]

Let me try to indicate the reasons against the proposed choice. It is generally admitted, at any rate in social anthropology, that particular features must be seen in their relations with other particular features. There follows, to my mind, a radical consequence—that a particular feature, if taken not in itself but in its concrete position within a system (what is sometimes called its "function"), can have a totally different meaning according to the position it occupies. That is to say, from a sociological standpoint it is *actually different*. Thus as regards the endogamy of a group: it is not sufficient to say that the group is "closed," for this very closure is perhaps not, sociologically speaking, the same thing in all cases; in itself it is the same thing, but in itself it is simply not a sociological fact, as it is not, in the first place, a conscious fact. One is led inevitably to the ideology, overlooked in the behavioristic sociology of Warner and others, which implicitly posits that, among the particular features to be seen in relation to each other, ideological features do not have the same status as the others. Nevertheless a great part of the effort of Durkheim (and of Max Weber as well) bore on the necessity of recognizing in them the same objectivity as in other aspects of social life. Of course this is not to claim that ideology is necessarily the ultimate reality of social facts and delivers their "explanation," but only that it is the condition of their existence.

The case of endogamy shows very clearly how social facts are distorted through a certain approach. Warner and Allison treat it as a fact of behaviour and not as a fact of values. As such it would be the same as the factual endogamy of a tribe having no prejudice against intermarriage with another tribe, but which given circumstances alone prevent from practicing it. If, on the contrary, endogamy is a fact of values, we are not justified in separating it in the analysis from other facts of values, and particularly—though not solely—from the justifications of it the people give. It is only by neglecting this that racial discrimination and the caste system can be confused. But, one might say, is it not possible that analysis may reveal a close kinship between social facts outwardly similar and ideologically different? The possibility can be readily admitted, but only to insist the more vigorously that we are as yet very far indeed from having reached that point, and that the task for the moment is to take social facts as they are given, without imposing upon them a discrimination scientifically as unwarrantable as is, in American society, the discrimination which these authors attack. The main point is that the refusal to allow their legitimate place to facts of consciousness makes true sociological comparison impossible, because it carries with it a sociocentric attitude. In order to see one's own society from without, one must become conscious of its values and their implications. Difficult as this always is, it becomes impossible if values are neglected. This is confirmed here from the fact that, in Warner's conceptual scheme, the continuity between class and caste proceeds, as we have seen, from an unsuspected relation to the egalitarian norm, while it is presented as a matter of behavior.

The criticism of the "Caste School of Race Relations" has been remarkably carried out by Oliver C. Cox (1918; 1945). From the same sources as Warner, Cox, with admirable insight, has evolved a picture of the caste system which is infinitely truer than that with which Warner was satisfied. It is true that one cannot everywhere agree with Cox, but we must remember that he was working at second and even at third hand (for instance, from Bouglé). Even the limits of Cox's understanding show up precisely our most rooted Western prejudices. He is insufficient mainly in what regards the religious moorings of the system (purity and impurity); because for the Westerner society exists independently of religion and he hardly imagines that it could be otherwise. On the other hand, Cox sees that one should not speak of the individual caste but of the system (pp. 3–4), and that it is not a matter of racial ideology: " . . . Although the individual is born heir to his caste, his identification with it is assumed to be based upon some sort of psychological and moral heritage which does not go back to any fundamental somatic determinant" (p. 5).

Elsewhere he writes (p. 14): "Social inequality is the keynote of the system . . . there is a fundamental creed or presumption (of inequality) . . . antithesis of the Stoic doctrine of human equality . . ." We see here how Cox strikes on important and incontrovertible points whenever he wishes to emphasize the difference between India and America. I will not enlarge on his criticism of Warner and his school; we have already seen that he makes the essential point: the Indian system is a coherent social system based on the principle of inequality, while the American "colour bar" contradicts the egalitarian system within which it occurs and of which it is a kind of disease.[11]

The use of the word "caste" to designate American racial segregation has led some authors, in an effort to recognize at the same time the ideological difference, to make a secondary distinction. Already in 1937 John Dollard was writing: "American caste is pinned not to cultural but to biological factors" (Dollard 1937; Davis 1941). In 1941, in an article called "Intermarriage in Caste Society" in which he was considering, besides India, the Natchez and the society of the Southern United States, Kingsley Davis asked: how is marriage between different units possible in these societies, while stratification into castes is closely dependent on caste endogamy? His answer was, in the main, that a distinction must be made between a "racial caste system" in which hybrids present an acute problem, and a "nonracial caste system" where this is not so. In India, hypergamy as defined by Blunt for the north of India, i.e., marriage between a man of an upper subcaste and a woman of a lower subcaste within the same caste can be understood in particular as a factor of "vertical solidarity" and as allowing for the exchange of prestige in return for goods (p. 386). (The last point actually marks an essential aspect of true hypergamy, in which the status or prestige of the husband as well as the sons is not affected by the relatively inferior status of the wife or mother.) Another difference between the two kinds of "caste systems" is that the "racial" systems rather oppose two groups only, whereas the other systems distinguish a great number of "strata." Finally, K. Davis remarks that the hypothesis of the racial origin of the Indian caste system is not proven and that at any rate it is not racial today (n. 22). It is strange that all this did not lead Davis to reflect upon the inappropriateness of using the same word to denote so widely different facts. For him caste, whatever its content may be, is "an extreme form of stratification," as for others it was an extreme case of class. This brings us to the question of the nature of this category of "stratification."

"Social Stratification"

Though the expression deserves attention in view of the proliferation of studies published under this title in the United States and the theoretical discussions to which it has given rise, it does not in effect introduce anything new on the point with which we are here concerned. We meet again the same attitude of mind we have already encountered, but here it runs up against difficulties. As Pfautz acknowledges in his critical bibliography of works published between 1945 and 1952, it is essentially a matter of "class."[12] However, Weber's distinction has made its way in the world: one can distinguish types of social stratification according to whether the basis of inequality is power, or prestige, or a combination of both, and classes are usually conceived of as implying a hierarchy of power (political as well as economic), castes and "estates" a hierarchy of prestige (pp. 392–93). One notes however that the community studies of Warner and others conclude that the status hierarchy is a matter of prestige and not of power. Let us stress here the use of the word "hierarchy," which appears to be introduced in order to allow different species to be distinguished within the genus "stratification." But here are two strikingly different concepts: should the quasi-geological impassibility suggested by the latter give way to the consideration of values?

A theoretical controversy in the columns of the *American Sociological Review* is very interesting for the light it throws on the preoccupations and implicit postulates of some sociologists (Davis 1942; Davis and Moore 1945; Buckley 1958; Davis 1959; Wrong 1959). The starting point was an article published in 1945 by Kingsley Davis and Wilbert E. Moore. Davis had, three years earlier, given basic definitions for the study of stratification (*status, stratum,* etc.). Here the authors raised the question of the "function" of stratification. How is it that such palpable inequalities as those referred to under the name of social classes are encountered in a society whose acknowledged norm is equality? Davis and Moore formulate the hypothesis that it is the result of a mechanism comparable to that of the market: inequality of rewards is necessary in a differentiated society in order that the more difficult or important occupations, those demanding a long training in special skills or involving heavy responsibilities, can be effectively carried out. Buckley objected that Davis and Moore had confused true stratification and pure and simple differentiation: the problem of stratification is not, or is not only, one of knowing how individuals potentially equal at the start find themselves in unequal positions ("achieved inequality"), but of discovering how inequality is maintained, since terms like stratum or stratification are generally taken as implying permanent, hereditary, "ascribed" inequality. In a rejoinder to Buckley, Davis admitted the difference of points of view; he added that the critic's animosity seemed to him to be directed against the attempt to explain inequality functionally. In my opinion, Davis was right in raising the question of inequality; he was wrong, as Buckley seems to imply, in raising it where inequality is weakest instead of tackling it where it is strongest and most articulate. But in so doing he remained within the tradition we have observed here, which always implicitly refers itself to equality as the norm, as this controversy and the very use of the term "inequality" show.

In a recent article Dennis H. Wrong sums up the debate. He points out the limitations of Davis's and Moore's theory and quotes from a work of the former a passage which again shows his pursuit of the functional necessity of stratification, as illustrated for instance by the fact that sweepers tend to have an inferior status in all societies (he is thinking of India).[13] In the end, Wrong asks for studies on certain relations between the egalitarian ideal and other aspects of society, such as the undesirable consequences of extreme equality or mobility (p. 780). It appears that equality and inequality are considered here as opposite tendencies to be studied on the functional level. Referring to the Utopians, Wrong recalls the difficulty of "making the leap from history into freedom" (p. 775).

Something has happened then in this branch of American sociology. With the multiplication of studies on social classes, one has been led to introduce values and that value-charged word, "hierarchy"; one has been led to search for the functions (and disfunctions) of what our societies valorize as well as of what they do not valorize ("in-equality") and which had been called for that reason by a neutral and even pejorative term, "stratification." What is in fact set against the egalitarian norm is not, as the term suggests, a kind of residue, a precipitate, a geological legacy, but actual forces, factors, or functions. These are negated by the norm, but they nevertheless exist; to express them, the term "stratification" is altogether inadequate. Nelson N. Foote wrote in a preface to a series of studies: "The dialectical theme of American history . . . has been a counterpoint of the principles of hierarchy and equality" (Foote 1953:325–26). The "problem" of social classes, or of "social stratification" as it appears to our sociologists springs from the contradiction between the egalitarian ideal, accepted by all these scholars as by the society to which they belong, and an array of facts showing that difference, differentiation, tends even among us to assume a hierarchical aspect, and to become permanent or hereditary inequality, or discrimination. As Raymond Aron says: "At the heart of the problem of classes I perceive the antinomy between the fact of differentiation and the ideal of equality" (Aron 1960:14). There are here realities which are made obscure to us by the fact that our values and the forms of our consciousness reject or ignore them. (This is probably still more so for Americans.) In order to understand them better, it is advantageous to turn to those societies which on the contrary approve and emphasize them. In so doing we shall move from "stratification" to hierarchy.

Hierarchy in India

It is impossible to describe the caste system in detail here. Rather, after briefly recalling its main features, I shall isolate more or less arbitrarily the aspect which concerns us. Bouglé's definition can be the starting point: the society is divided into a large number of permanent groups which are at once specialized, hierarchized, and separated (in matter of marriage, food, physical contact) in relation to each other.[14] It is sufficient to add that the common basis of these three features is the opposition of pure and impure, an opposition of a hierarchical nature which implies separation and, on the professional level, specialization of the occupations relevant to the opposition; that this basic opposition can segment itself without limit; finally, if one likes, that the con-

ceptual reality of the system lies in this opposition, and not in the groups which it opposes—this accounts for the structural character of these groups, caste and subcaste being the same thing seen from different points of view.

It has been acknowledged that hierarchy is thus rendered perfectly univocal in principle (Parsons 1953). Unfortunately, there has sometimes been a tendency to obscure the issue by speaking of not only religious (or "ritual") status, but also "secular" (or "social") status based upon power, wealth, etc., which Indians would also take into consideration. Naturally Indians do not confuse a rich man with a poor man but, as specialists seem to become increasingly aware, it is necessary to distinguish between two very different things: the scale of statuses (called "religious") which I name hierarchy and which is absolutely distinct from the fact of power; and the distribution of power, economic and political, which is very important in practice but is distinct from, and subordinate to, hierarchy. It will be asked then how power and hierarchy are related to each other. Precisely, Indian society answers this question in a very explicit manner.[15] Hierarchy culminates in the Brahman, or priest; it is the Brahman who consecrates the king's power, which otherwise depends entirely on force (this results from the dichotomy). From very early times, the relationships between Brahman and king or Kshatriya are fixed. While the Brahman is spiritually or absolutely supreme, he is materially dependent; whilst the king is materially the master, he is spiritually subordinate. A similar relation distinguishes one from the other the two superior "human ends," *dharma* (action conforming to) universal order and *artha* (action conforming to) selfish interest, which are also hierarchized in such a way that the latter is legitimate only within the limits set by the former. Again, the theory of the *gift* made to Brahmans, a preeminently meritorious action, can be regarded as establishing a means of transportation of material goods into values (see hypergamy, mentioned above, p. 79: one gets prestige from the gift of a girl to superiors).

This disjunction of power and status illustrates perfectly Weber's analytical distinction; its interest for comparison is great, for it presents an unmixed form, it realizes an "ideal type." Two features stand out: first, in India, any totality is expressed in the form of a hierarchical enumeration of its components (thus of the state or kingdom, for example), hierarchy marks the conceptual integration of a whole, it is, so to say, its intellectual cement. Secondly, if we are to generalize, it can be supposed that hierarchy, in the sense that we are using the word here, and in accord with its etymology, never attaches itself to power as such, but always to religious functions, because religion is the form that the universally true assumes in these societies. For example, when the king has the supreme rank, as is generally the case, it is very likely not by reason of his power but by reason of the religious nature of his function. From the point of view of rank at any rate, it is the opposite to what one most often supposes, namely that power is the essential which then attracts to itself religious dignities or finds in them support and justification.

One may see in the hierarchical principle, as it appears in India in its pure state, a fundamental feature of complex societies other than our own, and a principle of their unity; not their material, but their conceptual or symbolic unity. That is the essential "function" of hierarchy: it expresses the unity of such a society while connecting it to what appears to it to be universal, namely a conception of the cosmic order, whether or not it includes a God, or a king as mediator. If one likes, hierarchy integrates the society by reference to its values. Apart from the general reluctance which searching for social functions at this level is likely to encounter, it will be objected that there are societies without hierarchy, or else societies in which hierarchy does not play the part described above. It is true for example that tribes, while they are not entirely devoid of inequalities, may have neither a king nor, say, a secret society with successive grades. But that applies to relatively simple societies, with few people, and where the division of labor is little developed.

The Modern Revolution

There remain the societies of the modern Western type, which go so far as to inscribe the principle of equality in their constitutions. It is indeed true that, if values and not behavior alone are considered, a profound gap has to be acknowledged between the two kinds. What has happened? Is it possible to take a simple view of it? The societies of the past, most societies, have believed themselves to be based on the order of things, natural as well as social; they thought they were copying or designing their very conventions after the principles of life and the world. Modern society wants to be "rational," to break away from nature in order to set up an autonomous human order. To that end, it is enough to take the true measure of man and from it deduce the human order. No gap between the ideal and the real: like an engineer's blueprint, the representation will create the actuality. At this point society, the old mediator between man in his particularity and nature, disappears. There are but human individuals, and the problem is how to make them all fit together. Man will now draw from himself an order which is sure to satisfy him. As the source of this rationality, Hobbes posits not an ideal, always open to question, but the most general passion, the common generator of human actions, the most assured human reality. The individual becomes the measure of all things, the source of all "rationality"; the egalitarian principle is the outcome of this attitude, for it conforms to reason, being the simplest view of the matter, while it most directly negates the old hierarchies.[16]

As against the societies which believed themselves to be natural, here is the society which wants itself to be rational. While the "natural" society was hierarchized, finding its rationality in setting itself as a whole within a vaster whole, and was unaware of the "individual," the "rational" society on the other hand, recognizing only the individual, i.e., seeing universality, or reason, only in the particular man, places itself under the standard of equality and is unaware of itself as hierarchized whole. In a sense, the "leap from history into freedom" has already been made, and we live in a realized Utopia.

Between these two types which it is convenient to contrast directly, there should probably be located an intermediary type, in which nature and convention are distinguished and social conventions are susceptible of being judged by reference to an ideal model accessible to reason alone. But whatever may be the transitions which make for the evolution of the second type from the first, it is in the modern revolution which separates the two types, really the two leaves of the same diptych, that the central problem of comparative sociology most probably lies: how can we describe in the same language two "choices" so diametrically opposed to each other, how can we take into account at once the revolution in values which has transformed modern societies as well as the "unity of anthropology"? Certainly this cannot be done by refusing to acknowledge the change and reducing everything to "behavior," nor by extending the obscurity from one side to the other, as we should by talking of "social stratification" in general. But we remark that where one of the leaves of the diptych is obscure and blurred, the other is clear and distinct; use can be made of what is conscious in one of the two types of society in order to decipher what is not conscious in the other.

From Hierarchy to Discrimination

One can attempt, in broad terms, to apply this comparative perspective to the American racist phenomenon. It is obvious on the one hand that society did not completely cease to be society, as a hierarchized whole, on the day it willed itself to be simply a collection of individuals. In particular, the tendency to make hierarchical distinctions continued. On the other hand racism is more often than not understood to be a modern phenomenon. (Economic causes of its emergence have sometimes been sought, while much closer and more probable ideological connections were neglected.) The simplest hypothesis therefore is to assume that racism fulfills an old function under a new form. It is as if it were representing in an egalitarian society a resurgence of what was differently and more directly and naturally expressed in a hierarchical society. Make distinction illegitimate, and you get discrimination; suppress the former modes of distinction and you have a racist ideology. Can this view be made more precise and confirmed? Societies of the past knew a hierarchy of status bringing with it privileges and disabilities, among others the total juridical disability of slavery. Now the history of the United States tells us just this, that racial discrimination succeeded the slavery of the Negro people once the latter was abolished. (One is tempted to wonder why this all important transition has not been more systematically studied, from a sociological point of view, than it seems to have been, but perhaps one's ignorance is the answer.[17]) The distinction between master and slave was succeeded by discrimination by White against Black. To ask why racism appears is already to have in part answered the question: the essence of the distinction was juridical; by suppressing it the transforation of its racial attribute into racist substance was encouraged. For things to have been otherwise the distinction itself should have been overcome.

In general, racism certainly has more complex roots. Besides the internal difference of status, traditional societies knew an external difference, itself colored by hierarchy, between the "we" and the others. It was normally social and cultural. For the Greeks as for others, foreigners were barbarians, strangers to the civilization and society of the "we"; for that reason they could be enslaved. In the modern Western world not only are citizens free and equal before the law, but a transition develops, at least in popular mentality, from the moral principle of equality to the belief in the basic identity of all men, because they are no longer taken as samples of a culture, a society, or a social group, but as *individuals* existing in and for themselves.[18] In other words, the recognition of a cultural difference can no longer ethnocentrically justify inequality. But it is observed that in certain circumstances, which it would be necessary to describe, a hierarchical difference continues to be posited, which is this time attached to somatic characteristics, physiognomy, color of the skin, "blood." No doubt, these were at all times marks of distinction, but they have now become the essence of it. How is this to be explained? It is perhaps apposite to recall that we are heirs to a dualistic religion and philosophy: the distinction between matter and spirit, body and soul, permeates our entire culture and especially the popular mentality. Everything looks as if the egalitarian-identitarian mentality was situated within this dualism, as if once equality and identity bear on the individual *souls,* distinction could only be effected with regard to the *bodies.* What is more, discrimination is collective; it is as if only physical characteristics were essentially collective where everything mental tends to be primarily individual. (Thus mental differences are attributed to physical types). Is this far-fetched? It is only emphasizing the Christian ancestry of modern individualism and egalitarianism: the individual has only fellow-men (even his enemies are considered, not only as objects, but also as subjects), and he believes in the fundamental equality of all men taken severally; at the same time, for him, the collective inferiority of a category of men, when it is in his interest to state it, is expressed and justified in terms of what physically differentiates them from himself and people of his group. To sum up, the proclamation of equality has burst asunder a mode of distinction centered upon the social, but in which physical, cultural, and social characteristics were indiscriminately mixed. To reaffirm inequality, the underlying dualism demanded that physical characteristics be brought to the fore. While in India heredity is an attribute of status, the racist attributes status to "race."

All this may be regarded as an arbitrary view of the abstract intellect. Yet, the hypothesis is confirmed at least in part in Myrdal's work. Dealing with the American facts, this author discovers a close connection between egalitarianism and racism. To begin with, he notes in the philosophy of the enlightenment the tendency to minimize innate differences; then, generally everywhere and especially in America, the essentially moral doctrine of the "natural rights" of man rests on a biological egalitarianism: all men are "created equal." The period 1830–60 sees the development of an ideology for the defense of slavery: slavery being condemned in the name of natural equality, its champions argue against this the doctrine of the inequality of races; later the argument is used to justify discrimination, which becomes established from the moment when, about 1877, the North gives up enforcing assimilation. The author's conclusions are worth pondering upon: "The dogma of racial inequality may, in a sense, be regarded as a strange fruit of the Enlightenment . . . The race dogma is

nearly the only way out for a people so moralistically egalitarian, if it is not prepared to live up to its faith. A nation less fervently committed to democracy could probably live happily in a caste system . . . race prejudice is, in a sense, a function (a perversion) of egalitarianism."[19]

If this is so, it is permissible to doubt whether, in the fight against racism in general, the mere recall of the egalitarian ideal, however solemn it may be, and even though accompanied by a scientific criticism of racist prejudices, will be really efficient. It would be better to prevent the passage from the moral principle of equality to the notion that all men are identical. One feels sure that equality can, in our day, be combined with the recognition of differences, so long as such differences are morally neutral. People must be provided with the means for conceptualizing differences. The diffusion of the pluralistic notions of culture, society, etc., affording a counterweight and setting bounds to individualism, is the obvious thing (see Lévi-Strauss 1952). Finally, if the tendency to hierarchize still exists, if the affirmation of the modern ideal is not sufficient to make it disappear but, on the contrary, by a complicated mechanism, can on occasion make it ferocious and morbid, the antagonisms and interests which exploit it should not be lost sight of—but this is beyond our subject.

Cutting short here the attempt to define racism comparatively, I should like to recall, albeit too briefly, a structural relation which is essential to the possible developments of comparison. Equality and hierarchy are not, in fact, opposed to each other in the mechanical way which the exclusive consideration of values might lead one to suppose: the pole of the opposition which is not valorized is none the less present, each implies the other and is supported by it. Talcott Parsons draws attention, at the very beginning of his study, to the fact that distinction of statuses carries with it and presupposes equality within each status (1953:1). Conversely, where equality is affirmed, it is within a group which is hierarchized in relation to others, as in the Greek cities or, in the modern world, in British democracy and imperialism, the latter being tinged with hierarchy (e.g., incipient racism in India in the second half of the nineteenth century).[20] It is this structural relation that the egalitarian ideal tends to destroy, the result of its action being what is most often studied under the name of "social stratification." In the first place the relation is inverted: equality contains inequalities instead of being contained in a hierarchy. In the second place a whole series of transformations happen which can perhaps be summarized by saying that hierarchy is repressed, made nonconscious: it is replaced by a manifold network of inequalities, matters of fact instead of right, of quantity and gradualness instead of quality and discontinuity. Hence, in part, the well-known difficulty of defining social classes.

Conclusion

To conclude in general terms, comparative sociology requires concepts which take into account the values that different societies have, so to speak, chosen for themselves. A consequence of this choice of values is that certain aspects of social reality are clearly and consciously elaborated, while others are left in the dark. In order to express what a given society does not express, the sociologist cannot invent concepts, for when he attempts to do so he only manages, as in the case of "social stratification," to translate in a way at once pretentious and obscure the prejudices of his own society. He must therefore have recourse to societies which have expressed those same aspects. A general theory of "inequality," if it is deemed necessary, must be centered upon those societies which give it a meaning and not upon those which, while presenting certain forms of it, have chosen to disavow it. It must be a theory of hierarchy in its valorized, or simple and direct forms, as well as in its nonvalorized or devalorized, or complex, hybrid, covert forms. (Let us note, following Talcott Parsons,[21] that such a theory is only one particular way of considering the total social system.) In so doing one will of course in no way impose upon one society the values of another, but only endeavour to set mutually "in perspective" (Evans-Pritchard 1951:129) the various types of societies. One will try to see each society in the light not only of itself but of the others. From the point of view of social anthropology at any rate, this appears to be not only the formula for an objective comparison, but even the condition for understanding each particular society.

Notes

1. The tendency, which its only systematic opponent, O. C. Cox, has called "the Caste School of Race Relations," seems to have won the day. Another, more moderate, tendency consists in applying the word "caste" to the U.S.A. in a monographic manner, without comparative prejudice (Myrdal, etc., see below). The dictionaries give, besides the proper sense of the word, the extended meaning, e.g., *Shorter Oxford*

English Dictionary, s.v.: "3. *fig.* A class who keep themselves socially distinct, or inherit exclusive privileges 1807." (The French text has here a reference to Littre instead of O.S.D.)

2. Yet, among recent authors who are familiar with the Indian system, a sociologist working in Ceylon insists on the fundamental difference between India and the U.S. (Ryan 1953:18, n.), while F. G. Bailey asserts *a priori* that this comparison must take place under the word "caste" (*Contributions,* III, 90). Morris Carstairs is less categorical, but he accepts, with Kroeber's definition (below), the American usage, because of its advantages as compared with "race" (1957:23). Much earlier an Indian author, Ketkar, insisted on a hierarchical division of American society based on race and occupation, and he enumerated ten groups (based in fact on the country of origin). He did not use the word "caste" but he underlined with some relish the features which in his view were reminiscent of the Indian system (Ketkar 1909:100 n; 102 n; 115 n. 5). The general question has recently been discussed in Leach (ed.), 1960, esp. p. 5.

3. (Warner 1941, ed. 1946:9). G. S. Ghurye's position is close to that of Kroeber: well-marked status groups are common in Indo-European cultures; comparatively, the Indian caste system represents only an extreme case (untouchability, etc.), see *Caste and Race in India* (1932), pp. 140, 142.

4. Max Weber, *Wirtschaft und Gesellschaft,* II, 635–37. Discussed by Cox, *Caste, Class and Race,* p. 287, and "Max Weber on Social Stratification," *American Sociological Review,* 11 (1950), 223–27; see also Hans Gerth, "Max Weber vs. Oliver C. Cox," *American Sociological Review,* ibid., pp. 557–58 (as regards Jews and castes).

5. Sorokin 1947:259. (The "order" or "estate" as a "diluted caste," cf. what has been said above about class and caste.) Max Weber distinguishes between open and closed status groups (*Ges. Aufs. z. Religionssoziologie,* II, ed. 1920, 41–42). It is to be noted that a recent work recognizes two fundamental types of "social stratification," the caste type which comprises "orders" or "estates," and the open class type, related respectively to the poles of Talcott Parsons' alternative of particularism-universalism (Barber 1957).

6. Gunnar Myrdal et al. 1944:675; *stet* 668: "The scientifically important difference between the terms caste and class as we are using them is, from this point of view, *a relatively large difference in freedom of movement between groups"*(his italics). Same justification for the use of the term (practical reasons, not indicating identity with the Indian facts), in Westie and Westie 1957:192, n. 5.

7. Myrdal., pp. 667–68. In a footnote, Myrdal takes up an objection made in particular by Charles S. Johnson: the word "caste" connotes an invariable and stable system in which the tensions and frictions which characterize the relations between Whites and Blacks in the United States are not found; he replies that he does not believe that a caste system having such characteristics

exists anywhere (pp. 1374–75, n. 2) and says earlier (p. 668) that Hindu society today does not show that "stable equilibrium" that American sociologists, observing from a distance, have been inclined to attribute to it. We see here some trace of the egalitarian Creed. The author has, since, had first-hand experience of India and one wonders whether he would maintain this today, whether, even, he would continue to use the word "caste" for American phenomena.

8. Myrdal, pp. 670–71. There is here an interesting judgment on the Lloyd Warner school: according to Myrdal, one must take account of the extreme egalitarianism in the "popular national theory" in order to understand both the tendency among these authors to exaggerate the rigidity of distinctions of class and caste in America, and the interest aroused by their works, which has been greater than their strictly scientific novelty.

9. It is a little surprising to find, next to the ideas here summarized, a rather narrow idea of the place of concepts in science: "Concepts are our created instruments and have no other form of reality than in our usage. Their purpose is to help make our thinking clear and our observations accurate" (p. 667).

10. The operation of this choice is clear in principle: the caste system of India has been characterized by only those of its traits that it is thought may be found in America, where however they do not constitute a complete system but only part of a system which is called a class-and-caste system.

11. Cox's thesis appears to have had little effect. Sorokin however refers to his article and takes a similar position: the relation between Blacks and Whites has some of the elements of relations between castes but it differs fundamentally (1947:258, n. 12).

12. Pfautz 1953:391–418. The theory of stratification is approached, not starting from class, but from an absolutely general point of view, by Talcott Parsons in "A Revised Theoretical Approach to the Theory of Social Stratification" (Bendix and Lipset, ed., 1953). While it adopts the same label, the work is outside the current here criticized; the general conception *(in fine)* removes the habitual implications of the word. The argument proceeds from values and the hierarchy which necessarily results from them. The conceptual framework is that of the general theory.

13. I was unfortunately unable to consult during the preparation of this article Kingsley Davis' book, *Human Society,* New York, 1949, quoted by Wrong, and which would have been of particular interest since the author was concerned with India at that time (see *The Population of India and Pakistan,* Princeton, 1951).

14. Bouglé, *Essais sur le régime des castes* (1908:4). The English translation of Bouglé's thesis, and a commentary on his book together with that of Hocart, which poses the problem of power, is in *Contributions,* II, 1958.

15. What follows is summarized from my chapter on the conception of kingship in ancient India, to appear in L. Renou and J. Filliozat, *L'Inde classique,* III.

16. On Hobbes and the artificial society, "rational" in the sense of being devised according to the reality of man (the individual) and not inspired by an ideal order, see Strauss 1953, ch. 5; Halévy, *La Formation du radicalisme philosophique,* 1901–04, I, 3, 41, 53, 90; III, 347–48, etc.

17. The reaction to the abolition of slavery was not immediate but developed slowly. Discrimination appears as simple separation under the slogan "separate but equal." For the period before the Civil War also, Myrdal gives a succinct history, but the analysis, apparently, remains to be done. It promises to be fruitful, see for example the declarations of Jefferson and Lincoln (see *Times Literary Supplement,* July 22, 1960, pp. 457–58, according to J. W. Schulte-Nordholt, *The People That Walk in Darkness,* 1960). Recent articles by P. L. Van den Berghe partly satisfy my wish: 1960, pp. 47–56. According to this author, segregation has replaced etiquette as mode of social distance. The change would correspond to the movement from slavery to racism.

18. The fact that the transition from "equality" to "identity" operates chiefly at the level of popular mentality makes it more difficult to seize on than if it were present in the great authors. I propose nevertheless to study elsewhere more closely this particular complementarity between egalitarianism and racism.

19. Gunnar Myrdal 1944:83 ff., the quotations are from p. 89. Myrdal also takes account of the development of the biological view of man: *Homo sapiens* as a species in the animal world; see also p. 591: "The persistent preoccupation with sex and marriage in the rationalization . . . is, to this extent, an irrational escape on the part of the whites from voicing an open demand for difference in social status . . . for its own sake."

20. Machiavelli observes that a "republic" which wishes to extend its empire and not remain small and stagnant, should like Rome confide the defence of liberty to the people and not, like Sparta and Venice, to the great. (*Discourses on the First Decade of T. Livy,* I, Chs. V–VI.)

21. See n. 12 above.

THREE

"Art"

FOUR

Cézanne's Doubt

Maurice Merleau-Ponty

Consciousness of the human body (as *both* subject and object) was posited as the anchor of all awareness in Merleau-Ponty's phenomenology of culture. This phenomenology is both dialectical and perspectival, although, like hermeneutic studies in general (see the comments on Geertz's paper in this volume, and Ricoeur's *Freud and Philosophy*), the methodology calls for the arbitrary bounding of texts as the objects for study and analysis. Here, Cézanne's paintings are interpreted in the light of the "accidents" of the artist's personal history, but cannot be seen as caused by that history; each creates the other, forming a whole which becomes comprehensible when viewed through a multiplicity of frames: thus the Other becomes necessary for the affirmation of the Self and its products, including those products which, like paintings, forever "express what exists."

Merleau-Ponty's analysis is limited, however, by his relegation of the artist's personal history to the realm of "accident": that is, his failure to see the artist's life as shaped by concrete historical and cultural forces and to include these forces as part of the artist's world and the tools used to portray that world. On the surface, this appears to be an extreme form of relativism, which grants—virtually to the form of fetishism—the uniqueness of the artist. There is evidence that this was Merleau-Ponty's view: for example, Sartre says that Merleau-Ponty was co-director of the radical journal *Les Temps Modernes,* but would not have his name listed with Sartre's on the masthead. This Sartre attributes to Merleau-Ponty's distrust of Sartre's politics, and thus as a preparation for an easy dissociation (which, by the way, never occurred). Merleau-Ponty, Sartre says, "found his security in a multiplicity of perspectives." But at base his phenomenology, despite the implication that there is no uniquely privileged analytical perspective, by setting aside historical and cultural factors, *assumes* a universal existential dilemma.

HE NEEDED ONE HUNDRED working sessions for a still life, one hundred and fifty sittings for a portrait. What we call his work was, for him, only an essay, an approach to painting. In September, 1906, at the age of 67—one month

Reprinted by permission of the publisher, from Maurice Merleau-Ponty, *Sense and Non-Sense* (Evanston, Ill.: Northwestern University Press, copyright © 1964), pp. 9–26.

before his death—he wrote: "I was in such a state of mental agitation, in such great confusion that for a time I feared my weak reason would not survive. . . . Now it seems I am better and that I see more clearly the direction my studies are taking. Will I ever arrive at the goal, so intensely sought and so long pursued? I am still learning from nature, and it seems to me I am making slow progress." Painting was his world and his way of life. He worked alone, without students, without admiration from his family, without encouragement from the critics. He painted on the afternoon of the day his mother died. In 1870 he was painting at l'Estaque while the police were after him for dodging the draft. And still he had moments of doubt about this vocation. As he grew old, he wondered whether the novelty of his painting might not come from trouble with his eyes, whether his whole life had not been based upon an accident of his body. The uncertainty or stupidity of his contemporaries correspond to this effort and this doubt. "The painting of a drunken privy cleaner," said a critic in 1905. Even today, C. Mauclair finds Cézanne's admissions of powerlessness an argument against him. Meanwhile, Cézanne's paintings have spread throughout the world. Why so much uncertainty, so much labor, so many failures, and, suddenly, the greatest success?

Zola, Cézanne's friend from childhood, was the first to find genius in him and the first to speak of him as a "genius gone wrong." An observer of Cézanne's life such as Zola, more concerned with his character than with the meaning of his painting, might well consider it a manifestation of ill-health.

For as far back as 1852, upon entering the Collège Bourbon at Aix, Cézanne worried his friends with his fits of temper and depression. Seven years later, having decided to become an artist, he doubted his talent and did not dare to ask his father—a hatter and later a banker—to send him to Paris. Zola's letters reproach him for his instability, his weakness, and his indecision. When finally he came to Paris, he wrote: "The only thing I have changed is my location: my ennui has followed me." He could not tolerate discussions, because they wore him out and because he could never give arguments. His nature was basically anxious. Thinking that he would die young, he made his will at the age of 42; at 46 he was for six months the victim of a violent, tormented, overwhelming passion of which no one knows the outcome and to which he would never refer. At 51 he withdrew to Aix, where he found landscape best suited to his genius but where also he returned to the world of his childhood, his mother and his sister. After the death of his mother, Cézanne turned to his son for support. "Life is terrifying," he would often say. Religion, which he then set about practicing for the first time, began for him in the fear of life and the fear of death. "It is fear," he explained to a friend; "I feel I will be on earth for another four days—what then? I believe in life after death, and I don't want to risk roasting *in aeternum*." Although his religion later deepened, its original motivation was the need to put his life in order and to be relieved of it. He became more and more timid, mistrustful, and sensitive: on his occasional visits to Paris he motioned his friends, when still far away, not to approach him. In 1903, after his pictures had begun to sell in Paris at twice the price of Monet's and when young men like Joachim Gasquet and Emile Bernard came to see him and ask him questions, he unbent a little. But his fits of anger continued. (In Aix a child once hit him as he passed by; after that he could not bear any contact.) One day when Cézanne was quite old, Emile Bernard supported him as he stumbled. Cézanne flew into a rage. He could be heard striding around his studio and shouting that he wouldn't let anybody "get his hooks into me." Because of these "hooks" he pushed women who could have modeled for him out of his studio, priests, whom he called "sticky," out of his life, and Emile Bernard's theories out of his mind, when they became too insistent.

This loss of flexible human contact; this inability to master new situations; this flight into established habits, in an atmosphere which presented no problems; this rigid opposition in theory and practice of the "hook" versus the freedom of a recluse—all these symptoms permit one to speak of a morbid constitution and more precisely, as, for example, in the case of El Greco, of schizophrenia. The notion of painting "from nature" could be said to arise from the same weakness. His extremely close attention to nature and to color, the inhuman character of his paintings (he said that a face should be painted as an object), his devotion to the visible world: all of these would then only represent a flight from the human world, the alienation of his humanity.

These conjectures nevertheless do not give any idea of the positive side of his work; one cannot thereby conclude that his painting is a phenomenon of decadence and what Nietzsche called "impoverished" life or that it has nothing to say to the educated man. Zola's and Emile Bernard's belief in Cézanne's failure probably arises from their having put too much emphasis on psychology and their personal knowledge of Cézanne. It is quite possible that, on the basis of his nervous weaknesses, Cézanne conceived a form of art which is valid for everyone. Left to himself, he could look at nature as only a human being can. The meaning of his work cannot be determined from his life.

This meaning will not become any clearer in the light of art history—that is, by bringing in the influences on Cézanne's methods (the Italian school and Tintoretto, Delacroix, Courbet, and the Impressionists)—or even by drawing on his own judgment of his work.

His first pictures—up to about 1870—are painted fantasies: a rape, a murder. They are therefore almost always executed in broad strokes and present the moral physiognomy of the actions rather than their visible aspect. It is thanks to the Impressionists, and particularly to Pissarro, that Cézanne later conceived painting not as the incarnation of imagined scenes, the projection of dreams outward, but as the exact study of appearances: less a work of the studio than a working from nature. Thanks to the Impressionists, he abandoned the baroque technique, whose primary aim is to capture movement, for small dabs placed close together and for patient hatchings.

He quickly parted ways with the Impressionists, however. Impressionism tries to capture, in the painting, the very way in which objects strike our eyes and attack our senses. Objects are depicted as they appear to instantaneous perception, without fixed contours, bound together by light and air. To capture this envelope of light, one had to exclude siennas, ochres, and black and use only the seven colors of the spectrum. The color of objects could not be represented simply by putting on the canvas their local tone, that is, the color they take on isolated from their surroundings; one also had to pay attention to the phenomena of contrast which modify local colors in nature. Furthermore, by a sort of reversal, every color we perceive in nature elicits the appearance of its complement; and these complementaries heighten one another. To achieve sunlit colors in a picture which will be seen in the dim light of apartments, not only must there be a green— if you are painting grass—but also the complementary red which will make it vibrate. Finally, the Impressionists break down the local tone itself. One can generally obtain any color by juxtaposing rather than mixing the colors which make it up, thereby achieving a more vibrant hue. The result of these procedures is that the canvas—which no longer corresponds point by point to nature—affords a generally true impression through the action of the separate parts upon one another. But at the same time, depicting the atmosphere and breaking up the tones submerges the object and causes it to lose its proper weight. The composition of Cézanne's palette leads one to suppose that he had another aim. Instead of the seven colors of the spectrum, one finds eighteen colors—six reds, five yellows, three blues, three greens, and black. The use of warm colors and black shows that Cézanne wants to represent the object, to find it again behind the atmosphere. Likewise, he does not break up the tone; rather, he replaces this technique with graduated colors, a progression of chromatic nuances across the object, a modulation of colors which stays close to the object's form and to the light it receives. Doing away with exact contours in certain cases, giving color priority over the outline—these obviously mean different things for Cézanne and for the Impres-

sionists. The object is no longer covered by reflections and lost in its relationships to the atmosphere and to other objects: it seems subtly illuminated from within, light emanates from it, and the result is an impression of solidity and material substance. Moreover, Cézanne does not give up making the warm colors vibrate but achieves this chromatic sensation through the use of blue.

One must therefore say that Cézanne wished to return to the object without abandoning the Impressionist aesthetic which takes nature as its model. Emile Bernard reminded him that, for the classical artists, painting demanded outline, composition, and distribution of light. Cézanne replied: "They created pictures; we are attempting a piece of nature." He said of the old masters that they "replaced reality by imagination and by the abstraction which accompanies it." Of nature, he said that "the artist must conform to this perfect work of art. Everything comes to us from nature; we exist through it; nothing else is worth remembering." He stated that he wanted to make of Impressionism "something solid, like the art in the museums." His painting was paradoxical: he was pursuing reality without giving up the sensuous surface, with no other guide than the immediate impression of nature, without following the contours, with no outline to enclose the color, with no perspectival or pictorial arrangement. This is what Bernard called Cézanne's suicide: aiming for reality while denying himself the means to attain it. This is the reason for his difficulties and for the distortions one finds in his pictures between 1870 and 1890. Cups and saucers on a table seen from the side should be elliptical, but Cézanne paints the two ends of the ellipse swollen and expanded. The work table in his portrait of Gustave Geoffrey stretches, contrary to the laws of perspective, into the lower part of the picture. In giving up the outline Cézanne was abandoning himself to the chaos of sensations, which would upset the objects and constantly suggest illusions, as, for example, the illusion we have when we move our head that objects themselves are moving—if our judgment did not constantly set these appearances straight. According to Bernard, Cézanne "submerged his painting in ignorance and his mind in shadows." But one cannot really judge his painting in this way except by closing one's mind to half of what he said and one's eyes to what he painted.

It is clear from his conversations with Emile Bernard that Cézanne was always seeking to avoid the ready-made alternatives suggested to him: sensation versus judgment; the painter who sees against the painter who thinks; nature versus composition; primitivism as opposed to tradition. "We have to develop an optics," and Cézanne, "by which I mean a logical vision—that is, one with no element of the absurd." "Are you speaking of our nature?" asked Bernard. Cézanne: "It has to do with both." "But aren't nature and art different?" "I want to make them the same. Art is a personal apperception, which I embody in sensations and which I ask the understanding to organize into a painting" (recorded in Bernard 1912). But even these formulas put too much emphasis on the ordinary notions of "sensitivity" or "sensations" and "understanding"—which is why Cézanne could not convince by his arguments and preferred to paint instead. Rather than apply to his work dichoto-mies more appropriate to those who sustain traditions than to those men, philosophers or painters, who initiate these traditions, he preferred to search for the true meaning of painting, which is continually to question tradition. Cézanne did not think he had to choose between feeling and thought, between order and chaos. He did not want to separate the stable things which we see and the shifting way in which they appear; he wanted to depict matter as it takes on form, the birth of order through spontaneous organization. He makes a basic distinction not between "the senses" and "the understanding" but rather between the spontaneous organization of the things we perceive and the human organization of ideas and sciences. We see things; we agree about them; we are anchored in them; and it is with "nature" as our base that we construct our sciences. Cézanne wanted to paint this primordial world, and his pictures therefore seem to show nature pure, while photographs of the same landscapes suggest man's works, conveniences, and imminent presence. Cézanne never wished to "paint like a savage." He wanted to put intelligence, ideas, sciences, perspective, and tradition back in touch with the world of nature which they must comprehend. He wished, as he said, to confront the sciences with the nature "from which they came."

By remaining faithful to the phenomena in his investigations of perspective, Cézanne discovered what recent psychologists have come to formulate: the lived perspective, that which we actually perceive, is not a geometric or photographic one. The objects we see close at hand appear smaller, those far away seem larger than they do in a photograph. (This can be seen in a movie, where a train approaches and gets bigger much faster than a real train would under the same circumstances.) To say that a circle seen obliquely is seen as an ellipse is to substitute for our actual perception what we would see if we were cameras: in reality we see a form which oscillates around the ellipse without being an ellipse. In a portrait of Mme Cézanne, the border of the wallpaper on one side of her body does not form a straight line with that on the other: and indeed it is known that if a line passes beneath a wide strip of paper, the two visible segments appear dislocated. Gustave Geoffrey's table stretches into the bottom of the picture, and indeed, when our eye runs over a large surface, the images it successively receives are taken from different points of view, and the whole surface is warped. It is true that I freeze these distortions in repainting them on the canvas; I stop the spontaneous movement in which they pile up in perception and in which they tend toward the geometric perspective. This is also what happens with colors. Pink upon gray paper colors the background green. Academic painting shows the background as gray, assuming that the picture will produce the same effect of contrast as the real object. Impressionist painting uses green in the background in order to achieve a contrast as brilliant as that of objects in nature. Doesn't this falsify the color relationship? It would if it stopped there, but the painter's task is to modify all the other colors in the picture so that they take away from the green background its characteristics of a real color. Similarly, it is Cézanne's genius that when the over-all composition of the picture is seen globally, perspectival distortions are no longer visible in their own right but rather contribute, as they do in natural vision,

to the impression of an emerging order, of an object in the act of appearing, organizing itself before our eyes. In the same way, the contour of an object conceived as a line encircling the object belongs not to the visible world but to geometry. If one outlines the shape of an apple with a continuous line, one makes an object of the shape, whereas the contour is rather the ideal limit toward which the sides of the apple recede in depth. Not to indicate any shape would be to deprive the objects of their identity. To trace just a single outline sacrifices depth—that is, the dimension in which the thing is presented not as spread out before us but as an inexhaustible reality full of reserves. That is why Cézanne follows the swelling of the object in modulated colors and indicates *several* outlines in blue. Rebounding among these, one's glance captures a shape that emerges from among them all, just as it does in perception. Nothing could be less arbitrary than these famous distortions which, moreover, Cézanne abandoned in his last period, after 1890, when he no longer filled his canvases with colors and when he gave up the closely-woven texture of his still lifes.

The outline should therefore be a result of the colors if the world is to be given in its true density. For the world is a mass without gaps, a system of colors across which the receding perspective, the outlines, angles and curves are inscribed like lines of force; the spatial structure vibrates as it is formed. "The outline and the colors are no longer distinct from each other. To the extent that one paints, one outlines; the more the colors harmonize, the more the outline becomes precise. . . . When the color is at its richest, the form has reached plenitude." Cézanne does not try to use color to *suggest* the tactile sensations which would give shape and depth. These distinctions between touch and sight are unknown in primordial perception. It is only as a result of a science of the human body that we finally learn to distinguish between our senses. The lived object is not rediscovered or constructed on the basis of the contributions of the senses; rather, it presents itself to us from the start as the center from which these contributions radiate. We *see* the depth, the smoothness, the softness, the hardness of objects; Cézanne even claimed that we see their odor. If the painter is to express the world, the arrangement of his colors must carry with it this indivisible whole, or else his picture will only hint at things and will not give them in the imperious unity, the presence, the insurpassable plenitude which is for us the definition of the real. That is why each brushstroke must satisfy an infinite number of conditions. Cézanne sometimes pondered hours at a time before putting down a certain stroke, for, as Bernard said, each stroke must "contain the air, the light, the object, the composition, the character, the outline, and the style." Expressing what *exists* is an endless task.

Nor did Cézanne neglect the physiognomy of objects and faces: he simply wanted to capture it emerging from the color. Painting a face "as an object" is not to strip it of its "thought." "I realize that the painter interprets it," said Cézanne. "The painter is not an imbecile." But this interpretation should not be a reflection distinct from the act of seeing. "If I paint all the little blues and all the little maroons, I capture and convey his glance. Who gives a damn if they want to dispute how one can sadden a-mouth or make a cheek smile by wedding a shaded green to a red." One's

personality is seen and grasped in one's glance, which is, however, no more than a combination of colors. Other minds are given to us only as incarnate, as belonging to faces and gestures. Countering with the distinctions of soul and body, thought and vision is of no use here, for Cézanne returns to just that primordial experience from which these notions are derived and in which they are inseparable. The painter who conceptualizes and seeks the expression first misses the mystery—renewed every time we look at someone—of a person's appearing in nature. In *La Peau de chagrin* Balzac described a "tablecloth white as a layer of newly fallen snow, upon which the place-settings rise symmetrically, crowned with blond rolls." "All through youth," said Cézanne, "I wanted to paint that, that tablecloth of new snow. . . . Now I know that one must will only to paint the place-settings rising symmetrically and the blond rolls. If I paint 'crowned' I've had it, you understand? But if I really balance and shade my place-settings and rolls as they are in nature, then you can be sure that the crowns, the snow, and all the excitement will be there too."

We live in the midst of man-made objects, among tools, in houses, streets, cities, and most of the time we see them only through the human actions which put them to use. We become used to thinking that all of this exists necessarily and unshakeably. Cézanne's painting suspends these habits of thought and reveals the base of inhuman nature upon which man has installed himself. This is why Cézanne's people are strange, as if viewed by a creature of another species. Nature itself is stripped of the attributes which make it ready for animistic communions: there is no wind in the landscape, no movement on the Lac d'Annecy; the frozen objects hesitate as at the beginning of the world. It is an unfamiliar world in which one is uncomfortable and which forbids all human effusiveness. If one looks at the work of other painters after seeing Cézanne's paintings, one feels somehow relaxed, just as conversations resumed after a period of mourning mask the absolute change and give back to the survivors their solidity. But indeed only a human being is capable of such a vision which penetrates right to the root of things beneath the imposed order of humanity. Everything indicates that animals cannot *look at* things, cannot penetrate them in expectation of nothing but the truth. Emile Bernard's statement that a realistic painter is only an ape is therefore precisely the opposite of the truth, and one sees how Cézanne was able to revive the classical definition of art: man added to nature.

Cézanne's painting denies neither science nor tradition. He went to the Louvre every day when he was in Paris. He believed that one must learn how to paint and that the geometric study of planes and forms is a necessary part of this learning process. He inquired about the geological structure of his landscapes, convinced that these abstract relationships, expressed, however, in terms of the visible world, should affect the act of painting. The rules of anatomy and design are present in each stroke of his brush just as the rules of the game underlie each stroke of a tennis match. But what motivates the painter's movement can never be simply perspective or geometry or the laws governing color, or, for that matter, particular knowledge. Motivating all the movements from which a picture gradually emerges there can be only one thing: the landscape in its totality and in its absolute fullness, precisely what Cézanne called a "motif." He would start by discovering the geological foundations of the landscape; then, according to Mme Cézanne, he would halt and look at everything with widened eyes, "germinating" with the countryside. The task before him was, first to forget all he had ever learned from science and, second *through* these sciences to recapture the structure of the landscape as an emerging organism. To do this, all the partial views one catches sight of must be welded together; all that the eye's versatility disperses must be reunited; one must, as Gasquet put it, "join the wandering hands of nature." "A minute of the world is going by which must be painted in its full reality." His meditation would suddenly be consummated: "I have my *motif*," Cézanne would say, and he would explain that the landscape had to be centered neither too high nor too low, caught alive in a net which would let nothing escape. Then he began to paint all parts of the painting at the same time, using patches of color to surround his original charcoal sketch of the geological skeleton. The picture took on fullness and density; it grew in structure and balance; it came to maturity all at once. "The landscape thinks itself in me," he said, "and I am its consciousness." Nothing could be farther from naturalism than this intuitive science. Art is not imitation, nor is it something manufactured according to the wishes of instinct or good taste. It is a process of expressing. Just as the function of words is to name—that is, to grasp the nature of what appears to us in a confused way and to place it before us as a recognizable object—so it is up to the painter, said Gasquet, to "objectify," "project," and "arrest." Words do not *look like* the things they designate; and a picture is not a *trompe-l'oeil*. Cézanne, in his own words, "wrote in painting what had never yet been painted, and turned it into painting once and for all." Forgetting the viscous, equivocal appearances, we go through them straight to the things they present. The painter recaptures and converts into visible objects what would, without him, remain walled up in the separate life of each consciousness: the vibration of appearances which is the cradle of things. Only one emotion is possible for this painter—the feeling of strangeness—and only one lyricism—that of the continual rebirth of existence.

Leonardo de Vinci's motto was persistent rigor, and all the classical works on the art of poetry tell us that the creation of art is no easy matter. Cézanne's difficulties—like those of Balzac or Mallarmé—are of a different nature. Balzac (probably taking Delacroix for his model) imagined a painter who wants to express life through the use of color alone and who keeps his masterpiece hidden. When Frenhofer dies, his friends find nothing but a chaos of colors and elusive lines, a wall of painting. Cézanne was moved to tears when he read *Le Chef-d'oeuvre inconnu* and declared that he himself was Frenhofer. The effort made by Balzac, himself obsessed with "realization," sheds light on Cézanne's. In *La Peau de chagrin* Balzac speaks of "a thought to be expressed," "a system to be built," "a science to be explained." He makes Louis Lambert, one of the abortive geniuses of the Comédie Humaine, say: "I am heading toward certain discoveries . . . , but how shall I describe the power which binds my hands, stops my mouth, and drags me in the opposite direction from my vocation?" To say that Balzac set himself to understand the society of his time is not sufficient. It is no superhuman task to describe the typical traveling salesman, to "dissect the teaching profession," or even to lay the foundations of a sociology. Once he had named the visible forces such as money and passion, once he had described the way they evidently work, Balzac wondered where it all led, what was the impetus behind it, what was the *meaning* of, for example, a Europe "whose efforts tend toward some unknown mystery of civilization." In short, he wanted to understand what interior force holds the world together and causes the proliferation of visible forms. Frenhofer had the same idea about the meaning of painting: "A hand is not simply part of the body, but the expression and continuation of a thought which must be captured and conveyed. . . . That is the real struggle! Many painters triumph instinctively, unaware of this theme of art. You draw a woman, but you do not see her." The artist is the one who arrests the spectacle in which most men take part without really seeing it and who makes it visible to the most "human" among them.

There is thus no art for pleasure's sake alone. One can invent pleasurable objects by linking old ideas in a new way and by presenting forms that have been seen before. This way of painting or speaking at second hand is what is generally meant by culture. Cézanne's or Balzac's artist is not satisfied to be a cultured animal but assimilates the culture down to its very foundations and gives it a new structure: he speaks as the first man spoke and paints as if no one had ever painted before. What he expresses cannot, therefore, be the translation of a clearly defined thought, since such clear thoughts are those which have already been uttered by ourselves or by others. "Conception" cannot precede "execution." There is nothing but a vague fever before the act of artistic expression, and only the work itself, completed and understood, is proof that there was *something* rather than *nothing* to be said. Because he returns to the source of silent and solitary experience on which culture and the exchange of ideas have been built in order to know it, the artist launches his work just as a man once launched the first word, not knowing whether it will be anything more than a shout, whether it can detach itself from the flow of individual life in which it originates and give the independent existence of an identifiable *meaning* either to the future of that same individual life or to the monads coexisting with it or to the open community of future monads. The meaning of what the artist is going to say *does not exist* anywhere—not in things, which as yet have no meaning, nor in the artist himself, in his unformulated life. It summons one away from the already constituted reason in which "cultured men" are content to shut themselves, toward a reason which contains its own origins.

To Bernard's attempt to bring him back to human intelligence, Cézanne replied: "I am oriented toward the intelligence of the *Pater Omnipotens*." He was, in any case, oriented toward the idea or the project of an infinite Logos. Cézanne's uncertainty and solitude are not essentially explained by his nervous temperament but by the purpose of his work. Heredity may well have given him rich sensations, strong emotions, and a vague feeling of anguish or mystery which upset the life he might have wished for himself and which cut him off from men; but these qualities cannot create a work of art without the expressive act, and they can no more account for the difficulties than for the virtues of that act. Cézanne's difficulties are those of the first word. He considered himself powerless because he was not omnipotent, because he was not God and wanted nevertheless to portray the world, to change it completely into a spectacle, to make *visible* how the world *touches* us. A new theory of physics can be proven because calculations connect the idea or meaning of it with standards of measurement already common to all men. It is not enough for a painter like Cézanne, an artist, or a philosopher, to create and express an idea; they must also awaken the experiences which will make their idea take root in the consciousness of others. A successful work has the strange power to teach its own lesson. The reader or spectator who follows the clues of the book or painting, by setting up stepping stones and rebounding from side to side guided by the obscure clarity of a particular style, will end by discovering what the artist wanted to communicate. The painter can do no more than construct an image; he must wait for this image to come to life for other people. When it does, the work of art will have united these separate lives; it will no longer exist in only one of them like a stubborn dream or a persistent delirium, nor will it exist only in space as a colored piece of canvas. It will dwell undivided in several minds, with a claim on every possible mind like a perennial acquisition.

Thus, the "hereditary traits," the "influences"—the accidents in Cézanne's life—are the text which nature and history gave him to decipher. They give only the literal meaning of his work. But an artist's creations, like a man's free decisions, impose on this given a figurative sense which did not pre-exist them. If Cézanne's life seems to us to carry the seeds of his work within it, it is because we get to know his work first and see the circumstances of his life through it, charging them with a meaning borrowed from that work. If the givens for Cézanne which we have been enumerating, and which we spoke of as pressing conditions, were to figure in the web of projects which he was, they could have done so only by presenting themselves to him as *what* he had to live, leaving *how* to live it undetermined. An imposed theme at the start, they become, when replaced in the existence of which they are part, the monogram and the symbol of a life which freely interpreted itself.

But let us make no mistake about this freedom. Let us not imagine an abstract force which could superimpose its effects on life's "givens" or which cause breaches in life's development. Although it is certain that a man's life does not *explain* his work, it is equally certain that the two are connected. The truth is that *this work to be done called for this life*. From the very start, the only equilibrium in Cézanne's life came from the support of his future work. His life was the projection of his future work. The work to come is hinted at, but it would be wrong to take these hints for causes, although they do make a single adventure of his life and work. Here we are beyond causes and effects; both come together in the simultaneity of an eternal Cézanne who is at the same time the formula of what he wanted to be and what he wanted to do. There is a rapport between Cézanne's schizoid temperament and his work because the work reveals a metaphysical sense of the disease: a way of seeing the world reduced to the totality of frozen appearances, with all expressive values suspended. Thus the illness ceases to be an absurd fact and a fate and becomes a general possibility of human existence. It becomes so when this existence bravely faces one of its paradoxes, the phenomenon of expression. In this sense to be schizoid and to be Cézanne come to the same thing. It is therefore impossible to separate creative liberty from that behavior, as far as possible from deliberate, already evident in Cézanne's first gestures as a child and in the way he reacted to things. The meaning Cézanne gave to objects and faces in his paintings presented itself to him in the world as it appeared to him. Cézanne simply released this meaning: it was the objects and the faces themselves as he saw them which demanded to be painted, and Cézanne simply expressed what they *wanted* to say. How, then, can any freedom be involved? True, the conditions of existence can only affect consciousness by way of a detour through the *raisons d'être* and the justifications consciousness offers to itself. We can only see what we are by looking ahead of ourselves, through the lens of our aims, and so our life always has the form of a project or of a choice and therefore seems spontaneous. But to say that we are from the start our way of aiming at a particular future would be to say that our project has already stopped with our first ways of being, that the choice has already been made for us with our first breath. If we experience no external constraints, it is because we are our whole exterior. That eternal Cézanne whom we first saw emerge and who then brought upon the human Cézanne the events and influences which seemed *exterior* to him, and who planned all that happened to him—that attitude toward men and toward the world which was not chosen through deliberation—free as it is from external causes, is it free in respect to itself? Is the choice not pushed back beyond life, and can a choice exist where there is as yet no clearly articulated field of possibilities, only one probability and, as it were, only one temptation? If I am a certain project from birth, the given and the created are indistinguishable in me, and it is therefore impossible to name a single gesture which is merely hereditary or innate, a single gesture which is not spontaneous—but also impossible to name a single gesture which is absolutely new in regard to that way of being in the world which, from the very beginning, is myself. There is no difference between saying that our life is completely constructed and that it is completely given. If there is a true liberty, it can only come about in the course of our life by our going beyond our original situation and yet not ceasing to be the same: this is the problem. Two things are certain about freedom: that we are never determined and yet that we never change, since, looking back on what we were, we can always find hints of what we have become. It is up to us to understand both these things simultaneously, as well as the way freedom dawns in us without breaking our bonds with the world.

Such bonds are always there, even and above all when we refuse to admit they exist. Inspired by the paintings of Da Vinci, Valéry described a monster of pure freedom, without mistresses, credi-

tors, anecdotes, or adventures. No dream intervenes between himself and the things themselves; nothing taken for granted supports his certainties; and he does not read his fate in any favorite image, such as Pascal's abyss. Instead of struggling against the monsters he has understood what makes them tick, has disarmed them by his attention, and has reduced them to the state of known things. "Nothing could be more free, that is, less human, than his judgments on love and death. He hints at them in a few fragments from his notebooks: 'In the full force of its passion,' he says more or less explicitly, 'love is something so ugly that the human race would die out *(la natural si perderebbe)* if lovers could see what they were doing.' This contempt is brought out in various sketches, since the leisurely examination of certain things is, after all, the height of scorn. Thus, he now and again draws anatomical unions, frightful cross-sections of love's very act." (Valéry, trans. T. McGreevy 1929:185). He has complete mastery of his means, he does what he wants, going at will from knowledge to life with a superior elegance. Everything he did was done knowingly, and the artistic process, like the act of breathing or living, does not go beyond his knowledge. He has discovered the "central attitude," on the basis of what it is equally possible to know, to act, and to create because action and life, when turned into exercises, are not contrary to detached knowledge. He is an "intellectual power"; he is a "man of the mind."

Let us look more closely. For Leonardo there was no revelation; as Valéry said, no abyss yawned at his right hand. Undoubtedly true. But in "Saint Anne, the Virgin, and Child," the Virgin's cloak suggests a vulture where it touches the face of the Child. There is that fragment on the flight of birds where Da Vinci suddenly interrupts himself to pursue a childhood memory: "I seem to have been destined to be especially concerned with the vulture, for one of the first things I remember about my childhood is how a vulture came to me when I was still in the cradle, forced open my mouth with its tail, and struck me several times between the lips with it," (Freud 1916:33). So even this transparent consciousness has its enigma, whether truly a child's memory or a fantasy of the grown man. It does not come out of nowhere, nor does it sustain itself alone. We are caught in a secret history, in a forest of symbols. One would surely protest if Freud were to decipher the riddle from what we know about the meaning of the flight of birds and about *fellatio* fantasies and their relation to the period of nursing. But it is still a fact that to the ancient Egyptians the vulture was the symbol of maternity because they believed all vultures were female and that they were impregnated by the wind. It is also a fact that the Church Fathers used this legend to refute, on the grounds of natural history, those who were unwilling to believe in a virgin birth, and it is probable that Leonardo came across the legend in the course of his endless reading. He found in it the symbol of his own fate: he was the illegitimate son of a rich notary who married the noble Donna Albiera the very year Leonardo was born. Having no children by her, he took Leonardo into his home when the boy was five. Thus Leonardo spent the first four years of his life with his mother, the deserted peasant girl; he was a child without a father, and he got to know the world in the sole company of that unhappy mother who seemed to have miraculously created him. If we now recall that he was never known to have a mistress or even to have felt anything like passion; that he was accused—but acquitted—of homosexuality; that his diary, which tells us nothing about many other, larger expenses, notes with meticulous detail the costs of his mother's burial, as well as the cost of linen and clothing for two of his students—then we are on the verge of saying that Leonardo loved only one woman, his mother, and that this love left no room for anything but the platonic tenderness he felt for the young boys surrounding him. In the four decisive years of his childhood he formed a basic attachment which he had to give up when he was recalled to his father's home and into which he had poured all his resources of love and all his power of abandon. His thirst for life could only be turned toward the investigation and knowledge of the world, and, since he himself had been "*detached,*" he had to become that intellectual power, that man who was all mind, that stranger among men. Indifferent, incapable of any strong indignation, love or hate, he left his paintings unfinished to devote his time to bizarre experiments; he became a person in whom his contemporaries sensed a mystery. It was as if Leonardo had never quite grown up, as if all the places in his heart had already been spoken for, as if the spirit of investigation was a way for him to escape from life, as if he had invested all his power of assent in the first years of his life and had remained true to his childhood right to the end. His games were those of a child. Vasari tells how "he made up a wax paste and, during his walks, he would model from it very delicate animals, hollow and filled with air; when he breathed into them, they would float; when the air had escaped, they would fall to the ground. When the wine-grower from Belvedere found a very unusual lizard, Leonardo made wings for it out of the skin of other lizards and filled these wings with mercury so that they waved and quivered whenever the lizard moved; he likewise made eyes, a beard, and horns for it in the same way, tamed it, put it in a box, and used this lizard to terrify his friends," (Freud 1916:33). He left his work unfinished, just as his father had abandoned him. He paid no heed to authority and trusted only nature and his own judgment in matters of knowledge, as is often the case with people who have not been raised in the shadow of a father's intimidating and protective power. Thus even this pure power of examination, this solitude, this curiosity—which are the essence of mind—became Leonardo's only in reference to his history. At the height of his freedom he was, *in that very freedom,* the child he had been; he was detached in one way only because he was attached in another. Becoming a pure consciousness is just another way of taking a stand about the world and other people; Leonardo learned this attitude in assimilating the situation which his birth and childhood had made for him. There can be no consciousness that is not sustained by its primordial involvement in life and by the manner of this involvement.

Whatever is arbitrary in Freud's *explanations* cannot in this context discredit *psychoanalytical intuition.* True, the reader is stopped more than once by the lack of evidence. Why this and not something else? The question seems all the more pressing since Freud often offers several interpretations, each symptom being "over-determined" according to him. Finally, it is obvious that a doctrine which brings in sexuality everywhere cannot, by the rules of inductive logic, establish its effectiveness anywhere, since, excluding all differential cases beforehand, it deprives itself of any counter-evidence. This is how one triumphs over psychoanalysis, but only on paper. For if the suggestions of the analyst can never be proven, neither can they be eliminated: how would it be possible to credit chance with the complex correspondences which the psychoanalyst discovers between the child and the adult? How can we deny that psychoanalysis has taught us to notice echoes, allusions, repetitions from one moment of life to another—a concatenation we would not dream of doubting if Freud had stated the theory behind it correctly? Unlike the natural sciences, psychoanalysis was not meant to give us necessary relations of cause and effect but to point to motivational relationships which are in principle simply possible. We should not take Leonardo's fantasy of the vulture, or the infantile past which it masks, for a force which determined his future. Rather, it is like the words of the oracle, an ambiguous symbol which applies in advance to several possible chains of events. To be more precise: in every life, one's birth and one's past define categories or basic dimensions which do not impose any particular act but which can be found in all. Whether Leonardo yielded to his childhood or whether he wished to flee from it, he could never have been other than he was. The very decisions which transform us are always made in reference to a factual situation; such a situation can of course be accepted or refused, but it cannot fail to give us our impetus nor to be for us, as a situation "to be accepted" or "to be refused," the incarnation for us of the value we give to it. If it is the aim of psychoanalysis to describe this exchange between future and past and to show how each life muses over riddles whose final meaning is nowhere written down, then we have no right to demand inductive rigor from it. The psychoanalyst's hermeneutic musing, which multiplies the communications between us and ourselves, which takes sexuality as the symbol of existence and existence as symbol of sexuality, and which looks in the past for the meaning of the future and in the future for the meaning of the past, is better suited than rigorous induction to the circular movement of our lives, where the future rests on the past, the past on the future, and where everything symbolizes everything else. Psychoanalysis does not make freedom impossible; it teaches us to think of this freedom concretely, as a creative repetition of ourselves, always, in retrospect, faithful to ourselves.

Thus it is true both that the life of an author can teach us nothing and that—if we know how to interpret it—we can find everything in it, since it opens onto his work. Just as we may observe the movements of an unknown animal without understanding the law which inhabits and controls them, so Cézanne's observers did not guess the transmutations which he imposed on events and experiences; they were blind to *his* significance, to that glow from out of nowhere which surrounded him from time to time. But he himself was never at the center of himself: nine days out of ten all he saw around him was the wretchedness of his empirical life and of his unsuccessful attempts, the leftovers of an unknown party. Yet it was in the world that he had to realize his freedom, with colors upon a canvas. It was on the approval of others that he had to wait for the proof of his worth. That is the reason he questioned the picture emerging beneath his hand, why he hung on the glances other people directed toward his canvas. That is the reason he never finished working. We never get away from our life. We never see our ideas or our freedom face to face.

FIVE

Making Music Together
A Study in Social Relationship

ALFRED SCHUTZ

The sociological phenomenology of Alfred Schutz, indebted to Weber's sociology, Husserl's philosophy, and the thought of the American pragmatists, especially Dewey and James, forms a critique of and an alternative to positivist sociology; for Schutz, objectivity is not absolute, but the subjectivity of the outsider.

In this paper, Schutz presents his notion of the "mutual tuning-in relationship" which he posed as basic to communication. The construction of reality is conceived from the perspective of the active subject who defines his or her actions in the context of the given "stock of knowledge." Here Schutz examines the links between a musical culture and a musical performance, seeing the musical culture as the context in which a particular performance makes sense—the performance being, of course, a part of its own context; in this sense, the treatment is dialectical.

However, Schutz's insistence on the constitution of meaning *by people* is set in a theoretical frame which cannot offer any privileged analytic position, and is thus not able, ultimately, to consider thought as *praxis*. Schutz's work, along with that of other phenomenologists, does not deal with the historic production of ideological forms; rather, history becomes, itself, a self-conscious reification (another text). The interested student will find Schutz's longer work, *The Phenomenology of the Social World,* and Peter Berger's and Thomas Luckman's *The Social Construction of Reality,* helpful introductions to this viewpoint (see also Geertz in this volume, and Geertz, *The Interpretation of Cultures,* especially "Thick Description").

MUSIC IS A MEANINGFUL CONTEXT which is not bound to a conceptual scheme. Yet this meaningful context can be communicated. The process of communication between composer and listener normally requires an intermediary: an individual performer or a group of coperformers. Among all these partici-pants there prevail social relations of a highly complicated structure.

To analyze certain elements of this structure is the purpose of this paper. The discussion is not aimed at problems commonly relegated to the realm of the so-called sociology of music, although it is believed that an investigation of the social relationships among the participants in the musical process is a prerequisite for any research in this field; nor is

Reprinted by permission from *Social Research,* 1951, vol. 18, no. 1, pp. 76–97.

it concerned with a phenomenology of musical experience, although some elementary observations regarding the structure of music will have to be made. The chief interest of our analysis consists in the particular character of all social interactions connected with the musical process: they are doubtless meaningful to the actor as well as to the addressee, but this meaning structure is not capable of being expressed in conceptual terms; they are founded upon communication, but not *primarily* upon a semantic system used by the communicator as a scheme of expression and by his partner as a scheme of interpretation.[1] For this very reason it can be hoped that a study of the social relationships connected with the musical process may lead to some insights valid for many other forms of social intercourse, perhaps even to illumination of a certain aspect of the structure of social interaction as such that has not so far attracted from social scientists the attention it deserves. This introductory statement requires some clarification.

When sociologists speak of social interaction they usually have in mind a set of interdependent actions of several human beings, mutually related by the meaning which the actor bestows upon his action and which he supposes to be understood by his partner. To use Max Weber's terminology, these actions have to be oriented in their course with reference to one another. In studying the process of communication as such, most sociologists have taken as a model either the interplay of significative gestures or language in the broadest sense of this term. G. H. Mead, for example, finds that two wrestlers communicate with each other by a "conversation of gestures" which enables either of the participants to anticipate the other's behavior and to orient his own behavior by means of such anticipation, (Mead 1937:14, 63, 253 ff.). We may also say that two chess players who both know the functional significance of each chessman in general, as well as within the unique concrete constellation at any given moment of a particular game, communicate their thoughts to each other in terms of the "vocabulary" and "syntax" of the scheme of expression and interpretation common to both of them, which is determined by the body of the "rules of the game." In the case of ordinary speech or the use of written symbols, it is assumed that each partner interprets his own behavior as well as that of the other in conceptual terms which can be translated and conveyed to the other partner by way of a common semantic system.

In any of these cases the existence of a semantic system—be it the "conversation of significant gestures," the "rules of the game," or "language proper"—is simply presupposed as something given from the outset and the problem of "significance" remains unquestioned. The reason for this is quite clear: in the social world into which we are born, language (in the broadest sense) is admittedly the paramount vehicle of communication; its conceptual structure and its power of typification make it the outstanding tool for the conveying of meaning. There is even a strong tendency in contemporary thought to identify meaning with its semantic expression and to consider language, speech, symbols, significant gestures, as the fundamental condition of social intercourse as such. Even Mead's highly original endeavor to explain the origin of language by an interplay of significant gestures—his famous example of the dogfight—starts from the supposition that a prelinguistic "conversation" of "attitudes" is possible. It is not necessary to accept Mead's basic position of "social behaviorism" in order to admit that, as has so often happened, he has seen a crucial problem more clearly than others. Nevertheless, the solution he offers only appears to remove the difficulties connected with the basic issue, namely, whether the communicative process is really the foundation of all possible social relationships, or whether, on the contrary, all communication presupposes the existence of some kind of social interaction which, though it is an indispensable condition of all possible communication, does not enter the communicative process and is not capable of being grasped by it. It is currently rather fashionable to dismiss problems of this kind with a haughty reference to the question of the priority of the chicken or the egg. Such an attitude not only reflects an unfamiliarity with the philosophical issue discussed by the Schoolmen under the heading of priority, but also constitutes a self-made obstacle to a serious analysis of the various problems of foundation important especially for the social sciences.

As far as the question under scrutiny is concerned, the concrete researches of many sociologists and philosophers have aimed at certain forms of social intercourse which necessarily precede all communication. Wiese's "contact-situations," Scheler's perceptual theory of the alter ego, to a certain extent Cooley's concept of the face-to-face relationship, Malinowski's interpretation of speech as originating within the situation determined by social interaction, Sartre's basic concept of "looking at the Other and being looked at by the Other" *(le regard),* all these are just a few examples of the endeavor to investigate what might be called the "mutual tuning-in relationship" upon which alone all communication is founded. It is precisely this mutual tuning-in relationship by which the "I" and the "Thou" are experienced by both participants as a "We" in vivid presence.

Instead of entering here into the complicated philosophical analysis of this problem, it may be permissible to refer to a series of well-known phenomena in the social world in which this precommunicative social relationship comes to the foreground. Mead's example of wrestlers has already been mentioned. It is typical for a set of similar interrelated activities such as the relationship between pitcher and catcher, tennis players, fencers, and so on; we find the same features in marching together, dancing together, making love together, or making music together, and this last-named activity will serve as an example for analysis in the following pages. It is hoped that this analysis will in some measure contribute to clarification of the structure of the mutual tuning-in relationship, which originates in the possibility of living together simultaneously in specific dimensions of time. It is also hoped that the study of the particular communicative situation within the musical process will shed some light on the nonconceptual aspect involved in any kind of communication.

Certain elements of the social structure of the musical process were analyzed in one of the later writings of the famous French sociologist, Maurice Halbwachs (1939). The paper in question deserves special attention because it was written as a kind of introduction to a major study on the nature of time, which was unfortunately never completed owing to the author's tragic death in the concentration camp of Buchenwald in July 1944.

Halbwachs' basic position is well known. He assumed that all kinds of memory are determined by a social framework and that individual memory cannot be conceived of without the assumption of a collective memory from which all individual recollection derives. This basic principle—which it is not our concern to criticize here—was applied to the problem of musical communication because the author felt that the very structure of music—its development within the flux of time, its detachment from anything that lasts, its realization by re-creation—offers an excellent opportunity for demonstrating that there is no other possibility of preserving a set of recollections with all their shades and details except by recourse to the collective memory. In other words, Halbwachs was primarily concerned with analyzing the social structure of music. Curiously enough, he divided the realm of music into two distinct parts: music as experienced by the educated musician and music as experienced by the layman. With regard to the former, Halbwachs came to the conclusion that it is first of all the possibility of translating music into visual symbols—that is, the system of musical notation—which makes transmission of music possible. To be sure, the signs of musical notation are not images of the sounds. They are, however, means of expressing in a conventional language all the commands which the musician must obey if he wants to reproduce a piece of music properly. The conventional character of

the signs of musical notation and their combination consists in the fact that they have meaning merely by continuous reference to the group which invented and adopted them. This group, the "society" of educated musicians, lives in a world exclusively filled with sounds and is interested in nothing else but creating or listening to a combination of sounds. Even the invention of new combinations of sounds is possible only within the framework of the socially conditioned musical language (which, for Halbwachs, was identical with the system of musical notation). The creative act of the composer is merely a discovery in the same world of sounds that is accessible exclusively to the society of musicians. It is precisely because the composer accepts the conventions of this society and because he penetrates more deeply into them than others that he can make his discoveries. The musical language is not an instrument invented afterward in order to put down and to transmit to other musicians what one of them has spontaneously invented. On the contrary, it is this very language which creates music.

This is roughly Halbwachs' main argument for the social character of the musician's music. Yet the child or the musically uneducated person learns nursery rhymes, anthems, popular songs, dance or march melodies by rote without any knowledge of musical notation. How is this possible and how can this kind of memory for sound combinations be referred to the collective memory? Halbwachs' answer is that the layman's memory of musical events is also founded upon the collective memory but always attached to metamusical experiences.[2] The melody of a song is remembered because the words—a social product—are remembered. As for dances or marches or other pieces of music dissociated from words, it is the rhythm of marching, dancing, speaking, that serves as the carrier of the musical recollection. Yet rhythm does not exist in nature; it, too, is a result of our living in society. The insulated individual could not discover rhythm. No evidence is offered for this statement (which I believe to be wrong) except reference to the rhythmical character of work songs and of our speech. Both words and rhythms are of social origin and so, consequently, are the layman's musical experiences. But they refer to a world in which other than exclusively sonorous events exist and to a society not exclusively interested in musical texture. So much for Halbwachs.

Interesting as Halbwachs' analysis is, it suffers from various shortcomings. In the first place, it seems to me that the distinction between a musician's music and music accessible to the layman is without any foundation in fact. But postponing the discussion of this question and restricting ourselves for the time being to the province of music allegedly accessible only to the educated musician, the following objections to Halbwachs' theory must be raised: (1) He identifies the musical thought with its communication. (2) He identifies musical communication with musical language which to him is the system of musical notation. (3) He identifies musical notation with the social background of the musical process.

In regard to the first objection, it is clear that from the point of view of the composer a musical thought may be conceived without any intention of communication. This thought may be a perfect piece of music, having its specific meaning structure; it may be remembered at will without being translated into actual sounds or into the visible form of notation. This is, of course, not a particularity of the musical process. It has been said that Raphael would have been one of the greatest painters even if he had been born without arms. In general, all kinds of mental activities performed in phantasy may be perfectly meaningful and capable of being mentally reproduced within the solitude of the individual consciousness. All our unexpressed thoughts, our day dreams as well as projects for future action never carried out, show these features. But any kind of communication between man and his fellow-man and therefore the communication of musical thoughts presupposes an event or a series of events in the outer world which functions, on the one hand, as a scheme of expression of the communicator's thought and, on the other hand, as a scheme of interpretation of such thought by the addressee. Musical thoughts can be transmitted to others either by the mechanics of audible sound or by the symbols of musical notation.

It is hard to understand why Halbwachs regarded only the latter as the appropriate form of musical communication. Obviously he took as a model of his analysis the situation in which the composer has to communicate his musical idea to the performer by way of a system of visible signs before the performer can translate these ideas into sounds to be grasped by the listener. But this procedure has nothing to do with the particularities of musical communication as such; it is a more or less technical question. We may perfectly well understand an improvisation executed by one or several instrumentalists. Or we may, with Tovey, foresee a revolution in the process of musical communication by means of the microscopic study of phonographic records. "There is nothing to prevent the individual production of music directly in terms of the phonographic needle. That is to say, the composer, untrammeled by the technique of instruments, will prescribe all producible timbre in whatever pitches and rhythms he pleases, and will have no more direct cooperation with the craftsman who models the phonographic wave-lines, than the violinist may with Stradivarius" (Tovey 1929).

Musical notation is, therefore, just one among several vehicles of communicating musical thought. But musical notation is by no means identical with musical language. Its semantic system is of quite another kind than that of ideograms, letters, or mathematical or chemical symbols. The ideogram refers immediately to the represented concept and so does the mathematical or chemical symbol. The written word in our alphabetic languages refers to the sound of the spoken word and through it as an intermediary to the concept it conveys. As stated above, the meaning of a musical process cannot be related to a conceptual scheme, and the particular function of musical notation today as well as in its historical development reflects this situation. The musical sign is nothing but instruction to the performer to produce by means of his voice or his instrument a sound of a particular pitch and duration, giving in addition, at certain historical periods, suggestions as to tempo, dynamics, and expression, or directions as to the connection with other sounds (by such devices as ties, slurs, and the like). All these elements of the tonal material can only be approximately prescribed and the way to obtain the indicated effect is left to the performer. "The composer's specific indications are themselves not always a part of his original creation but rather one musician's message to another about it, a hint about how to secure in performance a convincing transmission of the work's feeling content without destroying its emotional and intellectual community," says a well-known composer and critic (Thompson 1948:296). And the conductor, Furtwängler, is certainly right in stating that the composer's text "cannot give any indication as to the really intended volume of a *forte,* the really intended speed of a *tempo,* since every *forte* and every *tempo* has to be modified in practice in accordance with the place of the performance and the setting and the strength of the performing group" and that "the expression marks have intentionally a merely symbolic value with respect to the whole work and are not intended to be valid for the single instrument, wherefore an '*ff*' for the bassoon has quite another meaning than for the trombone" (Furtwängler 1934:609 ff.).

Thus, all musical notation remains of necessity vague and open to manifold interpretations, and it is up to the reader or performer to decipher the hints in the score and to define the approximations. These limits vary widely in the course of the historical development of musical culture. The more closely we approach the present in the study of the history of music, the lower the level of the general musical culture of performers and of listeners, and the stronger the tendency of the composer to make his system of notation as exact and precise as possible, that is, to limit more and more the performer's freedom of interpretation.

To be sure, all signs of musical notation are conventional; but, as has been shown, the system of musical notation is more or less accidental to the process of musical communication. A social theory of music therefore does not have to be founded on the conventional character of the visual signs but rather on the sum total of what we have just called musical culture against the background of which the reader's or performer's interpretation of these signs takes place.

To make this web of social relationships called musical culture clearer, let us imagine a lonely performer of a piece of music sitting at his piano before the score of a sonata by a minor master of the nineteenth century which, we assume, is entirely unknown to him. Furthermore, we assume that our piano player is equally proficient as a technician and sight reader and that consequently no mechanical or other external obstacle will hinder the flux of his performance.

Yet, having hardly made these two assumptions, we hesitate. Are they indeed compatible with each other? Can we really maintain that the sonata in question is *entirely* unknown to our performer? He could not be an accomplished technician and sight reader without having attained a certain level of musical culture enabling him to read off-hand a piece of music of the *type* of that before him. Consequently, although this particular sonata and perhaps all the other works of this particular composer might be unknown to him, he will nevertheless have a well-founded knowledge of the type of musical form called "sonata within the meaning of nineteenth century piano music," of the type of themes and harmonies used in such compositions of that period, of the

expressional contents he may expect to find in them—in sum, of the typical "style" in which music of this kind is written and in which it has to be executed. Even before starting to play or to read the first chord our musician is referred to a more or less clearly organized, more or less coherent, more or less distinct set of his previous experiences, which constitute in their totality a kind of preknowledge of the piece of music at hand. To be sure, this preknowledge refers merely to the *type* to which this individual piece of music belongs and not to its particular and unique individuality. But the player's general preknowledge of its typicality becomes the scheme of reference for his interpretation of its particularity. This scheme of reference determines, in a general way, the player's anticipations of what he may or may not find in the composition before him. Such anticipations are more or less empty; they may be fulfilled and justified by the musical events he will experience when he starts to play the sonata or they may "explode" and be annihilated.

In more general terms, the player approaching a so-called unknown piece of music does so from a historically—in one's own case, autobiographically—determined situation, determined by his stock of musical experiences at hand in so far as they are typically relevant to the anticipated novel experience before him.[3] This stock of experiences refers indirectly to all his past and present fellow-men whose acts or thoughts have contributed to the building up of his knowledge. This includes what he has learned from his teachers, and his teachers from their teachers; what he has taken in from other players' execution; and what he has appropriated from the manifestations of the musical thought of the composer. Thus, the bulk of musical knowledge—as of knowledge in general—is socially derived. And within this socially derived knowledge there stands out the knowledge transmitted from those upon whom the prestige of authenticity and authority has been bestowed, that is, from the great masters among the composers and the acknowledged interpreters of their work. Musical knowledge transmitted by them is not only socially derived; it is also socially approved[4] being regarded as authentic and therefore more qualified to become a pattern for others than knowledge originating elsewhere.

In the situation we have chosen to investigate—the actual performance of a piece of music—the genesis of the stock of knowledge at hand with all its hidden social references is, so to speak, prehistoric. The web of socially derived and socially approved knowledge constitutes merely the setting for the main social relationship into which our piano player (and also any listener or mere reader of music) will enter: that with the composer of the sonata before him. It is the grasping of the composer's musical thought and its interpretation by re-creation which stand in the center of the player's field of consciousness or, to use a phenomenological term, which become "thematic" for his ongoing activity. This thematic kernel stands out against the horizon of preacquired knowledge, which knowledge functions as a scheme of reference and interpretation for the grasping of the composer's thought. It is now necessary to describe the structure of this social relationship between composer and beholder,[5] but before entering into its analysis it might

be well to forestall a possible misunderstanding. It is by no means our thesis that a work of music (or of art in general) cannot be understood except by reference to its individual author or to the circumstances—biographical or other—in which he created this particular work. It is certainly not a prerequisite for the understanding of the musical content of the so-called Moonlight Sonata to take cognizance of the silly anecdotes which popular belief attaches to the creation of this work; it is not even indispensable to know that the sonata was composed by a man called Beethoven who lived then and there and went through such and such personal experiences. Any work of art, once accomplished, exists as a meaningful entity independent of the personal life of its creator.[6] The social relationship between composer and beholder as it is understood here is established exclusively by the fact that a beholder of a piece of music participates in and to a certain extent re-creates the experiences of the—let us suppose, anonymous—fellow-man who created this work not only as an expression of his musical thoughts but with communicative intent.

For our purposes a piece of music may be defined[7]—very roughly and tentatively, indeed—as a meaningful arrangement of tones in inner time. It is the occurrence in inner time, Bergson's *durée,* which is the very form of existence of music. The flux of tones unrolling in inner time is an arrangement meaningful to both the composer and the beholder, because and in so far as it evokes in the stream of consciousness participating in it an interplay of recollections, retentions, protensions, and anticipations which interrelate the successive elements. To be sure, the sequence of tones occurs in the irreversible direction of inner time, in the direction, as it were, from the first bar to the last. But this irreversible flux is not irretrievable. The composer, by the specific means of his art,[8] has arranged it in such a way that the consciousness of the beholder is led to refer what he actually hears to what he anticipates will follow and also to what he has just been hearing and what he has heard ever since this piece of music began. The hearer, therefore, listens to the ongoing flux of music, so to speak, not only in the direction from the first to the last bar but simultaneously in a reverse direction back to the first one.[9]

It is essential for our problem to gain a clearer understanding of the time dimension in which music occurs. It was stated above that the inner time, the *durée*, is the very form of existence of music. Of course, playing an instrument, listening to a record, reading a page of music, all these are events occurring in outer time, the time that can be measured by metronomes and clocks, that is, the time that the musician "counts" in order to assure the correct "tempo." But to make clear why we consider inner time the very medium within which the musical flow occurs, let us imagine that the slow and the fast movement of a symphony each fill a twelve-inch record. Our watches show that the playing of either record takes about three and a half minutes. This is a fact which might possibly interest the program maker of a broadcasting station. To the beholder it means nothing. To him it is not true that the time he lived through while listening to the slow movement was of "equal length" with that which he dedicated to the fast one. While listening he lives in a dimension of time incomparable with that which can be subdivided into homo-geneous parts. The outer time is measurable; there are pieces of equal length; there are minutes and hours and the length of the groove to be traversed by the needle of the record player. There is no such yardstick for the dimension of inner time the listener lives in; there is no equality between its pieces, if pieces there were at all.[10] It may come as a complete surprise to him that the main theme of the second movement of Beethoven's Pianoforte Sonata in d-minor, Op. 31, No. 2, takes as much time in the mere clock sense—namely, one minute—as the last movement of the same sonata up to the end of the exposition (Tovey 1945:57).

The preceding remarks serve to clarify the particular social relationship between composer and beholder. Although separated by hundreds of years, the latter participates with quasi simultaneity in the former's stream of consciousness by performing with him step by step the ongoing articulation of his musical thought. The beholder, thus, is united with the composer by a time dimension common to both, which is nothing other than a derived form of the vivid present shared by the partners in a genuine face-to-face relation[11] such as prevails between speaker and listener.

But is this reconstruction of a vivid present, this establishment of a quasi simultaneity, specific to the relationship between the stream of consciousness of the composer and that of the beholder? Can it not also be found in the relationship between the reader of a letter with its writer, the student of a scientific book with its author, the high-school boy who learns the demonstration of the rule of the hypotenuse with Pythagoras? Certainly, in all these cases the single phases of the author's articulated thought are polythetically—that is, step by step—coperformed or reperformed by the recipient, and thus a quasi simultaneity of both streams of thought takes place. The reader of a scientific book, for instance, builds up word by word the meaning of a sentence, sentence by sentence that of a paragraph, paragraph by paragraph that of a chapter. But once having coperformed these polythetic steps of constituting the conceptual meaning of this sentence (paragraph, chapter), the reader may grasp the outcome of this constitutive process, the resulting conceptual meaning, in a single glance—monothetically, as Husserl puts it (Husserl 1931:§§118, 119; pp. 334 ff.)—that is, independently of the polythetic steps in which and by which this meaning has been constituted. In the same way I may grasp monothetically the meaning of the Pythagorean theorem $a^2 + b^2 = c^2$, without restarting to perform the single mental operations of deriving it step by step from certain assured premises, and I may do so even if I have forgotten how to demonstrate the theorem.

The meaning of a musical work,[12] however, is essentially of a polythetical structure. It cannot be grasped monothetically. It consists in the articulated step-by-step occurrence in inner time, in the very polythetic constitutional process itself. I may give a name to a specific piece of music, calling it "Moonlight Sonata" or "Ninth Symphony"; I may even say, "These were variations with a finale in the form of a passacaglia," or characterize, as certain program notes are prone to do, the particular mood or emotion this piece of music is supposed to have evoked in me. But the musical content itself, its very meaning, can be grasped merely by reimmersing oneself in the ongoing flux, by reproducing thus the articulated musical occurrence as it

unfolds in polythetic steps in inner time, a process itself belonging to the dimension of inner time. And it will "take as much time" to reconstitute the work in recollection as to experience it for the first time. In both cases I have to reestablish the quasi simultaneity of my stream of consciousness with that of the composer described herein before.[13]

We have therefore the following situation: two series of events in inner time, one belonging to the stream of consciousness of the composer, the other to the stream of consciousness of the beholder, are lived through in simultaneity, which simultaneity is created by the ongoing flux of the musical process. It is the thesis of the present paper that this sharing of the other's flux of experiences in inner time, this living through a vivid present in common, constitutes what we called in our introductory paragraphs the mutual tuning-in relationship, the experience of the "We," which is at the foundation of all possible communication. The peculiarity of the musical process of communication consists in the essentially polythetic character of the communicated content, that is to say, in the fact that both the flux of the musical events and the activities by which they are communicated, belong to the dimension of inner time. This statement seems to hold good for any kind of music. There is, however, one kind of music—the polyphonic music of the western world—which has the magic power of realizing by its specific musical means the possibility of living simultaneously in two or more fluxes of events. In polyphonic writing each voice has its particular meaning; each represents a series of, so to speak, autarchic musical events; but this flux is designed to roll on in simultaneity with other series of musical events, not less autarchic in themselves, but coexisting with the former and combining with them by this very simultaneity into a new meaningful arrangement.[14]

So far we have investigated the social relationship between composer and beholder. What we have found to be the outstanding feature of musical communication—that is, the sharing of the ongoing flux of the musical content—holds good whether this process occurs merely in the beholder's recollection,[15] or through his reading the score, or with the help of audible sounds. To believe that the visible signs of musical notation are essential to this process is no more erroneous than to assert, as even Husserl does, that a symphony exists merely in its performance by an orchestra. To be sure, the participation in the process of musical communication by means other than audible sounds requires either a certain natural gift or special training on the part of the beholder. It is the eminent social function of the performer—the singer or player of an instrument—to be the intermediary between composer and listener. By his re-creation of the musical process the performer partakes in the stream of consciousness of the composer as well as of the listener. He thereby enables the latter to become immersed in the particular articulation of the flux of inner time which is the specific meaning of the piece of music in question. It is of no great importance whether performer and listener share together a vivid present in face-to-face relation or whether through the interposition of mechanical devices, such as records, only a quasi simultaneity between the stream of consciousness of the mediator and the listener has been established. The latter case always refers to the former. The difference between the two shows merely that the

relationship between performer and audience is subject to all variations of intensity, intimacy, and anonymity. This can be easily seen by imagining the audience as consisting of one single person, a small group of persons in a private room, a crowd filling a big concert hall, or the entirely unknown listeners of a radio performance or a commercially distributed record. In all these circumstances performer and listener are "tuned-in" to one another, are living together through the same flux, are growing older together while the musical process lasts. This statement applies not only to the fifteen or twenty minutes of measurable outer time required for the performance of this particular piece of music, but primarily to the coperformance in simultaneity of the polythetic steps by which the musical content articulates itself in inner time. Since, however, all performance as an act of communication is based upon a series of events in the outer world—in our case the flux of audible sounds—it can be said that the social relationship between performer and listener is founded upon the common experience of living simultaneously in several dimensions of time.

The same situation, the pluridimensionality of time simultaneously lived through by man and fellow-man, occurs in the relationship between two or more individuals making music together, which we are now prepared to investigate. If we accept Max Weber's famous definition, according to which a social relationship is "the conduct of a plurality of persons which according to their subjective meaning are mutually concerned with each other and oriented by virtue of this fact," then both the relationship prevailing between intermediary and listener and that prevailing between coperformers fall under this definition. But there is an important difference between them. The listener's coperforming of the polythetic steps in which the musical content unfolds is merely an internal activity (although as an "action involving the action of Others and being oriented by them in its course" undoubtedly a social action within Weber's definition). The coperformers (let us say a soloist accompanied by a keyboard instrument) have to execute activities gearing into the outer world and thus occurring in spatialized outer time. Consequently, each coperformer's action is oriented not only by the composer's thought and his relationship to the audience but also reciprocally by the experiences in inner and outer time of his fellow performer. Technically, each of them finds in the music sheet before him only that portion of the musical content which the composer has assigned to his instrument for translation into sound. Each of them has, therefore, to take into account what the other has to execute in simultaneity. He has not only to interpret his own part which as such remains necessarily fragmentary, but he has also to anticipate the other player's interpretation of his—the Other's—part and, even more, the Other's anticipations of his own execution. Either's freedom of interpreting the composer's thought is restrained by the freedom granted to the Other. Either has to foresee by listening to the Other, by protensions and anticipations, any turn the Other's interpretation may take and has to be prepared at any time to be leader or follower. Both share not only the inner *durée* in which the content of the music played actualizes itself; each, simultaneously, shares in vivid present the Other's stream of consciousness in immediacy. This is possible because

making music together occurs in a true face-to-face relationship—inasmuch as the participants are sharing not only a section of time but also a sector of space. The Other's facial expressions, his gestures in handling his instrument, in short all the activities of performing, gear into the outer world and can be grasped by the partner in immediacy. Even if performed without communicative intent, these activities are interpreted by him as indications of what the Other is going to do and therefore as suggestions or even commands for his own behavior. Any chamber musician knows how disturbing an arrangement that prevents the coperformers from seeing each other can be. Moreover, all the activities of performing occur in outer time, the time which can be measured by counting or the metronome or the beat of the conductor's baton. The coperformers may have recourse to these devices when for one reason or another the flux of inner time in which the musical content unfolds has been interrupted.

Such a close face-to-face relationship can be established in immediacy only among a small number of coperformers. Where a larger number of executants is required, one of them—a song leader, concert master, or continuo player—has to assume the leadership, that is, to establish with each of the performers the contact which they are unable to find with one another in immediacy. Or a nonexecutant, the conductor, has to assume this function. He does so by action in the outer world, and his evocative gestures into which he translates the musical events going on in inner time, replace for each performer the immediate grasping of the expressive activities of all his coperformers.

Our analysis of making music together

has been restricted to what Halbwachs calls the musician's music. Yet there is in principle no difference between the performance of a modern orchestra or chorus and people sitting around a campfire and singing to the strumming of a guitar or a congregation singing hymns under the leadership of the organ. And there is no difference in principle between the performance of a string quartet and the improvisations at a jam session of accomplished jazz players. These examples simply give additional support to our thesis that the system of musical notation is merely a technical device and accidental to the social relationship prevailing among the performers. This social relationship is founded upon the partaking in common of different dimensions of time simultaneously lived through by the participants. On the one hand, there is the inner time in which the flux of the musical events unfolds, a dimension in which each performer re-creates in polythetic steps the musical thought of the (possibly anonymous) composer and by which he is also connected with the listener. On the other hand, making music together is an event in outer time, presupposing also a face-to-face relationship, that is, a community of space, and it is this dimension which unifies the fluxes of inner time and warrants their synchronization into a vivid present.

At the beginning of this paper the hope was expressed that the analysis of the social relationship involved in making music together might contribute to a clarification of the tuning-in relationship and the process of communication as such. It appears that all possible communication presupposes a mutual tuning-in relationship between the communicator and the addressee of the communication. This relationship is established by the reciprocal sharing of the Other's flux of experiences in inner time, by living through a vivid present together, by experiencing this togetherness as a "We." Only within this experience does the Other's conduct become meaningful to the partner tuned in on him—that is, the Other's body and its movements can be and are interpreted as a field of expression of events within his inner life. Yet not everything that is interpreted by the partner as an expression of an event in the Other's inner life is meant by the Other to express—that is, to communicate to the partner—such an event. Facial expressions, gait, posture, ways of handling tools and instruments, without communicative intent, are examples of such a situation. The process of communication proper is bound to an occurrence in the outer world, which has the structure of a series of events polythetically built up in outer time. This series of events is intended by the communicator as a scheme of expression open to adequate interpretation by the addressee. Its very polythetic character warrants the simultaneity of the ongoing flux of the communicator's experiences in inner time with the occurrences in the outer world, as well as the simultaneity of these polythetic occurrences in the outer world with the addressee's interpreting experiences in inner time. Communicating with one another presupposes, therefore, the simultaneous partaking of the partners in various dimensions of outer and inner time—in short in growing older together. This seems to be valid for all kinds of communication, the *essentially* polythetic ones as well as those conveying meaning in conceptual terms—that is, those in which the result of the communicative process can be grasped monothetically.

It is hardly necessary to point out that the remarks in the preceding paragraph refer to communication within the face-to-face relationship. It can, however, be shown that all the other forms of possible communication can be explained as derived from this paramount situation. But this, as well as the elaboration of the theory of the tuning-in relationship, must be reserved for another occasion.

Notes

1. The system of musical notation, as will be shown, has quite another function and a merely secondary one.
2. This term is not used by Halbwachs, but probably renders what he meant.
3. All this is by no means limited to the situation under scrutiny. Indeed, our analysis has so far been merely an application of Husserl's masterful investigations into the structure of our experience. According to him the factual world is always experienced as a world of preconstituted types. To embark upon the importance of this discovery by Husserl, especially for the concept of type, so fundamental for all social sciences, is not within the scope of the present paper. This theory has been touched upon in Husserl's *Ideas: General Introduction to Pure Phenomenology* (1931) and has been fully developed in his *Erfahrung und Urteil* (1939).
4. With regard to the concepts of socially derived and socially approved knowledge, see Schutz's paper, "The Well-Informed Citizen" (1946).
5. The term "beholder" shall include the player, listener, and reader of music.
6. This problem has been discussed for the realm of poetry by E. M. W. Tillyard and C. S. Lewis, in their witty and profound book, *The Personal Heresy, A Controversy* (1939).
7. An excellent survey of philosophical theories of music can be found in Suzanne K. Langer's *Philosophy in a New Key* (1942), Chs. 8 and 9, although the author's own position seems unsatisfactory. It may be summed up in the following quotation: "Music has all the earmarks of a true symbolism, except one: the existence of an *assigned connotation*. . . . It is a limited idiom like an artifical language, *only even less successful; for music at its highest, though clearly a symbolic form, is an unconsummated symbol*. Articulation is its life but not assertion; expressiveness, but not expression."
8. Some of these specific means are essential to any kind of music, others belong merely to a particular musical culture. Rhythm, melody, tonal harmony, technique of diminution, and the so-called forms based on what Tovey calls the larger harmony, such as Sonata, Rondo, Variations, and so on, are certainly characteristics of the musical culture of the nineteenth century. It may be hoped that intensified research in the phenomenology of musical experience will shed some light upon the difficult problem as to which of these means of musical arrangement of tones is essential to music in general, regardless of what its particular historical setting may be.
9. This insight has been formulated in an unsurpassable way by St. Augustine in Book XI, Ch. 38, of his *Confessions*.
10. We do not need the reference to the specific experience of listening to music in order to understand the incommensurability of inner and outer time. The hand of our watch may run equally over half the dial, whether we wait before the door of a surgeon operating on a person dear to us or whether we are having a good time in congenial company. All these are well-known facts.
11. This term, here and in the following paragraphs, is not used in the sense that Charles Horton Cooley used it in *Social Organization* (1937); it signifies merely that the participants in such a relation share time and space while it lasts. An analysis of Cooley's concept can be found in Schutz's "The Homecomer" (1945).
12. Also of other time-objects such as dance or poetry (see n. 13 below).
13. This thesis is simply a corollary to the other—that the meaning context of music is not related to a conceptual scheme. A poem, for instance, may *also* have a conceptual content, and this, of course, may be grasped monothetically. I can tell in one or two sentences the story of the ancient mariner, and in fact this is done in the author's gloss. But in so far as the poetical meaning of Coleridge's poem surpasses the conceptual meaning—that is, in so far as it *is* poetry—I can only bring it before my mind by reciting or reading it from beginning to end.
14. See, for instance, the Brahms song, *"Wir wandelten wir zwei zusammen,"* in the introduction of which the walking together of the two lovers is expressed by the specific musical means of a canon, or the same device used in the Credo of Bach's *B-minor Mass* for expressing the mystery of the Trinity (*"Et in unum"*).
15. In this connection, one recalls Brahms' dictum: "If I want to listen to a fine peformance of *Don Giovanni,* I light a good cigar and stretch out on my sofa."

SIX

Lévi-Strauss, Literarily

JAMES A. BOON

This selection from James Boon's *From Symbolism to Structuralism* combines an exposition of basic structuralist ideas with an analysis which goes part of the way toward situating structuralism in a cultural framework.

The crux of Boon's presentation is Lévi-Strauss's notion that "there are . . . no substantive others," that people cannot be "approached as objects." Instead, "in the absence of simple, whole man-objects, we must proceed by translating any texts *they* provide into structures which can then be related to the structure of the text that is ourselves." This is one of the clearest presentations of the structuralist viewpoint available.

But in order to understand it, it must be contrasted with another view: for example, the notion (deriving from George Herbert Mead and Phenomenology) that a person's life is a process of self-construction, in which the person strives toward his own integration, both internal and external, through the medium of his or her relations to others, which are visible, to the analyst and the person, as the person's actions and products. Note that, in contrast to this view (articulated at more length in the General Introduction), structuralism makes "objects" of people's products and the processes (rendered by structuralism as "structures") of production. Thus, the de-objectification of the other is accomplished at the cost of another objectification: of *both* the other and the self, and the acts which bring them together.

WHAT ARE THE UNIFYING FEATURES of the series of critical ramifications extending from novelistic Lévi-Strauss to anthropological Proust?

One such theme is the use of *distance* as an analytic and poetic device—distance being that removal from the event itself, which facilitates determining the significance of the event. Rousseau has been hailed as "the first critic of alienation, the first unmasker of culture" (Becker 1968:32). He recognized that to analyze behavior, one must stand abstracted from it, whether it is the behavior of others or of oneself. Even in daily experience, Rousseau confesses how he had to wait until *after* any personal confrontation to think of what he should have said. For, only in the distance of retrospect can the significant features of the whole event (along with

Reprinted by permission of the publishers from James A. Boon, *From Symbolism to Structuralism: Lévi-Strauss in a Literary Tradition,* copyright © 1972 (New York: Harper & Row; Oxford: Basil Blackwell, 1972), pp. 197–208.

the most appropriate response to them) be discerned. That is why he writes. Proust too makes of temporal removal an operational principle for disclosing the meanings and interrelationships of the everyday; and he at last translates this *time* into his work's final metaphor of spatial elevation on a pair of stilts— from which vantage point he attains his vision of unity. What Proust does for the experience of personalities, Lévi-Strauss envisions comparative human science doing for grouped man, by adding cross-cultural space to history's time:

It was necessary to await anthropologists in order to discover that social phenomena obey structural arrangements. The reason is simple: it is that structures appear only through observation practiced from outside. Inversely, this observation can never grasp processes, which are not analytic objects, but the particular fashion in which a temporality is lived by a subject. This is to say, on the one hand, that process exists only for a subject engaged in his own historical becoming, or more exactly in that of the group to which he belongs; and, on the other hand, that in a given group, processes are numerous enough—and sufficiently different from each other—for there to exist sub-groups of identification: for an aristocrat and a *sans-culotte,* the Revolution of 1789 is not the same process. And there exists a "meta-process" integrating these irreducible experiences only for historically posterior thinking . . . (Lévi-Strauss 1962b:44–45; my trans.)

Ideally anthropology employs both sorts of distance—spatial (cross-cultural) and temporal. History's procedural drawback is that historians generally study their own societies, thus lacking comparative perspective. Anthropology's circumstantial drawback is that preliterate groups lack historical records. But ideally anthropology should utilize both

varieties of distance in discerning the structure of cultural experience, just as Proust's narrative technique does so by establishing the point of view of a narrator who is both outside and later than the changing self of the novel's hero. As Richard Macksey observes:

The point of view from which the action is seen is curiously divided between the Marcel of past time who acts and grows old through the course of the narrative, and the Marcel who recollects him from the distant vantage and is at last joined by him to pass, with the final footfall, into time regained. The situation is not unlike that of "Rousseau juge de Jean-Jacques". . . . Thus the action can be likened to an odyssey or pilgrimage where the traveller in time has forgotten the location of the homeland or the significance of the shrine. (Macksey 1962:108)

The traveller of *Tristes Tropiques* adopts a similar technique but incorporates into the procedure the rescue of *other* cultural forms; for, the self cannot be rescued from time unless articulated into distinct relief by the *other*. Lévi-Strauss chooses man and tries to rescue the other, too.

Related to this theme of analytic distance, is the increasing denial of what might be called *substance* (as contrasted to *structure*). Simply and schematically, Rousseau showed how there was no substance to the self which must be reconstructed *ex post facto*. Then, Mein observes: "Baudelaire and Proust, with their conception of personality as a series of successive states, are prone to analyze ways of escaping the fate of even appearing to have a single, official identity" (Mein 1962:124).

Then, too, Mallarmé evokes the lack of substantive contact between ourselves and the ordinary aspects comprising the experience of our surroundings.

In fact, the hazy web of astoundingly could-be relationship which makes up his "Afternoon of a Faun" is a pristine embodiment of Lévi-Strauss's savage thought which "does not distinguish the moment of observation and that of interpretation" (Lévi-Strauss 1966:223). At last, Proust literally demonstrates that just as there is no self nor substantive *milieu,* there are likewise no substantive *others,* no archetypical incarnations of certain, fixed personalities along life's path. His finale likewise demonstrates what to do about this problem, as he induces us to realize that the very stuff of interpersonal experience must be reconstituted through time.

Yet a literary finale is not the only kind. And Lévi-Strauss goes on from that moment in *Tristes Tropiques* where he stared mutely into the incommunicable eye of primitive man to argue that there are likewise no substantive others in other milieus, even though many observers had assumed the contrary, thinking that men could be approached as objects. Yet, even in the absence of simple, whole man-objects, we must proceed by translating any texts *they* provide into structures which can then be related to the structure of the text that is ourself (cf. Rousseau), everything being just a matter of corresponding sets of relationships from semantic universes that have come into confrontation. Moreover, Lévi-Strauss argues that this conceptualization in terms of bundles of relationships (rather than in terms of fixed labels for substantive objects) is precisely what is manifested in many of the modes of communication that anthropology studies. And no more than a Symbolist work could be understood by assigning specific designata to the terms composing it, can many varieties of anthropological data be approached as statements about substantive things. Louis Dumont discusses this issue in terms of "traditional mentality" versus "modern mentality." On the one hand there is the modern way, whereby

. . . a system is conceived of as formed of objects, all of which have their own being (*être*) and act on each other by reason of this being and through a law of determined interaction; for example, physical bodies all have their own mass and act on each other in a measure determined by this mass and their relative position. This manner of thinking, which separates individual being and relation, is principally modern. It can no doubt be found elsewhere, but it is modern in its full development and its exclusion of the following. (Dumont 1967:60–61; my trans.)

The following is, then, traditional:

Or indeed to the contrary, an abstraction can be made of the "elements" in themselves, of which the system seems to be composed, and they can be considered as merely resulting from the network of relations of which the system would thus be constituted. A phoneme has only the characteristics which oppose it to other phonemes; it is not some thing but only the other from the others, thanks to which it signifies some thing. We will talk of structure exclusively in this case: when the interdependence of the elements of a system is so tight that they disappear without residue as soon as the inventory of the relations among them is made—in sum a system of relations and no longer a system of elements. The passage from one mentality or from one *esprit* to the other, from the world of structure to the world of substance, is no doubt the major problem for the comparison of societies. (Dumont 1967:61; my trans.)

Elsewhere Dumont argues for the logical priority of traditional mentality, i.e. structure: " . . . *structure or complementarity is neccessarily and historically prior to substance and individuality,* and in that sense complexity is prior to, and more explanatory than, simplicity'' (Dumont 1966: 238). Clearly then, structure as contrasted to substance parallels ''wild thinking'' *(pensée sauvage)* as contrasted with technological (I would add therapeutic) thinking. Moreover, according to Lévi-Strauss, if the human sciences want to be comparative, the only way to approach an unbiased comparison of different systems is by structural methods. Thus, ''traditional mentality,'' i.e. the world of structure, i.e. *pensée sauvage* wins out in the final analysis. And the circle is complete.

Finally, the relevancy of this discussion to that general tendency in communication theory to disregard problems concerning the source of phenomenal data should be pointed out. In the first place the self is *known* only insofar as it communicates to itself. Gilbert Ryle emphasized this point from ordinary language philosophy in his famous treatise against Cartesian dualism's doctrine that some ghostly ''mind'' must be assumed to lie behind mental activity as manifested through acts of the bodily machine. During the course of his argument that any data indicative of ''mind'' should be accepted without worrying where it comes from, Ryle states the following: ''The way in which a person discovers his own long-term motives is the same as the way in which he discovers those of others. The quantity and quality of the information accessible to him differs in the two inquiries, but its items are in general of the same sort'' (Ryle 1949: 90). The point is that there is no privileged source of information about the self or about where it is going. As Rousseau, Baudelaire, and Proust wrote, all there is is an input of data, better seen through hindsight, which makes it appear as if one had been moving towards something. For, even if one were to assume that there exists some noumenal self-mind, it would not enter (communicably) into communication:

Speaking to others (or to myself), I do not speak *of* my thoughts; I *speak them,* and what is between them—my after-thoughts and under-thoughts. (Merleau-Ponty 1964a: 19)

Or, with more specific reference to society:

Communication between individuals or groups is not, in effect, a consequence of life in society, it is this life itself, on the condition, of course, that it is not limited solely to oral or written communication. (Pouillon: 1956:158; my trans.)

This variety of reflection is generally summarized in communication theory through the assertion that, while *messages* can be assumed to be conveyed from a sender to a receiver, really all we have to go on are the messages themselves. For the sender and receiver can only be known across their messages, which is likewise true of oneself, at least in the view of Symbolists and structuralists. Yet the disintegration of ''self'' or ''person'' or ''substantive object'' is no cause for alarm, since there still remain, existentially, worlds of translatable (interrelatable) messages—messages which, remembering music and myth, are *both* formally regulated *and* sensory-bound. And even if the course of the messages lies beyond us, even if progress through time toward truth from message to message cannot be demonstrated, it is still to be assumed that we can achieve greater understanding of the messages by inter-translating them more and more.

This view has been with us from the start of this study. It lies behind the loose usage of "text" according to which our experiences of "self," of "anthropological and poetic writings" and of "other cultures" are all epistemologically par. All these things are more or less "texts"—sensory-bound systematic messages—that are there for the assimilation. This same view of experience was seen in Baudelaire's "Correspondances," one line of which also shows the key to expressing the view in French. The line is this: "Les parfums, les couleurs et les sons se répondent." And the key is the French reflexive. This particular verb form affords a ready means of suggesting interrelationship without having to specify either of the following: first, the locus of the relationship need not be determined; second, the reflexive form does not automatically imply the existence of some agent behind the state described analogous to the "by whom or what" expected of the English passive often used to translate the reflexive. Thus, a condition of intertwined existence can be simply and satisfyingly stated as unelliptically there. Contrasted with this subtle reflexive is the neccessarily cumbersome English translation of the above line: "Perfumes, sounds, and colors answer each to each" (Scarfe's *Baudelaire:* 1964:37).

Nor are the consequences of the reflexive mode of organization restricted to poetry. In fact, I would say that such readily stated, ungroundable, existentially given, reciprocal *being* is a cornerstone of French *sociologie*. Take, for example, the following evidence from Durkheim's discussion of the role of a clan's mythic ancestor as a means of expressing "the collective unity" characteristic of the clan:

Masse homogène et compacte où il n'existe pas, pour ainsi dire, de parties différenciées, où chacun vit comme tous, ressemble à tous, un tel groupe *se représente à lui-même* cette faible individuation, dont il a confusément conscience, en imaginant que ses membres sont des incarnations à peine différentes d'un seul et même principe, des aspects divers d'une même réalité, une même âme en plusieurs corps. (Durkheim 1897:52; my emphasis)

Sagarin's translation skirts the difficulty by imposing a transitive, thus diminishing any sense of cognition:

A homogenous and compact mass where there exists, so to speak, no differentiated parts, where each one lives like all and each resembles all—this is the clan. Such a group *sees its own image* in terms of a feeble individuation, of which it has a vague consciousness, by imagining that its members are incarnations, hardly at all different, from one and the same principle; they are various aspects of the same reality, a single soul in several bodies. (Sagarin trans. 1963:88; my emphasis)

Durkheim's whole point is right there in the untranslatable reflexive. He is talking about a phenomenon which—like "exchange" or the "social"—most basically involves *two* and cannot be reduced to anything individual (such as one acting on another). And this whole notion simply comes out more easily, thanks to the French reflexive—e.g.: ". . . la musique se vit en moi, je m'écoute à travers elle" (Lévi-Strauss 1964:25).

Regardless of how pervasive such thinking has been throughout French *sociologie,* it is central in Lévi-Strauss. As we have already detected, as far as he can know, men and mankind are a composition of messages—manifestations of communicative thought. He expresses the limits of his knowledge by means of the reflexive, especially when asserting that he seeks to show "how myths think themselves in men." While this particular assertion by Lévi-Strauss has aroused considerable controversy, there have been similar statements by other modern students of perception and conceptualization. For example, in *Sense and Non-Sense* Merleau-Ponty describes the creative process of Cézanne:

The picture took on fullness and density; it grew in structure and balance; it came to maturity all at once. "The landscape thinks itself in me," he said, "and I am its consciousness." (Merleau-Ponty 1964c:17)

This is Cézanne's way of stating that he himself exists in the forms his brush applies; they are evidence of him. He might exist through other forms as well—e.g., words he utters about his work. But at the moment of creating the painting Cézanne's being is a function of the landscape; and his vision derives from a perceptual grammar which cannot be solely his. This is very important to Merleau-Ponty, because he sees such painting as a representation of creative perception (the only kind) which in its simplest form still contains all those differential additives from which the whole of experience is built. In Merleau-Ponty's phenomenological view nothing is perceived without all sorts of suprasensory qualities—such as back-sidedness—being attributed to it. Thus, perception can claim primacy since it contains from the start all those mental complexities characteristic of the highest philosophies. For Merleau-Ponty perception itself is message (rather than something sensed by another thing), and a painting is a picture of message, of interrelationship irrespective of the sender or receiver. This is true both of the painting being painted and of the painting being seen:

I would be at great pains to say *where* is the painting I am looking at. For I do not look at it as I do at a thing; I do not fix it in its place. My gaze wanders in it as in the halos of Being. It is more accurate to say that I see according to it, or with it, than that I *see it*. (1964b:164)

And concerning Cézanne's art he maintains that it is neither imitation nor tasteful or instinctual construction; rather: "IT IS A PROCESS OF EXPRESSING," (1964c:17; my capitals). We can be satisfied with painting as ungrounded message, as a picture of a process of expressing, regardless of *by* whom or *of* what, because of the following notion:

Ultimately the painting relates to nothing at all among experienced things unless it is first of all "autofigurative." It is a spectacle of something only by being a "spectacle of nothing," by breaking "the skin of things" to show how the things become things, how the world becomes world. (1964b:181)

How like Lévi-Strauss. For that is exactly what human social experience is: a process of expressing. And myth is a picture of that process (showing how intersensory order *becomes* intersensory order), and must be understood as such. Elsewhere Merleau-Ponty offers this clarification:

Expressive operations take place between thinking language and speaking thought; not, as we thoughtlessly say, between thought and language. It is not because they are parallel that we speak; it is because we speak that they are parallel.
  The weakness of every "parallelism" is that it provides itself with correspondences between the two orders and conceals the operations which produced these correspondences by encroachment to begin with. (Merleau-Ponty 1964a:18)

In this anti-parallelism view, then, what matter are the processes interrelating analytically isolated orders of expression. The different orders cannot be distinguished, and labeled as substantial things (since, remembering Saussure, there is *nothing* to label until at least two orders are in *fact* interrelated). And in the absence of substance there can be no directional determinism between orders. Thus, unlike material-oriented Marxists, idea-oriented Hegelians, or transcendental Baudelaire, Lévi-Strauss leaves us with message—in texts—alone. Experience, including change, stands as a concert of interpenetrating, cross-referring orders, all of which can be rewritten somewhat differently in the others' terms. Change is a variation, to and fro, on a set of principles, which are themselves the structure that summarizes the relationship of the differences in a series of similar events. In other words and in reverse: if we take an object or event, it is known by means of a sensory-based *system;* take a similar object or event, likewise known, and detect its differences from the first. Then, state the relationship between the two sets of differences, and you have the *structure* of a series which might represent, for example, an earlier and a later view of the same 'object,' or *our* and *their* view of the same 'event,' and so forth. All of this is highlighted in anthropology because the *our* and *their,* and sometimes the earlier and later, are intrinsic to the nature of the inquiry. But two points must be borne in mind: first, that there can be no perception without differentiation among a series (i.e. without the stuff of *structure*); second, the differences between members of a series of systematic perceptions (i.e. the elements of the members' *structure*) are at first selected *arbitrarily* (whether by natives during perception or by anthropologists during comparative conceptualization).

In this light we can see the answer to a rhetorical queston recently posed in irony by Korn:

How can it be that "structure" is "the very content" but at the same time "is not related to empirical reality"? How can it be that it is "the very content" and it is also "rather a method"? (Korn 1969:6; my trans. of Korn's quotations from Lévi-Strauss's French)

This assortment of features attributed to "structure" appears outlandish only if one fails to note how much Lévi-Strauss's work is involved with theories concerning the grounds of perception and communication, as well as our limitations in arriving at an understanding of these processes. While a structure is built up from differences selected from empirical reality, it need in no way directly relate to whatever that "reality" might be, even if the reality could be directly *known.* For to order empirical reality is to transcend it or at least to *deny it as a feasible category.* Moreover, structure can indeed be "the very content" and also "rather a method" because (à la Proust and Merleau-Ponty on Cézanne) content is really relationship mistakenly substantized; and relationship is only communicably experienced as a systematic process (one might say, methodically). Proust offers a similar version of "reality":

An hour is not merely an hour. It is a vase filled with perfumes, sounds, plans and climates. What we call reality is a certain reltionship between these sensations and the memories which surround us at the same time (a relationship that is destroyed by a bare cinematographic presentation, which gets further away from the truth the more closely it claims to adhere to it) the only true relationship, which the writer must recapture so that he may forever link together in his phrase its two distinct elements. One may list in an interminable description the objects that figured in the place described, but truth will begin only when the writer takes two different objects, establishes their relationship—analogous in the world of art to the sole relationship in the world of science, the law of cause and effect—and encloses them in the neccessary rings of a beautiful style, or even when, like life itself, comparing similar qualities in two sensations, he makes their essential nature stand out more clearly by joining them in a metaphor, in order to remove them from the contingencies of time, and links them together with the indescribable bond of an alliance of words. From this point of view regarding the true path of art, was not nature herself a beginning of art . . . ? *(The Past Regained)*

Lévi-Strauss thinks so, precisely. Furthermore, not only does the anthropologist argue that it is pointless to seek as final aim the reality behind the process of expression; he also denies the utility of any hard and fast analytic differentiation of various orders of expression, since any such order is always *becoming* in a continual dialectic of inter-signification with all the other orders, simultaneously. This, then, is the savage mind; and in face of such mind about all one can do is delineate structures, thereby effecting correspondences among sensory systems and only (if ever) *finally* determining their logic.

FOUR

The Organization of Perception

SEVEN

Cultural Factors in Spatial Orientation

A. Irving Hallowell

Whatever the natural aspects of space, it is, like every other part of nature, given meaningful configuration in the culture of any people, and different peoples construct space differently, to a greater or lesser degree. Hallowell describes vividly and clearly the way in which the Saulteaux, a North American Indian tribe, conceive of space, the way in which they order it, and the way in which that ordering in turn becomes part of their experience of it. Descriptions of such subtlety and sensitivity as Hallowell's are less common than one might like, and so this paper becomes all the more valuable for the very clear and precise way in which he is able to translate the Saulteaux conceptions into terms we, with entirely different notions of space, can easily comprehend.

SPATIALLY, LIKE TEMPORALLY, coordinated patterns of behavior are basic to the personal adjustment of all human beings. They involve fundamental dimensions of experience and are a necessary condition of psychological maturity and social living. Without the capacity for space perception, spatial orientation and the manipulation of spatial concepts, the human being would be incapable of effective locomotion, to say nothing of being unable to coordinate other aspects of his behavior with that of his fellows in a common social life.[1] In addition to the psychophysical and psychophysiological conditions of human space perception, we know that varia-

tions occur, between one culture and another, with respect to the selective emphasis given to the spatial relations and attributes of things, the degree of refinement that occurs in the concepts employed, and the reference points that are selected for spatial orientation. The human individual is always provided with some culturally constituted means that are among the conditions which enable him to participate with his fellows in a world whose spatial attributes are, in part, conceptualized and expressed in common terms. Ontogenetically, self-orientation, object-orientation, and spatio-temporal orientation are concomitantly developed during the process of socialization.

Long ago Poincaré pointed out that the notion of space must be understood as a function of objects and all their relations. There is no such thing as space independent of objects. Relations among objects and the movements of objects are a necessary condition of space perception. More recently, James J. Gibson, approaching the problem from the standpoint of psychophysics, has developed the hypothesis "that space is constituted of the same variables as things . . . that surfaces and margins are what we see, not air. Space must be filled to be visible; empty space is an abstraction" (Gibson, p. 228). This author distinguishes problems concerned with (a) "the perception of the substantial or spatial world," "the world of colors, textures, surfaces, edges, slopes, shapes, and interspaces," what he calls *literal* perception, from (b) "the perception of the world of useful and significant things to which we ordinarily attend." He calls the latter *schematic* perception (p.10).

While it remains an open question how far the purely psychophysical dimensions of perception may be influenced by culturally constituted experiential factors, schematic perception, involving the meaningful aspects of experience, can hardly be understood without reference to an articulated world of objects whose relations and attributes become meaningful for the individual, not simply through the innate psychological potentialities he brings to experience but, above all, through the significance for experience that the development, patterning, transmission, and accumulation of past experience, in the form of a cultural heritage, have come to imply. The question: Is space perception native or acquired? though once hotly debated, is in actuality a pseudo-problem.[2] What Gibson argues against is an extreme form of perceptual relativism: "that perception is inevitably a constructive process which creates the world to suit the perceiver; that we see things not as they are but as we are." While "it is perfectly true," he says, "that perception can be fluid, subjective, creative, and inexact . . . it can also be literal . . . the student of human nature and society needs to remember this when he is in danger of assuming that men are the passive victims of their stereotypes and perceptual customs (pp. 210–11)".

Psychologists repeatedly have emphasized that unlike other aspects of experience (e.g., color and sound), which are mediated through highly specialized sense organs, perception of space requires the participation of several sense modalities including, for instance, tactual kinesthetic components. There is no "spatial sense," equivalent to vision and hearing, by means of which we perceive such attributes of space as extension, shape, size, direction, locality, and distance. Such experience is "intersensory" by its very nature; yet is as primary as experience mediated by specialized sensory modalities (Stern 1938:99). Furthermore, the role that differential linguistic and cultural factors play in the processes through which the spatial attributes of things become abstracted, conceptualized, expressed in traditional forms of speech, and made the basis of action cannot be overlooked in this case any more than it can be in the functioning of perception mediated through specialized sense modalities.

There is an additional factor, however, that has been neglected in discussions of space perception and spatial orientation. This is the peculiarly human capacity of achieving a level of psychological organization that makes possible the perception of the self as an object in a world of objects other than self. In addition to reference points anchored in the objective world, the human being constantly makes use of himself as a reference point. "Perceiving the world has an obverse aspect, perceiving oneself."[3] While we may, perhaps, assume this, it should not be forgotten that self-awareness as a universal psychological attribute of man is no more given at birth than the traditional schema of reference points to be found in a culture or the vocabulary of spatial reference. Self-identification and the perception of self as an object in relation to other objects is the result of a long socialization process, just as the skills underlying the achievement of a "sense of direction" only emerge from a complicated learning process.

Furthermore, in order to be spatially oriented in the widest sense, that is, beyond the field of immediate perception, the individual must not only be aware of himself but of his own position in some *spatial schema*. At the same time he must be capable of maintaining awareness of his own changes in position, and be able to assume the position of others in the schema with reference to himself. What spatial orientation in man actually involves is a constant awareness of varying relations between the self and other objects in a spatial schema of traditionally defined reference points. If I have a destination, beyond my limited field of vision, for example, I not only have to know where I am going but I have to know where I am now in relation to my goal and, as I move toward it, I have to be aware of the changing relations involved. In order to reach my goal and return to my starting point, I have to make use of formal or informal refer-ence points. I may be guided, in part, by a "mental" map. But, in any case, I have to maintain some kind of topographical or astronomical (Goodenough 1953), if not directional, orientation, in which my own changing position must be appraised. Gibson points out that this type of locomotion—that is, "the act of going to an object or place beyond the range of vision"—represents a much higher and more complicated level of mobility than that confined to a spatial field where optical stimulation yields all the necessary cues because the goal-object lies within it (Gibson, pp. 229–30). What we take for granted, without a close analysis of all the necessary conditions involved, is that the human individual will necessarily advance from the simpler to the more complicated level of finding his way about during the course of ontogenetic development. Yet this is certainly one of the vital points where the cultural factors that are an integral part of the spatialization of the world of man play an outstanding role. The human being not only advances from a rudimentary to a more complex level of spatial orientation and mobility; the possibility is opened to him through various kinds of symbolic means to become oriented in a spatial world that transcends his personal experience. Place naming, star naming, maps, myth and tale, the orientation of buildings, the spatial implications in dances and ceremonies, all facilitate the construction and maintenance of the spatial patterns of the world in which the individual must live and act.

While striking cultural variations occur, possible universals should be looked for. Is there any culture, for instance, in which there are *no* names for places and topographical features in the environment of the people? From the standpoint of human mobility and spatial orientation this practice would appear to have a generic human function. When integrated with individual knowledge and experience of the terrain it affords a schema of reference points for topographical orientation. Such points are not only a guide to action but, once known, can be mentally manipulated and organized in the form of "mental maps," and the spatial schema inherent in them communicated.[4] Maps among nonliterate peoples are, of course, the projection in the form of graphic symbols of space relations abstracted from knowledge already available in these "mental maps" rather than the outcome of such sophisticated techniques as surveying, serial photography, etc.[5] It is amazing how accurate such maps can be.[6] While maps are of limited occurrence among nonliterate peoples, names of topographical features and places appear to be universal.

Perhaps the most striking feature of man's spatialization of his world is the fact that it never appears to be exclusively limited to the pragmatic level of action and perceptual experience.[7] Places and objects of various classes are conceptualized as having a real existence in distant regions. Even though the individual never experiences any direct perceptual knowledge of them— since information must be mediated through some symbolic means (the spoken or written word, graphic representation)—such regions are, nevertheless, an integral part of the total spatial world to which he is oriented by his culture. For man everywhere has cosmic concepts; he is oriented in a universe that has spatial dimensions. The individual not only has heard about other groups of human beings he may not have seen; they are given a *locale*. He knows *where* the land of the dead is and something about it even though he has not yet visited it. Gods and spirits are given an abode and mobility in space; they not only exist but they exist *somewhere;* they may be "here" now and later "there." Likewise in Western culture world explorations and science have accustomed us to accept as reliable all sorts of information about the location of distant peoples, about natural phenomena of various kinds, the location and contours of the land masses of the earth, and so on, all beyond our direct perceptual experience. Astronomers, too, tell us about the spatial relations of bodies in the far-flung stellar universe. We assume, of course, that our knowledge of distant regions is more dependable than that of the primitive peoples we study, and this is undoubtedly true. At the same time it should not be forgotten that it is acquired by most individuals through symbolic mediation and that the qualitative differences of this knowledge are extremely recent in our own culture. We need only to compare the spatial orientation and knowledge of medieval man in Europe with our modern outlook to appreciate this. In *The Other World,* Howard R. Patch devotes a chapter to "Journeys to Paradise," many descriptive accounts of which are to be found in medieval literature. This author points out that "The Garden of Eden was universally believed to exist, and, although cut off from ordinary approach, was supposed still to be waiting for the saints before their ascent to Heaven. Medieval maps often showed its location." (Patch 1950:134). In other words, it was a *place* located on the earth that might be visited by travelers, "even if they had to have recourse to supernatural means." (Patch, p. 153). Even subsequent to medieval times there are references to such journeys and the author notes that, "when Christopher Columbus discovered the New World, he thought he was close to the Garden of Eden. . . ." (p. 173). Today the Garden of Eden has disappeared from our universe; it has no spatial existence. Similarly, Dante could present to his readers an intelligible image of hell "pictured as a huge funnel-shaped pit, situated beneath the Northern Hemisphere and running down to the centre of the earth." If we now ask, *where* is hell, what answer can we give if the cosmographic picture of our universe, defined on the basis of scientific knowledge, is accepted? As *places* heaven and hell in this universe are "nowhere."

What appears to be particularly significant in our human adjustment to the world is that over and above pragmatic needs for orientation and without any pretense to reliable knowledge of regions of space outside their personal experience, human beings in all cultures have built up a frame of spatial reference that has included the farther as well as the more proximal, the spiritual as well as the mundane, regions of their universe. What the recent history of Western culture demonstrates is the revolutionary challenge offered to the spatial orientation embedded in an older tradition when more reliable knowledge of distant regions, combined with the development of abstract mathematical concepts of space, established the foundations of the qualitatively different type of spatial orientation that is now possible for us.

The unique combination of factors that account for the distinctive mode of human spatial orientation has not always been clearly recognized. For a long period, dating back to the late eigh-

teenth century when the idea of the Noble Savage had such a vogue, the problem was obscured because of the widespread notion that savages, as compared with civilized man, had an innate sense of direction. This notion was based to some extent on the exaggeration, if not misrepresentation, of the observations of early travelers and missionaries. Pierre Jaccard, in a book which should be better known, (Jaccard 1932), calls attention to the excellent observations of Père Lafitau (1724) on the Iroquois. Their later distortion by Charlevoix, he thinks, gave rise to "la legende de l'instinct d'orientation des sauvages." In the nineteenth century, after the concept of biological evolution took hold, one of the prevailing ideas was that the "senses" of primitive man were more acute than those of civilized man, even though he might be intellectually inferior. Indeed, "savages" and the lower animals were thought by some to be alike in many respects. Haeckel (1868) in his *Natural History of Creation* observed that if one compared African Negroes, Bushmen, and the Andamanese with apes, dogs, and elephants, on the one hand, and with civilized man, on the other, one would be compelled to make a distinction, not between man and animal, but between civilized peoples on the one side, and savages and animals on the other. The question then of an innate, or special, sense of direction in primitive peoples became entangled with the more general question whether "primitive" mind and "civilized" mind represented psychological categories that had an evolutionary significance. Jaccard concludes:

Si tous les sauvages possédaient des facultés de direction, inconnues de nous, on pourrait peut-être accepter provisoirement l'hypothèse d'une différence de nature entre leur psychologie et la nôtre. Mais cette supposition n'est plus même premise aujourd'hui : il est en effet démontré que la plupart des non-civilisés sont tout aussi embarrassés que nous lorsqu'ils se trouvent dans une région dépourvue de repères, loin des horizons familiers de leur pays natal . . . loin de montrer la bestialité des sauvages, les faits d'orientation lointaine témoignent de l'excellence des pouvoirs d'attention, de mémoire, et d'observation des plus intelligents d'entre eux . . . c'est de reconnaitre que les sauvages et les civilisés possèdent a des degrés divers une même aptitude, plus ou moins développée chez les différents individus, selon les circonstances . . . l'hypothèse d'un sens particulier de la direction, affiné chez le sauvage et émoussé chez le civilisé, par suite des conditions d'existence, n'est pas plus soutenable que les interprétations basées sur une opposition entre l'intelligence et l'instinct. Aucune différence appréciable n'apparait entre les capacités sensorielles et les fonctions mentales élémentaires des diverses races humaines : ce fait seul suffit à démontrer l'erreur de toutes les théories attribuant aux sauvages des facultés d'orientation inconnues des civilisés.

We now know, of course, that even in studying animal behavior, the concept of "instinct" is too categorical and affords us no help at all in explaining how animals find their way about. Despite the fact that we are still in the dark on many frontiers of this area of investigation, great progress has been made in our detailed knowledge of some of these determinants in vertebrates and insects (Beecher 1952, Bogert 1948, Wolfson 1952, Von Frisch 1950). Astonishing as the performance of some of these creatures is with respect to their mobility, we can be certain that the crucial determinants are of a different order than those in human spatial orientation. Consequently, although at a very rudimentary perceptual level, there certainly is some overlapping in the spatial

world of ourselves and other animals, the phenomenological differences must be very great indeed no matter what local cultural variables are among the human factors involved.[8]

The Spatial Orientation of the Saulteaux

Directional Orientation

From an abstract point of view it might appear that the basic directional orientation of the Saulteaux is equivalent to that of occidental culture, since they recognize four cardinal directions as fundamental reference points which can be roughly equated with north, south, east, and west. Actually, the equivalence is not only historically fortuitous, it differs from our own directional orientation qualitatively and functionally in important respects.

The occidental directional schema is based on scientific knowledge that the Saulteaux do not possess. In our schema "true" north is taken as an absolute reference point; it is determined precisely by mechanical means, and instrumental correction for possible error is made under certain circumstances. Furthermore, the possession of a magnetic compass and the knowledge of how to use it enables us to check our directional orientation exactly at any time.

The Saulteaux, on the other hand, rely exclusively upon the direct observation of natural phenomena in order to maintain their directional orientation. Their most inclusive reference points are the North Star, the movements of the sun, and the "homes" of the four winds. Sometimes to these are added "straight up" (zenith), and "down" (nadir). The standardized and linguistically formulated cardinal directions of their culture, however, refer only to the four winds. It is through the traditional emphasis upon these that the wider aspects of their spatial universe are defined.

In their mythology the winds are anthropomorphic beings each associated with a complementary direction. The winds are brothers who at birth enunciate their personal relations to humanity. The first-born was East Wind, who said, "I shall be fairly kind to human beings." The next was South Wind, who said, "I'll be very good and treat human beings well, as long as any exist on this earth." The third child born spoke and said, "Human beings shall call me West Wind. I'll be a little rough on them but I'll never be wicked." "Be easy on our mother," he went on as another boy popped out. This one said, "Human beings shall call me North Wind. I'll have no mercy on any human being. I'll treat him just the same as the animals." At this remark his brothers asked, "How do you expect human beings to exist if you are going to treat them like that?" (But no answer is given in the myth.) Shortly after this the brothers decided that they could not remain together any longer. The East Wind said, "I'll go to live in the east." The West Wind said, "I'll sit opposite you at the other end of the earth." The South Wind said, 'I'll go to the southern end of the earth," and the North Wind said, "I'll go to the northern end."

In another myth North Wind invites his brother South Wind to a trial of strength, but is unable to worst him. Then the South wind invites his brother North Wind to come south for a return contest. All the South Wind did was to blow on him. After the first couple of days North Wind could hardly hold his head up. One of his eyes drooped and then the other. Finally, on the sixth day he had to give up; he was beaten. The South Wind said, "Now you know you're not the boss of everything." "And we know he is not the boss," added the narrator, "for, if he were, we would never have any summer."

For the Saulteaux, direction is only partially abstracted from *place*. That is, their conception has more the meaning "in the direction of such and such a place," "toward *x*." What we refer to abstractly as the cardinal directions are to them the *homes* of the winds, the places they come from. Similarly, east is thought of as the place where the sun rises; west, the place where it sets; south is the place to which the souls of the dead travel, and the place from which the summer birds come. In a myth summer is stolen from a place in the south. Indeed, the Saulteaux equivalents for north, south, east, and west are *place names* in a very real sense, rather than abstract terms for direction. They are far, distant, it is true, but in myths at least, people have been there. They define the periphery of the Saulteaux world, being the "farthest" places, although not different except in generality of direction, from places in the immediate environment. Such a connotation exists in Western civilization side by side with the highly abstract one expressed in terms of angles and their measurement used in science. We say, "He lives in the West," or "The South grows cotton." The terms "Occident" and "Orient" are also used as nouns denoting places or regions. The latter arose at a period when, like the Saulteaux, the people employing them thought that the earth was flat.

I do not mean to imply that the Saulteaux terms are never used abstractly.

But the degree to which this occurs is a function of the social situation. Abstraction is at its highest level when directional terms are employed in finding one's way about or in constructing a ceremonial pavilion. This may happen similarly with direction toward any place: a place, *x,* may be defined as "on the way to" *y.*

Thus it is inevitable that the directional orientation of these Indians is more flexible and less exact than our own, and that they must rely upon cues from several different classes of natural phenomena. Such limitations are intrinsic to the traditional means with which their culture provides them for ascertaining directional orientation. There are many instances of these limitations. I have heard Indians refer to the Milky Way, which is considered the path the Summer Birds follow flying north, as running north and south. This is not the case, but the approximate direction satisfies them. Another example is to be found on a map of Eagle Lake drawn by Adam Keeper, an Indian at Grand Rapids. On it he marked the four directions, but he was not aware of the discrepancy between his directional orientation and the measured directions of our schema. This is demonstrated by the fact that while he included a neatly ruled line representing the boundary between the provinces of Manitoba and Ontario, he made no use of it as one of his directional coordinates. Every Indian knows this line because it is actually cut out through the woods for miles and miles, and it runs exactly north and south. The fact that Adam ignored this cue shows the extent to which he has clung to his culturally constituted orientation in drawing the map, and the extent to which the local spatial interrelations of

landmarks and contours predominated for him.

We can be certain, then, that the north of the Saulteaux is not our exact north and that the other directions they recognize are likewise approximate, more inclusive, than ours. For example, east means "in the general direction of east" and is closer to our everyday usage when exact reckoning is unnecessary. If an Indian is asked where the east is he will point to where the sun rises. From his point of view it is unnecessary to take into account the variations in the sun's positions at different seasons of the year and to arrive at a measured point on the horizon designated "due" east. What the range of their margin of error may be I do not know; but it is obvious that for the Saulteaux directions, unlike our own, are not fixed coordinates.

Qualitatively and functionally, therefore, the existence of a four-directional schema in Western culture, on the one hand, and in Saulteaux culture, on the other, presents only a superficial resemblance. The behavioral implications in the two societies are quite different. Western man has been freed from the direct observation of nature in so far as he depends upon mechanical instruments for the determination of direction, or does not need to maintain his orientation with respect to compass points at all so far as the pursuit of daily life is concerned. The latter is particularly true of urban populations where such directional orientation may be almost completely ignored.[9]

The Saulteaux, however, constantly maintain a directional orientation. Traveling in the open as they do at all seasons of the year, across lakes and through a network of waterways in the summer and over snowclad wastes in winter, the direction of the wind in particular is always noticed and their practical activities adjusted accordingly.

Knowledge of Terrain

This culturally defined framework of directional orientation, with its customary reference points in certain natural phenomena, exposes the basic and most inclusive schema through which the Saulteaux orient themselves in a world of space. Closely integrated with it, and overshadowing it in importance, is the direct knowledge through exprience of the topography of the country and the relations in space of one locality to another.

This direct experiential knowledge, however, varies greatly among individuals. Most of the Berens River Indians have never traveled any considerable distance from the locality in which they were born. There is also a marked sexual dichotomy in direct knowledge of the country. Women travel far less than men. There are certainly few, if any, women of the Pekangikum Band who have been to the mouth of the river and most of them have not been as far as Grand Rapids, halfway there. In contrast to this, most of the men of the Pekangikum Band have been both to the mouth of the river and Grand Rapids.[10] At any rate, it would be erroneous to assume that a first-hand, detailed knowledge of all parts of the river and its environs is possessed by any single individual. The terrain which is most familiar to these Indians is their winter hunting ground and the region surrounding the fishing settlement in which they live during the summer months. They are, in short, bound in their direct knowledge and experience to the areas with which

their major economic activities are connected, a narrowly circumscribed spatial world which, even under modern conditions, has expanded very little. But within these limits the individual often possesses a phenomenally rich knowledge of the details of the terrain that contrasts sharply with his ignorance of parts of the country about which he has no direct knowledge[11] and of the still wider spatial world regarding which he sometimes entertains fantastic ideas.

In functional terms, it is not only the direct experience of the terrain which assists the individual in building up his spatial world; language crystallizes this knowledge through the customary use of place names. These in turn act as geographical reference points by means of which localities of various classes may be organized in spatial terms. This is not to imply that in Saulteaux culture the range of their application is coextensive with the total number of lakes, islands, points, rivers, and streams that might be named. Place names function integrally with the geographical knowledge and experience of the individual. Consequently, the local place names referring to topographical features within the radius of a particular summer settlement[12] are not known to the Indians of other settlements and the same applies to those attached to the geographical features of the winter hunting grounds. On the other hand, the place names of the major lakes, rivers, etc., and a general knowledge of their directions from their home and vague distances such as "long journey," of the environs of the Berens River as a whole are known to every Indian, regardless of whether he has ever traveled them or not. Correlated with the directions, these reference points define the wider limits of the geographical environment in which these Indians think and act, just as the place names for more circumscribed localities serve to organize the space relations of their local environment.

Beyond the Berens River itself, and peripheral to it, only a few geographical localities are at all familiar to the average Indian. On the west side of Lake Winnipeg the names of the larger lakes are known and a few Indian reserves and trading posts. To the north, trading posts such as Norway House, Oxford, God's Lake, stand out, and such geographical points as Deer Lake and Island Lake. Of course, every Berens River Indian has heard of Hudson Bay and the rivers that flow into it. To the southeast Lake Seul is well known because long ago a number of Berens River families came from there. To the south there are a number of rivers that are familiar, particularly the Red River which flows north to Lake Winnipeg. Cities like Selkirk and Winnipeg are known, and Ottawa because the government is there. But no Indian has been to all these places, and I am sure that their location with respect to one another and to the Berens River district is not understood.

If any of these places is thought of spatially I am certain that it is only as the context of the reference requires it. Any idea of its relation to other places in a spatial schema that is conceived as a geographical continuation of the Berens River region itself is totally foreign to the minds of these people. This seems to indicate that without some graphic means as an aid, place names are only effective in organizing one's spatial knowledge within the limits of one's direct experience or through a limited extension to regions immediately peripheral to such experience. Outside of this they tend to become disparate and unorganized, verbally known places.

Native Maps

Within a familiar terrain, however, such as the part of the country which he has known since childhood, or his hunting ground, an individual clearly grasps the precise location and has some idea of the relative distances of every significant detail of the topography in relation to every other. When integrated with some inclusive directional orientation such knowledge needs only graphic projection, and we have a rudimentary *map*. It is significant, nevertheless, that this organization of the spatial perceptions of the individual into a coordinated whole, a "mental map" (Jaccard, p. 213), applies only within the narrow limits indicated. It is deeply imbedded in the "active" experience of the individual.

That such a well-integrated organization of the spatial relations of certain parts of their geographical environment exists in some terms in the minds of some individuals may be inferred in several ways. I had in my possession maps of the National Topographical Series which are based on airplane photographs and on which the smallest lakes, rivers, and creeks are represented. In the first place, a number of Indians who had never seen a detailed map of the part of the country with which they were most familiar almost immediately grasped the geographical relations on these once a few landmarks had been identified. But it was necessary to orient the map in relation to the observer. The

Indians could not adapt themselves to looking at it in the conventional manner familiar to us with north at the top. They always had to have north on the map matched with north as it actually was from their point of view at the moment. Once they were fully oriented, it appeared as if they rediscovered on the map what was already organized in their minds. Some of them felt so much at home that often when I was trying to get them to delineate their trap lines or the boundaries of their hunting territories on the map, they would delay the process by side conversations with other Indians present, pointing to the outlet of some little creek where a moose had been killed or where some other event of interest to them had taken place.

Still more convincing evidence of the organization of the details of geographical relations in the mind of the individual was demonstrated by the objectification of such information in the form of maps which certain individuals drew for me. I secured five of these from three different men. That there is considerable individual variation in the ability to project such knowledge in graphic form is suggested by the admiration of other Indians for these maps. They said that it would have been impossible for them to perform such a task. The making of maps, however, was known in aboriginal days.

These aboriginal maps were intended to guide the individual using them through territory unknown to him. Their purpose was not to delineate a section of the country as such, but to indicate a route to be followed, and the emphasis was upon a succession of landmarks roughly indicated in their relations to one another and with only such other details of the topography as were necessary for the identification of the landmarks of primary interest. This is a very rudimentary form of map which does not require the refined abstract coordination of place, direction, distance, area, and contour that we expect. Areas and distances might be only relatively proportional, for instance, and yet such a crude delineation would serve its purpose.[13] The graphic emphasis upon a succession of landmarks is worth noting because it bears a close correspondence to the actual method of traveling about, just as the very limited geographical region for which detailed special knowledge is organized in the minds of individuals.[14] As might be expected, the narrow geographical limits of such organized positive knowledge bears an inverse relation to the ignorance of the terrain outside of the experience of the individual.[15] In this connection it is well to remind ourselves that without maps it would likewise be impossible for us to obtain any exact comprehension of geographical relations outside our experience.[16]

A startling illustration of this intrinsic limitation upon realistic spatial concepts of an unknown region is illustrated by the following episode. All the Indians were interested in a series of photographs I had taken of them, and some of them also were intrigued by the large-scale maps of their country, to which I have already referred. So, when one old man asked me to send him a *photograph* of the United States, I thought my interpreter had misunderstood him and that what he referred to was a map. But no! What he wanted was a photograph of the United States. Evidently the United States was to him a place regarding which he had only the vaguest idea and no notion whatsoever of its spatial extensity.

Travel

There still remains the practical question: How *do* the Saulteaux find their way about and what cues do they employ? The answer is a simple one: by means of the directional cues already described, combined with the constant use of all the relevant knowledge of the topography of the country they possess.

In addition to standardized reference points, i.e., named places and named directions, this includes a mass of impressions undiscriminated in speech but immensely important nevertheless. The characteristic manner of their procedure at all seasons, and whether traveling on land or water, can be reduced to a common principle. They always move from one point to another, rather than in a given direction toward a goal.[17] Directional orientation usually functions as the wider frame of reference to facilitate the step by step procedure.

In principle, this step by step procedure emerges in certain mythological narratives where it takes the following form: The protagonist is directed from point to point in a strange country by a series of old women. The first old woman he encounters not only directs him on his way, she tells him what to look out for, how to avoid obstacles to his progress, and so on. And finally, she tells him that he will come upon another old woman on whom he can depend for directional advice for the next stage of his journey. Of course, events occur as anticipated; the second old woman is reached who directs him to a third. The analogy to actual travel should be clear.

Familiar landmarks in a journey correspond to the old women; they mark the nodal points in a geographical progression in space and while they fail to give advice in a literal sense, they are anticipatory signs of the particular features of the country in the ensuing segment of the journey that must be mentally prepared for before they are encountered.

A commonplace illustration of ordinary procedure is illustrated by the ascent of the Berens River from its mouth to Grand Rapids, a hundred miles inland from Lake Winnipeg. The river is not in its entire length the natural road we usually think a river to be, for in places it opens into lakes. On this portion of it there are approximately fifty rapids, all named, which function as the nodal points in the journey. It is these geographical items which are checked off, as it were, in traveling up and down the stream, and one's position on the river at any time, particularly when eating and sleeping, is always talked about with reference to this schema of rapids. They also function as anticipatory signs of the features of the country to be encountered between them. No wonder then that the local Indians thought it curious and even hazardous when some white men a few years ago ascended the river without a guide. They were probably equipped with the excellent maps that are available. To the Indians they would have no anticipatory signs to guide them; they would not know what to expect.

A journey I once made across Lake Winnipeg in a skiff with an improvised sail illustrates the step by step principle in terms of another mode of travel. It also happened that the early part of the trip was made in a heavy fog which obscured the ordinary visual cues. My guides were, of course, very familiar with the directions of landmarks. Leaving the reserve early in the morning we rowed along the shore to Flathead Point where we disembarked to eat breakfast. Pigeon Point was not visible, but we headed in that direction rowing all the way. The wind was from the northwest. We set sail for Commissioner's Island which we reached about two and a half hours later. The fog having lifted somewhat in the meantime, we were able to sight the island some distance away and adjust our course accordingly. From there we made for Sandhill Island which we reached in an hour and a half. We spent the night there. The next morning it was easy to reach Stony Point and then to follow the shore south to Jack Head.

An analogous principle of travel in winter is set up under quite different circumstances when an Indian lays his trap line and makes his rounds periodically. The relation of the traps to each other, to certain topographical features of the country, and to his camp define a spatial order in which he regularly moves from point to point.

In winter, however, during long journeys on snowshoes or with a dogsled, when darkness obscures familiar landmarks and a storm makes even the stars invisible, then directional orientation inferred from the wind must be depended upon as the main cue. Under these conditions one has no choice but to proceed in a given direction; it is impossible to follow the visible cues provided by a series of landmarks, and it is possible to lose one's way badly. If directional orientation by means of the wind fails, there is nothing to do but make camp and wait until weather conditions change and the usual cues can be picked up again.

Topographical cues are, in fact, so important that if masked by snow an individual may lose his way even on familiar ground. An Indian once told me of such an experience which he considered very humorous because the trail was one frequently traveled by everyone—I had often used it myself in summer. But my friend missed his way one winter night when the drifted snow had radically distorted cues familiar even at that season of the year. On the other hand, there are well-known general patterns in the topography of their country which are used by the Indians as cues. The rocky ridges as well as the muskegs east of Lake Winnipeg, for instance, run east to west like the rivers so that whether it is cloudy or misty, night or day, a general orientation is possible. This pattern also can be used as a cue in winter when snow is on the ground. A Berens River Indian once went to fight a forest fire on the west side of the lake. He got lost because he was not familiar with local topographical landmarks and the muskegs had a different directional pattern. Not being aware of this latter fact, he relied on the muskegs and became disoriented. To an outsider general topographical patterns would not be obvious so that without any explanation of the actual clues being used it might appear somewhat mysterious how the Indians familiar with the country did find their way about in stormy or snowy weather and without a compass.

In connection with this dependence upon topographical cues it is interesting to recall the predicament of Wisαked-jak, the culture hero of the Saulteaux, told in a myth. Wisαkedjak had been temporarily deprived of his sight by getting his head encased in a bear skull and the method he employed to find his way about was to ask each tree he bumped into what its name was. Wisαkedjak wished to reach a lake since he thought he might find some people there, and he accomplished this by differentiating between trees that grew near the water and those that did not, adjusting his course accordingly.

If, as sometimes is the case in winter, there is a well-marked trail in the snow to be followed, then travel is greatly simplified. Under such conditions the Indian participates in one of the amenities of Western culture, the road, which we take for granted and which so enormously facilitates our movements from place to place. Neither directional orientation nor the use of such cues as the Saulteaux are compelled to employ are necessary in following a modern road. The contrast between this method of getting about and the other procedures described brings into sharp relief a basic difference in the pragmatic aspects of spatial orientation as demanded by Saulteaux culture on the one hand and Western culture, on the other.

Fear of Disorientation

The sharp contrast between the extremely intimate knowledge of a familiar terrain and the very hazy ideas which are entertained about other regions is sufficient, I believe, to account for a certain timidity on the part of these Indians in venturing into unknown territory unless accompanied by someone who is already acquainted with the region. While directional orientation can be maintained in unknown regions, the lack of all the well-known landmarks inevitably must lead to a certain amount of spatial disorientation. And there is always the possibility that one may really become lost. Hence, there is rational ground for apprehension.

A feeling of satisfactory spatial orientation, then, probably is one of the basic ties that bind the individual to familiar territory. The Indian would not analyze or express his feelings in such terms, but I think that it is a legitimate inference we are enabled to make from the very nature and character of his spatial orientation. It is likewise consistent with the basic role played by spatial orientation in all human behavior. For we, too, feel some sense of spatial disorientation in a strange city or country even when such orientation is less vital to our activities than to those of the Saulteaux and under cultural conditions which offer an opportunity for a more immediate and adequate reorientation. Furthermore, the feeling of the Saulteaux themselves about the loss of an adequate spatial orientation was illustrated in their concern when on one occasion I had difficulty in finding my way back to our camp, and their admonitions on others to be careful and not to lose my way when I went about by myself. Since I never was lost and their concern at times seemed a bit silly to me, I think that their attitude in these situations is quite revealing.

The same apprehension on their part can be demonstrated in another way by the story of the Indian who found his way back home from a strange part of the country. Early in the nineteenth century, when the Hudson's Bay Company reigned supreme in western Canada, some Indians raided a post at Sandy Narrows in order to obtain knives, powder, etc. The leader of the party was a man called Brimmed Hat. After he was apprehended it was planned to send him to England where he could observe for himself the power and magnitude of the white man's civilization. On the way to York Factory where he was to be put on a ship, Brimmed Hat escaped. This was near White Mud Falls on the Hayes River. Later he showed up again at Sandy Narrows, a distance of approximately three hundred miles as the crow flies. To the Indians such a journey was miraculous, and they believed he must have had the aid of supernatural helpers. First of all, he could not proceed in the usual way from one known point to another in a strange country. From our standpoint a correct directional orientation might have been a sufficient guide to him, combined, perhaps, with some general knowledge of the watersheds since Hayes River drains into Hudson Bay and the Berens River is on a shed from which the rivers empty into Lake Winnipeg. Besides this, he had no gun, not even a knife, and no way to secure skins to make new moccasins.

Cosmic Space

The apprehension with which the Saulteaux individual views excursions into strange regions, combined with his lack of experience in any but a circumscribed environment, and the limitations imposed by his culture upon the acquisition of accurate knowledge of distant regions, offers him no critical basis for an evaluation of what is beyond his experience. It is no wonder, then, that the traditional dogmas of his native culture in regard to the wider reaches of the universe are so thoroughly reified and uncritically accepted as part of his spatial world.

There is the Land of the Dead, for instance, far to the south. There is a road which leads directly to it which deceased souls follow, and a few individuals are known to have visited the Land of the Dead and afterwards returned to their homes. They have given accounts of their journey and of what they saw there. I remember that my interpreter once told an old Indian that I came from the south and that the United States lay in that direction. The old man simply laughed in a wise way and made no comment.

The earth itself, according to Saulteaux belief, is flat, a notion that is, of course, supported rather than contradicted by the naïve observation and experience of all human beings. No Indian can be convinced that the earth is spherical. According to Saulteaux dogma the earth is also an island, and there is an account in mythology (the earth-diver motif) of how this island came into existence. Contacts with the whites and, in certain cases, acquaintance with maps in the geography texts of their children have strengthened rather than undermined this dogma. For many Indians have been told, and others have seen it indicated on the maps of the world, that the western hemisphere is surrounded by water.

A stratification of worlds within the cosmos is another item of Saulteaux dogma that defines certain space relations in their conceptual universe. Since the earth is flat, it is easy to understand how this additional feature fits the general scheme. While this idea of the stratification of worlds is developed in considerable detail in other parts of America and even among related Algonkian peoples (Alexander 1916:275), the Saulteaux emphasize only the lower world immediately below this one, although they assert that there are other worlds farther down as well as one or two above "the central plane" on which they live.

The world that lies just below is called *pitawákamik*. It is also peopled by *änicinábek, Indians*. These lower world people only differ from those living on this earth by being immortal. When they grow old, they then become young again. This underworld was once visited by some Berens River Indians. They went out hunting and saw some strangers whom they followed to the lower world. At first the people living there wanted to kill them. But when the lower world people found that the Berens River Indians were so much like themselves, their lives were spared. The same species of animals and plants are found in *pitawákamik* as up here, but when it is night there it is day here and vice versa.

I have never heard of a corresponding upper world inhabited by human beings. However, the idea of strata in the universe is exemplified in the account in one of the myths in which the youngest brother of *matcikiwis* climbs up a tree to Thunder Bird Land. Here the Thunder Birds appear in human guise. When the daughters of the "boss" of these creatures come to earth they appear as women and marry human beings.

Within this cosmic scheme certain spiritual entities are given a specific location. To some extent such cosmic positions are correlated with observable natural phenomena. Since thunder is heard only in the summer and usually towards the south, the Thunder Birds are associated with the south as the spiritual controllers of the summer birds and are believed to inhabit one of the upper strata of the universe. On the other hand, the controllers of the fur-bearing animals are given a northern position in the cosmic space. In other cases the cosmic position of certain entities seems arbitrary, and some have no determinate location.

From the standpoint of the Saulteaux themselves, these concepts of cosmic space and the position of the various spiritual entities and other inhabitants within it, all are articulated as parts of an integral whole. It is in terms of the full sweep of this schema that we must endeavor to comprehend the qualitative characteristics of the farther reaches of their spatial world, as well as the relevant features of the proximate geographical environment in which they live.

Directional Orientation in Ceremonialism

Directional orientation, however, is not altogether confined to situations in which individuals are moving from place to place. The lodge erected for the Midewiwin, rectangular in ground plan, was always built on an east-west axis, as are the Wabano pavilions seen today. The entrance to both types of structure is at the east although two or more doors are made. The "place of honor" where the leader or leaders sit in both cases is on the south side near the east entrance. Another ceremony I witnessed, which had no superstructure, took place within a square bounded by stakes. The sides of the square were deliberately oriented in the four directions. In this case the entrance used was on the north side and at the close of the ceremony everyone left by the south "door." Graves are likewise oriented north and south as a rule; the deceased faces the south which is the Land of the Dead. Elsie Clews Parsons reported that the Pueblo Indians usually avoid sleeping with the head in the orientation given the dead in burial. It never occurred to me to make inquiry on this point (1939:I, 98–99).

Dancing always has a conventional direction. It is what we call "clockwise," but the Indians think of it in directional terms, i.e., from east to south to west to north to east. This is likewise the order of birth of the four winds in the myth cited. In the smoking of a ceremonial pipe the leader turns the stem in a clockwise direction and sometimes pauses when the stem has faced in each direction. The symbolism of this act lies in the fact that by including all the directions all of the spiritual entities in the entire universe are the recipients of the smoke offering (Alexander 1916:286–87).

The pavilion is a structural representation, in one sense, of the directions so that the *opposites,* north-south, east-west, and the *order* about the horizon may be recognized, but no further use is made of this.

The directional ordering of the Saulteaux spatial universe, therefore, is one that penetrates religious as well as secular life. And it is obvious that it has psychological implications qualitatively different from directional orientation in Western culture. The build-up of associations of north, south, east, and west with symbolic and mythological meanings makes the directions meaningful places. It further integrates other aspects of the culture and behavior so that a "living in" the world is experienced which has its own peculiar character. In other cultures directional orien-tation may deeply penetrate still other spheres of life and give the spatial orientation of the people a distinctive psychological cast.[18]

Conclusions

The development of man's mastery of space and the abstract concepts that have evolved along with it cannot be explained in any psychological terms which ignore the cultural factors involved. Human space perception is biologically rooted, but the level at which it functions in the individual is not reducible to innate capacities or maturational development. The process of socialization contributes experiential components that must be considered. Some of these acquired components of space perception are a function of the cultural milieu in which the individual has been reared. The cultural patterns of different societies offer different means by which spatial perceptions are developed, refined, and ordered. The spatial concepts of different societies also vary with respect to the degree of abstraction attained. There is also inter- and intra-societal variation in the utilization of different degrees of refinement of spatial perception in connection with different life activities. The variability is correlated with the fact that one set of conditions may demand very little in the way of spatial discriminations of a certain order (e.g., measurement), but considerable refinement in other respects (e.g., directional orientation).

Such considerations point to a wider historical question: "How have the cultural means themselves developed?" This is a matter for actual investigation, but our analysis of Saulteaux culture is suggestive in a negative respect. The point was stressed that the Saulteaux culture provided no incentive that would lead to the development of an abstract concept of area. On the other hand, they did draw crude maps in aboriginal days. The motive here was a very simple one: to provide a guide for the traveler in a strange country. There was a demand for maps for this purpose.

If we could illuminate the conditions and purposes in any given society which are relevant to the refinement and development of space perception, we would approach an answer to the historical question.

Notes

1. In the Preface to his *Perception of the Visual World* (1950), James J. Gibson remarks (p. vii) that "The perception of what has been called space is the basic problem of all perception. We perceive a world whose fundamental variables are spatial and temporal—a world which extends and endures. Space perception (from which time is inseparable) is not, therefore, a division of the subject matter of perception but the first problem to be considered, without a solution for which other problems remain unclear. That a solution is lacking, most psychologists would agree. The existing theories to account for the spatial and temporal character of our perceptions are not very satisfactory."

2. See e.g., Vernon (1937:64), who says, "The problem, however, which today appears to us of greater importance is concerned with the relative importance of the various types of perceptual and ideational data which subserve spatial perception, and their mutual relationships and coordination."

3. Gibson, p. 225, "perceiving the environment includes the ego as part of the total process. In order to localize any object there must be a point of reference. An impression of 'there' implies an impression of 'here' and neither could exist without the other."

4. "The capacity of men for forming correct mental maps is very great," write the authors of *Psychology for the Armed Forces* (Boring, ed., 1945:158), "although most persons do not use their capacities to the limit. Roads and street signs are enough to get them around in civilized familiar regions, and they do not feel a constant need to put everything into precise spatial relation. If they had more need for constant orientation, they would practice more on the building of their mental maps, would more easily find new and better ways of getting to old familiar palces, would learn more rapidly to find their way around in new regions". The stress laid here upon the absence of need for orientation only serves to highlight the positive motivation that is found in many nonliterate cultures.

5. The most comprehensive work on such maps is in Russian: B. F. Adler, *Maps of Primitive Peoples* (St. Petersburg: Imperial Society of Students of Natural History, Anthropology, and Ethnography, *Bulletin,* cxix, 1910). An English resumé by H. D. Hutorowicz is to be found in *Bulletin of the American Geographical Society,* xlii (1911). Adler's work is based on 55 maps from Asia, 15 from America, 3 from Africa, 40 from Australia and Oceania, and 2 from the East Indies. There is an earlier, but less significant work (a doctoral dissertation): W. Drober, *Kartographie bei der Naturvölkern,* 1903.

6. Dr. E. S. Carpenter has called my attention to the maps obtained from Ookpuktowk and Amaulik Audlanat, two Eskimo of Southampton Island, by Sutton (see Sutton 1936). Sutton obtained these in 1929 when no accurate maps of the island were avalable. More than a decade later a modern map, prepared fro.n aerial photographs, was made. Although I cannot reproduce the three maps here, the level of accuracy is certainly high in the Eskimo maps. Dr. Carpenter says, "Certain digressions, often shared, are immediately apparent. . . . But the striking feature is certainly accuracy, especially in the details of the shoreline."

7. Cassirer, in *The Philosophy of Symbolic Forms.* i (1953), discusses the expression of space and spatial relations in language in brilliant fashion, and in *An Essay on Man* (1944), he devotes a chapter to "The Human World of Space and Time." In this chapter Cassirer differentiates (1) organic space, (2) perceptual space, (3) symbolic space, (4) abstract space. *Organic* space he conceives of as the "space of action," a level of spatial orientation that is nonideational and, in effect, is confined to animals . . . (p. 43). *Perceptual* space is more complex in nature; it involves "elements of all the different kinds of sense experience—optical, tactual, acoustic, and kinesthetic" (p. 43). When we reach the level of *symbolic* space, we are on the borderline between the human and animal worlds. At a still higher level of human reflection and experience *abstract* space, i.e., mathematical or geometric space (p. 44) emerges, but only after many intermediate stages. "In primitive life and under the conditions of primitive soci-

ety," Cassirer says, "we find scarcely any trace of the idea of an abstract space. Primitive space is a space of action; and the action is centered around immediate practical needs and interests. So far as we can speak of a primitive 'conception' of space, this conception is not of a purely theoretical character." While this latter point is true enough, the very fact that the cosmic aspects of the world views of primitive peoples involve spatial concepts, is sufficient to show that "practical needs and interests" are actually transcended.

8. Revez (1937:434 n.) expresses the opinion that "Although the experience of space and perception of objects of animals seem to agree with that of our own, the theory of a general phenomenal agreement between animal and human perception is highly disputable from a logical and theoretical angle. . . . Because of the lack of language and ideas, all animals must have a different space concept . . . their objects must be perceived in a fundamentally different configuration and order than ours. . . . This must be the case regardless of their particular stage of evolutionary development and their biological relationship to man."

9. Jaccard (1932:224–25) refers to a Malagasy who, traveling in Europe, was profoundly impressed with the ignorance of directional orientation he found. In contrast, he himself constantly endeavored to maintain his orientation.

10. These remarks refer to the period of my investigations (1930–40).

11. Explorers frequently give excellent testimony on this point by their reference to the need for changing guides in the course of their journey. (See Jaccard, pp. 217–19). Foureau, for example, who made the first journey from North Africa to the Congo via the Sahara and Lake Chad, complained that his high-priced guides "ne connaissaient pas le pays au dela de quelques journées de marche. Les uns après les autres, arrivés à la limite, cherchaient des indigènes pour les remplacer."

12. I possess an outline map of the Poplar Narrows settlement made by a local Indian which gives all the place names in the environs of this settlement.

13. H. D. Hutorowicz says (cf. n. 11), "Of course the fundamental purpose of all these primitive maps is to show routes to hunting grounds, fisheries, settlements, etc." The maps of primitive people are oriented in various ways. The Tungus do not employ the cardinal points but use the prevailing direction of a major waterway. The Turkoman peoples use the main direction of the mountain ranges. The comments of Steffansson on Eskimo maps are pertinent here. "These Eskimo maps are likely to be good if you interpret them rightly. Here are some of the points. They are more likely to have the right number of curves in a river and the right shape of the curves than the proper distance scale. They are most likely to emphasize things that are of more importance to themselves; for instance, portages they have to cross are of more significance to them than mountains that stand to one side. . . . Primitive men are likely to

confuse the time scale with the mileage scale—after a ten-day journey of say six hours each day, they are likely to dot these camps at equal intervals, although, because of better going, they may have made twice the average distance one day and half the average another." See Raisz 1938:9.

14. Hutorowicz (p. 672), "Like all maps of primitive or ancient peoples, a Tungus map is truest of the region best known to the map-maker, and this region is usually shown to the central part of the map, so that nearer the border, distances and surfaces are likely to be less accurately shown." The comparison of an early Roman map (p. 677), made in the reign of Augustus (the *Tabula Pentigernana*) with the maps of primitive peoples is interesting, "They differ greatly in the fact that the Roman map attempts to show the whole world as then known, while primitive map-makers confine themselves to regions with which they are acquainted; but both are alike in having no degree nets, and in being little more than sketches of routes; and in both cases, the author tries to present the information of greatest importance to himself, other facts being almost ignored."

15. This may explain, perhaps, the gegraphical ignorance of the natives in certain parts of Malekula referred to by Harrison (1936:100). "This difficulty of the natives not knowing a name or direction for any point a few miles away, this complete geographical ignorance of the Malekula . . . is a handicap in travel, and particularly in taking a census. It means that one must cover all the ground oneself, and accept no negative statement as to the absence of villages."

16. Raisz 1938:1, quotes a neat analogy of the geographer P. E. James who, speaking of the individual's direct knowledge of the earth's surface, writes: "Like an ant upon a rug he may know very exactly the nature of the fabric nearby, but the general design is beyond his range of vision. In order to reduce the larger patterns in the face of the Earth to such proportions that they can be comprehended in a single view, the geographer makes use of a map." From a psychological as well as from a historical point of view the last sentence of this quotation is of particular significance. Maps, by abstracting and transforming such spatial attributes as distance, direction, area, and contour into symbolic forms that are easily perceptible in all their spatial relations, not only enable the individual to comprehend these relations more abstractly; they enable him to make measurements and calculations and plan his practical activities in a wider spatial sphere. And in travel he need have no fear of disorientation. The importance of maps as basic instruments for a realistic mastery of space by man cannot be exaggerated.

17. Cf. H. St. J. Philby (1933:173), who describes the surprise of his Arab guides that he could march south on a compass course towards nothing, then turn due west and hit off the main camp that had been left the day before on a northeast course. Such a feat implies, of

course, a developed geometry and abstract space concepts.

18. Parsons 1939:1, 99, states that "the order of the cardinal directions establishes the conventional circuit which is the countersunwise or sinistral, whether in coiling baskets (Hopi second mesa) or in pottery design or in dancing, although now and again the sunwise circuit is followed. A striking illustration of how the circuit may be read into life is the view, held at Zuñi, that eagles nest successively in four places and then repeat their nesting round."

In China categorical-symbolical thinking as applied to space and time has deep implication for all sorts of actual behavior (see Granet 1934:86–114). Bodde states (1939:201) that the Chinese are constantly made aware of directional orientation not only "by the layout of city streets along north-south and east-west axes," but by habitually thinking of the relations of household objects in terms of the directions. "When in China, for example, one wishes to have a table moved into a different part of one's room, one does not tell the servant to shift it to his right or left, but to 'move it a little east,' or west, or whatever the direction may be, even if it is a matter of only two or three inches."

Such a custom is so strange to Western thinking that some years ago when a twelve-year-old boy was discovered who appeared to possess an unusual sense of directional orientation, the question arose whether this might not be an innate ability (de Silva 1931). Investigation of his personal history, however, gave the proper cue. The child's mother was left-handed and found it more convenient to substitute the cardinal directions for left and right in giving the boy directions about the locations of objects in the house. Consequently, he was brought up from babyhood to respond to orders such as "Get me the brush on the north side of the dresser; go sit on the chair on the east side of the porch," etc. Experiment showed that the child's ability depended altogether upon correct initial visual orientation. He was easily disoriented when rotated a few times in a dark room.

EIGHT

Lineal and Nonlineal Codifications of Reality

DOROTHY LEE

It is nice to think that one can just have an experience and be able to sense that experience completely, in all its many faceted detail. And if one is careful, and disciplines one's perception so that nothing is read into the experience, nor subtracted from it, then one should be able to perceive exactly what has happened to one—no more, no less, and in no different way. This illusory notion is at the base of much of Western philosophy (for example, the intuitionism of Kant, modern phenomenology), and often provides an ideal toward which analysts of culture strive (see Geertz's paper in this volume, for an example).

As the late Dorothy Lee was by no means the first to tell us, such a positivist's utopian dream is neither easy nor usual. Not only what we perceive, but the way in which those perceptions are codified in the concepts embodied in language become intervening "lenses" (to use the common metaphor) which help to define just what that experience was and how it is to be understood. This does not mean that we are blind to any reality except that which our cultural "lenses" show us. Indeed, the very fact that we can become aware of the ways in which we have learned to perceive reality, and the ways in which we have learned to codify our perception in a particular language, go a long way toward freeing us to appreciate other aspects than those we might perceive without such comparative insights. Nor does the notion of a cultural "lens" mean that reality is nothing more or less than what we see. But it does mean that we take as real what we see as real, and we talk about reality in ways which give that reality its special configuration for us—be it lineal, nonlineal, or however.

THE FOLLOWING STUDY is concerned with the codification of reality, and more particularly, with the nonlineal apprehension of reality among the people of the Trobriand Islands, in contrast to our own lineal phrasing. Basic to my investigation is the assumption that a member of a given society not only codifies experienced reality through the use of the specific language and other patterned behavior characteristic of his culture, but that he actually grasps reality only as it is presented to him in this code. The assumption is not that reality itself is relative; rather, that it is differently punctuated and categorized,* or that dif-

Reprinted by permission from *Psychosomatic Medicine*, 1950, vol. 12, pp. 89–97.

*I have taken over this special use of the terms *codification* and *punctuation* from Gregory Bateson.

ferent aspects of it are noticed by, or presented to the participants of different cultures. If reality itself were not absolute, then true communication of course would be impossible. My own position is that there is an absolute reality, and that communication is possible. If, then, that which the different codes refer to is ultimately the same, a careful study and analysis of a different code and of the culture to which it belongs, should lead us to concepts which are ultimately comprehensible, when translated into our own code. It may even, eventually, lead us to aspects of reality from which our own code excludes us.

It is a corollary of this assumption that the specific phrasing of reality can be discovered through intensive and detailed analysis of any aspect of culture. My own study was begun with an analysis of linguistic formulation, only because it is in language that I happen to be best able to discover my clues. To show how these clues can be discovered and used as guides to the apprehension of reality, as well as to show what I mean by codification, I shall present at first concrete material in the field of language.

Diversity of Codification

That a word is not the reality, not the thing which it represents, has long been a commonplace to all of us. The thing which I hold in my hand as I write, *is* not a pencil; I *call* it a pencil. And it remains the same whether I call it *pencil, molyvi, Bleistift,* or *siwiqoq.* These words are different sound-complexes applied to the same reality; but is the difference merely one of sound-complex? Do they refer to the same *per-*ceived reality? *Pencil* originally meant little tail; it delimited and named the reality according to form. *Molyvi* means lead and refers to the writing element. *Bleistift* refers both to the form and to the writing element. *Siwiqoq* means painting-stick and refers to observed function and form. Each culture has phrased the reality differently. To say that *pencil,* for example, applies primarily to form is no idle etymologic statement. When we use this word metaphorically, we refer neither to writing element nor to function, but to form alone; we speak of a pencil of light, or a styptic pencil.

When I used the four words for this object, we all knew what reality was referred to; we knew the meaning of the word. We could visualize the object in my hand, and the words all delimited it in the same way; for example, none of them implied that it was a continuation of my fist. But the student of ethnography often has to deal with words which punctuate reality into different phrasings from the ones with which he is familiar. Let us take, for instance, the words for "brother" and "sister." We go to the islands of Ontong Java to study the kinship system. We ask our informant what he calls his sister and he says *ave;* he calls his brother *kainga.* So we equate *ave* with "sister" and *kainga* with "brother." By way of checking our information we ask the sister what she calls her brother; it turns out that for her, *ave* is "brother," not "sister" as we were led to expect; and that it is her sister whom she calls *kainga.* The same reality, the same actual kinship is present there as with us; but we have chosen a different aspect for naming. We are prepared to account for this; we say that both cultures name according to what we would call a certain type of blood relationship; but whereas we make reference to absolute sex, they refer to relative sex. Further inquiry, however, discloses that in this, also, we are wrong. Because in our own culture we name relatives according to formal definition and biologic relationship, we have thought that this formulation represents reality; and we have tried to understand the Ontong Javanese relationship terms according to these distinctions which, we believe, are given in nature. But the Ontong Javanese classifies relatives according to a different aspect of reality, differently punctuated. And because of this, he applies *kainga* as well to a wife's sister and a husband's brother; to a man's brother's wife and a woman's sister's husband, as well as to a number of other individuals. Neither sex nor blood relationship, then, can be basic to this term. The Ontong Javanese name according to their everyday behavior and experience, not according to formal definition. A man shares the ordinary details of his living with his brothers and their wives for a large part of the year; he sleeps in the same large room, he eats with them, he jokes and works around the house with them; the rest of the year he spends with his wife's sisters and their husbands, in the same easy companionship. All these individuals are *kainga* to one another. The *ave,* on the other hand, names a behavior of great strain and propriety; it is based originally upon the relative sex of siblings, yes, but it does not signify biologic fact. It names a social relationship, a behavior, an emotional tone. *Ave* can never spend their adult life together, except on rare and temporary occasions. They can never be under the same roof alone together, cannot chat at ease together, cannot

refer even distantly to sex in the presence of each other, not even to one's sweetheart or spouse; more than that, everyone else must be circumspect when the *ave* of someone of the group is present. The *ave* relationship also carries special obligations toward a female *ave* and her children. *Kainga* means a relationship of ease, full of shared living, of informality, gaiety; *ave* names one of formality, prohibition, strain. These two cultures, theirs and our own, have phrased and formulated social reality in completely different ways, and have given their formulation different names. The word is merely the name of this specific cultural phrasing. From this one instance we might formulate the hypothesis—a very tentative one—that among the Ontong Javanese names describe emotive experiences, not observed forms or functions. But we cannot accept this as fact, unless further investigation shows it to be implicit in the rest of their patterned behavior, in their vocabulary and the morphology of their language, in their ritual and their other organized activity.

One more instance, this time from the language of the Wintu Indians of California, will deal with the varying aspect or segmentation of experience which is used as a basis of classification. To begin with, we take the stem *muk.* On the basis of this stem we form the word *mukeda,* which means: "I turned the basket bottom up"; we form *mukuhara,* which means: "The turtle is moving along"; and we form *mukurumas,* which means: "automobile". Upon what conceivable principle can an automobile be put in the same category as a turtle and a basket? There is such a principle, however, and it operates also when the Wintu calls the activity of

laundering, *to make foam continuously.*
According to this principle, he uses the
same stem (*puq* or *poq*) to form words
for the following:

puqeda: I just pushed a peg into the ground.
olpuqal: He is sitting on one haunch.
poqorahara: Birds are hopping along.
olpoqoyabe: There are mushrooms growing.
tunpoqoypoqoya: You walked shortskirted,
    stifflegged ahead of me.

It is difficult for us to discover the
common denominator in the different
formations from this one stem, or even
to believe that there can be one. Yet,
when we discover the principle underlying the classification, the categories
themselves are understandable. Basic to
the classification is the Wintu view of
himself as observer; he classifies as an
outsider. He passes no judgment on essence, and where we would have used
kinesthetic or participatory experience
as the basis of naming, he names as an
observer only, for the shape of the activity or the object. The turtle and the automobile can thus naturally be grouped
together with the inverted baskets. The
mushroom standing on its stem, the fist
grasping a peg against the ground, the
stiff leg topped by a short skirt, or by the
body of a bird or of a man resting on a
haunch, obviously all belong together in
one category. But the progress of a
grasshopper cannot be categorized with
that of a hopping bird. We, who classify
on a different basis, apprehend the hop
of the two kinesthetically and see it as
basically the same in both cases; but the
Wintu see the difference in recurrent
shape, which is all-important to them,
and so name the two by means of completely different stems. Again, when we
discover this principle, it is easy to see
that from the observer's point of view

laundering is the making of a lot of foam;
and to see why, when beer was introduced, it was named *laundry.*

An exhaustive study of the language
and other aspects of Wintu culture
shows that this principle is present in all
of the Wintu language, as well as in the
Wintu's conception of the self, of his
place in the universe, in his mythology,
and probably in other aspects of his
culture.

Nonlineality in Trobriand Language

I have discussed at length the diversity of codification of reality in general,
because it is the foundation of the specific study which I am about to present.
I shall speak of the formulation of experienced reality among the Trobriand
Islanders in comparison to our own; I
shall speak of the nature of expectancy,
of motivation, of satisfaction, as based
upon a reality which is differently apprehended and experienced in two different
societies; which is, in fact, for each, a
different reality. The Trobriand Islanders were studied by the late Bronislaw
Malinowski, who has given us the rich
and circumstantial material about them
which has made this study possible. I
have given a detailed presentation of
some implications of their language elsewhere; but since it was in their language
that I first noticed the absence of lineality, which led me to this study, I shall
give here a summary of the implications
of the language.

A Trobriand word refers to a self-
contained concept. What we consider an
attribute or a predicate is to the Trobriander an ingredient. Where I would
say, for example, "A good gardener,"
or "The gardener is good," the Tro-

briand word would include both "gardener" and "goodness"; if the gardener loses the goodness, he has lost a defining ingredient, he is something else, and he is named by means of a completely different word. A *taytu* (a species of yam) contains a certain degree of ripeness, bigness, roundedness, etc.; without one of these defining ingredients, it is something else, perhaps a *bwanawa* or a *yowana*. There are no adjectives in the language; the rare words dealing with qualities are substantivized. The term *to be* does not occur; it is used neither attributively nor existentially, since existence itself is contained; it is an ingredient of being.

Events and objects are self-contained points in another respect; there is a series of beings, but no becoming. There is no temporal connection between objects. The taytu always remains itself; it does not *become* over-ripe; over-ripeness is an ingredient of another, a different being. At some point, the taytu *turns into* a yowana, which contains over-ripeness. And the yowana, over-ripe as it is, does not put forth shoots, does not *become* a sprouting yowana. When sprouts appear, it ceases to be itself; in its place appears a *silasata*. Neither is there a temporal connection made—or, according to our own premises, perceived—between events; in fact, temporality is meaningless. There are no tenses, no linguistic distinction between past or present. There is no arrangement of activities or events into means and ends, no causal or teleologic relationships. What we consider a causal relationship in a sequence of connected events, is to the Trobriander an ingredient of a patterned whole. He names this ingredient *u'ula*. A tree has a trunk, u'ula; a house has u'ula, posts; a magi-

cal formula has u'ula, the first strophe; an expedition has u'ula, a manager or leader; and a quarrel contains an u'ula, what we would call a cause. There is no purposive *so as to;* no *for the purpose of;* there is no *why* and no *because*. The rarely used *pela* which Malinowski equates with *for,* means primarily *to jump*. In the culture, any deliberately purposive behavior—the kind of behavior to which we accord high status—is despised. There is no automatic relating of any kind in the language. Except for the rarely used verbal it-differents and it-sames, there are no terms of comparison whatever. And we find in an analysis of behavior that the standard for behavior and of evaluation is noncomparative.

These implications of the linguistic material suggest to my mind an absence of axiomatic lineal connection between events or objects in the Trobriand apprehension of reality, and this implication, as I shall attempt to show below, is reinforced in their definition of activity. In our own culture, the line is so basic, that we take it for granted, as given in reality. We see it in visible nature, between material points, and we see it between metaphorical points such as days or acts. It underlies not only our thinking, but also our aesthetic apprehension of the given; it is basic to the emotional climax which has so much value for us, and, in fact, to the meaning of life itself. In our thinking about personality and character, we have assumed the line as axiomatic.

In our academic work, we are constantly acting in terms of an implied line. When we speak of applying an attribute, for example, we visualize the process as lineal, coming from the outside. If I make a picture of an apple on the board, and want to show that one side is green and the other red, I connect these attributes with the pictured apple by means of lines, as a matter of course; how else would I do it? When I organize my data, I *draw* conclusions *from* them. I *trace* a relationship between my facts. I describe a pattern as a *web* of relationships. Look at a lecturer who makes use of gestures; he is constantly making lineal connections in the air. And a teacher with chalk in hand will be drawing lines on the board whether he be a psychologist, a historian, or a paleontologist.

Preoccupation with social facts merely as self-contained facts is mere antiquarianism. In my field, a student of this sort would be an amateur or a dilettante, not an anthropologist. To be an anthropologist, he can arrange his facts in an upward slanting line, in a *unilinear* or *multilinear course* of development, in *parallel lines* or *converging lines*. Or he may arrange them geographically, with *lines of diffusion* connecting them; or schematically, using *concentric circles*. Or, at least, he must indicate what his study *leads to,* what new insights we can *draw from it*. To be accorded status, he must use the guiding line as basic.

The line is found or presupposed in most of our scientific work. It is present in the *induction* and the *deduction* of science and logic. It is present in the philosopher's phrasing of means and ends as lineally connected. Our statistical facts are presented lineally as a *graph* or reduced to a normal *curve*. And all of us, I think, would be lost without our diagrams. We *trace* a historical development; we *follow the course* of history and evolution *down to* the present and *up from* the ape; and it is interesting to note, in passing, that whereas both evolution and history are

lineal, the first goes up the blackboard, the second goes down. Our psychologists picture motivation as external, connected with the act through a line, or, more recently, entering the organism through a lineal channel and emerging transformed, again lineally, as response. I have seen lineal pictures of nervous impulses and heartbeats, and with them I have seen pictured lineally a second of time. These were photographs, you will say, of existing fact, of reality; a proof that the line is present in reality. But I am not convinced, perhaps due to my ignorance of mechanics, that we have not created our recording instruments in such a way that they have to picture time and motion, light and sound, heartbeats and nerve impulses lineally, on the unquestioned assumption of the line as axiomatic. The line is omnipresent and inescapable, and so we are incapable of questioning the reality of its presence.

When we see a *line* of trees, or a *circle* of stones, we assume the presence of a connecting line which is not actually visible. And we assume it metaphorically when we follow a *line* of thought, a *course* of action or the *direction* of an argument; when we *bridge* a gap in the conversation, or speak of the *span* of life or of teaching a *course,* or lament our *interrupted career.* We make children's embroidery cards and puzzle cards on this assumption; our performance tests and even our tests for sanity often assume that the line is present in nature and, at most, to be discovered or given visual existence.

But is the line present in reality? Malinowski, writing for members of our culture and using idioms which would be comprehensible to them, describes the Trobriand village as follows: "Concentrically with the circular row of yam houses there runs a ring of dwelling huts." He saw, or at any rate, he represented the village as two circles. But in the texts which he recorded, we find that the Trobrianders at no time mention circles or rings or even rows when they refer to their villages. Any word which they use to refer to a village, such as *a* or *this,* is prefixed by the substantival element *kway* which means *bump* or *aggregate of bumps.* This is the element which they use when they refer to a pimple or a bulky rash; or to canoes loaded with yams. In their terms, a village is an aggregate of bumps; are they blind to the circles? Or did Malinowski create the circles himself, out of his cultural axiom?

Again, for us as well as in Malinowski's description of the Trobrianders, which was written necessarily in terms meaningful to us, all effective activity is certainly not a haphazard aggregate of acts, but a lineally planned series of acts leading to an envisioned end. Their gardening with all its specialized activities, both technical and magical, leading to a rich harvest; their *kula* involving the cutting down of trees, the communal dragging of the tree to the beach, the rebuilding or building of large sea-worthy canoes, the provisioning, the magical and ceremonial activities involved, surely all these can be carried through only if they are lineally conceived. But the Trobrianders do not describe their activity lineally; they do no dynamic relating of acts; they do not use even so innocuous a connective as *and.* Here is part of a description of the planting of coconut: "Thou-approach-there coconut thou-bring-here-we-plant-coconut thou-go thou-plant our coconut. This-here it-emerge sprout. We-push-away this we-push-away this-other coconut-

husk-fiber together sprout it-sit together root." We who are accustomed to seek lineal continuity, cannot help supplying it as we read this; but the continuity is not given in the Trobriand text; and all Trobriand speech, according to Malinowski, is "jerky," given in points, not in connecting lines. The only connective I know of in Trobriand is the *pela* which I mentioned above; a kind of preposition which also means "to jump." I am not maintaining here that the Trobrianders cannot see continuity; rather that lineal connection is not automatically made by them, as a matter of course. At Malinowski's persistent questioning, for example, they did attempt to explain their activities in terms of cause or motivation, by stating possible "results" of uncooperative action. But Malinowski found their answers confused, self-contradictory, inconsistent; their preferred answer was, "It was ordained of old"— pointing to an ingredient value of the act instead of giving an explanation based on lineal connection. And when they were not trying to find answers to leading questions, the Trobrianders made no such connections in their speech. They assumed, for example, that the validity of a magical spell lay, not in its results, not in proof, but in its very being; in the appropriateness of its inheritance, in its place within the patterned activity, in its being performed by the appropriate person, in its realization of its mythical basis. To seek validity through proof was foreign to their thinking, yet they attempted to do so at the ethnographer's request. I should add here that their names for constellations imply that here they see lineal figures; I cannot investigate the significance of this, as I have no contextual material. At any rate, I would like to emphasize that, even if the

Trobriander does occasionally supply connecting lines between points, his perception and experience do not automatically fall into a lineal framework.

The fact remains that Trobrianders embark on, what is certainly for us, a series of acts which "must require" planning and purposiveness. They engage in acts of gift-giving and gift-receiving which we can certainly see as an exchange of gifts. When we plot their journeys, we find that they do go from point to point, they do navigate a course, whether they say so or not. Do they merely refrain from giving linguistic expression to something which they actually recognize in nature? On the nonlinguistic level, do they act on an assumption of a lineality which is given no place in their linguistic formulation? I believe that, where valued activity is concerned, the Trobrianders do not act on an assumption of lineality at any level. There is organization or rather coherence in their acts because Trobriand activity is patterned activity. One act within this pattern gives rise to a preordained cluster of acts. Perhaps one might find a parallel in our culture in the making of a sweater. When I embark on knitting one, the ribbing at the bottom does not *cause* the making of the neckline, nor of the sleeves or the armholes; and it is not a part of a lineal series of acts. Rather it is an indispensable part of a patterned activity which includes all these other acts. Again, when I choose a dress pattern, the acts involved in the making of the dress are already present for me. They are embedded in the pattern which I have chosen. In this same way, I believe, can be seen the Trobriand insistence that though intercourse is a necessary preliminary to conception, it is not the cause of conception. There are a number of acts in the pattern

of procreating; one is intercourse, another the entrance of the spirit of a dead Trobriander into the womb. However, there is a further point here. The Trobrianders, when pressed by the ethnographer or teased by the neighboring Dobuans, showed signs of intense embarrassment, giving the impression that they were trying to maintain unquestionably a stand in which they had to believe. This, I think, is because pattern is truth and value for them; in fact, acts and being derive value from the embedding pattern.

So the question of perception of line remains. It is because they find value in pattern that the Trobrianders act according to nonlineal pattern; not because they do not perceive lineality.

But all Trobriand activity does not contain value; and when it does not, it assumes lineality, and is utterly despicable. For example, the pattern of sexual intercourse includes the giving of a gift from the boy to the girl; but if a boy gives a gift so as to win the girl's favor, he is despised. Again, the kula pattern includes the eventual reception of a gift from the original recipient; the pattern is such that it keeps the acts physically and temporally completely disparate. In spite of this, however, some men are accused of giving gifts as an inducement to their kula partner to give them a specially good kula gift. Such men are labeled with the vile phrase: he barters. But this means that, unvalued and despised, lineal behavior does exist. In fact, there are villages in the interior whose inhabitants live mainly by bartering manufactured articles for yams. The inhabitants of Omarakana, about whom Malinowski's work and this study are mainly concerned, will barter with them, but consider them pariahs.

This is to say that it is probable that

the Trobrianders experience reality in nonlineal pattern because this is the valued reality; and that they are capable of experiencing lineally, when value is absent or destroyed. It is not to say, however, that this, in itself, means that lineality is given, is present in nature, and that pattern is not. Our own insistence on the line, such as lineal causality, for example, is often based on unquestioned belief or value. To return to the subject of procreation, the husband in our culture, who has long hoped and tried in vain to beget children, will nevertheless maintain that intercourse causes conception; perhaps with the same stubbornness and embarrassment which the Trobrianders exhibited when maintaining the opposite.

Absence of Line as Guide

The line in our culture not only connects, but it moves. And as we think of a line moving from point to point, connecting one to the other, so we conceive of roads as *running from* locality *to* locality. A Trobriander does not speak of roads either as connecting two points, or as *running from* point *to* point. His paths are self-contained, named as independent units; they are not *to* and *from,* they are *at.* And he himself is *at;* he has no equivalent for our *to* or *from.* There is, for instance, the myth of Tudava, who goes—in our view—from village to village and from island to island planting and offering yams. The Trobriand texts puts it this way: "Kitava it-shine village already (i.e. completed) he-is-over. I-sail I-go Iwa; Iwa he-anchor he-go ashore . . . He-sail Digumenu . . . They-drive (him off) . . . he-go Kwaywata." Point after point is enumerated, but his sailing from and to is given as a discrete event. In our view, he is actually following a southeasterly course, more or less; but this is not given as course or line, and no directions are even mentioned. In fact, in the several texts referring to journeyings in the Archipelago, no words occur for the cardinal directions. In sailing, the "following" winds are named according to where they are *at,* the place where they strike the canoe, such as wind-striking-the-outrigger-beam; not according to where they *come from.* Otherwise, we find names for the southwest wind (*youyo*), and the northwest wind (*bombatu*), but these are merely substantival names which have nothing to do with direction; names for kinds of wind.

When a member of our society gives an unemotional description of a person, he follows an imaginary line, usually downward: from head to foot, from tip to toe, from hair to chin. The Navaho do the opposite, following a line upward. The Trobriander follows no line, at least none that I can see. "My head boils," says a kula spell; and it goes on to enumerate the parts of the head as follows: nose, occiput, tongue, larynx, speech, mouth. Another spell casting a protective fog, runs as follows: "I befog the hand, I befog the foot, I befog the head, I befog the shoulders . . ." There is a magic formula where we do recognize a line, but it is one which Malinowski did not record verbatim at the time, but which he put down later from memory; and it is not improbable that his memory edited the formula according to the lineality of his culture. When the Trobriander enumerates the parts of a canoe, he does not follow any recognizable lineal order: "Mist . . . surround me my mast . . . the nose of my canoe . . . my sail . . . my steering oar . . . my canoe-gunwale . . . my canoe-bottom . . . my prow . . . my rib . . . my threading-stick . . . my prowboard . . . my transverse stick . . . my canoe-side." Malinowski diagrams the garden site as a square piece of land subdivided into squares; the Trobrianders refer to it in the same terms as those which they use in referring to a village—a bulky object or an aggregate of bumps. When the plots in the garden site are apportioned to the gardeners, the named plots are assigned by name, the others by location along each named side of the garden. After this, the inner plots, the "belly" of the garden, are apportioned. Following along a physical rim is a procedure which we find elsewhere also. In a spell naming villages on the main island, there is a long list of villages which lie along the coast northward, then westward around the island, then south. To us, of course, this is lineal order. But we have no indication that the Trobrianders see other than geographical location, point after point, as they move over a physically continuous area; the line as a guide to procedure is not necessarily implied. No terms are used here which might be taken as an implication of continuity; no "along the coast" or "around" or "northward."

Line vs. Pattern

When we in our culture deal with events or experiences of the self, we use the line as guide for various reasons, two of which I shall take up here. First, we feel we must arrange events chronologically in a lineal order; how else could our historians discover the causes of a war or a revolution or a defeat? Among the Trobrianders, what corresponds to our history is an aggregate of anecdotes, that is, unconnected points, told without respect to chronological sequence, or development, or causal relationship; with no grammatical distinction made between words referring to past events, or to present or contemplated ones. And in telling an anecdote, they take no care that a temporal sequence should be followed. For instance, they said to Malinowski: "They-eat-taro, they-spew-taro, they-disgusted-taro"; but if time, as we believe, is a moving line, then the revulsion came first in time, the vomiting was the result, coming afterward. Again, they say, "This-here . . . ripes . . . falls-down truly gives-birth . . . sits seed in belly-his"; but certainly the seed is there first, and the birth follows in time, if time is lineal.

Secondly, we arrange events and objects in a sequence which is climactic, in size and intensity, in emotional meaning, or according to some other principle. We often arrange events from earlier to later, not because we are interested in historical causation, but because the present is the climax of our history. But when the Trobriander relates happenings, there is no developmental arrangement, no building up of emotional tone. His stories have no plot, no lineal development, no climax. And when he repeats his garden spell, his list is neither climactic, nor anticlimactic; it sounds merely untidy to us:

The belly of my garden lifts
The belly of my garden rises
The belly of my garden reclines
The belly of my garden is-a-bushhen's-nest-in-lifting
The belly of my garden is-an-anthill
The belly of my garden lifts-bends
The belly of my garden is-an-ironwood-tree-in-lifting
The belly of my garden lies-down
The belly of my garden burgeons.

When the Trobrianders set out on their great ceremonial kula expedition, they follow a preestablished order. First comes the canoe of the Tolabwaga, an obscure subclan. Next come the canoes of the great chiefs. But this is not climactic; after the great chiefs come the commoners. The order derives meaning not from lineal sequence, but from correspondence with a present, experienced, meaningful pattern, which is the recreation or realization of the mythical pattern; that which has been ordained of old and is forever. Its meaning does not lie in an item-to-item relationship, but in fitness, in the repetition of an established unit.

An ordering of this sort gives members of our society a certain esthetic disphoria except when, through deliberate training, we learn to go beyond our cultural expectation; or, when we are too young to have taken on the phrasings of our culture. When we manipulate objects naïvely, we arrange them on some climactic lineal principle. Think of a college commencement, with the faculty arranged in order of rank or length of tenure or other mark of importance; with the students arranged according to increasing physical height, from shortest to tallest, actually the one absolutely irrelevant principle as regards the completion of their college education, which is the occasion for the celebration. Even when the sophisticated avoid this principle, they are not unconscious of it; they are deliberately avoiding something which is there.

And our arrangement of history, when we ourselves are personally involved, is mainly climactic. My great grandmother sewed by candle light, my grandmother used a kerosene lamp, my mother did her studying by gaslight, I did it by a naked electric ceiling light, and my children have diffused fluorescent lighting. This is progress; this is the meaningful sequence. To the Trobriander, climax in history is abominable, a denial of all good, since it would imply not only the presence of change, but also that change increases the good; but to him value lies in sameness, in repeated pattern, in the incorporation of all time within the same point. What is good in life is exact identity with all past Trobriand experience, and all mythical experience. There is no boundary between past Trobriand existence and the present; he can indicate that an action is completed, but this does not mean that the action is past; it may be completed and present or timeless. Where we would say "Many years ago" and use the past tense, the Trobriander will say, "In my father's childhood" and use non-temporal verbs; he places the event situationally, not temporally. Past, present, and future are presented linguistically as the same, are present in his existence, and sameness with what we call the past and with myth, represents value to the Trobriander. Where we see a developmental line, the Trobriander sees a point, at most swelling in value. Where we find pleasure and satisfaction in moving away from the point, in change as variety or progress, the Trobriander finds it in the repetition of the known, in maintaining the point; that is, in what we call monotony. Esthetic validity, dignity, and value come to him not through arrangement into a climactic line, but rather in the undisturbed incorporation of the events within their original, nonlineal order. The only history which has meaning for him is that which evokes the value of the point, or which, in the repetition, swells the value of the point. For example, every occasion in which a kula object participates becomes an ingredient of its being and swells its value; all these occasions are enumerated with great satisfaction, but the lineal course of the traveling kula object is not important.

As we see our history climactically, so do we plan future experiences climactically, leading up to future satisfaction or meaning. Who but a very young child would think of starting a meal with strawberry shortcake and ending it with spinach? We have come to identify the end of the meal with the height of satisfaction, and we identify semantically the words dessert and reward, only because of the similarity of their positions in a climactic line. The Trobriand meal has no dessert, no line, no climax. The special bit, the relish, is eaten *with* the staple food; it is not something to "look *forward to*," while disposing of a meaningless staple.

None of the Trobriand activities are fitted into a climactic line. There is no job, no labor, no drudgery which finds its reward outside the act. All work contains its own satisfaction. We cannot speak of S—R here, as all action contains its own immanent "stimulus." The present is not a means to future satisfaction, but good in itself, as the future is also good in itself; neither better nor worse, neither climactic nor anticlimactic, in fact, not lineally connected nor removed. It follows that the present is not evaluated in terms of its place within a course of action leading upward to a worthy end. In our culture, we can rarely evaluate the present in itself. I tell you that Sally is selling notions at Woolworth's, but this in itself means nothing. It acquires some meaning when I add that she has recently graduated from Vassar. However, I go on to tell you that she has been assistant editor of *Vogue,* next a nursemaid, a charwoman, a public school teacher. But this is a mere jumble; it makes no sense and has no meaning, because the series leads to nothing. You cannot relate one job to another, and you are unable to see them discretely simply as part of her being. However, I now add that she is gathering material for a book on the working mother. Now all this falls in line, it makes sense in terms of a career. Now her job is good and it makes her happy, because it is part of a planned climactic line leading to more pay, increased recognition, higher rank. There was a story in a magazine about the college girl who fell in love with the milkman one summer; the reader felt tense until it was discovered that this was just a summer job, that it was only a means for the continuation of the man's education in the Columbia Law School. Our evaluation of happiness and unhappiness is bound with this motion along an envisioned line leading to a desired end. In the fulfillment of this course or career—not in the fulfillment of the self as point—do we find value. Our conception of freedom rests on the principle of noninterference with this moving line, noninterruption of the intended course of action.

It is difficult to tell whether climax is given in experience at all, or whether it is always imposed on the given. At a time when progress and evolution were assumed to be implicit in nature, our musicians and writers gave us climactic works. Nowadays, our more reflective art does not present experience climactically. Then, is emotion itself climactic?

Climax, for us, evokes "thrill" or "drama." But we have cultures, like the Tikopia, where life is lived on an even emotive plane without thrill or climax. Experiences which "we know to be" climactic, are described without climax by them. For example, they, as well as the Trobrianders, described intercourse as an aggregate of pleasurable experiences. But Malinowski is disturbed by this; he cannot place the erotic kiss in Trobriand experience, since it has no climactic function. Again, in our culture, childbearing is climactic. Pregnancy is represented by the usual obstetrician as an uncomfortable means to a dramatic end. For most women, all intensity of natural physical experience is nowadays removed from the actual birth itself; but the approach of birth nevertheless is a period of mounting tension, and drama is supplied by the intensive social recognition of the event, the dramatic accumulation of gifts, flowers, telegrams. A pregnancy is not formally announced since, if it does not eventuate in birth, it has failed to achieve its end; and failure to reach the climax brings shame. In its later stages, it may be marked with a shower; but the shower looks forward to the birth, it does not celebrate the pregnancy itself. Among the Trobrianders, pregnancy has meaning in itself as a state of being. At a first pregnancy, there is a long ceremonial involving "preparatory" work on the part of many people, which merely celebrates the pregnancy. It does not anchor the baby, it does not *have as its purpose* a more comfortable time during the pregnancy, it does not *lead to* an easier birth or a healthy baby. It makes the woman's skin white, and makes her be at her most beautiful; yet this *leads to* nothing, since she must not attract men, not even her own husband.

Conclusion

Are we then right in accepting without question the presence of a line in reality? Are we in a position to say with assurance that the Trobrianders are wrong and we are right? Much of our present-day thinking, and much of our evaluation, are based on the premise of the line and of the line as good. Students have been refused admittance to college because the autobiographic sketch accompanying their application showed absence of the line; they lacked purposefulness and ability to plan; they were inadequate as to character as well as intellectually. Our conception of personality formation, our stress on the significance of success and failure and of frustration in general, is based on the axiomatically postulated line. How can there be blocking without presupposed lineal motion or effort? If I walk along a path because I like the country, or if it is not important to get to a particular point at a particular time, then the insuperable puddle from the morning's shower is not frustrating; I throw stones into it and watch the ripples, and then choose another path. If the undertaking is of value in itself, a point good in itself, and not because it leads to something, then failure has no symbolic meaning; it merely results in no cake for supper, or less money in the family budget; it is not personally destructive. But failure is devastating in our culture, because it is not failure of the undertaking alone; it is the moving, becoming, lineally conceived self which has failed.

Ethnographers have occasionally remarked that the people whom they studied showed no annoyance when interrupted. Is this an indication of mild temper, or might it be the case that they were not interrupted at all, as there was no expectation of lineal continuity? Such questions are new in anthropology and most ethnographers therefore never thought of recording material which would answer them. However, we do have enough material to make us question the line as basic to all experience; whether it is actually present in given reality or not, it is not always present in experienced reality. We cannot even take it for granted as existing among those members of our society who are not completely or naïvely steeped in their culture, such as many of our artists, for example. And we should be very careful, in studying other cultures, to avoid the unexamined assumption that their actions are based on the prediction of a lineal reality.

NINE

Colors and Cultures

Marshall Sahlins

Among the more important classic controversies in anthropology is the famous Sapir-Whorf hypothesis, named after Edward Sapir, an early anthropologist and linguist, and Benjamin Lee Whorf. The hypothesis, put crudely, states that culture is completely relative, so that any given experience can be assigned any meaning by different cultures, or that any symbol is purely arbitrary, so that anything can, in a cultural context, be made to stand for anything else.

But in various ways the arbitrariness of the symbol has been brought into question. From one side comes the demonstration of certain psycho-biological constraints on both perception and experience. From another comes the fact that no collection of symbols for any culture or any segment of any culture is purely random; they form systems, and in forming systems a degree of determination is imposed just as it is when, for example, we divide the universe into two portions and know that one constitutes 40 percent. The other portion must constitute 60 percent: it cannot be anything else.

In this paper, Sahlins deals directly with the problem of the relationship between meaning, the constraints of human and physical nature, and the cultural constitution of meaning. He does so by building on the important work of Berlin and Kay in their study of *Basic Color Terms*. He states his conclusion at the outset: "It is not, then, that color terms have their meanings imposed by the constraints of human and physical nature; it is that they take such constraints insofar as they are meaningful." And then he proceeds, using the methods of structuralist analysis, to brilliantly demonstrate the validity of that conclusion.

IT SEEMS NO EXAGGERATION to claim for Berlin's and Kay's *Basic Color Terms* (1970) a place among the most remarkable discoveries of anthropological science.[1] If exaggeration there be, it would consist in attributing the results to the authors alone, without reference to the development of the methods by Lenneberg and Roberts (1956) or the anticipation of the conclusions in the early researches of Magnus and Rivers—the debt to all of whom Berlin and Kay generously acknowledge.

Within a few short years, knowledge of Berlin-Kay results has been widely diffused and intensely debated. For the purposes of the present commentary it will be sufficient to mention briefly the three findings of most general and fundamental import: First, that despite the proven ability of human subjects to dis-

Reprinted by permission of Mouton, The Hague, from *Semiotica*, 1976, vol. 16, pp. 1–22.

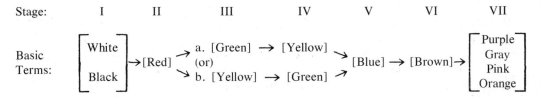

Figure 1. Progressive sequence of basic color in natural languages (Berlin and Kay, 1969)

criminate thousands of color percepts, natural languages manifest only a very limited number of "basic color terms," such as are applicable to a wide variety of objects; the number ranges from two to eleven, corresponding to English "black," "white," "red," "green," "yellow," "blue," "brown," "gray," "purple," "orange," and "pink." Secondly, these terms show a regular, cumulative order of appearance cross-culturally, such that natural languages can be arranged in a progressive sequence of color determinations, all those of any given stage discriminating the same basic hues (figure 9.1). Finally, the empirical referents of the basic terms on a spectrum of colors are very similar society to society: the most representative or focal "red," for example, is virtually the same for informants of different cultures, the agreement of average focal identifications between societies being generally greater than the range of experimental variation within a single society.

It is not necessary to suppose that the discoveries of *Basic Color Terms* are secure from further refinement or changes in detail. But on the evidence and in their essentials, the conclusions do seem beyond reach of the empiricist controversy they have occasioned—and beyond the misguided fears of an entrenched cultural relativism which, it is already possible to foresee, can only emerge from the encounter confirmed and enriched. Relativism will simply have to come to grips with the cross-cultural regularities of color categorization, though the unexpected findings challenge such basic doctrines as the arbitrary nature of the sign or, even more fundamental, the *sui generis* character of culture. It is not a question of salvaging a linguistic relativity of the kind usually attributed to Sapir and Whorf. Still less of defending the received wisdom that each society is at liberty to segment the spectrum as it were by its own lights, to impose its own particular discontinuities upon the continuum of color experience. Rather, in the face of the universals determined in *Basic Color Terms*, the decisive issue for relativism becomes synonymous with the autonomy of cultural activity as a symbolic valuation of natural fact. At stake is the understanding that each social group orders the objectivity of its experience, as the precipitate of a differential and meaningful logic, and so makes of human perception a historic conception. It is the essential problematic that the objectivity of objects is itself a cultural determination, dependent on the assignment of significance to certain "real" differences, while others are ignored (cf. Boas 1966 [1911], Saussure 1966 [1915]; Lévi-Strauss 1966; Douglas 1966; 1973). On the basis of this segmentation or *découpage*, the "real" is systematically constituted, i.e., in a given cultural mode. As Cassirer explains:

La représentation "objective"—c'est là ce que je veux essayer d'expliquer—n'est pas le point de départ du processus de formation du langage, mais le but auquel ce processus conduit; elle n'est pas son *terminus a quo*, mais son *terminus ad quem*. Le langage n'entre pas dans un monde de perceptions objectives achevées, pour adjoindre seulement à des objets individuels donnés des signes purement extérieurs et arbitraries; mais il est lui-même un médiateur par excellence, l'instrument le plus important et le plus précieux pour la conquête et pour la construction d'un vrai monde d'objets. (1933:23)

In this brief paper I would defend these conventional ideas, not as against Berlin's and Kay's results, but with their help. I argue that these results are consequent on the social use of color not merely to signify objective differences of nature but *in the first place* to communicate significant distinctions of culture. Colors are in practice semiotic codes. Everywhere, both as terms and concrete properties, colors are engaged as signs in vast schemes of social relations: meaningful structures by which persons and groups, objects and occasions, are differentiated and combined in cultural orders. My thesis is that because colors subserve this *cultural significance,* only certain color percepts are appropriately singled out as "basic," namely those that by their distinctive features and relations can function as signifiers in informational systems. For a crude example, if "yellow" is to be contrasted semantically to "red," the latter is not likely to be concretely identified as a form of orange (i.e., on pain of evident contradiction between concep-

tual and perceptual relations). *It is not, then, that color terms have their meanings imposed by the constraints of human and physical nature; it is that they take on such constraints insofar as they are meaningful.*

Accordingly, it is practicable to concede the strongest possible case to the naturalistic interpretation, for the same biological facts of color discrimination are not only accommodated by a semiotic theory, they are demanded by it. Evidence for a universal set of contrasts and combinations on the natural level, especially taken in conjunction with their differential realization in cultural systems, becomes testimony of a semiotic project, not unlike the diverse phonemic elaborations of a limited number of distinctive sound features by means of which perceptual distinctions are engaged as the support for conceptual constructions. Besides, the salience and generality of contrasts on the natural plane should help account for the progressive sequence we are now presented with on the cultural. Berlin and Kay themselves refrain from offering any grounds for their linguistic findings in perceptual psychology or physiology.[2] Yet consider, for example, the light/dark distinction comprising the starting-point (Stage I) of the series set forth in *Basic Color Terms* (hereafter *BCT*). This happens to be perceptually the most general of all "color" experiences, based on the most elementary physiological response to luminous flux: a contrast at once inclusive of hue and independent of it, as even complete color-blinds are able to perceive differences in this form. Apart from induction effects, the lightness/darkness distinction (or in direct light sources especially, "brightness" or "luminosity"), works on a simple sensitivity response, a "signaler" of achromatic light presence as opposed to the discriminatory contrast mechanisms ("modulators") of hue perception. The first stage in the evolution of basic categories determined by *BCT* thus corresponds to the most comprehensive "color" contrast the human eye can make, applicable panchromatically to all visible objects and lights (cf. Linksz 1952:72 ff; 1964; Hurvich and Jameson 1957; Padgham and Saunders 1975; Boynton 1970; Burnham, Hanes, and Bartleson 1963).

Parenthetically, a simple sensitivity to light is also older in the history of life than hue discrimination; it can thus be said that cultural ontogeny here recapitulates evolutionary phylogeny. In the terms Trubetskoy proposes for phonological oppositions, the luminosity response is on the physiological level "privative," a presence/absence mechanism; whereas the oppositions of hue discrimination are "equipollent" (Trubetskoy 1968 [1939]). On the perceptual level, however, the contrasts are more complex, as will be seen. It is important to reiterate that the light/dark distinction, although focused in white/black, is panchromatic. There is indeed a relative difference in lightness-effect by wavelength of the source, amounting to a parabolic "luminosity curve" with its peak in the yellow region—so that on an equal energy spectrum the yellows will appear brighter (and less saturated) than hues of long and short wavelengths (reds and violets). The brightness of a self-luminous source is also dependent, of course, on the absolute intensity. In the case of object-color, brightness depends on reflectance as well, which gives a sensation of whiteness and lightness to surfaces. The light/dark curve across the spectrum obtained by E. R. Heider (1972) for the Stage I Dani system is probably due to the differential reflectance of the Munsell red chips, which apparently give them in fact a greater brightness than greens or blues of the same low "values." (Red-and-green color blinds, when asked in casual trials to divide the light from the dark colors on the Berlin-Kay chart

likewise start low in the red range and move quickly up in the yellows [J. Pokorny, personal communication.].)

In the next stage (II) of the *BCT* series, a distinction of hue, represented by "red," is combined with the existing light/dark system. Why "red"? Once more it is possible to adduce biological grounds. Red is to the human eye the most salient of color experiences. At normal light levels, red stands out in relation to all other hues by virtue of a reciprocal heightening effect between saturation and brightness. On one hand, red will appear brighter or more luminous than other colors at the same level of saturation—an effect (the Helmholtz-Kohlrausch effect) that holds at all but the highest saturations, where blue and purple surpass red in brightness (cf. Padgham and Saunders 1975:135–37). This salience is given added perceptual significance by the fact that red appears to achieve a relatively high saturation over a greater variety of wavelength combinations than other colors. On the other hand and conversely, reds are perceived as purer or more saturated than other hues of the same brightness (Purdy 1930–31). But red not only "stands out," it stands closer: a direct spatial effect known as "chromatic aberration," which brings red surfaces subjectively nearer to the observer than objects of other hue situated at an equal distance (see Bidwell 1899:100 f.; Southall 1937:234). Red, simply, is the most color; hence its focal position in the contrast of hue to achromicity (lightness/darkness) at Stage II.

The advancing, attracting, or penetrating quality of red (as opposed especially to pale greens and blues) is commonly known to phenomenologists, as well as aestheticians and psychologists (cf. Merleau-Ponty 1962; Sargent 1923; Ellis 1900;

Graves 1951; Birren 1956; 1961; Spengler 1956; Bartley 1958.) Chromatic aberration is usually attributed physiologically to differences in focal points of different wavelengths, such that they are brought in or projected back for retinal focussing. As for saturation, blue ranks after red in capacity to maintain a relatively strong chroma level over a range of spectral combinations, followed by green, then yellow. As a rule, in object colors (as distinguished from the printed Munsell chips), red also achieves the highest absolute levels of saturation, along with blues and violets, these hues having the lowest coefficient of achromatic light response (see Hurvich and Jameson 1956; Burnham, Hanes, and Bartleson 1963; among others). In this connection, I should like to enter an objection to the use of "saturation" as an independent variable in perceptual tests—objection that, admittedly, is supported mainly by invocation of the emperor's clothes principle. Although it is evident that saturation enters into sensation as a function of definite physical properties of the radiant flux, it seems equally obvious that it does not do so independently, that is, as a distinctive-response variable correlated with one specific physiological channel. (This is already implied by the simultaneous variation of brightness and saturation in such phenomena as the Helmholtz-Kohlrausch effect, for which Padgham and Saunders suggest the explanation that, apparently, "luminance information [brightness] is transmitted to the brain along the nonopponent [degree of luminosity] channels, whereas the colour information is sent as colour difference opponent signals. It seems probable that when saturated colours are observed, the colour difference signals are very strong, and that perception of luminosity is involved in the brain from information received not only from the non-opponent channels but from the colour difference mechanisms" [1975:137].) In any case, *in a single percept,* it is impossible to differentiate the relative saturation of a color from its brightness value, as both may sensibly appear as a whitening or darkening of the hue. It is possible to train subjects (or oneself) to make the distinction between brightness and saturation in Munsell chips, for example, by holding the value constant and varying the chroma, or vice versa. But this discrimination is not a fact of naïve experience. It may thus very well be that the so-called "psychological color solid," constructed of the three equivalent dimensional coordinates of hue, brightness, and

saturation, is an egregious error: a purportedly "etic" grid which rests essentially if paradoxically on an "emic" determination of light as physical properties, and stems rather from the physical apparatus of color science than the experience of human color vision. Anyone who has had to make the distinction between saturation and brightness for himself, or teach it to others, can testify that it occasions no end of confusion—which, moreover, will not be easily resolved by the textbooks where "desaturation" is variously defined as the whiteness, paleness, dullness, darkness, greyness, shade, tint, impurity, or neutrality (at the same value) of the color. This confusion of the texts is itself testimony to an "ambiguity" of the folk categories—ambiguous, however, only so long as one continues to privilege the "reality" of physical descriptions over perceptual experience; "bright" and "brilliant" are especially applied indeterminately to highly luminous or highly saturated colors. ("The term luminosity is not normally used when dealing with surfaces, lightness being the preferred term. *Brightness, brilliance* and *value* also occur frequently. *Bright, brilliant, vivid* and *clear* are often used to describe highly saturated colours especially for objects of high reflectance" (Padgham and Saunders [1975:103].) Moreover, there are comparable problems in the tri-dimensional system with respect to hue and brightness, inasmuch as people's judgments of equal brightness are "very unreliable" if the light sources are different in wavelength—although such judgments are reliable in the reverse case (Cornsweet 1970:235–236). It seems to me that anthropology as well as other fields would be better served by a color-testing system constructed in closer accord with perceptual and physiological realities than those now in common use.

In *BCT* Stages III to V, red is joined by green, yellow, and blue to form a system of two complementary pairs whose privileged position in the evolutionary sequence again makes eminent natural sense. DaVinci had long ago called red, green, yellow, and blue (along with black and white) the "simple" colors, just as modern psychology considers them "primary" color experiences—or even more to the cross-cultural point, as the "primitives" or *Urfarben*. For on the level of perception (which is, of course, a different matter from mixing pigments), only these four colors are seen as unique, the percepts unalloyed with any other hue; even as all other colors, including the "basics" of later *BCT* stages, are perceived as some combination of two non-complementary "primitives." Thus purple appears as a mixture of red and blue, orange of red and yellow, and so forth. Unique yellow, green, blue, and red correspond to spectral loci of approximately 578 nm, 505 nm, 475 nm, and the complement of 495 nm, respectively. These *Urfarben* are not only perceptually elementary, but they alone remain constant in hue over variations in luminance; whereas other colors shift perceptibly toward one of their primitive components as they change in intensity (Bezold-Brücke phenomenon). It might be noted that brown, although physically analyzable as a dark yellow or dark red-yellow, appears to be an exception to the rule of compounded perception: like the *Urfarben,* it seems to be experientially unmixed (Padgham and Saunders 1975:143). Correspondingly, brown occupies a special position in the *BCT* sequence, marking Stage vi, which comes after the four elementary hues but before the several compound colors of Stage vii. The latter—purple, pink, and orange—emerge in no fixed order. Gray is also placed by Berlin and Kay in Stage vii, but on the evidence cited its position seems uncertain ethnographically, and it may evolve earlier. But then, as an intermediate of the "black" and "white" already present in Stage i, gray is not under the same ordering constraint (from simple to mixed) as the other hues of Stage vii, which would

have to wait until Stage v before their own constituents are available.

As complementary pairs of red and green, yellow and blue, the *Urfarben* moreover display certain relations of opposition and correlation: classic patterns of negation and evocation, well-known both to the logic of perception and the structure of conception. Green is never consubstantial with red, nor yellow with blue: complementaries cannot be seen together in the same time and space; yet each demands its opposite in such familiar effects as spatial induction and successive afterimage. Thus it becomes understandable why green should appear culturally in temporal proximity with red, as blue with yellow. Finally, the evolutionary priority of the four primitives, in conjunction with black and white, makes a neat connection on the physiological plane with the Hering "opponent process" theory of color vision—theory that has recently received support from electrophysiological study. In modern form, the Hering theory is that the neural processing of color sensation—as distinct from retinal photoreception—is organized as a triadic complex of binary contrastive processes: red-green, blue-yellow, and black-white. Impulses are fired to the brain from each of these processes in an oppositional manner, through cells that respond to one of the complementary hues but exclude the other; e.g., the red-green process is activated as $+R-G$ or $+G-R$, according to the wavelength composition of the sensation. Hence not only does the *BCT* series here find physiological support, but so also Lévi-Strauss in his observation (1972) that as binary coding is a structural mode already known to the body, we should not be surprised to find it manifested by the mind, thus to reappear as a fundamental principle of "objectified thought" (i.e., cultural order).

Authorities differ on whether the black/white response functions on the same neural mechanisms as the two pairs of primaries (red/green, blue/yellow). With regard to the latter, it is further pertinent to their early appearance in natural languages that they act in coupled and inverse manner under variations in intensity (the Bezold-Brücke effect, noted above) and changes in stimulus size. Again, the complementary pairs of *Urfarben* are linked in pathologies of color vision, i.e., as red-and-green or yellow-and-blue syndromes of color blindness. (On these and other perceptual and physiological qualities of the "primitives" noted above, see Hering 1964 [1920]; Linksz 1952; Hurvich 1960; Hurvich and Jameson 1957; Padgham and Saunders 1975; Pokorny and Smith 1972; Purdy 1931; Boynton 1971; Burnham, Hanes, and Bartleson 1963; Bornstein 1973; Cornsweet 1970; Durbin 1972.)

In sum, we can conclude that the emergence of basic color terms in natural languages follows a natural-perceptual logic. This logic is compounded of several broad evolutionary trends, most notably: (1) from general to specific, i.e., distinction of lightness/darkness to discriminations of hue; (2) from more to less salient, e.g., red before other hues; and (3) from simple to complex, i.e., from the unique to the mixed hues. Now given also the common average anthropological opinion that whatever is universal in human culture must find its explanation in human nature, it is difficult to escape the conclusion that the basic color categories are basically natural categories. Even a linguist can find in the *BCT* results the suggestion that, "the realm of semantics is based on species-specific biomorphological structures and that particular biological structures underlie what linguists generally call semantics" (Durbin 1972:269). Yet

the problem is precisely what is here being called semantics. And it is surprising nonetheless to find anthropology conspiring with a certain cognitive psychology to collapse the problem of meaning into the act of pointing, that is, the act of naming objective differences present to the senses. Curious also that the entire discussion of color categories, both before *BCT* and since, has chosen to relegate the true ethnographic existence of color terms and percepts—their actual cultural significance as codes of social, economic, and ritual value—to a secondary place of connotation. Instead, it is simply assumed that an empirical test of spectral referents is a determination of the essential meaning of color words. *A priori* we have understood the classification of color as the representation of experience, supposing the terms to intend and denote in the first instance the immanent properties of sensation.[3] It then became inevitable that Saussurean notions of the arbitrariness of the sign would be compromised by the results of the research—inasmuch as they had already been compromised in the premises. And Saussure himself foresaw, when language is thus taken for a mere nomenclature rather than a differential system of meaningful values, then cognition will be reduced to recognition, concept to percept, sign to signal—and in the end, culture to nature.

Phrased in another discourse, the semantic nominalism of the color test procedure comes to a confusion of "meaning" with "reference" (Quine 1963). As for the definition by ostension of any such object-attribute as color in a social situation, one could well ask, with Wittgenstein, " . . . what does 'pointing to the shape,' 'pointing to the colour' consist in? Point to a piece of paper.— And now point to its shape—now to its colour—

now to its number (that sounds queer).—How did you do it?—You will say that you 'meant' a different thing each time you pointed. And if I ask how that is done, you will say you concentrated your attention on the colour, the shape, etc. But I ask again: how is *that* done?" (Wittgenstein 1958:16).

One might have been alerted, on the other hand, by the logical paradox inherent in Berlin's and Kay's differentiation of "basic" from "secondary" color terms according to the freedom of the former from specific objective reference. Insofar as the "basic" terms are monolexemic and the "secondary" complex, the distinction may be morphologically justified. But insofar as the so-called "basic" terms are uniquely independent of the object, they are of higher logical type: thus not a discourse of particular experience but a metalanguage by which such experience is classified. It should be considered that except in the form of certain self-luminous sources, color is never a simple fact of naïve experience. As an object-property it has no more intrinsic claim to our attention than do shape, size, weight, texture, and many other coexisting attributes.[4] Hence basic color terms amount to the abstraction of perceptible features according to an arbitrary criterion of significance—which is then capable of achieving for society such miracles unknown to arithmetic as the conjoining of two apples, three cherries, and a pint of blood. Color in culture is indeed just this process of relating, not of recognizing. It cannot be, as Mauss says in a brilliant discussion of sympathetic magic, that the conceptual coupling of objects by similarities or differences in color is *sequitur* to the act of perception. For, "far from there being any association between the two objects due to their colour, we are dealing, on the contrary, with a formal convention, almost a law, whereby, out of a whole series of possible characteristics, colour is chosen to establish a relationship between two things" (Mauss 1972 [1902-03]:77; cf. Sperber 1975, on the arbitrariness of motivated relationships). "Basic" color terms testify to a selective ordering of experience: that kind of intervention in natural-perceptual fact whose presence is the certain indication of a cultural project.

To suppose color terms merely name differences suggested by the visible spectrum, their function being to articulate realities necessarily and already known as such, is something like the idea—to which Schneider (1968a; 1972) has taken valid exception—that genealogical relations comprise a *de facto* grid of "kinship types," inevitably taken in this significance by all societies, which differ merely in the way they classify (cope with) such universal facts of "relationship." The point, however, in color as in kinship, is that the terms stand in meaningful relations with other terms, and it is by the relations between terms within the global system that the character of objective reference is sedimented. Moreover, the concrete attributes thus singled out by the semantic differentiation of terms then function also as *signifiers* of social relations, not simply as the *signified* of the terms. In the event, it is not even necessary that those who participate in a given cultural order have the same substantive experience of the object, so long as they are capable of making some kind of sensory distinction at the semiotically pertinent boundaries. Hence the cultural facility of color blinds, functioning on differences in brightness—in a world that everyone else sees as differentiated by hue. "Red-and-green color-blind people talk of reds and greens and all shades of it [sic] using the same words most of us assign to objects of a certain color. They think and talk and act in terms of 'object color' and 'color constancy' as do the rest of us. They call leaves green, roses red. Variations in saturation and brilliance of their yellow gives [sic] them an amazing variety of impressions. While we learn to rely on differences of hue, their minds get trained in evaluating brilliance . . .

Most of the red-and-green blind do not know of their defect and think we see things in the same shades they do. They have no reason for sensing any conflict. If there is an argument, they find *us* fussy, not *themselves* defective. They heard us call the leaves green and whatever shade leaves have for them, they call it green. People of average intelligence never stop to analyze their sensations. *They are much too busy looking for what these sensations mean"* (Linksz 1952:119; last emphasis mine).

Another way of discussing the insufficiency of the naturalist interpretation is to note that by its commitment to empirical tests of color discrimination, it allows itself to be subsumed in a pre-anthropological, pre-symbolic epistemology of subject/object relations. Identifying "semantic category" as the verbal response to physical stimuli, naturalism would confine the problem of meaning within the endemic Western antinomy of a world-less subject confronting a thought-less object: antique dualism of mind and matter, between the poles of which 2,000 years of philosophy has succeeded in plausibly drawing the line of reality at every conceivable position from the idealism of Bishop Berkeley to the materialism of Vladimir Ilych. One of the apparent virtues of *BCT* is that it can be enlisted in a certain scientific resolution of the opposition—although at the expense of an anthropological consciousness of the symbolic. Only a century ago, Clark Maxwell could write: "In the eye we have on one hand light falling on this wonderful structure, and on the other we have the sensation of sight. We cannot compare these two things. The whole of metaphysics lies like a great gulf between them" (1970 [1872]:82). Yet today it seems that science has succeeded in bridging the gulf, passing safely over the metaphysical chasms of an age-old philosophy. Of course, no one can claim to have filled the space between sight and "light"; the qualitative difference subsists. But it is possible to say that human color sensations stand in specific correspondance to real differences in the world, the incomparability between stimulus and response reconciled by neuro-physiological processes, which here play the role of a kind of Kantian operator—yet not transcendentally, or beyond experience, as the neurological organization is itself product of natural selection (cf. Durbin 1972; Bornstein 1973). Given the universals of *BCT,* it follows that thought too shines with this borrowed light. The physical effect seems extendable now to cognition and culture, which apparently can do no more than translate into their own modalities the imperatives of a natural order.

Ironic, then, that the modern concept of culture should have been formulated out of Boas' discontent with just this mechanistic idea of subject/object relations (see Stocking 1968:133 ff.; 1974). Doubly, triply, infinitely ironic, as it all began with the very same problem of color: with the difficulties Boas encountered, during his doctoral research on the color of sea water, in judging the relative intensities of lights that differed slightly in hue. Boas was to pass on from physics to Fechnerian psycho-physics, then to geography, linguistics, and ethnology, but only to rediscover at each step the self-same discontinuity between the subjective and the objective. Quantitative differences in the stimulus did not evoke a corresponding gradation of response. Hence the organic could not be said to follow directly from the inorganic, the mind from the world nor, ultimately, culture from nature. Rather, the incommensurability in each case could only be comprehended by the existence of an interposed and third term, appropriate in form to the phenomenal level at issue. In the psychological experiments this would consist of a mental operation, contingent on the present situation and past experience of the subject, which transforms perception into apperception. On the ethnological plane, it would be the collective tradition or *Völkerge-danken,* which informs the subjective apperception by a historic conception. The set of understandings men entertain of themselves and the objects of their existence—this was the novel, specifically anthropological contribution to the venerable dualism of mind and matter: a *tertium quid,* culture, not merely mediating the human relation to the world by a logic of significance but constituting by that scheme the objective and subjective terms of the relationship. For Boas, as Benedict put it, the seeing eye was the organ of tradition.

How then to reconcile these two undeniable yet opposed understandings: that color distinctions are naturally based, albeit that natural distinctions are culturally constituted? The dilemma can only be solved, it seems to me, by reading from the cultural meaning of color to the empirical test of discrimination, rather than the other way round. We must give just due to this third term, culture, existing alongside subject and object, stimulus and response, and mediating between them by the construction of objectivity as significance. Moreover, a semiotic theory of color universals must take for "significance" exactly what colors do mean in human societies. They do not mean Munsell chips. Is it necessary to document that colors signify the differences between life and death, noble and common, pure and impure? that they distinguish moieties and clans, directions of the compass, and the exchange values of two otherwise similar strings of beads? I stress again that to adopt this point of semantic departure is not to ignore the biological facts of color naming; it is only to assign these facts their proper theoretical place. Information, as Bateson often says, is a difference that makes a difference. No less than any other code, a system of color meanings must be grounded in a corresponding set of distinctive perceptual properties. Hence the natural correlates of color words: they comprise the minimal *distinctive features* on the object plane—of lightness/darkness, hue/neutrality, uniqueness/admixture, and the like—by which differences in meaning are signalled.

This semiotic function of colors helps explain an important result of *BCT*—one which Berlin and Kay leave uninterpreted: the strong cross-cultural regularities in the foci of basic color categories, as determined in Munsell coordinates. Here one must disallow as in a way misleading the authors' claim that saturation is not a distinctive feature of color categories, especially as concerns the *Urfarben.* For given the identification of hue, saturation is *the* distinctive property of its focus—hence is the hue in its essential quality. Although in the construction of their chart, Berlin and Kay chose the maximum chroma for each brightness value, it cannot be said that saturation was thereby held constant, since these chroma maxima vary in absolute level according to hue and value. The *BCT* test spectrum accordingly shows a great range of saturation differences (from Munsell chromas of 2 to 16, in fact). And most important, these differences were decisive in informants' selections of category foci, which typically fall around the "home value" of the hue—i.e., the brightness value at which that particular hue attains its greatest saturation (e.g., Munsell value 4/ for "red," 5/ for "green," 8/ for "yellow"; cf. Evans 1928). This experimental result, I submit, is most consistent with the semiotic interpretation, for another way of describing it is to say that hues are socially relevant in their *most distinctive perceptible form,* where they are least subject to shading or tinting. And this because they mean something as such, and as distinct from black and white.

Yet the color code is more than an aggregate of distinctive features. A set of distinctive features will compose certain *perceptual relations,* and these in turn a specific totality or *structure* of a given type. By perceptual relations I mean the several types of contrast, complementarity and compatibility evident in ordinary color experience. Such relations are on the one hand ends of a natural process; yet on the other, they are means of a semiotic project, and so considered they permit a reading of the *BCT* sequence as something more than a progressive cumulation of individual elements. Berlin and Kay set out their findings as an evolutionary sequence from simple to complex, each stage typically defined by the emergence of a new basic term and percept. Seen in the semiotic vantage, however, what actually develops at each stage is not a new term or perceptual substance but a new perceptual relation. *The units of evolutionary differentiation are not terms but relations between terms.*

Hence what is found at the very beginning of the sequence, as the most elementary set, is a contrast of two categories. From a purely progressivist vantage there is no evident reason why the simplest color system should consist of two terms rather than one (cf. Berlin and Kay 1969:15). This circumstance only becomes reasonable when it is acknowledged that we are not confronted with the cumulative recognition of spectral differences in semantic categories, but with the meaningful differentiation of social categories in spectral terms. Therefore, contrast is from the beginning and throughout a necessary condition of color terminology and color discrimination, the most rudimentary code projecting the most general empirical distinction that can be made (light/dark). The elementary dualism of Stage I is of course preserved in more developed systems and always available for cultural use. (The use of the light/dark contrast is truly widespread in human societies, perhaps universally significant, and usually symbolic of fundamental oppositions of the social life—pure and unpure, life and death, sacred and profane, male and female, etc.).[5] Cross-cut and differentiated by other perceptual contrasts, however, the initial dualism is transformed at later stages into more complex structures of ternary, quaternary, and higher order, and of diverse logical type.

For example: the triad of red-white-black at *BCT* Stage II. This is the substantive perceptual result of the crossing of the basic dark/light dualism by a second contrast of hue/neutrality (see above on red as "the most color"). A distinction between these types of variation is easily made experientially, since neutrals vary only in one dimension, lightness, whereas hues differ in this respect as well as color. But precisely as red also varies in lightness/darkness, the triad of Stage II is not a simple order of three equivalent terms but a mediated opposition, i.e., of black and white by red. Red is particularly suited to this role because of its ability to maintain saturation over a wide range of brightness values, although reaching its strongest form at relatively low values. Therefore, red is especially like black in opposition to white, but occasionally like white in opposition to black. Where the complete triad is in cultural use, then, one can expect—as in all such cases of mediation—that certain meaningful values of red will themselves be opposed in moral sign, positive and negative. Furthermore, two additional dyads will be included in the structural set, red vs. white and red vs. black, the latter, because of the low brightness value of saturated red, probably the stronger or more marked opposition. In a classic work on Ndembu symbolism, V. Turner (1967) described a red-white-black trilogy of ritual values having many of these relations semantically, i.e., just those we discover perceptually. Turner goes on to document the widespread occurrence of the red-white-black triad in ritual systems—and to suggest an iconic and expressive interpretation of the symbolism different from the perspective adopted here.

In Stages IIIa and IIIb of *BCT,* the triad of Stage II is transformed into a four-part system. In IIIa, recall, green appears alongside red on the dimension of color; in IIIb, it is yellow instead of green. The consequent elementary structure is formally the same in both cases: a diagramatic set, A:B::C:D, matching two contrasting pairs by an analogous opposition. In Stage IIIa, the chromatic side has been factored by a complementary opposition, red/green, which is similar in induction effects to the achromatic black/white contrast. In IIIb, as focal yellow is a light value and red strongest at dark values, the colors reproduce on the side of hue the same distinction as characterizes the achromatic pair. (The actual color ethnography of such quaternary systems remains to be done. That it would prove fruitful is suggested by the ubiquity of diagramatic relations on such semiotic levels as kinship—cf. Lévi-Strauss 1963; Bourdieu 1971; Sahlins:in press).

Restricting ourselves to the hues, one encounters in Stage V of *BCT* a more complex kind of four-part system. In effect, I have already described this structure in discussing the Hering opponent-process theory of color vision and its phenomenal correlates. The four hues are the *Urfarben:* red, green, yellow, and blue. Each is opposed to its own complement experientially: red cannot coexist with green in the same percept, nor yellow with blue. But each demands its complement by simultaneous contrast in adjacent space, or successive afterimage. Each of the four "primitives," accordingly, can mix visually with only two of the remaining three. From such possible combinations of two *Urfarben,* all other hues are perceptibly composed. This structure of visual exclusion and compatibility among the *Urfarben* might be diagrammed as in the accompanying figure (figure 9.2).

In another essay (Sahlins:in press), I have suggested that the semantic relations of these colors in English—as may be gauged from the *OED* and dictionar-

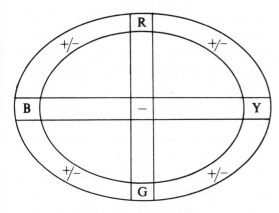

Figure 9.2. Perceptual structure of the *Urfarben*

ies of common usage—have the same general structure as their perceptual system. In several domains—politics, human bodily or mental states, religion, etc.—red, for instance, is like yellow in opposition to green (and blue) or like blue in opposition to yellow (and green). Note that the stop-light triad would be one derivation of these relations; indeed, it seems to reappear in a number of cultural contexts. As a flag of quarantine, yellow is, like red, a sign of danger; yet, specifically, the danger signalled by yellow is illness, which aligns it also with "sickly" or "bilious green" in contrast to "rosy red." Or to take another permutation: as compared with the positive sexuality of red (both male and female), green and yellow are forms of relative impotency, yet themselves at the opposite poles of immaturity and maturity—fresh, inexperienced youth (greenhorn), and a ripe old age whose course has been run ("My way of life is fallen into the seare, the yellow leaf"). Note, of course, the correlated domains of sex and vegetation, which may be rounded out with "ripe red." In all such semantic relations, the complementary *Urfarben* seem to have directly opposed meanings, as would be predicted from

the perceptual model. Blue is always different from yellow, for example: depressed ("the blues") where yellow is gay, loyal ("true blue") where yellow is cowardly, and the like. Blue has a similar meaning to yellow about once in a blue moon.

The *Urfarben,* of course, represent only a subsystem of *BCT* Stage v, and my intention here, as in the notices of other stages, has not been to provide a complete account of the several structures, their permutations and symbolizations. A lot more could easily be said, including some wild thought: ethnologists will not have failed to observe, for instance, that the structure of visual compatibilities and exclusions among these four "primitives" is the same as a system of marital exchanges among four groups divided into exogamous moieties (as Arunta). The purpose, however, was rather to suggest investigation than encourage speculation. It seems to me that *BCT* opens up very exciting prospects for an ethnography of color whose general aim, quite beyond the determination of the empirical correlates of semantic categories, might consist especially in the correlation of the semiotic and perceptual structures of color. For colors too are good to think (with).

It should be stressed that these perceptual structures are in themselves devoid of meaning, merely formal *combinatoires* of opposition and correlation. As such they are only the raw materials of cultural production, remaining latently available and incompletely realized until a meaningful content is attributed to the elements of the cultural set. Objectifying itself then in a system of colors, a human group accomplishes the essential cultural act of making a conceptual order out of a natural order. But such a code must be socially accessible: the success of the cultural project depends on the collective appropriation of objective features and relations that are generally present to the senses. Hence the biological correlates and cross-cultural regularities of basic color schemes.

As the perceptual structure of color has no meaning in itself, the content emanating rather from the culture than the color, this process of symbolic formation does not violate Saussurean principles of arbitrariness. However, if the perceptual set has no meaning, still it consists of marked contrasts of sensation, and it follows that for *any given culture* the choice of color meanings will not appear arbitrary but conditioned or motivated. In a universal sense, the iconicity is itself arbitrary, as it is relative to a specific cultural order and consists of a selection among all possible contrasts of color and social features in the interest of a particular relationship between them. But then, from within the system, the choice will seem motivated by analogy between color sensations and cultural relations—which may well have a common metaphoric base in the semantics of space (cf. Friedrich 1970b; Sahlins:in press). Consider, for example, that red is an experientially "advancing" color, as compared with the receding blues or whites. *Given* Western notions of sexuality, it will then hardly seem aleatory that red is harlotry as opposed to the prudery of blue or the purity of white (cf. Spengler 1956:256). This kind of ethnographic inevitability probably helps account for the popularity of iconic understandings of symbolic generation.

In interpreting color categories as the social appropriation of natural processes, I raise a central and contested issue of cultural theory. For this phrase, "social appropriation of natural processes," entails a certain reading of the famous structuralist invocation of "uni-versal laws that regulate the unconscious activities of the mind" (Lévi-Strauss 1963:59). No need on our part to clear Lévi-Strauss of the "biological reductionism" such statements have seemed to suggest. The burden of his own recent argument is that *no particular custom* will ever be accounted for by the nature of the human mind, for the double reason that in its cultural specificity it stands to mind as a difference does to a constant, and as a practice to a matrix (1966:130; 1971; 1972). One may thus understand his appeal to *l'esprit humain* not as an attempt to short-circuit the symbolic but to draw the full consequences of its ubiquity. The argument would seem simply to be that inasmuch as the human world is symbolically constituted, any similarities in the operations by which different groups construct or transform their cultural design can be attributed to the way the mind itself is constructed. By the same essential condition, that is symboling, "similarities" here cannot intend the content of that design, only the mode of ordering. It is never a question of specific meanings, which each group works out by its own lights, but the way meanings are systematically related, which in such forms as "binary opposition" may be observed to be general. Consequently, it is never a question either of biological reductionism. In *L'Homme nu,* Lévi-Strauss explains that the human nature which he invokes does not consist of an assemblage of substantial and fixed structures, "but the matrices from which structures belonging to the same ensemble are engendered" (1971:561). He characterizes the reductionist enterprise as an attempt to explain a given type of order by referring to a content which is not of the same nature but acts upon it from the outside. But such is not the structuralist's procedure:

An authentic structuralism, on the contrary, seeks above all to understand [*saisir*] the intrinsic properties of certain types of orders. *These properties express nothing which is outside of themselves.* But if one is compelled to refer them to something external, it shall be necessary to turn towards the cerebral organization, conceived as a network of which the most diverse ideologies, translating this or that property in terms of a particular structure, reveal in their own fashion the modes of interconnection, (Lévi-Strauss 1971:561; emphasis mine).

Perhaps, then, the problem of reductionism has resided mainly in a mode of discourse which, by giving mind all the powers of "law" and "limitation" has seemed to place culture in the position of submission and dependence. The whole vocabulary of "underlying" laws accords the mind all force of constraint, to which the cultural can only respond, as if the first was the active partner of the relation and the second passive. The interesting implication of a semiotic theory of color categories, however, is that the mind-culture relation is more adequately conceived the other way round. The structures of the mind here appear not as the imperatives of culture but as its implements. They constitute a set of organizational means and possibilities at the disposition of the human cultural enterprise, which remains at liberty to variously engage them or not, as also to variously invest them with meaningful content. How else to account for the presence in culture of universal structures that are nevertheless not universally present? And at another level, how else to deal, other than mystically, with such contradictions in terms as "collective consciousness," "collective representation" or "objectified thought," which attribute to an entity that is social a function patently individual? To answer all questions of this kind, it will be necessary to situate the human mental equipment as the instrument of culture instead of the determinant. Then, like Hegel's cunning of Reason, the wisdom of the cultural process would consist in putting to the service of its own intentions natural systems which have their own reasons.

Notes

1. I should like to thank Drs. Joel Pokorny and Vivienne Smith for generous technical help on problems of color perception. Any errors as well as outrageous opinions on these matters remaining in this paper are entirely my own.

2. *Faute de mieux,* I am obliged to make the case myself, within the range of my limited comprehension of the general texts, and without any claim to expertise in these matters. The same sort of apology must serve for the entire project of this essay, which I have felt impelled to undertake only because the central issues raised by *Basic Color Terms,* as it seemed to me, were not being considered in debates over the book. Again I can only claim the rankest amateur status with regard to the matters of linguistic and structuralist theory which, nonetheless, I am forced to discuss. I have waited a long time for someone more qualified to enter the lists, but so far in vain.

3. "Color categorization is the cultural classification of certain physical stimuli following their sensory reception and physical processing" (Conklin 1973:938; cf. Lenneberg and Roberts 1956).

4. There is indeed experimental evidence that shape is a more salient object-property than color for the very young and most age groups; besides, shape-constancy seems to be substantially greater in perception than color constancy (Arnheim 1974:335). Consider the difficulties Conklin had eliciting color identifications from

the Hanunoó in the absence of any general term for "color": "Except for leading questions (naming some visual-quality attribute as a possibility), only circumlocutions such as *kabitay tīda nu pagbantāyun?* 'How is it to look at?' are possible. If this results in description of spatial organization or form, the inquiry may be narrowed by the specification *bukun kay ?anyu?* 'not its shape (or form)'" (Conklin 1955:341 n.).

5. "With fine weather, and therefore with individual and social well-being, the Andamanese associate brightness and whiteness (for which they have only one word) and any bright or light colour. The association of light and dark with euphoric and dysphoric conditions respectively has a psychological basis, for it seems to be universal in human nature" (Radcliffe-Brown 1945 [1922]:316).

FIVE

Ritual and Myth

Symbols in African Ritual

Victor W. Turner

Although ostensibly a discussion of symbols in African ritual, Victor Turner's seminal paper can be taken as a model for the kind of symbolic analysis which he has undertaken with such signal success, showing its almost, if not indeed its truly, universal applicability and power. He suggests that ritual symbols may be investigated in three ways. Cultural actors may be asked to say what their "meanings"—their interpretations—are. Anthropologists may observe how symbols are manipulated, who manipulates them, and how actors interrelate as they use them. And finally, observers may find positional meaning in spatial and temporal relations among symbolic vehicles. Positional meaning also operates in the relationship between vehicle and symbol: thus, for example, metaphor and metonymy may be considered as instances of the positional dimension of meaning.

The central concepts of Turner's work are the multivocalic or polysemic nature of symbols, their capacity to unify apparently disparate significata and their capacity to condense—many ideas, relations between things, and so forth are represented simultaneously by the symbolic vehicle and the polarization of the referents assigned by custom to a major ritual symbol. Along with these aspects of the semantic structure of the symbol is the fact that certain symbols tend to be dominant; that the symbol's position is of crucial interpretive importance, and that actors experience symbols as power and as meanings.

NO ONE WHO HAS LIVED FOR LONG in rural sub-Saharan Africa can fail to be struck by the importance of ritual in the lives of villagers and homesteaders and by the fact that rituals are composed of symbols.

A ritual is a stereotyped sequence of activities involving gestures, words, and objects, performed in a sequestered place, and designed to influence preter-natural entities or forces on behalf of the actors' goals and interests. Rituals may be seasonal, hallowing a culturally defined moment of change in the climatic cycle or the inauguration of an activity such as planting, harvesting, or moving from winter to summer pasture; or they may be contingent, held in response to an individual or collective crisis. Contingent rituals may be further subdivided into life-crisis ceremonies, which are performed at birth, puberty, marriage, death, and so on, to demarcate the passage from one phase to

Reprinted by permission from *Science*, March 16, 1972, vol. 179, pp. 1100–05. Copyright © 1973 by the American Association for the Advancement of Science.

another in the individual's life-cycle, and rituals of affliction, which are performed to placate or exorcise preternatural beings or forces believed to have afflicted villagers with illness, bad luck, gynecological troubles, severe physical injuries, and the like. Other classes of rituals include divinatory rituals; ceremonies performed by political authorities to ensure the health and fertility of human beings, animals, and crops in their territories; initiation into priesthoods devoted to certain deities, into religious associations, or into secret societies; and those accompanying the daily offering of food and libations to deities or ancestral spirits or both. Africa is rich indeed in ritual genres, and each involves many specific performances.

Each rural African society (which is often, though not always, coterminous with a linguistic community) possesses a finite number of distinguishable rituals that may include all or some of the types listed above. At varying intervals, from a year to several decades, all of a society's rituals will be performed, the most important (for example, the symbolic transference of political authority from one generation to another, as among the Nyakyusa (Wilson 1959) of Tanzania) being performed perhaps the least often. Since societies are processes responsive to change, not fixed structures, new rituals are devised or borrowed, and old ones decline and disappear. Nevertheless, forms survive through flux, and new ritual items, even new ritual configurations, tend more often to be variants of old themes than radical novelties. Thus it is possible for anthropologists to describe the main features of a ritual system, or rather ritual round (successive ritual performances), in those parts of rural Africa where change is occurring slowly.

The Semantic Structure of the Symbol

The ritual symbol is "the smallest unit of ritual which still retains the specific properties of ritual behavior . . . the ultimate unit of specific structure in a ritual context." This structure is a semantic one (that is, it deals with relationships between signs and symbols and the things to which they refer) and has the following attributes: (i) multiple meanings (significata)—actions or objects perceived by the senses in ritual contexts (that is, symbol vehicles) have many meanings; (ii) unification of apparently disparate significata—the essentially distinct significata are interconnected by analogy or by association in fact or thought; (iii) condensation—many ideas, relations between things, actions, interactions, and transactions are represented simultaneously by the symbol vehicle (the ritual use of such a vehicle abridges what would verbally be a lengthy statement or argument); (iv) polarization of significata—the referents assigned by custom to a major ritual symbol tend frequently to be grouped at opposed semantic poles. At one pole of meaning, empirical research has shown that the significata tend to refer to components of the moral and social orders—this might be termed the ideological (or normative) pole of symbolic meaning; at the other, the sensory (or orectic) pole, are concentrated references to phenomena and processes that may be expected to stimulate desires and feelings. Thus, I have shown that the mudyi tree, or milk-tree *(Diplorrhyncus mossambicensis),* which is the focal symbol of the girls' puberty ritual of the Ndembu people of northwestern Zambia, at its normative pole represents womanhood, mother-hood, the mother-child bond, a novice ‚undergoing initiation into mature wom-anhood, a specific matrilineage, the principle of matriliny, the process of learning "women's wisdom," the unity and perdurance of Ndembu society, and all of the values and virtues inherent in the various relationships—domestic, legal, and political—controlled by matrilineal descent. Each of these aspects of its normative meaning becomes paramount in a specific epi-sode of the puberty ritual; together they form a condensed statement of the structural and communal importance of femaleness in Ndembu culture. At its sensory pole, the same symbol stands for breast milk (the tree exudes milky latex—indeed, the significata associated with the sensory pole often have a more or less direct connection with some sen-sorily perceptible attribute of the sym-bol), mother's breasts, and the bodily slenderness and mental pliancy of the novice (a young slender sapling of mudyi is used). The tree, situated a short distance from the novice's village, becomes the center of a sequence of ritual episodes rich in symbols (words, objects, and actions) that express impor-tant cultural themes.

Ritual Symbols and Cultural Themes

Opler has defined a theme as a part of a limited set of "dynamic affirmations" that "can be identified in every culture" (1945:198; 1968:215). In the "nature, expression, and relationship" of themes is to be found the "key to the character, structure, and direction of the specific culture" (ibid.). The term "theme" denotes "a postulate or position, declared or implied, and usually control-ling behavior or stimulating activity, which is tacitly approved or openly pro-moted in a society" (ibid.). Every cul-ture has multiple themes, and most themes have multiple expressions, some of which may be in one or more parts of the institutional culture. Ritual forms an important setting for the expression of themes, and ritual symbols transmit themes. Themes have multiple expres-sions, and ritual symbols, such as the mudyi tree (and thousands of others in the ethnographic literature of African ritual), have multiple significata (Turner 1974). The major difference between themes and symbols is that themes are postulates or ideas inferred by an observer from the data of a given cul-ture, while ritual symbols are one class of such data. Ritual symbols are multi-vocal—that is, each symbol expresses not one theme but many themes simulta-neously by the same perceptible object or activity (symbol vehicle). Symbols *have* significata, themes may *be* significata.

Themes, in their capacity as significa-ta (including both conceptions and images), may be disparate or grouped, as we have seen, at opposed semantic poles. Thus the mudyi signifies aspects of female bodily imagery (milk, suck-ling, breasts, girlish slenderness) and conceptions about standards of woman-hood and motherhood, as well as the normative ordering of these in relation to group membership, the inheritance of property, and succession to such political offices as chieftainship and village headmanship through matrilineal descent. There are rules of exclusion connected with the mudyi in this ritual context—all that is not concerned with the nurtural, procreative, and esthetic aspects of human femaleness and with their cultural control and structuring, is excluded from the semantic field of mudyi symbolism. This is a field of themes with varying degrees of concreteness, abstraction, and cognitive and orectic quality. The impulse that leads advanced cultures to the economical use of signs in mathematics finds its equivalent here in the use of a single symbol vehicle to represent simultaneously a variety of themes, most of which can be shown to be related, logically or pragmatically, but some of which depend for their association on a sensed likeness between variables rather than on cognitive criteria. One is dealing with a "mathematics" of sociocultural experience rather than with a mathematics of logical relationships.

Ritual symbols differ from other modes of thematic expression, particularly from those unformalized modes that arise in spontaneous behavior and allow for individual choice in expression (Opler 1945:200). Indeed, it might be argued that the more ritualized the expression, the wider the range of themes that may be signified by it. On the other hand, since a ritual symbol may represent disparate, even contradictory themes, the gain in economy may be offset by a loss in clarity of communication. This would be inevitable if such symbols existed in a vacuum, but they exist in cultural and operational contexts that to some extent overcome the loss in intelligibility and to some extent capitalize on it.

Dominant Symbols in Ritual Cycles

Rituals tend to be organized in a cycle of performances (annual, biennial, quinquennial, and so on); even in the case of contingent rituals, each is performed eventually. In each total assemblage, or system, there is a nucleus of dominant symbols, which are characterized by extreme multivocality (having many senses) and a central position in each ritual performance. Associated with this nucleus is a much larger number of enclitic (dependent) symbols. Some of these are univocal, while others, like prepositions in language, become mere relation or function signs that keep the ritual action going (for example, bowings, lustrations, sweepings, and objects indicative of joining or separation). Dominant symbols provide the fixed points of the total system and recur in many of its component rituals. For example, if 15 separate kinds of ritual can be empirically distinguished in a given ritual system, dominant symbol A may be found in 10 of them, B in 7, C in 5, and D in 12. The mudyi tree, for example, is found in boys' and girls' initiation ceremonies, in five rituals concerned with female reproductive disorders, in at least three rituals of the hunters' cults, and in various herbalistic practices of a magical cast. Other dominant symbols of Ndembu rituals, as I have shown elsewhere (Turner 1961; 1966; 1969a) recur almost as frequently in the ritual round. Each of these symbols, then, has multiple referents, but on each occasion that it is used—usually an episode within a ritual performance—only one or a related few of its referents are drawn to public attention. The process of "selectivity" consists in constructing around the dominant symbol a context of symbolic objects, activities, gestures, social relationships between actors of ritual roles, and verbal behavior (prayers, formulas, chants, songs, recitation of sacred narratives, and so on) that both bracket and underline those of its referents deemed pertinent in the given situation. Thus, only a portion of a dominant symbol's full semantic wealth is deployed in a single kind of ritual or in one of its episodes. The semantic structure of a dominant symbol may be compared with a ratchet wheel, each of whose teeth represents a conception or theme. The ritual context is like a pawl, which engages the notches. The point of engagement represents a meaning that is important in the particular situation. The wheel is the symbol's total meaning, and the complete range is only exposed when the whole cycle of rituals has been performed. Dominant symbols represent sets of fundamental themes. The symbol appears in many rituals, and its meanings are emphasized separately in many episodes. Since the settings in which the themes are ritually presented vary, and since themes are linked in different combinations in each setting, members of the culture who have been exposed to the entire ritual cycle gradually learn, through repetition, variation, and contrast of symbols and themes, what the values, rules, behavioral styles, and cognitive postulates of their culture are. Even more important, they learn in what cultural

domains and with what intensity in each domain the themes should apply.

Positional Role of Binary Opposition

The selection of a given theme from a symbol's theme assemblage is a function of positioning—that is, of the manner in which the object or activity assigned symbolic value is placed or arranged vis-à-vis similar objects or activities. One common mode of positioning is binary opposition, the relating of two symbol vehicles whose opposed perceptible qualities or quantities suggest, in terms of the associative rules of the culture, semantic opposition. Thus when a grass hut is made at the Ndembu girls' puberty ceremony for the seclusion of the novice for several months, the two principal laths of the wooden frame are made respectively from mudyi and mukula (blood tree) wood. Both species are dominant symbols. To the Ndembu, mukula represents the husband whom the girl will marry immediately after the puberty rites, and the mudyi stands for the bride, the novice herself. Yet when mukula is considered as a dominant symbol of the total ritual system, it is found to have a wide range (what has aptly been called a "fan") of significata (Turner 1967; 1968). Its primary and sensory meaning is blood—the Ndembu point to the dusky red gum secreted by the tree from cracks in its bark to justify their interpretation. But some bloods, they say, are masculine and some feminine. The former include blood shed by warriors, hunters, and circumcisers in the call of duty; the latter represents blood shown at menstruation and parturition. Another binary opposition within the semantic field of blood is between running blood and coagulating blood. The latter is good, the former is dangerous. Thus, prolonged menstruation means that a woman's blood is ebbing away uselessly; it should coagulate to form fetus and placenta. But since men are the dangerous sex, the blood they cause to flow in hunting and war may be good—that is, beneficial for their own group.

Mukula symbolism is adroitly manipulated in different rituals to express various aspects of the human condition as the Ndembu experience it. For example, in the *Nkula* ritual, performed to placate the spirit of a dead kinswoman afflicting the female patient with menstrual troubles causing barrenness, mukula and other red symbols are contextually connected with symbols characteristic of the male hunting cults to convey the message: the patient is behaving like a male shedder of blood, not like a female conserver of blood, as she should be. It is her "masculine protest" that the ritual is mainly directed at overcoming and domesticating into the service of her female role (Turner 1968:55–89). Mukula means many other things in other contexts, when used in religious ritual or in magical therapy. But the binary opposition of mudyi to mukula restricts the meaning of mudyi to young mature femininity and that of mukula restricts the meaning of mudyi to young mature masculinity, both of which are foundations of a hut, the prototypical domestic unit. The binding together of the laths taken from these trees is said to represent the sexual and the procreative union of the young couple. If these meanings form the sensory pole of the binary opposition as symbol, then the legitimated union by marriage represents the normative pole. In other words, even the binary opposition does not stand alone; it must be examined in the context of building the novice's seclusion hut and of the symbolic objects comprising the hut and its total meaning. There are, of course, many types of binary opposition. The members of pairs of symbols may be asymmetrical ($A > B$, $A < B$); they may be like or unlike but equal in value; they may be antithetical; one may be thought of as the product or offspring of the other; one may be active, the other passive; and so on. In this way, the Ndembu are induced to consider the nature and function of relationships as well as of the variables being related, for nonverbal symbol systems have the equivalents of grammar, syntax, accidence, and parts of speech.

Sometimes binary opposition may appear between complexes of symbol vehicles, each carrying a system of dominant and secondary symbols. Thus, in the circumcision rites of the Wiko, in Zambia (Gluckman 1949:165–67), one group of masked dancers may mime opposition to another group; each mask and headpiece is already a combination of multivocal symbols. Yet one team may represent protectiveness and the other, aggressiveness. It is, in fact, not uncommon to find complex symbol vehicles, such as statues or shrines, with simple meanings, while simple vehicles, such as marks drawn in white or red clay, may be highly multivocal in almost every ritual situation in which they are used. A simple vehicle, exhibiting some color, shape, texture, or contrast commonly found in one's experience (such as the whiteness of the mudyi or the redness of the mukula), can literally or metaphorically connect a great range of phenomena and ideas. By contrast, a complex vehicle is already committed, at the level of sensory perception, to a host of contrasts that narrow and specify its message. This is probably why the great religious symbol vehicles such as the cross, the lotus, the crescent moon, the ark, and so on are relatively simple, although their significata constitute whole theological systems and control liturgical and architectural structures of immense complexity. One might almost hypothesize that the more complex the ritual (many symbols, complex vehicles), the more particularistic, localized, and socially structured its message; the simpler the ritual (few symbols, simple vehicles), the more universalistic its message. Thus, ecumenical liturgiologists today are recommending that Christian ritual be essentially reduced to the blessing, distribution, and partaking of bread and wine, in order to provide most denominations with a common ground.

Actors Experience Symbols as Powers and as Meanings

The second characteristic of ritual condensation, which compensates in some measure for semantic obscurity, is its efficacy. Ritual is not just a concentration of referents, of messages about values and norms; nor is it simply a set of practical guidelines and a set of symbolic paradigms for everyday action, indicating how spouses should treat each other, how pastoralists should classify and regard cattle, how hunters should behave in different wild habitats, and so on. It is also a fusion of the powers believed to be inherent in the persons, objects, relationships, events,

and histories represented by ritual symbols. It is a mobilization of energies as well as messages.[1] In this respect, the objects and activities in point are not merely things that stand for other things or something abstract, they participate in the powers and virtues they represent. I use "virtue" advisedly, for many objects termed symbols are also termed medicines. Thus, scrapings and leaves from such trees as the mudyi and the mukula are pounded together in meal mortars, mixed with water, and given to the afflicted to drink or to wash with. Here there is direct communication of the life-giving powers thought to inhere in certain objects under ritual conditions (a consecrated site, invocations of preternatural entities, and so on). When an object is used analogously, it functions unambiguously as a symbol. Thus, when the mudyi tree is used in puberty rites it clearly *represents* mother's milk; here the association is through sight, not taste. But when the mudyi is used as medicine in ritual, it is felt that certain qualities of motherhood and nurturing are being communicated physically. In the first case, the mudyi is used because it is "good to think" rather than "good to eat";[2] in the second, it is used because it has maternal power. The same objects are used both as powers and symbols, metonymically and metaphorically—it is the context that distinguishes them. The power aspect of a symbol derives from its being a part of a physical whole, the ideational aspect from an analogy between a symbol vehicle and its principal significata.

Each symbol expresses many themes, and each theme is expressed by many symbols. The cultural weave is made up of symbolic warp and thematic weft. This weaving of symbols and themes serves as a rich store of information, not only about the natural environment as perceived and evaluated by the ritual actors, but also about their ethical, esthetic, political, legal, and ludic (the domain of play, sport, and so forth in a culture) ideas, ideals, and rules. Each symbol is a store of information, both for actors and investigators, but in order to specify just which set of themes any particular ritual or ritual episode contains, one must determine the relations between the ritual's symbols and their vehicles, including verbal symbolic behavior. The advantages of communication by means of rituals in nonliterate societies are clearly great, for the individual symbols and the patterned relations between them have a mnemonic function. The symbolic vocabulary and grammar to some extent make up for the lack of written records.

The Semantic Dimensions

Symbols have three especially significant dimensions: the exegetic, the operational, and the positional. The exegetic dimension consists of the explanations given the investigator by actors in the ritual system. Actors of different age, sex, ritual role, status, grade of esoteric knowledge, and so forth provide data of varying richness, explicitness, and internal coherence. The investigator should infer from this information how members of a given society think about ritual. Not all African societies contain persons who are ready to make verbal statements about ritual, and the percentage of those prepared to offer interpretations varies from group to group and within groups. But, as much ethno-graphic work attests,[3] many African societies are well endowed with exegetes.

In the operational dimension, the investigator equates a symbol's meaning with its use—he observes what actors do with it and how they relate to one another in this process. He also records their gestures, expressions, and other nonverbal aspects of behavior and discovers what values they represent—grief, joy, anger, triumph, modesty, and so on. Anthropologists are now studying several genres of nonverbal language, from iconography (the study of symbols whose vehicles picture the conceptions they signify, rather than being arbitrary, conventional signs for them) to kinesics (the study of bodily movements, facial expressions, and so forth as ways of communication or adjuncts and intensifiers of speech). Several of these fall under the rubric of a symbol's operational meaning. Nonexegetical, ritualized speech, such as formalized prayers or invocations, would also fall into this category. Here verbal symbols approximate nonverbal symbols. The investigator is interested not only in the social organization and structure of those individuals who operate with symbols on this level, but also in what persons, categories, and groups are absent from the situation, for formal exclusion would reveal social values and attitudes.

In the positional dimension, the observer finds in the relations between one symbol and other symbols an important source of its meaning. I have shown how binary opposition may, in context, highlight one (or more) of a symbol's many referents by contrasting it with one (or more) of another symbol's referents. When used in a ritual context with three or more other symbols, a particular symbol reveals further facets of its total "meaning." Groups of symbols may be so arrayed as to state a message, in which some symbols function analogously to parts of speech and in which there may be conventional rules of connection. The message is not about specific actions and circumstances, but the given culture's basic structures of thought, ethics, esthetics, law, and modes of speculation about new experience.

In several African cultures, particularly in West Africa, a complex system of rituals is associated with myths.[4] These tell of the origins of the gods, the cosmos, human types and groups, and the key institutions of culture and society. Some ritual episodes reenact primordial events, drawing on their inherent power to achieve the contemporary goals of the members of the culture (for example, adjustment to puberty and the healing of the sick). Ritual systems are sometimes based on myths. There may coexist with myths and rituals standardized schemata of interpretation that may amount to theological doctrine. But in wide areas of East and Central Africa, there may be few myths connected with rituals and no religious system interrelating myths, rituals, and doctrine. In compensation, there may be much piecemeal exegesis of particular symbols.

Foundations of Meaning

Most African languages have terms for ritual symbol. The Nyakyusa, for example, speak of *ififwani* (likenesses); the Ndembu use *chijikijilu* (a landmark, or blaze), which is derived from *kujikijila* (to blaze a trail or set up a landmark). The first connotes an association, a feeling of likeness between sign and signified, vehicle and concept; the second is a means of connecting known with unknown territory. (The Ndembu compare the ritual symbol to the trail a hunter blazes in order to find his way back from unexplored bush to his village.) Other languages possess similar terms. In societies that do not have myths, the meaning of a symbol is built up by analogy and association of three foundations—nominal, substantial, and artifactual—though in any given instance only one of these might be utilized. The nominal basis is the name of the symbol, an element in an acoustic system; the substantial basis is a symbol's sensorily perceptible physical or chemical properties as recognized by the culture; and its artifactual basis is the technical changing of an object used in ritual by human purposive activity.

For example: At the start of a girl's puberty ritual among the Nyakyusa of Tanzania (Wilson 1957), she is treated with a "medicine" called *undumila*. This medicine is also an elaborate symbol. Its nominal basis is the derivation of the term from *ukulumila,* meaning "to bite, to be painful." The substantial basis is a natural property of the root after which the medicine is named—it is pungent-tasting. As an artifact, the medicine is a composite of several symbolic substances. The total symbol involves action as well as a set of objects. Wilson writes (1957:87) that the root "is pushed through the tip of a funnel or cup made of a leaf of the bark-cloth tree, and salt is poured into the cup. The girl takes the tip of the root in her mouth and pulls it inward with her teeth, thus causing the salt to trickle into her mouth." The root and leaf funnel, together with their ritual use, constitute an artifact. These three bases of significance are substantiated by the Nyakyusa Wilson talked to. One woman told her (1957:102): "The pungent root is the penis of the husband, the cup is her vagina, the salt, also pungent, is the semen of her husband. Biting the root and eating the salt is copulation." Another woman confirmed this: "The *undumila* is put through the leaf of a bark-cloth tree, shaped into a cup, and it is a sign of man and woman, the penis in the vagina. It is similar to the plantains which we give her when we wash her. The plantains are a symbol of the husband. If we do not give her . . . the *undumila,* she constantly has periods and is barren." A third informant said: "It is the pain of periods that we symbolize in the sharpness of the *undumila* and salt." Thus *undumila* is at once a symbol of sexual intercourse, a prophylactic against pain in intercourse and against frequent or painful periods, and (according to other accounts) a ritual defense against those who are "heavy"—that is, those actively engaged in sexual intercourse, especially women who have just conceived. If a heavy person steps over the novice's footprints, the novice will not bear a child, but will menstruate continually. These explanations also demonstrate the multivocality and economy of reference of a single dominant symbol. The same symbol vehicles can represent different, even disparate, processes—marital intercourse and menstrual difficulty—although it may be argued that the Nyakyusa, at an unconscious level, regard a woman's "distaste" for inter-course as a cause of her barrenness or menorrhagia.

Symbols and Cosmologies

Similar examples abound in the ethnography of sub-Saharan Africa, but in the great West African cultures of the Fon, Ashanti, Yoruba, Dahomeyans, and Dogon, piecemeal exegesis gives way to explicit, complex cosmologies. Among the Dogon, for example (Calame-Griaule 1966; Dieterlen 1941 and 1963; Douglas 1968), a symbol becomes a fixed point of linkage between animal, vegetable, and mineral kingdoms, which are themselves regarded as parts of "un gigantesque organisme humaine." The doctrine of correspondences reigns—everything is a symbol of everything else, whether in ritual context or not. Thus the Dogon establish a correspondence between the different categories of mineral and the organs of the body. The various soils in the area are conceived of as the organs of "the interior of the stomach," rocks are regarded as the bones of the skeleton, and various hues of red clay are likened to the blood. Sometimes these correspondences are remarkably precise: one rock resting on another represents the chest; little white river pebbles stand for the toes of the feet. The same *parole du monde* principles hold true for the relationship between man and the vegetable kingdom. Man is not only the grain of the universe, but each distinct part of a single grain represents part of the human body. In fact, it is only science that has emancipated man from the complex weave of correspondences, based on analogy, metaphor, and mystical participation, and that enables him to regard all relations as problematical, not preordained, until they have been experimentally tested or systematically compared.

The Dogon further conceive of a subtle and finely wrought interplay between speech and the components of personality. The body constitutes a magnet or focus for man's spiritual principles, which nevertheless are capable of sustaining an independent existence. The Dogon contrast visible and invisible ("spiritual") components of the human personality. The body is made up of four elements: water (the blood and bodily fluids), earth (the skeleton), air (breath), and fire (animal warmth). There is a continuous interchange between these internal expressions of the elements and their external aspects. The body has 22 parts: feet, shins, thighs, lumbar region, stomach, chest, arms, neck, and head make up nine parts (it would seem that Dogon reckon double parts, as they do twins, as a unit); the fingers (each counting as a unit), make up ten parts; and the male genitals make up three parts. Further numerical symbolism is involved: there are believed to be eight symbolic grains—representing the principal cereal crops of the region—lodged in the collarbones of each Dogon. These grains represent the mystical bond between man and his crops. The *body* of speech itself is, like the human body, composed of four elements: water is saliva, without which speech is dry; air gives rise to sound vibrations; earth gives speech its weight and significance; and fire gives speech its warmth. There is not only homology between personality and speech, but also a sort of functional interdependence, for words are selected by the brain, stir up the liver, and rise as steam from the lungs to the clavicles, which decide ultimately whether the speech is to emerge from the mouth.

To the 22 parts of the personality must be added the 48 types of speech, which are divided into two sets of 24. Each set is under the sign of a supernatural being, one of the androgynous twins Nommo and Yourougou. Here I must draw on Griaule's and Dieterlen's extensive work on the Dogons' cosmogonic mythology (1963). The twins are the creations of Amma. Yourougou rebelled against Amma and had sexual relations with his mother—he was punished by being changed into a pale fox. Nommo saved the world by an act of self-sacrifice, brought humans, animals, and plants to the earth, and became the lord of speech. Nommo's speech is human and can be heard; the fox's is silent, a sign language made by his paw marks, and only diviners can interpret it. These myths provide a classification and taxonomy of cosmos and society; explain many details of ritual, including the forms and color symbolism of elaborate masks; and, indeed, determine where and how houses are constructed. Other West African cultures have equally elaborate cosmologies, which are manifested in ritual and divinatory symbolism. Their internal consistency and symmetry may be related to traditions of continuous residence and farming in a single habitat, combined with exposure to trans-Saharan cultural elements, including religious beliefs, for thousands of years—ancient Egyptian, Roman, Christian, Neo-Platonic, Gnostic, Islamic. The history of West Africa contrasts with that of Central Africa, where most societies descend from groups that migrated in a relatively short period of time across several distinct ecological habitats and that were then exposed to several centuries of slave raiding and slave trading. Groups were fragmented and then combined with the social detritus of other societies into new, temporary polities. There were conquest, assimilations, reconquests, the rise and fall of "kingdoms of the savannah," and temporary centralization followed by decentralization into localized clans. Swidden (slash-and-burn) agriculture kept people constantly on the move; hunting and pastoralism compounded the mobility. Because of these circumstances, there was less likelihood of complex, integrated religious and cosmological systems arising in Central Africa than in West Africa. Yet the needs and dangers of social and personal survival provided suitable conditions for the development of rituals as pragmatic instruments (from the standpoint of the actors) for coping with biological change, disease, and natural hazards of all kinds. Social action in response to material pressures was the systematic and systematizing factor. Order, cosmos, came from purpose, not from an elaborate and articulated cosmology. It is an order that accords well with human experience at preindustrial technological levels; even its discrepancies accurately reflect the "facts of life"—in contrast to consistent and harmonious cosmologies whose symbols and myths mask and cloak the basic contradictions between wishes and facts.

The Continuing Efficacy of African Ritual Symbols

Nevertheless, from the comparative viewpoint, there are remarkable similarities among symbols used in ritual throughout sub-Saharan Africa, in spite of differences in cosmological sophistication. The same ideas, analogies, and modes of association underlie symbol formation and manipulation from the Senegal River to the Cape of Good Hope. The same assumptions about powers prevail in kingdoms and nomadic bands. Whether these assemblages of similar symbols represent units of complex orders or the debris of formerly prevalent ones, the symbols remain extraordinarily viable and the themes they represent and embody tenaciously rooted. This may be because they arose in ecological and social experiences of a kind that still prevails in large areas of the continent. Since they are thus sustained and since there is a continuous flux and reflux of people between country and city, it is not surprising that much of the imagery found in the writings of modern African novelists and in the rhetoric of politicians is drawn from ritual symbolism—from which it derives its power to move and channel emotion.

Notes

1. This problem of the sources of the effectiveness of symbols has been discussed by Lévi-Strauss (1963:186–205), Munn (1969a). and myself (Turner 1969).

2. See Lévi-Strauss' formulation regarding "totemic" objects, countering the "common-sense" view of J. G. Frazer and other early twentieth-century anthropologists (Lévi-Strauss 1962a).

3. For example. Beattie (1968), Beidelman (1961), Evans-Pritchard (1956), Griaule (1965), Morton-Williams, Bascom, and McClelland (1966), Richards (1956), and Wilson (1954).

4. Examples of African cosmological systems may be found in D. Forde (1954). See also T. O. Beidelman on aspects of Swazi cosmology (1966).

ELEVEN

Ritual Communication: Some Considerations Regarding Meaning in Navajo Ceremonials

David W. Murray

The refinement of theories of signs and meanings, their development and increased sophistication, have contributed much to the growth of what is called "symbolic anthropology." It is not enough to say simply that "X = Y" and call that a theory of meaning; nor is it enough simply to say that one utterance can be understood in terms of another utterance.

Murray presents here a more detailed, elaborate, and well-developed theory of symbol and meaning, in which different kinds of signs are distinguished, and different kinds of meanings are discriminated, on the basis of their use, drawing on the work of Peirce, Morris, and Austin, and especially on Austin's notion of "performatives." He then applies this subtler, more precise theory of meaning to Navajo ceremonials and shows, thereby, its greatly increased analytic power. Not only is ritual seen as a mode of communication but a particular mode of communication which proceeds according to special forms of the use of signs. It is the display of the sophisticated analytic framework, which distinguishes different kinds of signs and meanings, and the ways in which this improves our understanding of the meaning of ritual, that makes this paper so compelling.

THIS PAPER WILL EXPLORE the type of theory of meaning presupposed by a notion of "ritual process." The data on Navajo ceremonial practice can be regarded as an exemplary instance of material most adequately handled by the approach to the meaning of ritual symbols discussed here. In addition, I will provide a more systematic terminology for considering the analysis of symbols in anthropology.

Published by permission of the author.

Clearly a great deal of trouble for the enterprise of symbolic anthropology devolves on terminological confusion and profusion. For instance, in a recent article by Victor Turner (1969a), we read of the properties of multivocal symbols as being: (1) possession of an iconic symbol vehicle, (2) a set of denotations (spoken of as "primary meanings," not as referents) and (3) a set of connotations, said to be implied in addition to the primary denotations. What one misses here is an explicitly defined concept of "designata." We must be able to deal with symbols which *lack* denotata or referents; this necessitates criteria for defining a set which may be empty (for example, the concepts "unicorn" or "ghost"). A theory of symbols which lacks the concept of designata must be *extensional* only, that is, it gives the meaning of a symbol only by enumerating a list of denotata, a series of referential objects. To be comprehensive, a theory of meaning must be *intentional* as well; it must have an idea of the characteristics or semantic features of the class to which the denotata belong. Designation in this sense is not equivalent to "connotation" noted above. Connotation, I contend, is best expressed as the felt relationship between different symbols, on the basis of regular association, temporal or causal, or suggested analogy. The connotation of a symbol is not inherent in the meaning of *one* symbol, it expresses a relationship *between* distinct symbols. They may shade into one another, or tender "prenumbra" of meaningful associations, or influence our understanding of and reaction to other symbols, but these are properties over and above the components of meaning that are primary for symbolic interpretation. *What* exactly symbols are and *how* they mean are issues never furnished with a rigorous and systematic language of discussion. In some measure, this is appropriate for a study finding its proper place to gnaw and digest a very enormous bone; in effect, most all of cultural life. Nevertheless, for convenience in our discussion, we should adopt by convention at least a common terminology for debate. In this interest, then, I shall adopt the following terminology, suggested by Charles Morris in his *Foundations of the Theory of Signs*.

Morris states; "The function of signs is, in general, a way in which certain existences take account of other existences through an intermediary class of existences." For Morris, signs (the most generic category of semiosis, or sign-use, to distinguish from de Saussure's usage) which refer to the same object need not have the same designata, since that which is taken account of in the object may differ for various interpreters. A sign of an object may, at one theoretical extreme, simply turn the interpreter of the sign upon the object, while at the other extreme it would allow the interpreter to take account of all the characteristics of the object in question, in the absence of the object itself. There is thus a potential sign continuum in which, with respect to every object or situation, all degrees of semiosis may be expressed, and the question as to what the designation of a sign is in any given situation is the question of what characteristics of the object or situation are actually taken account of when only the sign vehicle is present.

A sign must have a designatum, yet obviously every sign does not, in fact, refer to an actual, existent object. The *designatum* of a sign is the *kind* of object which the sign applies to, that is, those objects with the properties of which the interpreter takes account through the presence of the sign vehicle. And the taking-account-of may occur when there are no objects or situations with the characteristics taken account of. Where what is referred to actually exists as referred to, the object of reference is a *denotatum*. It thus becomes clear that, while every sign has a designatum, not every sign has a denotatum. A designatum is not a thing, but a kind of object or class of objects—and a class may have many members, or one member, or no members. The denotata are the members of the class.

Within semiosis, Morris tells us, a number of dyadic relations may be abstracted for study. One may study the relations of signs to the objects to which the signs are applicable. This relation is called the *semantic dimension.* Or the subject of study may be the relation of signs to interpreters. This relation is called the *pragmatic dimension.* Yet another is the formal relation of signs to one another. This, of course, is the relationship of *syntactics.* In general, the relation of signs to signs, of signs to objects and to interpreters can be correlated with a specific terminology, such that *implicates* is a term restricted to syntactics, *designates* and *denotes* to semantics, and *expresses* to pragmatics.

The focus of interest in this paper will be largely on pragmatics, broadly, the relations of signs to their users, and thus on explicating a theory of meaning that takes account of symbolic efficacy for users. More rigorously, pragmatics can be defined as the relation between a message fraction and variables specified in a "speech act function." Following Silverstein's usage, these variables would include interlocutors, referents, time of speech event, locus of interlocutors, and various socially significant relationships pertaining among them. Note that within one semiotic "level" we should expect a basic equivalence among the pragmatic, the operational, and the indexical (to be dealt with below) as dimensions of meaning in addition to the referential meanings of the sort that contribute to the propositional value of sentences (Silverstein, forthcoming).

One area of terminological under-brush has, I hope, been cleared for discussion, but I shall have to do this twice more before we can encounter the data of Navajo ceremonial practice. First, I shall have to establish a notion of *performatives,* then of *indexicality,* for my argument will seek to propound that ritual symbols are *performatives* with *indexical meaning* and *pragmatic efficacy.*

In his influential work *How to Do Things With Words,* the philosopher Austin developed the notion of a dichotomy between *performatives* and *constatives,* or statements of the propositional type. In effect, the distinction is not maintained by Austin's final work, where he states it is only a special case subsumed under the more generic trichotomy of locutionary, illocutionary, and perlocutionary acts. Much complexity and enrichment has been added to Austin's initial formulation by recent work, notably that of Searle and Sadock, yet his original distinctions can still serve us here.

Things that can go wrong on the occasion of performative utterances (which are not true or false, a quality of constatives only), Austin labels "infelicities." Consequently, the following are things he regards as necessary for the "happy" functioning of a performative (it should be noted that we can consider these criteria as applying to ritual acts as well):

(A.1.) There must be an accepted conventional procedure having a certain conventional effect, that procedure to include the uttering of certain words by certain persons in certain circumstances, and further,

(A.2.) the particular person and circumstances in a given case must be appropriate for the invocation of the particular procedure invoked.

(B.1.) The procedure must be executed by all participants both correctly and
(B.2.) completely.
(C.1.) Where, as often, the procedure is designed for use by persons having certain thoughts or feelings, or for the inauguration of certain consequential conduct on the part of any participant, then a person participating in and so invoking the procedure must in fact have those thoughts or feelings, and the participants must intend to so conduct themselves and further,
(C.2.) must actually so conduct themselves subsequently.

Now for locutionary, illocutionary, and perlocutionary. Locutionary acts, those with which we are most familiar, simply involve the speaker's act of saying whatever it is he says. Austin explains the performance of certain acts, however, in a new sense as the performing of an "illocutionary act," that is, performance of an act *in* saying something as opposed to performing an act *of* saying something. Performing an act *by* saying something, as in persuasion or argumentation, he calls perlocutionary, and considers the least important of his distinctions. Locutionary acts are acts performed in order to communicate. Perlocutionary acts are the by-products of acts of communication. The effects of a single perlocutionary act may be numerous or even unintended. Illocutionary acts are speech acts that we accomplish by communicating our intent to accomplish them. Thus, they are always interpreted as having been intended. "Performative" illocutionary acts are those that mention directly in the utterance the act that they accomplish. That is, they name themselves. Locutionary acts are roughly like constative statements and respond to analysis by traditional theories of meaning.

Illocutionary acts, however, *effect a state of affairs* in their performance as utterances. Examples would be "I marry you," "I declare war," "I promise," or "Be thou healed." Austin refers to the doctrine of the different types of function of language here in question as the doctrine of "illocutionary forces." For too long, philosophers have neglected this study, treating all problems as problems of "locutionary usage." They are coming now to a more clear realization that the *occasion* of an utterance matters seriously, and that the words used are to some extent to be explained by the context in which they are designed to be or have actually been spoken. Yet, Austin believes, we are still too prone to give these explanations in terms of "the meanings of words." Admittedly we can use "meaning" also with reference to illocutionary force— "He meant it as an order," for example. But we want here "to distinguish *force* and meaning in the sense in which meaning is equivalent to sense and reference, just as it has become essential to distinguish sense and reference within meaning" (Austin:100). He contends that the truth or falsity of statements depends not merely on the meanings of words but on what act is performed in what circumstances. "The total speech act in the total speech situation is the only actual phenomenon which, in the last resort, we are engaged in elucidating," he states (p. 147). The pertinent point for our discussion is the introduction of "illocutionary force" as an additional dimension of meaning; that is, meaning as function and effect, not just as semantic features, nor just the now-popular formula, "meaning is use," which is still limited to the locutionary.

If ritual language is to be treated in

terms of performatives, then there is a potential problem for the notion of native exegesis, which I shall mention later. Clearly, "illocutionary force" is a relevant concept for our understanding of native healing ceremonies, where transformation of at least the patient's subjective experience of illness or pain is effected by properly conducted "performatives."

The *locus classicus* of semiotic analysis has been the collected papers of C. S. Peirce, surely the most astute categorizer of signs in modern philosophy. It is to him I now turn, through a critical article by Arthur Burks, to establish my final terminological mapping of the symbolic terrain, in the relations of *icon, index,* and *symbol.*

Burks begins with a preliminary explanation of the three kinds of signs, the symbol, the index, and the icon, to be taken in that order. I shall summarize his argument in terms of the following examples: (1) the word "red," as used in the English sentence "The book is red"; (2) an act of pointing, used to call attention to some particular object, for example, a tree; (3) a scale drawing, used to communicate to a machinist the structure of a piece of machinery. All these are signs in the general sense in which this term is used by Peirce: each satisfies his definition of a sign as something which represents or signifies an object to some interpreter. In the above examples the objects are: the color red, the tree, and the structure of the machine, respectively; the interpreters are, in each case, the minds understanding the sign. But there are some important differences in the way in which these signs signify, or represent, their objects, and it is òn the basis of these differences that the classification is

made. A sign represents its object to its interpreter symbolically, indexically or iconically according to whether it does so (1) by being associated with its object by a conventional rule used by the interpreter (as in the case of "red"); (2) by being in existential relation with its object or a sign of this object (as in the case of the act of pointing); or (3) by exhibiting its object (as in the case of the diagram).

Burks next leads us to examine further the application of these criteria to our three examples. Consider first the word "red." The word "red" is a symbol because it stands for the quality red to an interpretant who interprets it in terms of the conventional linguistic rule of English establishing the meaning of this word. Thus any word is a symbol, including words that are indexical (for example, "this") and words that are iconic (for example, an onomatopoetic word).

Consider next the act of pointing. Its object is whatever is pointed to, that is, whatever is in a certain physical relation to the sign. Here the tree is selected or indicated by virtue of its being in the direction of the pointed finger, only a few yards away from it, and so on. Hence the act of pointing is an index, that is, a sign which determines its object on the basis of an existential connection. The symbol "this" is also an index, because (apart from the conventional element by virtue of which it is a symbol) it may function very much the same as the act of pointing, that is, instead of pointing to a tree, one may use the phrase "this tree." The object of a specific occurrence or token of "this" is determined or selected by virtue of its being in some existential relation to the occurrence of the sign itself.

Burks considers finally the diagram. The diagram is an icon because it represents the structure of the machine by exemplifying or exhibiting the same structure in some respects. The draftsman communicates to the machinist the fact that one wheel of the machine has twice the diameter of another by drawing the first wheel with twice the diameter of the second, and so on. In the same way the sound of an onomatopoetic word represents its sense. Icons or indices must, of course, have conventional (that is, symbolic) aspects to establish just what is iconic or indexical about the particular sign and the particular relevant parts of its object. They do not exist in "pure" form; the "symbolic" in this sense is more "basic" to our understanding of all types of signs, in that it is presupposed.

What is most relevant to us is the type of meaning associated with indexical signs. Peirce held that the function of an index is to refer to or call attention to some feature or object in the immediated environment of the interpretant. Peirce says: "If, for example, a man remarks, 'Why, it is raining' it is only by some such circumstances as that he is now standing here looking out at a window as he speaks, which would serve as an index" (in Burks: 677). The indexical element of this remark is implied in the speaker's use of the present tense, as well as in his bodily orientation, both of which give the meaning *here* and *now;* the sentence "It is raining" uttered under these cirumstances is equivalent in meaning to the sentence "It is raining here and now." Such time and place references as "here," "now," "there," "then," "yesterday," "tomorrow" are all indexical symbols. The pronouns "I," "you," "this," "that" and such expressions as "this city," "that bridge" are also indexical symbols.

It develops from his argument that the fundamental kind of indexical sign is the indexical symbol (rather than the pure index), and in presenting the concept of indexical-meaning we will need to analyze the distinction between indexical and non-indexical symbols. A clear formulation of this distinction requires the use of Peirce's type-token distinction. Burks invites us to consider a non-indexical symbol, for example "red." There are many occurrences of this word, each consisting of a written or printed pattern of a certain shape or a characteristic pattern of sound. Whenever such a pattern occurs in an appropriate context it is taken by the interpretant to signify the color red. Each occurrence of a pattern of "red" which is reacted to by an interpretant in this way is called a *token* of "red." A token of a non-indexical symbol is then an event of a certain character and so has a location in space and time. The class to which all tokens of a given word belong is called a *type*. There are two different tokens when a speaker uses "red" in two different sentences, and two more when "red" occurs once in a printed sentence but is read twice; and all of these tokens belong to the same type. A type will, of course, be without spatio-temporal location. The type-token distinction may be applied in the same way to indexical symbols. Each occurrence of the word "now" is a token, and the class of all tokens of "now" is a type.

Note, now, Burks's contention that the spatio-temporal location of a token of a non-indexical symbol is irrelevant to its meaning: "red" means the same thing when used at different times and places, each token signifying the same color. Moreover, the meaning of a token of a non-indexical symbol is always the same as the meaning of the type to which it belongs. The case is different with an indexical symbol, however, for the spatio-temporal location of a given token of such a symbol is relevant to the meaning of that token: "now" means two different things when it is uttered on two different days. Since the meaning of the type to which any symbol belongs (whether indexical or non-indexical) is always the same, it follows that the meaning of a token of an indexical symbol is different from the meaning of the type to which it belongs.

Yet even in the case of the indexical symbol, the meaning of the token clearly has something in common with the meaning of its type. For the meaning of a token of any kind of linguistic symbol is specified at least in part by a general linguistic rule applicable to all tokens of the type. Burks refers to the common element in the meaning of a token and the meaning of its type as the *symbolic-meaning* of the token or type. It is obvious that the complete meaning of a type (either indexical or non-indexical) is its symbolic meaning. Furthermore, the complete meaning of a token of a non-indexical symbol is also its symbolic meaning. But the symbolic meaning of a token of an indexical symbol is only part of its full meaning: he refers to its full meaning as its *indexical-meaning*. For example, every token of the type "now" has the same symbolic-meaning: "now" means *the time at which "now" is uttered*. But in order to know the indexical-meaning of a token of the type "now," one must know not only its symbolic-meaning but its temporal location as well. Morris, too, says of such signs, "An indexical symbol does not characterize what it denotes, except to indicate space-time coordinates" (1938).

To summarize the distinction between indexical and non-indexical symbols: Any two tokens of a given type of symbol have the same symbolic-meaning, but two tokens of a given type of indexical symbol may have different indexical meanings. The point for our discussion is the context-dependence of indexical symbols. Whatever types of symbolic usage that can be shown to be indexical must be treated to contextual analysis to be fully interpreted. The spatio-temporal context of their employment is a necessary additional dimension of their full meaning.

As Michael Silverstein has noted (forthcoming), the indexical role of language "meaning" as exemplified in rules of use has been sorely neglected. Not only such things as restricted codes, but also universal categories of language such as personal pronouns, syntactic markers of case, distinctive vocabulary sets, even such phonological indices as particular regional dialects or manners of speech that reflect social class (see Labov 1966) or distinctive patterns of use characteristic of a social role (judge, minister, drill sergeant) can all be demonstrated to "index" variables of social conditions that co-vary with message form and language use. Most significantly, however, ritual "language" symbols constitute a restricted code of meaning that is primarily indexical. This will be demonstrated at greater length in the conclusion. For now, however, I can conclude that an adequate analysis of ritual symbols must be predicted on their indexical relation to social conditions of the ritual occurrence and must include an awareness of their context-dependence.

Context and Function: Malinowski and Meaning

Many of the elements of the position with respect to meaning I have worked towards here have appeared in other guises, principly in the oft-maligned "ethnographic theory" of language advocated by Malinowski. Malinowski insisted we see language in the context of the situation. Speaking of the language of magic, he claimed, "The structure of linguistic material is inextricably mixed up with, and dependent upon, the course of the activity in which the utterances are embedded. The vocabulary, the meaning of the particular words used in their characteristic technicality is not less subordinate to action" (Malinowski 1923:311). He emphasized the dependence of the meaning of each word upon practical experience and of the structure of each utterance upon the momentary situation in which it is spoken. Primitive language he considered to be a mode of action and not an instrument of reflection. Language in its primitive function and original form was said to have an essentially pragmatic character; to be a mode of behavior, an indispensable element of concerted human action. And negatively: that to regard it as a means for the embodiment or expression of thought is to take a one-sided view of one of its most "derivate and specialized functions." Thus, for him, there can be no definition of a word without the reality which it means being present.

Jack Berry, in a critical introduction to *The Language of Magic and Gardening,* regards Malinowski's approach to language and the study of meaning in language as having much in common with behaviorist philosophers and, of course, psychologists (1965). The tradi-tional theory of meaning Malinowski challenged on the grounds of undue emphasis on the conceptual content of language and undue concern with communication of thought and expression of belief. It involves a metaphysical dualism between ideas and words, content and medium; which dichotomies he rejected.

Malinowski spurned this mentalist view of language and proposed a conception instead of language as active behavior, comparable to and interrelated with other bodily activities. It follows that language is most appropriately studied as "part of the act," not abstractly, as a discrete phenomenon. His "context of situation" is called by Berry "a sort of action-construct specifically developed for this purpose." Fundamentally, language was to "direct, control and correlate" human activity. Malinowski had a notion of the "instrumental meaning of words," based on a theory which goes back to James and the procedural theory of meaning of the pragmatists. Thus meaning, for Malinowski, turns out to be "function within the context of the situation," usually assumed to mean that the meaning of an utterance is its "observable effect" in a given situation. I suggest here that the notion of observable effect be limited to social realities, symbolically defined, for a particular type of speech activity only. Malinowski's excesses have been treated harshly, and his theory of meaning is certainly not adequate for the analysis of the *total* language of any group in its manifold situations of use. Criticism of such a contextual theory of meaning (offered by, among others, Berry himself) hinges on the fact of entailment of nominalist predicaments. An extreme contextualist position for the meaning of all language implies the need to enumerate an infinite number of contexts and to treat them "clinically" (as Berry calls it), below the level of general abstract theory. For the situational theory of meaning to be usable, it is necessary that we be able to recognize the identity or partial similarity of situations; this was claimed to be impossible for all of continuous social life. If, however, a functional, contextual theory of meaning be restricted in application to a special class of speech acts, such as those indexical ones I have been discussing that are employed in ritual situations, the very spatial and temporal location and well-defined boundaries of ritual occurrences provide a domain in which such a theory is again useful. Indeed, it would be the most adequate approach to meaning in these identifiable and finite contexts, for we would be dealing with Burks's "indexical-meaning" of a token. (I do not mean to throw out "traditional" theories of meaning for these situations, only to insist that they be complemented by this additional dimension.) We would be left mainly with the problem of the temporal axis of meaning in successive tokens of the same ritual symbol type; that is, of determining whether successive performances of a ritual can be said to have a meaning that is constant in a definable way. I have not eliminated Malinowski's problem, but surely greatly reduced the complexity of specifying contexts by restricting the application of the theory.

I should now make some attempt to grasp the relationship between context and meaning, thought of as sense or reference, to move towards an understanding of what it means to proffer a "communication" theory of ritual. I shall elaborate the manifold implications of context by the following example.

Let us suppose someone utters a bid of "one dollar" at an auction. To understand that utterance we need at least three notions of context for that utterance. The first is the context of previous utterances within the speech situation. This is an on-going, processual context that builds with every contribution. To understand "one dollar" we need to know that prior to this utterance other participants in the speech situation had emitted such utterances as "two bits," "four bits," and "six bits" in succession. We now have a clearer idea of why "one dollar" was said. In addition, however, we need to know the larger, spatio-temporal context of the occurrence of the utterance; we need the context of situation. This is a dimension of context that informs those utterances that are performatives. In our example, we need to know that this is a culturally-defined activity known as an auction, where certain types of behaviors are expected. It is an activity "bounded" by cultural definition, within which certain usual relationships of actors are prescribed. For instance, that the individual uttering "one dollar" be a legitimate, authorized bidder, standing in front of the auctioneer among other bidders, who, with serious intent, attempts to communicate his intention to the auctioneer within a defined time period (before the banging of the gavel). The third and largest context is analogous to encyclopedic knowledge of the culture. Context in this sense takes account of all cultural meanings that bear on the situation; for instance, that "one dollar" constitutes an offer of some unit of value, that money is an appropriate medium of exchange in this society, and that there exist cultural notions of property ownership and transaction of that ownership. To provide a "complete" analysis of the meaning of the utterance "one dollar" in the framework of an auction requires accounting of a set of cultural meanings connected to this utterance which are potentially infinitely expandable.

It is important to note here that the analysis of ritual symbols, indeed of symbols of any sort employed in a social context, is predicated on a cultural analysis of native categories of experience. The very existence of a domain of activity such as ritual within which certain symbolic meanings interplay is clearly an empirical question with respect to a particular culture. The analyst's imposition of *a priori* institutional frameworks and divisions on the flow of cultural life often leads to misapprehensions and the fruitless debating of spurious questions. Assuming that every culture categorizes and patterns experience in distinctive ways, it is these categories and their relationships that must constitute the initial ground for the interpretation of symbolic meanings. In particular, it is the native's apprehension of the classification and order of his world which informs the notion of "context" used here. Culture's role in establishing "context" is determinant. Cultural actors always find themselves interacting in manifold sets of circumstances. But not every feature of this environment of circumstances constitutes a relevant aspect of context. Certain features only are selected out as providing a significant contribution to the situation of interaction. Inasmuch as I have been stressing the role of context-dependence in the analysis of ritual symbols, we must bear in mind that these contexts are not "givens" in the material world, but rather are constituted as frameworks for social events. Thus it will be stressed

in subsequent sections that Navajo culture gives explicit and self-conscious recognition to the existence of a category of action I feel justified in calling "ritual." Further, the native theory of language and meaning seems quite congruent with the notions of symbolic efficacy discussed here. Symbols employed in ritual contexts are regarded as compelling and forceful agents in the creation and ordering of experience by the Navajos themselves.

John Lyons, in his book *Introduction to Theoretical Linguistics,* makes some similar statements about context, then notes, "on the basis of this intuitive notion of context we can now define 'having meaning' for utterances. An utterance has meaning only if its occurrence is not completely determined by its context. This definition rests upon the principle that 'meaningfulness implies choice.' If the hearer knows in advance that the speaker will inevitably produce a particular utterance in a particular context, then it is obvious that the utterance gives him no information, when it occurs: no 'communication' takes place" (1968). All that needs to be said about these utterances in a semantic description is that they are "used" in the situations in question. It would be futile to insist that they must "mean" something over and above their "use." This distinction is only theoretically absolute; we are really talking about quantifiability of meaning with respect to "expectancy" (or probability of occurrence) in context, as Lyons points out. The less probable a particular element is in a context, the more meaning it has in that context. So we see that "meaningfulness" of utterances varies in inverse proportion to their degree of "expectancy" in context. The point can be generalized to indicate that any semantic analysis of ritual language can validly include a "behavioristic" framework as an aspect of that analysis.

A Navajo singer may indeed make "choices" in the chant, song, and prayer material he wields; in fact, he is expected to do so. His choices do have "meaning," but it is indexical meaning primarily. The choices among alternatives are indices of relationships among certain social variables defined as relevant to the situation of the ceremonial performance. The only information communicated by the choice of one thematic subritual over another appropriate at this juncture is information about the cultural definition of this particular ritual situation. Change of message form covaries not with change in referential meaning so much as change in social conditions of use.

There is an inverse relationship between indexicality and what might be called "functional load." The higher the indexicality, the lower the functional, communicative load. Ritual language, to the extent that it is recital of a formula in a context, primarily only shows that such a ceremony is taking place. The semantic information being carried is minimal.

We can turn again to Silverstein's *Linguistics and Anthropology* to recount the position on "rules of use." Rules of use describe ways the message form covaries with social variables of the speech situation. Ritual language is a restrictive code of meaning and use, as opposed to the elaborated code of the full language employed in multiple situations. To the extent that we can correlate the employment of such subcodes with social conditions we can say that social conditions "mediate between the language as an abstract entity and speech. That is, we have a system of indexicality" (personal communication). A restricted code has low functional load, an elaborated code has higher. The higher the predictability of the message form through knowledge of the social conditions, then the lower the communicated information; the less "referential content." Communication in ritual situations is effected by other than linguistic acts; it is done by social conditions. In ritual speech, *to the extent that every syllable is performed according to a determined form,* the context of social conditions is the medium of successful communication.

Finally, I can present the following implications of some of the ideas I have introduced for ethnographic research, particularly the attempt to elicit "native categories."

"Performatives" can be viewed as predicates or "names" for cultural activities whose meaning is indexical only of the fact that the situation in question is defined as being an activity of this type. They are analogous to the role of "proper names," but in a religious, jural or other bounded sphere. The important point is that a particular performative predicate is dependent on a cultural "definition of a situation," defined in relation to a particular world view. For ethnographic investigation, these are powerful research cues, for knowing the situation in which a particular performative is employed is to get a native categorization of a situation or institutional activity, bounded in the culture's own terms and imbued with a native sense of value.

There is no internal (within language), structural way to distinguish ritual language, the specific illocutionary language of rigidly defined contexts, from ordinary language use. Even though a specialized vocabulary may be in effect, the same grammatical rules of construction apply. The difference lies in "rules of use," a theoretical construct for language analysis that "open-ends" grammar and links it with all cultural knowledge. The only criteria for typology, then, are external or *functional* ones, the criteria of culturally defined native interpretations of situations for proper use of such restricted codes. The operational presence of such restricted codes is a useful index of the way the culture defines social experience. Of the rules for such restricted codes, Silverstein has said: "Rules of use are not a description of actual linguistic behavior, so much as a *native model of behavior* in terms of the conditions in the speech act which are presupposed for the normal use of certain messages" (forthcoming).

When a Navajo singer selects certain elements from ritual complexes to apply in a particular situation, he is providing an index of the native definition and etiology of the current malady. The choice indicates the conception of the disease and its causal interconnection, the behavioral proscriptions violated, the relevant associated deities, and the social components of cure and restoration. I hope, in future research, to determine whether there may be coded as well social-organizational factors concerning the categories of personnel present.

In concluding this section, I can also make a possible contribution to the issue of the role of native exegesis. Recall Nadel's statement that "uncomprehended symbols have no part in social inquiry; their social effectiveness lies in their capacity to indicate, and if they

indicate nothing to the actors, they are, from our point of view, irrelevant, and indeed no longer symbols" (cited in Turner 1967:26). Yet it is frequently the case that Navajo singers, who must "purchase" their knowledge from a recognized authority, will economize by acquiring the "form" of the chant only, without even inquiring as to the meaning or interpretation of the symbols, which the established singer is reluctant to divulge. Thus, in their employment, we may indeed have "uncomprehended symbols" on the part of all participants. They really do not know the "meaning" of the symbols and do not consider them essential for the compelling, "illocutionary force" to take effect. This supports Turner's remarks that it is " . . . legitimate to include within the total meaning of a dominant ritual symbol, aspects of behavior associated with it which the actors themselves are unable to interpret, and indeed of which they may be unaware, if they are asked to interpret the symbol outside its activity context" (1967:27).

The ritual symbols of the chants may be broken into component units by native selection and usage. Each ritual passage or artifact has a range of inherent meanings, one (or more) aspects of which are brought to prominence and defined as being relevant to the situation at hand by the patterning of meanings of the other elements chosen in the ritual performance. Like syntagmatic chains of meaningful elements, a *constellation* of symbolic meanings, or distinctive configuration, effected by previous and subsequent choice of elements and their combinations, provide a contextual determination of *which* meanings of the range inherent in the symbol are to be effected. This construction of a context is, of course, a function of the on-going *ritual process*, which gives it the unique, characteristic reality of symbols in social life.

Healing and Symbolic Efficacy

In the consideration of the main tenets of Navajo religious belief and ceremonial practice which follows, I seek to focus in particular on the following aspects: the primacy of *action* or *effect* for establishing meaning and forming classifications; the exacting *formalism* and compulsion of ritual procedures; the role of *selection* and *combination of elements or units* in the ritual process; and the function of circumstantial *context* in defining the specific paramount meaning of symbols employed from among their range of possible "disparate significata." My main sources are Kluckhohn, Haile, Lamphere, Reichard, Witherspoon and Wyman.

Reichard states: "The Navajo dogma is based on a cosmogony that tries to account for everything in the universe by relating it to man and his activities." And later in the same work, "The universe is conceived as a place for man, and all natural phenomena are interpreted as his allies or his enemies" (Reichard 1950). Let us first regard Navajo categories of their world, derived primarily from articles by Kluckhohn (1964) and Wyman (1938).

The Navajo conception of Holy or Supernatural does not have its paired opposite to designate the phenomena of the mundane world. Earth-surface-people are regularly contrasted with supernatural people, but there is no general category embracing everything in ordinary experience. The universe is con-

ceived as a continuum. Lamphere (1969) remarks that the dichotomy between nature and society does not accurately reflect Navajo belief. "Nature" becomes an all-inclusive organizing device: a fusion of natural, supernatural and human or social elements. Humans, *diyin dine'e* or supernaturals, and natural phenomena all possess the same kinds of souls; each has an in-standing-one *(bii-siziini)* and breath *(nilchi)* by means of which it moves and has life (see Haile 1943). All elements of the Navajo universe share the same life-giving forces. Some natural phenomena and the *diyin dine'e,* though, share the quality of being dangerous *(bahadzid)* and are capable of causing illness to humans.

Ceremonial behavior, behavior directed towards the supernaturals, is purposively "restorative." Haile calls it, "an organized attempt . . . to influence the course of events through supernatural techniques" (1951). The Navajo word for such behavior is freely applied to a major ritual; a small ceremony; witchcraft; to ritual practices employed in trading or gambling; to events directed within the supernatural world by supernaturals. The behavior relating to the supernatural is dichotomized between the "good side" and the "bad side," the evil or the ugly. This latter refers to all culturally disapproved ritual activity, paramount of which is witchcraft, divided by technique into four distinct categorizations.

The "good side" is cut into a distinction between "chants" and all else. The Navajo word which means "chant" refers to those ceremonials differentiated by a simple and consistent operation: those which include singing accompanied by some kind of rattle. Chants are subdivided fundamentally in two ways. The first refers merely to duration, and one hears therefore of one-night, two-night, five-night and nine-night chants. Or a patient may have only an "excerpt" from a chant or ceremonial.

The other subdivision is according to the "ritual" (or *way-k'ejhi*) by which they are carried out: Holy Way, Ugly Way, or Life Way. Several chants provide for performance according to all three rituals; a much larger number for performance by Holy Way and Ugly Way only. The ritual is selected in accord with the assumed etiology of the disease of the patient being treated. If the illness is thought to be caused by angry supernaturals, Holy Way is appropriate. If the cause be the ghosts of fellow tribesmen or witches, Ugly Way is selected. The Life Way ceremonials are for those suffering from injuries attributed to accidents, either recent or past. Special circumstances may call for some combination of rituals within a performance of a single chant. Each ritual implies certain choices of procedures, equipment, songs, and symbolism. Thus in Angry Way subritual, reds are turned in, blues out; in Peaceful Way, blues are toward the figure, reds out. Holy Way ritual makes provision for three subrituals: Weapon Way, Angry Way, and Peaceful Way. Here likewise the decisive factor is the diagnosis of the origin of the illness.

The specific chants which may be conducted according to one or more of the rituals and subrituals are loosely associated by the Navajo into subgroups which are derived in the first instance from the particular corpus of mythology on which the chants are based, and, in the second instance, from well-known techniques or features prominent in, or distinctive of, these connected chants.

This does not exhaust the possibilities of Navajo classification of their ceremonials. For example, chants of a certain group may be given without masked impersonators, in which case they are called "just-visiting" chants. There are additional features such as sand painting, prayer sticks, jewels, and various other paraphernalia which may or may not be added. Kluckhohn relates that it is possible to get a chanter to specify the ceremony he is conducting in the following elaborate manner: "Holy Way, male shooting branch; nine nights; angry and peace way sub-rituals; Thunderstruck side: with Sun's house and Dark Circle of Branches" (1960).

The non-chants have the following groups: five varieties of Blessing Way, three main varieties of prayer ceremonials, two varieties of war ceremonials, many varieties of hunting ceremonials, and four types of divination rites.

Blessing Way is sung but not to the accompaniment of a rattle. Although it is short and of fixed duration (two nights), it is stated by almost all Navajos to be the very keystone of their whole ceremonial system. In addition to its existence as an independent ceremonial, each chant has its Blessing Way part, and many minor rites are essentially "built up" out of Blessing Way.

Prayer ceremonials are mainly associated with Blessing Way, but alone among Navajo ceremonials they have a duration of four nights. Prayer ceremonials are intended primarily for cure of witchcraft and for protection against witches. Likewise, most war ceremonials are felt to have a marked affiliation with Ugly Way ritual.

Types of divination are distinguished by technique: hand trembling, stargazing, listening, and *Datura* divination. In each case the practitioner goes into a kind of trance to diagnose the cause and history of an event (illness, loss, theft, adultery), and to make a prognostication of a favorable course of action (what ceremonial to have for an illness, for example). It is also relevant to remark that diagnosticians seldom carry out other ceremonials. Divination is a specialty, and Navajos generally assume implicitly it is an exclusive one. All other ceremonials are learned; one becomes a diagnostician by a sudden "gift."

Almost everything known to the Navajo is personalized in the supernatural context: animals, plants, mountains, winds, and rain. The personalized "inner forms" of animals, plants, and inanimate natural phenomena are addressed in prayers and mentioned in myths and ceremonials.

Kluckhohn goes on to note that Navajo "gods" are many. The sun appears really in three guises: as object, as "inner form" of this object ("one who carries a round object here and there in daytime"), and as a completely individualized being who is one of the major Navajo supernaturals. The wife of the sun, Changing Woman, is regarded by many as the principle Navajo divinity. In the main stream of Navajo thought, the principle divinities appear to be Sun and Changing Woman; their children, the Hero Twins; First Man and First Woman. Note that just as the dual form is prominent in the Navajo language, the main deities appear in pairs.

The divinities themselves are differentiated by terminology, each deity having an alias. Reichard asserts that the alternate terms are used when Navajo lore wishes to emphasize special manifestations of their "personalities." For the Navajo everything comes in twos, or its multiple, four, the paramount symbolic number of Navajo ritual. Many divinities appear in duplex or multiplex forms. How the Navajo classify a supernatural depends upon quite standardized features of context. The elder of the Hero Twins is called Monster Slayer when arrayed in armor, Holy Man otherwise (Reichard 1950). Place and situation are also determinative of the various appelations of the twins.

The category "Supernatural People" seems to be the most generic one which can be applied to all individual divinities and personalized powers, to all "people" of the pre-emergence world as contrasted with Earth-Surface-People, even to chanters when they are saturated with supernatural power at the height of a ceremonial.

Navajo deities are said to be strikingly less fully categorized than the ceremonials, though each ceremonial tends to be associated with a particular figure (Kluckhohn 1964). Changing Woman is, so to speak, patron of Blessing Way and the prayer ceremonials. The Sun is prominent in the Shooting Way complex. First Man and First Woman are connected with all evil magic. Breast-Grabber is first and foremost the tutelary deity of hunters. The Hero Twins, great warriors, stand large in most ceremonials telling of war. Black Supernatural, however, conducts Enemy Way.

Navajo sacred myths deal with the emergence from the eleven lower worlds (their number varies from eleven to four). There are, as well, myths that are the rationale for the various ceremonials. The emergence myth, or part of it, is incorporated into the justificatory legend of many ceremonials. In another class are legends of the wanderings and subsequent development of the various clans.

A Navajo talking about mythic material may say most definitely at a point that appears altogether arbitrary "here Blessing Way begins." The origin legends of numerous ceremonials may be almost identical up to a certain point and then branch off. Beauty Way and Mountain Top Way are independent continuations of the story of the war against the Pueblo Indians of Taos, a story which the Navajo seem to regard as having been begun in the myth of Monster Way, and that in turn in the emergence story.

Wyman states:

As more Navajo myths are recorded, the more apparent it becomes that the total mythology possesses a somewhat limited number of episodes and incidents of types thereof which can recur over and again in the origin legends of different chants. It is almost as in the construction of the chants themselves, where a limited number of types of ceremony are combined in different ways and with various individual minutiae. (1945)

From a Navajo viewpoint, everything is related to everything else. The beliefs and practices constitute a ramified system. Most chants are connected with particular animals. Many are related to specific mountains (especially the sacred mountains of the four directions) and to other localities. Each ceremonial has a color, directional, sex, number, and sound symbolism. The intricacies reminded Kluckhohn of the contrived, systematic symbolism of Joyce's *Ulysses*.

For the interrelationships, causation is said to be the keynote. You begin by finding out what "caused" your illness or who stole your property or indulged in adultery with your wife. A course of action is then indicated in "logical" terms. The system with its categorizations tells you. If the diagnostician maintains that you have "Thunderstruck" sickness, then obviously you must have recourse to a practitioner of one of the Shooting Ways. The chanter, on the basis of his information on what details divination has revealed and his knowledge of the full mechanics of etiology as set forth in the myth, will know what ritual, subritual, branch, and features of Shooting Way are indicated; what divinity or divinities must be given special attention in the symbolism of the chant. And at points almost inseparable, the keynote is origin. For example: Was there a failure in treatment because superficial diagnosis prescribed Enemy Way but, as the legends show, the story of Enemy Way begins "farther back" in the Monster Way and therefore it was this latter that was required? In general, categorizations of myth and supernatural beings are left implicit except for the degree to which they reflect the categories of the ceremonial system.

Kluckhohn (1960) suggests that this differential of categorical elaboration rests upon the pervasive theme of Navajo culture: action. The cases where the Navajo are least equivocal on their classifications involves operations of the observation of action. Navajos categorize ceremonialists as well as ceremonials, and here again they resort to observations of behavior. Navajos are interested in words insofar as they categorize events with some precision. The words of a chant myth must be just right because they prescribe a course of behavior that must be followed with minute exactness. But the test of correct behavior invariably stresses what is to be done and how it is to be done. The Navajo are not concerned with arguments over belief unless they were to be shown that accepting one or the other position inevitably involved different ritual practices. Myths and beings are important only insofar as they affect ceremonial action, and there is little probability of error here so long as rites are correctly classified.

The major ceremonies and their subdivisions, as well as the deities and their manifestations can be said to stand in paradigmatic relation one to another. A particular ritual occurrence, processually transpiring over an extended period of time, represents a selection of ceremonial elements from appropriate categories and their arrangement into a sequence. At junctions in the performance, there are criteria of substitutability considered and agreed upon by knowledgable practitioners. The choice of one ceremonial unit over another in a paradigmatic set is related to the social circumstances that impinge on the performance. Thus the "form" of the overall ritual message co-varies with other conditions of the culturally defined situation of performance. That is, there are "rules of use" for the ceremonial units that function indexically. The ceremonial units are constellations of ritual symbols, both verbal and non-verbal. Whether regarding song, prayer, prescribed action, and visual representation as justifiably one "ceremonial unit" is certainly a legitimate issue, one that I argue elsewhere. The crucial point is whether the Navajo regard these disparate media of ritual communication as "saying the same thing." The point here, however, is that the symbols of a ceremonial unit surely have meaning of one sort, and the choice among these in their employment surely has meaning of an additional sort. A comprehensive interpretation of the ritual process seems to me to require both dimensions of meaning.

This concludes a general overview of Navajo categorization of their cosmos. We have seen the primacy of effect or function for establishing the criteria on which categorization of the "supernatural" universe is based and indicated the importance of the context of action for defining the meaning of the categories. In the next section I will present the various themes and charters for Navajo healing ceremonies, as discussed by Lamphere and Witherspoon. The focus will be on the natural/supernatural world as related to the experience and cure of the patient.

In Navajo ritual, symbolic objects and actions used with reference to the patient's body effect a transformation from a state of "ugly" conditions to a state of "pleasant" conditions, if the proper chant is performed which acts against the "dangerous" factor and which involves the aid of the proper *diyin dine'e*.

V. Turner, T. Beidelman, and others find that bodily states provide a paradigm for the classification of nature and/or society. Body fluids constitute the basis for symbols which make the kind of communicative statements emphasized by Leach in his "Ritualization in Man" (1966). In her article "Symbolic Elements of Navajo Ritual," Lamphere claims that Navajo ritual symbolism represents the reverse process. Symbolic statements about the natural/supernatural world provide the basic paradigm for interpreting bodily processes of illness and health. Ritual does more than communicate the structure of the Navajo universe; as she attempts to show, natural materials become symbolic objects associated with supernaturals. These combine with symbolic action to express the themes of prestation, identification, and removal so that the relationship with the *diyin dine'e* is altered and the patient's body is transformed from a state of *hózhxǫ́* to a state of *hózhǫ́*.

Harmony is frequently the translation of *hózhǫ́*, which stresses the importance of "communion relationships," but Lamphere suggests that "manipulative relationships" are more characteristic of man-to-god transactions.

The myth which belongs to each chant and which validates its content (telling, as we say, of the incidents whereby the ritual procedures are acquired by the *diyin dine'e* and later transferred to the *nahokaa dine'e*) is said to be an aid to analyzing the ritual in three ways: it identifies the major supernaturals symbolized in the chant, it helps interpret the meaning of the song groups which accompany the ritual, and it explains the origin and significance of objects used during the ritual (Lamphere 1969). Particular supernaturals and objects can be traced to the accompanying myths; however, a Navajo chant is not a re-enactment of the myth story but has a structure of its own.

The chant setting corresponds to a "map" of the Navajo universe. The circular horizon, the two sexes, the four directions, the four colors, and the clockwise movement of the sun are the Navajo distinctions basic to the cosmological scheme. This is the scheme replicated in the chant setting.

Chant activities have implications beyond their use in communicating the structure of the natural/supernatural world; it is important to view the way in which they transform the patient's body state and his relation to the *diyin dine'e*. The four concepts *hózhxǫ́*, *hózhǫ́*, *diyin* and *'antí* (to act or do) summarize Navajo ritual action. The purpose of a chant is to counteract the "action against" the patient *('antí)* and remove ugly conditions *(hózhxǫ́)* and to produce immunity by making the patient *diyin* and thus create pleasant conditions *(hózhǫ́)*. Necessary to this process are the ritual objects used during the chant (Lamphere 1969).

For ritual objects, materials from the natural world are combined in ways specified by the chant myth so that objects associated with the *diyin dine'e* are produced. The same color and sex distinctions which characterize the cosmological scheme are also prominent in the materials used to construct an item and to associate it with a particular supernatural.

During the chant, ritual objects are combined with several kinds of ritual actions: (1) *prestations* from the patient to the supernaturals, (2) actions of *incorporation* which are directed to the patient's body and which identify the patient with the supernaturals, and (3) actions of *removal* which also involve the patient's body and which rid it of ugly conditions (Lamphere 1969).

If a prayer stick, a common ritual object, is presented correctly to the appropriate supernatural, he is *compelled* to aid the patient. In return for the correct prestation, the immunity producing quality of ritual objects and actions is ensured.

In addition to obtaining aid from the supernaturals by the presentation of the prayer stick, much ritual action associates the patient's body with the supernaturals by applying objects externally and administering medicines internally. The symbolism of identification by incorporation (both through "applying to" or "taking in") is contrasted with the symbolism of removal or "taking out" substances which are making the patient sick. The aim of "inward directed" activities is to identify the patient with the supernatural and to make him sacred. Bringing sacred objects derived from the supernaturals into direct contact with the patient's body sanctifies him (makes him *diyin*).

After applying sacred objects to the patient, the singer gives a call to each of the four cardinal directions which directs the attention of the supernaturals to the fact that the patient is being sanctified. Calling and motioning dramatize the reciprocal part of this transaction—they symbolize that the supernaturals are reacting by sanctifying the patient and making him immune. The patient's body is involved both externally and internally, whether the action is directed towards sanctification or towards removing agents which act against the patient.

The three themes noted by Lamphere of prestation, identification, and removal are repeated over and over during the entire chant. They recur in each sub-ceremony, in each prayer, and in each song set. However, one of these themes may be dominant or emphasized in a particular sub-ceremony. During the prayer stick ceremony, prestations are important; during the sweat and emetic ceremony, the removal of *hózhxǫ́* is crucial, and during a sand painting ceremony the identification of the patient with the *diyin* is the focus of effort.

There are many sand paintings used in certain chants. The singer can select among several appropriate to a particular day. Likewise, as we have seen, for the kind of ritual objects included, the duration of the ceremony, even which major segments from different "Ways," are all selected in substantially *ad hoc* fashion in response to the presumed etiology of the malady and the native definition of the current situation. The meaning of the various symbols and groups of symbols, I contend, is in large measure their effect in action. The choices made by ritual participants are *indexical* of a particular type of ritual and of a particular relationship with the supernatural. Their primary "meaning" is the *kind* of relationship specified for this occasion; they are indexical of cultural definitions of situations. There are dominant themes and sub-themes for each branch, segment, or unit of ritual. The definition of which meaning is paramount is a function of the *ritual process* which provides a relevant context for disambiguating among possible meanings of what are essentially multi-vocal symbols, selecting dominant meanings for this occasion, and combining them into a configuration. In addition, the symbols and symbolic actions of the chanter with respect to the patient *create a state of affairs;* effect a transformation of the patient's bodily state as they are enacted, and thus have *illocutionary force* as a dimension of their meaning.

Lamphere expands Leach's suggestion that rituals communicate information about the natural/supernatural world and suggests that Navajo ritual also provides a means for manipulating relationships within this structured universe. For her, the communication of a static cosmological model is only one aspect of Navajo ritual; transformation of the patient's relation to the supernaturals and changes in his body state are also crucial. (Note that this communication model is not at variance with my approach. The total meanings, use, and function of ritual symbols, taken together, do "communicate" models of the cosmos. But the propositional, semantic-feature meanings of the ritual symbols alone do not, indeed, in a sense, can not "communicate" information.)

Lamphere's discussion of identification and removal she considers to provide an interpretation of symbols which differs from Turner's analysis. In contrast with Ndembu, there is little stress in Navajo ritual on body emission of internal substances (for example, blood, milk, semen, urine, and feces). The body emissions which are important (vomit and sweat) are representative of something external and ugly which has been taken into the body and which must be removed. Objects which are simultaneously natural and supernatural are projected into or on the body rather than concepts derived from body states being projected into the natural or supernatural world.

To summarize, Lamphere suggests that Navajos derive the meanings of their symbols from their model of the natural-supernatural world and not from bodily experiences. She concludes: "In the Navajo case, it seems most appropriate to analyze chants as a system of symbolic objects and actions which both express cosmology and provide a means of dealing with individual illness through symbolic manipulation of man-to-god relationships and the patient's body state."

My first discussion was of Navajo cosmology and categorization. Then within the cosmological sphere I narrowed the focus to apprehend the way symbolic elements of Navajo religion are systematically interrelated into a ramified scheme in ritual practice. Now I wish to specify still more tightly and present a brief account of a single basic unit or "molecule" of specific ritual structure (albeit one that presumes the status of being "central," "core," "key," or "dominant" for Navajo culture), a ritual symbol. This symbol is an element of ritual language, a phrase discussed at length by Witherspoon, known as 'sa'ah naaghai bik'eh hózhǫ' (SNBH). For Witherspoon, this symbol is the central concept of Navajo world view (Witherspoon n.d.). His analysis engrosses us in a detailed discussion of Navajo linguistics which I will dispense with, yet his conclusions are helpful.

As we have seen, "restoration" is a particularly important concept in understanding the nature and purpose of curing rites. Illness occurs when the normal harmony of one's world becomes disrupted, and curing rites are designed to restore that harmony and, by doing so, to restore the health of the patient.

For Navajo, words, like thoughts, are considered to have creative power. In mythology things came into being or happened as people thought or talked about them. Repeating something four times will cause it to occur. A request made four times cannot easily be denied. At the end of each major portion of a ceremonial prayer, the phrase hózhǫ́ náhasdlį́į́ (roughly, hózhǫ́ 'it is becoming') is repeated four times. Lines in prayers and songs are repeated four times, and the rite itself is supposed to be done four times to be really effective. This is necessary to ensure "closure" or the conclusion of a restoration. Linguistically, the phrase SNBH has etymological implications of repetitive restoration or concluding closure. The world with which the patient must be harmonized operates, on a daily and yearly basis, on a four-fold cycle. *'Hózhǫ́ji'* or the state of being *hózhǫ́*, accomplished by harmonious, "closure" activities, is defined by Reichard as perfection as far as it is attainable by man; it represents the end to which not only men but also the Supernaturals and Time and Motion, institutions and behavior, strive (Reichard 1950).

Witherspoon, following Wyman (1970), says that in the explicit belief of the Navajo, *Sa'ah Naaghai* and *Bik'eh hózhǫ́* are personified as two beings who form an inseparable pair. When they arose out of First Man's medicine bundle, they were said to be without equal in their beauty and radiance. Their existence would always be manifested in the power of the earth to reproduce and sustain life.

The power of Changing Woman to restore her youth and of the earth to rejuvenate each spring comes from *SN*, who represents the inner form of the earth, and *BH*, the outer form, which is found in the beauty and happiness of plants, lakes, trees, and mountains. *SN* is also said to represent thought, while *BH* represents speech. Thus thought is the inner form and speech, the outer (Witherspoon n.d.).

SN and *BH* for Witherspoon are the central animating power of the universe, and, as such, they produce a world described as *hózhǫ́*, the ideal environment of beauty, harmony, and happiness. All living beings, including the earth, have inner and outer forms, and to achieve well-being these inner forms must harmonize and unify with *BH*. The desirable conditions of *SNBH* are disturbed and disrupted by improper or inastute contact with things that are defined as dangerous, and by the evil deeds of others. Curing rites re-enact the creation of the world through myth, song, prayer, and drama, and place the patient in this recreated world, closely identifying him with the good and power of various deities. In Kluckhohn's words, these deities are "charged with positive spiritual electricity" (1968). Ritual identification with them neutralizes the contaminating effect of dangerous things or evil deeds, and through symbols like the phrase *SNBH* restores one to the good and harmony of *hózhǫ́*. Witherspoon concludes by claiming that "the Holy People are supernaturals just because of their closeness to this 'power source' and because of their knowledge of the 'ways' (rituals) to connect and to harmonize with this central power source of *SNBH*."

A concern with the process of healing, ideally operating on both the physical and mental aspects of a person, should, I believe, prove to be a fruitful locus for the development of an anthropological approach to symbols. The patient in a rite becomes a nexus of intersection of the major theoretical components of human social life. Through the *societal relations* of community focus and interaction, *cultural symbolic structures* are brought to bear in an effort to transform *individual, subjective experience* and *biological states*. Symbols and symbolic usage mediate between the social and the individual, establishing an interface between them as well as being internalized into the constitution of the individual's action. They express relations between social beings and create new ones, being what Geertz and Kluckhohn and Kroeber call both "models of" and "models for" reality.

Curing rites we regard as symbolic manipulations and transformations of subjective experience. The meaning of the symbols employed in such rites must include their role in this manipulation; in the *act* of change and the re-ordering or creation of experience, not just their semantic components or definitional equations, which only give us the relationship between one symbol type in a system and other symbols within the same system. Definition of referential content is always circular within a system (though admittedly ultimately predicated on a *deictic* relationship with some existent referent); we must find a way to "open" meaning, to connect it on one hand with social circumstances of use through indexicality and, on the other, to pragmatic dimensions of use through function and illocutionary force. Symbols and their meanings are creating another nature, the longed-for lands where human values, morality and desires are momentarily realized.

Kaplan and Johnson in their article "The Social Meaning of Navajo Psychopathology and Psychotherapy" have approached the healing of "mental illness," an analysis which, though taking account of societal interaction of the community with the patient, nevertheless remains remarkably "psychological" in its analytic framework. They do not develop a general notion of the cultural meaning and use of the symbols of healing. Though, as they note, mental illness is not clearly distinguished in Navajo etiology from diseases in general, they begin by stating that where some conception of the etiology of psychopathology exists in a culture, therapeutic processes will be organized on the basis of this conception. As well, the illnesses themselves as they are subjectively experienced, will be oriented to and shaped by these conceptions.

As we have seen, all natural phenomena have an outer form and an inner form that exists independently of its outer shell and controls it. "That-which-stands within" human beings is the "wind soul." These are seven: white wind, blue wind, yellow wind, dark wind, small wind, left-handed wind and glossy-wind. Certain combinations or relationships of them determine personal characteristics. Certain events may change the deployment of the winds and so influence a person's character (Haile 1943). (We should note here a general congruence between Navajo conceptions of personality and the structure of the myth and ritual system.)

Kaplan and Johnson regard the most characteristic mental illnesses as having as their central element abdication of ego-control, effected by a notion of possession by an alien wind. Mental illness is usually the dire consequence of culturally undesirable behavior, such as incest. However, such diverse activities as having certain contact with bear, deer, or coyote (the breath of a bear being particularly dangerous), burning certain animals, or association with lightning strikes all may result in illness. The most potent causes, however, are those connected with witchcraft.

The main patterns of psychopathology are moth sickness, ghost sickness, and what they term crazy violence, generally associated with drunken behavior. In moth sickness, the specific causal agent of crazy behavior is a moth, crawling inside the head between the eyes. The moth grows bigger and bigger and flys around more and more violently, while the victim's behavior follows suit. In the end, the victim circles closer and closer to a fire and finally throws himself in. In moth sickness, the individual has committed a social wrong and suffers for it. The "treatment" involves repentance and promises not to transgress again. Kaplan and Johnson regard the illness, as a dramatic warning of transgression, as "part of the socialization apparatus of the society" (1964). In ghost sickness, the patient is a victim of the malevolence of others. In the curing process, the community is said to range itself on the side of the victim and to muster its strength for his support. For a patient to be helped, Kaplan and Johnson contend, he need only place himself within the curing system, which, once set in motion, proceeds almost automatically. Navajo mental illness they describe as "hysterical," and consider the curing practices, being themselves "hysterical," to be the most rational approach to cure.

Kluckhohn and Leighton have compared the singer's task in such cures to that of memorizing a Wagnerian opera (presumably also "hysterical"), including orchestral score, every vocal part, all details of the settings, stage business, and each requirement of costume (1962). Prayers and songs are used to invoke the deities, while sand paintings capture power and bring it nearer to the patient. The purification rituals of emetic, sweating, and continence help to prepare the patient to receive the benefit of the ceremony. The patient remains passive throughout, but is expected to have an attitude of acceptance and to focus his attention on the ceremony.

Kaplan and Johnson regard the effectiveness of curing ceremonies to reside in two processes. One of them is "suggestion" (whatever that could mean in a theory of symbolic behavior—it is left unanalyzed); the other, reaffirmation of the solidarity of the community and indeed the whole pantheon of Navajo deities with the patient. They are considered to reinforce each other psychologically.

The failings of the Kaplan and Johnson article lie principally in the fact that their analysis rests in no way on native categorization of disease and its cure. The psychoanalytic terminology and the notion of "etiology" are certainly suspect analytic constructs for understanding Navajo practice. As well, they apparently neglect the powerful role of symbols in ordering the meaning of disease and health that constitutes the real and only experience of a cultural actor. It is a tenet of cultural anthropology as I understand it that perception and evaluation are integrated. The symbolic language of a ritual performance alters and reorders the perception of a patient's experience and is thus capable of transfiguring the meaning of that experience. Lévi-Strauss in his essay "The Effectiveness of Symbols," based on a theory of individual interaction with cultural symbolic systems, notes the power of this ritual efficacy (1963). This material is elaborated on and generalized in Nancy Munn's "The Effectiveness of Symbols in Murngin Rite and Myth" (1969), which advocates an approach consonant with the Navajo ceremonial practice detailed here, invoking identification of the patient with mythic personae and a subsequent "objectification" of his experience through symbolic societal forms.

For Lévi-Strauss, the effectiveness of symbols consists in an "inductive property," by which formally homologous structures are related to one another. The primacy of "experience" and "action," developed from the employment of symbols, points out well the necessity for going beyond "sense and reference" to understand the meaning of the symbols in a healing process.

Nancy Munn's concern is with collective symbolic forms as instruments for transforming subjective experience. She suggests that rituals affect subjective experience by transforming the myth or "language" for these experiences. For her, a myth-ritual complex can function as a mechanism for social control through its provision of an external, regulatory system for states of bodily feeling. "Naming power" is significant in that it can "create" the world through imposing upon it a social identity, by socially objectifying it and giving it a power of its own. "Thus they can change the merely 'lived-in-world' into the 'thought-about-world'" (Munn 1969). Munn views the operation which a rite performs upon a myth from the perspective of the ritual process. The articulation of the myth and rite is said to be pivoted through the equation of actors with myth protagonists, and so of certain key myth events with the happenings on the ceremonial ground. She views the rite as a kind of electrical transformer through which currents of bodily destruction (themes found in the specific Murngin myth) are converted into currents of bodily health.

Munn's main contribution is to develop a diagram of the relationship between narrative code and a system of ritual action. The diagram describes a circuit from the subjective experience of an individual ego through the objectification of collective codes (myth codes) and back into individual experience via the social action of the rituals in which ego is identified with the persons in the myth. This circuit defines a symbolic space: it refers to the relative symbolic distance between ego (his subjective experience) and the persons and events of a narrative code. This "objectivization" of ego's experience is a requisite part of the mechanism for reformulating experience which is developed through the myth-ritual complex. She concludes with a statement pertinent to our purposes here:

The "effectiveness" of symbol systems derives in part from the fact that they are so structured as to provide the means for adjusting interior experience through external, societal forms. Analyses of symbolic structure should not simply be directed at abstracting underlying conceptual systems, *but should be concerned with symbols as mechanisms which regulate the orientations of actors to each other and to common situations.* [Emphasis added.]

Munn's remarks have striking applicability in the Navajo case, where elaborate attempts are made to "identify" the patient with the Holy people of myth and song. In the sand-painting phase, the patient is brought into direct physical contact with a representation of a *diyin dine'e* and is said to be directly empowered by him. In the songs of identification, the patient appears to acquire the attributes of mythic personae and to journey with them through mythic episodes. This is accomplished in every instance by a symbolic manipulation that is illocutionary in force. The meaning of this symbolism lies in the creation of new experience for the patient, the timeless experience of the *diyin dine'e.*

At this point I shall summarize some of the crucial ideas relevant to Navajo ritual practice. Reichard claims that Navajo religion is a synthetic whole in which each element involves an understanding of many other elements and their combinations into properties, rites, beliefs, and results (Reichard 1944). In Navajo categorization, there is a belief in the essential unity of all things which causes the association of diverse elements into classes on the basis of similarity of function. The associations are so extensive and range over such "disparate significata" that the categorizations are remarkably fluid. The categories operate according to what Reichard calls a "law of complements": if it includes something, it must also include its opposite. The categories are based on "inclusion," founded on similarity of function, done with such facility that it is often hard to determine the boundaries (indeed it seems to require a specific context for a category to be defined at all). The ceremonial system is treated as a whole which functions in different ways, the emphasis to depend on the circumstances. She states, "Within it is a huge compilation of elements from which any innovator may select and combine depending on his desired emphasis." ("Desired emphasis" is another unexamined term which should, I believe, interrelate with social factors of the situation of use.) Each myth includes incipient references to elements of all myths. A particular element appears as an independent unit of ceremony only for a specific emphasis or function; but it symbolically connotes all others in an interlocking fashion.

According to Reichard, the universe is not divided fundamentally into good versus evil. Rather, there is an elemental force or power, and the presence of *control* of that power is the difference between good and evil; ultimately, this depends on knowledge, for *control is*

ritual. Originally, the world was neutral, then some things allied with evil, so that today there is good, evil, and holy, which is some power manipulated for good. It takes more effort and knowledge to drive out evil than to attract good, but even evil can be sanctified by persuasion for a specific event, though it is dangerous to do so. Ritual causes an identification of the person afflicted with the powers that can cure him. To identify with a deity and his symbols is to acquire his powers, thus one may identify with a dangerous or evil deity in order to dissipate its power. Evil can be invoked and brought under control by ritualistic *compulsion*. It yields to compulsion and can work good (Reichard 1944). The implied mechanism of this compulsion is perhaps misleading. It seems more to be the case that when certain acts are performed, certain consequences must follow because they are returning to the way things *must be;* the *Way* that things are, not just what they ought to be; for human values are just part of the larger harmonious working of all life. This compulsion is wrought symbolically (as performatives, creating a world).

The Navajo are self-conscious about words and their combinations. A text of the origin legend gives "one word" as the name of the original state of the universe (which evidently consisted of water and darkness). Reichard claims that they believe thought is equivalent to or has the same potentiality as word. To this they also add deed. One should not try to differentiate reality along these axes, since they are an integrated unity. Thought may be a compulsive force even as symbol is, but words add to the force. With words, the result is prayer, a fully developed literary form that is formulaic in the sense that it is exacting and functions properly because of completeness and order. Within a defined unit of prayer, one cannot alter the order of the elements without extreme danger. Its effect is a result of compulsion by exactness of word. Reichard regards Navajo prayer as "an unending system of symbolic associations which can in no way be considered 'free' since they are too orderly and depend on decree. Besides the mental effort involved in the ritual there is the emotional pressure which ensues from the dictum that a single mistake not only renders the prayer void, but may bring upon the one praying the wrath, instead of the blessing, of the being implored." Prayer, I believe, is a highly significant special case of ritual language. Prayer is a constant, or fixed, reference point, in the shifting pattern of meanings in the whole ceremonial complex and, as such, is of central importance for Navajo ritual process. It will remain undeveloped here, but the eventual model of Navajo ceremonial towards which I am working is analogous in some features to a flow chart in which major symbols stand at the inception of the process and establish themes which prevail over the whole structure. There are subsequently "nodes" along "pathways" where medial symbols establish subritual themes, holding for the duration of specific episodes yet providing a context for all other symbols in the structure, all occurring in the ritual's processual, branching progression to some socially defined end.

For all the symbolic systematicity apparent in the Navajo cosmos, some problems remain to be worked out. For instance, do all the disparate media in which ritual meaning is expressed "say the same things"? Is there an effective theoretical way to establish the "translation" of meanings into different media? To do so, we would have to postulate a "meta-structure" of cultural action and rules of transformation. At least, we should be able to expect the various symbols to be altered in patterns, so long as the same structured relationship between certain symbolic elements is constant. Reichard seems to support such an interpretation (see the chart, Reichard 1945).

For instance, in research on a performance of the Male Shooting Chant it was determined that a regular, four-fold progression of verbal elements in songs, altering tense and aspect of verbs to move from an inceptive to a completed state for the patient, was paralleled by a congruent progression in the non-verbal symbolism. In dance, placement of sacred objects, relationship of patient to depicted mythic personae, and disposal of emesis, a four-fold symbolic structure was established in iconic relationship to the verbal symbolism. Further research along this line seems fruitful but requires elaboration of our notion of ritual meaning to enable us to go beyond the mere listing of concordances.

TWELVE

The "Wife" Who "Goes Out" Like a Man Reinterpretation of a Clackamas Chinook Myth

Dell H. Hymes

This paper by the noted anthropologist and linguist Dell Hymes is best understood in the context of the theory of myth advanced by Claude Lévi-Strauss. In a paper which has become a classic, "The Structural Study of Myth" (in *Structural Anthropology,* 1963), Lévi-Strauss uses some of the technical apparatus of de Saussure's structural linguistics to isolate cognitive oppositions—for example, between distance or closeness of kinship—which, taken together, reveal the cultural framework in which the myth takes place.

Or so Lévi-Strauss argues. Hymes shows in this paper, however, that a single myth cannot be taken to reveal the entire framework on which it rests: rather, a single myth is part of a set *(genre)* which constitutes an arena of choice for the narrator; and the individual myth becomes more fully comprehensible in this context. Much more importantly, however, the cultural framework to which the myth refers is seen as more complex and much less a static, cognitive thing, in Hymes's view; and the flexibility of myth is also shown: because a story is part of a set, and a particular story represents—to the audience as well as the speaker—a choice among possible statements, it is also *active:* not merely a passive reflection (or representation) of a cognitive field. Unfortunately, the limited contextual information we have from a culture with no living members limits the understanding of the range and nature of this active nature of story-telling we can get from Hymes's paper; but it provides an important and instructive methodological example.

I SHALL TAKE UP IN TURN the background of the paper; its methodological significance; a synopsis of the myth in question; the first interpretation of the myth; a reinterpretation of the myth; some further implications of the reinterpretation including application of the mode of analysis developed by Lévi-Strauss; and make a concluding remark.[1]

Reprinted by permission from *Essays in Semiotics,* Julia Kristeva, ed. (The Hague: Mouton, 1971), pp. 296–326.

Background

Melville Jacobs has given us one of the handful of major contributions to our knowledge and understanding of the literatures of the Indians of North America. The quality of the texts he so fortunately rescued a few months before the death of the last capable informant, and the quality of the insight and interpretation he has provided for them, make his series of monographs of Clackamas Chinook outstanding (Jacobs 1958, 1959a, 1959b, 1960). Perhaps no one can appreciate his contribution more than one who, like myself, also works with Chinookan materials. The field of Chinookan studies has engaged the energies of Franz Boas and Edward Sapir; within it Jacobs' accomplishment is the richest for oral literature, one which redounds to the value of the rest.

In the study of written literatures the work of interpretation is never complete. Major texts are regarded, not as closed, but as open to new insight and understanding. The case should be the same for aboriginal literatures. The significance of a body of work such as the Clackamas series will increase as others come to it and keep it vital by building on the basic contribution. Indeed, a secondary literature on Clackamas has already begun (Scharbach 1962). This paper adds to it by reinterpreting a particular Clackamas myth, "Seal and Her Younger Brother Dwelt There," published in *Clackamas Chinook Texts, Part II* (Jacobs 1959a:340–41, #37 in the collection), and first interpreted in *The People are Coming Soon* (Jacobs 1960:238–42).

Jacobs himself has remarked that the Clackamas myths are susceptible of a plurality of interpretations (personal communication). In keeping with that spirit, I wish to avoid the appearance of personal criticism that recurrent use of personal names and pronouns can suggest, and so shall generally refer simply to the "first interpretation" and the "second interpretation."

My title calls attention to an actor in the myth, the significance of whose role is a central difference between the two interpretations. The Chinookan idiom on which the title is based is explained in note two below; it is adapted to identify her because she is given no name in the myth itself.

Methodological Remarks

The two interpretations are alike in being philological in basis and structural in aim. Since the narrator of the myth and all other participants in Clackamas culture are dead, we cannot collect other variants, interrogate, experiment. Access to the form and meaning of the myth is only through a finite corpus of words; but both Jacobs and I believe it possible to bring to bear a body of knowledge and method that enables one to discern in the words a valid structure.

In practice the two interpretations differ. The first can be said to plunge to the heart of what is taken as the psychosocial core of the myth, and to view its structure as unfolding from that vantage point. The second does not discover an import for the myth until a series of lines of evidence as to its structure have been assembled.

The first interpretation might thus be said to practice philology in the spirit of Leo Spitzer's "philological circle" (Spitzer 1948:18–20), but that would not accurately distinguish it from the second. Either approach can hope to find a motivational core from which the whole might be satisfactorily viewed, and both should enjoin what good philological practice always entails: close reading of the verbal action as it develops sentence by sentence in the original text, and interpretation based on using cumulatively all there is to use, as to the significance of details, and as to the situation which implicitly poses the question to which the text is to be regarded as a strategic or stylized answer (Burke 1957: 3). The effective difference lies in the greater temptation to the first approach to take a shortcut, to assume that a purportedly universal theory, be it psychoanalytical (as in the present case), dialectical, or whatever, can go straight to the heart of a myth before having considered its place in a genre structurally defined and functionally integrated in ways perhaps particular to the culture in question.

In sum, the second interpretation undertakes philology in the spirit of the structural ethnography developed by Goodenough (1956, 1957), Conklin (1964), Frake (1962), and others (for discussion of other implications of such ethnography, cf. Hymes 1964a, 1964b, 1965a). One is asked to regard the study of a verbal genre as of a kind with the ethnographic study of kinship, residence rules, diagnosis of disease, firewood, or wedding ceremonies. One assumes that there is a native system to be discovered; that what is identified as the same genre, e.g., "myth," ethnologically (cross-culturally) may differ significantly in structural characteristics and functional role ethnographically (within individual cultures); that one thus must formulate a theory of the special case, defining a genre in terms of features and relationships valid for the individual culture; and that the meanings and uses of individual texts are to be interpreted in the light of the formal features and relations found for the native genre.

Put otherwise, one assumes that persons growing up in the community in question acquire a grasp of the structures and functions of the genre, such that they are able to judge instances as appropriate or inappropriate, not only in terms of overt formal features ("surface structure"), but also in terms of underlying relations ("deep structure"). One assumes that the structural analysis of a genre, like other structural ethnography, is in principle predictive (see Goodenough 1957). That such an approach is correct, that participants in a culture do in fact have the ability to use an implicit knowledge of genre structure, is attested by the assimilation of new materials, either through innovation (I take the Kathlamet Chinook "Myth of the Sun" to be a late Chinookan instance) or diffusion (see Dundes 1963). The point seems obvious, but it is important to stress it, because the nature of the usual emphasis in folklore research upon the traditional has cost heavily. (I pass by the question as to whether the object of folkloristic study should be defined as traditional material at all; for one aspect of the question see Hymes 1962).

Folklorists have commonly identified their object of study, traditional material, as a matter of texts, not of underlying rules. The frequent consequence has been that the very material which would decisively test a structural analysis has been disregarded. The occurrence of a reworked European tale in an Indian pueblo (say, *Beowulf*) may evoke amusement, or embarrassment, if one thinks of one's goal as autochthonous texts. If one thinks of one's goal as natively valid rules, such a case may be an invaluable opportunity to verify the principles of the native genre through an instance of their productivity. In one striking case, a collector discovered that some of his tapes represented songs his informant had herself composed to keep him working with her. The songs had seemed perfectly in keeping with all the others obtained from her; only when a later check found them to have no counterparts in other collections from the region was their status suspected. Confronted with the discrepancy, the informant confessed. Because the material (as text) was "non-traditional," the collector destroyed it. What he destroyed was from the standpoint of a structural ethnography the most valuable portion of his work: spontaneous evidence of the productivity of the rules of the genre. (I am indebted for this example to my colleague Kenneth Goldstein.)

In short, if structural analysis of myth, and of folklore generally, is to keep pace with ethnographic and linguistic theory, it must attempt to achieve what Chomsky (1964:923–25) has recently called "descriptive adequacy"; that is, to give a correct account of the implicit knowledge of the members of the culture competent in the genre, and to specify the observed texts in terms of underlying formal regularities.

The highest level of adequacy designated by Chomsky would be that of "explanatory adequacy." Adapted to the study of folklore, the notion would call for a concern with the capacities of persons to acquire a productive, theory-like grasp of genres, and to employ that grasp, that implicit sense of rules and appropriateness in judging performances and instances, in adapting them to social and personal needs, and in handling novel materials. In the sphere of linguistics Chomsky, Lenneberg, and others consider explanatory adequacy to involve innate, species-specific capacities of human beings, which entail quite specific universals of grammatical structure. In the sphere of folklore the capacities are no doubt derived from innate abilities, and the work of Lévi-Strauss would seem to point directly to what some of them might be; such innate abilities, however, are almost certainly not specific to folklore. My concern here is first of all with "descriptive adequacy," that is, with the culturally specific form taken by general capacities with respect to folkloristic genres through participation in a given community. It is at the level of "descriptive adequacy" that the study of folklore can now most profitably join with the recent parallel developments in structural linguistics and structural ethnography. (The concept of descriptive adequacy in linguistics is quite analogous to Goodenough's formulation [1957] of the criterion for adequate ethnographic description; cf. Hymes 1964a:10, 16–17, and especially 30–31).

Synopsis of the Myth

Of the myth Jacobs (1960:238) says aptly: "A remarkable quantity of expressive content is compacted in this short horror drama of an unnamed woman who comes to Seal Woman's younger brother."

This myth has a short prologue and three short scenes. The prologue introduces the actors as compresent in one setting. I present the myth in the form of a revised translation which differs from that in Jacobs (1959a:340–41) in its division into segments and in some points of verbal detail. The revised division into segments defines sharply the structure of the content (prologue, first scene, second scene, climax, denouement), but it has not been made in terms of content alone. Rather, considerations of content have been integrated with what are taken to be formal segment markers, that is, recurrent initial and final elements. The segment initial and segment final elements of the prologue and first two scenes have identical or partially identical form: "They lived there (. . .)", "Don't say that! (. . .)". The climax and denouement are marked most saliently by final elements of parallel content: "She screamed," "She wept," "She kept saying that," "The girl wept."

Points of verbal detail are revised partly in the light of grammatical and lexical analysis, aided by Wishram data. Such points are supported in footnotes. Other revisions are for the sake of following the Clackamas text as exactly as possible in form.

A later re-reading of the translation (ignoring the footnotes) may integrate the structures and effects analyzed separately in the paper.

Seal (and) Her Younger Brother Lived There[2]

They lived there, Seal, her daughter, her younger brother. I do not know when it was, but now a woman got to Seal's younger brother.

They lived there. They would go outside in the evening.[3] The girl would say, she would tell her mother, "Mother! There is something different about my uncle's wife. It sounds like a man when she 'goes out.'[4] "Don't say that! (She is) your uncle's[5] wife!"

They lived there like that for a long long time. They would "go out"[6] in the evening. And then she would tell her, "Mother! There is something different about my uncle's wife. When she 'goes out', it sound like a man." "Don't say that!"

Her uncle and his wife would "lie together" in bed.[7] Some time afterwards the two of them "lay" close to the fire, they "lay" close beside each other.[8] I do not know what time of night it was, but something dripped on her face. She shook her mother. She told her, "Mother! Something dripped on my face." "Hm . . . Don't say that. Your uncle (and his wife) are 'going.'"[9]

Presently then again she heard something dripping down. She told her, "Mother! Something is dripping, I hear something." "Don't say that. Your uncle (and his wife) are 'going.'"

The girl got up, she fixed the fire, she lit pitch, she looked where the two were lying.[10] Oh! Oh! She raised her light to it.[11] In his bed[12] her uncle's neck was cut. He was dead. She screamed.

She told her mother, "I told you something was dripping. You told me, Don't say that. They are 'going.' I had told you[13] there was something different about my uncle's wife. When she 'goes out,' it sounds like a man when she urinates. You told me, 'Don't say that!'" She wept.

Seal said, "Younger brother! My younger brother! They (his house posts) are valuable standing there.[14] My younger brother!" She kept saying that.[15]

But the girl herself wept. She said, "I tried in vain to tell you. My uncle's wife sounds like a man when she urinates, not like a woman. You told me, Don't say that! Oh oh my uncle!" The girl wept.

Now I remember only that far.[16]

First Interpretation

Most aspects of the myth are noticed in the interpretative discussion (Jacobs 1960:238–42), but the focus of attention can be said to be upon three themes. These are the implications of (1) transvestitism and "the horror reaction to homosexuals" (Jacobs 1960:239); (2) the "wife" and the "society's tense feelings about females" (including the girl) (Jacobs 1960:241); (3) tensions, and norms of conduct, among in-laws. The analysis concludes:

The myth is, in short, a drama whose nightmarish horror theme, murder of one's own kin by a sexually aberrant person who is an in-law, causes profound fear and revulsion as well as deep sympathy. The tension around in-laws is basic to the plot. Several implied moral lessons (one should not marry a wife in such a manner; one should not speak disparagingly of in-laws and others' sexual intimacy; one should heed one's daughter) somewhat relieve the awfulness of conflict with dangerous in-laws. (Jacobs 1960:242)

In terms of narrative action the fabric of the myth is said to be woven about the man and his shocking death (Jacobs 1960:239). The death itself is taken as motivated by the humiliation caused the "wife," who must avenge herself on a family whose daughter has cast aspersions upon her manner of urinating, that is (it is inferred) upon her sexuality (Jacobs 1960:241–2).

Form of the Myth

On this view of the basis of the plot one might expect murder to be followed by steps for revenge, as indeed commonly would have been the case in the aboriginal culture and as occurs in some other Clackamas myths (e.g., "Black Bear and Grizzly Woman and their Sons"). The absence of any indication of such steps in the final scene is suggested as one reason for thinking the present form of the myth to be truncated.

Significance of Actors

Little is said in the myth about any of the four actors (as is typical of Clackamas literature). Their nature and significance, on which the meaning of the myth turns, must be largely inferred from the action which symbolically manifests them in the text, from an understanding of the culture, and from assumptions with which one approaches all these. Having observed (1960:241) that "The drama provides no clear-cut delineations of characters," the first interpretation proceeds to find the significance of the three actors through their identification with social roles:

"Seal is nothing more than a mother and the older sister of the murdered man. He is only a rich gentleman who marries in a manner which occurred solely in the Myth Age and which symbolizes tensions between in-laws. The daughter is no more than a girl who possesses insight as do other girls, but she is not mature enough to know when to keep from saying things that might cause trouble with in-laws" (Jacobs 1960:241). The expressions "nothing more," "only," "no more" are in keeping with a view which subordinates all three actors in importance.

Seal's relative insignificance is further indicated in expressions such as "Seal does little more than . . ." (Jacobs 1960:241) and "all that Seal does in the myth as recorded is to . . ." (Jacobs 1960:241), as well as in the explanation, regarding the myth's Clackamas title, that "The only reason for naming Seal is to provide a convenient labeling of the myth" (Jacobs 1960:239).

The statement that the fabric of the myth is woven about the husband and his murder claims little place for him other than as a silent victim.

Seal's daughter receives more attention, but, as the preceding quotation has shown, essentially as a type labelled "youngest smartest," expressing underlying social tensions. Commenting on the girl as "youngest smartest", Jacobs suggests: "Chinooks appear to have thought, in effect, 'Set a young thief to catch an old thief!' Both are feminine! The society's tense feelings about females receive nice expression in this plot" (Jacobs 1960:241). With regard to her place in the narrative action, the daughter is regarded as having immaturely elicited the murder. Her conduct in the last scene is not discussed, except in the context of the speculation as to the absence of steps for revenge: "The daughter offers only, 'I warned you but you would not listen to me'" (Jacobs 1960:241).

The "wife" is interpreted most pointedly in terms of the projection of tensions and fears found to underlie the myth. The view of her and her importance is shown in the continuation of the passage about delineation of characters: "The murderess is both an anxiety-causing in-law and a female who hates. Such hate is symbolized by the murder. The cause of the hate is pointed to by the device of having her masquerade so as to appear feminine, while the sound of her urinating reveals masculinity . . ." (Jacobs 1960:241). (The sexual identification intended in the passage is unclear to me: the "wife" is referred to both as a female and as masquerading so as to appear feminine. Perhaps a hermaphrodite is envisaged.)

Clearly the "wife" is found to be the most significant actor. Of the rest, the girl seems to be most important, judging from the comment about her. The husband's role as victim might claim the next place for him. Seal is clearly considered less important than the "wife" and the girl, perhaps least important of all. This relative order of significance is confirmed by the order in which the actors are taken up in the passages quoted above; the discussion seems to proceed from least (Seal) to most significant (the "wife").

The first interpretation of the myth may be summarized as follows. The myth is in theme based on tensions concerning females and in-laws, expressed in terms of ambiguous and insulted sexuality. In plot its conflict is based on relations between in-laws; its climax is caused by the girl's rude speech to an in-law; and its denouement is incomplete from absence of steps towards revenge against in-laws. In significance the actors are first of all the "wife," then the girl, the husband, and Seal. Together these strands form a consistent whole; indeed, to a great extent they mutually imply each other.

Second Interpretation

The volume containing the first interpretation is self-sufficient, containing a plot summary with each analysis. Having read it, if one goes back to the Clackamas text, one is somewhat surprised. Each scene is actually a confrontation between Seal and the girl; the "wife" barely appears on stage, and has no lines whatever. Interpersonal tension is portrayed, not with regard to an in-law, but between two consanguineal relatives, a mother and daughter.

Such a discrepancy between interpretation and manifest verbal action gives pause. It need not, of course, be decisive. Myths have latent meanings not immediately given in surface structure. It ought to be possible, however, to specify the nature of the connection between the underlying and the manifest dimension of a myth; and it ought to be possible to do this in a way consistent with the nature of such connections in other myths of the same culture. To do this for the first interpretation does not seem possible. Rather, the various lines of evidence available combine to support a different interpretation of the focus of the myth, one for which the discrepancy with manifest structure does not arise, and one which is consistent with a provisional theory of the structuring of much of Chinookan myth as a whole.

Among the lines of evidence are the naming of actors in titles and myths; the structure of myth titles; the relation of myth titles to the body of a myth; the comparative evidence as to the tale type in question; verbal detail, particularly with regard to what is actually presented in Clackamas, overt expression of emotion, and a thread of imagery. In the use of the evidence there is a fundamental assumption that the genre embodies a coherent treatment of features and relations, so that parallels, contrasts, and covariation as between myths can be brought to bear.

In developing the second interpretation it will be best to reverse the order adopted for presenting the first, and to begin with questions of structure having to do with the nature of the actors, their roles and their relative import. Most of the evidence will be introduced in this connection. We shall then be able to reconsider the form of the myth, and some new dimensions of its underlying theme.

Titles and Named Actors

For the first interpretation, titles are to be explained by a need for unmistakeable identification of each myth; a particular title is chosen solely with an eye to mnemonic use and convenience of reference (Jacobs 1959b:258, 260; 1960:239). It is suggested that Seal is named in the title of the present myth because she is its only named actor, and because, there being no other myths in which she occurs that bear her name, no confusion could arise.

Such an approach assumes that facts as to names and titles are adventitiously,

not structurally, related to myths. One may indeed expect what is found to be important in a myth to be named and represented in its title. Thus Jacobs raises the question as to why the man, who with his murder is found to form the myth's fabric, is not named. If Seal is named and takes pride of place in the title, although an actor of no particular importance, then significance of role, so it would seem, can have nothing to do with the matter. A name is only a convenient peg on which to hang a story, the title only a convenient tag by which to recall it.

In contrast, I maintain that names and titles are structurally motivated, and give evidence of underlying relations implicitly grasped by the makers of the literature. To claim descriptive adequacy, an analysis must formulate a hypothesis that accounts for the facts as to a myth's names and titles. Such facts can disconfirm an interpretation.

This basis for this approach to Chinookan myths was developed first with regard to Kathlamet Chinook. The first insight had to do with the stem *-k'ani,* which occurs in the formal close of many Clackamas and Kathlamet myths, and which regularly occurs in Kathlamet myth titles together with the name of an actor. The aboriginal range of meaning of *-k'ani* is variously translatable into English as "myth; character; nature; customary traits, habits, ways." In effect,

. . . The title of a myth singles out from the set of supernatural dramatis personae one or two whose ways, innate nature *(-k'ani),* perhaps ultimate contribution to mankind, are to be defined by being exhibited in the action of the myth. The titled actor need not be the initiator of the myth's action, nor the protagonist. Often enough, the initiator or protagonist is an anonymous human . . . The title directs attention to the moral, rather than to the action, protagonist, or scene. In general, the telling of myths was an act of pedagogy, of cultural indoctrination, and it is in terms of this goal that the titles were selected. (Hymes 1959:143)

Generally the first or only named actor of two is the focus of the myth's attention.

If the Clackamas title "Seal Woman and her Younger Brother Dwelt There" is taken seriously in the way just indicated, the first interpretation is turned on its head. What had seemed the least important figure (Seal) becomes most important. Can such an interpretation actually be sustained? In point of fact, the title can be shown to be motivated in relation to the myth. Such a hypothesis makes coherent sense of the manifest structure of the myth, and of its place in a series of myths, leading to a new understanding of its theme. To show this we must reconsider the evidence as to the nature of the plot.

The Plot: The Girl's Culpability

We have seen that on the first interpretation the conflict central to the plot is one between in-laws, expressed by a climax (murder) caused by the girl's rude speech with regard to the "wife." In point of fact, the girl does not cause the murder.

Notice first that the girl's culpability must be localized in the first scene. In the second scene, the murder is already under way, if not complete. What she says is in response to evidence of the murder (the dripping); it cannot be its cause.

Notice second that the mother's response in both the first and second scenes is of closely parallel form. She replies, "ák'waška!" (Do not say that), followed by a phrase which begins with specification of "your uncle." (In the first scene it is "your-uncle his-wife," in the second, "your-uncle those-two-are-copulating-together"). The structural parallels suggest that both scenes make the same point, and that the focus of concern as to propriety in speech is in each case, not the "wife," but the uncle.

With regard to the first scene, the girl's culpability turns on the inference that her statements are heard by the "wife," and so provoke her to murder. If not heard, the statements could hardly provoke. Yet there is no evidence that the statements are heard by anyone ("wife" or uncle) other than the mother to whom they are explicitly addressed. That the audience for the girl's warnings is specifically the mother is indicated further by her remonstrance at the end of the myth: "I tried to tell *you* (my emphasis-D.H.) but in vain . . . You said to me . . ."

The text requires no inference other than that the mother shushes the daughter because one is not supposed to speak in such a way about matters related to one's uncle's private life. As noted, this is in fact what the mother does say: "Don't say that! Your uncle + X!" There is not, for example, a premonitory "Your uncle's wife will hear you," let alone a warning as to consequences of speaking so. In this connection consider the pattern of a myth and a tale in which a younger person is indeed warned not to say something, because bad consequences will befall ("Kušaydi and his older brother," Jacobs 1959a:354–55;

"A boy made bad weather," Jacobs 1959a:456). The identical shushing word (ák'waška!) is used as is used by Seal, *and* the bad consequences (which do occur) are stated in the warning. This partial identity and partial contrast indicate that bad consequences are *not* implicit in Seal's response.

Other facts are also at variance with interpretation of the girl as culprit. The motivation of the murder is not expressed in the text. The first interpretation comments that Clackamas would have rationalized the situation by blaming the girl (Jacobs 1960:241). Not only is there no reason to consider that the girl *could* have caused the murder, as we have seen, but also there is no reason to consider that the girl *need* have caused the murder.

First, murders are not necessarily motivated in Clackamas myths. They may be taken as expressions of the intrinsic character of an actor. Jacobs in fact observes that the "wife" acts as do dangerous, self-appointed wives who murder in other Clackamas myths (Jacobs 1960:241).

Second, the "wife" is in origin not a murderous transvestite or homosexual, but a trickster. The only known Northwest Coast parallel to the present myth consists of eight Tlingit, Haida, and Tsimshian versions involving the well-known figure of Raven (equivalent to Coyote in the Chinookan area). Boas (1916:692) comments as follows: "This tale occurs in a number of distinct forms. In the Tlingit group it leads up to the tale of how Raven kills the seal and eats it—an incident which is treated independently among the southern tribes." Boas notes that the Haida versions conclude with an account of how the true character of Raven is discovered (e.g., by his tail or gait; cf. Clackamas, sound of urination). A Tlingit version concluding with the killing of the husband (Seal) is abstracted as follows (Boas 1916:394):

Raven goes to visit the chief of the Seals. He assumes the shape of a woman and transforms a mink into a child. The chief's son marries her (Raven). The man goes out hunting, and on returning washes himself in the house. One day when he goes out, Raven pinches the child and makes it cry. The man hears it and returns at once. The woman remarks that this is an evil omen. At night she presses Mink on his mouth, and suffocates him; then she cries and wants him buried behind a point of land. She wails at the grave. Another man wants to marry her, and sees her sitting by the body and pecking at it. Then the people catch Raven, smoke him, and make him black.

References are given also by Thompson (1929:304, n. 109). Clearly the source of the story is a typical trickster tale in which the trickster assumes woman's form to seduce a victim. (The distribution of a cognate form of the story in the Eastern Woodlands suggests that the tale is an old one; there are possible parallels in Indic and Japanese traditions. I am indebted to Alan Dundes for these observations.)

Whether the "wife" in the Clackamas myth is still essentially a trickster, or has been assimilated implicitly to the role of ogre, "she" is entirely capable in Clackamas terms of compassing the death of her husband. No provocation is needed, and none is expressed.

Finally, the assignment of the girl to the "youngest smartest" type is justified precisely because she acts as do her parallels in other Chinookan myths, who sense that someone is a trickster and/or a danger. (Some of Jacobs' comments are to this effect.) It is contradictory and unparalleled to have "youngest smartest" responsible for tragedy in virtue of the very trait for which prized. In general, the girl's place in the myth simply is not that of a young person whose conduct has brought on catastrophe. When the Clackamas wish to make such a point in a story, they leave no doubt of it, as in "A boy made bad weather" (cited above), and other "Tales of transitional times" about children in the same collection.

The Plot: Seal's Culpability

It is not the girl, but Seal, whom the myth treats as culpable. Let us consider the most closely analogous myth in the Clackamas collection that of "Crawfish and her older sister (Seal)" (Jacobs 1959a:376–79, No. 43). There are a younger and an older woman; the younger woman is troublesome by talking too much about the wrong things; she brings a disaster upon herself and her sister by doing so; whe weeps; there is a speech of remonstrance. The differences, however, are instructive. Most important, the speech of remonstrance is made by, rather than to, Seal; and it is quite clear that the actor who receives the speech of remonstrance is taken as being in the wrong. If in the one case it is Crawfish, then in the myth being analyzed it is Seal.

Recall also the significance of the structure of titles. The myths under consideration are the only two whose titles focus on Seal and a younger woman. The myth whose title is "Crawfish and her older sister" clearly exhibits the consequences of acting as did Crawfish. "Seal and her younger brother dwelt there" must be taken as exhibiting the consequences of acting as did Seal. (Furthermore, the second person identi-fied in each title is one who suffers from the behavior of the named actor.)

The interpretation of the plot along these lines becomes especially clear when we see the situation of "Seal and her younger brother dwelt there" as part of a group of such situations in Clackamas myths. The trio of consanguineal relationships among actors, mother: mother's younger brother: mother's daughter, is in fact not isolated, but one of the recurrent patterns of relationship in Clackamas. It is found in three other myths, or a total of four of the forty-nine known to us. Let us consider the pertinent parts of the three additional myths in turn.

(a) "Grizzly Bear and Black Bear ran away with two girls" (Jacobs 1958:130–141, No. 14). The pertinent part (pp. 132–34) shows the trio and a dangerous spouse as well, this time a male (Grizzly). The wife he has obtained has born two children, first a girl, then a boy. Five times the mother and her daughter go rootdigging. Four times the girl urges her mother to hurry back home, but the mother will not do so; when they do return, the girl strikes her Grizzly brother and is stopped by the mother. The fifth time the girl forces the mother to return earlier, and proves (by forcing a still uneaten toe from the young Grizzly's mouth) that the Grizzlies, the younger one taking the lead, have killed and eaten the mother's five younger brothers, as each came in turn.

The myth as a whole has to do with complex relations between Grizzly nature and human identity, and the portion dealing with the consanguineal trio is not expressed in the title. The situation itself, however, is quite fully parallel to that of the Seal myth. The roles of the consanguineal trio relative to each other are quite the same, and there is no doubt but that the girl is correct in attempting to avert calamity, nor that the mother, by failing to respond, bears a responsibility for the deaths of her younger brothers. Indeed, as a direct parallel, this portion of the Grizzly myth might be said to clinch matters. There is something to be learned, however, by considering other myths as well.

(b) "Cock Robin, his older sister and his sister's daughter" (Jacobs 1959a:301–10, No. 31). The pertinent part (31A) shows only the consanguineal trio. The older sister instructs Cock Robin to bake roots for his niece (her daughter) when she cries; when the girl cries, he misrepeats the instructions to himself and bakes her instead, burning her to death. His sister returns to find him crying. He explains that he had done as told. She explains the actual instructions, and he replies that he had not comprehended.

Here the roles of the consanguineal trio relative to each other are changed. It is the younger brother who does not respond adequately to what is told, the older sister and mother who gives the information for dealing with a situation, and the daughter who suffers consequences. Such a change is extremely telling, however, for the structure of the title changes accordingly. The overt order, as between this myth and that of Seal, differs: here, younger brother, older sister, daughter; there, older sister, (daughter), younger brother. (The first sentence of the Seal myth introduces the actors with the daughter between the other two.) The functional order is the same: *Culpable actor : advising actor : victim.*

Thus, the two myths so far considered show one an exact parallel and one an exact covariation in support of the second interpretation of the role of Seal.

A Semantic Field of Myth Situations and Actors

The remaining myth having a situation involving the same consanguineal trio opens up a larger series, one which is in effect a small semantic field, or typology, of Clackamas myth situations and actors.

(c) The myth is "Blue Jay and his older sister" (Jacobs 1959a: 366–69, No. 41). Jacobs describes the latter part of the myth (which is a series of similar episodes) as garbled (the myth having been the first dictation taken from his informant), but the initial episode (41A), which is the only one showing the consanguineal trio as a whole, is clear. His older sister speaks to Blue Jay in jest. He responds as if the statement were an instruction, and copulates in the sweathouse with a corpse. The girl (his niece) hears him laughing and tells her mother. (Copulation is associated with laughter among the Indians of the area). Her mother considers the information, gives it a polite explanation, and cautions the girl not to go to the place (ak'wašga). The girl, noticing a foot sticking out from the sweathouse, goes to it anyway, pulls, and when the foot comes off, takes it to her mother. Blue Jay's older sister now runs, discloses the corpse inside the sweathouse, and tells Blue Jay to put it back, which he does.

The roles of the consanguineal trio relative to each other are the same as in the previous myth of Cock Robin, except for one notable fact: no injury is done to any of them (in particular, not to the girl). This myth might thus seem to count against, or be an exception to, the analysis given so far. The fact is that it, together with the other myths just discussed, is not an exception, but takes its place as a part of a larger set.

The existence of such a set was discovered by use of the method described by Lévi-Strauss (1963:16):

(1) define the phenomenon under study as a relation between two or more terms, real or supposed;
(2) construct a table of possible permutations between these terms;
(3) take this table as the general object of analysis . . .

The two terms from which the series is generated must obviously be defined in a way appropriate to the myth of Seal and her younger brother with which we have begun. If we consider the myth from the standpoint of Seal, she is seen to uphold a social norm (as to propriety of speech) at the expense of heeding and making adequate response to her daughter's attempts to inform her. Generalizing, we may say that the opposition is one between maintenance of formal expectations, general social roles, proprieties, on the one hand, and the heeding of or appropriate response to information about a particular empirical situation, on the other. If we summarize the two terms of the relation as the maintenance of two types of rationality, that of SOCIAL NORM, and that of EMPIRICAL SITUATION, each term can readily be seen as capable of two values. For SOCIAL NORM, the values are (+) *Upheld*, and (−) *Violated*. For EMPIRICAL SITUATION, the values are (+) *Adequate Response*, and (−) *Inadequate*

Response. The possible permutations give rise to a series:

	1	2	3	4
SOCIAL NORM	+	+	−	−
EMPIRICAL SITUATION	+	−	+	−

Of the myths containing the consanguineal trio in question, the first three (those of Seal, Grizzly, Cock Robin) are all of the type 2 (+ −). The case with regard to Seal has just been stated above. In the Grizzly myth the mother persists in her responsibility to provide food (replying to the girl, "Go dig roots!" and "We will be bringing nothing back" (if we return now) (Jacobs 1958:132, 133). The urging of her daughter, and the daughter's strange behavior on returning home, give her plenty of indication that something is wrong; but until actually forced by the daughter, she will not give up rootdigging to return in time to encounter the physical evidence which (by convention of the myth) is the only way she can be told exactly what is wrong. (A situation of the general type (+ −) also occurs with regard to the headman at the end of the myth (Jacobs 1958:140–41), when he disastrously ignores his children's warning of the changing nature of the wife who has come to him). In the Cock Robin myth Cock Robin perseveres in following his sister's instructions but without having understood what the particular instructions are and at the expense of the obvious consequences to be anticipated by so persevering. (The text makes clear that the misunderstanding of two similar words—more similar morphonemically even than phonemically—is involved: a-m-(a)-a-1-či-ya "you (m) will (a . . . ya) bake (či) it ((a)) for (1) her (a)" : a-m-(a)-u-ši-ya "you (m) will (a . . . ya) bake (ši) her ((a))."

In the myth of "Blue Jay and his older sister," there is no question of Blue Jay upholding social norms. Throughout Clackamas mythology he is variously cruel, thievish, stupid, a buffoon, and the like. Given that he also (as in all the episodes of the myth in question) responds incorrectly to what he is told to do at the expense of the obvious empirical consequences, the myth focussed upon him as first named character must be taken as being of type 4 (− −). (The situation is somewhat different as between this myth and the last. Cock Robin mistakes an actual word, and his sister explains to him what had actually been said; Blue Jay mistakes the import of words actually used [in the Clackamas version], as indicated by his sister's use of the introductory expression *wiska pu* and her admonishing use of *dnuči* "not ever"; she explains to him how what was said should have been taken. In this respect Blue Jay violates a social norm as to speech.) "Skunk was a married man" (Jacobs 1958: 179–80, No. 19) is a similar case. Skunk does not hunt as he should. When he does, he mistakes one homonym in his wife's complaint for another, and brings back, not *breast* of deer, but his own pulled teeth.

Other instances of type 4 (− −) are found in "She deceived herself with milt" (Jacobs 1959a:348–50, No. 39) and *"Kušaydi"* (Jacobs 1959a:350–65, No. 40). In the first a woman persists in insulting another woman whose (magically obtained) husband she has stolen, despite warning to desist, and in consequence she loses the husband. In the latter part of the second myth (Jacobs 1959a:365–65) the murderous hero *Kušaydi* insists upon eating something against which he has been warned by both his older brother and the woman preparing it; he dies in consequence, and his older brother pronounces that it shall be so for all killers. In both cases, thus, a person has not observed social norms (mate-stealing, murder), fails to heed sufficient warning, and suffers the consequences. (The case is the same with Fire's great grandsons at the end of the myth of "Fire and his son's son" (Jacobs 1959:129) and with Grizzly in the myth of "Grizzly and Black Bear ran away with the two girls." The actors in question participate in murder, fail to heed warnings, and die in consequence.)

Type 1 (+ +) is not common in the Clackamas collection. I suspect that myths told aboriginally by males might have had more examples of male heroes to whom the type would apply. We find it here in "Coyote and his son's son and their wives" (Jacobs 1958:19–20, No. 2), wherein Coyote acts to maintain social propriety and heeds his grandson's information and advice (not without some intervening humor before the correct outcome for the cultural period is laid down). In "Black Bear and Grizzly Woman and their sons" (Jacobs 1958:143–56, No. 16) Black Bear's sons behave, especially the named hero *wasgúkmayli*, responsibly, heed their mother's advice, and later Crane's, and succeed both in avenging her and outwitting Grizzly Woman. In "Greyback Louse" (Jacobs 1959a:334–40, No. 36) the youngest Grizzly behaves well toward Meadow Lark, heeds her advice, and succeeds in outwitting and transforming Greyback Louse so that she shall not kill people, only bite them.

Type 3 $(- +)$ is represented by the title character of "Crawfish and her older sister" (Jacobs 1959a:376–79, No. 43). While Crawfish misbehaves, she does respond properly to the consequent situation and her sister's instructions. The outcome is that the relation between the two is dissolved (at which Crawfish weeps), but without personal tragedy; each takes on its appropriate nature for the cultural period that is to come, and that of Crawfish is positively valued, as beneficial to mankind. (The second portion of the Cock Robin myth might invite the same interpretation, given its outcome with regard to him, which is quite parallel to that of Crawfish; but as he has both misbehaved [stealing fish and not sharing food with his siblings] and ignored the opportunity to behave correctly, the outcome is rather a matter of "just desserts" $[- -]$, modulated from incipient death by burning [cf. the fate of Grizzly] to transformation depriving him forever of what he had misappropriated.)

In "Seal took them to the ocean" the protagonist Seal Hunter has behaved meanly to his elder brother, but during the course of the adventures underwater consistently heeds Seal's advice, so that he and his fellows survive each test. They do not, however, return wealthy from their encounter with the supernatural, but poor (Jacobs 1958:226); later they become transformed. Notice that the otherwise puzzling outcome (Jacobs 1958:290, No. 226) of the one brother, Seal Hunter, being poor, fits his place as protagonist in the semantic field being analyzed $(- +)$.

In other myths the people at the end of "Tongue" (Jacobs 1959a:369–75, No. 52) and the wife (Sun) at the end of "The Basket Ogress took the child" (Jacobs 1959a:388–409, No. 46) fit the type. Misbehavior (insult in the one case, disobeying instructions in the other) is complemented by effort at correction ("Tongue") and positive deeds ("The Basket Ogress took the child"), with the result a mixed outcome in which actors are separated and transformed into the identities they will have in the cultural period.

A set of situations belonging to this type occur when a series of girls come to obtain a husband (improper behavior) and are killed except for the fifth and last, who receives and follows the advice of Meadow Lark, and so saves herself ("Snake Tail and her son's sons" (Jacobs 1958:194–99, No. 24); "Awl and her son's son" (Jacobs 1958:226–41, No. 27). In each the youngest girl weeps at the fate of her older sisters, but also puts an end to the danger (pronouncing that snakes will not kill people in the cultural period to come in the one case, returning Awl from temporary identity as a dangerous being to status as an inanimate object again in the other).

The contrasting values of the four types can be rather clearly seen. When social norm is observed, and when advice and circumstances are properly heeded, events come out as they should for the actors concerned and for the future state of the world (the cultural period in which the people will have come) (Type 1, + +). When social norm is observed at the expense of heeding an empirical situation, the result is death and even tragedy (Type 2, + −). When social norm is violated, but advice and circumstances are properly responded to, the outcome is mixed (Type 3, − +).

There is an ingredient of misfortune but it is not unrelieved. When social norm has not been observed, the consequences of not heeding advice and circumstances are effectively "just desserts" (Type 4, − −).

Second Interpretation (Resumed)

Significance of Actors

The manifest action of the myth, and a view of the structural role of titles, led to the hypothesis that the myth expressed first of all the nature (-k'ani), not of someone acting like the "wife," but of someone acting like Seal. Analysis of the place of the main actors in a larger series of myths and myth situations has confirmed the hypothesis. The leading theme of the myth is the conduct of Seal. The behavior of the girl is not a device to express the horror of an ambiguously sexed and hateful "female" in-law, but rather, an ambiguous "female" is a device to express the failure of a proper woman to relate to a danger threatening one she should protect. The myth uses a stock villain to dramatize a relationship subtler than villainy. The female figure whose nature is focussed upon in the title and disclosed in the action is not one who is feared for her violation of social norms, but one who is too fearful in her keeping of them.

The girl shares the stage with Seal, and as primary protagonist and most expressively characterized actor, ranks almost equal to her. (Her significance will be brought out further in the sections immediately following.) Although largely passive, the younger brother is important for the relationship identified in the title, and as object of the mourning of both Seal and the girl. He is the one whose fate exemplifies the nature of the actor the title first names. Notice, on this account, that he is presumably not homosexual. The trickster origin of the "wife" indicates that her female form is the result of transformation, not transvestitism or hermaphroditism, and that the urinating with the sound of a man is simply a clue to essential identity parallel to such clues in other North Coast analogues. It is indeed a difficulty with the first interpretation that a horror reaction to homosexuals should implicate the younger brother and uncle who is the object of the women's great concern. On the second interpretation the difficulty disappears, together with any significance of the "wife" as a focus of homosexual fears. The horror of the second scene is not the copulation, nor the murder (which is committed off stage, and never stated as occurring), but its discovery, and the retrospective realization of what has preceded its discovery, the enormous disparity between the reality of danger and Seal's response. As observed, the "wife" is significant only as a means of dramatizing the relations among the other three via the husband, as is shown by the fact that the denouement is one, not of revenge toward "her," but of grief for him. In the myth as we have it, "she" is least important, a mechanical villain.

Dialectics of Actors

A further richness of this short myth can be found by utilizing a second method demonstrated by Lévi-Strauss. It is that in which a myth is understood in terms of a progression from an initial opposition through a succession of mediating terms (Lévi-Strauss 1963:224). I am not able to provide an analysis precisely comparable to those achieved by Lévi-Strauss, but if one asks, what in the present myth answers to the form of the method, further insight emerges.

An initial opposition is given in the title of the myth. It is Seal : Younger Brother. A development of the initial pair in the form of a triad is given in the introductory sentence of the myth, which presents Seal, her daughter, her younger brother, in that order.

Several aspects of the relationship suggest themselves. Seal and her younger brother are both adult, but the one is female, socially responsible (as elder sibling and mother), and sexually experienced, while the other is male, not yet socially responsible (as younger sibling and bachelor), and as yet sexually inexperienced, although eligible for such experience. The girl is female, like her mother, but sexually inexperienced, like her uncle. She is, I would suggest, attentive both to the claims of social responsibility, such as her mother should show toward her (the mother's) younger brother, and of sexual maturity, such as her uncle embarks upon. Hence she may be seen as an appropriate potential mediator between what Seal and Seal's younger brother respectively express.

As we know, the girl's efforts are to fail. The myth develops in two scenes which present now the girl and her mother as the opposing terms. Between them in each are posed middle terms which are not so much mediational as ambivalent, ambiguous, susceptible of interpretation in the light of either of two prior concerns. The first is the "wife," presented as a bundle of two features: a socially proper role, that of "your uncle's wife," and a behaviorally incongruous fact, that of urinating with a sound like that of a man. The second is the dripping from the uncle's bed. As a result of marital copulation it is socially proper and not to be noticed. As a signal of danger, it is, as it proves to be, evidence of a murder. In each case the mother explains away in terms of social propriety what the girl has seized upon as experiential fact.

The final scene has also a triad, but perhaps only in narrative form. The girl remonstrates and mourns, then her mother mourns, then again the girl. Structurally there seems no middle term, unless it is the death to which each woman responds in character, but independently. Having remonstrated, the girl ends weeping alone; the mother ends repeating a formula.[17] The dialogue is dissolved, and with it the possibility of resolution of the opposition of the underlying terms.

In outline form, we have:

$$
\begin{array}{ccccccccc}
\text{ElSi} & & \text{ElSi/Mo} & & \text{Mo} & & \text{Mo} & & \text{Mo} \\
| & \longrightarrow & \begin{array}{c}\diagdown\\ \text{Da/SiDa}\\ \diagup\end{array} & \longrightarrow & \begin{array}{c}\diagdown\\ \text{``wife''}\\ \diagup\end{array} & \longrightarrow & \begin{array}{c}\diagdown\\ \text{dripping}\\ \diagup\end{array} & \longrightarrow & \begin{array}{c}\diagdown\kern-6pt\times\\ \text{death}\\ \diagup\kern-6pt\times\end{array} \\
\text{YoBr} & & \text{YoBr/MoBr} & & \text{Da} & & \text{Da} & & \text{Da}
\end{array}
$$

Given this formal development, what are we to make of it? In one sense, of course, it is another way of stating the place of the myth in the semantic field indicated above. In another sense, the dialectical form draws attention to implications of the myth which are matters not only of a place in a larger series, but also of individual qualities of imagery, tone, and expressive detail. In general, the structure and theme of the myth are as has been stated. In particular, they are something more.

Imagery

If the imagery of the myth had not been attended to before, the position of the dripping, correlative to that of the actors, would demand attention to it. In point of fact, three· strands of imagery are interwoven in this brief narrative. The first is one of light : darkness in a relation like that of figure to ground. All the dramatized action takes place at night (they go out at night to urinate; of the second scene the narrator remarks, before mentioning copulation, "I do not know what time of night it was . . ."). Darkness is to be presumed. As the climax is realized, the visual setting changes correlatively: the girl rises, fixes the fire, and lights pitch. When she looks by that light into her uncle's bed to discover the dripping from it to be his blood, the moment is quite literally one of truth, and light the appropriate symbol of its acquisition.

The second strand of imagery sets off the two main actors in terms of experience of wetness, on the one hand, and of speech exclusively, on the other. Each major scene involves the girl in experience of something having a liquid aspect: the "wife's" urination; the uncle's blood; her own tears. These sensory experiences are specific to the girl. The mother hushes report of the first two, and speaks, as against the girl's tears, in the last scene. Seal's relationship to speech is patently symbolic of social propriety. I suggest that the girl's

relationship to wetness expresses a different mode of experience, one in part at least sexual. (Compare, too, the concreteness of the girl's experience of urination, copulation, and ejaculation as against the euphemistic expression of each in ordinary Clackamas terms.)

The third strand of imagery focusses on the girl. She *hears* the urination. She then hears, but first *feels,* what drips down (on her face). At the climax she *sees* blood. In the denouement she herself *produces* tears. I suggest that this sequence of modes of sensory experience (hearing, feeling, seeing, weeping) progresses from the more passive and remote to the more active and immediate (indeed, internally caused). Quite literally, in bringing light into the darkness, the girl has been brought to a knowledge of blood and death. The final weeping represents full assumption of the mode of experience symbolized.

Tone and Expressive Detail

The tone and expressive detail of the narration confirm the imagery in pointing to a special concern with the figure of the girl, contrasted to that of the mother. Her effort to prevent tragedy is heightened in the second scene by the detail that not only does she warn her mother verbally, but first shakes her. The intensification of the confrontation between the two is heightened on the mother's side by the fact that she does not immediately respond with "ák'waška!," as in the first scene, but with "m̂ . . . ," as if hesitating or considering before deciding how to interpret the information as to dripping, and by the modulation of the hushing word here occurring without exclamation mark.

The denouement, one of the finest in Clackamas literature is, within its terse conventions not only well prepared for, but also highly dramatized as a contrast between the girl and mother that reaches into the verbal particulars of the lament of each. Seal exclaims: "Younger brother! My younger brother! They (his house posts) are valuable standing there. My younger brother!" The myth adds: "She kept saying that." There is a touch of personal feeling in the directness of the first word, the uninflective vocative *(awi)*, before the inflected term of reference (correspondingly used also by the girl). The statement as to the house posts may heighten the scene, showing the death to have been that of a rich and important man (as Jacobs observes); it also suggests that concern for social position dominates. We know from another myth (Jacobs 1959a:408) that a formal lament was proper at the death of someone. With Seal we seem to have here almost exclusively that, although repeated and repeated, in an implicit state of shock.

In its brevity and social reference Seal's lament sets in relief the extended laments of the girl which enclose it. Her first lament is the myth's longest speech, and an unusually long speech for any Clackamas myth. Its emotion is indicated in part by the adding of explicit reference to the urination like a man. (The precise words for "man-like" and "she urinated" are added here to the expression for "go out" with a sound like λ', a found in the first scene. Jacobs translates the two occurrences of the former addition "exactly (like)" and "just (like)" to convey that the use of the explicit term is forcefully expressive.)

The girl mingles remonstrance with remorse, throws back "åk'waška" at her mother, and weeps. After Seal's lament, it is said "But the girl herself

wept." She repeats her remorse in heightened form, adding "in vain" *(kin-wa)*, and ends with the kinship term preceded by a particle openly stating her emotion: "*áná* my uncle! *aná* my uncle!" (In Wishram the particle is glossed as expressing "grief, pain, pity, remorse".) Jacobs has observed that direct linguistic statement of grief is rare in Clackamas literature. Notice moreover that the use of the particle is modulated; first it is doubly stressed, then singly (Jacobs translates "Oh oh" then "Oh"), as if the words are descending into the tears that follow. It is only the girl who weeps, and it is with her weeping that the myth ends.

It is difficult to imagine a reading that does not find the denouement, like the scenes leading to the climax, a fabric woven about a character contrast between mother and girl, a contrast of which the girl is implicitly the heroine.

The Role of Women and the Form of the Myth

The myth, in short, has something more of significance as to feeling about women than its disclosure of Seal. To be sure, the girl is in part Cassandra in the first scene, part Greek chorus in the last. Her role fits the part of "youngest smartest," and represents as well the "immobilism," as Jacobs terms it (Jacobs 1959b:169–72) prescribed for Clackamas women—the expectation that women are not to take the lead and, although not passive, are to act through men if men in the correct social relationship are present. The girl can be seen to act properly by not going to the uncle herself, but trying to act through the only proper intermediary available to her, her mother, the uncle's older sister. Her discovery of the murder, when all has failed, may still be assigned to the "youngest smartest" role. The ending of that climax, however, on her scream, and the expressive detail and tone of the denouement suggest something more, something which is equally pointed to by the way in which the strands of imagery are woven about her. Over against the structural significance of Seal, there emerges something of an individual quality in the role of the girl. She seems the voice of a concern for personal loyalty as against social propriety; sensory experience as against verbal convention; personal feeling as against formal grief; of an existential situation.

Was this concern aboriginal? We cannot be sure. Two points, however, can be made. First, it would be foolish to assume that a uniform literary criticism and interpretation of myth prevailed among the Clackamas, or among any other "primitive" or "tribal" community. Indeed, the persistence of interpretative differences between men and women can be documented even today. I first heard a rather widespread plot as to how Coyote tricks a girl into intercourse from a man, who enjoyed telling it to me as a man's story at the expense of women. Later a woman mentioned it as a story her grandmother had told her to warn her against men.

An aboriginal male audience may well have had a special interest in the myth in its original form, an interest perhaps including a horror reaction to homosexuals. The myth as we have it titled and told now is testimony to the special interests of women. I myself see no reason to think that as much of the myth as we have does not tell something about the aboriginal society's feelings about females; only it does so, not from a male, but from a female standpoint.

Second, as reinterpreted as a confrontation between women, from the standpoint of women, the present myth makes sense in terms both of its history and its form. It has reached us through a line of women. (Jacobs' informant, Mrs. Howard, had her knowledge of myths from her mother-in-law and her mother's mother ("Seal and her younger brother dwelt there" from the former).[18] I find that transmission reflected in the detail of the handling of female actors, which is often more salient and moving than the handling of male actors; in the large proportion of myths which involve significant female actors; in the recurrent use of the rather matrilineal trio of Mo, MoDa, MoBr; and in the remembrance in some cases of only that portion of myths having to do with female actors. This last point applies to "Duck was a married woman" (Jacobs 1958:184–85; No. 21) and "Robin and her younger sister" (Jacobs 1959a:380; No. 44); and I believe it applies to "Seal and her younger brother dwelt there."

The selective retention and phrasing of tradition under acculturation by a sequence of women is reflected in the form of the present myth, not only quantitatively (how much is retained), but also qualitatively.[19] The present form of the myth is not as such incomplete; rather, it has remarkable unity. In terms of the structural analysis of the title's focus upon Seal, and of the place of that focus in a larger semantic field, the text is a complete expression. In terms of the dialectics, imagery, and expressive detail woven about the girl, the text is not only a whole, but an expression whose unity is complex and effective.

I take the possibility of explaining the form of the myth as strong support for the interpretation offered here.

Concluding Remark

The second interpretation gives the myth something of an Oedipal ring. It is perhaps ironic that the Oedipal theme, which the author of the first interpretation is quick to catch in his work with Clackamas literature, here is merely mentioned in passing (Jacobs 1960:239), whereas its pursuit might have led to a quite different understanding. Again, Seal Woman is discussed elsewhere in a tenor quite compatible with the second interpretation, indeed in a way that would seem almost to imply it. Discussing the occurrence of Seal in three myths, Jacobs finds no commonalty, but comments on her role in the myth in question here as that of

a woman who followed etiquette in being so circumspect and uncomprehending about perils in an in-law relationship that she did not act in time to save the life of her younger brother, whose wife decapitated him. The delineation was of a well-mannered and weak or frightened woman. (Jacobs 1958:161)

In a similar context Seal is referred to as

a woman who was so cautious about in-laws' feelings that she failed to act in time to save her brother's life (Jacobs 1958:162)

I had worked through my reinterpretation in relation to the text before coming to these passages. Obviously the statements apply brilliantly to the myth as reinterpreted here. Equally clearly, they were lost sight of in the actual formal interpretation of the myth in the volume devoted to such interpretation (Jacobs 1960:238–42), if indeed they do not contradict it.

The methodological point would seem to be this. Despite the richness a socio-psychological perspective provides, prior reliance upon its insights can override and even conceal the import of a myth. A structural analysis of the features and relationships of a myth must first be made and made in terms pertinent to genre in the culture in question. Focus first on what is essentially at best a latent content can lead interpretation far from actual dramatic poignancy and skill.

Notes

1. An earlier version of this paper was read at the annual meeting of the American Folklore Society, Denver, Colorado, November 21, 1965. I wish to thank Alan Dundes, John L. Fischer, Archie Green. David Mandelbaum, Warren Roberts, John Szwed, and Francis Lee Utley for comments. The myth is discussed briefly also in my general review of Jacobs' Clackamas Chinook work (Hymes 1965b:337–38).

2. The prefix *ł* - in "they lived there" already implies more than two present.

3. Literally so: *-y(a)* "to go," λáxuix "outside";

xabixix is better "evening" as contrasted with *-pul* "night" later on.

4. The text and translation require clarification here. Although the first scene is discussed in terms of the sound of the "wife's" urination, the translation contains no reference to a sound. Furthermore, the Clackamas verb in question (*-ba-y(a)*) does not refer to urination, but to going out. As to the sound, the text contains an untranslated element λ'a. In Wishram Chinook there is a particle λ'alalala . . . "the sound of water dripping, or as when it comes out of a hose." The use of the

recursively repeatable element -*la* for repetition of a sound is attested in Kathlamet Chinook, leaving Wishram and Clackamas λ'*a* presumably as equivalent in meaning. As to the "going out," the verb in question is attested as an idiom for urination among both the Kathlamet and Wishram (groups to the west and east, respectively, of the Clackamas). The test thus combines a euphemistic verb and an onomatopoetic particle, literally "a-dripping-sound some-man's-like she-'goes out.'" (A corroborative instance from our own society: in families with a boy and girl, mothers in bed may tell which of their children has gotten up during the night precisely from this auditory clue. I owe the observation to Archie Green.)

As adapted from the Chinookan expression, the title of the paper indicates the two features singled out by the first interpretation as crucial to the actor found focus of the myth: questionable sexual identity, and the clue disclosing it.

5. "Uncle" has expanded prefix *iwí*—(instead of *wi*-), perhaps for emphasis.

6. With distributive plural suffix -*w*.

7. The theme is -*x-kwš-it* "to be in bed," used in this construction as a euphemism analogous to English "go to bed." Here -*kwš* is preceded by *ga*-, apparently as an intensifier. In Wishram *ga*- and *da*- appear before other stem elements marking direction, and contribute the sense of "fast motion." "In bed" as a location is here marked explicitly *(wi-lxámit-ba)*. Hence the choice of "lie together" in quotation marks as translation.

8. Same theme as in n. 5, but without intensifying *ga*-. In the second occurrence -*š-gm*- indicates close beside each other (or beside some implied object with dual prefix *š*-), not beside "it" (the fire) as in the first translation. Such a form would have -*a-gm,* in concord with the prefix of *wa-tuɫ* "fire."

9. The form *š-x-l-ú-yǝ-m* seems literally to contain -*y(a)* "to come, go," and continuative suffix -*m,* so that in virtue of *u*- "direction away," it means "those two are going together," an apparent analogue to the English sexual idiom "to come." The concrete idiom heightens the scene.

10. Literally, either "she saw it (*i*-)," presumably the bed *(wi-lxamit),* or "she saw him (her uncle)" where the two were lying down.

11. Perhaps to be translated as "she looked at it thus" with accompanying gesture to indicate the raising of the light. In Wishram *iwi* may mean "thus" and the verb stem -*q'wma* suggests a diminutive form of -*quma* "to look." (The form -*q'wma* is not itself attested in Wishram.)

12. In his (*ya*-) bed, not merely "the" bed.

13. A change of tense is signaled by *n*- . . . *t*-.

14. The verb in the reference indicates that long objects stand in a line. The noun is paralleled in Wishram by a form meaning "a hardwood arrow forepiece, now also one of copper", or "ornaments of tin, funnel-shaped tied to belt, saddle." Presumably the Clackamas expression characterizes the value of the house posts in terms of ornamentation by objects of some such sort.

15. With intransitive -*kim,* continuative-repetitive -*niɫ,* perfective -*čk.*

16. A similar phrase occurs in a few other places in the collection. Notice the absence of a concluding formula, e.g., *k'ani k'ani.*

17. Notice that hitherto the speech acts of the two acts had been designated by the inherently transitive stem -*lxam* (rendered always "told" in the revised translation). The mother's words in the denouement are introduced and concluded, and the last words of the girl are introduced, with the inherently intransitive verb stem -*kim* (always rendered "said"). Choice of verb stem thus marks the final isolation of each speaker, speaking without addressee.

18. Hymes (1965b:338) inadvertently substitutes mother's mother as the source.

19. I have not succeeded in phrasing in English the exact effect the myth conveys to me. One component of that effect is that I feel there may somehow be something implicitly expressive of the acculturation situation in the contrast so thoroughly drawn between convention and experience—as if the mother accepts, or stands for the acceptance of, the strange newcomers, the whites (called *k'ani* for their marvelous customs, and *duxnipčk,* "they come up from the water," as ones with whom one can enter into conventional reciprocal relationships (i.e., trade), and as if the girl stands for a realization that the strange ways are not only different but dangerous and will destroy them (by destroying their men, who were the main casualty of the acculturation process). But all this is speculative.

SIX

Ideology and Myth

The Fetishism of Commodities and the Secret Thereof

KARL MARX

Every culture seems, to those who live in and through it, to be "natural," in two senses: first, in the sense that we cannot conceive the lives of those who do not live as we do (we, after all, are "doing what comes naturally"), and second, in the sense that we feel that our own world is not culturally-constructed, not the result and the distillate of a historical process: it is outside of those things, at least in its basic aspects.

Karl Marx was the first major figure in Western social thought to realize the significance of this aspect of culture. In this selection, which is his classic statement of the problem of "fetishism" or naturalization, he shows (1) how this attitude grows out of living within the cultural system; (2) how it takes its specific form from the specific nature of capitalist society; and (3) how working within this attitude—that is, in an ahistorical, non-comparative framework which makes *one* culture's "common sense" into basic laws of human nature—thwarts both the understanding of our own society and the possibility of creating a meaningful alternative to that society.

This is perhaps the most complex piece which Marx, an extremely difficult and complex writer, ever wrote. But following these three themes with care through Marx's exposition will enable the reader to grasp one of the most powerful analytic methods ever developed—and give a sense of the basic structure and limitations of our own society. Many students find that a "key" helps them to read Marx: we suggest the selection by Lefebvre in this volume, and also Bertell Ollman's *Alienation* and Istvan Mészárós' *Marx' Theory of Alienation*.

A COMMODITY APPEARS, at first sight, a very trivial thing, and easily understood. Its analysis shows that it is, in reality, a very queer thing, abounding in metaphysical subtleties and theological niceties. So far as it is a value in use, there is nothing mysterious about it, whether we consider it from the point of view that by its properties it is capable of satisfying human wants, or from the point that those properties are a product of human labor. It is as clear as noon-day, that man, by his industry, changes the forms of the materials furnished by Nature, in such a way as to make them useful to him. The form of wood, for instance, is altered, by making a table out of it. Yet, for all that, the table continues to be that common, everyday thing, wood. But, so

Published 1967 by International Publishers Co., Inc., New York, N.Y.

soon as it steps forth as a commodity, it is changed into something transcendent. It not only stands with its feet on the ground, but, in relation to all other commodities, it stands on its head, and evolves out of its wooden brain grotesque ideas, far more wonderful than "table-turning" ever was.

The mystical character of commodities does not originate, therefore, in their use-value. Just as little does it proceed from the nature of the determining factors of value. For, in the first place, however varied the useful kinds of labor, or productive activities, may be, it is a physiological fact, that they are functions of the human organism, and that each such function, whatever may be its nature or form, is essentially the expenditure of human brain, nerves, muscles, etc. Secondly, with regard to that which forms the ground-work for the quantitative determination of value, namely, the duration of that expenditure, or the quantity of labor, it is quite clear that there is a palpable difference between its quantity and quality. In all states of society, the labor-time that it costs to produce the means of subsistence, must necessarily be an object of interest to mankind, though not of equal interest in all stages of development. And lastly, from the moment that men in any way work for one another, their labor assumes a social form.

Whence, then, arises the enigmatical character of the product of labor, so soon as it assumes the form of commodities? Clearly from this form itself. The equality of all sorts of human labor is expressed objectively by their products all being, equally, values; the measure of the expenditure of labor-power by the duration of that expenditure, takes the form of the quantity of value of the products of labor; and, finally, the mutual relations of the producers, within which the social character of their labor affirms itself, take the form of a social relation between the products.

A commodity is therefore a mysterious thing, simply because in it the social character of men's labor appears to them as an objective character stamped upon the product of that labor: because the relation of the producers to the sum total of their own labor is presented to them as a social relation, existing not between themselves, but between the products of their labor. This is the reason why the products of labor become commodities, social things whose qualities are at the same time perceptible and imperceptible by the senses. In the same way the light from an object is perceived by us not as the subjective excitation of our optic nerves but as the objective form of something outside the eye itself. But, in the act of seeing, there is at all events, an actual passage of light from one thing to another, from the external object to the eye. But it is different with commodities. There, the existence of the things *qua* commodities, and the value-relation between the products of labor which stamps them as commodities, have absolutely no connection with their physical properties and with the material relations arising therefrom. There it is a definite social relation between men, that assumes, in their eyes, the fantastic form of a relation between things. In order, therefore, to find an analogy, we must have recourse to the mist-enveloped regions of the religious world. In that world the productions of the human brain appear as independent beings endowed with life, and entering into relation both with one another and with the human race. So it is in the world of commodities with the products of men's hands. This I call the Fetishism which attaches itself to the products of labor, so soon as they are produced as commodities, and which is therefore inseparable from the production of commodities.

This Fetishism has its origin, as the foregoing analysis has already shown, in the peculiar social character of the labor that produces them.

As a general rule, articles of utility become commodities, only because they are products of the labor of private individuals or groups of individuals who carry on their work independently of each other. The sum total of the labor of all these private individuals forms the aggregate labor of society. Since the producers do not come into social contact with each other until they exchange their products, the specific social character of each producer's labor does not show itself except in the act of exchange. In other words, the labor of the individual asserts itself as a part of the labor of society only by means of the relations which the act of exchange establishes directly between the products, and indirectly, through them, between the producers. To the latter, therefore, the relations connecting the labor of one individual with that of the rest appear, not as direct social relations between individuals at work, but as what they really are, material relations between persons and social relations between things. It is only by being exchanged that the products of labor acquire, as values, one uniform social status, distinct from their varied form of existence as objects of utility. This divi-

sion of a product into a useful thing and a value becomes practically important when exchange has acquired such an extension that useful articles are produced for the purpose of being exchanged, and their character as values has therefore to be taken into account, beforehand, during production. From this moment the labor of the individual producer acquires socially a two-fold character. On the one hand, it must, as a definite useful kind of labor, satisfy a definite social want, and thus hold its place as part and parcel of the collective labor of all, as a branch of a social division of labor that has sprung up spontaneously. On the other hand, it can satisfy the manifold wants of the individual producer himself, only in so far as the mutual exchangeability of all kinds of useful private labor is an established social fact, and therefore the private useful labor of each producer ranks on an equality with that of all others. The equalization of the most different kinds of labor can be the result only of an abstraction from their inequalities, or of reducing them to their common denominator, viz., expenditure of human labor-power or human labor in the abstract. The two-fold social character of the labor of the individual appears to him, when reflected in his brain, only under those forms which are impressed upon that labor in everyday practice by the exchange of products. In this way, the character that his own labor possesses of being socially useful takes the form of the condition, that the product must not only be useful, but useful for others, and the social character that his particular labor has of being the equal of all other particular kinds of labor, takes the form that all the physically different articles that are the products of labor, have one common quality, viz., that of having value.

Hence, when we bring the products of our labor into relation with each other as values, it is not because we see in these articles the material receptacles of homogeneous human labor. Quite the contrary: whenever, by an exchange, we equate as values our different products, by that very act, we also equate, as human labor, the different kinds of labor expended upon them. We are not aware of this, nevertheless we do it. Value, therefore, does not stalk about with a label describing what it is. It is value, rather, that converts every product into a social hieroglyphic. Later on, we try to decipher the hieroglyphic, to get behind the secret of our own social products; for to stamp an object of utility as a value, is just as much a social product as language. The recent scientific discovery, that the products of labor, so far as they are values, are but material expressions of the human labor spent in their production, marks, indeed, an epoch in the history of the development of the human race, but, by no means, dissipates the mist through which the social character of labor appears to us to be an objective character of the products themselves. The fact, that in the particular form of production with which we are dealing, viz., the production of commodities, the specific social character of private labor carried on independently, consists in the equality of every kind of that labor, by virtue of its being human labor, which character, therefore, assumes in the product the form of value—this fact appears to the producers, notwithstanding the discovery above referred to, to be just as real and final, as the fact that, after the discovery by sci-ence of the component gases of air, the atmosphere itself remained unaltered.

What, first of all, practically concerns producers when they make an exchange, is the question, how much of some other product they get for their own? in what proportions the products are exchangeable? When these proportions have, by custom, attained a certain stability, they appear to result from the nature of the products, so that, for instance, one ton of iron and two ounces of gold appear as naturally to be of equal value as a pound of gold and a pound of iron in spite of their different physical and chemical qualities appear to be of equal weight. The character of having value, when once impressed upon products, obtains fixity only by reason of their acting and re-acting upon each other as quantities of value. These quantities vary continually, independently of the will, foresight, and action of the producers. To them, their own social action takes the form of the action of objects, which rule the producers instead of being ruled by them. It requires a fully developed production of commodities before, from accumulated experience alone, the scientific conviction springs up, that all the different kinds of private labor, which are carried on independently of each other, and yet as spontaneously developed branches of the social division of labor, are continually being reduced to the quantitative proportions in which society requires them. And why? Because, in the midst of all the accidental and ever fluctuating exchange-relations between the products, the labor-time socially necessary for their production forcibly asserts itself like an over-riding law of Nature. The law of gravity thus asserts itself when a house falls about our ears. The determination of the magnitude of value by labor-time is therefore a secret, hidden under the apparent fluctuations in the relative values of commodities. Its discovery, while removing all appearance of mere accidentality from the determination of the magnitude of the values of products, yet in no way alters the mode in which that determination takes place.

Man's reflections on the forms of social life, and consequently, also, his scientific analyses of those forms, take a course directly opposite to that of their actual historical development. He begins, post festum, with the results of the process of development ready to hand before him. The characters that stamp products as commodities, and whose establishment is a necessary preliminary to the circulation of commodities, have already acquired the stability of natural, self-understood forms of social life, before man seeks to decipher, not their historical character, for in his eyes they are immutable, but their meaning. Consequently it was the analysis of the prices of commodities that alone led to the determination of the magnitude of value, and it was the common expression of all commodities in money that alone led to the establishment of their characters as values. It is, however, just this ultimate money-form of the world of commodities that actually conceals, instead of disclosing, the social character of private labor, and the social relations between the individual producers. When I state that coats or boots stand in a relation to linen, because it is the universal incarnation of abstract human labor, the absurdity of the statement is self-evident. Nevertheless, when the producers of coats and boots compare those articles with linen,

or, what is the same thing, with gold or silver, as the universal equivalent, they express the relation between their own private labor and the collective labor of society in the same absurd form.

The categories of bourgeois economy consist of such like forms. They are forms of thought expressing with social validity the conditions and relations of a definite, historically determined mode of production, viz., the production of commodities. The whole mystery of commodities, all the magic and necromancy that surrounds the products of labor as long as they take the form of commodities, vanishes therefore, as soon as we come to other forms of production.

Since Robinson Crusoe's experiences are a favorite theme with political economists, let us take a look at him on his island. Moderate though he be, yet some few wants he has to satisfy, and must therefore do a little useful work of various sorts, such as making tools and furniture, taming goats, fishing and hunting. Of his prayers and the like we take no account, since they are a source of pleasure to him, and he looks upon them as so much recreation. In spite of the variety of his work, he knows that his labor, whatever its form, is but the activity of one and the same Robinson, and consequently, that it consists of nothing but different modes of human labor. Neccessity itself compels him to apportion his time accurately between his different kinds of work. Whether one kind occupies a greater space in his general activity than another, depends on the difficulties, greater or less as the case may be, to overcome in attaining the useful effect aimed at. This our friend Robinson soon learns by experience, and having rescued a watch, ledger, and pen and ink from the wreck, commences, like a true-born Briton, to keep a set of books. His stock-book contains a list of the objects of utility that belong to him, of the operations neccessary for their production; and lastly, of the labor-time that definite quantities of those objects have, on the average, cost him. All the relations between Robinson and the objects that form this wealth of his own creation, are here so simple and clear as to be intelligible without exertion, even to Mr. Sedley Taylor. And yet those relations contain all that is essential to the determination of value.

Let us now transport ourselves from Robinson's island bathed in light to the European middle ages shrouded in darkness. Here, instead of the independent man, we find everyone dependent, serfs and lords, vassals and suzerains, laymen and clergy. Personal dependence here characterizes the social relations of production just as much as it does the other spheres of life organized on the basis of that production. But for the very reason that personal dependence forms the ground-work of society, there is no necessity for labor and its products to assume a fantastic form different from their reality. They take the shape, in the transactions of society, of services in kind and payments in kind. Here the particular and natural form of labor, and not, as in a society based on production of commodities, its general abstract form, is the immediate form of social labor. Compulsory labor is just as properly measured by time, as commodity-producing labor; but every serf knows that what he expends in the service of his lord, is a definite quantity of his own personal labor-power. The tithe to be rendered to the priest is more matter of fact than his blessing. No matter, then, what we may think of the parts played by the different classes of people themselves in this society, the social relations between individuals in the performance of their labor, appear at all events as their own mutual personal relations, and are not disguised under the shape of social relations between the products of labor.

For an example of labor in common or directly associated labor, we have no occasion to go back to that spontaneously developed form which we find on the threshold of the history of all civilized races. We have one close at hand in the patriarchal industries of a peasant family, that produces corn, cattle, yarn, linen, and clothing for home use. These different articles are, as regards the family, so many products of its labor, but as between themselves, they are not commodities. The different kinds of labor, such as tillage, cattle tending, spinning, weaving, and making clothes, which result in the various products, are in themselves, and such as they are, direct social functions, because functions of the family, which, just as much as a society based on the production of commodities, possesses a spontaneously developed system of division of labor. The distribution of the work within the family, and the regulation of the labor-time of the several members, depend as well upon differences of age and sex as upon natural conditions varying with the seasons. The labor-power of each individual, by its very nature, operates in this case merely as a definite portion of the whole labor-time of the family, and therefore, the measure of the expenditure of individual labor-power by its duration, appears here by its very nature as a social character of their labor.

Let us now picture to ourselves, by way of change, a community of free individuals, carrying on their work with the means of production in common, in which the labor-power of all the different individuals is consciously applied as the combined labor-power of the community. All the characteristics of Robinson's labor are here repeated, but with this difference, that they are social, instead of individual. Everything produced by him was exclusively the result of his own personal labor, and therefore simply an object of use for himself. The total product of our community is a social product. One portion serves as fresh means of production and remains social. But another portion is consumed by the members as means of subsistence. A distribution of this portion amongst them is consequently necessary. The mode of this distribution will vary with the productive organization of the community, and the degree of historical development attained by the producers. We will assume, but merely for the sake of a parallel with the production of commodities, that the share of each individual producer is determined by his labor-time. Labor-time would, in that case, play a double part. Its apportionment in accordance with a definite social plan maintains the proper proportions between the different kinds of work to be done and the various wants of the community. On the other hand, it also serves as a measure of the portion of the common labor borne by each individual, and of his share in the part of the total product destined for individual consumption. The social relations of the individual producers, with regard both to their labor and to its products, are in this case perfectly simple and intelligible, and that with regard not only to production but also to distribution.

The religious world is but the reflex of the real world. And for a society based upon the production of commodities, in which the producers in general enter into social relations with one another by treating their products as commodities and values, whereby they reduce their individual private labor to the standing of homogeneous human labor—for such a society, Christianity with its *cultus* of abstract man, more especially in its bourgeois developments, Protestantism, Deism, etc., is the most fitting form of religion. In the ancient Asiatic and other ancient modes of production, we find that the conversion of products into commodities, and therefore the conversion of men into producers of commodities, holds a subordinate place, which, however, increases in importance as the primitive communities approach nearer and nearer to their dissolution. Trading nations, properly so called, exist in the ancient world only in its interstices, like the gods of Epicurus in the Intermundia, or like Jews in the pores of Polish society. Those ancient social organisms of production are, as compared with bourgeois society, extremely simple and transparent. But they are founded either on the immature development of man individually, who has not yet severed the umbilical cord that unites him with his fellowmen in a primitive tribal community, or upon direct relations of subjection. They can arise and exist only when the development of the productive power of labor has not risen beyond a low stage, and when, therefore, the social relations within the sphere of material life, between man and man, and between man and Nature, are correspondingly narrow. This narrowness is reflected in the ancient worship of Nature, and in the other elements of popular religions. The religious reflex of the world can, in any case, only then finally vanish, when the practical relations of everyday life offer to man none but perfectly intelligible and reasonable relations with regard to his fellowmen and to Nature.

The life-process of society, which is based on the process of material production, does not strip off its mystical veil until it is treated as production by freely associated men, and is consciously regulated by them in accordance with a settled plan. This, however, demands for society a certain material ground-work or set of conditions of existence which in their turn are the spontaneous product of a long and painful process of development.

Political Economy has indeed analyzed, however incompletely,[1] value and its magnitude, and has discovered what lies beneath these forms. But it has never once asked the question why labor is represented by the value of its product and labor-time by the magnitude of that value.[2] These formulae, which bear it stamped upon them in unmistakeable letters that they belong to a state of society, in which the process of production has the mastery over man, instead of being controlled by him, such formulae appear to the bourgeois intellect to be as much a self-evident necessity imposed by Nature as productive labor itself. Hence forms of production that preceded the bourgeois form, are treated by the bourgeoisie in much the same way as the Fathers of the Church treated pre-Christian religions.

To what extent some economists are misled by the Fetishism inherent in commodities, or by the objective appearance of the social characteristics of labor, is shown, amongst other ways, in the formation of exchange-value. Since exchange-value is a definite social manner of expressing the amount of labor bestowed upon an object, Nature has no more to do with it, than it has in fixing the course of exchange.

The mode of production in which the product takes the form of a commodity, or is produced directly for exchange, is the most general and most embryonic form of bourgeois production. It therefore makes its appearance at an early date in history, though not in the same predominating and characteristic manner as now-a-days. Hence its Fetishistic character is comparatively easy to be seen through. But when we come to more concrete forms, even this appearance of simplicity vanishes. Whence arose the illusions of the monetary system? To it gold and silver, when serving as money, did not represent a social relation between producers, but were natural objects with strange social properties. And modern economy, which looks down with such disdain on the monetary system, does not its superstition come out as clear as noon-day, whenever it treats of capital? How long is it since economy discarded the physiocratic illusion, that rents grow out of the soil and not out of society?

But not to anticipate, we will content ourselves with yet another example relating to the commodity-form. Could commodities themselves speak, they would say: Our use-value may be a thing that interests men. It is no part of us as objects. What, however, does belong to us as objects, is our value. Our natural intercourse as commodities proves it. In the eyes of each other we are nothing but exchange-values. Now listen how those commodities speak through the mouth of the economist. "Value" (i.e., exchange-value) is a property of things, riches"—(i.e., use-value) "of man. Value, in this sense, necessarily implies exchanges, riches do not." "Riches" (use-value) "are the attribute of men, value is the attribute of commodities. A man or community is rich, a pearl or a diamond is valuable . . . A pearl or a diamond is valuable" as a pearl or diamond.[3] So far no chemist has ever discovered exchange-value in either a pearl or a diamond. The economic discoverers of this chemical element, who by-the-by lay special claim to critical acumen, find however that the use-value of objects belongs to them independently of their material properties, while their-value, on the other hand, forms a part of them as objects. What confirms them in this view, is the peculiar circumstance that the use-value of objects is realized without exchange, while, on the other hand, their exchange-value is realized only by exchange that is, by means of a social process. Who fails to call to mind here our good friend Dogberry, who informs neighbour Seacoal, that, "To be a well-favoured man is the gift of fortune; but reading and writing comes by Nature."

Notes

1. The insufficiency of Ricardo's analysis of the magnitude of value, and his analysis is by far the best, will appear from the 3rd and 4th books of this work. As regards value in general, it is the weak point of the classical school of Political Economy that it nowhere, expressly and with full consciousness, distinguishes between labor, as it appears in the value of a product, and the same labor, as it appears in the use-value of the products. Of course, the distinction is practically made, since this school treats labor, at one time under its quantitative aspect, at another under its qualitative aspects. But it has not the least idea, that when the difference between various kinds of labor is treated as purely quantitative, their qualitative unity or equality, and therefore their reduction to abstract human labor, is implied.

2. It is one of the chief failings of classical economy that it has never succeeded, by means of its analysis of commodities, and, in particular, of their value, in discovering that form under which value becomes exchange-value. Even Adam Smith and Ricardo, the best representatives of the school, treat the form of value as a thing of no importance, as having no connection with the inherent nature of commodities. The reason for this is not solely because their attention is entirely absorbed in the analysis of the magnitude of value. It lies deeper. The value-form of the product of labor is not only the most abstract, but is also the most universal form, taken by the product in bourgeois production, and thereby gives it its special historical character. If then we treat this mode of production as one eternally fixed by Nature for every state of society, we neccessarily overlook that which is the *differentia specifica* of the value-form, and consequently of the commodity-form, and of its further developments, money-form, capital-form, etc. We consequently find that economists, who are thoroughly agreed as to labor-time being the measure of the magnitude of value, have the most contradictory ideas of money, the perfected form of the general equivalent. This is seen in a striking manner when they treat of banking, where the commonplace definitions of money will no longer hold water.

3. Marx here cites two contemporary economists. Marx's citations of contemporary and classical economic authorities, and his discussions of faults of particular economic treatises, have been deleted here—EDITORS' NOTE.

FOURTEEN

Ideology and the Sociology of Knowledge

HENRI LEFEBVRE

This piece from Lefebvre's *The Sociology of Marx* is part of the author's "new reading of Marx," a reading which is intended to re-create and extend the thought behind Marx's works. "Marx," writes Lefebvre, "is not a sociologist; but there is a sociology in Marx." The continuation of that sociology entails the enquiry into "the genesis of so-called 'modern' society, its fragmentations and contradictions." The notion of ideology is particularly important in this endeavor.

Lefebvre notes that the generative process through which ideological forms are created in, and themselves affect, social relations, is central to the Marxist notion of ideology. Lefebvre depicts ideology as having a dual character: general and abstract, while at the same time tied to and representative of specific, determinative interests. According to Lefebvre, it is this dual characteristic, which mediates between modes of *praxis* ("reality") and its conscious understanding, for example, in the forms of language, that allows ideology to represent and *naturalize* extant modes of domination.

At issue here are the historical processes through which ideologies are reproduced and through which they may be replaced (by other ideologies and—as Lefebvre puts it—by "true theory"). Lefebvre's attempt to extend a reading of Marx to an analysis of culture is one of the clearest general statements of the neo-Marxist position shared by a number of schools which, however, take divergent approaches to the solution of the problems raised here, such as the Frankfurt School (especially Theodor Adorno, Max Horkheimer, and Herbert Marcuse) and "existential Marxists" such as Jean-Paul Sartre.

THE CONCEPT OF IDEOLOGY is one of the most original and most comprehensive concepts Marx introduced. It is also one of the most complex and most obscure, though the term is widely employed today. To clarify it, we shall begin with a few preliminary considerations.

Reprinted by permission of the publishers from Henri Lefebvre, *The Sociology of Marx* (New York: Random House, 1969), pp. 59–88; (Paris: Presses Universitaires de France).

a. It is well known that the term "ideology" originated with a philosophical school (empiricist and sensationalist, with a tendency to materialism) which enjoyed considerable influence in France at the close of the eighteenth and the beginning of the nineteenth century. According to the philosophers of this school (Destutt de Tracy is the best known), there is a science of ideas, i.e., of abstract concepts, which studies their genesis and can reconstruct it in full starting from sensations (a conception that goes back to Condillac). This science was called "ideology," and the philosophers who practiced it called themselves "ideologists" (*idéologues*).

Marx tranformed the meaning of the term—or, more accurately, he and Engels gave their approval to a transformation in meaning which the term underwent once the school of the *idéologues* died out. The term now became a pejorative one. Instead of denoting a theory, it came to denote a phenomenon the theory accounted for. This phenomenon now took on entirely different dimensions. As interpreted by the French ideologists, ideology was limited to accounting for individual representations by a causal psychology. To Marx and Engels, the phenomenon under study became a collection of representations characteristic of a given epoch and society. For example: *The German Ideology*. The original meaning was not entirely lost sight of: Marx aimed at formulating a theory of general, i.e., social representations; he defined the elements of an explanatory genesis of "ideologies" and related the latter to their historical and sociological conditions.

b. If we introduce terms such as "opacity" and "transparency" (of a given society) in our exposition, we may be charged with substituting images for scientific definitions. However, Marx himself uses such "images" and views them as elements of knowledge. "Transparency" stands for "immediate presence or intelligibility"—a quality that is not often found in "representations."

Since Robinson Crusoe's experiences are a favorite theme with political economists, let us take a look at him on his island. Moderate though he be, yet some few wants he has to satisfy, and must therefore do a little useful work of various sorts, such as making tools and furniture, taming goats, fishing and hunting. Of his prayers and the like we take no account, since they are a source of pleasure to him, and he looks upon them as so much recreation. . . . All the relations between Robinson Crusoe and the objects that form this wealth of his own creation, are . . . simple and transparent. . . .

Let us now transport ourselves from Robinson's island bathed in light to the European Middle Ages shrouded in darkness. . . . For the very reason that personal dependency forms the foundation of society, there is no necessity for labor and its products to assume a form different from their reality. They take the shape . . . of services in kind and payments in kind. Here the particular and natural form of labor—and not as in a society based on production of commodities, its general abstract form—is the immediate social form of labor. . . . In the patriarchal industries of a peasant family that produces corn, cattle, yarn, linen, and clothing for home use, these different articles are, as regards the family, so many products of its labor, but as between themselves, they are not commodities. . . .

Let us now picture to ourselves . . . a community of free individuals, carrying on their work with the means of production in common, in which the labor power of all the different individuals is consciously applied as the combined labor of the community. . . . The social relations of the individual producers, with regard both to their labor and to its products, are in this case perfectly simple and transparent, and that with regard not only to production but also to distribution. . . .

Trading nations properly so-called exist only in the Intermundia of the ancient world, like the gods of Epicurus or like Jews in the pores of Polish society. Those ancient social organisms of production are, as compared with bourgeois society, extremely simple and transparent. But they are founded either on the immature development of man individually, who has not yet severed the umbilical cord that unites him with his fellow men in a primitive tribal community, or upon direct relations of subjection. . . .

The life-process of society which is based

on the process of material production does not strip off its mystical veil until it is treated as production by freely associated men and is consciously regulated by them in accordance with a settled plan. . . ." (*Capital* I: 88–92)

Clearly, according to Marx, the social consciousness generated by a given praxis faithfully reflects it only in specific situations: namely, when the praxis is not shrouded in mystical veils, when interhuman relations are direct, without "opaque" intermediaries. The various types of social praxis within specific social structures and modes of production give rise to "representations." These representations increase or decrease the degree of a given society's "opacity." They illumine or obscure the society. Sometimes they illumine it with a false clarity and sometimes they plunge it into shadow or darkness in the name of a doctrine even obscurer than the reality generating it. Social reality, i.e. interacting human individuals and groups, produces *appearances* which are something more and else than mere illusions. Such appearances are the modes in which human activities manifest themselves within the whole they constitute at any given moment—call them modalities of consciousness. They have far greater consistency, let alone coherence, than mere illusions or ordinary lies. Appearances have reality, and reality involves appearances. In particular, the production of commodities is enveloped in a fog. We have to keep getting back to the commodity, for here we find the key to Marxian thought and sociology. In analytical reflection, the commodity is a pure form, hence something transparent. In practical everyday experience, on the other hand, it is opaque and a cause of opaqueness. The very existence of the commodity is strange, the more so because men are not aware of its strangeness.

A commodity appears, at first sight, a very trivial thing, and easily understood. Analysis shows that it is in reality a very peculiar thing, abounding in metaphysical subtleties and theological niceties. (*Capital* I: 81)

It has a "mystical character"; it exists only thanks to human beings in their interrelations, and yet it exists apart from them and modifies their relations, reifying the latter and making them abstract. Many centuries had to go by before critical thought would unmask this fetishism, revealing its mystery as the power of money and capital. Thus the commodity, as a form and a system implying the existence of money and capital, must inevitably give rise to an opaque society. In popular terms, the opaqueness is expressed in the fact that money holds sway over human beings: people with money intrigue their way to power, the powers-that-be constitute an occult order. The opaqueness or non-transparency of society is thus a social, or rather, a socio-economic fact. Only revolutionary praxis by articulating the (true) theory and furthering (practical, verifying) modes of action restores the conditions for transparency. Revolutionary praxis does away with the conditions illusory representations thrive on, brings about new conditions to dispel them.

This much is clear. However, Marx's writings contain two definitions of ideology sufficiently different to raise questions and call for an elucidation of the concept.

Ideology, we are told, is an inverted, truncated, distorted reflection of reality. In ideologies men and their conditions appear upside down like images on the lens of a camera; supposedly, this comes about as the result of a specific biological process, similar to the physical process which accounts for the way images are reversed on the retina. In their representations, individuals similarly grasp their own reality "upside down," and this fact is part of reality. Consciousness is no more or less than individual consciousness, yet one law of consciousness decrees that it must be perceived as a thing apart from the self. Human beings do not perceive themselves exactly as they are, but instead as projected upon a screen. Illusory representations of reality—the illusionism being ordained by this reality—refer either to nature and man's relations with nature or to interhuman relations. Ideologies, by this account, come down to false representations of history or to abstractions from history. Every ideology, then, is a collection of errors, illusions, mystifications, which can be accounted for by reference to the historical reality it distorts and transposes.

Study of ideologies thus leads to a critical view of history. General representations (philosophy, law, religion, art, knowledge itself)—cloudy precipitations rising from human brains—are superpositions over material and biological processes which can be empirically observed without them. Morals, religion, metaphysics, and the other aspects of ideology, and the corresponding forms of consciousness are only seemingly autonomous. "They have no history, no development," i.e., they cannot be understood unless they are related to the modes of production and exchange obtaining in a given society at a given moment. "It is not consciousness that determines life, but life that determines consciousness," according to the famous formula, so often quoted out of context. Actually, the context is very clear: it says that there are only two ways to understand history. Either we start from consciousness; in which case we fail to account for real life. Or we start from real life; then we come up against this ideological consciousness that has no reality, and must account for it. Historical materialism puts an end to the speculation which starts from consciousness, from representations, and hence from illusions: "Where speculation on real life stops, real and positive science begins. The object of such science is practical activity, the process of human development on the practical plane."

This process is self-sufficient. Reality and rationality are inherent in it. Knowledge puts an end to phraseology, to ideology. More particularly, when philosophy devotes itself to representation of reality, it loses its medium of existence. What takes the place of philosophy? Study of the results of historical development, which have no interest, no meaning, no value outside history. Inherited philosophical concepts can serve merely to facilitate the ordering of the historical materials, indicate the sequence of successive deposits.

What follows in the same work (*The German Ideology*) goes far to correct what is extremist in this theory. Once ideology is related to the real conditions that gave rise to it, it ceases to be completely illusory, entirely false. For what is ideology? Either it is a theory that is unconscious of its own presuppositions, its basis in reality, and true meaning, a theory unrelated to action, i.e., without consequences or with consequences different from those expected and foreseen. Or it is a theory that generalizes special interests—class interests—by such means as abstraction, incomplete or distorted representations, appeals to fetishism.

If so, it is erroneous to maintain that every ideology is pure illusion. It appears that ideology is not, after all, to be accounted for by a sort of ontological fate that compels consciousness to differ from being. Ideologies have truly historical and sociological foundations, in the division of labor on the one hand, in language on the other.

Man possesses consciousness; on this score the philosophers who formulated and elucidated the concept of consciousness were right. Where the philosophers went astray was when they isolated consciousness from the conditions and objects of consciousness, from its diverse and contradictory relations with all that is not consciousness, when they conceived of consciousness as "pure," but above all when they ascribed "purity" to the historically earliest forms of consciousness. In this way they raised insoluble speculative problems. For from the outset the supposed purity of consciousness is tainted with original sin. It cannot escape the curse of "being soiled with a matter that here takes the form of agitated layers of air, in short, language." Language is as old as consciousness. There is no consciousness without language, for language is the real, practical consciousness, which exists for other human beings, and hence for beings that have become conscious. Marx discovers that language is not merely the instrument of a pre-existing consciousness. It is at once the natural and the social medium of consciousness, its mode of existence. It comes into being with the need for communica-

tion, with human intercourse in the broadest sense. Consequently, being inseparable from language, consciousness is a social creation.

It remains to note what human beings communicate to one another, what they have to say. To begin with, the objects of their communications include the sensorily perceived environment and their immediate ties with other human beings. They also refer to nature in so far as it is a hostile power before which man feels helpless. Human consciousness begins with an animal, sensuous awareness of nature, though even at this stage it is already social. This gives rise to a first misrepresentation: a religion of nature which mistakes *social* relations (however elementary) for *natural* relations, and vice versa. What we might call "tribal consciousness" emerges out of earlier barbarism, earlier illusions, as productivity expands, as tools are perfected, and as needs and population increase. What had hitherto been a purely biological division of labor (based on sex, age, physical strength, etc.) begins to become a technological and social division of labor. As the society develops, it takes on ever new forms and subdivisions (city *vs.* countryside, social *vs.* political functions, trade *vs.* production—not to mention the ever sharper distinction that comes to be drawn between individual and social labor, partial and over-all labor, etc.). So far as the development of ideologies is concerned, the most important division is that between physical and intellectual labor, between creative action (operations upon things with the aid of tools and machines) and action on human beings by means of nonmaterial instruments, the primary and most important of which is language. *From this point forward, consciousness becomes capable of detachment from reality,* may now begin to construct abstractions, to create a "pure theory." Theology supplants the religion of nature, philosophy supplants religion, morality supplants traditional manners and customs, etc. Ever more elaborate representations are built up, and overlay the direct, immediate consciousness, now felt to be at once crude and deluded, for having remained at the natural, sensorial level. When these abstract representations come into conflict with reality, i.e., with existing social relations, the social relations themselves have become contradictory, both as between themselves and between them and their social base—namely, the productive forces (the technological division and the social organization of labor).

These representations give rise to theories. Consequently, what we are dealing with is not detached, isolated representations, but ideas given coherent form by "ideologists," a new kind of specialist. Those who wield material (economic and political) power within the established social and juridical order also wield "spiritual" power. The representations, i.e., the consciousness of society, are elaborated into a systematic idealizing of existing conditions, those conditions that make possible the economic, social, and political primacy of a given group or class. Individuals active on the plane of praxis play an important part in forming the general consciousness and in excluding representations contrary to the interest of the ruling groups. As a result, "their ideas are the dominant ideas of their epoch," but in a way which leaves room for invention. For instance, when the king, the nobili-

ty, and the bourgeoisie are striving with one another for dominance, we find a political theory of the separation of powers. To understand a given ideology, we have to take into account everything that is going on in the higher circles of the society in question—classes, fractions of classes, institutions, power struggles, diverging and converging interests. It must also be kept in mind that the "ideologists" themselves are rarely active as members of their given class or group. This detachment on their part is passed on in their "treatments" of the realities they represent, whether in justification or condemnation. The theoretical conflicts are not unrelated to the actual conflicts discussed, but the verbalizations do not accurately, point by point, reflect the realities they represent. This leaves room for revolutionary ideas when a revolutionary group or class actually exists in the society, with a practical end in view: namely, the transformation of society through solving its problems, resolving existing contradictions.

According to Marx (and Engels), ideologies possess the following characteristics:

1 Their starting point is reality, but a fragmentary, partial reality; in its totality it escapes the ideological consciousness because the conditions of this consciousness are limited and limiting, and the historical process eludes the human will under such conditions of intervention.

2 They refract (rather than reflect) reality via preexisting representations, selected by the dominant groups and acceptable to them. Old problems, old points of view, old vocabularies, traditional modes of expression thus come to stand in the way of the new elements in

society and new approaches to its problems.

3 Ideological representations, though distorted and distorting not because of some mysterious fate but as a result of the historical process within which they become a factor, tend to constitute a self-sufficient whole and lay claim to be such. The whole, however, comprises praxis, and it is precisely this that ideologies distort by constructing an abstract, unreal, fictitious theory of the whole. The degrees of reality and unreality in any ideology vary with the historical era, the class relations, and other conditions obtaining at a given moment. Ideologies operate by extrapolating the reality they interpret and transpose. They culminate in systems (theoretical, philosophical, political, juridical), all of which are characterized by the fact that they lay behind the actual movement of history. At the same time it must be admitted that every ideology worthy of the name is characterized by a certain breadth and a real effort at rationality. One typical example studied by Marx and Engels is German philosophy between the end of the eighteenth and the middle of the nineteenth century. Every great ideology strives to achieve universality. The claim to universality is unjustified, however, save when the ideology represents a revolutionary class during the time it serves as the vehicle of historical interests and goals with genuinely universal significance. This was the case with the middle classes in the period of their rise to power.

4 Consequently, ideologies have two aspects. On the one hand, they are general, speculative, abstract; on the other, they are representative of determinate, limited, special interests. In setting out to answer all questions, all problems, they create a comprehensive view of the world. At the same time they reinforce specific ways of life, behavior patterns, "values" (if we may use here a terminology that does not occur in Marx's writings).

Ideologies are thus ignorant of the exact nature of their relations with praxis—do not really understand their own conditions and presuppositions, nor the actual consequences to which they are leading. Ignorant of the implications of their own theories, they comprehend neither the causes of which they are effects, nor the effects which they are actually causing; the real why and how escapes them. At the same time they are inescapably involved in praxis. They are at once starting points and results of action in the world (however effective or ineffectual). Ideological representations invariably serve as instruments in the struggles between groups (peoples, nations) and classes (and fractions of classes). But their intervention in such struggles takes the form of masking the true interests and aspirations of the groups involved, universalizing the particular and mistaking the part for the whole.

5 Since they have a starting point and a foothold in reality (in praxis), or rather to the extent that they do, ideologies are not altogether false. According to Marx, we have to distinguish among ideology, illusion, and lies, on the one hand, and ideology, myths, and utopias on the other hand. Ideologies may contain class illusions, have recourse to outright lying in political struggles and yet be related to myths and utopias. Historically, all sorts of illusory, deceptive representations have been inextricably mixed up in ideological thinking with real concepts—i.e. scientific insights. Some-

times the ideology has served as the vehicle of sound thinking, sometimes as agent of its distortion or supression. The evaluation of ideological thinking can only be done *post facto,* patiently, with the aid of some more or less radical critical thought. The typical example cited by Marx and Engels is German philosophy. Thanks to Germany's economic and social backwardness, its thinkers were capable of speculative thought in the first half of the nineteenth century, whereas in the same period English thinkers were creating theories of political economy (the theory of competitive capitalism) and the French were operating on the plane of direct political action (making revolutions). The Germans transposed praxis to the realm of metaphysics. In their systems it is so heavily disguised as to be all but unrecognizable. This was perfectly in keeping with the actual prospects of their nation, which were at once limitless (in the abstract) and severely limited (practically speaking). At the same time, however, they did give expression to some new concepts—among others, the concept of dialectical change—which were eventually integrated in scientific theory and revolutionary praxis. It is incumbent on critical thought and revolutionary action to salvage what is valid from the wreckage of collapsing systems and crumbling ideologies.

6 Thus it may be said that ideologies make room for nonscientific abstractions, whereas concepts are scientific abstractions (for instance, the concepts of use value and of the commodity). Such concepts do not remain forever shrouded in the mists of abstraction; as we have seen, they are integrated in praxis, though we still have to specify just how. They enter into praxis in two ways: as a constraining factor, and as a form of persuasion. Abstract ideas have no power in themselves, but people who hold power (economic or political) make use of representations in order to justify their actions. Moreover, and this is the main point, the most completely elaborated ideological representations find their way into language, become a permanent part of it. They supply vocabularies, formulations, turns of thought which are also turns of phrase. Social consciousness, awareness of how multifarious and contradictory social action can be, changes only in this way: by acquiring new terms and idioms to supplant obsolete linguistic structures. Thus it is not language that generates what people say. Language does not possess this magical power or possesses it only fitfully and dubiously. What people say derives from praxis—from the performance of tasks, from the division of labor—arises out of real actions, real struggles in the world. What they actually do, however, enters consciousness only by way of language, by being said. Ideologies mediate between praxis and consciousness (i.e., language). This mediation can also serve as a screen, as a barrier, as a brake on consciousness. Consider the words, symbols, expressions that religions have created. Revolutionary theory, too, has created its own language and introduced it into the social consciousness; the most favorable conditions for this occur when a rising class is mature enough to take in new terms and assimilate new concepts. Even then we must expect to run into formidable obstacles. These are created not only by voluntary actions of contemporaries, but also by long-accepted ideas reflecting contemporaries' limited horizons. An individual member of the

middle class is not necessarily malicious or stupid, but he is incapable of rising above the mental horizon of his class. His outlook is formulated in the medium of language, which moreover is the language of society as a whole. Now, language—not only the language of ideologists (e.g., philosophers) but also of all those who speak—distorts practical reality. According to Marx, neither thought nor language forms an autonomous domain. Language, this repository of ideas in the keeping of society as a whole, is full of errors and illusions, trivial truths as well as profound ones. There is always the problem of making the transition from the world of representations (ideas) to the real world, and this problem is none other than that of making the transition from language to life. The problem thus has multiple aspects—the actually existing language, ideologies, praxis, the class situation, the struggles actually going on. When the bourgeois speaks of "human" rights, "human" conditions, etc., he actually means bourgeois conditions, bourgeois rights, etc. He does not distinguish between the two because his very language has been fashioned by the bourgeoisie.

Marx, then, tries to situate language within praxis, in relation to ideologies, classes, and social relationships. Language is important, but is not by itself the crucial factor. Let us go back briefly to the commodity. In one sense, every commodity is a sign: *qua* exchange value it is only the outward and visible sign of the human labor expended to produce it. However, "If it be declared that the social characters assumed by objects, or the material form assumed by the social qualities of labor under the regime of a definite mode of production, are mere signs, it is in the same breath also declared that these characteristics are arbitrary fictions sanctioned by the so-called universal consent of mankind" (*Capital* I: 103).

This view, according to which every commodity is a sign and which was much in favor during the eighteenth century, is ideological; it is not a conceptual, scientific account of the puzzling forms assumed by social relations (*Capital* I: 103). In analyzing language or this other form, the commodity, we must isolate its formal character, but we must never separate it from its other aspects—content, development, history, social relations, praxis.

To gain a better understanding of the Marxian concept of ideology, we may compare it with the "collective representations" of the Durkheim school. In a way, every ideology is a "collective representation," but whereas to Durkheim society is an abstract entity, to Marx it results from practical interactions among groups and individuals. Thus a given ideology does not characterize a society as a whole; it arises out of individual inventions made within the social framework in which groups, whether castes or classes, struggle to assert themselves and gain dominance. On the other hand, ideologies do not affect individual minds from the outside, for they are not extraneous to the real life of individuals. Ideologies utilize the language of real life, and hence are not vehicles of the coercive pressure society exerts on the individual (according to Durkheim's sociology). Those who use ideologies rarely hesitate to resort to force when this is justified by the same ideologies, in which case we have brutal constraint exercised by the powers-that-be. Ideologies as such, however, as instruments of persuasion, guide the individual and give him a sense of purpose. Viewed from outside, ideologies seem self-contained, rational systems; viewed from inside, they imply faith, conviction, adherence. In pledging his allegiance to a given ideology the individual believes he is fulfilling himself. In actual fact he does not fulfill himself, he loses himself, he becomes alienated, though this is not immediately apparent to him, and when it does become apparent it is often too late. Thus ideologies impose certain obligations on individuals, but these obligations are voluntarily accepted. The inner or outer penalties imposed by ideologies are expected, demanded by the individuals concerned. Thus the power of ideologies is very different from that of Durkheim's "collective representations."

Every society, every authority has to be accepted. A given social structure, with its specific social and juridical relations, must obtain the consensus of a majority, if not the totality of its members. No social group, no constituted society is possible without such adherence, and sociologists are justified in stressing this consensus. But how is the consensus arrived at? How do conquerors, rulers, masters, those in power make oppression acceptable? Marx and Engels have repeatedly emphasized the fact that no society is based on sheer brute force alone. Every social form finds its rationale in the society's growth and development, in the level its productive forces and social relations have attained. It is the role of ideologies to secure the assent of the oppressed and exploited. Ideologies represent the latter to themselves in such a way as to wrest from them, in addition to material wealth, their "spiritual" acceptance of this situation, even their support. Class ideologies create three images of the class that is struggling for dominance: an image for itself; an image of itself for other classes, which exalts it; an image of itself for other classes, which devalues them in their own eyes, drags them down, tries to defeat them, so to speak, without a shot being fired. Thus the feudal nobility put forward an image of itself—a multiple image with multiple facets: the knight, the nobleman, the lord. Similarly the middle class elaborated an image of itself for its own use: as the bearer of human reason in history, as uniquely endowed with good and honorable intentions, finally as alone possessed with capacity for efficient organization. It also has its own images of the other classes: the good worker, the bad worker, the agitator, the rabble-rouser. Lastly it puts forward a self-image for the use of other classes: how its money serves the general good, promotes human happiness, how the middle-class organization of society promotes population growth and material progress.

No historical situation can ever be stabilized once and for all, though that is what ideologies aim at. Other forms of consciousness and rival ideologies make their appearance and join the fray. Only another ideology or a true theory can struggle against an ideology. No form of consciousness ever constitutes a last, last word, no ideology ever manages to transform itself into a permanent system. Why? Because praxis always looks forward to new possibilities, a future different from the present. The consensus an ideology succeeds in bringing about in its heyday, when it is still growing and militant, eventually crumbles away. It is supplanted by another ideology, one that brings fresh criticism to bear on the existing state of affairs and promises something new.

When we analyze more closely the views on ideology propounded by Marx and Engels, we make out the elements for an orderly outline of its origin and development.

a. First of all, some representations are illusory, for they arise prior to the conditions under which concepts can be formed. Thus, before the concept of historical time had arisen, there were representations concerning the succession of events, how the undertakings of a given society or group and its leaders were initiated and succeeded or failed as they did. Such representations had a mythical, legendary, epical, heroic character. Elaborated by still relatively undifferentiated social groups, they were refined by priests and poets. The same is true of the earliest representations of natural forces and of the few human acts as yet capable of modifying natural processes. Such representations ascribed to human beings, or rather to certain individuals, a fictitious power of control over the unknown, and so accounted for the lesser ability and inability of other men and of society as a whole to do as much.

b. Related to these elaborations are the early cosmogonies and theogonies, images of the world which were often projected against a background of the actual life of social groups, and the actual organization in villages and towns. These great constructions included interpretations of the sexes (masculinity, femininity), of the family (according to division of labor, age), of the elements (often presented in pairs—earth and air, fire and water), of the

relationship between leaders and subordinates, of life and death.

Were these grandiose images of society, time and space, a history scarcely begun, the prehistory of the race—were they ideologies? Yes and no. Yes, to the degree they justified the nascent inequalities among men, including possession (primitive appropriation) of a territory by a single group and seizure of the group resources—the scanty surplus product—by its leaders. No, because it is not yet possible to speak at this stage of classes or even of castes. No, because these constructions of the mind are works of art—more like monuments than abstract systems. They belong to the same category as styles in art history, compendia of moral wisdom, "cultures." They show to what extent rulers feel the need to justify themselves in the eyes of the vanquished and the oppressed: such works serve both to justify and to consolidate their rule.

c. It does not seem that in Marx's view mythologies can be regarded as ideologies. They are much closer to genuine poetry than to formal constructions. Marx thought that Greek mythology, the soil that nourished Greek art, was an expression of the real life of the people, an ever fresh source of the "eternal" charm of this art. The Greek myths and the Greek gods were symbols of man or rather of his powers. They gave in magnified form a picture of how human beings appropriate their own nature—in the various activities of their own lives (warfare, metal working), in games, love, and enjoyment.

Cosmogonies, myths, and mythologies are turned into ideologies only when they become ingredients in religion, especially in the great religions that lay claim to universality. Then the images and tales are cut off from the soil that nourished them, the beauty of which they represented to the eye and mind. Now they take on different meaning. The great religions' all-inclusive character and claim to universality are marked on the one hand by abstractness and by loss of their original local flavor, and on the other by an ever growing gap between individuals, between groups, between peoples, and between classes. The great religions were born concomitantly with consolidation of the power of the state, the formation of nations, and the rise of class antagonisms. Religions make use not of a knowledge freed of illusion, but of illusions antedating knowledge. To these they add unmistakably ideological representations, i.e., representations elaborated in order to disguise praxis and to give it a specific direction. As theoretical constructions they alternate between a kind of poetry borrowed from the earlier cosmogonies and sheer mystification intended to justify the acts of the powers-that-be.

Incontestably, according to Marx, religion in general (religion to the extent it lays claim to universality, to representing the fate of mankind, of the human species) is the prototype and model of all ideology. All criticism begins and is renewed again with the criticism of religion. Radical criticism, i.e., criticism that goes to the roots, tirelessly keeps going back to the analysis of religious alienation.

Summing up Marx's thought, we can now formulate the sociological features of any ideology. It deals with a segment of reality, namely, human weakness: death, suffering, helplessness. It includes interpretations of the wretched portion of reality, consciousness of which, if taken in isolation and overemphasized, acts as a brake on all creation, all progress. By virtue of their link with "reality"—a reality transposed and interpreted—ideologies can affect reality by imposing rules and limitations on actually living men. In other words, ideologies can be part of actual experience, even though they are unreal and formal, reflect only a portion of human reality. They offer a way of seeing the world and of living, that is to say, up to a certain point, a praxis which is at once illusory and efficacious, fictitious and real.

Ideologies account for and justify a certain number of actions and situations which need to be accounted for and justified, the more so the wronger and more absurd they are (i.e., in process of being surmounted and superseded). Thus every ideology represents a vision or conception of the world, a *Weltanschauung* based on extrapolations and interpretations.

Another feature of ideologies is their perfectibility. An ideology may encounter problems, but not of a kind to shake it fundamentally. Adjustment is made, details are altered, but the essentials are left intact. This gives rise to passionate and passionately interesting discussions between conservatives and innovators, dogmatists and heretics, champions of the past and champions of the future. As a result, a given ideology becomes associated with a group (or a class, but always a group active within a class: other groups within this class may remain ideologically passive, though they may be most active in other respects). Within the group that takes up the ideology, it serves as pretext for zealousness, sense of common purpose, and then the group tends to become a sect. Adherence to the ideology makes it possible to despise those who do not adhere to it, and, needless to say, leads to their conversion or condemnation. It becomes a pseudo-totality which closes in upon itself the moment it runs into its external or internal boundaries, whether limitations or outside resistances. In short, it becomes a *system*.

Man has emerged from nature in the course of the historical process of production—production of himself and of material goods. Consciousness, as we have seen, emerges at the level of the sensuous, and then rises above it without being cut off from it. This practical relationship, which is essentially and initially based upon labor, is consequently broadened to include the entire praxis of a society in which the various kinds of labor become differentiated and unequal. At this point, objects, situations, actions acquire specific "meanings" in relation to the over-all "meaning" of social life and the course it follows. However, the human groups assigned to perform productive physical labor were unable for many a long century to elaborate a conception adequate to their situation, to the part they actually played in social praxis, which is the essence of their activity. Multiple conflicts are caused by the scarcity of goods, poverty, and bitter struggles over the tiny surplus of wealth produced. In the course of these conflicts, the conditions that made possible production of a surplus, however small, and sometimes production itself, were destroyed. In peace as in war, the interests of the productive groups were sacrificed. On the symbolic plane of ideology, these sacrifices were given an aura of ideality and spirituality.

In actual fact, there was nothing mysterious about the sacrifice: the oppressed were sacrificed to the oppressors, and the oppressors to the very conditions of oppression—the gods, the Fates, the goals of their political actions. As a result, products and works acquired a transcendent significance, which amounted to an ideological and symbolic negation of their actual significance. All this served to justify the actions of the ruling groups and classes seeking to control the means of production and lay hands on the surplus product. Man's appropriation of nature took place within the framework of ownership, that is, the privative appropriation of the social surplus by privileged groups, to the exclusion of other groups, whether within the given society or outside it, and so gave rise to endless tension and struggle. Religion expressed this general attitude of the privileged groups and classes, which was broadened into an ideology that held out to other groups and classes the hope either of oppression eventually coming to an end one day or of being allowed to share in the advantages of oppression themselves.

The features we have just stressed in religion (or, more accurately, in religions which have theoretical systems) are also to be found in philosophy, though there are certain differences. The philosophers elaborate the incomplete rationality which is present in social praxis and confusedly expressed in language—the logos. Thus philosophy breaks off in turn from religion, from poetry, from politics, and finally from scientific knowledge, and as against these more or less specialized domains, claims to express totality. But religion, the state, and even art and science make the same claim. The difference is that, whereas the latter merely use the concept of totality for their own purposes, philosophy also refines it. Unlike the other ideological activities, philosophy contains a self-transcending principle. Philosophical systems reflect human aspirations, they aim at rigorous demonstrations, they express symbols of human reality. The systems eventually disintegrate, but the problems they raised, the concepts they formulated, the themes they treated do not disappear. They enter into culture, affect all thought, in short, become part of consciousness. The relationship between philosophy and praxis (including the consciousness of praxis) is thus more complex and far more fruitful than that between religion or the state and the same praxis.

Among the philosophical attempts at totality, i.e., at achieving a system at once closed and encompassing all "existents," the systems of morals are the most ideological in character. They set themselves above praxis, promulgating absolute principles and eternal "ethical" truths. They prescribe sacrifice for the oppressed, promising them compensations. They also prescribe sacrifice for the oppressors, when the conditions of their dominance are threatened. Consequently, every morality is dictated by the ruling class, according to its needs and interests in a given situation; the generality it claims is dubious, its universality illusory. It is not on the moral (ethical) plane that the universal is concretely realized. Morality substitutes fictitious needs and aspirations reflecting the constant pressure of the ruling class for the real needs and aspirations of the oppressed. More particularly, under capitalism human needs diverge sharply into highly refined, abstract needs on the one hand, and crude, grossly simplified needs on the other. This dissociation is sanctioned and consecrated by the bourgeois moralities. The latter go so far as to justify the state of non-having—the situation of man separated from objects and works which are meaningful themselves and give concrete, practical meaning to life.

The state of non-having is the extremest form of spiritualism, a state in which man is totally unreal and inhumanity totally real: it is a state of very positive having—the having of hunger, cold, sickness, crime, degradation, stupor, every conceivable inhuman and anti-natural thing (Marx 1844:42)

Now, objects, i.e., goods, products, and works of social man, are the foundation of social man's objective being, his being for himself as well as for others. To be deprived of objects is to be deprived of social existence, of human relations with others and with oneself. Morality *qua* ideology masks this privation and even substitutes a fictitious plenitude for it: a sense of righteousness, a mistaken, factitious satisfaction in nonfulfillment of the self.

Political economy (at least in its beginnings) elaborates scientific concepts—social labor, exchange value, distribution of the over-all income, etc. At the same time it contains an ideology. It is a "true moral science," even "the most moral of all the sciences." Its gospel is saving, i.e., abstinence. "The less you are . . . the more you have. . . . All the things you cannot do, your money can do." Thus scientific concepts are all mixed up with a moralistic ideology, in a way its own authors do not notice. The wheat is separated from the chaff only later, in the name of radical criticism, in connection with revolutionary praxis.

Summing up: as Marx saw it, ideology involves the old problem of error and its relation to the truth. Marx does not formulate this problem in abstract, speculative, philosophical terms, but in concrete historical terms with reference to praxis. Unlike philosophy, the Marxian theory of ideology tries to get back to the origin of representations. It retains one essential philosophical contribution: emergent truth is always mixed up with illusion and error. The theory discards the view that error, illusion, falsity, stand off in sharp and obvious distinction from knowledge, truth, certainty. There is continual two-way dialectical movement between the true and the false, which transcends the historical situation that gave rise to these representations. As Hegel had seen, error and illusion are "moments" of knowledge, out of which the truth emerges. But truth does not reside in the Hegelian "spirit." It does not precede its historical and social conditions, even though it may be anticipated. Thus Hegel's philosophical—i.e., speculative, abstract—theory is transformed into a historical and sociological theory, a continuation of philosophy in the sense that it preserves the latter's universal character.

The representations men form of the world, of society, of groups and individuals, remain illusory as long as the conditions for real representation have not ripened. One notable example is how time was represented—a sense of society, of the city-state, as existing in time—prior to the emergence of fully elaborated concepts of history and historical knowledge. These last are rooted in an active social consciousness of the changes taking place within the praxis. While the mists surrounding natural phenomena are being dispelled, the mystery (the opacity) of social life keeps thickening. While increasing human control over nature (technology, the division of labor) makes it possible to elaborate nonideological concepts of physical nature, the actions of the ruling classes throw a veil of obscurity over social life. Praxis expands in scope, grows more complex and harder to grasp, while consciousness and science play an increasingly effective part in it. Thus it has been possible for illusory representations (mythologies, cosmogonies) to become an integral part of styles and cultures (including Greek culture). They must now give way to knowledge. Revolutionary praxis and Marxism *qua* knowledge do away with the ideologies. According to Marx, Marxism has gone beyond ideology—it signals and hastens the end of ideology. Nor is it a philosophy, for it goes beyond philosophy and translates it into practice. It is not a morality, but a theory of moralities. It is not an aesthetics, but it contains a theory of works of art, of the conditions for their production, how they originate and how they pass away. It discloses—not by some power of "pure" thought but by deeds (the revolutionary praxis)—the conditions under which ideologies and works of man generally, including whole cultures or civilizations, are produced, run their course, and pass away.

It is on the basis of conscious revolutionary praxis that thought and action are articulated dialectically, and that knowledge "reflects" praxis, i.e., is constituted as reflection on praxis. Until then knowledge was characterized precisely by its failure to "reflect" reality, namely, praxis, could only transpose it, distort it, confuse it with illusions—in short, knowledge was ideological.

At the height of its development, ideology becomes a weapon deliberately used in the class struggle. It is a mystifying representation of social reality, or the process of change, of its latent tendencies and its future. At this stage—in contemporary racism, for instance—the "real" element is present; the human species does in fact include varieties and variations, ethnic groups and ethnic differences. But in racism extrapolation and transposition are carried to fantastic lengths; the extrapolation of a real element is combined with "values," and the whole systematized with extreme rigidity. Consequently racist ideology can hardly be mentioned in the same breath with such a philosophy, say, as Kant's. In the twentieth century, ideologizing has reached a sort of apogee within the framework of imperialism, world wars, and a monopolistic capitalism linked with the state. At the same time and because of this, ideology is discredited: extreme ideologizing is accompanied by a certain conviction that "the end of ideology" has been reached. But ideology is not so easily eliminated; to the contrary, it is marked by sudden flare-ups and makes surprising comebacks. Aversion from ideological excess is no more than a pale foretaste of the transparency still to be achieved by revolutionary praxis and its theoretical elaboration on the basis of Marx's work.

In this situation, a sociology inspired by Marxism might well address itself to the relations between the following concepts, which are still insufficiently distinguished: ideology and knowledge, utopia and anticipation of the future, poetry and myth. Such a critical study needs to be taken up again in our changing world. Here is a choice theme for the sociologist, one with plenty of scope both for critical thought and for the most "positive" findings: the distance between ideology and practice, between current representations of reality and the reality itself. . . .

FIFTEEN

Identity Choice and Caste Ideology in Contemporary South India

STEVE BARNETT

As Barnett writes in the introductory pages of this essay, theoretical paradigms within anthropology have largely failed to comprehend societies totalistically and have, particularly, replaced historical, generative studies with transcendental-formalist analyses. Barnett suggests that the apparently different endeavors of structuralism (for example, the work of Lévi-Strauss) and "etic" anthropology (the cultural materialism of Marvin Harris, for example) are similarly reductionistic.

Barnett uses a consideration of the character of social change in India to illustrate a powerful general model of how ideological forms are created or transformed and how they are generative in and of social action. Barnett, like Dumont, on whom he draws a good deal, locates change in contemporary India in the shift from the holistic universe of caste hierarchy to the substantial, individualistic universe of class in which castes have become "ethnic" groups. But Barnett's study does this in the context of an extension of Marx's concepts of the relative opacity and transparency of ideologies and, correlatively our understanding of symbolic dominance. In these respects, Barnett's paper furnishes the bases of a radical anthropological theory at the same time that it is an illuminating instance of the theoretical insights which can come with a critical anthropology of everyday life.

WHAT IS HAPPENING to contemporary caste is the central question for Indian anthropology. Much of our research bears on caste organization and recent changes given state capitalism, urbanization, wage labor, etc. Unfortunately, we tend to freeze local trends as global directions and so anthropologists have suggested that castes are now compartmentalizing traditional and modern com-

Reprinted by permission of the publisher from *The New Wind: Changing Identities in South Asia*, Kenneth David, ed. (The Hague: Mouton, World Anthropology Series).

ponents—that castes are being superseded by class orientations—that castes are adapting to modern conditions by mobilizing members to vote for particular political candidates—etc. Since all these are co-occurring, middle-range theories that purport to account for each are inadequate and misleading.

This paper will outline recent changes in one South Indian caste as an illustration of a broad approach to contemporary caste ideology. The approach focuses on identity and identity choice as the central problem in situating caste today. Since South Indians live in a world where identity choices based on caste, class, ethnicity, cultural nationalism, and "race" are possible, such an approach must include these within one analytic frame.

This analytic approach is a synthesis of recent anthropological work in symbolic analysis (especially that of G. Bateson, L. Dumont, C. Geertz, D. Schneider, and C. Lévi-Strauss) and in neo-Marxist theories of superstructure (L. Althusser, H. Lefebvre, G. Lukács, and J.-P. Sartre).[1] It attempts to provide an understanding of ideology that does not make self-serving distinctions between science and ideology, or "explain" ideology only as a cultural system (bracketing base and infrastructure relations). Given the rapid and profound changes in caste in this century, Indians can choose among a number of identities and the relation of these choices to caste is central to understanding the operation of ideologies in everyday life. Placing ideological choice in the domain of everyday life poses most clearly questions of ideological mechanisms: how do people assert and argue over particular identity choices? And therefore the orientation of this analytic frame is: how do symbols symbolize in ideologies; what is the relation of ideology to action; how can ideologies compete; what are the interconnections among ideologies within one society; and what is the form of the relation between control over production and ideological control? Basically, we must focus on caste ideology and how changes in that ideology allowed and shaped the other ideological developments of class, cultural nationalism, etc.

This synthetic approach to meaning in ideological form is prompted by a sense of anthropological malaise: while numerous new "schools" attempt to totalize their very partial understandings of social formations, there is a corresponding lack of critical dialogue across "schools." Without trying to prove an impression, there are signs of a kind of flatness within the discipline. Despite the recent exponential rise in Ph.D.'s, there is no theoretical ferment; most younger anthropologists seem content to do "normal science," but in this case, a filling in of paradigms that do not genuinely excite or capture the imagination. Anthropological schools (materialist, ethnoscience, structuralist, whatever) tend doggedly to defend their territory, never admitting the slightest chink in their armor, rather than engage in serious theoretical struggle.

Of course, we have learned much but our attempts to expand partial understandings into global theories have run into the epistemological conundrum of our time: how to link thought and action. And anthropologists have filled in the cells created by their philosophical predecessors—reduce ideas to action, or action to ideas, or bounce them off one another in an endless hall of mirrors, or separate them entirely. Within the discipline, we are reaping the consequences of a naïve epistemology, elaborated most clearly after World War II but already present in the works of Tylor, Frazer, and Radcliffe-Brown. Taking other societies as the object of investigation was made possible as an activity by a strong sense that analysis was modeled on natural science and that categories of analysis in fact existed in an objective sense in a real world. The problem then became forms of ordering within these analytical categories, whether Tylor's "species" or Radcliffe-

Brown's "typological classification." This stance, while guaranteeing the Archimedean Point of anthropological analysis, concealed the anthropologist's historicity and his imbeddedness in a culture-specific theory of knowledge.

But "other societies" as object has not delivered anthropology from a more general critique. Unlike the genuine creation of an object for a genuinely new scientific exploration (say, as Althusser points out, the unconscious in Freudian psychiatry) where that new object is central and well-integrated in a complex array of theoretical constructions, the idea of "other societies" (or more generally and more vacuously "man") is a spurious object. "Spurious" because we have never provided a place for that object: the hallowed four fields of anthropology remain separate; the pious phrase, "the psychic unity of mankind," is just that. The inductive assumption that our various investigations would somehow sum to a significant totality inverts the nature of a scientific effort that simultaneously creates and integrates its object.

Few anthropologists now accept as innocently as did their ancestors that categories are "given" and that we are doing something directly akin to natural science, but there has been a determined effort to preserve either an ahistorical stance or a "rational" theory of knowledge. But, crucially, the fundamental link between them is severed, especially in the two serious attempts to redefine anthropological inquiry, one at the level of the nature of categories (structuralism) and the other at the level of natural science as a model (etic, ecological, or biological anthropology). Structuralism sees surface categories as aimed at reproducing a system, not analyzing it,

and therefore seeks an analytic structure that crosscuts ("underlies") these surface categories. In the work of Lévi-Strauss and others, however, there is a question about their ultimate reliance on surface categories (most importantly, kinship) (Schneider and Boon 1974). And beyond that, to the extent that structuralist analysis restricts itself to a resorting of lexically given data, it cannot address the meta-structuralist question: are the results a tautological artifact of the method? If one searches lexically given data carefully enough, one can find alternate orderings: the metaquery—whence any particular order—cannot be addressed (and Lévi-Strauss has said that he is writing myths about myths). Since there is no way, internal to structuralism, to ground an order in something outside itself, form becomes ahistorical, with history filling in the content of that form. (Of course, I am being extreme here to make an epistemological point; it is not as if structuralists select orderings at random, rather they have provided us with elaborated and, in many cases, sensitive accounts of meaning in particular settings. But, as in any pathbreaking endeavor, this has brought to light new problems. For example, what are we to make of Lévi-Strauss's brilliant transformation of totemic structures to caste structures when he omits, since it doesn't correspond to the elements of the transformation, any reference to rank and hierarchy in caste?) (Lévi-Strauss 1966: Ch. 4).

The general structuralist dilemma results in an abstract accounting of possibilities within structures of meaning as the analyst, his ideology, his historicity are not included within the analysis. The older anthropological Archimedean

Point, modeled on the natural sciences, was grounded in a "rationality" that by its very nature was ahistorical; one could, at least there was no inherent *methodological* obstacle, develop truths that spanned historical epochs. For structuralists, since surface categories are not "given," positivist rationality also vanishes but an ahistorical pose remains, here justified by a total imbeddedness in mythological thought. The "rationality" of mythological thought can never get outside itself to "truth" and so history becomes just another mythological category.

Etic, ecological, and biological anthropologists, responding to a deep ideological concern to extend the "objectivity" of natural science to all inquiry (a concern that directly parallels the general constitution of bourgeois ideology: Lukács 1971: Ch 1), attempt to situate the construction of meaning in symbolic form in terms of environmental *cum* physiological ("material") constraints. "Scientific method" is here preserved and reified by a simple bracketing artifice: elements of meaning do not relate to each other systematically. Rather, each particular element can be related to a particular "material" constraint (e.g., Marvin Harris' relating the sacredness of cows in India, and not considering Hindu sacredness in general, to efficient energy utilization, and then thinking he had said something about the nature of ideology: Harris 1966). Meaning, as discrete elements, can be understood in terms of something outside itself, but structures of meaning cannot since such structures do not have direct behavioral or "material" referents. What crosscuts surface categories is not deep structures of meaning, but similar "material" requisites (typically,

in terms of ratios of caloric intake and caloric expenditure). This reductionist rationality (reductionist because it cannot comprehend ideological form as such) allows historical speculation in terms of utilization (control and techniques) of a "material" base.

For these anthropologists, a theory of knowledge, a purified "operational" positivism, provides the path to history. But the path vanishes before the destination is reached, vanishes the moment we ask for the historical genesis of operational positivism itself. Following Marx, history is not a chronological retelling of what happened, but the evolution of the totality (as praxis—action in ideological form) of particular epochs. But the idea of ideological form, totality as praxis, has already been bracketed by operational positivism and so operational positivism, *from a perspective internal to the method,* can only be seen in terms of the abstract development of a non-culture specific, rational theory of knowledge. That is, it cannot be seen in relation to an encompassing ideological field. (To the extent that etic anthropologists distinguish "idealist" from "materialist" analysis as a kind of recognition of ideological struggle, they fail to recognize the idealism of a materialism that cannot justify itself either in theory or in praxis, a point made long ago by Marx himself.) But the abstract growth of rationality as a kind of thing-in-itself amounts to a teleology not clearly related to calories or statistical summaries of bits of behavior. Again history fills in the content of ahistorical form; in structuralism this is transparent, in etic anthropology the same configuration is opaque.

Let us make the critique more general: a serious consideration of the nature of meaning implies that whatever approach we develop, it will include the analyst's own method as well.[2] Unlike physics for example, where quantum mechanics need not explain its own genesis, any approach to socially given forms of meaning must either imbed its own method in those social forms (i.e., account for itself) or found an inquiry into social forms on de-socialized individual imagination. And so the scope of the "scientific method" as appropriated by social scientists must be questioned rather than embraced as the final arbiter and guarantor of rigor. Methodological discussions in etic anthropology (and the "new archeology") do not address these issues, instead they castigate "idealism" in the name of what Marx deridingly called "mechanical materialism." And so it is no surprise that dialectics is to be purged from anthropological Marxism. But the purge also includes ideology as form and there are those who seek the final biological reduction of the problem of meaning by asking such questions as, "Do apes have a kinship system."[3]

My aim is not to provide a definitive critique of structuralism or etic anthropology, only to suggest in outline how they seek to preserve aspects of a once coherent anthropological problematic that attempted to provide an answer to the anthropological extension of the "other minds" problem. The object, other societies (or simply, man), was to be comprehended as a totality through the activity of participant observation (however light on the "participant" and heavy on the "observation"). But the totality was both thought and action, and ultimately anthropologists were forced to recapture the sense of the possibility of perceiving this totality by the fiat of reduction, either in terms of

reducing meaning to action or action to meaning. (As a necessary aside, we must also situate another attempt to work through this problem: the Parsonian strategy of analytically semi-autonomous "systems"—cultural, social, psychological—linked by a complex web of "levels." This served the immediate purpose of providing a ready justification for business as usual—analysis in each "system" could proceed as before with the added security that it was contributing to a totalistic integration. But more importantly, it provided the rationale for the abandonment of theoretical holism as the initial object of research. The totality became given in the sense that "sense-data" was given for British positivists: an immediate out-there that for that very reason could not be analyzed as such. Analytically, the totality could only be reconstructed, built up later from its parts [the systems]. The justificatory aspect of Parsonian sociology is apparent in the lack of fit of the "parts" and the eventual drowning of the whole in the infinite complexity of the "levels.")

The relative clarity of the anthropological problematic in a period of theoretical crisis defines contemporary attempts to carry on within those limits and suggests the potential of a radical anthropology. Such an anthropology would return to the object, the totality of a social formation, in a non-reductionistic way, including ideology as form and non-ideological constraints that do not allow that form to be directly enacted in the world. Ideological form is itself structured by non-ideological constraints (it is not an abstract accounting of symbolic possibilities with all possibilities equally given) and non-ideological constraints develop, not simply as external impingements, but in terms of a particular social formation. The whole is thus brought back into primary focus and the analytic distinctions of thought and action are seen in terms of their dialectical relation within that whole.

A return to theoretical holism also implies a shift in the anthropological problematic away from "rationality" as ahistoric toward a limited rationality that is fundamentally tied to a particular epoch. As L. Dumont has explicitly recognized (Dumont 1970a) we see what is stressed in one ideology by comparing it with what is unstressed in another (initially our own). But it is not just a matter of a free floating stressed/unstressed opposition, but that opposition in history (as contradiction): why is something stressed here and not there? In order to recapture a non-reductionist whole in history, we must focus on the general concept of the problematic, not just within anthropology, but underlying an entire social formation (and, interestingly, this provides the beginning of self-reflexivity to the extent that we can develop forms of analysis that include both the traditional data of anthropology and the internal history and structure of the discipline). "Problematic" (Althusser 1970) refers to what an ideology places outside itself as part of that which is simply given; that givenness is central to the reproduction of a social formation by making dispute over the basis of symbolic constructions out of bounds. Seeing symbolic form as grounded in a problematic also implies that we move beyond the analysis of lexical form. Although lexical form relates to a problematic, resortings of that form will not get us to the problematic since it cannot assign weight to alternate possibilities (as Lévi-Strauss could not reach the

problematic of caste—hierarchy—through transformations of totemism) and fundamentally since a problematic is also characterized by an *absence* of problems posed within an ideology.

By asking how a social formation reproduces itself, we also move to the heart of the dynamics of change and thereby to historical form, not merely history as content. Fundamental change becomes the replacement of one problematic by another, not the surface alterations that are grounded within a single problematic and, to that extent, serve to reproduce a social formation, however modified. (The tendency of anthropologists of change to see change all over the place interestingly parallels a general ideological tendency to see progress in incremental "changes.") Further, focusing on an ideological problematic enables us to relate non-ideological constraints, not to isolated symbolic elements, but to the basis of the reproduction of a social formation. Finally, through seeing other problematics, we come to be more aware of our ideology and can then relate to our own forms of repression in ways that creatively link the activities of anthropologist and citizen.

The nine starting points below elaborate this radical anthropological alternative in terms of the nature of identity in a profoundly changing South India. They enable an understanding of that moment of transformation when two ideologies co-exist and allow us to see why one ideology can structure action to a greater extent than another; that is, how non-ideological constraints affect the possibility of ideological enactment.

1. Persons and groups act on partial understandings of their world and these understandings are structured and

altered by acts. This praxis creates the need for interpretation (connecting understanding and act) and situates conflict (differing understandings, differing acts).

2. In order to act (for an act to have meaning, to make sense), a person must situate himself in terms of some construction of the world (ideology). Or, he must be "interior" to an ideology—it must be a construction that defines the "real." And since we are talking of "reality," a person interior to a particular ideology cannot consciously manipulate its most basic points. These points are accepted; they are seen by the interior person as *outside* the ideology, as part of a putative natural (vs. constructed) world. An ideology thus grounds "reality" as well as providing the range of manipulation of that "reality." A definition of ideology should include this double distortion: that it has a "natural" ground and that its limits are "real." This definition locates the tension between ideology and history (the paradoxical replacement of ideologies which in their own terms are irreplaceable) and provides an opening for the generation of new symbolic formations.

3. At the same time a person is interior to an ideology, he is exterior to other ideologies (sex, class, race, kin, etc.) in the same society (all such ideologies constituting an ideological field). These exterior ideologies are at least partially understandable (sharing global symbols common to the whole society) but do not provide a direct frame for action. Placement (interior vs. exterior) is therefore critical and moves praxis to the center of the analytical stage.

4. Since ideologies are partial understandings (or, distortions given symbolic domination and control) yet at the same time implicated in concrete action,

action both proceeds from and informs ideology. An act relates to an interior ideological position and is also an additional fact in the world, open to counter-interpretation from an external perspective (can be seen as interior for more than one ideology). A person may shift ideological stance given the cumulative effect of new acts and persuasive counter-interpretations and so action can restructure positions of interiority and exteriority for particular persons (identity choice).

5. All symbols and meanings in an ideology or an ideological field are not equally restructured through changes in personal identity. There is some relation between kinds of action and kinds of ideological consequence. Since ideologies have form (meanings embodied in symbols are interconnected, are structured) as well as content, this form conditions the action-ideology dialectic.

6. Symbolic structure is not an abstract set of binary oppositions or taxonomic configurations or whatever, but is fundamentally tied to action. Ideologies are "structures-in-dominance": symbols are asymmetrically related, with certain symbols in a dominant position (they inform central domains of action and can articulate basic propositions about reality). To understand symbolic meaning in ideological form, we must direct attention to symbolic dominance (the particular form of distortion). Oppositions, taxonomic relations, etc., emerge as significant as they articulate interiority and exteriority, forcing choice and action. An abstract configuration of symbols can reveal possibilities for manipulation and future direction but only if imbedded in a discussion of dominance. This moves us toward *mechanisms* of ideological change (changes in dominance within an ideo-

logical field, quantitative change, and changes of the ideological field itself, qualitative change).

7. Symbols embody, in their range of possible meanings, meanings which specify contradictions (such global symbols may, at the same time, be central to two or more ideologies in fundamental conflict). Here a stress on certain possibilities within a range of meaning (and a devaluation of other possibilities) defines a person's place (interiority) in an ideological field. The symbolic stress of groups controlling resources and use of resources defines an overall structure-in-dominance and opposition to that structure. An abstract accounting of all metaphorical possibilities of meaning without regard for stressed and unstressed aspects defines the range of options within an ideological field (but *not* the field itself since it always has dominance aspects).

8. Shifts in stressed and unstressed meanings can also relate to levels of meaning, or where a symbol's meaning is located in a particular ideological structure. (''Levels'' is another word for disputes over kinds of reification.) Since there may be much overlap from one ideology to another in an ideological field, location characterizes an interior vs. exterior placement with regard to a particular ideology. Whether a symbol is seen as central or peripheral can determine one or another identity choice.

9. These starting points are directed to processual change, to the differing viewpoints and identities found in complex societies and to the ways they interrelate. We are directed to forms of ideological struggle (what might be called ''theoretical practice'').

Identity and identity choice is the central form of ideological struggle in South India. The ideological field of caste hierarchy has been (is being) replaced by a field where caste has a fundamentally altered significance and the options of ethnicity, cultural nationalism, class, and race become viable. This replacement revolves around the meanings assigned by South Indians to the symbol, blood purity; a stress on blood as embodying a castewide code for conduct reproduces caste hierarchy, a stress on blood as embodying natural substance opens the ideological field to other identity choices. Within particular castes, caste members now can hold widely differing views on what it means to belong to that caste and these differences often result in verbal quarrels, factions, isolation, marriage partner choice, and physical fights. A controversial act by a caste member becomes a fact differently understood by these antagonists and is endlessly recounted, revised, and debated.

The analytic frame in points 1–9 is designed to help understand these struggles and to move them into ethnographic focus as generators of new ideological forms (instead of the usual ploy of using struggle and conflict to illustrate some functionalist-oriented regularity). In terms of current anthropological discussions of ''idealism'' and ''materialism,'' it avoids both the idealism of divorcing culture from all else and the materialism that sees culture as epiphenomena. The basic issue is the structure of ideology: anthropological idealists would have it that this structure is intelligible at the level of abstract meaning, anthropological materialists that there is no symbolic structure at all. The task of a truly radical anthropology is not to reify form or content but to follow through the implications of their connectedness.

A striking fact of South Indian life today is the range of identity choices open to people, rural and urban, wealthy and poor. It is possible to keep up caste appearances, deny them, stress a commonality with all "Dravidians," change the focus of caste ties from local to regional, join a union and strike against a factory owned by a man of your caste, or adopt racist attitudes toward lower castes (especially Adi-Dravidas). These choices relate to, but also cut across, divisions of rural-urban, class, and education. And their manifest complexity seems to defy such analytic simplifications as modern caste is declining, modern caste is adapting to new conditions, or modern caste is compartmentalizing new and old lifeways. Theorists tend to offer replacement (caste is becoming class) or additive (caste plus class) solutions without being fully aware of the "apples and pears" nature of the problem.

There are two (potentially complementary) versions of an additive solution that deserve immediate attention. One suggests "compartmentalization" (Singer 1972), the separation of conflicting domains and behaviors (e.g., home—office). The other hypothesizes the "interpenetration" of those aspects of modernity and tradition that do not directly clash and that contribute to the development of a modern state (Rudolph and Rudolph 1967).

But these solutions simplify too soon and categorize too sharply. Take the compartmentalization illustration of a Brahman businessman who eats with lower castes at the office (and who may eat meat on trips abroad) but whose wife and mother keep an orthodox kitchen at home. The rub is for that kitchen and home to be truly orthodox (adhering say, to the standards of traditional Iyer Brahman purity), the businessman

should be outcaste and barred from eating in his own home. The rules of orthodoxy and concepts of purity are being importantly modified rather than being maintained through compartmentalization.[4]

Take the political activities of caste associations as an example of interpenetration, of the adaptability of caste to parliamentary democracy. To what extent do regional, named groups called castes have anything to do with localized caste principles of hierarchical organization? Vote mobilization is an activity that, on the surface, seems not involved with relative purity or transactional rank and presupposes basic shifts in rank principles and purity components. To reify the category "caste" without probing the ideological organization of caste conceals the significance of recent caste change.

So, these additive solutions, while initially compelling, really serve as stimulants to further speculative effort. And such effort should focus on present struggle, for identity choice seen in terms of the political and economic appeals of class alliances, cultural nationalism, and racism are profound matters that will determine the proximate course of Indian society. This last sentence is not what anthropologists usually think about when considering identity matters, but it is time we risked a bit more theoretically to speak to concerns of much of the world's population.

A Caste Substantialization in Contemporary South India

Louis Dumont, not especially concerned with recent developments in

India and surely no Marxist, has nonetheless put his finger on the basic change in twentieth-century caste—substantialization (Dumont 1970a).

I will illustrate this discussion of ideology, identity, and recent caste change by detailing this process for an upper non-Brahman, landowning caste in Tamilnadu State—KoNTaikaTTi VeLaLar (hereafter KV). To begin to understand the roots of identity, we must ask what makes a person a KV. An older KV will reply, "*maTi*" (purity). Purity concepts are, of course, complex, but importantly characterize a flow of material through a person's body. This flow includes food, semen, water, and excreta. Parts of the body retain purity or pollution such as hair and fingernails and must be handled with caution. And so the person may be considered a kind of bag or vessel in which, through which, and around which this flow of relatively pure or polluted material occurs. An individual KV may at any one moment be more or less pure than other KVs depending on whether he has eaten, just taken a bath, is observing death impurity for a close relative, etc.

But this relatively small range of purity occurs within the purity boundaries of the KV caste as a whole. And this overarching KV purity is what makes a KV a KV. For KVs, this purity is located in a person's blood (*irattam*). Blood is transmitted from both parents to their children,[5] from the father through the concentrated blood that is semen and from the mother through the concentrated blood that is breast milk (or as an occasional KV woman said, directly through uterine blood).[6] This blood purity is not fixed for life at birth but is affected by life style (the flow of material). KVs are extremely orthodox (resembling Brah-

mans more than other less concerned upper non-Brahman castes) and say, for example, that eating meat lowers blood purity. Since many other actions may raise or lower blood purity, a caste-wide "code for conduct" (Schneider 1968a) is enjoined by the definition of caste identity in terms of purity given at birth but alterable in everyday life. The traditional possibility of outcasting for serious violations of the KV code for conduct by the KV *panchayat* institutionalizes this dual aspect of blood purity. Blood purity, as substance enjoining a code for conduct, defines what it is to be a KV—how a person becomes a KV and what he must do to remain a KV.

Within the KV caste as a whole (with members in almost all Tamilnadu districts), there are distinct village clusters seemingly preserving the boundaries of tax-collection units in ancient Tamil kingdoms, and within most village clusters, KVs break down into ranked, non-intermarrying, bilateral kindreds (*vakaiyara*).[7] KVs say that these kindreds are ranked by life style; lower kindreds are slightly looser about purity requirements and therefore pass on slightly lower blood purity to their children. When pushed by a persistent anthropologist, some KVs make this quantitative: there is a small range of purity for all KVs but within this range there is still room for distinctions.

This structure—the caste as a whole, village clusters, ranked kindreds within clusters—unified by an indigenous theory of purity and conception, roughly summarizes important levels of KV identity during British Rule at least until the early 1920s. Until then, caste hierarchy was intact as a structure stressing holism, interdependence of its parts, and rank corroborated through asymmetric intercaste transactions. Here, in Dumont's phrase, there is no "privileged level"; we cannot talk of an inviolable caste substance apart from codes for conduct that structure intercaste relations. Castes, subcastes, and kindreds emerge as plateaus which temporarily freeze the constant flow of relatively pure and polluting material in particular contexts within local wholes.

By the turn of the century, things were beginning to change and the focus of activity was the development of the South Indian cultural nationalist movement (M. R. Barnett 1972). Early on, South Indian cultural nationalism was anti-Brahman, reflecting in part the privileged position of Brahmans in governmental bureaucracy. KVs traditionally were close to Brahmans in orthodoxy and rank (just below Brahmans but above other upper non-Brahmans) and also were dominant landowners. If the non-Brahman movement was successful, KV leaders hoped their caste might assume leadership in South India along with other vegetarian VeLaLar castes. But they needed greater visibility— Brahmans were recognized throughout India but KVs were numerically small and known as a distinct caste only where they controlled significant village clusters. More optimistic KV leaders hoped that all six vegetarian VeLaLar castes could unite, forming a powerful bloc in what was then Madras Presidency.

In addition, Madras City emerged as a center of government, education, and small-scale indigenous industrial and entrepreneurial activities. Educated, wealthy KVs from all districts began to move to Madras City, meeting other KVs from widely separate village clusters. KVs from villages near the City

also began to urbanize, taking clerical posts and working for the railroad. A very few KVs had been to England and began to question caste customs in light of their own experiences bolstered by appeals to a transplanted Utilitarian rationality.

These KV reformers saw intermarriage across village clusters and among kindreds within village clusters as basic to KV political identity and to KV advance in the urban setting. (Some hoped that eventually all vegetarian VeLaLars might intermarry.) Intermarriage would contribute to the creation of an all South Indian identity and would allow educated, urban KVs to form new, advantageous alliances with other urban KVs from different village clusters. After a prolonged struggle, these reformers mustered enough votes at a late 1920s KV caste association meeting to pass a resolution endorsing interdistrict marriage. (Similar resolutions have been reported throughout India, but their significance is obscured by assumptions that widening marriage networks is an adaptive mechanism, allowing the continuation of caste forms of organization in the modern world.)

Copies of minutes of that KV caste association meeting plus recollections by participants convey the tenor of the debate over passage. Orthodox KVs were shocked at the prospect of wider alliance possibilities, arguing that a person was not simply a KV but a KV of a certain *vakaiyara* in a certain village cluster. These *vakaiyaras* were transactionally ranked; upper *vakaiyara* KVs would not, for example, take cooked food or water from lower *vakaiyara* KVs since the lower *vakaiyara* KVs were thought to be less strict in observing purity standards embodied in codes for conduct. Interdistrict or inter-*vakaiyara* marriage would mean that such codes for conduct were no longer stressed since, without a transactional ranking frame, how could one know the relative purity of a KV living four hundred miles away.

KV reformers countered by arguing that nowadays a KV is a KV solely by virtue of birth (his parents were KV)— since the caste *panchayat* no longer functions to outcaste, the way a KV lived was essentially his own business as far as marriage or caste membership was concerned. These reformers invoked the Kali Yuga to justify this line of thought, suggesting that this was a general era of gathering chaos and moral laxity. Of course, they did not envisage KVs eating beef or inviting Untouchables to their homes; rather, they argued for a general KV way of life (often on health, not religious, grounds) objecting to minute distinctions and the previous emphasis on subdividing the caste as a whole.

The implications of the reformers' logic are profound and ultimately confront the entire ideological field of caste hierarchy. Blood purity, including in its range of meaning heritable substance enjoining a code for conduct as co-definers of KV caste identity, is now altered so that substance is stressed, code for conduct unstressed. This does not imply that KVs have no concern for how they act, only that particular acts are no longer coterminous with *being* a KV. If codes for conduct are not definers of caste identity, then the range of personal choice opens (including codes for conduct related to class, bourgeois westernization, Tamil cultural nationalism, etc.). Transactional caste ranking is no longer central to fixing a caste's position since the behavior of one caste member

no longer redounds to the rank of the caste as a whole. The hierarchical interdependence of castes so central to a holistic ideology is similarly challenged. Before, KVs could not perform all the tasks necessary to sustain life; they required the labor of service and untouchable castes. Now, since adhering to a castewide code for conduct is not part of being a KV, KVs do more for themselves now than before. Many KVs have "self-respect" marriages, using KV leaders to officiate at the ceremony rather than rely on Brahman priests.

Since passage of this resolution, there have been important changes in KV kinship patterns. Rather than different levels of caste organization appearing or vanishing in different contexts there is now a privileged level—KVs as a regional caste bloc. For rural, poorer KVs kindred affiliation may be kept up but is desultory; alliances within a kindred may continue as a path of least resistance but people of different kindreds regularly eat together and it is very poor taste to talk publicly of kindred rank. The KV regional caste bloc is layered roughly into an elite at the top composed of educated, mostly urban, KVs from all districts; a mass at the bottom, usually marrying within their kindred and village cluster; and a linking group with ties in both directions. This organization is well-suited to cope with increased KV demands for education, jobs, and other favors since members of the mass can reach the elite through the linking group.

What I have described is the process of what Dumont calls the substantialization of caste. This may also be understood as the transition from caste to ethnic-like regional caste blocs. "Ethnic-like" because each such unit is potentially independent of other such units, defined and characterized by a heritable substance internal to the unit itself and not affected (in terms of membership in the unit) by transactions with others outside the unit. Rather than the conceptual holism of caste, we begin to see the antecedent autonomy of its component parts. In an ethnic-like situation, transactional ranking no longer orders the parts of the whole and caste interdependence is replaced by regional caste bloc independence. This qualitative change in the ideological field of caste (summarized in the table below) is possible (it can motivate action, it makes some sense to the actors even if they do not see or accept its ramifications) to the extent that it is expressed in terms of *the* symbol of traditional caste identity—blood purity. A shift in stress from code for conduct to inviolable substance at once seems to preserve the trappings of caste and provides a surface ideological continuity while undercutting caste ideology at its root:

Stressed and Unstressed Aspects of Caste and Class

CASTE	*CLASS (ETHNICITY)*
1. Hierarchy—structural logic of interdependence	1. Stratification—substantialist logic of independent units
2. Holism—sacred order (pure-impure)	2. Individualism—secular order
3. Controlled imitation	3. Imitative order—reference group behavior
4. Multiplicity of units—expansion primarily by fission at the subcaste level	4. Fewer units—expansion by fusion
5. Social order as part of nature	5. Social order as rational—distinct from nature

I emphasize the qualitativeness of this change because caste substantialization opens the way for competing and complementary identity claims. Once codes for conduct can cross caste lines, other identity possibilities arise in South Indian ideology. KVness, rather than providing an overriding structure for one's identity and actions, becomes one among a number of identity elements in a historical period of great flux. This crossing of caste lines allows the South Indian ideological field to be divided in any number of ways. I have already discussed KV "ethnicity" and will only add there is strong evidence that other castes (especially other upper non-Brahman castes) have developed similar ethnic-like structures. Tamil cultural nationalism (the non-Brahman movement from the Justice Party to the DK to the DMK and now, given the recent split, the Anna DMK) suggests that all Tamils (alternatively all South Indians) participate in the same Dravidian culture (casteless and classless in its pristine state in ancient Dravidanadu, so the argument goes) and that this culture provides an overriding and basic identity for all Tamils. M. R. Barnett and I have suggested (Barnett and Barnett), that caste substantialization is an important prerequisite for the ideological appeal of Tamil cultural nationalism. If codes for conduct can cross caste lines, it becomes possible to suggest one code for conduct (Dravidian culture) for all castes, for all South Indians. In caste society, the idea of a basic commonality from upper to lower castes would have seemed absurd.

Racism, a stress on physical features

to determine rank, is not a clear feature of traditional caste rank. While traditional texts do write of skin color, facial construction, body proportions, etc., these are not used to rank castes in particular villages or localities. One can however see evidence for an emerging racism in contemporary South India, although this is a sensitive matter and the data are not conclusive. South Indian racism takes the form of emphasizing supposed differences in the physiology of Untouchables to account for their oppressed condition. The development of ethnic-like caste blocs, and the concomitant de-emphasis on transactional ranking, has qualitatively demarcated the one group for whom transactional ranking and residential segregation have been assiduously maintained—Untouchables. Untouchable bottom rank, poverty, menial work, and their general state of opprobrium were as severe as can be imagined in caste society, but they were at the bottom of a conceptual continuum that, in terms of purity, form of ranking, and holism, included all castes. Now all castes keep up asymmetric transactions with Untouchables, even where they abandon them with other castes. Given this qualitative distinction, Untouchables are coming to be seen as a separate "race." A survey I conducted in Madras with heads of KV households revealed that most older and rural KVs felt Untouchables were different because they *behave* differently, while most younger and urban KVs felt Untouchables were different because they *look* differently (Barnett and Barnett).

Caste substantialization, seen for KVs first in a change in marriage possibilities presaging a fundamental shift in the basis of caste ideology, has consequences for diverging identities among members of the KV regional caste bloc. The shift from holism to pluralism, from transactional rank to attributional rank, from interdependence to independence, is made real for South Indians because they see it in terms of those symbols that define a person's identity. Previously, blood purity defined membership in a caste by establishing a link with caste ancestors (ultimately those created in the KV origin myth) through heritable substance, and by establishing a code for conduct that sustained that link. A stress on blood purity as substance changes all this. Just as caste blocs can be seen as independent of other caste blocs, persons in caste blocs can see themselves as independent. Their actions are no longer subject to the scrutiny of a caste *panchayat* with the power to outcaste. They become involved in the crosscutting, multiple identity claims of modern life—ethnicity, class, cultural nationalism, and race.

This summary of KV caste change in the twentieth century would totally miss the point if it suggested that these choices were unambiguous. Contemporary South Indian life is rather one of contention, with people putting forth competing identity claims. Members of the same family, kindred, and caste can hold basically different views of who they are and these differences may emerge in family and public fights (verbal and physical). Identity theorists tend to see ethnic groups as monoliths espousing some ideological uniformity. Alternatively, ethnic groups can be understood as forums where people contend (feel that contending is necessary) and therefore are arenas for the presentation of diverse ideological poses.

Implicit here is a heretical view of the way symbols symbolize. Symbolic anthropologists either elide past concretely linking culture to action (much structuralist work) or fall back on some Parsonian construction of levels (Schneider and C. Geertz in their very different ways). The levels approach tends to rely on external criteria ("distinctive features") to establish levels that purportedly hold throughout a society. But those distinctive features which separate levels derive from an antiseptic form of anthropological questioning; in the course of everyday life just what is a level (what will pass for a distinctive feature) is precisely up for grabs. It involves symbolic domination and manipulation since different understandings of levels articulate different identity choices and these choices shape political and economic struggle. I read much current anthropology by unfreezing levels—whenever an anthropologist establishes them, I see instead a set of abstract possibilities to be fought over. The levels do not exist "out there," "out there" is structured by power, dominance, and control: who has the power to define levels (symbolic dominance), what is the consciousness of those being opressed by that definition, and what courses of resistance (how can they alter the definition) are open to them.

So also for identity choice in South India. KVs are KVs and also workers, bosses, racists, communists, Tamil nationalists, followers of Gandhi, atheists, and pious Hindus. These possibilities can be found within families, kindreds, and neighborhoods. When disputes occur, they are over level, over the implications of being a KV and simultaneously being whatever else.

Let me illustrate with an instance from Madras City.[8] A traditionally orthodox KV refused to invite a reformist KV (a longtime Tamil nationalist who had eaten with lower castes at political meetings) to his daughter's wedding feast. When KV caste leaders heard of this, they told the orthodox KV that they would boycott the wedding meal unless he rescinded and invited the reformist.

The orthodox KV was using the traditional ploy of refusing to interdine with those of lower blood purity (here because of the reformist's particular code for conduct) to enforce his sense of what it means to be a KV. The caste leaders used the same ploy to suggest an alternate sense of KV identity (disputing the salience of the reformist's code for conduct). This is not all, for the orthdox KV was caught in a double-bind: since orthodoxy in caste society is defined by a castewide code for conduct, when caste leaders refused to attend the wedding feast they were redefining orthodoxy itself, denying an orthodox pose to the father of the bride.

This revealingly simple incident revolved around levels of determining KV identity. For the orthodox KV, the distinctive feature of caste membership was a code for conduct enjoined by KV blood purity. For the KV caste leaders, only ancestry counts and that ancestry is distinct from a particular code for conduct. This was not, however, a contest of equivalent, opposing views for to the extent that the orthodox KV's sense of what it means to be a KV depends on castewide consensus, it has no standing as an individual statement of belief. Accordingly, he eventually invited the reformist KV but remained genuinely confused and a bit forlorn, understanding that his sense of KV identity was superseded, but feeling it was a "fast one," a kind of shell game (popular in Madras as one of many street magicians' hustles).

Another incident, having to do with a possible strike in a Madras City factory where a number of KVs are employed, extends the idea of levels of meaning relating to identity choice as being up for grabs.[9] During a week-long discussion on strike issues, all KV workers decided to meet to formulate a single position. Without elaborating in detail, the issue of that meeting was the relation of being a KV to being a worker. One man suggested KV workers oppose the strike, "After all, most of us own some land [village land] and have PaRaiyan workers there so that we are bosses as well as workers. What if those PaRaiyans decided to strike?" Another countered, "It is our custom to own paddy land, but what is KV factory custom. We should lead the strike and lead other workers just as we lead other castes in the village." A third said, "How can we lead others if we ourselves are being commanded by the factory foremen at the same time. We are simply workers like other workers. Maybe we can use our caste to contact KVs who know the factory owner, but those KVs have nothing in common with us anyway."

Finally, someone asked, "Why are we here? If we are KVs we should have one position." However, unanimity could not be reached and at the end of the meeting a young KV said in disgust, "Being a KV is like being fat: you can recognize other fat people, but the only thing you have in common is eating. All we have in common is a name; either we are workers or scabs, nothing else."

What is being debated here is the centrality of KV ethnicity. Are general characteristics of KV ethnicity (landowning, links with KVs of other classes, etc.) relevant to the strike and to being a worker? Appeals to traditional prerogatives are countered with denials of relevance and, in one sense, the importance of being a KV, what does it entail, is at issue.

In addition to double-binding and centrality as mechanisms of ideological struggle around matters of identity, another possibility is hedging.[10] KVs in one urban neighborhood in Madras City strive to maintain transactional rank with other castes to retain their position above other upper non-Brahman castes, while at the same time they deny that a caste-wide code for conduct has anything to do with being a KV. They are presenting one face to themselves (KV identity as ancestral KV substance) and another to other castes (KV identity as enjoining a code for conduct).

This hedging (presenting two contradictory identities in two contexts) is really a kind of holding action and cannot be sustained in the urban setting. At a local non-Brahman temple, the priest offers *viputi* (sacred ash) to KVs before offering it to members of other castes. In 1968, some worshippers objected, asking why should one caste be privileged. The temple priest, mindful that temple donations are his basic income, went to KV leaders and suggested a compromise: KVs could get *viputi* first if they came to temple before other castes so that no one else could see and possibly object. KVs adamantly refused, saying that the point of priority was precisely its publicity so that other castes knew KV transactional privileges. (The issue was unsettled and remained tense when I left Tamilnadu in 1969.) In this incident, a KV attempt at hedging is being challenged and could turn into a double-bind for them.

Once the analytic frame is understood, almost any conflict can be seen as one of identity choice, over the symbols of identity and their placement (levels) in an ideology. Let me offer one more illustration; this time a rural case.[11] In one KV village, another upper non-Brahman caste asked local Untouchables to perform the same ritual service for them as they performed for any KV, and they offered a bribe of paddy as inducement. The Untouchables, aware that KVs still exercised important village control, refused; but since they desired the paddy, suggested that they would perform this service for *some* members of this other caste, but not *all* members. The Untouchables were suggesting two levels of caste identity: for KVs, substance enjoining code for conduct (and therefore including all KVs); for the other caste, individual wealth and merit (interestingly, Untouchables were willing to perform the service for important members of a number of upper castes). The other caste, of course, was unhappy since they hoped to challenge KV rank and could only do so if they *as a caste* were treated equivalently.

Untouchables hoped to play both ends against the middle by hedging—offering two criteria for caste identity, hopefully, in two arenas. But the other caste wanted to change transactional rank and so required the same criteria as applied to KVs. They hoped to make the best of what they could get by eventually accepting the Untouchable offer and suggesting that since some caste members were being treated like KVs, all were equivalent to KVs, following the logic that the behavior and treatment of one caste member redounds to the caste as a whole. KVs ridiculed this, saying that since some were *not* treated equivalently, the caste as a whole had no claim to change rank.[12]

These incidents point up essential features of contemporary life in South India seen in identity choices and the consequence of those choices. To understand traditional KV caste identity, we first noted their structural position, ranking between Brahmans and other upper non-Brahmans, combining a concern for orthodoxy with local dominance (the ability to command other castes without being commanded in turn). KVs see orthodoxy dictated by KV blood purity, a purity derived from KV ancestors and transmitted as substance, and maintained by a castewide code for conduct enjoined by that substance.

Given urbanization, the development of the non-Brahman movement, occupational diversification, and the introduction of Western forms of education (all given basic form by the nature of British imperialism and independent India's present political and economic structure), KV reformers persuaded the caste association to endorse interdistrict (and interkindred) marriage. The rationale for and effect of this decision was to alter the stress in the range of meaning of blood purity from code for conduct enjoined by substance to heritable substance itself. KV identity seen as this heritable, inviolable substance really changed KV caste to a KV ethnic-like regional caste bloc, a transition from caste as a holistic, interdependent, transactionally ranked hierarchy to caste blocs as substantial (in Dumont's sense), independent, attributionally ranked units in a plurality. Since codes for conduct could now cross caste lines, this allowed the development of other identity choices, most importantly those of class, ethnicity, Tamil cultural nationalism, and race.

This set of choices, corresponding to the ideological emergence of the person as antecedent and autonomous (as the agent of choice), is the focus of present-day South Indian ideological struggle. The *form* of that struggle has to do with disputes over levels, over the import and placement of one or another symbol of identity.

The form of double-binding is a counterexample to the additive solution of "interpenetration." Recalling the incident of the wedding feast, the orthodox KV attempted to push KV identity as substance enjoining code in a context where there was no agreement on what is entailed by KV substance. Since code must be castewide, he had no orthodox move left when caste leaders threatened not to attend the feast. Here modern and traditional elements did not so much interpenetrate as confound the orthodox KV in a situation of rapid and profound change.

The form of hedging is a counterexample to the additive solution of compartmentalization. The KVs who changed the basis of identity within the caste yet attempted to enforce urban transactional rank in *viputi* distribution are stressing *both* substance *and* code for conduct, but in different arenas. But the idea of distinct arenas (vs. substance enjoining code across the board) is *itself* a conceptual innovation, forced by the multiplicity of identity possibilities. The separation of arenas is open to the challenge that each arena affects the other— in the long run, KVs cannot sustain the contradiction inherent in separating and simultaneously stressing substance and code (just as, in the Brahman businessman example mentioned at the outset, the Brahman family cannot sustain the contradiction of simultaneously having and violating a single standard of purity).

Conclusion

This summary of the bases of KV caste identity and recent changes in that identity depends for its direction on the nine starting points given earlier in this paper. KV caste ideology was sufficient to order caste relations in pre-1920 villages but was inadequate to cope with twentieth-century economic and political developments. KVs were interior to this ideology: blood purity was not, in their eyes, something to be argued about or altered; it was the way the world was. That world was the ideological field of caste hierarchy. Structured by ideas of blood purity as substance enjoining a code for conduct, ideological stress was placed on holism, interdependence, and transactional rank. The foreign exposure of early KV reformers is crucial in confronting that interiority, since these KVs directly experienced alternate ideological stances. Most Europeans, especially the English, lumped all Indians together (and, as the Victorian use of "nigger" indicates, all nonwhites) in a racist ideology quite distinct from the KVs' understanding of caste hierarchy. But these same KVs also came into contact with English reformers with utilitarian underpinnings and learned biological theories of descent and biochemical approaches to the constitution of living organisms.

These contacts fundamentally altered

the scope of caste hierarchy; no longer was it the only natural vision of the world, it was now one among many, and a conquered one at that. These reformers eventually challenged the particular structure-in-dominance of caste hierarchy by altering the stress on the range of meaning of blood purity (stressing an inviolable, heritable substance that does not necessarily enjoin a particular code for conduct).[13] The new stress qualitatively changed the ideological field of caste hierarchy, but not as a conscious act. KV reformers hoped to preserve caste and did not foresee KV ethnicity. KV blood purity was still "natural," as was caste hierarchy. I have summarized the effects of that change, the development of a new structure-in-dominance: ethniclike, regional caste blocs. This ethniclike structure-in-dominance, with its individualist bias, allowed ideological struggles to take form around identity choices.

South Indians now live in a world where the options of caste, ethnic, class, cultural nationalist, or racial bases of personal identity coexist. Contemporary ideological struggle is focused on either the caste ideological field versus the ethniclike ideological field, or the various ideologies of identity within the ethnic-like ideological field. In this light, the incidents adumbrated above work concretely through the set of abstract possibilities that is the range of meaning of blood purity. The orthodox KV in the wedding-feast incident was interior to an ideology of caste hierarchy, while the reformer and the caste leaders were interior to an ideology of KV ethnicity. Blood purity was the key symbol for both ideologies but, given a different stress in each case, it specified the contradictions between them. Commensality,

withheld first by the orthodox KV and then by caste leaders, pinpointed these contradictions. The orthodox KV's sense of KV identity depended on caste-wide agreement, so he was moved out of cast interiority when caste leaders expressed disagreement. The fact of commensality is basic to new interpretation given another ideology (a legitimation of individual codes for conduct, eliminating transactional rank where one person's behavior has caste-wide consequences). In this alternate ideology, commensality was withheld, not because of purity danger, but as an insult. The orthodox KV's action (refusal to invite) proceeded from his sense of what it means to be a KV. The consequences of that action, counteraction by caste leaders, confounded that identity since he could no longer argue that his personal orthodoxy had caste-wide implications.

The incident over priority of *viputi* distribution illustrates the same points. Here, the significance and the arena of KV priority is interpreted differently given different positions of interiority. KVs want public distribution so all castes can understand KV rank in a caste ideological field. Other persons want *viputi* distributed on a first-come-first-served basis, given an individualistic perspective. The temple priest will give KVs *viputi* first, but privately, granting KV ethnicity but not the KV caste identity. There is no Solomon-like solution; one or another presentation of self and caste must give way.

We have just skimmed the surface of identity choice in contemporary South India as structured by the form of competing ideologies. But an elaboration of the form of ideological competition is not closed; to approach the basic question of symbolic dominance, we must expand our analysis to include those forces that, although not internal to an ideology and its problematic, by that very fact shape its power to motivate and sow the seeds of its eventual replacement. Why is it that holism structures less and less action in South Indian society? Surely not because, on the analogy of chess, another ideology magically appears with superior "moves." Rather, to anticipate our answer, because one ideology expresses what has become necessary to express—it constructs that new reality needed to reproduce a new social formation.

Starting with colonization, and perhaps earlier given recent revisionist views of the development of factories in pre-British India, we are directed to new forms of labor outside the structure of work as ordered within caste society (generally glossed in India studies as the *jajmani* system). This is a specific case of a general process: the transition to contractual forms of labor, and the separation of the domains of home and work. Rather than the interpenetration of substance and code in caste so that doing and being become aspects of the same structural position, substance is associated with home and code for conduct (as a particular kind of performance: contractual) is associated with work. Or, doing and being become ideologically distinct.

Ideologically, the prior condition for the separation of substance and code as contract is a stress on individualism. In a holistic hierarchical ideology, the merging of substance and code *provides* an explanation of difference: members of a caste do what they do because they are who they are (and vice versa). The whole is composed of these differentiated castes acting toward the same end.

Given individualism, the merging of substance and code *prevents* an explanation of difference: if individuals are autonomous and equivalent, the merging of substance and code implies a society composed of persons each doing the same thing. Demarcating code as contract, on the other hand, allows for (creates) difference as the application of "reason" (allocating tasks, organizing functions, etc.) in society. Substance as shared by all serves to set up the possibility of different codes where difference does not, ideologically at least, immediately imply ranked distinctions.

British imperialism and Indian capitalism after political independence create the environment in which caste becomes substantialized through the introduction of a nascent individualism and the consequent separation of substance and code. Symbolic dominance is seen in the simultaneous presence of two ideologies—caste and non-caste. These ideological fields are not simply juxtaposed, rather the caste ideological field can no longer structure and integrate basic life experiences. Once the individual becomes the basic unit of contractual codes for conduct, the individual is valorized ideologically as those contractual codes are perceived as part of the ways things are.

Further, we can only reach an understanding of symbolic dominance (as opposed to an abstract formal account of symbolic possibilities) by focusing on the problematic of an ideological field; those propositions, often unstated (that is, *supplied* by the analyst in the movement from what is stressed in one ideological field to what is unstressed in the other), that undergird actual ideological discourse. In this paper, there has been a double movement: the ideological field of holism is seen against Euro-American individualism, and then that ideological holism allows the breakdown of the individual into substance and code aspects. It is the particular relation of substance and code in the two ideological fields that allows us to speak of their respective problematics and to understand the dominance of one field over the other.

Present caste substantialization develops as labor shifts from a holistic orientation to contractual forms. Contractual labor stresses the parties (persons) involved in a specific contract; ideologically, each party is an independent entity engaging in "natural intercourse" with other entities by contract (Marx 1971: 17). As ideological struggle formed around the nature of contractual labor (glossed in the literature on "modernization" as "occupational diversification"), identity became substantialized in ethnic, in cultural nationalist, and in class terms (symbolic dominance). This processual replacement of one ideological field by another becomes at any one moment the competition of these two fields. The Marxist idea of cultural "lag" is just this overlap of cultural fields. But the overlap conceals a vector, since the ideological field of caste cannot sustain itself given ethniclike caste blocs (structure-in-dominance); or the stance of caste internality requires the related operations of double-binding and hedging (the form of contradiction between fields): the orthodoxy of the orthodox KV depends on the absence of a competing ideological field, Double-binding and hedging reveal the dominance of one ideological field over another—the inability of symbols of one field to structure activity to the extent that these symbols no longer allow or justify the reproduction of present base and infrastructure relations.

Within a single ideological field, it is difficult to see vectors, for we are now talking of some projection of where a society is going, not simply its present configuration. Here, praxis is a constant reordering and reassessing of the centrality of certain symbols (recall the example of the KV strikers).

What stands out in South Indian political and cultural life is the tension between class-based alliances and ethnic, racial, or cultural nationalist alliances. That non-Marxist political parties should try to blunt organization along class lines is not surprising and suggests cross-cultural comparisons. Harris (1970: 12) has suggestively argued that "ambiguity in Brazilian racial identity" and the

prevention of the development of racial ideology may very well be a reflex of the conditions which control the development of class confrontations. In the United States, racism and racial caste divisions have split and fragmented the lower class. In Brazil, racism and caste formation would unite the lower class (since there is a close correlation in Brazil between the class and race). "Black power" in the United States lacks the revolutionary potential of the preponderant mass; 'black power' in Brazil contains this potential. The ambiguity built into the Brazilian calculus of racial identity is thus, speculatively at least, as intelligible as the relative precision with which blacks and whites identify each other in the United States.

In India, racial identification is redundant in the caste system, in which intercaste transactions structure relationships in particular villages and in village clusters. Further, a stress on racial identity would dichotomize the "divide, rule, and isolate" aspects of caste rank. Where regional caste blocs cross class lines, physical differentiation among these blocs is not claimed by Tamils.

With the breakdown of uniform transactions among the members of these blocs, it is difficult to guess a person's affiliation. Such ambiguity allows the blocs to continue while at the same time suggesting the possibility for commonality across the blocs (i.e., the development of Tamil cultural nationalism).

The ideological raciation of untouchables inhibits the revolutionary development of the lower classes since, as in America, it fragments the lower classes. While most Untouchables are lower class, they do not comprise a majority of that class, which includes members of all castes, with a skewing in favor of lower castes. If other members of the lower classes come to regard Untouchables as a separate race, organization along class lines is, at least temporarily, blocked.

Symbolic dominance is thus an aspect of power defined as allowing the reproduction of a particular social formation despite clear inequity and oppression (differential allocation of control and resources) within that social formation. Ideologically, this reproduction takes place through structures-in-dominance (false consciousness) which define the limits of human action within that social formation.

Notes

1. This list obviously includes writers who disagree with each other. Here, I am not so much concerned with that as with a selection of aspects of these approaches that does not imply full agreement with any author. I do think that potential syntheses have been hampered by partisan debate. While I will enumerate the points of selection below, I reserve a detailed discussion for a future paper. Bateson (1972) has elaborated an approach to schizophrenia based on a theory of double binding which I extend to ideology as a whole. Dumont's (1970) notions of hierarchy and substance are basic to my understanding of South Indian culture. Geertz's (1964) paper is a basic critical foil. Schneider's (1968) concepts of substance and code for conduct enable me to make a link between an abstract understanding of South Indian ideology and everyday life. Lévi-Strauss of course has developed the most suggestive approach to abstract symbolic possibilities.

Althusser (1972, 1973) has most seriously tried to extend Marx's concepts and superstructure through an understanding of ideological fields and structures-in-dominance. Lefebvre (1971) has pointed to the crucial importance of the domain of everyday life for a Marxist interpretation of ideology. Lukács (1972) has decisively rejected the science/ideology dichotomy. Sartre (1968) has focused on the significance of the actor's position (internal, external) for analyzing ideological action. J. Dolgin, J. Magdoff, M. Silverman contributed to these points. This paper has also been importantly aided through discussion with P. Rabinow and P. Seitel.

2. For an expansion of this point, see Wellmer 1971, esp. Ch. 1.

3. N. Bukharin (1925:72) wrote of earlier biological reductions, "The dog state, the capitalist ape, and the imperialist chicken are an excellent indication of the level of modern bourgeois science."

4. I am here restating a point made for Chinese society by Levenson (1958).

5. There is evidence that for some castes blood is seen as passing from father only to children, or even from mother only to children. Correlating this with caste kinship differences (KVs emphasizing bilateral kindreds, Brahmans lineages, etc.) may prove fruitful.

6. The matter is much more complex. The "child" is not seen as a simple unit but has components that derive from either mother or father. The question of mother's blood is tricky: does she take on her husband's blood as she becomes part of his descent group on marriage? These questions would require another paper and are not directly relevant to recent caste change.

7. I use "bilateral kindred" in Yalman's somewhat unorthodox sense. See Yalman 1962.

8. For more detail, see my earlier paper (Barnett 1973a).

9. For more detail, see my forthcoming "Class Struggles in South India."

10. A graduate student in anthropology at Princeton, Fred D'Agostino, first brought the philosophical literature on hedging to my attention.

11. For more detail, see my earlier paper (Barnett, 1973b).

12. The decision to accept the Untouchable offer was made after I left Tamilnadu, and subsequent events were reported to me by letter.

13. Once substance is recast this way, it becomes possible for a well-educated, younger KV to say to me, "Why bother with this blood nonsense; KVs really share chromosomes—that is what makes me a KV."

SIXTEEN

Sexuality as a Social Form: Performance and Anxiety in America

David S. Kemnitzer

An anthropology of *praxis* sees a people's appropriation of ideology as occurring in *praxis*. Thought must be understood (and analyzed) as action; or, as Kemnitzer puts it here, symbolic processes *are* social. Through the concrete study of the creation of the ideology of the "new" sexuality in the contemporary United States, Kemnitzer's paper examines the production of "self" as an ideological process and situates this constitution of the "person" within the larger social order. In documenting the substitutability within American culture of relations based on "substance" and relations based on "code" (see Schneider, in this volume)—as well as the substitutability of the native domains of "home" and "work"—the analysis reveals the complex symbolic processes entailed in the manipulation of new ideological forms by the dominant society and locates the creation of new forms within the existing social order. Kemnitzer depicts how modes of domination (in this instance sexism) can be preserved, but in such a way that the fact that old forms of social relations have been maintained is masked. The analysis indicates the social dynamics underlying absorption in the United States from the perspective of the intentional actor and of the social system and is thus an important addition to Marcuse's presentation of the ideological processes manifest in the workings of late capitalist society.

THIS PAPER IS AN ATTEMPT to analyze the cultural construction of the "person" in American culture through the analysis of an action-domain, sexual relations.[1] In anthropological parlance, a "domain" is a subsystem of a larger symbolic unity, the "cultural order" (see Schneider 1969 in this volume). As such, a domain is a *native* category or metacategory: it exists in native thought, its boundaries and its usage are defined in native terms, rather than in terms derived from an *a priori* set of analytical concepts. Thus, for example,

we can make a distinction between kinship as the theoretically-defined set of relations of consanguinity and affinity and "kinship" as the cultural definition of the field of "relatives" and the relationships between them (see Schneider 1968 and 1969).

At the same time, this paper is about a social process, social differentiation and absorption, and about the way in which that process acquires meaning for the participants. Thus, while this paper does not do history, it views its materials through time. The purpose is to exempli-

Published by permission of the author.

fy a historical-analytical method which is, in my opinion, a way to handle contemporary problems as to the nature of metaphor or the relations between "culture" and social system. The paper also suggests, as the basic ground for cultural analysis, the study of symbolic processes as *social* processes: the dialectic of absorption, substitution, and social control. For a fuller discussion of this topic, see Kemnitzer, forthcoming.

It might be argued that this project should include detailed historical analysis; but culture-history rarely yields a systematic account without mystifying oversimplification. A more effective way to integrate the historical and the systematic viewpoints is to confront the process of differentiation and absorption through the study of "deviance." I want to emphasize, however, the negative consequences of the normative implications of that term: when we study deviance, we in fact study unsuccessful rebellion—the systematic absorption of differentiation and rebellion to the constituted order of power and authority.

Finally, this paper is about a new cultural construction of sex by a substantially new population in America, the young professionals and white-collar workers in a new kind of city environment, working at new kinds of jobs, and acting on a different action-set than their predecessors. The definition of sexual relations in a domain for action is a way whereby I try to approach the cultural constitution of the person, and of what it means to have relationships in this environment. The construction of sex in this regard is particularly important because it is the focal point of personal identity in American culture; and because an increased understanding of the relationships between men and women may be useful to a movement which can transform our "freedom"—which is now in fact merely our separation from a *previous* form of oppression—into our liberation.

I

What is the new sexuality? I should stress that the phenomena discussed here are, for the most part, cultural—that is, they are *ideological* insofar as they are significations of sexual behavior and not necessarily that behavior itself. (In Section III, I shall discuss some *social* processes, but the distinction should be kept clear, as an analytical, though not a principled, contrast.) My analysis is not based on data as to who actually does what to whom under what circumstances. Rather, I am concerned here with *ideas about* sex and even more particularly with the concepts employed in the construction of ideas about sex. The concern is with the natives' *interpretation* of their sexual behavior, its meaning *to them,* and with how that meaning takes its shape.

The meaning of any phenomenon is complex, and this fact produces two problems. The first is that the necessarily schematic character of any analysis such as this means that whole dimensions of meaning, the particularity, the implications, the concrete, human richness, of these phenomena, are lost.

Second, it is difficult to isolate a meaning-complex or domain, to say this is where it stops and this is where it begins. Sexuality—in American culture at least—is perhaps more complex in this way than other domains of American culture, and my decisions as to the direction and limits of the meaning-complex I discuss here are dictated largely by concerns which lie outside the data.

Part of the complexity of American sexuality is the centrality given to sexual relations throughout the culture, particularly with regard to the establishment of a field for social relations (Schneider 1968), but also with regard to the differentiation between the natural and the cultural (or "human"), between men and women. But in a sense, this is precisely the point of this paper: for in traditional or mainstream American culture, sexual relations and sexuality are an omnipresent but submerged and encapsulated aspect of social relations in general, domestic and interpersonal relations in particular. On the other hand, in the "new sexuality," sexual relations have become (or are becoming) a *domain* unto themselves (although a domain which constitutes a subset of a larger domain which has become similarly extracted from a more general social-cultural milieu).[2]

Associated with the encapsulation and omnipresence of sexuality in traditional/mainstream American culture is the special-ness of sex as an activity— sex is normatively restricted to a certain kind of relationship, between husband and wife, and to certain places, times, and acts. Sex is powerful, demi-mystical, and "dirty." It is neither an admitted aspect of other relationships, nor is it something which is properly discussed. By contrast, in the new construction, sex is practially *all* one can talk about: sexual relationships are an aspect of *all* relationships—among many, whether or not these relationships are heterosexual (and homosexual *feelings,* if not acts, are normatively found in all same-sex relations). Sexual relations are considered to be merely one of a large number of types of relationship and, in fact, to be incumbent upon the partners to an increasingly wide spectrum of (friendly) relationships, many if not most of them casual.[3] The following analysis will focus around one aspect—perhaps it is a consequence, but I doubt it[4]—of this construction: the notion that doing sex "properly" (itself a new notion), which is measurable in terms of both partners "achieving" orgasm of a particular sort and intensity as well as in terms of regularity, intensity, and variety of sexual activity, is a function of skill or technique: that fucking is a *performance,* subject to criteria of competence, which can be mastered as a skill (one can learn to be "a good fuck"). On this view, a "good fuck," a good performance, is the product of the competence of the partners.

There are a variety of "cultural" influences—the effects of psychoanalysis and "sexology," the increasing independence of women—which are part of the cause of this phenomenon and are to be found associated with it. I shall not deal with many of these, nor in much detail, for they speak, by and large, to aspects of relationships which are *content* to the social-cultural *forms* under analysis here. I might note, though, that while many of these things seem to have had quite an effect, the essential formal characteristic of the sex act in American society—which is the exploitation of women by men—has not changed. For example, notions of the nature of female sexual pleasure in the old ideology denied women pleasure by denying them clitoral stimulation, duration of coitus, and duration of "foreplay" (itself an instructive concept), and by placing the sex act within a fundamentally exploitative relationship, marriage. A friend of mine once illustrated that, for all the "technical" information available to men now, this has not changed: "They think it's a god-damned *button*, for Christ's sake! One kiss, they push it, and you're supposed to come." This, of course, does not gainsay the benefits, to both women and men, of increased knowledge about sex; it merely points out that technical expertise is not a substitute for human sensitivity and response. And it dramatizes, I think, the fact that the fetishism of technique in the new sexuality is a substitute for, and not a transcendence of, the clumsy brutality and selfishness which previously denied women sexual pleasure.

I want to begin my analysis with two approaches to the problem of the nature of the person in bourgeois society—approaches which are directly relevant here because they take as their core the sexuality of the person. Part of the purpose of this discussion will be to show the weakness of a cultural analysis which derives from psychology (that is, from either the concerns of psychotherapy or from metapsychological theory); but also, in differentiating myself from two positions—one advanced by Rollo May and the other by Herbert Marcuse—I shall better be able to begin my own analysis.

Rollo May has analyzed the fetishism of sexual technique, in his book *Love and Will* (1969), in terms of a concept derived from his earlier work (see 1950, esp. pp. 6–7), that of "normal anxiety." May uses his notion to characterize the "problems" of a culture as they are lived by its members and in particular by the neurotic and psychotic members of a culture, who live them unsuccessfully (1969: Introd.). He illustrates this con-

cept with a contrast between Victorian and contemporary culture, noting that the neurotic disorders treated by Victorian psychotherapists (Freud in particular) stemmed from the excessive repression of all forms of sexual or sensual enjoyment and the guilt that derived from these repressed desires. For moderns, by contrast, anxiety is shaped by the demand *for* sexual activity, sexual enjoyment, and associated problems.

May adduces a good deal of data to provide an excellent impressionistic account of these problems. For example, he presents one of his patients' dreams:

A knowledgeable medical student, one of whose reasons for coming into analysis was his sexual impotence, had a revealing dream. He was asking me in the dream to put a pipe in his head that would go down through his body and come out of the other end as his penis. He was confident in the dream that the pipe would serve as an admirable erection . . . [he had] an image of himself as a "screwing machine."

(1969:56)

As an interpretation of this and other data, May offers the following:

. . . the excessive concern with technical performance in sex is correlated with the reduction of sexual feeling. The techniques of achieving this approach the ludicrous: one is that an anaesthetic is applied to the penis before intercourse . . . Making one's self *feel less* in order to *perform better!*

(1969:54-55)

Again, May notes that "the distinguishing characteristic of the machine is that it can go through all the *motions* but it never *feels*" (1969:56). The "normal anxiety" of modern actors, then, is defined by May as a function of a "non-feeling" construction of the sex act. However, rather than a "non-feeling" construction, it is a function of the actors' inability to *conceive* of "feeling" in relation to a certain kind of act. The problem with May's "normal anxiety" notion is that it sees this inability as being a confrontation between the cultural order and human psychic nature; as the analysis which follows should make clear, it is far more productive to see the problem as a contradiction in the culture, a cultural double-bind, which is, for some, paralytic.

And yet, May has produced a powerful model of sex in this cultural construction which, had he accompanied his psychological analysis with a social analysis, he might have been better able to exploit. This is the image of the *machine*. Or, rather, production with machines: May's patients have the same attitude of self-sacrifice to the machine (or to the productive act) as do workers on an assembly line; sexuality is similarly the satisfaction of a separate and alien Other (in this case, the Other is an abstract standard, or myth, of competence and performance: how many men feel inadequate because their partners have not had orgasms resembling a *grand mal* seizure? and how many women have *faked* a *grand mal* seizure to spare men this "mortification"? and how many women feel inadequate *themselves* for not having such seizures?). And yet, at the same time that people sacrifice themselves to it, their sexuality is, they think, the supreme self-gratification, the final and most complete subjectivity. Again, I would suggest that this is the (cultural) contradiction which is paralytic.

Marcuse's formulation of the nature of sexuality in American culture is formulated on two levels, one meta-psychological, the other a philosophical analysis of contemporary society (*Eros and Civilization,* 1955; *One-Dimensional Man,* 1964). In the first, a "philosophical inquiry into Freud," Marcuse introduces the ideas of "surplus-repression" and "performance-principle" as modifications of the Freudian theory. Freud felt that civilization rested on the repression of the naturally-free sexuality of the individual (which is the *libidinal energy* of the biological organism, as well as the social energy of the political animal). This is accomplished through the channeling of libidinal energy into forms of activity conducive to cooperation and thus to social life. This channeling—which is the psychological introjection of socio-historical forms of the sublimation of sexuality into *work*— takes the form of the individual's self-repression, the censorship of unmitigated and immediate Desire (the Pleasure Principle) by a Reality Principle. Marcuse suggests that a differentiation be made between the repression necessary to *social life as such,* and the repression necessary to maintain a *particular social order.* This distinction is analogous to Marx's distinction between socially "necessary" and "surplus" product (value)—because a particular social order is a system of domination: because surplus-repression varies with the extent to which energy—*labor,* or work in its social form—is a process of self-fulfillment, or conversely, with the extent to which labor is alienated or expropriated (see 1955: 80 ff.).[5] Marcuse sees the form of basic repression as universal—and on a symbolic level it would take the form of the distinction between "nature" and "culture." Surplus-repression take its form from other aspects of the social organization. In American culture (or bourgeois culture generally), surplus-repression takes the form of a performance principle, which is a particular form of the Reality Principle: an individual is supposed to be possessed of capacities, and his place in the social order and all rewards are a direct function of his ability to utilize these capacities in more or less predetermined ways, for the accumulation of wealth and honor (and, in theory, for the good of the system as a whole). This is the philosophy of possessive individualism (MacPherson 1962; Halévy 1955), the philosophy of capitalism, internalized as personal imperatives (Marcuse 1955:40).

The point of this is that this particular form of the Reality Principle is not universal, but historically-conditioned. Surplus-repression constitutes an absorption of the energies and drives of the individual, not merely by Society in the abstract, but by a particular social order. As an aspect of a particular social order, surplus-repression thus has both a function and a form. And in the case of the performance-principle, this form is the contrast between "work" and "home," in which work is the site of performance in the competitive-individualist sense, and home the site of respite and personal fulfillment. In other terms, work is self-negation (and thus alienation, self-sacrifice), while home is the place where erotic tendencies (in the Platonic sense of the term, which was the sense in which Freud used it), subjectivity, can be realized. But this work-home distinction is not invulnerable within the culture.

Quite to the contrary, in fact: "leisure," the world of home, has the status, under the performance principle, of a remnant, and it is possible that the world of work may invade the world of home. And in *One-Dimensional Man*,

Marcuse claims that this is precisely what has happened: with the extension of commodity-production and the cash nexus, which are the essence of a "consumption-oriented" society and economy, the individual differentiation and autonomy which are supposed to characterize the domain of the home are eroded—*absorbed* by a mechanism which renders individuality specious, differentiation a farce, because they can only be expressed in terms of selection among products which render the personal a token of the general processes of production.

Marcuse's analysis, I think, is correct: the new "sexual freedom" is, in many ways, a means whereby people themselves become commodities, the objects of labor and acquisition. But it seems that Marcuse's argument is overly abstract and general, and that some attention must be paid to the symbolic and meaning-creating processes whereby people do this—to themselves. It is generally valid, I think, to be skeptical of any sociological explanation—regardless of its evocative power—which relies on "basic" psychobiological, evolutionary, functional, or even symbolic "laws," rather than on the concrete *practice* of people.

II

In American culture, the division of the individual's action-orientation into work and home obtains. One's own gratification—and by extension, the gratification of the members of one's family, for family and self are indeed considered to be one cultural unit established through "shared substance"—is paramount in the home, while at work, one sacrifices one's self to the demands of others. Things are done for ulterior motives—or indeed, for a reason—at work, while at home things are their own justification and are done for their "intrinsic" value.

"Economics" is a category of the world of work. The home—and other social spaces which share its characteristics, such as clubs, churches, lodges— is where people have *relationships,* which are not based on the "rational" calculations which typify economic action. Relationships exist between people who are, for all intents and purposes, equal (this is even true for the relationship between father and son: insofar as they "have a relationship," it is one of camaraderie and mutual respect, shared pleasure or shared activities; the same would apply to other parent-child relations, or to those between spouses or siblings). In this view, relationships are not an arena for competence—one may "be a good father" or a good daughter, but one may not be good at "being a father," and father and daughter may not be "good at relating": they either "have a good relationship" or they don't. (This is changing somewhat: see below, Section IV). The same is true of friends, comrades, and relatives in general.

"Competence" is a description of one's ability to do a job, to execute a task properly (there being standards for such execution implicit in each task, or those standards being competitive and relative). A "job" is something done to "things" and not to people. If people are to be manipulated, they must be redefined (for example, in terms of a stereotype) as things (that is, as mere tokens of a group or class): since manipulated people are people stripped of their particularity and their individuali-ty, one does not manipulate one's family or friends, only those to whom one is opposed in some way. "Things" have no individual characteristics, only attributes which are representative of the class of which a given item is a token: things are passive, and one relates to them with tools.

Sex, in this complex, is the most private of private activities, the most home-like of the activities of the home. It is, first of all, the way in which the home is founded (a man and a woman are married, and as husband and wife have intercourse and children). Sex is also the essence of the bond between man and wife—although in this regard it is an outcome and a distillate of a generalized "compatibility." This is because sexuality is the most subjective of subjectivities: compatibility in intercourse is a product of "love," that is, generalized compatibility and intersubjectivity. The exclusivity, privacy, and encompassed-ness of sex (by other forms of affection, by the overall relationship between man and wife) is expressed by the saying "a house is not a home," which draws a contrast between a house of prostitution (in which sex is there for the taking, or the paying, is public, and is not embedded in any other relationship between partners) and the home. It is considered *foolish* to "marry for sex"; but it is genuinely *despicable* to "marry for money." "Marrying for sex" is foolish because while sexual compatibility may betoken compatibility in other regards, it is not a guarantee of it (sex, like money, "isn't everything," although, like money, it is "way ahead of anything in second place"—sex and money are symbols of and for different and contrasted domains); "marrying for money" is despicable because it is a travesty on the idea of the home. It allows the pecuniary motives and the symbolism of the world of work and economics to intrude into relationships within the family.

Personal sex is not a subject for public discussion; indeed, it is more a subject of intra-sex than inter-sex conversation, and even partners may find it difficult or repugnant to discuss their sexual relationship. The affairs of the house or the home generally are not discussed in front of "outsiders" to it—and there is a specific prohibition against discussing particularly private or disturbing matters of the home (especially those which might undermine the façade of solidarity which one should always maintain): one does not "wash one's dirty linen in public." Sexual activity is typically portrayed as going on in the dark, "behind closed doors"; married couples are often portrayed (on television, in films, and in stories) as sleeping in separate rooms or beds, as sleeping fully clothed (indeed, sleeping nude is considered to be salacious). Informants report regularly engaging in intercourse while partially dressed; and, of course, the prohibitions on who may do what, on the variety of expression and action in intercourse, are well-known. (On this point, I would suggest that these prohibitions, for example on oral or anal sex, are contradicted by the common desire, especially among men, to have them done to one. The prohibitions serve to *ritualize* the sex act, to draw a line between the things one does with one's *wife* [mother; Virgin] and what one does or would do with a *whore* [Magdalene figure].)

This special-ness, restrictedness, and highly-charged (and perhaps *therefore* ritualized?) nature of the sex act is due at least in part to the fact that intercourse is potentially an animal act: and seen in this light as stark and uncivilized (the integration of love and hate, tenderness and brutality, in sex is a common feature of American cultural statements), representing the more base— that is, the more "basic" and the "lower"—characteristics of men and women as zoological specimens. This animality is transformed by the affection and the ongoing relationship which should accompany the act of intercourse, as well as by the limitations as to what constitutes the "proper way" to engage in intercourse. But passion is always associated with violence, domination, loss of the will, hunger—animal characteristics ("love" is the lack of self-control). Since sex and passion are so "animalistic" (and since "men are animals" while female "animal instincts" are motherly and protective), women enjoy sex less than men. This is in part because women are potentially *more* animalistic than men, and their animal nature should be controlled:[6] but regardless of this, it is held that women derive their sexual pleasure primarily from pleasing their partners and submitting to their demands and desires. (A woman who enjoys sex as sex is a "hellcat," a "wildcat," a "tiger"—a rapacious beast; all terms applied to violent women as well— and a woman who appears, on stereotypical grounds, as though she will enjoy the sexual act itself (as opposed to flirting or "succumbing" to a man's passion) is a "fox"; women at the point of orgasm supposedly make animalistic noises—whimpers, mewls, squeals, cries, and groans—or utter obscenities, which of course they never do otherwise. All of these images recur throughout the representational and conversational forms of the culture.)

On the other hand, mutual discovery of sex is supposed to be one of the stronger bonds between husband and wife (that is, in their younger years, since Americans mistakenly believe that couples enjoy sex less as they have been together longer, and that old people don't enjoy sex). The husband should have had some sexual experience before marriage (although not too much), while the wife should be a virgin; the husband is thus something of a teacher, and his status as mediator between his wife and the outside world, from which he derives his personal authority over her, is thus extended. One of the chief features of the honeymoon is that a recently-married couple should "get used to each other" sexually during this period; then, of course, the "honeymoon is over," and sex takes a back seat to other considerations of life and love (and the young wife ceases to really enjoy sex, since the romance of submission and mystery is over). This period of mutual discovery is more or less necessitated by the absence of public sex education (in the schools, for example), although this only serves to make the honeymoon *special,* since any partners will require a time of mutual discovery and a period of accomodation. But in American culture, if it is "really love," no period of adjustment is necessary, compatibility is instantaneous and is not based upon knowledge of the other person or on communication and response. It is therefore felt that there *should* be no sex education in the schools, not because sex is too dirty to discuss with children, but because it is private and mysterious and should be relegated to the home and the honeymoon. Sex education would replace mystery with "being jaded" about sex, it would "take the romance out of marriage," and thereby threaten the institution itself.

The dirtiness of sex is exemplified by the attitudes toward contraception, even among those who are not opposed to contraception on religious or other grounds. Condoms are "sold under the counter"; the paraphernalia of other forms of contraception (diaphragms, for example) are mysterious and should on no account be seen by or discussed with one's husband (or lover: this attitude prevails amongst practitioners of the "new sexuality" as well). This is even more true of menstruation; a surprising number of otherwise educated and sophisticated men do not know what menstruation *is* (based on a survey at a Planned Parenthood Clinic in Palo Alto, California, about 25 percent); and very few men are aware of their wife's or lover's menstrual cycle, birth-control problems, or "female disorders." And this is not merely callousness or irresponsibility on their part—women don't want them to know.

III

I have of course presented only a small part of American ideas about sex; the reasons for my selection will become apparent in a moment. This "traditional" or "mainstream" construction exists as part of a larger cultural milieu, two aspects of which I want to discuss here. One is an ideology of particularism, and the other is the clear dominance in traditional American culture of relationships of "shared substance" as against relationships established by virtue of a "code for conduct" (Schneider 1969).

"Particularism," as I use it here, refers to the fact that people had, or have, identities, visions of themselves, which *mediate* between their conscious ness of themselves as individuals and their consciousness of themselves as one of a type—for example, as Americans or as human beings. Again, I would stress that mediate identities are, or have been, purely ideological, and not necessarily a reflection of determinants of observable action.[7]

"Mediate identities" is a jargonistic phrase to indicate the prevalence of voluntary organizations, viable neighborhoods, extended families, highly-developed ethnic consciousness and organization,[8] and the like. They often have concrete organizational reflections as well as a strong ideological aspect. On this sort of ideology, one does not exist solely as an individual and as a citizen or a member of a species; the gap between the two is filled by other group memberships of a particular sort: families, ethnic groups, and so on, to which one is recruited "by birth" (which is *by blood:* a sharing of substance, of being, between people), and voluntary organizations of which one is a member because of the kind of person one is (lodges are a good example; I might add parenthetically that occupational groups have a similar character, in part because one follows one's kin into a profession or trade, and in part because one should earn one's living by using one's talents, which is by doing "what comes naturally"; and I should note as well that trade unions, whose members call each other "brother" or "sister" are an organizational reflection of the substantial bonds between co-workers as much as they are pragmatically-oriented pressure groups, which might help explain the conservatism and lack of cross-trade organization in the American labor movement).

Now, it might be noted that this ideology of particularism is a consciousness which is suited to—and derives from—small towns or cities composed of groups of immigrants; and that it represents a conservative form of resistance to what is called, in Marxist jargon, *proletarianization* or massification.

Proletarianization refers to the lack of mediation between the person and the polity; as "massification" or "modernization" the idea has been used by sociology to denote the primacy of "civil" ties as against "primordial sentiments" (the sloppy term Geertz uses to denote the relationships I term "relations of substance"; see Geertz 1963). This idea derives, through Sorokin, from Ferdinand Tönnies' distinction between *Gemeinschaft* (community) and *Gesellschaft* (society) (see Tönnies 1887/1957; Pappenheim 1959), and has had a long and checkered history. For my purposes here, I need only point out that the formula is merely *structural.* Marx's idea of proletarianization, however, was historical as well and as such offers an explanation, as opposed to a mere description or a psychological reduction, of the phenomena to which it is applied.

In the *Grundrisse,* Marx sketched the historical genesis of the proletariat in the development of capitalism, in what is by now a familiar formula: the workers must be rendered *propertyless* (p. 514) and then *concentrated* around means of production which are not in their hands (p. 528): in the terms of the later formulation in *Capital* I, the worker must be separated from the conditions (means) of production, which are individual, and integrated with a production process which is general or collective.

The motive force for this transition is the extension of commodity production (production for sale as against production for use, which is production of exchange value, which is abstract, as against production of use-values, which are particular), and this requires the extension of the cash nexus. All products, if capitalism is to flourish, must be commensurable against a single standard, money (see *Pre-Capitalist Economic Formations,* esp. pp. 88–116; 127 ff.; Polanyi 1944). The demand for commensurability necessitates that the labor of workers be standardized (*at least* within an industry); which, in turn, implies that the labor of discrete individuals be stripped of its uniqueness and be rendered abstract: production itself is standardized, and the worker in his labor becomes an appendage of a general production process; and the value of labor, which must be equally standardized, becomes a simple function of time.

It is in this formula, I think, that the advantage of Marx's method is revealed: not only are concrete forms of social relationships related to ideological phenomena (thus, property ownership and the distribution of wealth, the organization of work and the distribution of the population are associated with possessive individualism and formal [legalistic] egalitarianism), but these are unified in a historical development which, while it may not have in all times and places a single cause, does have a central (overdetermined) indicator. That the progress of capitalism is the history of the steady expansion of the cash nexus is not, to my knowledge, seriously debated in either the economic or the historical literature. And one of the general characteristics of this advancement has been the steady growth of what economists call the "tertiary sector," the service sector of the economy, not only in absolute size (for pre-capitalist

and pre-industrial bureaucracies also have a large service sector), but in a steadily expanding range of "services" offered for sale (see Baran and Sweezy 1966; Kuznets 1966). This tendency, marked in the United States since the Progressive Era (ca. 1900-ca. 1916), has accelerated rapidly since the end of World War II. It is associated with a dramatic change in the occupational structure, an increase in the percentage of the population with college (or professional-trade) educations, increased individual (geographical and social) mobility, an accelerated nuclearization of the residential or co-acting family, and a shift in migration patterns away from blue-collar centers toward centers of white-collar employment.

One way to sum up these developments would be to note a change in "life style" and "values." But such a summary is insubstantial in comparison to another. The trends noted above have a variety of consequences. These, in concert with the increased standardization and centralization of modes of entertainment—consonant with the growth of television and "free time" industries, the monopolization of the mass media (the lack of local programming), and the development of a specious hedonism as a stimulus to the consumption of "fun" as *commodities*—have weakened particularistic ties, both on a concrete, sociological, *relational* level, and on a psychological, identificational-cultural level. Substituted for mediate identities, which have a concrete, "substantial" character, are the abstract identities of age group, socio-economic status, and class. This fact is dramatized by the proliferation of ideological and cultural fads (religions, diets, therapies) which people can share as codes, and which are mass-produced mediate identities, equivalent to the identities established on the basis of shared taste for standardized products and hobbies.[9] Indeed, the production of such ideologies, tastes, and hobbies, the production of "fun," has become a flourishing "glamour" industry.[10]

The basic organization of the social order, the organization of production, thus provides (1) the basic conceptual scheme, the opposition between work and home, which appears to the natives as "given," and in terms of which "new" concepts are developed;[11] (2) the situation to which a new cultural formation will be a response; (3) the communicative means by which this response is expressed, elucidated, and controlled; (4) the formal characteristics (abstraction of social relations) of the "new" formulation. In this view, the cultural facts are accounted for without necessitating psychological reductions. What is isolated is a form for *praxis* (meaningful action) which derives from a contradiction within a previously constituted form for meaningful action (the contradiction between the particularity of the subject guaranteed by the contrast between work and home, and the abstractness—generality, substitutability—of the subject which is a feature of the cash nexus and commodity exchange).

The explanation is not strictly deterministic: it allows for another turn of events. In fact, much of the analysis of what *has* happened hinges on an evaluation of the *potential developments present* in the characteristic contradictions of the previous order. The "new sexuality" is a response to a new social situation which is, in fact, an extension of the basic form of alienation (surplus-repres-

sion) which characterized the old social order. Thus, technique-fetishism and swinger-ism are not necessary constructions of a *sui generis* cultural code, but a response to a situation. The expansion of the cash nexus has broken the back of the work/home distinction, both as a viable ideological construct and as a mode of social action. This establishes a new arena of *freedom*, especially for women, who were previously the slaves of that over rigid dichotomy, and makes *possible* the transformation of freedom, which is merely *negative,* in this instance merely the lack of a restraint, into *liberation,* the self-conscious construction of a new and higher mode of life. But this would entail the infusion of "home" values (broadly speaking, Erotic values, the values and relations of a heightened and actualized Subjectivity) into the world of work. As yet, the women's movement has not made the political alliances nor the ideological commitments necessary to accomplish this, but has instead allowed itself to become one of a series of substitutable "pressure groups" within the purview of relations defined by the imperatives of production (the consciousness-raising movement may turn out to be an exception to this, especially if it is able to constitute itself as a political—that is, a subversive—movement, rather than as a substitute for the "home" for women in the old construction).

IV

What, then, is the sense in which the "new sexuality" represents an expansion of the cash nexus? If my argument here is correct, it will be precisely in the terms of the traditional/mainstream culture. But this does not mean that the mechanical nature of the "new" sexuality will be *apparent* to the natives. On the contrary, the process is again one of substitution: in this case, the mechanical (code-prescribed) is substituted for the relational (substantial bond-derived) but it is still *called* "relating." Indeed, as relations become more mechanical, and more subject to the conscious application of technique, the verbal use of "relate" increases: the language itself becomes stripped of the contrasts which might give it the potential for criticism or for posing substantially utopian possibilities against the constituted order.

The process of the construction of sexuality takes place in the context of a differentiation between "nature" (the world of animals and plants, of processes which are not "rational," and which are uncontrollable, though they may be ordered) and "culture." Lévi-Strauss has argued that this is a universal feature—and a biologically necessary one—of all cultural systems (1969), and Schneider has shown its centrality to the construction of "kinship" in American culture (1968:21 ff.); and, as I noted above, the symbolization of basic repression (as against surplus-repression) takes the form of a differentiation between "nature" and "culture." The problem with Lévi-Strauss's and Marcuse's formulations is that the differentiation between "nature" and "culture" has a *form*, a socially determined form: it is not merely a simple contrast.

Sex, in American culture, is a *"natural"* fact, and this is even more true in the "new sexuality." Sex is a feature and an activity of the *natural* man and woman. *As such, it is to be transformed into a cultural fact.* This represents a general characteristic of the American constitution of the person (ersatz "natu-

ralness" notwithstanding), whereby the zoological, the "natural," becomes "personal" (that is, general characteristics of the species become differentiating aspects of the individual existence).

Now, in American culture generally, there are two ways in which "nature" can be transformed or controlled: the "natural" can be a *thing*, in which case it is controlled through *technique*, or it can be a person (or embodiment of a person, or an attribute of the species character of persons), in which case it is transformed by being encapsulated within some sort of relationship *between* persons. This appears to be a rather rigid metaphysical dichotomy within American culture—an example of its rigidity might be the application of technique to environmental-ecological problems. As biologists are fond of pointing out *ad nauseum*, ecological problems are problems of *relationship*—between a mode of social life and natural resources, land configurations, and biological processes (a good introduction is to be had from Shepard and McKinley 1969). However, ecological problems are approached by Americans as though they were problems of a machine—even among those genuinely concerned with ecological problems, like R. Buckminster Fuller. Thus, for example, the problems associated with the production of electrical power—air and water pollution, fuel shortages, damages to water basins and to land, and the constant demand for more and more power—are a feature of the unnecessary overconcentration of the population, but more importantly of the constant demands for growth in production of a capitalist economy, which *demands* the wasteful use of raw materials in general, the proliferation of "convenient" gadgetry, and display uses of electricity. But the solutions—if one can call them that—which are offered tend to concentrate on ways to produce more power, or to reduce the sulfur content of bituminous coal, or to "conserve" power: fine tunings on the machine, but no question about whether the *relationship* we have with our environment, the constant demand for *more* on which our society is built, should be changed (see Bookchin 1971).

There are two associated features of the "new sexuality" which inform—and are informed by—the nature/culture contrast. The first is the predominate tendency to look upon sexual activity as a biological, rather than social, activity (this despite the fact that one's sexual activity might be referred to euphemistically as one's "social life" or one's "love life"). Perhaps the clearest example of this is the Masters and Johnson study, *Human Sexual Response,* which was such a popular best seller, and which purported to tell us, by virtue of results gained from monitoring subjects' physiological functions in an artificial "sex" environment, what "sexual response" was. The authors have also established a "sexual therapy" clinic in St. Louis, and they conduct seminars around the country. One of these was recently the subject of a report in a Chicago newspaper, which offered a list of some of the Masters and Johnson terminology: impotence is referred to as "sexual dysfunction," a marriage constitutes a "committed unit," an orgasm is "sexual effectiveness" (two orgasms indicates a "return to sexual effectiveness" in the male) (Goldstein 1974). Technique and zoology are closely connected.

This contrasts with the traditional/mainstream view of sex, in which the physiological aspect is overcome by the encapsulation of sexuality in a particular sort of relationship, an encapsulation which is represented by the sequestering of sex in the bed in the bedroom in the home, as well as its sequestering in time. Note that even sexual relations which are not in harmony with the norms embody this same encapsulation, although here, because of the highly charged nature of adulterous or "adventurous" sexual encounters, most especially for women (and in literature for women), the encapsulation is more extreme. The relationship which encapsulates the sexual act (indeed, sexual feelings, or "passion," itself) is not marriage but "love." And in the literature of sexual adventure—the Sunday-supplement romances, confession stories, women's magazine fiction—the adulterous or "romantic" relationship, often undertaken by a neurasthenic, "strange" girl or a giddy wife, happen in peculiar, marked surroundings, such as vacation spots (and note the similarity to pornographic plots, as well). In this fashion, the "tabu" character of the extra-marital sexual encounter, the dangerous (because somehow "out" of the world of culture) aspect of passion, is overcome by its placement in a context of (psychological, spatial, temporal, or existential) liminality, and the cultural code survives the (natural) transgression against the norm. (In a similar vein, informants' reports and popular literature lead me to think that if a person were to find that his or her spouse had been having an affair, the reaction would be far stronger if the rendezvous took place in the home which they shared than if it were to take place in a motel.)

The emphasis on sex as biology is also interesting because it represents an *absorption* of a radical cultural and political movement of the pre-World War I era and the Twenties. In the early part of this century, to affirm the biological in man was to affirm his *particularity* and his freedom against the banality and the repression of Victorian and Edwardian middle-class culture. The novels of Henry Miller, for example (especially *Black Spring*), not only celebrate the biological sensations and urges of the sexual man, but his *iconoclasm* and his outrageousness vis-à-vis his asexual fellows. The same could be said of D. H. Lawrence, although his place in this movement was mitigated by his fascination with power (and his confusion of masculinity with aggression and dominance): his fascism, his male chauvinism; and it is certainly characteristic of the cultural radicalism associated with such figures as the early Freudians, Malinowski, Havelock Ellis, Virginia Woolf, and Gertrude Stein. This affirmation of the biological *as revolt* and refusal was also a major part of the ideology of the Surrealists, who consciously tried to fuse "biological radicalism" and radical politics (see Marcuse 1972). The "new sexuality" is an acting out of the dynamic which caused the Surrealists, who once stormed the Bastille of the museums and galleries to return art to the daily life, to become amongst those museums' most prized possessions.

But the "new sexuality" not only renders sex immutably biological, it wrests it from any relational context. This can be well seen in the literature (I use the term advisedly), film, and so on, which is expressive of this sexual form and which plays such an important part in shaping and inculcating it. Typically, sexual encounters in these media take place between strangers (either in a chance encounter or between virtual strangers whose interaction suddenly and inexplicably changes). For example, the film *Deep Throat* has two expressive scenes near the beginning: in the first scene of the film, the heroine enters to find a delivery boy engaging in cunnilingus with her roommate. Although she has never met the boy, she goes off at the end of the scene "to slide down the bannister in case he wants a hot lunch." The third scene of the film is an attempt to find sexual satisfaction for the frustrated heroine: the means is an assemblage of men "with different specialties" and each, upon arrival at the house, takes a number and is called in turn, whereupon he enters the heroine's bedroom and plies his trade (interestingly enough, unsuccessfully: but note that the solution to the heroine's problem—"inability to achieve orgasm"—is a *technical* one: she discovers that her clitoris is in her throat).

Most pornographic films—whether the sordid little "shorts" or the more lavish "features," and including non-pornographic, "X-rated" films, such as those by Russ Meyer—have much the same character. Indeed, in one film, *The Telephone Book,* a fairly funny satire on the genre, the central character, a woman, falls in love with an obscene telephone caller: the film is the story of her exploits as she wanders through the city searching for her "lover" (this is particularly interesting because the central character has the least possible relation, not only to her "lover," but to *herself:* for she is defined solely as the Object of his perversion). One of the more striking features of this anonymity is its close association with sado-masochism: an association generally characteristic of French pornography (particularly *The*

Story of O), but present in many, if not most, pornographic novels.

While there are few people—including, to the best that I have been able to discover, those who perform in them—who live the life of the fuck flick (just as there are few who live the life of the "sort of man who reads *Playboy*"), there *are* forms of association, increasing in popularity throughout the country, which share the essential feature—anonymity and generality—of pornographic sex. Here, the anonymity is largely a function of circumstance: sexual encounters typically begin in "singles bars" which have proliferated in the past few years, and whose sole reason for existence (since the drinks are weak and over-priced, the atmosphere tacky, and the entertainment fifth-rate) is to provide a place *to* initiate sexual encounters. And, having done so, these couples have in common only a common taste for a bar: which is to say they are over eighteen, like rock music (like fifty or sixty million others) and don't work on Saturday night. "Singles clubs," which have the same restricted function, and singles "communities," housing developments, apartments, or condominium complexes which allow no children and discourage couples, have also proliferated: these last are the epitome of the entire construction, for these are "communities" in which the sole bond is the sex drive, hardly a differentiating characteristic. Similarly, advertisements for sex and sexual relations seem to be spreading through periodicals ranging from the raunchy to the effete: from *Screw* and the San Francisco *Ball* ("To ball is to live; everything else is just waiting"), to underground, "radical" papers such as the Berkeley *Barb* or the Los Angeles *Free Press* (which has so many sex ads that they constitute a separate section of the newspaper), to the *New York Review of Books*. Of course, the character of the ads changes: advertising for someone interested in Greek culture means something different in *Screw* than it means in the *New York Review*—I think.

This construction of sex—anonymity, instant (though ersatz) intimacy, the elevation of technique, and the mistaken idea that "you don't fuck their minds"—is not only characteristic of "swingers" and the "underground." It obtains as well, in only slightly attenuated form, in popular culture. Masters and Johnson's *Human Sexual Response* dominated the New York *Times* bestseller lists for months, despite its turgid prose, outlandish price, and lack of pictures. So have a variety of other "how to" books, most of which merely repeat the same barely reasonable platitudes in banal and unimaginative ways. When a sex manual has imaginative and tasteful illustrations, such as *The Joy of Sex*, or some other distinguishing characteristic, it becomes a major publishing sensation. And there are literally hundreds of them; a list, from memory: *The Sensuous Woman, The Sensuous Man, The Sensuous Couple, Everything You Always Wanted to Know About Sex . . . , Any Woman Can!* And books which, while not being manuals for sexual technique, *are* manuals for how to use sex *as* a technique: *Sex and the Single Girl, The Intimate Enemy*. And the immensely popular magazines whose existence is devoted to this "new sexuality" and the image of the "good life" (as *good consumer*) associated with it, like *Cosmopolitan, Playboy, Penthouse,* and *Oui*. And the instant culture heroes: like Linda Lovelace, who has managed to transform a routine accomplishment into a career, or Xaviera Hollander (the "happy hooker") who has recently become something of a *cause célèbre*.

Associated with and encompassing this phenomenon is the proliferation of books, magazine articles, and ersatz institutions of various kinds which teach "techniques" for relationships in general. These are literally too numerous to mention: I alluded to the proliferation of "therapies" before, and these, with their technical language for social relations (like Transactional Analysis, which is literally a foreign language, incomprehensible without a guide), their conscious manipulation of self (neo-Reichianism) and others (Family Therapy, t-groups) are as much a part of the fetishism of technique as is the *Kama Sutra*.

In a culture, people *constitute* themselves and others, their actions, as a meaningful framework in which to view themselves and their actions, and apply significance to them. In American culture, the "new sexuality" is such a framework, and it is a means whereby people create themselves as *abstractions*. They are generalized (as biological creatures, they are reduced to their species-being; as anonymous creatures, their particularity becomes only a style off an assembly line). For sex to be a matter of technique, a form of *work* an arena for *competence,* the partner—and ultimately, like Mozart's Don Juan, *oneself*—must be rendered a *thing,* rather than a person: an Object rather than an Other. In terms of American culture, this represents an *economization* of domestic ("home") relations and an alienation from one's own body (as it becomes the instrument of labor and the means whereby one sacrifices one's self to *a priori* standards of performance). This is a feature (mystified by its being called "relationships": a fetishistic transformation of relations between people into relations between things), of the actual and material economization of the private spheres of human existence, of the breakdown of the work/home distinction *in fact* through the development of "consumer" capitalism.

Notes

1. The analysis presented here was worked out in conversations with Janet L. Dolgin, John T. Kirkpatrick, and my wife, Stephanie Massey. Janet L. Dolgin, John T. Kirkpatrick, Stephanie Massey, and David M. Schneider commented substantially and helpfully on previous drafts of this paper. Susan P. Montague helped me place some limits on my natural pomposity and verbosity—I hope to some avail. This paper was inspired by my acquaintance with Herbert Marcuse and his works, which stand as shining examples of committed scholarship and intellectual courage, of which I hope I am worthy. The responsibility for the views here, however, is strictly my own.

2. Whether or not this separation of sexuality as a "domain" has anything to do with the change in relationships between "shared substance" and "code for conduct" as bases for the establishment of a field for social relations, is an interesting question which I can only touch on here. It will, however, be the subject of a forthcoming paper, on the symbolic constitution of the feminist identity in American culture.

3. The pressure to engage in sexual relations can have two discrete sources; it can come from partners within the relationship in question, and from friends—often members of one's same sex—outside of it.

4. In other cultures in which sexual relationships are considered proper, or even incumbent, among a wide range of relationship-types, there is no evidence of the high valuation of sexual technique which is to be found in American culture—examples are the Marquesas Islands (see Suggs) and the Trobriands (see Malinowski).

5. Marcuse draws this comparison explicitly: 1964:22-27.

6. This matter of the animal nature of women is discussed by Ortner (1973), who feels that the low status of women vis-à-vis men is in part a function of the closer identification of women with the "natural" (i.e., because of the inescapability of menstruation which is a purely biological thing, because women are the reproducers of the race, etc.). I disagree with Ortner's interpretation, in part for reasons which are discussed in the text—I think it is simplistic and largely inaccurate. My views on this matter will be discussed at length in the aforementioned paper on feminist identities in American culture.

7. To some extent, the quite considerable gap between the ideological construction of mediate identities and behavior has been a function of a transition in the character of American society which has taken a good deal of time—the period which can roughly be marked by the two World Wars, or by the advent of the Progressive Era just before World War I, although some of these trends predate this century and some are not yet fully developed.

8. We witness now, of course, a resurgence of an ethnic consciousness which has been for a time submerged or devalued—largely as a result of "melting pot" propaganda. But I would argue that this is a form of absorption, rather than resistance: see Dolgin 1973, and Magdoff and Dolgin 1974.

9. These "codes" are also subject to a certain reification, whereby they become substantialized, and often serve in the classification of people to relational fields in a manner somewhat similar to that described for "blood" by Schneider (1968).

10. As Baran and Sweezy (1966) and Marcuse (1964) among others have pointed out, this development whereby ideology—or "meaning"—becomes a commodity is not a feature of *demand* in an economic sense, either *per se* or as a configuration of demand, nor is it an attribute of a "culture" or a "cultural logic" in any meaningful (i.e., precise) sense of the term. Instead, it is a feature of production and production relations: in particular, the capitalist imperative for a continually expanding production, for needs which grow faster than the means to meet them.

11. And one might note as well that, besides being a representation of the conflict between Eros (Subjectivity) and the performance principle, this is also a representation of the central, "explosive" contradiction of capitalism, namely that between the social (collective) production of wealth and its private appropriation (by the owners of capital).

SEVENTEEN

Person, Hierarchy, and Autonomy in Traditional Yapese Theory

John T. Kirkpatrick

In the Introduction, we noted two kinds of oscillation between alternative ways a situation can be "expressed" or an action defined: the action of "epitomizing" symbols and the oscillation between two codes for the description of the same thing. Obviously, these can be two ways to describe the same process: the investment of an event with meaning in the context of potential or actual social conflict and consequent divergent interpretations of events.

Kirkpatrick's paper documents and analyzes an instance of this sort of oscillation and shows its relation to political dominance and social hierarchy for the island of Yap.

One interesting aspect of this analysis is the fact that "everybody knows" that a decision *announced* as being for one reason was actually *made* for a different, though known, reason. In this case, then, the oscillation between everyday life and the language of domination is *transparent;* and the enactment of political domination in language is itself "epitomizing," in that it summarizes an event or result which has already taken place. In some situations, however—most notably in our own society—the enactment of political domination in language is *opaque* to the domination itself, and the language is thus "elaborating," in that it is part of the creation of the very event it characterizes. An interesting question, which Kirkpatrick does not deal with, is what sorts of social and cultural structures produce these two different forms.

IN A FAMOUS ESSAY, Mauss (1950) drew attention to the different assumptions accepted in various societies concerning the nature and possibilities of persons. His intention was to scrutinize the "floating, delicate" category of the self in the contemporary West, showing it to be far from securely rooted in either history or its own approach toward consistency. Mauss shows the notion of the person as an autonomous individual to be a social product, just as are alternate conceptions. Louis Dumont has carried the question further by claiming that cultures may order social reality through emphasis on autonomous units—persons or groups—or the whole, but not both. His claim is not that cultural stress on the one rules out the appearance of the other, but that the other may appear only in a special, marked relation—e.g., as external or deviant—to the social order. Dumont distinguishes the "empirical agent," the actor in any soci-

Published by permission of the author.

ety, from the "normative subject," the unit or whole to which such concepts as order or liberty are addressed and in terms of which a social ideology is constructed (1970a:9).[1]

This paper faces Mauss's question through attention to Dumont's. A discussion of traditional ideology indicates the presence of a hierarchically ordered orientation to the social whole on Yap. Yap in the Western Carolines is not India, and Yapese society is not and has not been caste society, yet Yapese social theory falls into Dumont's class of holistic ideologies. No point by point comparison of Yap to India is attempted; rather Yapese data are presented in order to deepen our understanding of the social and cultural possibilities of hierarchic orders.[2] The Yapese case seems apposite because Yap combines a stress on rank differentiation with a cultural recognition of personal isolation at certain points which arguably may go beyond that of Dumont's "empirical agent" to a notion of personal autonomy.[3] On Yap, it may be that autonomous units are recurrently created at the center of a hierarchic social order, a possibility excluded, it seems, by Dumont.

By traditional theory or ideology is meant Yapese understandings of social order as recorded by ethnographers. Greatest stress is placed on the explanations of people held to be expert in traditional matters, weighing later statements on the basis of their fit with those reported in earlier accounts (Müller 1918; Furness 1910). The work of David Labby in gathering and synthesizing such data is of prime importance: I follow Labby's data and many of his formulations concerning the ordering of traditional theory. Later in the paper I draw on case data collected by David M. Schneider, Charles Broder, and myself. The data include both modern cases and accounts of events *circa* 1930. By "traditional Yap" I rather arbitrarily mean Yapese society before the late 1930's, when Japanese colonial rule limited the exercise of many Yapese activities. Modern data serve in the absence of earlier accounts of particular matters and are used selectively. Despite the use of the ethnographic present, I do not argue that this paper applies to contemporary Yap.

As an inquiry into traditional theory, this paper is concerned with understandings that are questioned or little known on Yap today. Whether they ever went unquestioned in all contexts may be doubted.

Basic Tenets of Traditional Yapese Ideology

Yapese social organization is complex, involving what has been termed double descent; village political organization by both chiefly offices and what look like age grades; multiple levels of areal organization, crosscut by a division between "sides" that apparently allocates different political roles and styles to different villages; and a high degree of integration of these units at the top of the political hierarchy through the meetings of chiefs for deliberations and ritual. Labby has shown that all this may be understood in terms of a synthetic Yapese ideological model, a Yapese theory which delineates the nature and potentials of persons and relationships (1972). In this section some of the basic tenets of that ideology are noted. A useful starting point is a distinction between ahistoric and historically developed units. While this might be taken to be the familiar nature/culture distinction, we note the Yapese phrasing in terms of process.

People are ahistorically related through mother-child links: children of one mother are "of one belly" as are all people who presumptively might trace ancestry through women to a common bearer. Even in the most ancient of days it appears that people of a number of matrilineal clans (*ganung*) lived on Yap. They did not, however, originate there: founding ancestresses came to Yap, often in the shape of fish or vermin, became tied to the land through marriage and cultivation and have, through their progeny, remained as people ever since.

Land and sea existed from the beginning, and it appears that the land was not all the same: plots differed in the crops they might bear. People without land are scavengers; land without people is wild. It is through work that land takes on value and, with it, people take on value as members of Yapese society.

Work on the land is not done simply by clan sub-units; the clan founders came to live with men and ever since the land has been held and worked by people of different clans. Land is passed from generation to generation between people of different clans, e.g., from father to son. The continuity of such transmission of cultivated land involves a continuity of worthwhile work, of value in the land and the people on it. Thus the highest ranking landholding units on Yap are held to have been inhabited since the time when humans and those "half-spirit, half-human" commingled on Yap (Uag 1969).[4] Work on the land is transformed into the rank of the land; at

the same time it shows the worth of the worker. Similarly, the acquisition of a skill, e.g. canoe-building, has impact on the position of a landholding unit in which it is transmitted. Prowess in war brings repute not only to the champion but to his landholding unit, and is held to be service for the "land," i.e., the village or areal political unit.

People and land unite in landholding units, *tabinaw*, often glossed as 'estates,' and larger political units (villages, networks of varying scope). Such units all include people of differentiated rank.[5] Thus the lands held by one *tabinaw* may vary from the highest house platform of the village to newly gardened plots to forested stretches upland. Alongside distinction among lands goes distinction among people, for the highest taro land of a *tabinaw* provides food for older men, lesser lands feeding older women, younger men, women and children and, lowest of all, girls just after menarche. People eat food from appropriate lands cultivated by the appropriate people, cooked in the appropriate pots on separate hearths by women wearing the appropriate skirts. An older man may "throw down" food to those below him, but should a lower person work land which is too high, the land will be polluted, dirty (*taay*).

Yapese application of the concept of pollution supplements informants' statements about the ordering of rankings. Polluted land within a *tabinaw* is low, but it is simply the lowest in the *tabinaw:* it in principle is still higher than land in lower ranking villages. Informants currently claim that all the people of the highest municipalities—an administrative unit including parallel traditional network segments—are above all the people of lesser municipalities; all the people of the highest village in a municipality above all the people of lesser villages. Within villages—or between villages of the same village rank level—land is still ranked but the scaling is in principle village-wide.

The land and clans have been affected by historical process. The forty or so dispersed clans include people of all ranks; land is differentiated into variously ranked house platforms, walled taro patches, gardens, sacred sites on which magicians may practice their inherited skills, and so forth. Work on the land has resulted, in the ideological view, in the establishment of such special qualities *in* the land. Thus political office is in the land, to be exercised by a landholder *(tafen)* or landholder's representative who carries the *lungun* 'voice' of the land into deliberations:

While it was generally not remembered how a given land-estate [*tabinaw*] came to have its particular 'voice,' there was no question but that it had been a result of the efforts of the ancestors. The 'voice' of the land was the voice of the ancestors, those who had lived and worked on the land before and were seen to continue to reside in it as spirits after they had died (Labby 1972:44).

As historic associations of ahistoric units (land, people), *tabinaw* must be maintained. Continuity depends on the movement of people of different clans over the land. Each new generation to come to *tabinaw* office is of a different clan from its immediate predecessors: in Yapese terms, *tabinaw* are not descent units but loci for transactions between units, loci which at the same time carry the outcomes of past transactions as rank.

The inter-clan transactions of the *tabi-naw* are understood as long-term exchange of control over land for labor. A woman marries away from her natal lands, works her husband's land, and, by her labor, gains a foothold for her children. Labor demonstrates the worth of mother and children, the fit of their rank with the land. The son, if all goes well, comes to hold the land and in turn pass it on to newcomers. The daughter marries out, preferably onto higher ranking land, continuing the clan.

This highly general presentation of traditional belief has certain implications. Clans are coded as ranked to the extent that they are implicated in particular transactions, unranked or multi-ranked to the extent that their members are involved in many transactions at any one time. While Yapese may speak vaguely of a "branch of a clan," no easily isolable segment is thus labelled. Clans are, as the ideology implies, dispersed units with ambiguous ranking, if any.

Personal isolation is coded into the view of history as the project of work on the land. People are differentiated by clan, *tabinaw,* and sexual identity. These dimensions separate all persons except for same-sex full siblings. So long as such siblings eat from the same land they remain undifferentiated by the terms sketched out in this section. But not for long: sisters marry to different *tabinaw;* brothers enter into village eating grades at different times, eating food from land appropriate to their separate grades, and hold separate positions as household heads, *tabinaw* and village office-holders. Ahistorically, people are separated by sex and clan identity; as members of society all persons are isolated in distinct social positions. Certain positions may be held equivalent, to the extent that their holders may share food, but this results from equivalence of positions in different hierarchies of land-and-people (*tabinaw*, village, political network).

Personal Development in Traditional Ideology

The distinction between the ahistoric and the historic units of Yapese society separates units which must be continually maintained as social from those which simultaneously serve as context for the work of maintenance and as reservoir of the outcome of past work. People were on Yap, it is said, before clan exogamy and such features of social order were decided on; people and the land are both units needing maintenance and the maintainers of the social order.

Traditional notions of conception are complex; in one version *tabinaw* ghosts *(thagith)* decide that a woman of the *tabinaw*, presumably one married into the *tabinaw*, has done worthy work and impregnate her. A spirit shapes the child in the womb and the ghosts oversee the work, instructing the shaping spirit *(mam)* to disfigure the child should the parents ignore prohibitions (Schneider 1968). In another version, a woman's labor on her husband's land is parallelled by his "working" of her reproductive "land" (Labby 1972, 1976). These accounts agree in seeing conception as rooted in *tabinaw* work, and in opposing a woman's reproductive resources to action on those resources from her husband's *tabinaw*.

After birth, a mother and child go to the village menstrual area for a short period. Meanwhile authorities of the husband's *tabinaw* meet and choose a name which is preferably first called out in public by the child's father's sister or father's father's sister. Until the name is announced, the child has been termed Sogaw (m.) or Ligaw (f.). Names are "in the land"; male names are recycled within *tabinaw* while female names pass from *tabinaw* to *tabinaw* as women marry and develop membership in their marital *tabinaw*. Names may not be given without, minimally, the knowledge of both resident *tabinaw* authorities and non-resident ones, the matrilineal descendants of past landholders' sisters.

Children are nurtured by their parents, the father providing the appropriate male-gathered products (fish, coconuts, betel nut and leaf), the mother giving and cooking produce (taro, vegetables). Children eat with their mothers. Young girls learn to work with their mothers from an early age: boys may wander farther from the home, e.g., entering the *faluw* (young men's house) and listening to old men, but appear both slower to enter into production activities and to be socialized into them by older brothers and peers more than by their fathers.

At puberty a girl becomes full of menstrual blood, which is highly polluting. In traditional terms, a woman loses menstrual blood through her adult life until, with the end of menstruation, she no longer threatens to pollute high lands and is a *pilibithir* 'old person,' like an elderly man. Girls go first to the menstrual area, then to the *tarugod* 'place for girls' where they primp and entertain lovers. No such speedy transition is evident for young men; they come to sleep in the *faluw* or in temporary houses about the age of puberty, may provide a bit more labor for their *tabinaw* than they did as boys of age ten or so, and pursue lovers (see Schneider 1955).

Marriage comes when a girl stays the night at a boy's temporary house, is found there, and her father, informed, raises no objection. Unions of young persons are not expected to be lasting and may be ended easily by either party. When a child is born, however, the situation changes, and a woman who leaves her husband has "thrown down" her child. Should she take the child, she has cut it off from her husband's *tabinaw*, where it might hope to succeed to office; if the child remains with the father, as is expected, his mother, who has abandoned it, has still not demonstrated the fit of her and her people's value with the rank of the land.

As men grow older they ascend through the system of eating grades of their villages. A young man takes part in village projects with others under the chief of the young men *(lanan pagal)*; if his *tabinaw* has land from which he can eat as a member of a man's eating grade, he will at some point join the lowest men's eating grade, ascending to the higher grade or grades as land becomes available in his *tabinaw*, i.e., as the landholder *(tafen)* allocates such land to him or names him to succeed him. (Some *tabinaw* in a village may even lack land to feed an adult male, so the male *tabinaw* head of such would receive food at distributions with the old women of the village.) Women also pass from being "young women" to "women" to "old people" but they lack eating grades which meet for feasts and their changes in age categories are said to correlate with the amount of menstrual blood they have and with the birth of children.

As people grow older they become wiser. The young are held to know little about matters of importance and often will not admit knowledge. With age and *tabinaw* office as a household head or *tabinaw* landholder comes responsibility for the planning of production activities. Landholders or their representatives take their *tabinaw's* place in the council of village men and whatever office is "in the land" of the *tabinaw*. With wisdom comes authority over those under a person, ranging from a child's duty to care for a younger sibling, to a landholder's right to remove a *tabinaw* name and/or access to land from one under him, to a chief's right to seize land for offences against the "peace of the village."

At death a person's ghost wanders for a short time and then returns to his *tabinaw*, joining the pool of ghosts which may be contacted by a landholder at the high ranking platform(s) of a *tabinaw*. Male ghosts stay with the *tabinaw* of naming; female ghosts stay with the *tabinaw* to which they have married and lived. (Unmarried ghosts presumably stay with their original *tabinaw*.) Ghosts supervise the life of the *tabinaw*, guarding it against evil forces from outside (malevolent spirits, sorcery) and granting benefits. When angered by the residents' behavior, they may withhold their favor, guaranteeing thereby the infertility of the *tabinaw's* land and people. *Tabinaw* ghosts act forcefully, if at all, only against those outside the *tabinaw*.

Holism and Hierarchy

For Dumont, Indian society is ordered in terms of three ideological principles noted by Bouglé (1908): gradation of status; rules insuring separation of units; interdependence among units. Underlying and aligning these principles is the opposition of pure and impure: "it is by implicit reference to this opposition that the society of castes appears consistent and rational to those who live in it" (1970a:43,44). Hierarchy is not understood by Dumont simply as differential status but *"the principle by which the elements of the whole are ranked in relation to the whole"*; since it is an ideological principle, hierarchy need not result in unilineal gradations of power or wealth or any such single variable (1970a:66). Indeed, Dumont finds religious status to be separate from and to encompass power in Indian ideology.

The presence of status gradations and rules for separation on Yap should by now be clear. Interdependence of people and land, of male and female, of *tabinaw* office, of the chiefly offices of a village and of the political networks of Yap may also be found. Yapese use the metaphor of *ngucol*, three rocks which constitute a hearth, to stress interdependence: if one is removed, no pot can be balanced on the hearth and nothing is accomplished. The landholder and two types of non-resident *tabinaw* authority (both *m'fen,* discussed below) are compared to *ngucol*, as are three chiefly offices which Yapese say are found in every village. The chiefs of the three major political networks are termed *dalip e ngucol* 'three stones,' emphasizing that they are in balanced opposition; were they not opposed, Yapese say, one might dominate and all order be abolished. At least at this level, hierarchy on Yap is without question "in relation to the whole." Notions of accumulated labor as value apply widely, being used in the explanation of the nature of all social units and relations. Personal purity and pollution appear as a minor instance of the opposition of historic cultivation to the wild and natural. Whether a Yapese equivalent to the separation of status and power (priest and king, *dharma* and *artha*) may be found is problematic: a distinction between supervision and action is notable and may be homologous. This may be seen in *tabinaw,* villages, and Yap-wide relations.

Tabinaw authorities include ghosts,

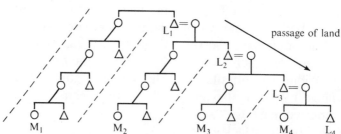

Figure 17.1 L_1, L_2, L_3, L_4 are successive landholders of a *tabinaw*. M_1, M_2, M_3, M_4 are *m'fen* lines over that *tabinaw*. Succession to landholder status is shown as father to son for simplification; that is not necessary, even in Yapese theory. Similarly, not all *m'fen* lines which might possibly be formed in four generations are shown. When L_3 is landholder, M_2 would be the 'new' and most authoritative *m'fen;* M_3 would be 'new' *m'fen* over L_4. In some areas M_3, M_2 and M_1 would all be active *m'fen* (of diminishing involvement in the *tabinaw*) over L_4; in other areas *m'fen* are thought to 'fall' after two generations. Adapted from Labby (1972).

landholders, and *m'fen*. *M'fen* are matrilineal descendants of the sisters of prior landholders. (See figure 17.1; for *m'fen* recruitment in various situations: cf. Schneider 1962.) *M'fen* have a claim on the *tabinaw* because the founder of a *m'fen* line was 'formed on the land' *(sum ko binaw)*. As she is from the *tabinaw*, a *m'fen* line founder has a claim resulting from her matriline's work, yet she marries elsewhere; renouncing use of the land. Instead, she and her descendants have authority over the "people of the *tabinaw*" until the work of their forebears is matched by that of later inhabitants of the *tabinaw*. The "new *m'fen*," sister to the immediately previous landholder, may exile any and all people from the *tabinaw* for certain offences, while *m'fen* linked to earlier landholders have less voice, figuring largely in distributions at ceremonies such as may attend marriage or death. When the forbears of a *m'fen* line have rendered signal service to a *tabinaw*, e.g., bringing large amounts of land to it, the *m'fen* line may not "fall," lose its relation to the *tabinaw*, after two or three generations but last as long as seven generations. When no *m'fen* founder is recruited from one landholder's generation to be "new *m'fen*" over his successor, the previous *m'fen* line retains the authority it had as "new *m'fen*" since, Yapese say, the point is not so much a precise calculation as to maintain the *tabinaw* in balance. In a similar vein, men who have inherited land from their mothers may say that they are both landholder *(tafen)* and *m'fen* of the *tabinaw*, not deeming the office of *m'fen* to lapse.

M'fen oversee the conduct of the *tabinaw* in general with an eye toward respect to previous landholders. The prototypical act of *m'fen* is extreme, expulsion of the "people of the *tabinaw*." *M'fen* are not expected to interfere daily but to safeguard the *tabinaw* heritage against the whims of its current inhabitants. Similarly, landholders have diffuse authority and superior rank over other *tabinaw* members, while household heads retain the right to organize specific projects. Men, the expected household heads and landholders, work away from the land, while supervising the work of their wives and children on the land. At each step, diffuse authority and more specific work on the land are contrasted. It is notable that among the authorities who are not living "people of the *tabinaw*," ghosts are largely passive, punishing by relaxing their guard against evil, while *m'fen* take specific action against particular offenders. Authority is hence spread among all the matrilines which have worked the land, with those most distant from current workers having general supervision, and more proximate authorities more specific authority.

Within the village, the office of "old person of the village" is highest although its attendant powers appear vague. In contrast, the "chief of the village" has supervisory rights over the maintenance of large taro patches in which different *tabinaw* have sections. This chief may transfer unused sections to particular *tabinaw* without consulting the current holders, in order to insure continuity of production. The chief is not said to own such sections but the recipient *tabinaw* take full rights over them. The "chief of the young men" organizes work on a variety of projects agreed on by the chiefs and people of a village such as road maintenance and policing activity. Other *tabinaw* may hold offices having the right to organize specific sorts of fishing expeditions or exchanges; the line between chiefs and specialists is far from clear except in the theoretical emphasis on the above-mentioned triad of chiefs.

M'fen may exile *tabinaw* inhabitants but should find new workers, not use the land themselves. The chiefs may have a plot of land seized in retribution for offences, but must leave the land untouched until apology is made with Yapese valuables. (In one case a net was seized when men of one village fished in another's preserve; the men of the seizing village used the net and, forced to admit this impropriety, had to return it although no apology was made.)

All villagers—in some cases particular village sections—are *baan pilung* 'chiefly side' or *baan pagal* 'young men's side.' Each political network involves separate 'strands' (*tha' e nugh*) of the two sides with a *baan pilung* and a *baan pagal* village paired as complementary at the top under a highest village or *tabinaw*. *Baan pagal* are deemed somewhat below *baan pilung* in the abstract, and to the two sides are attributed contrasting styles of activity. *Baan pagal* are active and impetuous, while *baan pilung* 'sit,' are wise and order *baan pagal* to act. The highest chiefs (*baan pilung*, probably with the agreement of the highest *baan pagal*) permit wars between those below them in order to maintain balance, just as the leaders of the three major networks combine and recombine against each other to insure against dominance by any one of them. Although Arib *tabinaw* in T'eb (Tomil municipality) is sometimes said to be the single highest *tabinaw* of all Yap, it is so as "old person" of all Yap, not as most powerful or

active; the landholder of Arib may foretell political changes and is above all a source of legitimation for them.[6]

This summary review leads us to see Yapese theory as hierarchic in precisely Dumont's terms. People and land have value in relation to histories of cultivation, themselves arranged with regard to the history of all Yap. The continuing land-and-people units emerge as association of differentially ranked, separate and interdependent people and land. Such units are the focus in every generation for action to maintain value under the supervision of all predecessors on the land.

Yet a problem may be glimpsed in this summary. We see the highest men on Yap *deciding* on the conduct of wars, even adjusting the rankings of villages. The order of villages and, within villages, of *tabinaw* appears fixed at any moment but may be changed as hierarchical superiors deem current action valuable. At the very summit of Yapese belief may be a god so *otiosus,* so distant, that he goes unmentioned in this account, but among men we find persons acting decisively in their capacities as authorities to alter orderings below them. This is visible in such simple cases as a landholder's allotting land of a high eating grade to a man previously in a lower grade.

In India, Dumont emphasizes, interested action (*artha*) is coded as encompassed by duty (*dharma*) (1970b). The distinction between moral and interested action is visible on Yap, but it is a complex one as we might expect when we deal with succession to offices, not simply the separation of offices such as those of king and priest.[7] To set the stage, I recount a story known across Yap. Its most limited point is to explain the ranking of two villages. Its popularity suggests that a more general moral is to be drawn from it.

The Okaw War

Okaw was one of the seven highest villages of Yap (of the *bulce* category of *baan pilung*). A man of Okaw had by virtue of his *tabinaw* office the duty of opening a major ceremony involving people from a number of villages. On one occasion he failed to appear and, after a long wait, others decided to start without him. He arrived to see another man receiving goods which were to go to him and speared his substitute. Pandemonium ensued.

His offence placed the highest leaders of Yap in a quandry; how should a *bulce* official be punished for killing another high ranking man, when the killing was done in defense of the offender's ceremonial position? The chiefs met for days at T'eb, returning nightly to their homes. One day the lowly man who poled one chief across the bay to T'eb complained that he would die of fatigue should the deliberations continue and asked what they concerned. When told, he offered to kill the offender. The chiefs accepted this proposal as a solution. Accordingly, the people of Kanif, the servant's low ranking village, attacked Okaw. Only one or two children were left alive in Okaw, and they only because they recognized clansmen among the attackers and begged for mercy.

The chiefs of Yap decided that Kanif had served them so well that it should replace Okaw among the seven *bulce* villages. Okaw lost rank: it is usually said to have been one of the seven

bulce, its rank subsequent to the battle being uncertain.

Rank is shown here as involving not only the continuity of proper action, e.g., the ceremonial role of the Okaw chief, but the approval of higher authorities. The highest chiefs of Yap, holding office as from the highest *tabinaw* of Yap, may not only find a war an appropriate solution but raise a village from the bottom to the top of village rankings. As Yapese explain matters, this is highly unusual, but not contradictory to the view of rank as the outcome of work on the land. Because the initial killing posed a problem involving the stability of relations among the highest villages of Yap, solving the problem entailed exceptional labor on behalf of all Yap. The chiefs' decision was theirs to make; it is not explained as precedented or decreed to them by tradition, but neither was it made without reason acceptable to Yapese audiences.

The Whole vs. the Part?

Such decision-making displays a recurrent anomaly: the differentiation of rank, authority, and wisdom positions certain persons so that they may rule not only on the validity of work done by persons under them but on the hierarchic order under their sway. The extreme case is a decision said by Yapese to have been made by the highest chiefs *circa* 1943. The population had been declining for at least fifty years; Japanese rule was harsh; all men's houses had been destroyed; the consensus appears to have been that survival, much less proper maintenance of the social order, was of great difficulty. The chiefs are said to have decided to put aside sexual prohibitions on men connected with fishing and the seclusion of menstruating women, in hope that the people might increase (D. M. Schneider: personal communication). With the second relaxation came a weakening, perhaps the abolition, of eating rules, since the presence of menstruating women would previously be understood to pollute the land. Henceforth the maintenance of eating restrictions to the full was a private matter, good Yapese 'tradition' (*yalen*) but not prescribed. At one stroke, the chiefs are believed to have *legitimately* abolished the framework of separation that ordered relations of persons and land throughout Yap.

The proof that such a stroke was legitimate has come and been widely recognized: the population is rising. Were the abolition distasteful to *tabinaw* ghosts, they would, sooner or later, withdraw their protection, allowing infertility to ensue (see Schneider 1957). Were the population steady or decreasing, matters would be more opaque; as it is, bitter elders might suspect that the ghosts are momentarily showing compassion *(renguy)* and will exact punishment later. All agree that these are difficult times but do not publicly blame the chiefs.

But the decision was made—or believed to have been made—by the proper persons and supported by their hierarchic superiors. It was made for the benefit of society although it entails reordering much of the social order: as Dumont says in a different context, "hierarchy culminates in its contrary . . ." (1970a:194).

A holistic ideology need not suppress or make impossible action against the social order by its proponents. Instead we see the reduction of hierarchy and separation affirmed in terms of holistic values.[8] If such decisions are admissible, has a view of the actor on Yap as, at bottom, relationally coded lost its persuasion?

When the question is thus radically posed, the answer is obvious: it is because chiefs and the like take their authority and wisdom in a relational universe that they may legitimately revise its order of the moment. To see the chiefs acting as individuals, as the "normative subject" is to misconstrue Yapese understandings of both the event in question and the historical whole. The more interesting and problematic question is rather whether historic rank constitutes such chiefs as autonomous vis-à-vis all other persons, while still not "normative subjects." If history makes unprecedented action legitimate, at the very least we must come to understand action as developing not from single norms or statements about "the way the world is" but as a selection of a strategy from a range admissible in a situation defined by tradition. The range of such strategies may be outlined in some situations (see Kirkpatrick and Broder, 1976, for adoption decisions). A few options open to *m'fen* and landholders are examined.

Phrasings of Recruitment

Naming necessitates decision by *tabinaw* authorities. A child must be named to be truly a Yapese person, and the name must be given by *tabinaw* authorities. If the *m'fen* of the child's *tabinaw* are not informed of the choice of a name, the naming is invalid. Ghosts are consulted through divination and show their approval or disapproval of a selected name. The father's sister is the preferred candidate to make the name public: the whole range of actual and imminent *tabinaw* authorities is involved.

In one informant's phrase, a name is a "stamp" in, I think, two senses: as needed to send a person through the *tabinaw* mails and as the seal put on the person by the *tabinaw*. Names *(ngacal)* are likened to the hearthstones *(ngucol):* they support people on the land (Labby 1972:73). Their importance was demonstrated to Schneider (1968) when he named a dog Maria; Maria, he learned was not a fit name for a dog since dogs are not people. Yapese are amazed by Palauan names which translate as "pig" or the like. Yapese names are handed down in and between *tabinaw* or, on occasion, given by spirits *(kan)* through mediums; they are hardly to be chosen or adapted by their carriers.

As "stamp" a name does not commit a person unequivocally to a particular *tabinaw* so much as point him towards life in one. As names are granted, so may they be removed or changed by *tabinaw* authorities: above all else a name marks its carrier as currently in relation with *tabinaw* authorities somewhere on Yap and hence as Yapese.

Although a name neither commits a person to lifetime *tabinaw* membership nor *tabinaw* authorities to care for him, the choice of a name may be the occasion for delicate negotiations among authorities pursuing various interests. A contemporary example illustrates some of the issues involved.

A widow gave birth, to the anger of many people connected to her husband.

A man related to the husband wished to have a child and so adopted *(pof)* hers. This did not settle matters entirely: in the view of some he should have married the woman, which he had no wish to do. Since he was soon to leave Yap he wanted to be momentarily unattached and the child to be nurtured by the natal mother. Since he hoped to marry later, he feared that children born to a future wife would ally against his adopted child and cast the adoptee off after the man's death. To placate the members of his *tabinaw,* he suggested that the child be named for his father. To insure the child's future security, he gave another name as well, taken from a separate *tabinaw* for which he was landholder. When his suggestions were accepted, he had accomplished complex adjustments in the relations of all people connected with the *tabinaw* through three generations.

M'fen may call on their authority over one *tabinaw* to give a name from the *tabinaw* in which they actually reside. This naming may imply that the child will be affiliated to the *m'fen's* own *tabinaw* or it may not, depending on agreements among authorities. Thus a *m'fen* may simply wish to see a name given and have no intention of taking the child. Often a *tabinaw* authority wishes to give a name not out of interest in the child but in remembrance of the last carrier. In other cases the *m'fen* may indeed wish to gain a potential junior *tabinaw* member, perhaps as worker, perhaps in order to warn a person who is already presumptive successor to the *m'fen* in the latter's *tabinaw* that he may have a competitor, and succession is assured only by work. *M'fen* may exercise authority at naming and afterwards to separate a child from his natal parents against their will (see Kirkpatrick and Broder, 1976: case I), although such behavior is improper as "greedy."

One justification may cover a variety of modes of attaching children, names, parents, and land: keeping a *tabinaw* together. Since a *tabinaw* is a historic association of people and land, and only derivatively a bounded group or set of lands, the reference to "a *tabinaw*" may be adjusted at times to validate adoption of a particular strategy. Examination of an extended case brings out the vagaries of reference (figure 17.2).

Figure 17.2 shows the people of two *tabinaw,* X and Y. Informants in the neighborhood cited the naming practices of all the people related to X as admirable—A2 and B2, I was told, "exchanged names." The naming of A2 and his chil-

dren is unexceptional, as A2 discusses it: all were given names from X and their names were chosen or called out by *tabinaw* elders. A2 explained the choice of name D2 for his first daughter: D1 had been like a mother to him so the child was named after her even though E1 was still alive (and would have been pleased to see a girl named for her). He did not stress the fact that, by his own testimony, C1 picked the name.

B1 had searched for a worthy successor as landholder of Y. His adopted son, M, turned out to be incompetent, so he expected his lands to pass to people of X through D1. The "people of Y"—B1 and perhaps C1 and D1—feared that A1 would, as landholder of X, try to merge Y with the lands of X should Y be passed to a member of X *tabinaw*. B2 was named from Y and later designated as successor on Y to avoid this eventual-

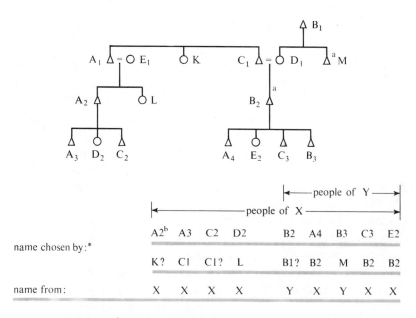

	A2[b]	A3	C2	D2		B2	A4	B3	C3	E2
name chosen by:*	K?	C1	C1?	L		B1?	B2	M	B2	B2
name from:	X	X	X	X		Y	X	Y	X	X

a: adopted. b: numbers indicate order of name-giving.

* Data as recounted by A2 and B2: possibly chosen or called out.

Figure 17.2

ity. To my limited knowledge, B2 has never placed himself in a public context where A1 or A2 (as successor to C1 who succeeded A1 as landholder of X) may be seen to be higher than him, although he states that he is of X and A2 carries the "voice" of X. B2 says that he did not have his children named in the traditional manner but, instead, he "just put the name on paper." Of his four children, the first two were given names held previously by members of A1's household. The third child was also named from X, but after C1, who had raised B2. B2's children are all younger than those who share their names in the other household: he chose names in such an order that his children are "small" A and C, while A2's children are "middle" A and "big" C. Only with his fourth child did B2 have a name from Y given, and this name alone was given "traditionally" by M.

In maintaining the integrity of both X and Y *tabinaw,* B2 has avoided A2 in some interactional contexts and has not named his children according to the "traditional" manner—avoiding one such context—just as his elders successfully shortcircuited A1 in the matter of B2's naming. The result is that the naming is exemplary, the unity of each *tabinaw* is not contradicted by action, and it will little matter in the long run whether there is great distrust and avoidance between the two households. All these namings are accepted as proper both because no one would object and because they help to "keep the *tabinaw* together."

An analytic problem remains. We may discuss various practices as subsumed under the modes of reference possible in the legitimating claim to "keep the *tabinaw* together," but not all

decisions by *tabinaw* authorities are so validated, although they may be accepted as legitimate.

M'fen exile the "people of the *tabinaw*" for one prototypical offence above all others: taking food from land reserved at the death of a landholder. Should a *m'fen* order the "people of the *tabinaw*" off the *tabinaw* land, they may only ask for cause to be publicly cited. Yapese admit that a "greedy *m'fen*" might lie in claiming that this offence had occurred. The "people of the *tabinaw*" may not appeal to outside authorities: it is purely a matter for those connected with the *tabinaw* to handle. "People of the *tabinaw*" may not publicly contradict the *m'fen*: such impudence would be cause for exile. There is hence no recognized recourse against the whims of *m'fen* in such an extreme situation and, in public discourse at least, the *m'fen's* decision to punish is of necessity proper.

These examples suggest that, when we distinguish personal strategies on the one hand from evidence of them in public discourse, the decisions of authorities are consistently legitimate *in public discourse* and untainted by any hint of antisocial interests. The deliberations in which names are chosen are private, so the only public fact is that negotiations have ended with a chosen name on which all authorities, including ghosts, have agreed. A "greedy *m'fen*" who uses her authority to take a child acts quite improperly but goes unchallenged by the child's parents. All may agree that she abused her authority, but no one may properly state that opinion in public contexts.

The full range of decisions which may be taken by Yapese authorities obviously cannot be examined, but more instances might be given of what I take to be a fundamental fact of Yapese society: authorities are so empowered and public discourse is so structured that those people who have authority as the outcome of histories of cultivation cannot help but act in ways which *in public discourse* are always either traditionally valid or highly improper as opposed to a higher authority whose action is inevitably valid (e.g., a landholder accusing a *m'fen* of lying).

Two results emerge. Authorities hold and exercise their offices in relation to the whole and the presentation of their decisions in public is in terms of such holistic relations. That presentation does not rule out the exercise of private interests but shows apparently any outcome of negotiations among authorities as holistically oriented. Either it is legitimate and publicly unquestionable or it is an affront to particular superiors. There is no middle ground.[9]

Secondly, the relation between traditional ideology and public discourse needs specification for both ethnographic and theoretical purposes. Since I have not observed traditional Yap at first hand, I can hardly provide rules to discriminate between public and private discourse. Yapese clearly do make such discriminations when, e.g., they term succession "something of the *tabinaw*" not open to public examination. The political networks, in which messengers each move only from one particular chief to certain recipients in other villages, both organize private discourse in the deliberations of the office holders of one village or of the leaders of one confederation or all Yap, and carry public discourse in its most influential form, the 'word of the chiefs' *(thin ko pilung)*.

As Lingenfelter (1971) has shown, when messages pass properly from point to point in political networks (along the *tha' e nug*) they may not be disregarded without opposing the authority of all those who have passed the messages. Directives, requests, and apologies properly sent hence achieve their ends quickly.

Despite the limits on our knowledge of traditional Yapese discourse, the point seems clear: talk is managed on Yap so as to separate public and private discourse. Much of the work of the political system is accomplished in small meetings, secret rituals, plots and counter-plots; all this is hidden from the public sphere in which the results may be announced, but they are hardly debated. Traditional theory is repeatedly validated in public discourse, but the two are not equivalent: e.g., the promotion of Kanif to *bulce* rank emphasized continuity in that there were and are seven *bulce,* as everyone knows, but the decision taken was without precedent. The handling of incest clarifies the distinction between ideology and public discourse: incest is an abomination, the confusion of men with beasts, but punishment is left to *tabinaw* ghosts (Schneider 1957; Labby, 1976). Sooner or later they withhold their protection and harm comes to the clan and/or *tabinaw* in which the offence occurred. The *tabinaw* is threatened, but active punishment by *tabinaw* authorities would parallel the offence by opposing *tabinaw* members, not linking them as senior and junior. *Tabinaw* authorities may attempt to mollify the ghosts, but do not cast off the offenders. In the end, i.e., in public notice, punishment comes from the ghosts or is allayed through gifts to them, but the nature and gravity of incest are clear.[10]

The relation of the ideology to public discourse may help to clarify a somewhat opaque concept in Dumont's work, that of the "threshold." Dumont emphasizes that ideology orders but does not subsume a society: much remains which people may or may not notice but do not seem to take as fundamental. Such matters, which the ideology can only explicate in an *ad hoc,* stumbling way, are beyond a threshold of social *conscience* (Dumont 1970a:36–39, 232–39). Without denying the ideology its function of orienting the social order, we may avoid such question-begging formulations as a "threshold of consciousness" by hypothesizing the existence of rules delimiting modes of discourse. The ideology is thereby made more accessible to inquiry as discovered in certain discourse modes and no suggestion is made that alternate orders are unthinkable. Certainly Yapese are aware of the exercise of personal interests and often willing to gossip about them. Anecdotes, like foreigners, pass away in time, unlike the public discourse in which the continuity of land and people, as resource and as project, is affirmed.[11]

Finally, this view of discourse modes as carriers of ideology may permit us to pose comparative questions in a clearcut, if hardly easy manner: may differences in the negotiability and variation of social action in holistic societies be correlated with differences in the encoding of ideology in discourse modes? The Yapese example, in which restrictions on public discourse allow much activity to occur behind the scenes, makes this suggestion plausible. Recent papers by Rosaldo (1973) and Keenan (1973) suggest it may apply to situations in which ideological combat of perceived old and new ways is dominant.

Conclusion: The Notion of the Person

In Yapese theory a person unites both ahistoric clan membership and a historic identity as named, in a *tabinaw,* holding office. Out of history he threatens assimilation with animals: clan totems are, after all, "siblings" to clanspeople. In history a person is differentiated from all others and develops a biography. Aging while in hierarchic relation to authorities, a person gains wisdom and rights to have his opinions translated into what is publicly known and stated. With age, he retreats from action to supervision. At any point, however, a person may displease higher authorities and either lose name and *tabinaw* or bring infertility to his people and land. When a person loses his name he may look elsewhere for a name and *tabinaw* membership. In the background, then, is the specter of not only natural or wild persons but alternate affiliations.

In public discourse, people are not said to be developing alternate ties. Wrongful actions are the occasion for compassion and rebuke from authorities or explusion from *tabinaw* identity and/or membership. A person was born to a *tabinaw,* grows in a *tabinaw,* not necessarily the same one, dies and becomes a ghost. Complex relations recede from view as attention is publicly focussed on the achieved continuity of relations to the whole.

When Schneider was on Yap in 1947–

48, a man who was younger brother to the landholder of one *tabinaw* lived with an elder in an adjacent village. Because he cared diligently for the old man, he was expected to succeed as landholder to the old man's *tabinaw* and was spoken of as the old man's "child." The old man had an adopted son, but the latter was deemed irresponsible and lived elsewhere. It was entirely proper that such a man not succeed to the status of landholder. Soon after, the adopted son returned, settled his differences with the old man, and succeeded as landholder. When I visited in 1972, the son's peregrinations were forgotten and no one mentioned the dutiful man's tie to the elder. The dutiful man was a "person of" his natal *tabinaw* and village, and now is a ghost of that *tabinaw*. All three men's remembered course through life was uneventful and undistinguished.

Yapese say that they can identify any person's village, given his name, and often they can. The name signals to others the complex biography of a consociate, yet it functions as "stamp": personal biographies are derivative of *tabinaw* and village histories. All the people of a high *tabinaw* may be seen as generous, and people count on those from the lowest villages to engage in repulsive practices. Elders and ghosts may change a person's name at will. People may achieve autonomy, but they do so in the sight of hierarchic authorities, within larger units, and not in opposition to them.

In public discourse, the person appears as both speaker and topic, as hierarchically integrated and, when rebuked, as *ufanthin* 'arrogant' (literally: proud of his own words). The unmarked form of the person is in relation to the whole; the marked and exceptional form is in rebellion to that historic whole. When Yapese elders explain traditional theory to ethnographers they stress the contrast between the project of keeping and improving rank in which every unit enters and reversion to the wild (Labby 1972, 1976); in the announcements of authorities the same opposition is encoded.

A person or group may reach what all know to be unprecedented decisions and enforce them while remaining within the traditional whole. Yapese do not need formal rules such as genealogical criteria for succession to statuses in order that a succession conform to tradition: the decision of a landholder as announced by others after his death is assured to be proper. (Whether it is the landholder's actual choice that is announced is another problem, as Yapese are aware.) Indeed, we may take Yapese rules for succession to *m'fen* rights and landholding as a commentary on the point: since *m'fen* rights derive from the work of *clanspeople,* they are "naturally" passed by a rule of descent; since succession to landholding involves recognition of rank, work on the project of social reproduction, and so forth, it is a matter of choice by authority. The choice of a landholder's successor is publicly appropriate after the fact even when it was highly unexpected beforehand. Yapese theory would seem to agree with American ideology in separating natural laws from social rules and probabilities. Precisely because people are bound in social hierarchy, they may and do take autonomous action without any threat to the "normative subject" of the whole. Holistic society hence does not enslave its members to tradition, excluding any and all innovation, but orders autonomy and dependence, and a variety of action strategies under its expansive cloak of relationship.

Notes

1. All quotations from Dumont's work are taken from the English translation, although the original French was consulted.

This paper has been improved by criticism from David M. Schneider, Janet Dolgin, David Kemnitzer, Ben Lee, and Terry Strauss.

Fieldwork on Yap was conducted in June–November 1972 and June–September 1973 with the support of the National Institute of Mental Health and the Lichtstern Fund through the University of Chicago and D. M. Schneider.

Yapese orthography is not yet standardized; the spellings used here approximate Rumung municipality dialect. "C" is used for /č/.

2. The terms "society" and "culture" are separated in conformity with Kroeber and Parsons (1958), referring to an organized population and a system of symbols, respectively.

3. In Dumont's work and subsequent debates (see Madan 1971), many terms have been given limited usages with reference to Indian ethnography and its theory. Such terms as "rank" are used here in an attempt to avoid most of the controversy. It should be noted that no equation is made in this paper between Indian caste and what, in the Yapese ethnography, has been called "caste."

4. The terms "rank" and "position" are used somewhat loosely at this point, following the Yapese practice of indicating that one unit is comparable to but 'higher than' (toolang ko) another.

5. The discussion of tabinaw and political organization in this paper is sketchy. For more detail, see Schneider (1953, 1957, 1962), Lingenfelter (1971), Defngin (1958, 1966) and Mahoney (1958). The stress placed on alternative recruitment outcomes in this paper supplements these sources; much that Defngin and Mahoney treat as land transfer I would also handle in its aspect of recruitment.

"Political" is not used here in the limited sense of Dumont (1970c) but with reference to village and areal organization on Yap. "Political" matters traditionally include the giving of tribute, feasts, magical protection, as well as wars and the sending of typhoons; no domain restricted to one mode of action is denoted by the term in this paper.

Some reflective Yapese students, on reading an earlier paper (Kirkpatrick and Broder, 1976), found that undue emphasis had been placed on notions of work, and not enough on renguy ('compassion, love'). It

appears that renguy is most salient in precisely those relations of inequality in which work is performed and judged: these critics may be emphasizing the higher partner's role and I the lower one's. Whether or not our disagreement is thus a limited one, I must admit that I have devoted extra attention to explicating the notion of work in tabinaw contexts, simply because such a cultural operator is not usually expected in the context of what, previously, was seen as a partrilineage.

6. The argument here is that Yap is homologous to India as a society hierarchically ordered by a holistic ideology, not that it is isomorphic with Indian society. The data given to make this point beg full description of social organization and raise many questions left unansered here, e.g., the recurrence of triads in Yapese phrasings of interdependence and hierarchy. For a partial answer to that problem, see Labby 1972.

7. The supervision/work distinction visible in m'fen/ landholder relations and 'sitting' baan pilung/ 'going' baan pagal interdependence is reminiscent of the action implications of dharma/artha. It is not clear whether other systems of interdependence could be arrayed in terms of a supervision/work distinction, although it is suggestive that such commonly used objects demanding specialized skills in manufacture as pots and woven cinctures (baguy), found in every household, were produced by the lowest political units, pimilingay villages and tributary atoll dwellers to the east, respectively.

In order to press the comparison of Yapese theory with Dumont's version of Indian ideology home, a parallel to the dimension of purity/pollution in India should be suggested. This is not attempted here, partly out of uncertainty whether such a single dimension along which hierarchical distinctions can be arrayed was ever posited on Yap. Were such to be posited, it would have to encompass such recurrently found Yapese orderings as high/low, supervision/work, and pure/impure.

8. This is hardly the place to debate the complex issue of whether hierarchy is still regnant on Yap, and so such ambiguous phrases as "reduction of hierarchy" are used to avoid prejudging the issue.

9. The Yapese data converge with Weber's ideal type of traditional authority. Weber stressed that the traditional chief rules partly in terms of traditions which set forth precisely his authority and its proper objects, party by "free, personal decision" since obedience to the chief is nearly without limit (1947:341). For Yap, the distinction does not lie between delimited and extensive powers: an operational definition of "keeping the tabi-

naw together" is out of the question. Rather the decisions of traditional authorities are so taken and announced that they are always in conformity with tradition or, unambiguously, incursions into the preserve of other authorities. Tradition does not direct deliberations so efficiently and univocally as it formulates an inevitable code for their announcement. The difference between Yapese authority and Weber's ideal type seems to parallel the difference between holistic and individualistic models of relationship noted by Dumont (1970a: Appendix): the ordering of interactional protocol effaces the distinction between delimited and free authority that is so striking when Weber concentrates on the powers of an individual actor.

10. Similar public recognition of offence and punishment may be noted in politics. Typhoons are sent by magicians on the orders of chiefs who are displeased with their subordinates. After the typhoon has hit, there is *voiced* agreement that people have no food, rather than that the chief has acted against the people. People agree that they are destitute and lacking the basic medium of social exchange; at this point they are fit objects for the compassion of their superordinates.

11. Recognition that certain relations and modes of interaction are ideologically stressed and bulwarked by discourse constraints may be of help in connection with problems outside Yap. To sketch the way in which such analysis might proceed, I hazard an answer to the problem of the Maori *hau*, the "spirit of the gift."

I suspect that the *hau* is proof that gift and countergift were just that, and not some less valued sort of transaction. Sahlins stresses that the Maori countergift is "customarily larger than the initial gift" and would hence gloss the *hau* in the countergift, with some qualification, as "profit" (1972:160–61). In contrast, I would stress

that the gift need be shown to be gift, and find the countergift to serve this function, i.e., to be both *taonga* gift and *hau* validation. That such validation takes the form of an increased return is of interest, but not, I think, as important as its function of defining the sort of transaction taking place. This would seem to fit with Ranapiri's statements that "We have no agreement about payment" for the initial prestation—its return will be delayed and the suspicion may arise that there will be no return—and that the return valuable, which functions as *hau*, may not be kept "whether it is something very good, or bad" (Ranapiri's explanation to Best as retranslated in Sahlins 1972:152). Similarly, the ceremony in analogy to which Ranapiri mentions the *hau* of the gift involves a validation of ideological truth: when priests eat forest birds they demonstrate that their skills have indeed brought abundance to the forest. It seems incautious to claim that when Ranapiri said that "These birds are the property of, or belong to, the *mauri*, the *tohunga*, and the forest" (Best, qu. ibid.: 158), he meant that they demonstrate the intimacy of relation of these three. Rather it may be that an explanation of *hau* as the validation of action as ideologically proper and hence as the proof of the ideology is more powerful and suggestive than Sahlins' analogy to economics or Lévi-Strauss's insistence on the value of exchange *per se*. *Contra* Lévi-Strauss, I doubt that the *hau* is an unnecessary elaboration merely because lending and borrowing, buying and selling are covered by a single term (1950:xl). In social life, the question may arise whether lending or the imposition of humiliation, borrowing or barely masked theft occurred. The *hau* of the gift affirms gift, giver, recipient, and the value of giving without denying the existence of improper transactions in social intercourse.

EIGHTEEN

The Whiteness of the Whale

Herman Melville

Were there no understanding of the "whiteness" of the whale, Melville tells us, the sense of *Moby Dick* would be lost, and with that the meaning of the beast. In giving "comprehensible form" to this "mystical and well nigh ineffable" whiteness of the whale, Melville provides an exceedingly masterful symbolic analysis. As he documents—and creates—the complexities of meaning in "whiteness," in the processes through which particular symbols appear in a multitude of meaningful structures (associations), Melville shows these symbols (even that of "nature" itself) to be comprehended ideologically. Consideration of the gap between appearance and reality stands behind Melville's examination of those things which share "whiteness"—japonicas, pearls, and kings, the Albatross, albinos, the pallor of the dead, New Hampshire's mountains, Lima, and the veil of the Christian God.

WHAT THE WHITE WHALE was to Ahab, has been hinted; what, at times, he was to me, as yet remains unsaid.

Aside from those more obvious considerations touching Moby Dick, which could not but occasionally awaken in any man's soul some alarm, there was another thought, or rather vague, nameless horror concerning him, which at times by its intensity completely overpowered all the rest; and yet so mystical and well nigh ineffable was it, that I almost despair of putting it in a comprehensible form. It was the whiteness of the whale that above all things appalled me. But how can I hope to explain myself here; and yet, in some dim, random way, explain myself I must, else all these chapters might be naught.

Though in many natural objects, whiteness refiningly enhances beauty, as if imparting some special virtue of its own, as in marbles, japonicas, and pearls; and though various nations have in some way recognised a certain royal pre-eminence in this hue; even the barbaric, grand old kings of Pegu placing the title "Lord of the White Elephants" above all their other magniloquent ascriptions of dominion; and the modern kings of Siam unfurling the same snow-white quadruped in the royal standard; and the Hanoverian flag bearing the one figure of a snow-white charger; and the great Austrian Empire, Caesarian, heir to overlording Rome, having for the imperial color the same imperial hue; and though this pre-eminence in it applies to the human race itself, giving the white man ideal mastership over every dusky tribe; and though, besides, all this, whiteness has been even made significant of gladness, for among the Romans a white stone marked a joyful day; and though in other mortal sympathies and symbolizings, this same hue is made the emblem of many touching, noble things—the innocence of brides, the benignity of age; though among the Red Men of America the giving of the white belt of wampum was the deepest pledge of honor; though in many climes, whiteness typifies the majesty of Justice in the ermine of the Judge, and contributes to the daily state of kings and queens drawn by milk-white steeds; though even in the higher mysteries of the most august religions it has been made the symbol of the divine spotlessness and power; by the Persian fire worshippers, the white forked flame being held the holiest on the altar; and in the Greek mythologies, Great Jove himself being made incarnate in a snow-white bull; and though to the noble Iroquois, the midwinter sacrifice of the sacred White Dog was by far the holiest festival of their theology, that spotless, faithful creature being held the purest envoy they could send to the Great Spirit with the annual tidings of their own fidelity; and though directly from the Latin word for white, all Christian priests derive the name of one part of their sacred vesture, the alb or tunic, worn beneath the cassock; and though among the holy pomps of the Romish faith, white is specially employed in the celebration of the Passion of our Lord; though in the Vision of St. John, white robes are given to the redeemed, and the four-and-twenty elders stand clothed in white before the great white throne, and the Holy One that sitteth there white like wool; yet for all these accumulated associations, with whatever is sweet, and honorable, and sublime, there yet lurks an elusive something in the innermost idea of this hue, which strikes more of panic to the soul than that redness which affrights in blood.

This elusive quality it is, which causes the thought of whiteness, when divorced from more kindly associations, and coupled with any object terrible in itself, to heighten that terror to the furthest bounds. Witness the white bear of the poles, and the white shark of the tropics; what but their smooth, flaky whiteness makes them the transcendent horrors they are? That ghastly whiteness it is which imparts such an abhorrent mildness, even more loathsome than terrific, to the dumb gloating of their aspect. So that not the fierce-fanged tiger in his heraldic coat can so stagger courage as the white-shrouded bear or shark.[1]

Bethink thee of the albatross, whence come those clouds of spiritual wonderment and pale dread, in which that white phantom sails in all imaginations? Not Coleridge first threw that spell; but God's great, unflattering laureate, Nature.[2]

Most famous in our Western annals and Indian traditions is that of the White Steed of the Prairies; a magnificent milk-white charger, larged-eyed, small-headed, bluff-chested, and with the dignity of a thousand monarchs in his lofty, over-scorning carriage. He was the elected Xerxes of vast herds of wild horses, whose pastures in those days were only fenced by the Rocky Mountains and the Alleghanies. At their flaming head he westward trooped it like that chosen star which every evening leads on the hosts of light. The flashing cascade of his mane, the curving comet of his tail, invested him with housings more resplendent than gold and silver-beaters could have furnished him. A most imperial and archangelical apparition of that unfallen, western world, which to the eyes of the old trappers and hunters revived the glories of those primeval times when Adam walked majestic as a god, bluff-browed and fearless as this mighty steed. Whether marching amid his aides and marshals in the van of countless cohorts that endlessly streamed it over the plains, like an Ohio; or whether with his circumambient subjects browsing all around at the horizon, the White Steed gallopingly reviewed them with warm nostrils reddening through his cool milkiness; in whatever aspect he presented himself, always to the bravest Indians he was the object of trembling reverence and awe. Nor can it be questioned from what stands on legendary record of this noble horse, that it was his spiritual whiteness chiefly, which so clothed him with divineness; and that this divineness had that in it which, though commanding worship, at the same time enforced a certain nameless terror.

But there are other instances where this whiteness loses all that accessory and strange glory which invests it in the White Steed and Albatross.

What is it that in the Albino man so peculiarly repels and often shocks the eye, as that sometimes he is loathed by own own kith and kin! It is that whiteness which invests him, a thing expressed by the name he bears. The Albino is as well made as other men— has no substantive deformity—and yet this mere aspect of all-pervading whiteness makes him more strangely hideous than the ugliest abortion. Why should this be so?

Nor, in quite other aspects, does Nature in her least palpable but not the less malicious agencies, fail to enlist among her forces this crowning attribute of the terrible. From its snowy aspect, the gauntleted ghost of the Southern Seas has been denominated the White Squall. Nor, in some historic instances, has the art of human malice omitted so potent an auxiliary. How wildly it heightens the effect of that passage in Froissart, when, masked in the snowy symbol of their faction, the desperate White Hoods of Ghent murder their bailiff in the market-place!

Nor, in some things, does the common, hereditary experience of all mankind fail to bear witness to the supernaturalism of this hue. It cannot well be doubted, that the one visible quality in the aspect of the dead which most appals the gazer, is the marble pallor lingering there; as if indeed that pallor were as much like the badge of consternation in the other world, as of mortal trepidation here. And from that pallor of the dead, we borrow the expressive hue of the shroud in which we wrap them. Nor even in our superstitions do we fail to throw the same snowy mantle round our phantoms; all ghosts rising in the milk-white fog—Yea, while these terrors seize us, let us add, that even the king of terrors, when personified by the evangelist, rides on his pallid horse.

Therefore, in his other moods, symbolize whatever grand or gracious thing he will by whiteness, no man can deny that in its profoundest idealized significance it calls up a peculiar apparition to the soul.

But though without dissent this point be fixed, how is mortal man to account for it? To analyze it, would seem impossible. Can we, then, by the citation of some of those instances wherein this thing of whiteness—though for the time either wholly or in great part stripped of all direct associations calculated to import to it aught fearful, but nevertheless, is found to exert over us the same sorcery, however modified;—can we thus hope to light upon some chance clue to conduct us to the hidden cause we seek?

Let us try. But in a manner like this, subtlety appeals to subtlety, and without imagination no man can follow another into these halls. And though, doubtless, some at least of the imaginative impressions about to be presented may have been shared by most men, yet few perhaps were entirely conscious of them at the time, and therefore may not be able to recall them now.

Why to the man of untutored ideality, who happens to be but loosely acquainted with the peculiar character of the day, does the bare mention of Whitsuntide marshal in the fancy such long, dreary, speechless processions of slow-pacing pilgrims, down-cast and hooded with new-fallen snow? Or to the unread, unsophisticated Protestant of the Middle American States, why does the passing mention of a White Friar or a White Nun, evoke such an eyeless statue in the soul?

Or what is there apart from the traditions of dungeoned warriors and kings (which will not wholly account for it) that makes the White Tower of London tell so much more strongly on the imagination of an untravelled American, than those other storied structures, its neighbors—the Byward Tower, or even the Bloody? And those sublimer towers, the White Mountains of New Hampshire, whence, in peculiar moods, comes that gigantic ghostliness over the soul at the bare mention of that name, while the thought of Virginia's Blue Ridge is full of a soft, dewy, distant dreaminess? Or why, irrespective of all latitudes and longitudes, does the name of the White Sea exert such a spectralness over the fancy, while that of the Yellow Sea lulls us with mortal thoughts of long lacquered mild afternoons on the waves, followed by the gaudiest and yet sleepiest of sunsets? Or, to choose a wholly unsubstantial instance, purely addressed to the fancy, why, in reading the old fairy tales of Central Europe, does "the tall pale man" of the Hartz forests, whose changeless pallor unrustingly glides through the green of the groves— why is this phantom more terrible than all the whooping imps of the Blocksburg?

Nor is it, altogether, the remembrance of her cathedral-toppling earthquakes; nor the stampedoes of her frantic seas; nor the tearlessness of arid skies that never rain; nor the sight of her wide field of leaning spires, wrenched copestones, and crosses all adroop (like canted yards of anchored fleets); and her suburban avenues of house-walls lying over upon each other, as a tossed pack of cards;—it is not these things alone which make tearless Lima, the strangest, saddest city thou can'st see. For Lima has taken the white veil; and there is a higher horror in this whiteness of her woe. Old as Pizarro, this whiteness keeps her ruins for ever new; admits not the cheerful greenness of complete decay; spreads over her broken ramparts the rigid pallor of an apoplexy that fixes its own distortions.

I know that, to the common apprehension, this phenomenon of whiteness is not confessed to be the prime agent in exaggerating the terror of objects otherwise terrible; not to the unimaginative mind is there aught of terror in those appearances whose awfulness to another mind almost solely consists in this one phenomenon, especially when exhibited under any form at all approaching to muteness or universality. What I mean by these two statements may perhaps be respectively elucidated by the following examples.

First: The mariner, when drawing nigh the coasts of foreign lands, if by night he hear the roar of breakers, starts to vigilance, and feels just enough of trepidation to sharpen all his faculties; but under precisely similar circumstances, let him be called from his hammock to view his ship sailing through a midnight sea of milky whiteness—as if from encircling headlands shoals of combed white bears were swimming round him, then he feels a silent, superstitious dread; the shrouded phantom of the whitened waters is horrible to him as a real ghost; in vain the lead assures him he is still off soundings; heart and helm they both go down; he never rests till blue water is under him again. Yet where is the mariner who will tell thee, "Sir, it was not so much the fear of striking hidden rocks, as the fear of that hideous whiteness that so stirred me?"

Second: To the native Indian of Peru, the continual sight of the snow-howdahed Andes conveys naught of dread, except, perhaps, in the mere fancying of the eternal frosted desolateness reigning at such vast altitudes, and the natural conceit of what a fearfulness it would be to lose oneself in such inhuman solitude. Much the same is it with the backwoodsman of the West, who with comparative indifference views an unbounded prairie sheeted with driven snow, no shadow of tree or twig to break the fixed trance of whiteness. Not so the sailor, beholding the scenery of the Antarctic seas; where at times, by some infernal trick of legerdemain in the powers of frost and air, he, shivering and half shipwrecked, instead of rainbows speaking hope and solace to his misery, views what seems a boundless churchyard grinning upon him with its lean ice monuments and splintered crosses.

But thou sayest, methinks this white-lead chapter about whiteness is but a white flag hung out from a craven soul; thou surrenderest to a hypo, Ishmael.

Tell me, why this strong young colt, foaled in some peaceful valley of Vermont, far removed from all beasts of prey—why is it that upon the sunniest day, if you but shake a fresh buffalo robe behind him, so that he cannot even see it, but only smells its wild animal muskiness—why will he start, snort, and with bursting eyes paw the ground in phrensies of affright? There is no remembrance in him of any gorings of wild creatures in his green northern home, so that the strange muskiness he smells cannot recall to him anything associated with the experience of former perils; for what knows he, this New England colt, of the black bisons of distant Oregon?

No; but here thou beholdest even in a dumb brute, the instinct of the knowledge of the demonism in the world. Though thousands of miles from Oregon, still when he smells that savage musk, the rending, goring bison herds are as present as to the deserted wild foal of the prairies, which this instant they may be trampling into dust.

Thus, then, the muffled rollings of a milky sea; the bleak rustlings of the festooned frosts of mountains, the desolate shiftings of the windrowed snows of prairies; all these, to Ishmael, are as the shaking of that buffalo robe to the frightened colt!

Though neither knows where lie the nameless things of which the mystic sign gives forth such hints; yet with me, as with the colt, somewhere those things must exist. Though in many of its aspects this visible world seems formed in love, the invisible spheres were formed in fright.

But not yet have we solved the incantation of this whiteness, and learned why it appeals with such power to the soul; and more strange and far more portentous—why, as we have seen, it is at once the most meaning symbol of spiritual things, nay, the very veil of the Christian's Deity; and yet should be as it is, the intensifying agent in things the most appalling to mankind.

Is it that by its indefiniteness it shadows forth the heartless voids and immensities of the universe, and thus stabs us from behind with the thought of annihilation, when beholding the white depths of the milky way? Or is it, that as in essence whiteness is not so much a color as the visible absence of color; and at the same time the concrete of all colors; is it for these reasons that there is such a dumb blankness, full of meaning, in a wide landscape of snows—a colorless, all-color of atheism from which we shrink? And when we consider that other theory of the natural philosophers, that all other earthly hues—every stately or lovely emblazoning—the sweet tinges of sunset skies and woods; yea, and the gilded velvets of butterflies, and the butterfly cheeks of young girls; all these are but subtile deceits, not actually inherent in substances, but only laid on from without; so that all deified Nature absolutely paints like the harlot, whose allurements cover nothing but the charnel-house within; and when we proceed further, and consider that the mystical cosmetic which produces every one of her hues, the great principle of light, for ever remains white or colorless in itself, and if operating without medium upon matter, would touch all objects, even tulips and hoses, with its own blank tinge—pondering all this, the palsied universe lies before us a leper; and like wilful travellers in Lapland, who refuse to wear colored and coloring glasses upon their eyes, so the wretched infidel gazes himself blind at the monumental white shroud that wraps all the prospect around him. And of all these things the Albino whale was the symbol. Wonder ye then at the fiery hunt?

Notes

1. With reference to the Polar bear, it may possibly be urged by him who would fain go still deeper into this matter, that it is not the whiteness, separately regarded, which heightens the intolerable hideousness of that brute; for, analysed, that heightened hideousness, it might be said, only rises from the circumstance, that the irresponsible ferociousness of the creature stands invested in the fleece of celestial innocence and love; and hence, by bringing together two such opposite emotions in our minds, the Polar bear frightens us with so unnatural a contrast. But even assuming all this to be true; yet, were it not for the whiteness, you would not have that intensified terror.

As for the white shark, the white gliding ghostliness of repose in that creature, when beheld in his ordinary moods, strangely tallies with the same quality in the Polar quadruped. This peculiarity is most vividly hit by the French in the name they bestow upon that fish. The Romish mass for the dead begins with "Requiem eternam" (eternal rest), whence Requiem denominating the mass itself, and any other funeral music. Now, in allusion to the white, silent stillness of death in this shark, and the mild deadliness of his habits, the French call him *Requin*.

2. I remember the first albatross I ever saw. It was during a prolonged gale, in waters hard upon the Antarctic seas. From my forenoon watch below, I ascended to the overclouded deck; and there, dashed upon the main hatches, I saw a regal, feathery thing of unspotted whiteness, and with a hooked, Roman bill sublime. At intervals, it arched forth its vast archangel wings, as if to embrace some holy ark. Wondrous flutterings and throbbings shook it. Though bodily unharmed, it uttered cries, as some king's ghost in supernatural distress. Through its inexpressible, strange eyes, methought I peeped to secrets which took hold of God. As Abraham before the angels, I bowed myself; the white thing was so white, its wings so wide, and in those for ever exiled waters, I had lost the miserable warping memories of traditions and of towns. Long I gazed at that prodigy of plumage. I cannot tell, can only hint, the things that darted through me then. But at last I awoke; and turning, asked a sailor what bird was this. A goney, he replied. Goney! I never had heard that name before; is it conceivable that this glorious thing is utterly unknown to men ashore! never! But some time after, I learned that goney was some seaman's name for albatross. So that by no possibility could Coleridge's wild Rhyme have had aught to do with those mystical impressions which were mine, when I saw that bird upon our deck. For neither had I then read the Rhyme, nor knew the bird to be an albatross. Yet, in saying this, I do but indirectly burnish a little brighter the noble merit of the poem and the poet.

I assert, then, that in the wondrous bodily whiteness of the bird chiefly lurks the secret of the spell; a truth the more evinced in this, that by a solecism of terms there are birds called grey albatrosses; and these I have frequently seen, but never with such emotions as when I beheld the Antarctic fowl.

But how had the mystic thing been caught? Whisper it not, and I will tell; with a treacherous hook and line, as the fowl floated on the sea. At last the Captain made a postman of it; tying a lettered, leathern tally round its neck, with the ship's time and place; and then letting it escape. But I doubt not, that leathern tally, meant for man, was taken off in Heaven, when the white fowl flew to join the wing-folding, the invoking, and adoring cherubim!

NINETEEN

Role Models

ESTHER NEWTON

Sex identity is normatively considered a natural thing in American culture; it is simply biological and depends entirely on whether the person has one or another kind of genitalia. There is even a term, "secondary sex characteristics," which reinforces the stress on the genitalia and their quality as the defining criterion of sex identity.

Yet, as Newton shows so clearly here, sex identity is no such simple thing. Not only is "the natural" an elaborate cultural construct built in opposition to an equally elaborate cultural construct, "the cultural," but it is crosscut by an inside-outside opposition, so that what may be male inside is female outside, female inside is male outside, and the manipulation of the symbols outside purport to state conditions on the inside.

Further, "camp" is the concept which covers the manipulation of the symbols—the self-conscious, creative, and indeed often euphoric manipulation of the symbols—of outside and inside which state sex identity. Camp is the strategy for a situation, how to play the role so that it is felt as genuine by both player and beholder and becomes, therefore, perfectly genuine. Newton explores these matters with a subtlety and sensitivity, and understanding based on intensive fieldwork.

The Actress

FEMALE IMPERSONATORS, particularly the stage impersonators, identify strongly with professional performers. Their special, but not exclusive, idols are female entertainers. Street impersonators usually try to model themselves on movie stars rather than on stage actresses and nightclub performers. Stage impersonators are quite conversant with the language of the theaters and the

Reprinted by permission of the publisher from Esther Newton, *Mother Camp: Female Impersonators in America* (Englewood Cliffs, N.J.: Prentice-Hall, copyright © 1972), pp. 97–111.

nightclubs, while the street impersonators are not. In Kansas City, the stage impersonators frequently talked with avid interest about stage and nightclub "personalities." The street impersonators could not join in these discussions for lack of knowledge.

Stage impersonators very often told me that they considered themselves to be nightclub performers or to be in the nightclub business, "just like other [straight] performers."

When impersonators criticized each other's on- or off-stage conduct as "unprofessional," this was a direct appeal to norms of show business. Certain show business phrases such as "break a leg" (for good luck) were used routinely, and I was admonished not to whistle backstage. The following response of a stage impersonator shows this emphasis in response to my question, "What's the difference between professionals and street fairies?" This impersonator was a "headliner" (had top billing) at a club in New York:

"Well (laughs), simply saying . . . well, I can leave that up to you. You have seen the show. You see the difference between *me* and some of these other people (his voice makes it sound as if this point is utterly self-evident) who are working in this left field of show business, and I'm quite sure that you see a *distinct* difference. I am more conscious of being a performer, and I think generally speaking, most, or a lot, of other people who are appearing in the same show are doing it, not as a lark—we won't say that it's a lark—but they're doing it because it's something they can drop in and out of. They have fun, they laugh, have drinks, and play around, and just have a good time. But to *me,* now, playing around and having a good time is [sic] important to me also; but primarily my interest from the time I arrive at the club till the end of the evening—I am there as a performer, as an entertainer, and this to me is the most important thing. And I dare say that if needs be, I probably could do it, and be just as good an entertainer . . . I don't know if I would be any more successful if I were working in men's clothes than I am working as a woman. But comparing myself to some of the people that I would consider real professional entertainers— people who are genuinely interested in the show as a show, and not just as I say, a street fairy, who wants to put on a dress and a pair of high heels to be seen and show off in public."

The stage performers are interested in "billings" and publicity, in lighting and make-up and stage effects, in "timing" and "stage presence." The quality by which they measure performers and per-formances is "talent." Their models in these matters are established performers, both in their performances and in their off-stage lives, insofar as the impersonators are familiar with the latter. The practice of doing "impressions" is, of course, a very direct expression of this role modeling.

From this perspective, female impersonators are simply nightclub performers who happen to use impersonation as a medium. It will be recalled (Chapter One [of *Mother Camp*]) that many performers are drab in appearance (and sometimes in manner) off stage. These men often say that drag is simply a medium or mask that allows them to perform. The mask is borrowed from female performers, the ethos of performance from show business norms in general.

The stated aspiration of almost all stage impersonators is to "go legit," that is, to play in movies, television, and on stage or in respectable nightclubs, either in drag *or* (some say) in men's clothes. Failing this, they would like to see the whole profession "upgraded," made more legitimate and professional (and to this end they would like to see all street impersonators barred from working, for they claim that the street performers downgrade the profession). T. C. Jones is universally accorded highest status among impersonators because he has appeared on Broadway (*New Faces of 1956*) and on television (Alfred Hitchcock) and plays only high-status nightclubs.

The Drag Queen

Professionally, impersonators place themselves as a group at the bottom of the show-business world. But socially, their self-image can be represented (without the moral implications; see Chapter Six [*Mother Camp*]) in its simplest form as three concentric circles. The impersonators, or drag queens, are the inner circle. Surrounding them are the queens, ordinary gay men. The straights are the outer circle. In this way, impersonators are "a society within a society within a society," as one impersonator told me.

A few impersonators deny publicly that they are gay. These impersonators are married, and some have children. Of course, being married and having children constitute no barrier to participation in the homosexual subculture. But whatever may be the actual case with these few, the impersonators I knew universally described such public statements as "cover." One impersonator's statement was particularly revealing. He said that "in practice" perhaps some impersonators were straight, but "in theory" they could not be. "How can a man perform in female attire and not have something wrong with him?" he asked.

The role of the female impersonator is directly related to both the drag queen and camp roles in the homosexual subculture. In gay life, the two roles are strongly associated. In homosexual terminology, a drag queen is a homosexual who often, or habitually, dresses in female attire. (A drag butch is a lesbian who often, or habitually, dresses in male attire). Drag and camp are the most representative and widely used symbols of homosexuality in the English speaking world. This is true even though many homosexuals would never wear drag or go to a drag party and even though most homosexuals who do wear drag do so only in special contexts, such as private parties and costume balls.[1] At the middle-class level, it is common to give "costume" parties at which those who want to wear drag can do so, and the others can wear a costume appropriate to their gender.

The principle opposition around which the gay world revolves is masculine-feminine. There are a number of ways of representing this opposition through one's own person, where it also becomes an opposition of "inside" = "outside" or "underneath" = "outside." Ultimately, all drag symbolism opposes the "inner" or "real" self (subjective self) to the "outer" self (social self). For the great majority of homosexuals, the social self is often a calculated respectability and the subjective or real self is stigmatized. The "inner" = "outer" opposition is almost parallel to "back" = "front." In fact, the social self is usually described as "front" and social relationships (especially with women) designed to support the veracity of the "front" are called "cover." The "front" = "back" opposition also has a direct tie-in with the body: "Front" = "face"; "back" = "ass."

There are two different levels on which the oppositions can be played out. One is *within* the sartorial system itself,[2] that is, wearing feminine clothing "underneath" and masculine clothing "outside." (This method seems to be used more by heterosexual transvestites.) It symbolizes that the visible, social, masculine clothing is a costume, which in turn symbolizes that the entire sex-role behavior is a role—an act. Conversely, stage impersonators sometimes wear jockey shorts underneath full stage drag, symbolizing that the feminine clothing is a costume.

A second "internal" method is to mix

sex-role referents *within* the visible sartorial system. This generally involves some "outside" items from the feminine sartorial system, such as earrings, lipstick, high-heeled shoes, a necklace, etc., worn *with* masculine clothing. This kind of opposition is used very frequently in informal camping by homosexuals. The feminine item stands out so glaringly that it "undermines" the masculine system and proclaims that the inner identification is feminine.[3] When this method is used on stage, it is called "working with (feminine) pieces." The performer generally works in a tuxedo or business suit and woman's large hat and earrings.

The second level poses an opposition between a one-sex sartorial system and the "self," whose identity has to be indicated in some other way. Thus when impersonators are performing, the oppositional play is between "appearance" which is female, and "reality" or "essence" which is male. One way to do this is to show that the appearance is an illusion; for instance, a standard impersonation maneuver is to pull out one "breast" and show it to the audience. A more drastic step is taking off the wig. Strippers actually routinize the progression from "outside" to "inside" visually, by starting in a full stripping costume and ending by taking off the bra and showing the audience the flat chest. Another method is to demonstrate "maleness" verbally or vocally by suddenly dropping the vocal level or by some direct reference. One impersonator routinely tells the audience: "Have a ball. I have two." (But genitals must *never* be seen.) Another tells unruly members of the audience that he will "put on my men's clothes and beat you up."

Impersonators play on the opposition to varying extents, but most experienced stage impersonators have a characteristic method of doing it. Generally speaking, the desire and ability to break the illusion of femininity is the mark of an experienced impersonator who has freed himself from other impersonators as the immediate reference group and is working fully to the audience. Even so, some stage impersonators admitted that it is difficult to break the unity of the feminine sartorial system. For instance, they said that is difficult, subjectively, to speak in a deep tone of voice while on stage and especially while wearing a wig. The "breasts" especially seem to symbolize the entire feminine sartorial system and role. This is shown not only by the very common device of removing them in order to break the illusion, but in the command, "tits up!" meaning "get into the role" or "get into feminine character."

The tension between the masculine-feminine and inside-outside opposition pervades the homosexual subculture at all class and status levels. In a sense the different class and status levels consist of different ways of balancing these oppositions. Low-status homosexuals (both male and female) characteristically insist on very strong dichotomization between masculine-feminine so that people must play out one principle or the other exclusively. Low-status queens are expected to be very nellie, always, and low-status butch men as so "masculine" that they very often consider themselves straight.[4] (Although as mentioned in Chapter Four, [*Mother Camp*] the queens say in private that "today's butch is tomorrow's sister.") Nevertheless, in the most nellie queen the opposition is still implicitly there, since to participate in the male homosexual subculture as a peer, one must be male inside (psychologically).

Recently, this principle has begun to be challenged by hormone use and by the sex-changing operation. The use of these techniques as a final resolution of the masculine-feminine opposition is hotly discussed in the homosexual subculture. A very significant proportion of the impersonators, and especially the street impersonators, have used or are using hormone shots or plastic inserts to create artificial breasts and change the shape of their bodies. This development is strongly deplored by the stage impersonators who say that the whole point of female impersonation depends on maleness. They further say that these "hormone queens" are placing themselves out of the homosexual subculture, since, by definition, a homosexual man wants to sleep with other *men* (i.e., no gay man would want to sleep with these "hormone queens").

In carrying the transformation even farther, to "become a woman" is approved by the stage impersonators, with the provision that the "sex changes" should get out of gay life altogether and go straight. The "sex changes" do not always comply, however. One quite successful impersonator in Chicago had the operation but continued to perform in a straight club with other impersonators. Some impersonators in Chicago told me that this person was now considered "out of gay life" by the homosexuals and could not perform in a gay club. I also heard a persistent rumor that "she" now liked to sleep with lesbians!

It should be readily apparent why drag is such an effective symbol of both the outside-inside and masculine-feminine oppositions. There are relatively few ascribed roles in American culture and sex role is one of them; sex role radiates a complex and ubiquitous system of typing achieved roles. Obvious examples are in the kinship system (wife, mother, etc.) but sex typing also extends far out into the occupational-role system (airline stewardess, waitress, policeman, etc.). The effect of the drag system is to wrench the sex roles loose from that which supposedly determines them, that is, genital sex. Gay people know that sex-typed behavior can be achieved, contrary to what is popularly believed. They know that the possession of one type of genital equipment by no means guarantees the "naturally appropriate" behavior.

Thus drag in the homosexual subculture symbolizes two somewhat conflicting statements concerning the sex-role system. The first statement symbolized by drag is that the sex-role system is natural: therefore homosexuals are unnatural (typical responses: "I am physically abnormal"; "I can't help it, I was born with the wrong hormone balance"; "I am really a woman who was born with the wrong equipment"; "I am psychologically sick").

The second symbolic statement of drag questions the "naturalness" of the sex-role system *in toto;* if sex-role behavior can be achieved by the "wrong" sex, it logically follows that it is in reality also achieved, not inherited, by the "right" sex. Anthropologists say that sex-role behavior is learned. The gay world, via drag, says that sex-role behavior is an appearance; it is "outside." It can be manipulated at will.

Drag symbolizes both these assertions in a complex way. At the simplest level, drag signifies that the person wearing it is a homosexual, that he is a male who is behaving in a specifically inappropriate way, that he is a male who places himself as a woman in relation to other men. In this sense it signifies a stigma. At the most complex, it is a double inversion that says "appearance is an illusion." Drag says, "my 'outside' appearance is feminine, but my essence 'inside' [the body] is masculine." At the same time it symbolizes the opposite inversion: "my appearance 'outside' [my body, my gender] is masculine, but my essence 'inside' [myself] is feminine."

In the context of the homosexual subculture, all professional female impersonators are "drag queens." Drag is always worn for performance in any case; the female impersonator has simply professionalized this subcultural role. Among themselves and in conversation with other homosexuals, impersonators usually call themselves and are called drag queens. In the same way, their performances are usually referred to by themselves and others as drag shows.

But when the varied meanings of drag are taken into consideration, it should be obvious why the drag queen is an ambivalent figure in the gay world. The drag queen symbolizes all that homosexuals say they fear most in themselves, all that they say they feel guilty about; he symbolizes, in fact, *the* stigma. In this way, the term "drag queen" is comparable to "nigger." And like that word, it may be all right in an ingroup context but not in an outgroup one. Those who do not want to think of themselves or be identified as drag queens under any circumstances attempt to dissociate themselves from "drag" completely. These homosexuals deplore drag shows and profess total lack of interest in them.

Their attitude toward drag queens is one of condemnation combined with the expression of vast social distances between themselves and the drag queen.

Other homosexuals enjoy being queens among themselves, but do not want to be stigmatized by the heterosexual culture. These homosexuals admire drag and drag queens in homosexual contexts, but deplore female impersonators and street fairies for "giving us a bad name" or "projecting the wrong image" to the heterosexual culture. The drag queen is definitely a marked man in the subculture.

Homosexuality consists of sex-role deviation made up of two related but distinct parts: "wrong" sexual objects and "wrong" sex-role presentation of self.[5] The first deviation is shared by all homosexuals, but it can be hidden best. The second deviation logically (in this culture) corresponds with the first, which it symbolizes. But it cannot be hidden, and it actually compounds the stigma.

Thus, insofar as female impersonators are professional drag queens, they are evaluated positively by gay people to the extent that they have perfected a subcultural skill and to the extent that gay people are willing to oppose the heterosexual culture directly (in much the same way the Negroes now call themselves Blacks). On the other hand, they are despised because they symbolize and embody the stigma. At present, the balance is far on the negative side, although this varies by context and by the position of the observer (relative to the stigma). This explains the impersonators' negative identification with the term drag queen when it is used by outsiders. (In the same way, they at first used masculine pronouns of address and

The Camp

While all female impersonators are drag queens in the gay world, by no means are all of them "camps." Both the drag queen and the camp are expressive performing roles, and both specialize in transformation. But the drag queen is concerned with the masculine-feminine transformation, while the camp is concerned with what might be called a philosophy of transformation and incongruity. Certainly the two roles are intimately related, since to be a feminine man is by definition incongruous. But strictly speaking, the drag queen simply expresses the incongruity while the camp actually uses it to achieve a higher synthesis. To the extent that a drag queen does this, he is called "campy." The drag queen role is emotionally charged and connotes low status for most homosexuals because it bears the visible stigmata of homosexuality; camps, however, are found at all levels in the homosexual subculture and are very often the center of primary group organization.[6]

The camp is the central figure in the subcultural ideology of camp. The camp ethos or style plays a role analogous to "soul" in the Negro subculture (Keil 1966:164–90). Like soul, camp is a "strategy for a situation."[7] The special perspective of the female impersonators is a case of a broader homosexual ethos. This is the perspective of moral deviance and, consequently, of a "spoiled identity" in Goffman's terms (Goffman 1963). Like the Negro problem, the homosexual problem centers on self-hatred and the lack of self-esteem.[8] But if "the soul ideology ministers to the needs for an identity" (Keil 1966:165), the camp ideology ministers to the needs for dealing with an identity that is well defined but loaded with contempt. As one impersonator who was also a well-known camp told me, "No one is more miserable about homosexuality than the homosexual."

Camp is not a thing. Most broadly, it signifies a *relationship between* things, people, and activities or qualities, and homosexuality. In this sense, "camp taste," for instance, is synonymous with homosexual taste. Informants stressed that even between individuals there is very little agreement on what is camp because camp is in the eye of the beholder, that is, different homosexuals like different things, and because of the spontaneity and individuality of camp, camp taste is always changing. This has the advantage, recognized by informants, that a clear division can always be maintained between homosexual and "straight" taste.

He said Susan Sontag was wrong about camp's being a cult,[9] and the moment it becomes a public cult, you watch the queens stop it. Because if it becomes the squares', it doesn't belong to them any more. And what will be "camp art," no queen will own. It's like taking off the work clothes and putting on the home clothes. When the queen is coming home, she wants to come home to a campy apartment that's hers—it's very queer—because all day long she's been very straight. So when it all of a sudden becomes very straight—to come home to an apartment that any square could have—she's not going to have it any more.[10]

While camp is in the eye of the homosexual beholder, it is assumed that there is an underlying unity of perspective among homosexuals that gives any particular campy thing its special flavor. It is possible to discern strong themes in any particular campy thing or event. The three that seemed most recurrent and characteristic to me were *incongruity, theatricality,* and *humor.* All three are intimately related to the homosexual situation and strategy. Incongruity is the subject matter of camp, theatricality its style, and humor its strategy.

Camp usually depends on the perception or creation of *incongruous juxtapositions.* Either way, the homosexual "creates" the camp, by pointing out the incongruity or by devising it. For instance, one informant said that the campiest thing he had seen recently was a Midwestern football player in high drag at a Halloween ball. He pointed out that the football player was seriously trying to be a lady, and so his intent was not camp, but that the *effect* to the observer was campy. (The informant went on to say that it would have been even campier if the football player had been picked up by the police and had his picture published in the paper the next day.) This is an example of unintentional camp, in that the campy person or thing does not perceive the incongruity.

Created camp also depends on transformations and juxtapositions, but there the effect is intentional. The most concrete examples can be seen in the apartments of campy queens, for instance, in the idea of growing plants in the toilet tank. One queen said that *TV Guide* had described a little Mexican horse statue as campy. He said there was nothing campy about this at all, but if you put a nude cut-out of Bette Davis on it, it would be campy. Masculine-feminine

juxtapositons are, of course, the most characteristic kind of camp, but any very incongruous contrast can be campy. For instance, juxtapositions of high and low status, youth and old age, profane and sacred functions or symbols, cheap and expensive articles are frequently used for camp purposes. Objects or people are often said to be campy, but the camp inheres not in the person or thing itself but in the tension between that person or thing and the context or association. For instance, I was told by impersonators that a homosexual clothes designer made himself a beautiful Halloween ball gown. After the ball he sold it to a wealthy society lady. It was said that when he wore it, it was very campy, but when she wore it, it was just an expensive gown, unless she had run around her ball saying she was really not herself but her faggot dress designer.

The nexus of this perception by incongruity lies in the basic homosexual experience, that is, squarely on the moral deviation. One informant said, "Camp is all based on homosexual thought. It is all based on the idea of two men or two women in bed. It's incongruous and it's funny." If moral deviation is the locus of the perception of incongruity, it is more specifically role deviation and role manipulation that are at the core of the second property of camp, *theatricality.*

Camp is theatrical in three interlocking ways. First of all, camp is style. Importance tends to shift from what a thing *is* to how it *looks,* from *what* is done to *how* it is done. It has been remarked that homosexuals excel in the decorative arts. The kind of incongruities that are campy are very often created by adornment or stylization of a well-defined thing or symbol. But the emphasis on style goes further than this in that camp is exaggerated, consciously "stagey," specifically theatrical. This is especially true of *the* camp, who is definitely a performer.

The second aspect of theatricality in camp is its dramatic form. Camp, like drag, always involves a performer or performers and an audience. This is its structure. It is only stretching the point a little to say that even in unintentional camp, this interaction is maintained. In the case of the football player, his behavior was transformed by his audience into a performance. In many cases of unintentional camp, the camp performs to his audience by commenting on the behavior or appearance of "the scene," which is then described as "campy." In intentional camp, the structure of performance and audience is almost always clearly defined. This point will be elaborated below.

Third, camp is suffused with the perception of "being as playing a role" and "life as theatre" (Sontag 1964:529). It is at this point that drag and camp merge and augment each other. I was led to an appreciation of this while reading Parker Tyler's appraisal of Greta Garbo. Garbo is generally regarded in the homosexual community as "high camp." Tyler stated that "'Drag acts,' I believe, are not confined to the declassed sexes, Garbo 'got in drag' whenever she took some heavy glamour part, whenever she melted in or out of a man's arms, whenever she simply let that heavenly-flexed neck . . . bear the weight of her thrown-back head" (Tyler, n.d.:12). He concludes, "How resplendent seems the art of acting! It is all *impersonation,* whether the sex underneath is true or not" (ibid.:28).

We have to take the long way around to get at the real relationship between Garbo and camp. The homosexual is stigmatized, but his stigma can be hidden. In Goffman's terminology, information about his stigma can be managed. Therefore, of crucial importance to homosexuals themselves and to non-homosexuals is whether the stigma is displayed so that one is immediately recognizable or is hidden so that he can pass to the world at large as a respectable citizen. The covert half (conceptually, not necessarily numerically) of the homosexual community is engaged in "impersonating" respectable citizenry, at least some of the time. What is being impersonated?

The stigma essentially lies in being less than a man and in doing something that is unnatural (wrong) for a man to do. Surrounding this essence is a halo effect: violation of culturally standardized canons of taste, behavior, speech, and so on, rigorously associated (prescribed) with the male role (e.g., fanciful or decorative clothing styles, "effeminate" speech and manner, expressed disinterest in women as sexual objects, expressed interest in men as sexual objects, unseemly concern with personal appearance, etc.). The covert homosexual must therefore do two things: first, he must conceal the fact that he sleeps with men. But concealing this *fact* is far less difficult than his second problem, which is controlling the *halo effect* or signals that would announce that he sleeps with men. The covert homosexual must in fact impersonate a *man,* that is, he must *appear* to the "straight" world to be fulfilling (or not violating) all the requisites of the male role as defined by the "straight" world.

The immediate relationship about Tyler's point about Garbo and camp/

drag is this: if Garbo playing women is drag, then homosexuals "passing" are playing men; they are in drag. This is the larger implication of drag/camp. In fact, gay people often use the word "drag" in this broader sense, even to include role playing which most people simply take for granted: role playing in school, at the office, at parties, and so on. In fact, all of life is role and theatre—appearance.

But granted that all acting is impersonation, what moved Tyler to designate Garbo's acting specifically as "drag"? Drag means, first of all, role playing. The way in which it defines role playing contains its implicit attitude. The word "drag" attaches specifically to the outward, visible appurtenances of a role. In the type case, sex role, drag primarily refers to the wearing apparel and accessories that designate a human being as male or female, when it is worn by the opposite sex. By focusing on the outward appearance of role, drag implies that sex role and, by extension, role in general is something superficial, which can be manipulated, put on and off again at will. The drag concept implies *distance* between the actor and the role or "act." But drag also means "costume." This theatrical referent is the key to the attitude toward role playing embodied in drag as camp. Role playing is *play;* it is an act or show. The neccessity to play at life, living role after superficial role, should not be the cause of bitterness or despair. Most of the sex role and other impersonations that male homosexuals do are done with ease, grace, and especially humor. The actor should throw himself into it; he should put on a good show; he should view the whole experience as fun, as camp.[11]

The double stance toward role, putting on a good show while indicating distance (showing that it is a show) is the heart of drag as camp. Garbo's acting was thought to be "drag" because it was considered markedly androgynous, and because she played (even overplayed) the role of *femme fatale* with style. No man (in her movies) and very few audiences (judging by her success) could resist her allure. And yet most of the men she seduced were her victims because she was only playing at love— only acting. This is made quite explicit in the film *Mata Hari,* in which Garbo the spy seduces men to get information from them.

The third quality of camp is its *humor.* Camp is for fun; the aim of camp is to make an audience laugh. In fact, it is a *system* of humor. Camp humor is a system of laughing at one's incongruous position instead of crying.[12] That is, the humor does not cover up, it transforms. I saw the reverse transformation—from laughter to pathos—often enough, and it is axiomatic among the impersonators that when the camp cannot laugh, he dissolves into a maudlin bundle of self-pity.

One of the most confounding aspects of my interaction with the impersonators was their tendency to laugh at situations that to me were horrifying or tragic. I was amazed, for instance, when one impersonator described as "very campy" the scene in *Whatever Happened to Baby Jane?* in which Bette Davis served Joan Crawford a rat, or the scene in which Bette Davis makes her "comeback" in the parlor with the piano player.

Of course, not all impersonators and not all homosexuals are campy. *The* camp is a homosexual wit and clown; his campy productions and performances are a continuous creative strategy for dealing with the homosexual situation, and, in the process, defining a positive homosexual identity. As one performer summed it up for me, "Homosexuality is a way of life that is against all ways of life, including nature's. And no one is more aware of that than the homosexual. The camp accepts his role as a homosexual and flaunts his homosexuality. He makes the other homosexuals laugh; he makes life a little brighter for them. And he builds a bridge to the straight people by getting them to laugh with him." The same man described the role of the camp more concretely in an interview:

"Well, 'to camp' actually means 'to sit in front of a group of people' . . . not on-stage, but you *can* camp on-stage . . . I think that I do that when I talk to the audience. I think I'm camping with 'em. But a 'camp' herself is a queen who sits and starts entertaining a group of people at a bar around her. They all start listening to what she's got to say. And she says campy things. Oh, somebody smarts off at her and she gives 'em a very flip answer. A camp is a flip person who has declared emotional freedom. She is going to say to the world, 'I'm queer.' Although she may not do this all the time, but most of the time a camp queen will. She'll walk down the street and she'll see you and say, 'Hi, Mary, how are you?' right in the busiest part of town . . . she'll actually camp, right there. And she'll swish down the street. And she may be in a business suit; she doesn't have to be dressed outlandishly. Even at work the people figure that she's a camp. They don't know what to *call* her, but they hire her 'cause she's a good kid, keeps the office laughing, doesn't bother anybody, and everyone'll say, 'Oh, running around with Georgie's more fun! He's just more fun!' The squares are saying this. And the other ones [homosexuals] are saying, 'Oh, you've got to know George, she's a camp.' Because the whole time she's lighthearted. Very seldom is a camp sad. Camp has got to be flip. A camp queen's got to think faster than other queens. *This* makes her camp. She's got to have an answer to anything that's put to her. . . . [13]

"Now *homosexuality* is *not* camp. But you take a camp, and she turns around and she makes homosexuality funny, but not ludicrous; funny but not ridiculous . . . this is a great, great art. This is a fine thing . . . Now when it suddenly became the word . . . became like . . . it's like the word 'Mary.' Everybody's 'Mary.' 'Hi Mary. How are you Mary.' And like 'girl.' You may be talking to one of the butchest queens in the world, but you still say, 'Oh, girl.' And sometimes they say, 'Well, don't call me "she" and don't call me "girl." I don't feel like a girl. I'm a *man.* I just like to go to bed with you *girls.* I don't want to go to bed with another man.' And you say, 'Oh, girl, get you. Now she's turned butch.' And so you camp about it. It's sort of laughing at yourself instead of crying. And a good camp will make you laugh along with her, to where you suddenly feel . . . you don't feel like she's made fun of you. She's sort of made light of a bad situation."

The camp queen makes no bones about it; to him the gay world is the "sisterhood." By accepting his homosexuality and flaunting it, the camp undercuts all homosexuals who won't accept the stigmatized identity. Only by fully embracing the stigma itself can one neutralize the sting and make it laughable.[14] Not all references to the stigma are campy, however. Only if it is pointed out as a joke is it camp, although there is no requirement that the jokes be gentle or friendly. A lot of camping is extremely hostile; it is almost always sarcastic. But its intent is humorous as well. Campy queens are very often said to be "bitches" just as campy humor is said to be "bitchy."[15] The campy queen who can "read" (put down) all challengers and cut everyone down to size is admired. Humor is the campy queen's weapon. A camp queen in good form can come out on top (by group consensus) against all the competition.

Female impersonators who use drag in a comic way or are themselves comics are considered camps by gay people. (Serious glamour drag is considered campy by many homosexuals, but it is unintentional camp. Those who see glamour drag as a serious business do not consider it to be campy. Those who think it is ludicrous for drag queens to take themselves seriously see the whole business as a campy incongruity.) Since the camp role is a positive one, many impersonators take pride in being camps, at least on stage.[16] Since the camp role depends to such a large extent on verbal agility, it reinforces the superiority of the live performers over record performers[17] who, even if they are comic, must depend wholly on visual effects.

Notes

1. In two Broadway plays (since made into movies) dealing with English homosexuals, *The Killing of Sister George* (lesbians) and *Staircase* (male homosexuals), drag played a prominent role. In *George,* an entire scene shows George and her lover dressed in tuxedos and top hats on their way to a drag party. In *Staircase,* the entire plot turns on the fact that one of the characters has been arrested for "going in drag" to the local pub. Throughout the second act, this character wears a black shawl over his shoulders. This item of clothing is symbolic of full drag. This same character is a camp and, in my opinion, George was a very rare bird, a lesbian camp. Both plays, at any rate, abounded in camp humor. *The Boys in the Band,* another recent play and movie, doesn't feature drag as prominently but has two camp roles and much camp humor.

2. This concept was developed and suggested to me by Julian Pitt-Rivers.

3. Even one feminine item ruins the integrity of the masculine system; the male loses his caste honor. The superordinate role in a hierarchy is more fragile than the subordinate. Manhood must be achieved, and once achieved, guarded and protected.

4. The middle-class idea tends to be that any man who has had sexual relations with men is queer. The lower classes strip down to "essentials" and the man who is "dominant" can be normal (masculine). Lower-class men give themselves a bit more leeway before they consider themselves to be gay.

5. It becomes clear that the core of the stigma is in "wrong" sexual object when it is considered that there is little stigma in simply being effeminate, or even in wearing feminine apparel in some contexts, as long as the male is known to be heterosexual, that is, known to sleep with women or, rather, not to sleep with men. But when I say that sleeping with men is the core of the stigma, or that feminine behavior logically corresponds with this, I do not mean it in any causal sense. In fact, I

have an impression that some homosexual men sleep with men *because* it strengthens their identification with the feminine role, rather than the other way around. This makes a lot of sense developmentally, if one assumes, as I do, that children learn sex-role identity before they learn any strictly sexual object choices. In other words, I think that children learn they are boys or girls before they are made to understand that boys love *only* girls and vice versa.

6. The role of the "pretty boy" is also a very positive one, and in some ways the camp is an alternative for those who are not pretty. However, the pretty boy is subject to the depredations of aging, which in the subculture is thought to set in at thirty (at the latest). Because the camp depends on inventiveness and wit rather than on physical beauty, he is ageless.

7. This phrase is used by Kenneth Burke in reference to poetry and is used by Keil in a sociological sense.

8. I would say that the main problem today is heterosexuals, just as the main problem for Blacks is Whites.

9. I don't want to pass over the implication here that female impersonators keep up with Susan Sontag. Generally, they don't. I had given him Sontag's "Notes on Camp" (1964) to see what he would say. He was college-educated, and perfectly able to get through it. He was enraged (justifiably, I felt) that she had almost edited homosexuals out of camp.

10. Informants said that many ideas had been taken over by straights through the mass media, but that the moment this happened the idea would no longer be campy. For instance, one man said that a queen he knew had gotten the idea of growing plants in the water tank of the toilet. But the idea is no longer campy because it is being advertised through such mass media as *Family Circle* magazine.

How to defend *any* symbols or values from the absorbing powers of the mass media? Jules Henry, I believe, was one of the first to point to the power of advertising to subvert traditional values by appropriating them for commercial purposes (Henry 1963). But subcultural symbols and values lose their integrity in the same way. Although Sontag's New York *avant garde* had already appropriated camp from homosexuals, they did so in the effort to create their own aristocracy or integrity of taste as against the mass culture.

11. It is clear to me now how camp undercuts rage and therefore rebellion by ridiculing serious and concentrated bitterness.

12. It would be worthwhile to compare camp humor with the humor systems of other oppressed people (Eastern European Jewish, Negro, etc.).

13. Speed and spontaneity are of the essence. For instance, at a dinner party someone said, "Oh, we forgot to say grace." One woman folded her hands without missing a beat and intoned, "Thank God everyone at this table is gay."

14. It's important to stress again that camp is a pre- or proto-political phenomenon. The anti-camp in this system is the person who wants to dissociate from the stigma to be like the oppressors. The camp says, "I am not like the oppressors." But in so doing he agrees with the oppressors' definition of who he is. The new radicals deny the stigma in a different way, by saying that the oppressors are illegitimate. This step is only foreshadowed in camp. It is also interesting that the lesbian wing of the radical homosexuals has come to women's meetings holding signs saying "We are the women your parents warned you against."

15. The "bitch," as I see it, is a woman who *accepts* her inferior status, but refuses to do so gracefully or without fighting back. Women and homosexual men are oppressed by straight men, and it is no accident that both are beginning to move beyond bitchiness toward refusal of inferior status.

16. Many impersonators told me that they got tired of being camps for their friends, lovers, and acquaintances. They often felt they were asked to gay parties simply to entertain and camp it up, and said they did not feel like camping off stage, or didn't feel competent when out of drag. This broadens out into the social problem of all clowns and entertainers, or, even further, to anyone with a talent. He will often wonder if he is loved for himself.

17. A "record performer" is a female impersonator who accompanies another (usually famous or popular) artist's recording with an impersonation of the other artist's act—EDITOR'S NOTE.

SEVEN

History and Myth (Time) as Cultural Categories

The Invisible Event

Janet L. Dolgin and JoAnn Magdoff

In the concluding chapter to *The Savage Mind*, Lévi-Strauss attempts to formulate the relationship between events and structures—or between history, taken as a succession of events, and "myth," taken as a temporally flattened structure of meaning—in general terms. There, he suggests that events are always subsidiary to structures as determinants of social form: that events do not affect social form except insofar as they are given significance by structures of symbols. Lévi-Strauss has been much taken to task for this argument; and in an extended interview with a French journalist, Claude Charbonnier, he revised his position somewhat, claiming that the relation between structure and event he described in *The Savage Mind* obtains in "primitive" societies, while events have a more independent impact on social form in the more advanced or modern societies.

In this paper, Dolgin and Magdoff examine the relations between structure and event, history and myth, in our own culture. Their analysis casts these relationships on more dynamic terms: structure and event, history and myth, cease being absolute polar types and are shown to be, in effect, rhetorical types, articulated as part of a people's reification of itself. This reformulation of these relations could be extended, as well, to the analysis of the ideology of pre-industrial or "primitive" societies with equally productive results.

"THE VERY PRINCIPLE OF MYTH" writes Roland Barthes is that "it transforms history into nature. . . . [myth] is not read as motive, but as reason" (1972:129). What Barthes calls "myth" is the essence of reification: the course through which the histories that people make are naturalized. In critically approaching cultures which are in anthropological terms historic, the sense of history can become a subject of analysis. Some events (the signing of the Declaration of Independence in the United States, for example) are at the time of happening framed as significant. Such occurrences are accepted as "events" and provide a historic past which grounds subsequent history, simultaneously providing a model of and for the conceptualization of experiences of newer history—itself comprised of "events." In reflection, as an act assumes concreteness, it becomes conceptually defined and, presumably, bounded. Events are naturalized through placement in history. History may be naturalized through the accretion of events.

As time passes, events of import to a people, redolent with detail, retain only the skeleton of their significance or, having lost much of their previous content, these events become vehicles for new significations (see Geertz 1973). At the same time, such events embody contemporary meanings, legitimated by an implicit reference to a historic past; simultaneously, they (event-meaning) legitimate the past by exemplifying its continuity in the present.

The continuity of societies is made possible by the institutionalization of social form (Weber 1968). These forms presuppose (and reify) varying conceptions of the "natural," the taken-for-granted,[1] the valorized[2] in these societies. At the bottom in the West stands the notion of the person.[3] Our analysis proceeds from a consideration of the person embedded in group and history. The concept of the individual varies from place to place; correlatively the particular form which alienation takes in each place varies. Rather than proceed with an analysis of alienation along lines familiar to European scholars we have chosen an approach which is situated anthropologically, relying on an analysis of forms of the interrelation of people, presupposing differing definitions of the individual which emerge in and define various contemporary societies.

That a people considers history to be commonly shared indicates their perception of a mutual (ancestral and contemporary) identity which, locatable in varying substances, is often correlated with blood or land (see D. M. Schneider 1968a, 1969). The ways in which history is naturalized enjoin, preeminently, a people's notion of "person" and of the group. Through the concept of the nation, group (and person) may be metonymized[4] in substance, emerging from and providing the metaphor for history.[5]

For an act to be an event of historic significance, it must in some way define or limit the identity of a group. In the modern world the identity of a group (e.g., its ethnicity, its religion) may or may not be in potential conflict with its identity as part of a nation. The process by which the historic is made real in the present, and the present is grounded in the past, is seen as an aspect of the cultural construction of reality.[6] The concept of a nation is concretized, is predicated in terms of ethnicity, through reference to what is considered "naturally real"—blood, land, the events of history.

Each of the events of history—a revolution, the founding of a state, the coronation of a monarch—is constantly redefined, through the redefinitions of successive moments, of the ongoing, the unnoticed, the history of everyday life. An "event," meaningful in reflection, in comparison to the past, itself becomes the object of future comparisons once it is historic.

In France, the Revolution has become a condensed symbol, standing simultaneously for all and each of the "events" which the period encompassed. The Revolution is no longer (merely) history, but myth; the condensed symbol of France itself. The inevitability of the past—once perceived it had to have been—is posited against the knowledge that it always could have been otherwise. This contradiction simultaneously confirms and negates the "naturalness" of "history." In France, the events of recent history are naturalized and enjoined with and by the remainder of French history.

On the streets of Paris a part of French history is inscribed. Metal plaques, attached to the outer walls of buildings, at times near a door, sometimes near street signs, commemorate the Resistance, naming the times and places of the deaths of those who combatted Fascism. There is an implicit congruence of identity of contemporary French people with the heroes of the Resistance, as evidenced by the signs. The Resistance is thereby incorporated as an authorized and generalized part of French nationality. From the present, and in retrospect, it was a resistance not of the few but of the whole.

The identity of a group is effected through metonymizations, the creation of accepted contiguities among and between people with the correlative construction of the Other, of those who are external to the metonymized group. Such contiguities can occur through the structural reification of substance and relations or through historicization. In a society where identity is based within notions of substance, the individual person becomes the unit through and in which the "natural" and the worthwhile is conceived and contained; this is what Louis Dumont calls the unit of valorization.

Where there is a predominantly egalitarian ideology, as in the United States, any individual is posited as "equal" of any other; that is, any person may serve as metaphor for any other. It is because the individual is the unit of reference that more encompassing identities, as David M. Schneider has shown in the domains of American kinship, nationality, and religion, are patterned similarly (1969; and in this volume). Each person, the family, the nation, the church are all imagined in terms of the antecedent individual.

In illustrating the process undergirding various forms of identity *within* the egalitarian society of the United States we use the three cases of American Jews, Mormon Americans, and a small town in New England. In each case we use examples of "events" enacted by the group. These events, each of which explicates the group's notion of its own history, illustrate how differences and similarities in identity as Americans are manifested through variant uses of history.

In the United States the egalitarian ideology of the West finds virtually unopposed expression.[7] Ideological forms, historically rooted, provide the groundings of reality. People tend to be unaware of the ideological forms within which they think and act, for these forms are taken to be "natural." The acceptance of egalitarianism in the United States presupposes and reifies the notion of the autonomous individual. The concept of the national collectivity, of consenting, free people joined together as a nation depends, in turn, upon the reification of the autonomous individual. Or in other words, the nation is metaphor for the individual.[8] The pattern for nationhood arose from the Western idea of State, based within an egalitarian, universalistic ideology. In the United States, since the Civil War, ethnic and racial groups represent the concretization of difference through substance (blood). Metaphors of concretization (e.g., blood, land) are potentially substitutable; they function primarily as reifications creating the groundings of reality. The imputed substitutability of American ethnic groups is founded on the assumption of the equality of any individual and of any ethnic group. Certain ethnic minorities are perforce excluded from one or more aspects of the attainment of unmarked American ethnicity.[9]

Contradictions which may arise because of identity as an American and simultaneous identity as a member of an ethnic minority may manifest themselves obviously or may be contained and masked. As Martin Silverman notes, it is possible to maintain identities which may be in potential conflict by "isolating a symbolic form to a particular practice, or making the meanings appear more abstract so that the contradictions appear resolved. Thus the 'transcendentalization' of meaning and the specialization of meaning are different facets of the same process" (Manuscript, n.d.).[10] The possibility of locating ethnicity on one level and nationalism on another (generally more encompassing) level is shared by American ethnic minorities who, in this respect, may be seen to be substitutable for one another. The process through which potentially conflicting identities can appear harmonious by the allocation of different aspects of identity to different domains is well illustrated by the history of American Jews.

Throughout their history, Jews have variously been designated a religion, a race, a nationality, and an ethnic group. For the Jews, as for other peoples, what they stress in their history changes over time. Unlike Israeli Jews and Mormon Americans, American Jews are not afforded a congruence of ethnic and national identification. The existence of the state of Israel endows Jewishness itself with the substance of normality in that by locating Jewishness in a concrete territory, historically legitimated and/or divinely granted, the State enables the Jew of the American diaspora to be an ethnic like any ethnic—the curse of homelessness may now be replaced with a land of historic origin. For American Jews the new metaphor of the state of Israel can remain as metaphor. The security that comes with this normalization allows a spiritual identification in conjunction with physical distance, particularly for the non-religious Jew.

When the Jewish Defense League, an American-based movement of activist Jews, tried to "become" "Israelis in the Exile," they were quickly faced with the impossibility of maintaining this position. JDLers attempted to forge a new image of the Jew, both for American Jewry and for the American public, by resurrecting models from the heroic past of the Bible, and by appropriating heroic images of contemporary Israel. "Let my people go," a ubiquitous cry of demonstrating JDLers resounded in the streets of New York and Washington, peopled in the name of Soviet Jewry. Techniques of mass demonstrations among activist dissident American groups were appropriated by JDL and codified to suit the movement's particular cause. Instead of the slogans of Black Power, JDLers (afforded the title of "Jewish Panthers") used phrases from the Bible and from the history of Jewish struggle.

For JDLers, the cry "Let my people go" signalled the plight of Soviet Jewry and JDL's efforts on behalf of those Jews. After prayers one Saturday afternoon (1972), a group of young JDLers jointed in discussion of the Old Testament. Someone began to peruse the Book of Exodus and discussion turned to the Jewish departure from ancient Egypt. "Let my people go," read the JDLer from the Biblical text. "Let my people go?" repeated one of the young participants in the conversation with astonishment. The speaker, a League member who had chanted that slogan uncounted times, continued: "*They* said that *too?*" A metaphor which had been carefully selected to provide JDL with the aura of authenticity had been so well appropriated that its original power was obscured. In the rediscovery, the two metaphors, that of the Biblical activist and that of the contemporary Jewish activist, were again placed apart but now the Bible was made "real," for in the end, Moses existed for JDLers because JDL did, rather than the other way around.

The conscious construction of ethnic identity through historicization faces the dominant ideology, among other things, with the gap between egalitarianism and the actual consequences of difference. The correlate of the egalitarian ideology in terms of relation to the nation is precisely the presumption that the nation's history is "naturally" there, that the concept of the history and the history itself are identical. By constructing a separate ethnic history, JDLers, themselves entwined within the universe of American ideology which they verbally rejected, employed and tacitly augmented the dominant forms. The movement was created, and ultimately limited, in using the specific content of Jewish history within a generalizable American form of ideology.

In the dominant American ideology, form and content are without tension; history is "natural" and "naturalizing." An egalitarian ideology was a clear foundation of the Declaration of Independence and the revolutionary war. The idea that "no taxation" would be tolerated "without representation" rests upon a conceptualization of peoples in question (here people in England and America) as equals. The explicit location of equality within the individual has as its corollary the implicit "sameness" of the respective populations.[11]

Throughout America the revolution of 1776 provides images of an American history. In general, Independence Day can be analytically thought of as a signal in form and content of the individualist ideology of modern America. For most Americans on July Fourth, history is submerged in a more general celebration of "everyday life." Fireworks, rodeos, clam bakes, parades, and picnics mark the unquestioned acceptance of the idea of the Nation. The celebration of the Fourth of July had, as its initial referent, the signing of the Declaration of Independence, which event rapidly became a symbol for the whole of the Revolutionary War and the creation of the United States. Through the workings of history, the recurrent event of the Fourth is no longer merely the metaphor for American Independence, but for the more encompassing concept of the nation. "Independence," no longer exclusively considered an act of historic liberation from the British "Other," has come to stand for a personal attribute, concretized in the individual. The metaphor of independence is retained as real, though often in its celebration it has been submerged in the metaphor of nationhood. The nation, in its turn, has come to represent not Independence, but a collectivity of equal individuals. Americans consider themselves connected to each other through their imputed participation in a celebrated history, a bounded territory.

On Independence Day (1974) the commemoration in Bridgton, Maine, included a parade down the center street, followed by competitive games and demonstrations by local fire and police departments, a clam bake, and fireworks. Among a cavalcade of antique autos, Boy and Girl Scouts, and the local high school ("blue jeans") band, two set-pieces were paraded. One, labelled "Snoopy's Christmas," starred half a dozen children, dressed as "Snoopies" in Dr. Denton pajamas,[12] white hoods, black ears and tails and whiskered faces, seated around several plastic, tinselled Christmas trees and throwing wrapped bubble gum to the spectators. The appearance of a "Christmas" float in July at a parade celebrating independence was not perceived by the crowd as out of joint.[13]

The most dramatic float in the parade carried a simulated house which became the setting for a "family" saved from fire. On the "house's" porch a young woman with a head of curlers and a red-painted face, pillow-pregnant, sat rocking. Smoke poured from the house—a local fire engine drove up and firemen "rescued" a toy child and "put out" the fire, pulling the obviously embarrassed woman off the porch and shoving the "child" into her arms to the amusement and applause of the spectators. The theme of fire and the fire company dominated the day. After the parade, a "water barrel fight" was staged between the police department and several companies of local fire departments.[14]

On a narrow street perpendicular to Main Street the adversaries squared off. Each team of three men held a fire hose pointed, ostensibly, at a barrel placed on the street between the sides. At a signal, the game was a contest in mutual dousing, with a by-play of gallons of water hosed on delighted, howling bystanders.

As a contest it was a failure. When, bemused, we asked the fire chief which side, in fact, had won, he replied "Uh, I don't know. I guess the police did." The sport between firemen and police, although not ending in a decisive victory for either side was nonetheless highly competitive. Freudian implications of fire hosing notwithstanding, the event, billed as a "battle" was an institutionalized (and thereby contained) competition among (perforce male) equals. The prevalent metaphor of fire was never totally submerged. "Reacting quickly, the police returned the fire—er, water," reported the Bridgton News, "and both teams charged at each other, spraying like mad" (July 11, 1974). The paper continued: "Water sprayed, helmets flew and spectators laughed . . . the firemen were employing free substitution, but all that meant was that they had more different people who got wet." To don either uniform was the prerequisite for "free substitution" among the players. Any fireman, presumably, could take the place of any other in this battle between the prototypical forces of law and order. Each "team" was posed as the valorized whole equivalent to the other team. Any "person" (implicitly "adult" male) was presented as the equivalent of any other—equally "free to compete as 'equals.'"

American Mormon communities exemplify the working out of the egalitarian ideology in a community defining itself as both quintessentially "American" and substantially distinct (sharing "substance" with other Mormons and not with the nation as a whole). Mormons are a separate ethnic minority whose recapitulation of American sociocultural forms and processes allows periods of identification with broader American culture to alternate with periods of isolationism (see Leone 1969). The assumption of American cultural forms with the maintenance of separate Mormon identity is made possible by the Mormon belief that the continent of America will house the millenium and that, in fact, the Garden of Eden was situated in Jackson County, Missouri. For Mormons, "America" is conceptually encompassed by Mormonism. While professing a divine relation to the American continent and the United States Government—the Constitution is a divine document for Mormons—in the nineteenth century Mormons were accepted neither by the United States government nor by most of the towns in which they lived during their journey West from New York to Utah. Today the relation between the Mormons and the larger society is less precarious, and Mormon communities throughout the Western United States, particularly, have been able to join Mormonism with patriotism.

The Mormon celebration of July Fourth is followed by the celebration of Mormon Pioneer Day on July twenty-fourth. During the celebrations in several small towns along the Little Colorado River, Arizona, in 1970, symbolisms normally associated exclusively with Mormonism (e.g., the singing of Mormon hymns, the use of Church liturgy) prevailed during the celebration of the national holiday, and symbolisms normally exclusively identified with American expressions of patriotism (e.g., the wearing of red, white, and blue; the widespread display of the national flag) prevailed during the celebration of the Mormon holiday. The Fourth of July was, if you will, "Mormonized," and Mormon Pioneer Day, "Americanized" (Dolgin 1974).

The selection of Mormon events celebrating American nationalism presents an example of the ways in which the domains of ethnicity and nationalism may interpenetrate. The celebration of Mormon Pioneer Day would be recognized in small towns throughout America as typical fare for the Fourth of July. To celebrate American nationalism on July twenty-fourth is to celebrate not merely the national holiday of independence, but the relation of Mormons to their own and other Americans' national identity. Mormons' relation to themselves as Americans allows stress on either the inherent conjunction of the nation and the individual Mormon or on Mormons as distinct from the larger whole. Mormonism conceives of blood as a definitive substance, dividing humanity into three broad groups: the blood of the House of Israel, the blood of the Gentile, and the blood of the Negro (Book of Mormon; Pratt 1855; J. F. Smith 1966–70; Whitehead 1947). The American public allows a contentually different division of humanity. Mormons' claim for privileged (i.e., different) substance is not shared by the dominant society which considers Mormons to be the descendents of North European settlers—prototypically American substance. American incorporation of Mormons is echoed by Mormons' acceptance of themselves as Americans, yet each group considers that it encompasses the other.

Insofar as Mormons have been able to achieve a flexible relation between themselves and other Americans, it is, in large part, dependent upon their being substantially unmarked. For the inhabitants of Bridgton, their own ethnicity (blood) is not an issue. They enact an identification with the history/nation of America by virtue of (and in turn reifying) territory, historically "won" and inhabited. Mormons appear to have a similar relation to territory. From the vantage of American culture there is a felt congruence of substance with the

Mormons. This is made possible, in part, by the similarity of Mormon cultural forms to those of America—not surprising since Mormonism had its roots in nineteenth-century America. The situation is different for American Jews who do not share substance (blood) with other Americans. As the ethnic group is not defined as a community, sharing one geographic space, its relation to American territory varies greatly. On the one hand, Jews may identify themselves as Americans, accepting the idea of the nation (along with the territory) as home. On the other hand, identification with the Jewish nation as a nation of people living in many countries who share a common substance, can more easily co-exist with an identification with an American nationalism concretized territorially than a definition of Jewish identity concretized through the identification with the "land" of Israel. Israel as a State provides a possibly conflicting identity for Jews who reside in America (or elsewhere in the diaspora). They are spread over too much territory, so to speak.

It is as the metaphor of the Jewish nation, conceptualized in terms of "blood" that Israel is not in conflict with America as a source of identity. A potential conflict arises in the same allocation of Jewish identity in terms of shared "blood" since, for American Jews to be an ethnic group like any other American ethnic group, Israel must be at least, in spirit, a land of origin; it must be able to stand as one state among many.

In America, where the construct of the nation is reified through metaphors of substance (e.g., blood, land), identities tend to be expressed according to an ethnic model.[15] As we have said the generalization of ethnicity promotes the process through which American groups become substitutable for each other. (Magdoff and Dolgin 1974). Following Dumont, the structural universe of Indian caste provides an alternative form to that found in America. With Hindu caste, the structural whole, understood through the opposition between purity and impurity is definitively and *a priori* metonymic. Preliminary analysis suggests that a third form is found in contemporary Italy where metonymizations occur as well through the reifications of relations which are substantialized. Locatable within the historic and substantial Western universe, Italy presents a case of metonymization of relations, finding its prototype in the image of the family and within regionalism which identifies an idealized, historic past. The ahistoric Madonna and child acts as a religious referent for the family, the unit of Italian valorization.[16] The image of the Madonna with child supports an identity through positing as natural a relation whose historicity is definitionally transcended; it does not amalgamate national identity through a historic past.

"You Americans have a strange idea of being American," said a Roman informant. "We Italians think about it differently. For one thing we have not been a nation very long. We think more of ourselves as each coming from different regions. And yet we are still Italians. So that when we are away, out of Italy, we miss our home. We miss the food. It is important for a man to eat the food of his home. Those are his roots." Through food, among other things, relations are concretized in Italy, providing the metonymy of identity. As noted above, the relational metonymy of Italy differs from the universe of caste in being substantial rather than structural and in partaking of the Western individualistic, hence metaphoric, ideology.

Although of recent origin, the Italian state offers an overarching, if vague category of identity. Identification with one's natal region and further with the nearest city or town is paramount; however the explanation offered for such regionalism is exactly the recency of Italian unification and the historic battling of previously independent city-states.

In the thirteenth century a Tuscan town was designed by an architect as a fortified outpost of Florence; the village structure today remains basically unchanged. Although legally within the region administered by Arezzo, the town's inhabitants identified themselves and their village with Florence—and its history is invoked to make the identification "natural." In addition, inhabitants cite the closeness of their quasi-dialect to contemporary Florentine and simultaneously downgrade Aretine Italian. "Land" is not substantialized as such except by a few farmers who identify themselves with a specific plot of "their" land. Dwelling within the same historic unit, however, is seen to bind people together. Reference to Medici history gives an "ancestral" reality to contemporary identity, notwithstanding the particular origin of any family. That is, beyond three antecedent generations, the region of origin of a family is in no way seen to conflict with identity with the community in which they currently live nor with its history.

"We are all one family here" said the priest, not a native of the town. Almost all inhabitants with the exception of the priest, the doctor—the only "rich" man

fully integrated into community life— and the pharmacist, follow familial and friendship forms of address and use the familiar form of the verb with one another.

Metaphors stemming from familial relations are of two types: parent-child (almost always mother-child with mother-son as the unmarked category) and fraternal (used to name brother-sister or sister-sister relations as well). A business partnership is not described, as it might be in the United States, as a marriage, but as a contract of brothers. Competition is considered a salient aspect of fraternal relations while it is affirmed to be absent between mothers and children. And competition is generally discouraged within the familial setting among children. In general, one child, usually the youngest son, is the parents' acknowledged favorite. Manifestation of existing tension between husband and wife may take the form of divergent preference for offspring. Outside the family, competition is limitedly encouraged. Both men and women, when asked to describe Italian culture say that to understand it one must understand "calcio, caccia e la politica" (soccer, hunting, and politics). All are male domains. Soccer and politics are avowedly competitive and are described as enacted by groups or teams of brothers.

The 1975 regional elections framed notions of Italian politics. In towns of under 5,000 population the tendency is for two parties to form in correspondence to the pattern of majority and minority representatives in the town council. Incumbents and opposition are created out of all or some of the eight national parliamentary political parties. When the mayor in one such Tuscan town (a fifty-eight-year-old ex-fascist and in the leadership of the Christian Democrat party, dominant in the town) was asked, prior to the election, to describe what the elections would be like, he said, "They are a contest, a match between two teams—like soccer." He further added that "a political party is like a family." And described the family as composed of a father, his brothers and his sons, and stated that party discipline should mirror familial discipline: a strong authoritarian structure should be maintained both for the unity of the party and because the rank and file are not in a position to make decisions. When asked who the mother of the political family was, he responded, "Women are not interested in politics."

A member of the secretariat of the town's Communist Party (a professional in his fifties) said that his party, like all political parties, was like a family. Echoing the Christian Democrat, he elaborated the metaphor: the party is composed of fathers and sons. Grandfathers were added in spirit, however, in the personnae of Gramsci and Togliatti, the two most often mentioned founders of the Italian Communist Party. In response to a query as to the location of the party's mothers and wives, he responded, "My wife [a Socialist] is in the kitchen; as for my mother, well, you take everything too literally."

The thirty-year-old recently elected head of the left-dominated opposition in the town was enthusiastic about a proposed debate with the incumbents. "We'll destroy them," he said, grinning. (The debate never took place.) When it was remarked that he seemed to be enjoying the prospect of the debate, he remarked, "Yes. In a way it's like a game, a contest between rival teams—like soccer."

Neither the Mayor nor his opponent would deny the un-gamelike nature of the election's outcome: the town was due, presumably, to continue along the lines it had followed since the elections of 1948, or to change its administrative point of view dramatically. And yet, the metaphors of each side were the same: a soccer match, a male-composed family. The use of the symbols however is not the same. "Soccer," a competitive match, is the encompassing metaphor for the enactment of a political election for the Mayor. And while it is employed by the secretary of the Communist Party, his use of it is limited to a specific aspect of the election campaign. In an extendedly fraternal definition, the family is the metaphor for relations within a political party for both incumbents and opposition. However, the explicit content of "brotherhood" varies markedly from group to group. It is exactly the process of defining the family as an authoritarian and rigid structure, or as a flexible and kindly (authoritarian) structure that demonstrates how symbols work in Italy, where absorption is possible and also open to contestation. The model of the family, unlike the ethnic model prevalent in the United States, is based within a society which lacks the substantially defined Other found in North America.

Of the three previously mentioned activities, soccer, hunting, and politics, only hunting is not described in metaphors of the family (that is, fraternally). Although it is generally conducted by small groups of young and middle-aged men, it is also possible for a man to go out alone with a dog. Hunting exists, above all, in a realm inhabited by man and animal. It is the single most often used metaphor to describe sexual pursuit and conquest. Occasionally it is used in a condemnatory sense to describe a woman who is sexually active outside marriage or engagement, or who takes an active role in trying to marry or "trap" a man. Several times a day one hears "Man is a hunter." The unspoken correlate is that woman is the hunted, the animal.

Identification of woman as animal serves to point out a primary "difference that makes a difference" (Bateson 1972) in Italian ideology: women are substantially different from men. Described as biological in origin, the difference is not correlated directly with blood but with relation: "Women are naturally different," and further, the difference is referred to the mother-child relation: "If a child is hurt anywhere in the world, even 10,000 kilometers away, a mother, if she is a real mother, knows." and "No one can understand a baby's sayings except its mother; she knows instinctively what its noises mean." The nature of mother-child relations is metonymic both in the contiguity of the womb and of breast feeding, but the metonymy is explicitly located in action. It is not only mother's milk which provides shared substance, but the act of feeding—relation as relation. The relation is temporally ongoing and, insofar as it participates in and mirrors the sacred image of Mary and the infant Jesus, eternal.

In one Tuscan village, and in the area in general, spiritual intercession was effected through the figure of Mary.[17] Mary is the mother of God and of all human beings. As one Tuscan remarked, "You must go to Mass on the day of the Assumption because Mary is taken up to heaven. This is important because we are all her children and a mother wouldn't go to heaven and leave her children behind—it isn't logical![18] What kind of a mother would that be? No. We are all saved because of Mary."

Queried about the proposed abortion referendum, Italians say that many will not vote for it because "a mother and child are sacred; it would be interfering with God to have an abortion." Women as mothers participate in Mary and, to the extent that they do, they are identified with the divine. The same informants, along with the majority of Italian voters, lined up behind laic forces in 1974 to institute divorce for the first time in Italy. Many said "I am a devout Catholic, but what can a priest know about having a family? He is not a real man." Priests are, in popular conception, however, only too real: divorce is voted for in part because priests are not fully identified with God, but are "just men" or "not even men."

Catholic hierarchy operates directly on the everyday life experience of Italian people through Mary, the mediator between God and the world, and is daily manifest in the conception and valorization of the family as understood particularly in the mother-child relation.

The veil of relational metonymy, the possibility of reification through relation rather than through substance alone, allows the Italians to avoid the overarching substitutability resulting from the substantialization of the individual in the United States. That is to say, alienation in Italy differs from alienation in the United States where any identity is formulated through individuals each of whom unavoidably becomes metaphor for each other. In Italy the metonymies sustained in and by religious images *are* enacted but that enactment is ultimately in contradiction with the larger situation of Italian life in the industrialized West. In the United States, even when embedded in larger groups, the individual remains the metaphoric substitutable referent of identity so that, like individuals, larger groups are substitutable for one another.

The reification and naturalization of history is accomplished in part through the relating of events to objects and/or recurrences in the world which are already accepted as given. The domains and categories of everyday life are a backdrop for the events of history. Everyday life is itself apparently a recurrent series of insignificant, taken-for-granted, events whose occasional non-enactment is barely noticed. The contiguous processes of the everyday may be perceived as meaningful through recourse to the historic metaphor. Everyday life is itself unsubstantial: That is, a non-substitutable union of signifier and signified is currently replaced by a "system of floating signs" (Lefebvre 1971), in which, at its logical extreme, anything can be made to stand for anything else (see Magdoff and Dolgin 1974)—understood as a universe of alienation. According to Steve Barnett, "alienation" occurs in the replacement of (the metaphor of) metonymy by (the metaphor of) metaphor, signalled by the replacement of use value by exchange value.

Within the West, where ideology is, at base, enacted metaphorically, metaphor or metonymy may appear to predominate; the level of alienation varies correspondingly. Where metonymy is stressed, when, that is, substance is not the primary locus of identity, as in Italy, the "fact" of relations are concretized with reference to a form of recurrent patterns. This form is ideally represented by parables used in Church sermons and which, formally shared with history, can serve to place history within a structural, i.e. repeatable and thus ahistoric, framework.

Events may become the substance of ideas and relations may become the content of events: in either case, whether events are enacted relationally or substantially, they become metonymizable foundations of everyday life. In the one case, the illusion of metaphor prevails; in the other case, that of metonymy. Within the historic West, the metonymization of metaphor and the metonymization of metonymy are both fundamentally metaphoric forms of reification. Sartre writes, "the possibility of reification is given in all human relations—even in a precapitalist period, even in relations between family members or friends" (1965:449).

This process of reification, of making metaphor contiguous and real, is not contingent upon alienation. As Sartre suggests, the process of reification pertains as well in a non-alienated universe. The problem remains as to whether the modes of reification in a non-alienated universe are the same as those operative in the West.

Notes

1. What a society takes for granted, regards as "natural," has been posed as a primary focus of anthropological analysis by S. Barnett.

2. Following L. Dumont (1970a) we use "valorize" to indicate the level of social "value." In a culture in which individualism is the dominant ideology, the key metaphor in whose terms other things and relations are conceptualized is the individual.

3. Focus on the "person" as a basic unit to be analyzed in any society has been suggested by D. M. Schneider (1968a, 1969) and M. G. Silverman (1971).

4. Our use of metaphor and metonymy is based on the definitions offered by P. Seitel (1972): "Metaphor, in the most general sense, is the relationship which obtains between entities of separate domains by virtue of the relationship each has with entities in its own domain" (29). "Metonymy, in the most general sense, is any relationship which obtains between entities by virtue of their inclusion within the same domain" (32). (Both definitions are underlined in original.)

5. In addition to our use of European source material, the data for this analysis stem from our field experiences in Israel, Italy, and the United States (and our personal histories as natives of the U.S.).

6. The position that "reality" is to a large extent culturally created we share with Schutz and other phenomenologists. However, as this paper shows, the process of reification is rarely conscious; cultural constructions come in and from action quite as much as actions are consciously predicated upon thought.

7. Our use of ideology follows Barnett (1973c) and Dumont (1970a): in any society there are pervasive forms within which what it means to be human is understood and enacted.

8. Contrasting constructions of "nations" have entailed the subjugation of autonomous peoples. Correspondingly, the creation of an American national identity depended upon stressing the opposition to the British nation and equally upon the attempted deculturalization of the autocthonous population, the Indian. We are indebted to personal communication with Professor Alfonso Ortiz.

9. This category includes groups whose members are considered different in substance (e.g., Blacks, Jews), groups whose members have a non-Christian, specifically non-Protestant, religion (e.g., Jews, Catholics), groups whose relation to land is somehow ambiguous (e.g., American Indians, a particularly complex example in that their land of origin is precisely the place where they are unwelcomed and where furthermore recognition of this situation puts in question the historic legitimacy of the American claim; Blacks whose "land" of origin is misty—African nationalism notwithstanding—and who share with diaspora Jewry the "memory" of an unwilled exile; Jews, whose relation to the newly reconstituted Israeli state is multi-dimensional and varied.)

10. Identification as "otherness" may in effect be isolated in a special domain—ethnicity, religion, race—while identification as an "American" is both more and less abstract—as an expression of the ideology in which the activities and meanings of everyday life are grounded. The creation of two domains provides apparent flexibility in that the relation of each to the other can be articulated in several ways. The notion of domains, employed by systems theorists is, we feel, useful as a description of American modes of conceptualization. Some of its limitations as an analytic tool are discussed below.

11. Certainly, not all were equal in an era of black slavery, "no representation" for American Indians and neither representation nor suffrage for women—black, white, or American Indian.

12. Dr. Denton pajamas, generally made of flannel, consist of one piece from neck to toes. They are often snapped down the front and include soft soles at the feet end which serve as slippers.

13. For most Americans, Christmas is perceived not only as an important holiday, but as standing prototypically for the Idea of holiday and therefore the elements of Christmas become the elements of celebration. We are grateful to Claude Swanson for pointing this out to us.

14. The Bridgton fire companies are composed of local adult male residents who volunteer and receive remuneration only when they are called into service.

15. The use of the "ethnic" model is illustrated by JDL's appropriation of forms of black identity and by American feminists' definition of the position of women through analogy to oppressed "ethnic" minorities.

16. Representations of the Madonna, often of the Madonna with child, adorn the buildings of Rome and other Italian cities, or inhabit niches arched in the walls. Occasionally, in Rome, flowers dress the inscriptions, but most of the time, they appear to be received as part of the landscape. The image of the Madonna with child is both a religious symbol and the distilled representation within Italy of the valorization and essence of the family.

17. The figure of Jesus as adult interceder is not invoked often in Italian Catholicism. The image of Jesus as adult corresponds with the rise of individualism and is associated with Protestantism (see Weber 1968 and Dumont 1970a).

18. "Logical" is locally used as North Americans use "natural" or the French use "c'est normale."

TWENTY-ONE

Industrialization and Capitalism in the Work of Max Weber

Herbert Marcuse

One of the common assumptions of social inquiry is that there is a form of rationality which transcends cultural boundaries and provides a privileged viewpoint, so that the social scientist can discover—given enough time and data—the "truth" of a society or the basic "laws" which govern all societies. This rationality is difficult to define briefly and precisely, but it is the rationality of Science; and the assumption that this form somehow provides a privileged position runs through most contemporary schools of social thought.

Max Weber, the great German sociologist, was one of the first to inquire into the relationship between this form of rationality and modern industrial capitalism and the bureaucratic state. Weber felt that every system of social relations was an instance of one or another form of rationality—true rationality, in which both ends and means were subjected to criticism, "directed" rationality, in which the means to accomplish an otherwise determined end were the object of maximization, "traditional" rationality, in which things were done the way they were and for the reasons they were out of affection for or attachment to a traditional viewpoint, and "patriarchal" rationality, in which things were done because an authority figure ordered it that way. Weber felt that modern society was an instance of "true" rationality.

In this article, written in the 1930's, Herbert Marcuse subjects Weber's argument to a penetrating and trenchant criticism. He shows that the formal rationality which we usually think of as somehow transcendent or privileged is in fact merely another social form; that it is part of a more general and basic mode of life; and that the notion that it is somehow privileged is an instance of what Marx called "fetishism" (see the selections by Marx and Lefebvre in this volume).

INDUSTRIALIZATION and capitalism become problematic in Max Weber's work in two respects: as the historical fate of the West, and as the contemporary fate of the Germany created by Bismarck. As the fate of the West, they are the decisive realizations of that Western rationality, that idea of reason, which Weber traces in its open and veiled, progressive and repressive, manifestations. As the fate of modern Germany, these manifestations determine for him the politics of the Reich, primarily as the historical task of the German bourgeoisie—in the transformation of the conservative-feudal state, then in democratization, finally in the struggle against revolution and socialism. It is essentially the idea of a fateful connection between industrialization, capitalism, and national self-preservation that motivates Max Weber's passionate and—let us be frank—spiteful fight against the socialist efforts of 1918. According to him, socialism contradicts the idea of occidental reason, as well as that of the national state; hence it is a world-historical error, if not a world-historical crime. (We might ask, what Max Weber would have said had he lived to see that it is not the West, but the East, which, in the name of socialism, has developed modern occidental rationality in its extreme form.) Whatever capitalism may do to man, it must, according to Weber, first and before all evaluation, be understood as necessary reason.

Philosophical, sociological-historical, and political motives are fundamentally connected in Weber's analysis of industrial capitalism. His theory of the intrinsic value-freedom, or ethical neutrality, of science reveals itself as that which it is in practice: an attempt to make science "free" to accept obligatory valuations that are imposed on it from the outside. This function of Weber's theory of knowledge has been clear ever since his inaugural address at Freiburg in 1895, which with ruthless frankness subordinates value-free economics to the claims of national power politics. Sometime later (at the meeting of the *Verein für Sozialpolitik* in 1909) he himself made it as explicit as possible:

The reason why I argue on every occasion so sharply and even, perhaps, pedantically against the fusion of Is and Ought is not because I underestimate Ought questions, but, on the contrary, because I cannot stand it when problems of world-moving importance, of the greatest intellectual and spiritual bearing, in a certain sense the highest problems that can move a human breast are transformed here into questions of technical-economic "productivity" and are made into the topic of discussion of a *technical* discipline, such as economics is. (*GASS*:419)[1]

But the Ought that is thus taken out of science (a mere "technical discipline") is thereby simultaneously protected from science and shielded from scientific criticism: the "value of that ideal itself can never be derived" (*GASS*:402) from the material of scientific work itself.

It is precisely Max Weber's analysis of industrial capitalism, however, which shows that the concept of scientific neutrality, or, better, impotence, vis-à-vis the Ought, cannot be maintained: pure value-free philosophical-sociological concept formation becomes, *through its own process,* value criticism. Inversely, the pure value-free scientific concepts reveal the valuation that is contained in them: they become the critique of the given, in the light of what the given does to men (and things). The Ought shows itself in the Is: the indefatigable effort of conceptual thinking makes it appear. In *Wirtschaft und Gesellschaft,* that work of Max Weber which is most free from values and where the method of formal definitions, classifications, and typologies celebrates true orgies, formalism attains the incisiveness of content. This authentic concretion is the result of Weber's mastery of an immense material, of scholarship that seems unimaginable today, of knowledge that can afford to abstract because it can distinguish the essential from the inessential and reality from appearance. With its abstract concepts, formal theory reaches the goal at which a positivistic, pseudoempirical sociology hostile to theory aims in vain: the real definition of reality. The concept of industrial capitalism thus becomes concrete in the formal theory of *rationality* and of *domination* which are the two fundamental themes of *Wirtschaft und Gesellschaft*.

Let us try first to present the connection between capitalism, rationality, and domination in the work of Max Weber. In its most general form this connection may be formulated as follows: the specifically Western idea of reason realizes itself in a system of material and intellectual culture (economy, technology, "conduct of life," science, art) that develops to the full in industrial capitalism, and this system tends toward a specific type of domination which becomes the fate of the contemporary period: total bureaucracy. The comprehensive and basic concept is the idea of reason as Western rationality. We begin with this concept.

For Weber, there is a rationality that has come into effect only in the West, that has formed (or has at least helped form) capitalism, and that has decided our foreseeable future. The effort to determine this rationality in its many (and often contradictory) manifestations occupies a large part of Weber's work. The "spirit of capitalism," as described in the first volume of his collected essays in the sociology of religion, is one of these manifestations; the preface to this work points out programmatically that the rationality formulated and acted on in capitalism fundamentally distinguishes Western industrialization from all other forms of economy and technology.

Let us first list the elements that are characteristic of Max Weber's concept of reason. (1) There is the progressive mathematization of experience and knowledge, a mathematization which, starting from the natural sciences and their extraordinary successes, extends to the other sciences and to the "conduct of life" itself (universal quantification). (2) There is the insistence on the necessity of rational experiments and rational proofs in the organization of science as well as in the conduct of life. (3) There is the result of this organization which is decisive for Weber, namely, the genesis and solidification of a universal, technically trained organization of officials that becomes the "absolutely *inescapable* condition of our entire existence" (*GAR*:1ff.). With this last characteristic, the transition from theoretical to practical reason, to the historical form of reason is effected. The consciousness of its specific historicity was contained in the beginning in Weber's conception of reason, with, or precisely due to, its abstractness. However, we shall see that it is not sustained in the entire course of his analysis and miscarries at the decisive point. In his sociology, formal rationality turns into *capitalist* rationality. Thus it appears as the methodical taming of the irrational "acquisitive drive," the taming that finds its typical expression in "inner-worldly asceticism."

In this "taming," occidental reason becomes the *economic* reason of capitalism, that is, the striving for ever renewed gain within the continuous, rational, capitalist enterprise. Rationality thus becomes the condition of profitability, which in turn is oriented toward systematic, methodical calculation, "capital accounting" (*GAR*:4–5).

The basis of this rationality is abstraction which, at once theoretical and practical, the work of both scientific and social organization, determines the capitalist period: through the reduction of quality to quantity. As universal functionalization (which finds its economic expression in exchange value), it becomes the precondition of calculable *efficiency*—of universal efficiency, insofar as functionalization makes possible the domination of all particular cases and relations (through their reduction to quantities and exchange values). Abstract reason becomes concrete in the calculable and calculated *domination* of nature and man. The reason envisaged by Weber thus is revealed as *technical* reason, as the production and transformation of material (things and men) through the methodical-scientific apparatus. This apparatus has been built with the aim of calculable efficiency; its rationality organizes and controls things and men, factory and bureaucracy, work and leisure. But *to what purpose* does it control them? Up to this point, Weber's concept of reason has been "formal," that is, has been defined as quantifying abstraction from all particulars, an abstraction that rendered possible the universally calculable efficiency of the capitalist apparatus. But now the limits of formal reason emerge: neither the specific purpose of the scientific-technical construction nor its material (its subjects and its objects) can be deduced from the concept of reason; they explode from the start this formal, "value-free" concept.

In capitalist rationality, as analyzed by Weber, these elements that are prior and "external" to reason and that thus materially delimit it appear in two historical facts: (1) provision for human needs—the aim of economic activity—is carried out in the framework of *private enterprise* and its calculable chances of gain, that is, within the framework of the *profit* of the individual entrepreneur or enterprise; (2) consequently, the existence of those whose needs are to be satisfied depends on the profit opportunities of the capitalist enterprise. This dependence is embodied, in its extreme form, in the "free" labor that is at the disposal of the entrepreneur.

In terms of Weber's conception, these facts are pregiven to formal reason from the outside, but as historical facts, they limit the general validity of the concept itself. According to Weber, the focal reality of capitalist rationality is the *private* enterprise; the entrepreneur is a free person, responsible by and to himself for his calculations and their risks. In this function, he is *bourgeois*, and the bourgeois conduct of life finds its representative expression in innerworldly asceticism. Is this conception still valid today? Is the bourgeoisie, in which Weber saw the bearer of industrial development, still its bearer in the late capitalist phase? Is late capitalist rationality still that which derives from innerworldly asceticism? I think the answer to these questions must be in the negative. In the development of capitalistic rationality itself, the forms ascribed to it by Weber have disintegrated and become obsolete, and their disintegration makes the rationality of capitalistic industrialization appear in a very different light: in the light of its *ir*rationality. To mention only one aspect: "innerworldly asceticism" is no longer a motivating force in late capitalism; it has become a fetter that serves the maintenance of the system. Keynes denounced it as such, and it is a danger to the "affluent society" wherever it could hinder the production and consumption of superfluous goods. To be sure, even late capitalism is built on "renunciation": the struggle for existence and the exploitation of labor must be intensified more and more if increased accumulation is to be possible. "Planned obsolescence," methodical irrationality, becomes a social necessity. But this is no longer the conduct of life of the bourgeoisie as the class that develops the productive forces. It is rather the stigma of productive destruction under total administration. And the capital accounting of mathematized profitability and efficiency celebrates its greatest triumphs in the calculation of kill and overkill, of the risk of our own annihilation compared with that of the annihilation of the enemy.

In the unfolding of capitalist rationality, *irrationality* becomes *reason:* reason as frantic development of productivity, conquest of nature, enlargement of the mass of goods (and their accessibility for broad strata of the population); irrational because higher productivity, domination of nature, and social wealth become destructive forces. This destruction is not only figurative, as in the betrayal of so-called higher cultural values, but literal: the struggle for existence intensifies both within national states and internationally, and pent-up aggression is discharged in the legitimation of medieval cruelty (torture) and in the scientifically organized destruction of men. Did Max Weber foretell this development? The answer is No if the accent is placed on "tell." But this development is implied in his conceptual scheme— implied at such a deep level that it appears as inexorable, final, and thereby, in turn (in the bad sense), rational.

In the course of Weber's analysis, the value-free concept of capitalist rationality becomes a critical concept—critical in the sense not only of "pure science," but also of an evaluative, goal-posting critique of reification.

But then the critique stops, accepts the allegedly inexorable, and turns into apologetics—worse, into the denunciation of the possible alternative, that is, of a qualitatively different historical rationality. With clairvoyance, Weber himself recognized the limit of his conceptual scheme. He defined himself as a "bourgeois" and identified his work with the historical mission of the bourgeoisie; in the name of this alleged mission, he accepted the alliance of representative strata of the German bourgeoisie with the organizers of reaction and repression. For political adversaries on the radical left, he recommended the lunatic asylum, the zoo, and the revolver shot. He raged against the intellectuals who had sacrificed their lives for the revolution.[2] The personal serves us here only as illustration of the conceptual; it serves to show how the concept of reason itself, in its critical content, remains ultimately tied to its origin: "reason" remains *bourgeois* reason, and, indeed, only one part of the latter, viz. capitalist technical reason.

Let us try now to reconstruct the inner development of the Weberian concept of capitalist reason. The Freiburg inaugural address envisions capitalist industrialization wholly as a form of power politics, that is, as imperialism. Only the development of large-scale industry can guarantee the independence of the nation in the ever more intense international competitive struggle. Imperialist power politics requires intensive and extensive industrialization, and vice versa. The economy must serve the *raison d'état* of the national state and must work with the latter's means. Such means are colonization and military power, means for the realization of the extrascientific aims and values to which value-free economics must subordinate itself. As historical reason, the reason of state demands rule by that class which is capable of carrying out industrialization and thus effecting the growth of the nation, i.e. rule by the *bourgeoisie*. It is dangerous when an "economically declining class is in power" (*GpS*:20–21) (as the Junkers in Germany). Under the pressure of extrascientific, political valuation, economic science thus becomes, with Weber, the political-sociological critique of the state erected by Bismarck. And this critique anticipates the future in an unheard-of way: in Germany, the historically appointed class, the bourgeoisie, is "immature"; in its weakness it longs for a new Caesar who would do the deed for it (*GpS*:27).

The coming to power of the bourgeois class meant, at that time, the democratization of the still prebourgeois state. But, owing to its political immaturity, the German bourgeoisie can neither realize nor hinder this democratization and calls for caesarism. Democracy, the political form corresponding to capitalist industrialization, threatens to change into plebiscitary dictatorship; bourgeois reason conjures up irrational *charisma*. This dialectic of bourgeois democracy if not of bourgeois reason continued to trouble Weber, and is incisively expressed in *Wirtschaft und Gesellschaft*. We shall return to it. Here it should be observed that Weber, more correctly than most contemporary socialists, also foresaw the later development of the other class that underlies

capitalism, the proletariat, and therewith repeated almost unchanged what Bismarck had said as early as 1865. "The danger does not lie with the masses" (*GpS*:29), Weber declared in his 1895 inaugural address. It is not the ruled classes who will hinder imperialistic politics, let alone cause it to fail. It is rather "the ruling and rising classes" who represent this threat to the nation's chances for survival in international competition.

The conservative character of the masses, the caesaristic tendencies of the ruling classes: *these* changes of late capitalism Max Weber did foresee. He did not, as Marxist theory does, root them in the structure of capitalism itself. "Political immaturity" is a poor category as long as it does not define the factors behind the fact—in this case the impossibility for capitalist production of preserving the free market through free competition. Capitalist production itself runs up against its limits in the democratic institutions of the market society. Domination is concentrated in and above the bureaucracy, as the necessary apex of regimentation. What appeared as political immaturity within the context of liberalistic capitalism becomes, in organized capitalism, political maturity.

And the harmlessness of the ruled classes? Even while Weber was still living, they were, for a historical instant, ready to cause imperialistic politics to fail. After that, however, the political maturity of the bourgeoisie and the intellectual efficiency of capitalist productivity took things in hand and confirmed Weber's prediction.

Let us now look at his concept of capitalism where (apparently) it is removed from the concrete context of imperialistic power politics and developed in its value-free scientific purity: in *Wirtschaft und Gesellschaft*. Here capitalism, as a form of "rational economic acquisition," is defined in the first instance as a "particular form of monetary calculation":

Capital accounting is the valuation and calculation of profit opportunities and . . . proceeds by means of comparing the respective monetary values of total (fixed and liquid) assets at the beginning and end of a single profit-oriented undertaking or, in the case of a continuous profit-making enterprise, of comparing the initial and final balance sheets for an accounting period. (*WuG*:48; *TSEO*:191–92)

The effort—one is tempted to say the provocative effort—to define capitalism in a purely scientific manner and to abstract from everything human and historical shows forth even in the forbidding syntax (at least in German). What is at issue here is business and nothing else. In contrast to this attitude, Weber's emphasis on the next page seems almost shocking: "Capital accounting in its *formally* most rational mode thus presupposes *the struggle of man with man*."[3] What capital accounting does to men finds sharper expression in its abstract definition than in the latter's concretion: inhumanity is included in the rationality of the initial and final balance sheets.

The "formally most rational" mode of capital accounting is the one into which man and his "purposes" enter only as variables in the calculation of the chances of gain and profit. In this formal rationality, mathematization is carried to the point of the calculus with the real *negation of life* itself; at the extreme, risk of death from hunger, it becomes a motive for economic activity on the part of those who have nothing:

. . . decisive as [an] element of the motivation of economic activity under the conditions of a market economy [is] *normally* . . . for those without property . . . the fact that they run the risk both for themselves and their personal dependents, such as children, wives, sometimes parents, whose maintenance the individual typically takes over, of going without any provision . . . (*WuG*:60; *TSEO*:213–14)

Again and again, Weber defines *formal* rationality in contrast to a *material* (substantive) rationality, in which the economic maintenance of men is considered "from the point of view of certain valuational postulates (of whatever kind)."[4]

Formal rationality is thus in conflict not only with "traditional" value orientations and goals, but also with revolutionary ones. As an example, Max Weber mentions the antinomy between formal rationality on the one hand and, on the other, of attempts to abolish the separation of powers ("soviet republic, government by a convention or committee of public safety": *WuG*:167; *TSEO*:406–07) of attempts, in other words, to change radically the existing form of domination. But is the formal rationality that finds expression in a capitalist economy really so formal? Here, once more, is its definition:

The term "formal rationality of economic action" will be used to designate the extent of quantitative calculation or accounting which is technically possible and which is actually applied. A system of economic activity will be called "formally" rational according to the degree in which the provision for needs, which is essential to every rational economy, is capable of being expressed in numerical, calculable terms, and is so expressed. (*WuG*:44–45; *TSEO*:184–85)

According to this definition, a totally planned economy, that is, a noncapitalist economy, would evidently be *more* rational, in the sense of formal rationality, than the capitalist economy. For the latter sets itself the limits of calculability in the particular interest of the private enterprise and in the "freedom" (however regimented) of the market. If Weber declares such a planned economy retrogressive or even realistically impossible, he does so in the first place for a technological reason: in modern industrial society, the separation of the workers from the means of production has become a *technical* necessity requiring the individual and private direction and control of the means of production, that is, the authority of the personally responsible entrepreneur in the enterprise. The highly *material,* historical fact of the private-capitalist enterprise thus becomes (in Weber's sense) a *formal* structural element of capitalism and of *rational* economic activity itself.

But the rational social function of individual control of production that is based on the separation of labor from the means of production goes beyond this. For Max Weber, it is the guarantor of technically and economically necessary organizational *discipline,* which then becomes the model of the entire discipline required by modern industrial society. Even socialism, according to Weber, has its origin in factory discipline: "From this life situation, from the discipline of the factory, was modern socialism born" (*GASS*:501).

The "subjection to work discipline" characteristic of free enterprise is thus, on the one hand, the rationality of a *personal hierarchy,* but on the other hand, the rational domination of things over man, that is, "of the means over the end (the satisfaction of needs)." In these words, Weber quotes a socialist thesis (*GASS*:502). He does not contest it but believes that not even a socialist society will change the fundamental fact of the worker's separation from the means of production, because this separation is simply the form of technical progress, of industrialization. Even socialism remains subject to its rationality, for otherwise it cannot remain faithful to its own promise of the general satisfaction of needs and the pacification of the struggle for existence. The control of man by things can be deprived of its irrationality only through the rational control of man by man. The question, therefore, is for socialism, too: "Who, then, is supposed to take over and direct this new economy?" (*GASS*:511).

Industrialization is thus seen as the fate of the modern world, and the fateful question for both capitalist and socialist industrialization is only this: What is the most rational form of dominating industrialization and hence society? ("Most rational" is still used in the sense of that *formal* rationality which is determined only by the calculable and regulated functioning of its own system.) But this formal rationality seems to have changed imperceptibly in the course of the logical development of Weber's analysis. In becoming a question of domination, of control, this rationality subordinates itself, by virtue of its own inner dynamic, to another, namely, to the rationality of domination. Precisely insofar as this formal rationality does not go beyond its own structure and has nothing but its own system as the norm of its calculations and calculating actions, it is as a whole dependent, determined "from the outside" by something older than itself; in this fashion reason becomes, in Weber's own definition, "material."

Industrialization as "fate," domination as "fate"—Max Weber's concept of "fate" shows in exemplary fashion the material content of his formal analysis. "Fate" is the law of an economy and society which are largely independent of individuals, and violation of this law would mean self-destruction. But society is not "nature." Who decrees the fate? Industrialization is a phase in the development of men's capacities and needs, a phase in their struggle with nature and with themselves. This development can proceed in very different forms and with very different aims; not only the forms of control but also those of technology and hence of needs and of their satisfactions are in no way "fatal," but rather *become* such only when they are socially sanctioned, that is, as the result of material, economic, and psychological coercion. Weber's concept of fate is construed "after the fact" of such coercion: he generalizes the blindness of a society which reproduces itself behind the back of the individuals, of a society in which the law of domination appears as objective technological law. However, in fact, this law is neither "fatal" nor "formal." The context of Weber's analysis is the historical context in which economic reason became the reason of domination—domination at almost any price. This fate has *become* a fate and inasmuch as it has become a fate it can also be *abolished*. Any scientific analysis that is not committed to this possibility is pledged, not to reason, but to the reason of established domination. For there is no structure that has not been *posited* or *made* and is not as such dependent. In the continuum of history, in which all economic action takes place, all economic reason is always the reason of domination, which historically and socially determines economic action. Capitalism, no matter how mathematized and "scientific," remains the mathematized, technological *domination* of men; and socialism, no matter how scientific and technological, is the construction or demolition of domination.

If in Weber's work the formal analysis of capitalism thus becomes the analysis of forms of domination, this is not due to a discontinuity in concept or method; their purity itself shows itself impure. And this is so, not because Max Weber was a bad or inconsistent sociologist, but because he knew his subject matter: Truth becomes critique and accusation, and accusation becomes the function of true science. If he subjected the science of economics to politics as early as in the inaugural address, this tour de force shows itself, in the light of the whole of Weber's work, as the inner logic of his method. Your science must remain "pure"; only thus can you remain faithful to the truth. But this truth forces you to recognize what determines the objects of your science "from the outside." Over this you have no power. Your freedom from value judgments is as necessary as it is mere appearance. For neutrality is *real* only when it has the power of resisting interference. Otherwise it becomes the victim, as well as the aid, of every power that wants to use it.

The formal rationality of capitalism comes up against its internal limit in two places: in the fact of *private enterprise,* or the private entrepreneur as the actual subject of the calculated nature of economic activity; and in the fact of the worker's separation from the means of production, of *free labor.*

These two facts belong, for Max Weber, to the specific rationality of capitalism (*WuG*:19–23; *TSEO*:130–39):

they are technological necessities. For him, they thus are the basis for domination as an integral element of capitalist (and even of economic) rationality in modern industrial society. If this is so, then domination itself must be demonstrated as the form of modern economic rationality; and this is what Weber tries to do in his analysis of *bureaucracy*.

Bureaucratic control is inseparable from increasing industrialization; it extends the maximally intensified efficiency of industrial organization to society as a whole. It is the formally most rational form of control, thanks to its "precision, steadfastness, discipline, rigor, and dependability, in short calculability for both the head [of the organization] and for those having to do with it . . . " (*WuG*:128; *TSEO*:337); and it is all this because it is "domination by virtue of knowledge," ascertainable, calculable, calculating knowledge, specialized knowledge. Properly speaking, it is the *apparatus* that dominates, for the control of this apparatus, based on specialized knowledge, is such only if it is fully adjusted to its technical demands and potentialities. For this reason, domination of the apparatus is "possible for the layman only within limits: in the long run, the technically trained permanent official is usually superior to the layman as a [government] minister" (*WuG*:128–29; *TSEO*:338).

Again Weber stresses that any "rational socialism" "would simply have to take over and would intensify" bureaucratic administration since this administration is nothing but purely *objective* domination, demanded by the objective circumstances themselves, and equally valid for the most varied political, cultural, and moral aims and institutions. And the objective circumstances themselves are the given, ever more productively and efficiently developing, ever more precisely calculable apparatus.

The specialized scientific administration of the apparatus as formally rational domination: this is the reification of reason, reification *as* reason, the apotheosis of reification. But the apotheosis turns into its negation, is bound to turn into its negation. For the apparatus, which dictates its own objective administration, is itself instrument, means— and there is no such thing as a means "as such." Even the most productive, most reified apparatus is a means to an end outside itself. As far as the economic apparatus of capitalism is concerned, it is not enough to say that this end is the satisfaction of needs. Such a concept is too general, too abstract, in the bad sense of the word. For, as Max Weber himself realized, the satisfaction of needs is far more the by-product than the end of capitalist economic activity. Human needs are necessary and "formally rational" as long as living human beings are still required as consumers (as producers they already are partly unnecessary), and already much is sold to warehouses—stockpiling for annihilation and a subhuman subterranean life. But if the bureaucratic administration of the capitalist apparatus, with all its rationality, remains a means, and thus dependent, then it has, as rationality, its own limit. The bureaucracy subjects itself to an extra- and suprabureaucratic power—to an "unbusinesslike" power. And if rationality is embodied in administration, and *only* in administration, then this legislative power must be irrational. The Weberian conception of reason ends in irrational *charisma*.

Among all of Weber's concepts, that of charisma is perhaps the most questionable. Even as a term it contains the bias that gives every kind of successful, allegedly personal domination an almost religious consecration. The concept itself is under discussion here only insofar as it can illuminate the dialectic of rationality and irrationality in modern society. Charismatic domination appears as a phase in a twofold process of development. On the one hand, charisma tends to turn into the solidified domination of interests and their bureaucratic organization; on the other hand, bureaucratic organization tends to submit to a charismatic leader.

In the chapter "Transformation of Charisma" Max Weber describes how pure charismatic domination tends to transform itself into a "permanent possession"; in this process "it is given over to the conditions of everyday life and to the powers that dominate it, above all to economic interests" (*WuG*:762). What begins as the charisma of the single individual and his personal following ends in domination by a bureaucratic apparatus that has acquired rights and functions and in which the charismatically dominated individuals become regular, tax-paying, dutiful "subjects."

But this rational administration of masses and things cannot do without the irrational charismatic leader. For the administration would tend, precisely to the degree to which it is really rational, to the abolition of domination (and to the administration of *things*). Yet the administrative apparatus has always been built on the basis of domination and has been established to maintain and strengthen domination. To the democratization required by rational administration thus corresponds a parallel limitation and manipulation of democratization. Domination as the privilege of particular interests and self-determination as an expression of the general interest are brought into forced unity. This violent and simultaneously formally rational, i.e. technically efficient, solution of the contradiction has its classical manifestation in plebiscitary democracy (*WuG*:156–57; 174; 763 ff.), in which the masses periodically depose their leaders and determine their policies—under previously established conditions well controlled by the leaders. For Max Weber, universal suffrage thus is not only the result of domination but also its instrument in the period of its technical perfection. Plebiscitary democracy is the political expression of irrationality-become-reason.

In what way does this dialectic of reason (that is, of *formal* reason) show forth in the development of capitalism? The latter's profane power resists the idea of charisma, and Weber is rather timid when it comes to the application of this term to contemporary industrial society, even though his attitude and even his language during World War I and against the revolution often came very close to succumbing to charismatic illusions. But the actual trend is clearly exhibited by his analysis: the formal reason of the technically perfect administrative apparatus is subordinated to the irrational. Max Weber's analysis of bureaucracy breaks through the ideological camouflage. Far ahead of his time, he showed the illusory character of modern mass democracy with its pretended equalization and adjustment of class conflicts. The bureaucratic administration of industrial capitalism is indeed a "leveling," but what is decisive here is exclusively the *leveling of the dominated* vis-à-vis the ruling, bureaucratically organized group, which may actually, and often even formally, occupy a wholly autocratic position (*WuG*:667). He stresses again and again that precisely the technically perfect administrative apparatus, *by virtue of its formal rationality,* is a "means of power of the very first rank for him who has the bureaucratic apparatus at his disposal."

The dependence of the material fate of the mass on the continuous, correct functioning of the increasingly bureaucratically organized private-capitalist organizations increases continuously, and the thought of the possibility of their elimination thus becomes ever more utopian (*WuG*:669).

Total dependence on the functioning of an omnipresent apparatus becomes the "basis of all order" so that the apparatus itself is no longer questioned. "Trained orientation toward obedient subjection to those orders" becomes the cement of a subjugation of which people are no longer conscious because the order to which they subordinate themselves is itself so terrifyingly rational; that is, because it administers so efficiently and puts at one's calculable disposal the world of goods and performances of which the single individual no longer has an overview or a comprehension. Max Weber did not live long enough to see how mature capitalism, in the efficiency of its reason, makes even the planned annihilation of millions of human beings and the planned destruction of human labor the fountainhead of a bigger and better prosperity, how even sheer insanity becomes the basis, not only of the continuation of life, but of the more comfortable life. He did not live to see the "affluent society," in the face of inhuman misery and methodical cruelty outside its borders, squander its unimaginable technical, material, and intellectual power and abuse its power for the purposes of permanent mobilization. Even before the unfolding of the power of this reason he called attention to the danger present in the submission of the rational bureaucratic administrative apparatus, by virtue of its own rationality, to an irrational supreme authority.

In the first place, in the framework of Weber's conceptual scheme, it is almost self-evident that the administration of industrial society requires outside and superior direction: "Every administration requires some kind of domination, since, for its direction, some commanding powers must always be placed in someone's hands" (*WuG*:607). The capitalist entrepreneur is "in the material sense" as little of a trained official as the monarch at the head of the empire. No specialized qualities are required of him: "Bureaucratic domination thus inevitably has at its apex an element that is at least not purely bureaucratic" (*WuG*:127). "Inevitably," because the value-free rationality of administration is dependent upon values and goals that come to it from the outside. In his inaugural address, Weber had defined the power politics of the nation-state as giving economics its values and goals. Capitalism was therewith defined as *imperialism*.

In *Wirtschaft und Gesellschaft* some characteristics of the imperialistic economy are called by their names and summed up in the concept of "politically oriented capitalism." Weber then states: "It is clear from the start that those politically oriented events that offer these (political) possibilities for gain are economically irrational when viewed from the point of view of orientation toward market chances. . . ."

(*WuG*:96). As irrational, they can be replaced by others. Control of the capitalistic economy not only requires no specialized qualification, it is also to a great degree fungible.

Capitalism, with all its rationality (or rather just because of its specific rationality), thus terminates in an irrational, "accidental" head—not only in the economy, but also in the control of the bureaucratic administration itself, in governmental administration. (It is difficult not to think here of Hegel's *Philosophy of Right* where the state of civil society, the rational state, culminates in the "accidental" person of the monarch who is determined only by the contingency of birth: in Hegel as in Weber, the analysis of bourgeois reason reveals the latter's limits: bourgeois reason negates itself in its consummation.)

Let us look back briefly at the stages in the development of Weber's concepts (and of their objects). Western capitalism originated under the specific social, political, and economic conditions of the waning Middle Ages and of the Reformation. It developed its "spirit" in that formal rationality that realized itself in the psychological as well as the economic orientation and action of the originators (but not the objects!) of the process of capital. Industrialization has been carried out under this formal reason: technical progress and progressive satisfaction of needs, whatever needs they may be. We have seen that this formal rationality develops on the basis of two very *material* historical facts, which maintain themselves in its progress and which (according to Max Weber) are *conditions* of capitalism, namely (1) the private enterprise and (2) "free labor," the existence of a class that "economically," "under the compulsion of the lash of hunger," is forced to sell its services (*WuG*:240). As productive forces, these material conditions enter into formal reason. Capitalism expands in the competitive struggle of unequal (but formally free) powers: the struggle for existence of persons, nation-states, and international alliances.

For Max Weber, the contemporary phase of capitalism is dominated by national power politics: capitalism is imperialism. But its administration remains formally rational, i.e. bureaucratic domination. It administers the control of men by things; rational, "value-free" technology is the separation of man from the means of production and his subordination to technical efficiency and necessity—all this within the framework of private enterprise. The machine is the determining factor, but the "lifeless machine is congealed spirit *(Geist)*. Only by being this has it the power to force men into its service. . . ." (*GpS*:151). Yet because it is "congealed spirit," it also is domination of man by man; thus *this* technical reason reproduces enslavement. Subordination to technology becomes subordination to domination as such; formal technical rationality turns into material political rationality (or is it the other way around, inasmuch as technical reason was from the beginning the control of "free" labor by private enterprise?). Under the compulsion of reason, the fate is fulfilled that Weber foresaw with remarkable clarity in one of his most telling passages:

Joined to the dead machine, [bureaucratic organization] is at work to erect the shell of that future bondage to which one day men will perhaps be forced to submit in impotence, as once the fellahs in the ancient Egyptian state—*if a purely, technically good, that is, rational bureaucratic adminis-*

tration and maintenance is the last and only value which is to decide on the manner in which their affairs are directed. (*GpS*:151)

But it is precisely here, at this most decisive point, where Weber's analysis becomes self-criticism, that one can see how much this analysis has fallen prey to the identification of technical reason with bourgeois capitalist reason. This identification prevents him from seeing that not "pure," formal, technical reason but the reason of domination erects the "shell of bondage," and that the consummation of technical reason can well become the instrument for the *liberation* of man. Put differently: Max Weber's analysis of capitalism was not sufficiently value-free, inasmuch as it took into its "pure" definitions of formal rationality valuations peculiar to capitalism. On this basis, the contradiction developed between formal and material (or substantive) rationality, whose obverse is the "neutrality" of technical reason vis-à-vis all outside material valuations. This neutrality, in turn, made it possible for Weber to accept the *(reified)* interest of the nation and its political power as the values that determine technical reason.

The very concept of technical reason is perhaps ideological. Not only the application of technology but technology itself is domination (of nature and men)—methodical, scientific, calculated, calculating control. Specific purposes and interests of domination are not foisted upon technology "subsequently" and from the outside; they enter the very construction of the technical apparatus. Technology is always a historical-social *project:* in it is projected what a society and its ruling interests intend to do with men and things. Such a "purpose" of domination is "substantive" and to this extent belongs to the very form of technical reason.

Weber abstracted from this ineluctable social material. We have emphasized the right to this abstraction in the analysis of capitalist reason: abstraction becomes *critical* of this reason insofar as it shows the degree to which capitalist rationality itself abstracts from man, to whose needs it is "indifferent," and in this indifference becomes ever more productive and efficient, calculating and methodical, thus erecting the "shell of bondage," furnishing it (quite luxuriously), and universalizing it. Weber's abstractness is so saturated with his material that it pronounces rational judgment on the rational exchange society. In the course of its development, however, this society tends to abolish its own material prerequisites: the private entrepreneur is no longer the subject of economic rationality, answering only to himself, and "free labor" is no longer the enslavement enforced by the threatening "lash of hunger." The exchange society, where everything proceeds so freely and rationally, comes under the control of economic and political monopolies. The market and its liberties, whose ideological character Max Weber demonstrated often enough, is now subjected to frightfully efficient regulation, in which the general interest is markedly shaped by the ruling particular interests. Reification is abolished, but in a very deceptive manner. The separation from the means of production, in which Weber rightly saw a technical necessity, turns into the subjection of the whole to its calculating managers. The formal rationality of capitalism celebrates its triumph in electronic computers, which calculate everything, no matter what the purpose, and which are put to use as mighty instruments of political manipulation, reliably calculating the chances of profit and loss, including the chance of the annihilation of the whole, with the consent of the likewise calculated and obedient population. Mass democracy becomes plebiscitary even within the economy and the sciences: the masses themselves elect their leaders into the shell of bondage.

But if technical reason thus reveals itself as political reason, it does so only because from the beginning it was this technical reason and this political reason, that is, limited in the specific interest of domination. As political reason, technical reason is *historical*. If separation from the means of production is a technical necessity, the bondage that it organizes is *not*. On the basis of its own achievements, that is, of productive and calculable mechanization, this separation contains the potentiality of a qualitatively different rationality, in which separation from the means of production becomes the separation of man from socially necessary labor; were that

potential realized, that depurposiveness would be no longer "antinomical"; nor would administer automated production, formal and substantive purposiveness would be no longer "antinomical"; nor would formal reason prevail indifferently among and over men. For, as "congealed spirit," the machine is *not neutral;* technical reason is the social reason ruling a given society and can be changed in its very structure. As technical reason, it can become the technique of liberation.

For Max Weber this possibility was utopian. Today it looks as if he was right. But if contemporary industrial society defeats and triumphs over its own potentialities, then this triumph is no longer that of Max Weber's bourgeois reason. It is difficult to see reason at all in the ever more solid "shell of bondage" which is being constructed. Or is there perhaps already in Max Weber's concept of reason the irony that understands but disavows? Does he by any chance mean to say: And this you call "reason"?

Notes

1. *Editor's note:* Marcuse uses Weber's originals. *Gesammelte Aufsätze zur Soziologie und Sozialpolitik* (Weber 1924) is cited in the text as *GASS; Gesammelte Aufsätze zur Religionssoziologie* is cited as *GAR; Gesammelte politischen Schriften* is cited as *GpS; Wirtschaft und Gesellschaft* as *WuG*. Portions of the latter were translated by Henderson and Parsons as *The Theory of Social and Economic Organization*. Where Marcuse cites a passage from Weber which is in that selection, it will be cited as *WuG*:00; *TSEO*:00.

2. For documentation, see Mommsen (1959), where the documentation is collected and analyzed in an exemplary manner.

3. Weber, *Wirtschaft und Gesellschaft,* p. 49 [original italics]. Henderson and Parsons translate the passage as follows (1947:185): "Thus the highest degree of rational capital accounting presupposes the existence of competition on a large scale."

4. *Wirtschaft und Gesellschaft,* p. 44 (Henderson and Parsons 1947:185). *Translator's note:* Weber's term *"materiale rationalität"* is rendered by Henderson and Parsons as "substantive rationality." Here, both "material" and "substantive" are used.

EIGHT

Language and Codes

Shape in Grammar

PAUL FRIEDRICH

> The structure of language often forces an assemblage of concepts
> that impresses us as a stylistic discovery. Single Algonkin
> words are like tiny imagist poems.
>
> EDWARD SAPIR (*Language* 1921:244)

Paul Friedrich is one of the more provocative of those anthropological linguists who are concerned with the interplay of culture, cognition, and language—with what Friedrich here calls "the human experience that is immanent in the linguistic code."

Here, in an abridged version of a longer paper (Friedrich 1970b), Friedrich uses an unusual type of linguistic feature to explore the various ways in which the phenomena of shape are experienced and expressed; in this respect, his project here is similar to that of Sahlins in this volume. Friedrich's approach is through linguistic analysis, however.

It is important to note—as doubtless Friedrich himself would—that, although the burden of this paper is to suggest the existence of universals in the human experience which are reflected in language, the *forms* in which these are expressed—and therefore, their relations to other aspects of experience—differ widely from culture to culture.

THIS PAPER IS ABOUT the semantic substructure of language, roughly as the idea was launched by Humboldt (1836), and has been developed since by Whorf (1964), Benveniste (1966), Jakobson (1957), Berlin (1968), Filmore (1968), and many others. More particularly, it is about the so-called "numeral classifiers," "classificatory verbs," and "body part suffixes" in the Tarascan language.

Reprinted by permission of Mouton, The Hague, from *Linguistics,* vol. 75, pp. 5–22.

Before continuing, I would like to allude to an interesting fact of intellectual history: the phenomena of shape in grammar to be discussed below are characteristically ignored or perfunctorily dismissed with a sentence or a paragraph in authoritative works on grammatical theory, whether traditional, structural, descriptive, generative, or eclectic. They go nearly or wholly unmentioned in Saussure, Bloomfield, Jespersen, Jakobson, and Chomsky, and Lyons in his superb general text dismisses them in two paragraphs

(1968:288, 300). This neglect presumably mirrors an Indo-European bias (although Yuen Ren Chao refers to classifiers only once in his recent text book, and then in a single sentence devoted to illustrating "selection" (1968b:60)). If the following discussion looks unfamiliar, therefore, it is partly because the territory, although discovered and provisionally mapped by linguistic anthropologists, still remains to be explored in a more thoroughly theoretical manner. With this next goal in mind, the present article presents the first relatively systematic account of the actual covariation and intersection between the several semantic features of shape as they are coded in the grammar of one language.

Three sets in Tarascan grammar are shown to be partially coordinated morphological operators that relate thousands of concrete and often earthy or colorful Tarascan-specific referents to a much smaller number of semantic features of dimension and shape, which, in turn, are part of the geometrical semantics of Tarascan. This component in the grammar forces the speaker and hearer to code numerous and subtle decisions about shape. Shape-differentiation appears to be part of an integrated semantic style (cf. Hymes 1961) which "cuts across typical grammatical classifications" (Whorf 1964).

Turning from an intensive analysis of one part of the total semantic substructure of Tarascan, the final sections on wider implications review the global distribution of such obligatory morphological operators. The category of shape appears to be a typological universal in grammar and of not inconsiderable significance for a theory of semantics in grammar.

Numeral Classifiers

The Tarascan language contains three statistically frequent morphemes that, like the rest of the lexicon, are governed by inextricably interconnected semantic and syntactic patterns. Semantically, they imply classes of non-rational or pre-rational things with shape, usually visual shape—such as a pot. Both Tarascan Indians and Amerind grammarians tend to label such shapes as "longish, flattish, and roundish," or even "sticklike, tortilla-like, and ball-like." Their more essential features are saliency or emphasis of one, two, or three dimensions.

The Meaning of the Classifiers

What is the meaning of the numeral classifiers? In one sense, they mean the words they replace, and this is often the only kind of meaning provided by linguists discussing similar phenomena in other languages. In Tarascan, the one-dimensional classifier regularly replaces words such as those meaning "tree, worm, penis, corncob, key," and most animal names. The same classifier replaces the word for "story," presumably because of some mental image of protraction. The two-dimensional classifier similarly replaces words for "cloth, hide, shingle, tortilla," and the like—but is also substituted for "valley bottom," possibly because of the flat visual impression. The three-dimensional classifier, finally, replaces words for cubic shapes, such as "house," and for round things such as "pot" and "ball," as well as other saliently three-dimensional shapes such as "eyeball, turtle, and buttocks." But the same classifier also subsumes letters of the alphabet, testicles, and stars; when questioned, a Tarascan would normally rejoin that these things "look round." This brief and partial itemization of an illustrative sample of nominal expressions indicates—particularly in the case of stars—that dimension itself is defined in terms of physical (often visual) impression.

What are some of the patterns of paradigmatic replacement that reflect the meaning of the classifiers? First of all, the Tarascan classifier can replace not only a name, but also the entire set of more specific, subordinate taxa that a given name subsumes. For example, the words for "bird" and "flower," and for all the hundreds of species-level taxa of birds and flowers, and also all the words for seed grains, are obligatorily replaced by the three-dimensional classifier. This particular rule of obligatory replacement operates even where one- or two-dimensionality may be salient; for example, the Mexican broadbean, like all seeds, is replaced by the three dimensional classifier *(irá-ku)*, although it is saliently flat and broad. In these cases of obligatory substitution for any member of a definable set, just as in the anaphoric answer formulae, the classifiers resemble grammatical substitutes.

In a second type of pattern, a relatively inclusive term may be classified as one-, two-, or three-dimensional, but the classification of taxonomically subordinate terms will depend on the Tarascan perception of the referent; in such cases, the salient dimension of the more inclusive term differs from that of the included term. For example, fruits and insects are normally classified as three-dimensional, but a banana or a "walking-stick" insect are always coded as one-dimensional (even when the speaker does not know the name for the latter). Animals are normally coded as one-dimensional, but frogs and toads are classed as three-dimensional because, as Tarascans say, they may get round; a fixed epithet is, "to be fat-lipped and swell up like an angry toad." In these and many other cases the correct application of the classifiers depends on culturally established features of shape.

The meaning of the classifier often depends on the shape as perceived in the context of a particular speech situation, or class of such situations. This shape or the perception of it may change through time, as when a long balloon is inflated to roundness. Facetious or idiosyncratic usage also may be involved. For example, humans after infancy are normally classified as speech-capable, rather than as shaped objects. But if asked, "How many women does Panchu have?" the answer could be, "Three *irá-hku,*" thereby implicitly classing his plump mistresses with pots because of their three-dimensional bottoms. These examples indicate that the meaning of the classifiers involves a specifically Tarascan perception of what is "out there," and that these percepts are concatenated with diverse connotations and cultural implications.

The meaning of the classifiers is further disclosed by cases of dynamic usage, of categorizations that alter and conflict with each other. Ribbons are normally both saliently long and saliently flat, and this inherent ambiguity is reflected in their varying classification. Yet more interesting are the ambiguities that generate subconscious suppressions. Birds and flowers, as already noted, are coded as three-dimensional. But the speaker seems to avoid using a classifier for them—he tends not to classify them at all—when they have been painted on the girth of a pot, with its invariably bulging exterior. This suppression presumably reflects the perceptual confusion caused by the double ambiguity of mapping an ambiguously three-dimensional shape onto an ambiguously two-dimensional surface. The application of the classifiers, far from being a superficial matter, involves decisions at a relatively deep level of semantic structure—assuming, as I do, that the semantic system has a hierarchy of its own, partly independent of syntax, the weighting and evaluation of which is often connected with the premises of the cultural system.

The classifiers are also verbal roots and can be discussed by many speakers of Tarascan, usually without any particular strain. On occasion I heard jests or comments about misusage by children or myself, and my questionnaire about the classification of nouns caused hesitation or uncertainty only where the referents themselves were typically ambiguous. As already indicated, classifier usage can be humorous, although these usages, I think, are largely governed by subconscious factors. Of the classifiers one can ask, "What do you mean, *irá-ku*? or "What does *irá-ku* mean?" Such seemingly natural questions are normally answered by one of the standard glosses (see below), such as "Something round" *(ambé-ma, eng-uólin-há-ši-ka),* or by naming an illustrative object such as a pot. The classifiers, in short, can be talked about, and ideas about them consequently form part of the native speaker's model of his language. In this they differ from the classifiers in Mayan languages such as Tzeltal, where speakers find it difficult or impossible to generate glosses or to discuss the meanings in an explicit manner. A paradigm of roots, glosses, and illustrative words is presented below.

Verbal Root	Usual Tarascan Gloss	Standard Token	Illustrative Form
ičá-	*ió-(s-ka-)*	animal, especially horse, cow	*ičá-ndi-ti-ni,* "long object on shoulder"
ičú-	*kó-(s-ka-)*	tortilla	*ičú-hpa-ni,* "to pat out (make) tortillas"
irá	*uólin-há-ši, wirí-pi-ti*	pot or jug	*irá-ndi-ti-ni,* "roundish object on shoulder"

Table 22:1

Although they can be discussed, the classifiers do not normally occur alone, but always in morphophonemically close combination with an adjacent number or some other type of grammatical substitute.

Individuals vary considerably in how they apply the classifiers. For example, cars are generally one-dimensional, but one speaker classified a Volkswagen as three-dimensional because of its roundish, bug-like quality. Ears are normally two-dimensional, but several Tarascans classed as one-dimensional the erect ears of a donkey, and, when questioned, referred to the elongated shape. Furthermore, the usage obviously depends on individual intelligence and character, and might well serve as an index in studies of personality and bilingualism; one neurotic young bilingual, for instance, insisted that turtles were one-dimensional, and devils three-dimensional! To sum up, the classifiers involve various levels and dimensions of meaning, and of cultural, situational, and individual variables.

Covertly Classificatory Verbs

Let us now turn to the second shape-oriented set in Tarascan grammar. A considerable number of verbal roots are marked covertly for various features, notably smallness and the three dimensions of "longish, flattish, and roundish." A few verbal roots (e.g., *kúkú-*, "to carry something roundish and small") are simultaneously marked for two of these features. These covert features are thought to be "real" for two main reasons. First, in recorded utterances containing the roots in question, one or more of the features is generally a property of the subject or object—the subject of a verbal expression in the middle voice, or the object of a verbal expression in the active voice. Second, when defining a verbal root and its derivatives, whether by Tarascan paraphrase or Spanish translation, the more able speakers will normally volunteer that the subject or object belongs to one or the other of these categories (e.g., "something roundish," *irá-k-ambé*). The verbal roots are classificatory, then, in that the speaker must make decisions about the shape of their referents and the shape of the referents of the co-occuring subjects and objects.

The clearest evidence is afforded by the minimal pairs where what appears to denote roughly the same concept such as "to carry" or "to be thick," is conveyed by two or more shape-specific roots. The table gives some of these pairs and triads in order of increasing differentiation (moving downwards). It shows that there is less differentiation by roots as the number of dimensions increases from one to three, and that there is least differentiation for the feature of smallness. Where a slot contains two or more verbal roots, there is further subdifferentiation on the basis of

Verbal Concept	"Longish"	"Flattish"	"Roundish"	"Smallness"
		Features		
1. "throw to ground"	*wás-atá-*		*thúm-/póm-atá-*	
2. "pile on ground"	*ekwá-*	*kápa-, takú-*		
3. "twisted, bent"	*khunčú-*	*pheŋé-*		
4. "cut"	*kačú-, katú-, karú-, tuná-*			
5. "lie, rest on"	*ičá-*		*irá-, umbá-*	*eté-*
6. "carry"	*ičá-*		*kirá-, pará-, kúkú-, irá-*	*kunú-*
7. "thin"	*ȼhawá-*	*ȼhirí-*		
8. "fat, thick"	*tepá-*	*tayá-*	*poṛé-, toyó-*	
9. "pat out, flatten"		*ičú-*		

Table 22:2

features not discussed here (although some are dealt with in the text that immediately follows).

The verbal roots (see table 22:2) should be differentiated from the cases where the nature of the action or state expressed by the root necessarily calls for a subject or object of a certain shape. These inherently classificatory verbs are of several kinds in Tarascan (and have English analogues in some cases). One kind is the middle voice stems that call for longish subjects or objects: *aŋá-*, "erect," *čáŋa-*, "straighten up," *čotó-*, "lack prominence," *čukwi-* "protrude," and *čhumbí-*, "pointed." Of a different order is a second set that involves notions of poking, stabbing, or sticking into, and forms such as *má-h-pa-ta-ni*, "to stab in by a thrust," *theŋá-ni*, "to stab superficially," *čhoṛi-*, *čuṛú-*, *tešá-*, or *tišó-*, "poke or prod, without actually penetrating," and *phó-*, *sú-*, or *taṛá-*, "insert, stick into." The subjects or specified instruments co-occurring with roots of this kind are differentiated from each other in terms of bluntness of point, depth of penetration, and other features that need not be spelled out here. The critical fact is that speakers often define these inherently classificatory roots in terms of shape, as specified by numeral classifiers ("to insert *something long*"), thereby relating them to the other, covertly classificatory roots, discussed earlier, where a semantic feature that is entirely arbitrary requires that the subject or object be of a particular shape class.

The Suffixes of Locative Space

The meaning of sets such as the numeral classifiers and the classificatory verbs is partly a matter of their intersec-

tion with other, semantically connected ones. The third major part of this paper concerns the underlying semantics of a distinct set of morphemes, the thirty-two suffixes of locative space, and, more particularly, the subset of the so-called "body part suffixes."

The thirty-two suffixes of locative space occur in the third position of a complex word, after the root and certain adverbial suffixes, and before others of voice, type of motion, and inflection, nominalization, and so forth. In semantic terms, these morphemes signify the features of a location, often including its dimension and shape; in the most general terms, these are features of space, as contrasted with those of number, aspect, tense, and the like; the spatial features apparently lack temporal implications. Some of the thirty-two suffixes refer to body parts pure and simple, such as the hand and the "bottom." Others refer mainly or entirely to certain other kinds of non-corporeal location, often of a certain shape, as in the suffixes for "flat (artifactual) surface" and "flat (earthen) surface." Fourteen of these suffixes, however, are more complex semantically in that they combine corporeal with non-corporeal referents; also, they are defined by abstract features which yield sets of empirical referents that are potentially infinite in number. These suffixes of space are largely obligatory when discussing any one of their wide range of referents; one is forced to code the location of the action in terms of spatial features, many of which are shape-differentiated.

The spatial suffixes are numerous and frequent. They constitute a substantial fraction of the suffixes in the morphology and enter into construction types that range from frozen idioms to regular productive formations to idiosyncratic innovations. A total of 484 verbal roots can take at least one spatial suffix with a corporeal meaning, and about two hundred can take any one of the complex body part suffixes. The suffixes occur throughout many narrative tales, frequently in punch lines, since the theme or focus is often the body or its functions. Since they are employed to denote the shape of parts of observable objects, they pervade some kinds of discourse; some of these suffixes may occur dozens of times during one morning of pottery moulding or mule packing. In these terms, the spatial suffixes are prominent in *parole*.

The spatial suffixes are also structurally covert. While a Tarascan can discuss words, including numeral classifiers, it is just as true that he categorically never uses a spatial suffix in isolation—in fact, about half of them in their full phonemic form begin with phonemes and phoneme clusters that are not permitted initially. When asked to discuss a spatial as such, the Tarascan speaker is typically baffled, troubled, or puzzled, often remarking that "it isn't a word," or turning to the nearest-sounding verbal root. Nor does the Tarascan have any conscious idea of the subsets of these suffixes, with their concatenations of distinctive features. The units, relations, and rules of the spatial suffixes, despite their productivity, are almost totally covert and implicit. In this they contrast with the relatively explicit Tarascan knowledge of the numeral classifiers and the verbal roots. Let us now turn to an abbreviated review of the meanings of just one of these complex suffixes—of a suffix that is patently appropriate in an article addressed to linguists.

The frequent suffix; *mu,* and four semantically allied suffixes that also begin with *m,* such as *mi* and *marú,* are usually defined by the feature of "orifice" and the referent of "mouth." In fact, the primary referent (*Hauptbedeutung*) probably *is* mouth in a fairly general sense that may include the lips, as after the root for "kiss" (*putí-mu-ku-ni,* "to kiss another"), or the teeth, as in the stem for "to have missing or broken teeth" (*tokó-mu-ni*). The root for "taste well" (*áspi-*) can only take *mu,* and occasionally does so, with the combined meaning of "to taste well in the mouth" (*áspi-mu-ni*). Still within the corporeal domain, *mu* also names the female orifice in derisively used stems such as *čapé-mu-ni,* "to have wide-open genitals." One of the m-stems is used exclusively for the crotch or inner thighs, especially of a female, as in the mocking *čakwá-maru-ni,* "to be seated with the legs spread."

M-stems are also applied to the tongue, as in the *kwatá-pi-mu-ni,* "to be nimble-tongued, to possess the gift of gab"; as one might suspect, many other m-stems have a transferred reference to language or speaking, as in *phindé-mu-ni,* "to adjust verbally, to learn a new dialect." M-stems figure in the idiom of social and religious ritual, as in *sɨtá-maṛi-ku-ni,* "to suspect the gossip of another," or *šačó-mu-ku-ni,* "to take the Host." The root for "to enjoy" plus *mu* yields *ȼí-ȼí-mu-ni,* "to enjoy the food one is eating," whereas the same root plus *mi* yields *ȼí-ȼí-mi-ni,* "to sing happily," as of a bird at dawn.

Other m-stems involve metaphor-like transfers into a physical but non-corporeal sphere. The standard m-referent of "bud" appears in *ȼipá-mu-ni,* "to flower from the bud"—leaving one to infer either the image of a puckered mouth, or of the inner orifice of an opening bud. Similarly, one stage in the maize cycle is when the leaves grow into a twisting shape on top of the plant, over the upward-thrusting tassel; this is called *phará-mu-ni*.

Some of these non-corporeal referents are actually more routine than the corporeal ones. M-stems recur frequently to denote any kind of door or doorway area, as in *haćí-mu-ta-ni*, "to place (something) in the door." They also are used for the opening or orifice of any container such as the lip of a pot, in about fifteen stems that are highly frequent in ceramics contexts: *picí-mu-ku-ni* means "to smoothen the inside of the attached lip of a pot."

M suffixes enter into a large number of other stems involving the edge of a field, of clothing, of a town, or of a body of water. Some good examples of this are:

ha-mú-ku-ti-ni, "edge, especially of a town or field"
ú- or *kará-mu-ku-kata,* "embroidered," of cuffs, hems, and other borders and edges of clothing
thirí-ra-mu-ni, "to break away from the edge of a crowd" (San José dialect)
šaṛía-mu-ku-ni, "shore of river, lake, or other body of water"

M-stems also serve to denote various working edges, as in *réh-huká-mu-kwa*, the name for the tip of a wooden plow, to which one attaches the iron point (San José). *Waṛá-mu-ku-ni* means "to sharpen a knife blade," or similar working edge. Both "edge" and "orifice" seem to be implied by the numerous stems involving cuffs, hems, and the opening of containers, and both of these semantic features certainly are concatenated in "to toll a bell" (*wá-mu-ku-ni*, where the clapper hits *(wá-)* the edge of the bell's orifice).

Let us infer the general meaning of "sense" from these various referents.

Since no orifice actually lacks an edge, and since Tarascan m-stems also denote edges that are not orifices (as of a knife), the underlying general meaning is probably "edge, usually of an orifice or some similar curved or rounded shape." This definition covers referents as diverse as bud, bell, vagina, and blade of knife, is a reasonable characterization of the general meaning, and does enable one to predict the many hundreds of regular m-stems. Its vagueness may be a fact about this part of the semantic system.

Shape as a Feature Underlying Other Spatial Suffixes

Semantic analysis of a large sample of usage in the principal contexts or domains of life, as defined by the culture, has yielded shape-oriented definitions for the remaining twelve complex suffixes of locative space. The so-called "neck" suffix, for example, is applied to diverse classes of shapes, such as the section of a peg above where it enters a beam, and may be characterized abstractly as "juncture of a longish object." The "ear-shoulder" suffix also has diverse classes of referents, including the juncture area of a floor and wall, or of earth and sky—which lead ultimately to a general definition of "inner surfaces of an angle on a vertical axis." The "face-eye" suffix also comprises such referential concepts as cliff, shin, female groin, and kernelled cob beneath the husk—leading eventually to a definition of "interior surface, usually flattish." The conceptually complementary "back" suffix, in turn, comprises referential concepts such as roof, penis shaft, and the exterior of an unhusked corn cob—leading eventually to the distinc-

Complex	Relational	Simple
basicness, centrality (2)	intersection (2)	long (4)
orifice-edge	lateral	interior (3)
	narrowing	flat (2)
	projection	exterior (2)
	vertical angle	bottom (2)
	top, upper surface	

Table 22:3

tive features of "exterior surface, usually long, and always convex."[1]

In Table 22.3 there appear the thirteen principal semantic features, which I take to be geometrical primitives in the Tarascan code. Seven of them function as definers of more than one suffix, as is indicated by the numbers in parentheses. These features have been classified on purely semantic grounds into those that are highly complex, and those that obviously involve relations with two or more others, and third, those that are relatively simple.

First Conclusions

This concludes my preliminary analysis of the coding of the semantic category of shape in Tarascan. It has been shown that the numeral classifiers, classificatory verbs, and spatial suffixes share two main kinds of implications. In the first place, these symbols, many of them rather complex, have implications "downwards" to sets of finely differentiated referential categories, both perceptive and cognitive. The categories are "empirical" in the specific sense that, like the lip of a pot or a mouth, they relate to physical experience—above all, visual experience. The suffixes of locative space, in particular, suggest that the grammatical code compels or

encourages the speaker or hearer to verbalize and conceptualize in terms of a stream of abutting shapes and adjoining surfaces and lines that is reminiscent of Cézanne's dismembership of objects into their geometrical components, or, following Sapir, of "a tiny imagist poem." In the "upwards" direction these symbols imply a set of abstract geometrical features such as "projection" and "edge-orifice." These features belong to the geometry of formal principles in Tarascan, and also to the formal principles of the geometry in Tarascan semantic structure. In sum, the partly intersecting grammatical operators of classifier, root, and suffix, mediate between an abstract geometry of signification and a concrete map or geography of language-specific reference (Lévi-Strauss 1963:III, v). A future analysis in fuller scale may lead to an adequate description of the semantic geometry of this language.

Wider Implications

The partly obligatory semantic categories of shape discussed above are not limited to one genetically unaffiliated language of some 40,000 speakers in the mountains of southwestern Mexico. On the contrary, the perspective emerging from Tarascan can be greatly widened by a cursory review of some of the information available on other languages and of a few of the intensive studies dealing with shape categories, notably those by Berlin, Boas, Haas, Hoijer, and Malinowski.

To begin with, a wider import is suggested by the presence of similar patterns in other languages of North and South America. The Nambiquara dialects of Brazil have a number of grammatically obligatory nominal suffixes pertaining to shape, size, and physical condition, and including the features of "wavy, flexible" (e.g., rope, trail), "container" (ear, pot, rectum, etc.), "flat" (earth, sky, and the like), "orifice" (mouth, vagina, door), and "round, long/seedlike, generative" (as illustrated by fruit, navel, heart, star, head, breast, year, penis, seed). The parallels with Tarascan are obvious, as are a number of striking differences, such as the concatenation of "round" and "long" into one image. Other Nambiquara suffixes occurring in this position include "water," "mother/big/female," "child/small," "doughy/powdery," and "open/spreading" (P. David Price, personal communication). Many other examples could be cited from other indigenous languages of this continent.

The Tzeltal Indian language of southeastern Mexico, has about 528 numeral classifiers, which fall into eighty "semantic domains" defined by a much larger number of geometrical and other features as in "balls of soft, pliable flexible materials" and "cylindrical shaped solid objects," and so forth (Berlin 1968).

For the Kwakiutl of the Pacific Northwest, Boas' highly original monograph (1911:475–84) provided a full listing of twenty-eight suffixes called "parts of space as body limitations," and three others for "special organs" (499); interestingly enough, it is the "eye" suffix which includes the referents of "door" and "round opening like an eye," whereas the "mouth" suffix comprises the expectable oral and verbal meanings, "narrow and outward" openings, and the not-so-expectable but logical one of "wife" (!). Finally, the four main Kwakiutl suffixes for what Boas calls "limitations of form" (484) are "long, flat, round," and "human"—identical to the four major Tarascan features as defined above.

Another Amerind language, Takelma, was described by Sapir (1922:72–86) as containing a substantial paradigm of seventeen body part suffixes that "have, besides their literal, also a more formal, local value" (e.g., di^e-, "anus, in the rear"). These suffixes are interpreted by Sapir as semantically complementary and coordinate to the sixteen "purely local" prefixes (e.g., han-, "across, through"). Despite the superficiality of his semantics at this point, Sapir's skeleton of forms and glosses does give glimmerings of a latent and more interesting world of shapes; for example, his evidence on the "mouth" suffix (da-) comprises not only the familiar oral and verbal referents, but also the outlet of a stream, as indicated by his gloss of one word: "(creek) going into (river) (literally, in-mouth-being)."

Many American Indian languages show types of obligatory co-variation between verbal roots and nominal expressions, on the basis of semantic features of number, texture, and shape; unlike the covert categories of Tarascan, these classificatory verbs are marked by formal particles. One recent areal study of the Athapascan languages has demonstrated the ubiquity of such classificatory verbs throughout the family, and a Pan-Athapascan inventory of eight shared categories: "round, long, living, container, fabriclike, bulky mass, ropelike, mudlike" (Davison et al. 1963:40). Other studies attest the presence of similar features in Eyak and Tlingit (Krauss 1968). Hoijer's pioneer article on classificatory verbs revealed that the Navaho language has thirteen such categories, including (1) "single, round, solid," (2) "long, slender, rigid," (3) "zoological," (4) "fabriclike (i.e., flat)," (5) "parallel, long, rigid."[2] Probably the most differentiated of these Nadéné systems is Haida, for which Swanton (1911:34) lists thirty-six classes, "most of which refer to the physical shape of objects, apparently largely predictable, and in some cases very specialized" (Krauss 1968:203). Mary Haas has discussed the classifiers in genetically unaffiliated languages of California and concluded that the underlying feature is shape; in particular, she pointed out that the Yurok (Algon-Ritwan) classifiers and the Hupa (Athapascan) classificatory verbs share the following basic features: sticklike, round, ropelike, and human (in addition, there is a Yurok classifier for "animals"). Clearly then, obligatory processes for coding shape are very widespread in native America, although no language I have discovered equals Tarascan in combining numeral classifiers, classificatory verbs, and body part suffixes. Tarascan concepts of shape not only strike us as a "stylistic discovery," but force us to consider their grammatical functioning.

Similar processes for the coding of shape are common if by no means ubiquitous in the Old World. The Kiriwina language of the Trobriand Islands, made famous through the ethnographic analyses of Bronislaw Malinowski, contains a set of obligatory "classificatory particles" which serve to indicate "the class of object numbered, pointed at, or qualified." The major categories of this system are: (1) human being, (2) female human and animal, (3) trees and plants, wooden things, and long objects, (4) round, bulky objects, stones, and abstract nouns, and (5) leaves, fibers, and other flat or thin objects (Malinowski 1920; 1935:33–36). The reader will surely have noted the striking resemblance of these categories to those of Kwakiutl and Tarascan—although Malinowski failed to describe properly the relation of the abstract shape classes to other, more specific categories such as wood, stone, and fiber. The major contrast of the shape concepts, furthermore, is not with "rational," but with a zoological class which in turn breaks down into human versus female and animal. Malinowski concludes about the classificatory particles, "I have enlarged on this subject because it is unquestionably the most exotic feature of the Trobriand language" (1935:36).

The Trobriand particles are "exotic" only from the point of view of Indo-European and other languages where shape is relatively peripheral or unimportant among the obligatory, overt morpho-syntactic categories. In the first place, they obtain in other parts of Oceania. Second, the numerous dialects of Chinese have elaborate systems of classifiers, many of which involve shape. Spoken Mandarin shows twenty-one such classifiers, involving shapes such as "round, top, sheet-like, opening," and "tube-like" (Chao 1968a:590–93). The Mandarin classifiers are part of a larger taxonomic set of seven major dimensions that also includes group measures, container measures, and temporary measures (the latter including body parts such as the hand). A highly developed system obtains in Thai (Haas 1942).

The Burmese inventory of "about 200" classifiers has been analyzed by Burling into fourteen "semantic groups," of which the second, concerning "dimension in time or space," includes (1) "long, slender objects," (2) "thin, flat objects," (3) "very thin and flat objects," (4) "spherical or cubical objects," (5) "objects which come in symmetrical pairs," (6) "holes," (7) "loop-shaped objects," and (8) "long, slender living, or recently living things, which are vertical or perpendicular to the object to which they are attached" (1965:251). Classifiers for events which occur in time and others for objects occurring in space are also found. Furthermore, the twelve classifiers of time and space include some of the most frequently used, and clearly imply a concern with the basic trichotomy of long, flat, and round, or one-, two-, and three-dimensional.

Let us conclude this cursory review with Africa. In all African languages there are probably the usual body part words with routinized, metaphor-like extensions on the basis of shape. Perhaps the most interesting data—which ties back to the earlier Tarascan example—comes from Luo, one of the Nilotic languages. Some of the so-called prefixing forms of Luo are almost isomorphic semantically with their suffixal counterparts in Tarascan. One Luo prefixing form, for example, lumps together not only "mouth" and associated oral concepts such as language, but also (1) the opening of any container, and the outer surfaces of the lip of any container, and (2) the edge and outer rim surface of any flat object, such as a plateau, and (3) the edge of a town, and (4) the shoreland of a lake or other body of water, and finally (5), the gateway of a homestead, the doorway of a house, and also the ground extending outwards and the wall extending backwards from such entries.[3]

The incomplete distributional and taxonomic facts can now be summarized in a paradigm, as follows (counting only overt signaling in general, but overt or covert categorization in Tarascan):

Morphological Pattern	Language or Language Family
1. numeral classifier	Kiriwina, Chinese, Mayan, Tarascan
2. classificatory verbs	Nadéné, Penutian, Mayan, Tarascan
3. locative shape affixes	Kwakiutl, Takelma, Tarascan

In more general terms, I think that the foregoing discussion has demonstrated that obligatory categories of shape are salient in some grammars and probably operative to some extent in all. Several of the concepts of shape treated above should certainly figure in any general theory of grammatical semantics, and these include: (1) the complex concept of orifice-(curved) edge, (2) the trichotomy of "long, flat, and round," or, as has been explicated above, the relative salience of one, two, and three dimensions, and (3) the overall shape of the zoological body, particularly the human body, as an abstract model of anatomical relations (as contrasted with taxonomic or paradigmatic ones) that can be mapped onto other corpora (cf. Basso 1967). More intensive studies and a wider typological base would lead to greater insight into these probabilities. It has been suggested that shape ranks with time, aspect, and the like as one of the fundamental ideas in grammar and, by implication, in the mind of the speakers of natural language. Both sensuous perceptual categories of shape and covert geometrical features are part of the human experience that is immanent in the linguistic code.

Notes

1. I basically sympathize with Jakobson (e.g., 1936) in the sense that a determined and systematic search for conjunctive, intensional, significational definitions *(Gesamtbedeutungen)* almost inevitably leads to insights into semantic features, semantic structures, and so forth.

2. The thirteen Navajo categories generally have parallels in Tarascan, although they are not all coded the same way. The glaring exceptions would be Navajo V, "rigid container and its contents," although it resembles the Tarascan spatial suffix for "cavity" *(n)*, which is used for the interior of canoes, houses, tree trunks, thoraces, and so forth.

3. The standard references for Luo, such as Tucker or Bryan, contain little or no information on the forms cited. The data above comes via a personal communication from William Sytek, a social anthropologist with a good command of the language. The Bantu languages, of course, employ obligatory prefixes to signal the gender of nominals, and of adjectives and verbs in construction with them; these gender categories, however, involve categories of "inanimate, non-human, abstract, common," and the like, and do not appear to be defined in terms of shape.

TWENTY-THREE

The Semantics of Money-Uses

Karl Polanyi

We have noted several times in this book that the tendency to try to understand the actions of members of other cultures as if they were actions of members of our own creates problems for understanding and analysis. One of the areas where this problem is most clearly evident—and where the use of Western categories and concepts to describe non-Western peoples' actions is most controversial—is in the study of primitive or non-capitalist economics. This is because, in classical economics, the economy is considered to be the primary focus of rational optimization of material ends, regulated by basic attributes of human nature (the desire to maximize individual consumption) and the material (ecological) characteristics of the environment.

Karl Polanyi was an economic historian who, in the 1940s and '50s, worked with a number of anthropologists at Columbia University. Polanyi's argument was that the economy was an "instituted process"—that is, it was a social form. He and his co-workers and students found a number of instances of economies in which the principles of individual (or even group) maximization were not in effect, and they isolated a number of other forms which economies could take. The classic statement of their position is *Trade and Market in the Early Empires* (Polanyi et al. 1957). The position is controversial: many economic anthropologists feel that analytic categories derived from market-type economies can be made to apply to other sorts of economies—this is the "formalist" position, in contrast to Polanyi's "substantivism"; Marxists generally criticize Polanyi for his exclusive concentration on systems of exchange and his tendency to ignore production, although they accept Polanyi's work to a large degree.

BECAUSE OF THE EXCHANGE-USE of money under our market organization of economic life we are apt to think of money in too narrow terms. No object is money per se, and any object in an appropriate field can function as money. In truth, money is a system of symbols similar to language, writing, or weights and measures. These differ from one another mainly in the purpose served, the actual symbols employed, and the degree to which they display a single unified purpose.

Pseudo-Philosophies of Money

Money is an incompletely unified system, a search for its single purpose a blind alley. This accounts for the many,

Reprinted by permission of H. M. McLuhan, Centre for Culture and Technology, University of Toronto, from *Explorations*, October 1957.

unavailing attempts at determining the "nature and essence" of money. We must be content with listing the purposes to which the quantifiable objects actually called money are put. This is achieved by pointing to the *situation* in which we operate those objects and with what effect. We will find them called money, when used in any one of the following ways: for payment; as a standard; as a means of indirect exchange. The human situation is, of course, given independently of the notion of money, just as the handling of the objects is described in operational terms independently of that notion. Payment occurs in a situation of obligation, and a handing over of the objects has the effect of wiping out the obligation. Money used as a standard is a quantitative tag attached to units of goods of different kinds, either for the purpose of barter with the effect that, by adding up the numerals, we can readily equalize the two sides in the exchange, or for budgeting and balancing stores of different staples, thus producing staple finance. Finally, there is the exchange use of such objects, that is, acquiring them in order to acquire other objects through a further act of exchange. The objects employed in direct exchange thereby gain the character of money. They become symbols through their participation in a definite human situation.

A few sidelines are here avoided. First: The distinction between tokens and what they "represent" is ignored. Either function as money objects and form part of the symbolic system. No difference is therefore made between barley money, gold money or paper money. To confuse the basic problem of money with that of token money is a source of frequent misunderstandings.

Tokens as such are no novelty—fiction and abstraction belong to the original endowment of man. In Herodotus' well-known story of compulsory temple prostitution in Babylonia, he records this operational detail: "The silver coin may be of any size; it cannot be refused for that is forbidden by the law, since, once thrown, it is sacred." Nor are mere tokens unknown in the primitive societies of our ethnographers. Some peoples of the Congo employ "simply as a token" straw mats or grass cloth originally of square shape, but eventually reduced to a tangle of hay, "practically of no value at all." Strips of blue cloth of standard width that had become in time useless rags were current as token money in parts of the Western Sudan. Since paper money came to the fore, however, scholars felt induced to focus on the tokens instead of on the massive physical objects themselves. This modernizing fashion carried the day. The latest outstanding work of an ethnographer, Mrs. Quiggin (1949), takes the token to be the true money and accordingly dubs the actual money objects that it describes exhaustively, "money substitutes."

Historians of antiquity have proved hardly less susceptible to modernizing on the matter of money. Since third millennium Babylonia possessed no paper money, the metals were regarded by historians as the orthodox money material. Actually, all payments were made in barley. Bruno Meissner, the Assyriologist, put this in the terms "Money was primarily replaced by grain." His colleague Lutz thought that the scarcity of silver "necessitated the use of a substitute. Thus grain often took the place of metals." Throughout, token money ranks as true money, since it is the most abstract and the least useful; next comes gold and silver, as substitutes; in their absence, even grain will do. This is a consistent reversal of the sequence in which the physical money objects are primary empirical evidence. Yet the existence of tokens should cause no complications; it is a matter of course in a monetary system. If paper money viewed as a token, "symbolizes" coins, then in our terms it symbolizes that which is already a symbol, namely, money. Symbols do not merely "represent" something. They are material, oral, visual, or purely imaginary signs that form part of the definite situation in which they participate; thus they acquire meaning.

Second, a similar disregard of the semantics of economic theory is forced upon us in the choice of terms when referring to the various money-uses. Payment, standard, and means of exchange are distinctions originally developed by classical economists. Hence the understandable belief of some anthropologists that their application to primitive money implies an economistic bias. The reverse would be truer. Actually, modern economics does not rely for its monetary theories on such distinctions at all. Archaic society, on the other hand, shows an institutional setting where the use of quantifiable objects typically occurs in precisely those three ways.

All-Purpose and Special-Purpose Money

From a formal angle, modern money, in contrast to primitive money, offers a striking resemblance to both language and writing. They all possess a uniform grammar. All three are organized in an elaborate code of rules concerning the correct way of employing the symbols— and general rules applicable to all the symbols. Archaic society did not know "all-purpose" money. Various money-uses may be supplied here by different money objects. Consequently, there is no grammar with which all money-uses must comply. No one kind of object deserves the distinctive name of money; rather the term applies to a small group of objects, each of which may serve as money in a different way. While in modern society the money employed as a means of exchange is endowed with the capacity of performing all the other functions as well, in early society the position is rather the reverse. One encounters slaves or horses or cattle used as a standard when judging of prestige conveying wealth, or anyway of large amounts, while cowrie shells are solely employed for small amounts. (Eventually, the unit slave or horse may stand for a conventional value representing a mere unit of account, real slaves and horses being actually sold at varying prices.) We might also find that while real slaves are a means of payment of tribute to a foreign overlord, cowrie shells function as a domestic means of payment or even as a medium of exchange. This may not exclude the use of precious metals for hoarding wealth, while such metals may not otherwise serve as money except perhaps as a standard, and in exchange for imports. Where the market habit is fairly widespread money might, moreover, serve as a means of exchange to which end several trade goods might be in use, which otherwise are not employed as money at all. Numerous combinations of these variants occur. No *one* rule is universally valid, except for the very general, but no less significant, rule that money-uses are distributed between a multiplicity of different objects.

No such fragmentation in the use of sounds is known in any language. In speech all articulate oral sounds, in script all letters of the alphabet are eligible for use in all types of words, while archaic money in extreme cases employs one kind of object as means of payment, another as a standard of value, a third for storing wealth, and a fourth for exchange purposes—like a language where verbs consisted of one group of letters, nouns of another, adjectives of a third, and adverbs of yet a fourth.

Moreover, in primitive society [commercial] exchange is not the fundamental money-use. If any one be more "basic" than another it is rather the use for [non-commercial] payment or standard. These are common even where the exchange-use of money is not practiced. Accordingly, while in modern society the unification of the various uses of money happened on the basis of its exchange-use, in early communities we find the different money-uses institutionalized separately from one another. Insofar as there is interdependence between them, we find use for payment or as a standard or for storing wealth, having precedence over use for exchange. Thus nineteenth-century money, employing exchange symbols for various other uses, appears as an almost complete parallel to language and writing with its all-purpose sounds and signs. But to some extent the analogy holds also for primitive and archaic money, which differs from its modern counterpart only in the lesser degree to which the systems are unified. Since the second quarter of the twentieth century,

however, starting with Nazi Germany, "modern" money begins to show a definite tendency toward a reverting to disunification. Half a dozen "marks" were current under Hitler and each of them restricted to some special purpose or other.

Exchange-Money

"Money is a means of exchange." This presumption belongs among the most powerful in the field of modern thought. Its authority may be gauged by the axiomatic manner in which it was formulated to cover the whole course of human history and even extended by anthropologists to primitive society. It is forcefully expressed in the following quotation: "In any economic system, however primitive, an article can only be regarded as true money," Professor Raymond Firth declares, "when it acts as a definite and common medium of exchange, as a convenient stepping stone in obtaining one type of goods for another. However, in so doing, it serves as a measure of value, allowing the worth of all other articles to be expressed in terms of itself. Again, it is a standard of value, with reference to past or future payments, while as a store of value it allows wealth to be condensed and held in reserve." (1929)

According to this still current view, the exchange-use to which money can be put is its essential criterion, not only in modern, but also in primitive society. Even under primitive conditions the various money-uses are asserted to be inseparable. Only quantifiable objects serving as means of exchange can, therefore, be regarded as money. Their functioning as means of payment, as standard of value, or as means of hoarding wealth, is not decisive for their character as money, unless it implies their use as media of exchange. For it is this use that logically unifies the system, since it allows a consistent linking up of the various functions of money. Without it there cannot be true money. Such a modernizing approach to the problem, we submit, is largely responsible for the obscurity in which the characteristics of primitive money still abide.

The Payment-Use of Money

Payment is the discharge of an obligation through the handing-over of quantifiable objects, which then function as money. The connectedness of payment with money and of obligations with economic transactions appears to the modern mind self-evident. Yet the quantification, which we associate with payment, operated already at a time when the obligations discharged were quite unconnected with economic transactions. The story starts with the propinquity of payment and punishment on the one hand, obligation and guilt on the other. No unilineal development should be inferred, however. Rather, obligations may have origins different from guilt and crime, such as wooing and marriage; punishment may spring from other than sacral sources, such as prestige and precedence; eventual payment, then, with its quantitative connotation, may include operational elements not entailed in punishment as such.

It is only broadly true that civil law followed on penal law, penal law on sacral law. Payment was due alike from the guilty, the defiled, the impure, the weak and the lowly; it was owed to the gods and their priests, the honored, the pure, and the strong. Punishment, accordingly, aimed at diminution in power, sanctity, prestige, status, or wealth of the payer, not stopping at his physical destruction.

Pre-legal obligations mostly spring from custom and give rise to an offense only in case of default. Even so the restoring of the balance need not involve payment. Obligations are, as a rule, specific, and their fulfilment is a qualitative affair, thus lacking an essential of payment—its quantitative character. Infringement of sacral and social obligations, whether toward god, tribe, kin, totem, village, age-group, caste, or guild, is repaired not through payment but by action of the right *quality*. Wooing, marrying, avoiding, dancing, singing, dressing, feasting, lamenting, lacerating, or even killing oneself may occur in discharge of an obligation, but they are not for that reason payments.

The specific characteristic in the payment-use of money is quantification. Punishment approximates payment when the process of riddance of guilt is numerable, as when lashes of the whip, turns of the praying mill, or days of fasting dispose of the offense. But though it has now become an "obligation to pay," the offense is atoned for not by depriving one's self of quantifiable objects, but primarily by a loss of personal qualitative values or sacral and social status.

The payment-use of money links up with the economy when the units discharged by the person under obligation happen to be physical objects such as sacrificial animals, slaves, ornamental shells, or measures of food stuffs. The obligations may still be predominantly non-transactional, such as paying a fine, composition,* tax, tribute, making gifts and counter-gifts, honoring the gods, ancestors, or the dead. There is now, however, a significant difference. For the payee does gain what the payer loses—the effect of the operation fits the legal concept of payment.

The ultimate intent of the obligation to pay may still be the diminution in power and status of the payer. In archaic society an exorbitant fine did not only bankrupt but politically degraded the victim. For a long time power and status in this way retained their precedence over economic possessions as such. The political and social importance of accumulated wealth under these conditions lay in the rich man's capacity of making a big payment without undermining his status. (This is the condition of affairs in archaic democracies where political confiscation takes the form of exorbitant fines.) Treasure gains great political importance, as witness Thucydides' memorable passages in the Archeology. Wealth is here directly transmuted into power. It is a self-maintaining institution. Because the rich man is powerful and honored he receives payments: gifts and dues are showered upon him without his having to use power to torture and kill. Yet his wealth, used as a fund for gifts, would procure him a sufficiency of power to do so.

Once money as a means of exchange is established in society, the practice of payment spreads far and wide. For with the introduction of markets as the physical locus of exchange a new type of obligation comes into prominence as the legal residue of transactions. Payment appears as the counterpart of some

*In this context, composition means payment as part of an agreement for cessation of hostilities. EDITORS' NOTE

material advantage gained in the transaction. Formerly a man was made to pay taxes, rent, fines, or blood-money. Now he pays for the goods he bought. Money is now means of payment *because* it is means of exchange. The notion of an independent origin of payment fades, and the millennia in which it sprang not from economic transactions, but directly from religious, social, or political obligations, are forgotten.

Hoarding or Storage-Use of Money

A subordinate money-use—storing of wealth—has its origin largely in the need for payments. Payment is not primarily an economic phenomenon. Neither is wealth. In early society it consisted largely of treasure, which is again rather a social than a subsistence category. The subsistence connotation of wealth (as of payment) derives from the frequency with which wealth is accumulated in the form of cattle, slaves, and non-perishable goods of common consumption. Both that which feeds the store of wealth and that which is disbursed from it gains then a subsistence significance. Only within limits, however, since payments are still made, as a rule, for non-transactional reasons. This is true both of the rich who own the store of wealth, and the subjects who fill the store by their payments. He who owns wealth is thereby enabled to pay fines, composition, taxes, etc., for sacral, political, and social ends. The payments, which he receives from his subjects, high or low, are paid to him as taxes, rents, gifts, etc., not for transactional but for social and political reasons ranging from pure gratitude for protection or admiration of superior endowment, to stark fear of enslavement and death. This, again, is not to deny that once exchange-money is present money will readily lend itself as a store of wealth. But, as in the case of payment, the condition is the previous establishment of quantifiable objects as media of exchange.

Use of Money as a Standard

Money as a standard of value seems more closely linked with the exchange use of money than is either payment or hoarding. For barter and storage of staples are the two very different sources from which the need for a standard springs. At first sight the two have little in common. The first is akin to transaction, the other to administration and disposal. Yet neither can be effectively carried out in the absence of some standard. For how otherwise than with the help of computation could, for instance, a piece of land be bartered against an assortment consisting of a chariot, horse-harness, asses, ass-harness, oxen, oil, clothes and other minor items? In the absence of a means of exchange the account in a well-known case of barter in ancient Babylonia shaped up like this. The land was valued at 816 shekels of silver, while the articles given in exchange were valued in shekels of silver as follows: chariot 100, 6 horse-harnesses 300, an ass 130, ass-harness 50, and ox 30, the rest were distributed over the smaller items.

The same principle applied, in the absence of exchange, to the administration of vast palace and temple stores (staple finance). Their keeper handled subsistence goods under conditions which, from more than one angle, required a gauging of the relative importance of these goods. Hence the famed rule of accountancy of "one unit of silver = one unit of barley" on the stele of Manistusu as well as at the head of the Laws of Eshnunna.

Research data reveal that the exchange-use of money cannot have given rise to the other money-uses. On the contrary, the payment, storage, and accountancy uses of money had their separate origins and were institutionalized independently of one another.

Elite Circulation and Staple Finance

It seems almost self-contradictory to expect that one could pay with money with which one cannot buy. Yet that precisely is implied in the assertion that money was not used as a medium of exchange and still was used as a means of payment. Two institutions of early society offer a partial explanation: treasure and staple finance.

Treasure, as we saw, should be distinguished from other forms of stored wealth. The difference lies mainly in its relation to subsistence. In the proper sense of the term, treasure is formed of prestige goods, including "valuables" and ceremonial objects, the mere possession of which endows the holder with social weight, power, and influence. It is, then, a peculiarity of treasure that both the giving and the receiving enhances prestige; it largely circulates for the sake of the turnover, which is its proper use. Even when food is "treasured" it is liable to pass backward and forward between the parties, however absurd this might appear from the subsistence point of view. But food rarely functions as treasure, for interesting food, like slaughtered pigs, does not keep, and that which keeps, such as barley or oil, is not exciting. The precious metals, on the other hand, which are almost universally valued as treasure, cannot readily be exchanged for subsistence, since apart from exceptionally auriferous regions such as the Gold Coast or Lydia, display of gold by the common people is opprobrious.

Nevertheless, treasure, like other sources of power, may be of great economic importance, since gods, kings, and chiefs can be made to put the services of their dependents at the disposal of the giver, thus indirectly securing for him food, raw materials, and labor services, on a large scale. Ultimately, this power of indirect disposal, which may comprise the important power of taxation, arises, of course, from the enhanced influence exerted by the recipient of treasure over his tribe or people.

All this holds good, whether the treasure consists of quantifiable units or not. If it does, the handling of treasure may give rise to something in the nature of finance. In archaic Greece, for instance, he who owned treasure employed it to gain the favor of gods and chiefs or other politically influential agents, by forming the gold and silver into conventionally acceptable gifts, such as tripods or bowls. But this did not make tripods into money, for only by an artificial construction could such an honorific gift-use be subsumed under either payment or exchange. Transactions of treasure finance were restricted to the narrow circle of the gods and chiefs. While some things could be paid for with treasure, very many more could not be bought with it.

Storage of wealth as an institution of the subsistence economy starts from the collecting and stacking of *staples*. While treasure and treasure finance do not, as a rule, belong to the subsistence economy, the storing of staples represents an accumulation of subsistence goods involving, as a rule, their use as a means of payment. For once staples are stored on a large scale by temple, palace, or manor, this must be accompanied by such a use. Thus treasure-finance is replaced by staple-finance.

Most archaic societies possess an organization of staple-finance of some kind or other. It was in the framework of the planned transfer and investment of staples stored on a gigantic scale that the accounting devices were first developed, which characterized the redistributive economies of the ancient empires over long periods of time. For only well after the introduction of coined money in Greece some six centuries before our era, did money-finance begin to supersede staple-finance in these empires, especially in the Roman Republic. Nevertheless, even later, Ptolemaic Egypt continued in the traditions of staple-finance, which it raised to unparalleled levels of efficiency.

Redistribution as a form of integration often involves under primitive conditions the storage of goods at a center, whence they are distributed and fall out of circulation. Goods passed on as payment to the center are passed out from there and are consumed. They provide subsistence for army, bureaucracy and labor force, whether paid out in wages, in soldiers' pay or in other forms. The personnel of the temples consumes a large part of the payments made to the temple in kind. The raw materials are required for the equipment of the army, for public works and government exports; wool and cloth are exported too; barley, oil, wine, dates, garlic, and so on, are distributed and consumed. Thus the means of payment are destroyed. Maybe some of them are eventually bartered privately by their recipients. To that extent a "secondary circulation" is started, which might even become the mainspring of local markets, without disrupting the redistributive economy. Actually, no evidence of the existence of such markets has yet turned up. The relevance of treasure and staple to the question of money-uses is therefore that they explain the functioning of the various money-uses in the absence of the market system.

Treasure goods, which happen to be quantifiable, may be used for payment. Yet such elite goods are not normally exchanged and cannot be used for purchase except in the sacral and foreign policy spheres. The much larger sector of payments concerns, of course, subsistence goods. Such objects, when used for the discharge of obligations, i.e., for payment, are stored at the center whence they revert through redistributive payment and are consumed.

Treasure and staples, between them, offer therefore broadly the answer to the institutional problem set by the conditions of early society, where means of payment may be independent of the exchange use of money. The absence of money as a means of exchange in the irrigational empires helped to develop a kind of banking enterprise—actually large estate managements practicing staple finance—in order to facilitate transfer and clearing in kind. It might be added that similar methods were employed by the administrations of the larger temples. Thus clearing, book-transfer and non-transferable checks were first developed, not as expedients in a money economy, but on the contrary, as administrative devices designed to make barter more effective and therefore the developing of market methods unnecessary.

Babylonia and Dahomey

In regard to its monetary organization, Hammurabi's Babylonia, in spite of its complex economic administration and elaborate operational practices, was typically "primitive," for the principle of differentiation of money-objects was firmly established. With many important reservations as to detail, the following broad generalization can be made: rents, wages, and taxes were paid in barley, while the standard of value was universally silver. The total system was governed by the rule of accountancy, unshakably grounded on the equation "1 *shekel* of silver = 1 *gur* of barley." In case of a permanent improvement in the average yield of the land (as would be caused by large-scale irrigational works), the barley content of the *gur* was raised by solemn proclamation. The general use of silver as money of account facilitated barter enormously; the equally general employment of barley as a means of domestic payment made the storage system possible on which the redistributive economy of the country rested.

It appears that all the important staples functioned to some extent as means of exchange, none of them being permitted to attain the status of "money" (as opposed to goods). This may also be put in the following terms: an elaborate system of barter was practiced, which was based on the function of silver as money of account; the use of barley as means of payment; and the simultaneous employment of a number of staples such as oil, wool, dates, bricks, etc. as means of exchange. Amongst the latter should be counted barley and silver, care being taken to prevent these or any other staple developing into a "preferred means of exchange," or, as we should say, money. These safeguards included the avoidance of coined money, the hoarding of precious metals in palace and temple treasury, and, more effective than all, strict legal provisions as to the documentation of transactions. The outstanding provision appears to have been the restriction of formal "sale-purchase" transactions to *specific* goods such as a plot of land, a house, heads of cattle, individual slaves, a boat—all of them specimens which might be designated by a name. In regard to staples or fungible goods, such as barley, oil, wool, or dates, no documentation of exchange against each other is in evidence during the millennia of cuneiform civilization.

On a very much smaller scale the eighteenth-century Negro kingdom of Dahomey shows monetary conditions not so dissimilar to those of Babylonia. Cowries were used as domestic currency in all four uses, but as a standard of value they were supplemented by slaves, which served as money of account for larger amounts. Accordingly, the wealth of rich persons, the customs payments of foreign ships to the king, tribute to foreign sovereigns, were reckoned (but only in this last instance, paid) in slaves. These did not, however, here serve as a means of exchange, as in some Hausa regions. In this latter use cowrie was supplemented by gold dust,

which was especially employed in ports of trade and other foreign contacts. As to storage of wealth, not only cowrie but also slaves were used. It is reminiscent of Babylonia that the rule of accountancy governing the system involved equation between slaves and cowrie, which it seems, was a matter of public proclamation; so was the export price of slaves, which was reckoned in ounces of gold dust.

Appendix: Notes on Primitive Money*

I. General Propositions on Trade, Money, and Markets

(1) Trade and money originate separately and independently of markets. They do not arise, as has been thought, from individual barter and exchange. Trade and money are much more widely spread institutions than markets. The various forms of trade and the different money-uses should be regarded, therefore, independently of markets and market elements. Much of economic history consists precisely in the linking up of trade and money-uses with market elements, thus leading to market-trade and exchange-money. All this may be subsumed under the thesis of the *independent origins of trade and money from markets*.

(2) The development of trade, money, and markets follows different lines according to whether these institutions

---

*This appendix was compiled by George Dalton, editor of Polanyi's papers, from unpublished memoranda Polanyi wrote between 1947 and 1950 and distributed as mimeographed notes to his students in courses in economic history at Columbia University. The unpublished material is printed by permission of Ilona Polanyi and Kari Polanyi Levitt. EDITORS' NOTE

are primarily external or internal to the community. One of the characteristics of the nineteenth-century type of economy [laissez-faire capitalism] was the almost complete obliteration of this distinction. We may call this the thesis of the *separate origins of external and internal trade, money, and markets.*

(3) We are familiar with the manner in which trade, money uses and market elements are integrated under a market system. Their manner of integration, however, in the absence of a dominant market system is obscure. It is submitted that it is explained through the part played in the process by non-economic institutions, more especially by the reciprocating and redistributive elements comprised in (a) basic social organization and (b) political administration. The latter has a predominant role in archaic society. This may be referred to as the thesis of the *integrative role of reciprocity and redistribution in non-market societies.*

II. Propositions in Regard to Primitive Money

Money Uses

(1) In modern society the distinction between the various money uses is of hardly more than a historical or theoretical, but rarely of practical interest. The reason is that modern money, at least up to recently, was all-purpose money—i.e., the medium of exchange was also employed for the other money uses. Primitive money, on the contrary, is special-purpose money—i.e., different objects are, as a rule, employed in different money uses. The various money uses are, therefore, institutionalized separately and, mostly, independently from one another. Consequently, the distinction between the various money uses is here of utmost practical importance for the understanding of the money use of quantifiable objects.

(2) The definition of primitive money is derived from its uses. The money uses are payment, standard, hoarding, and exchange. Money is defined as quantifiable objects employed for any of the above uses.

(3) Thus the emphasis shifts to the definition of the various money uses. They should contain (a) the sociological situation in which the use arises and (b) the operation performed with the objects in that situation.

(a) Payment is the discharging of obligations through the handing over of quantifiable objects or, in the case of "ideal units," of some definite manipulation of debt accounts. The "sociological situation" refers here not to one single use but to a number of them, for only in regard to different obligations can we speak of "payment" in the distinctive sense of the term, i.e., as involving a money use. If only one type of obligation is involved, its discharge through the handing over of quantifiable objects may well be a non-monetary operation, as when an obligation is discharged "in kind."

(b) Standard, or Accounting, use of money is the equating of amounts of different goods either for the purposes of barter or in any other situation involving the need for accountancy. The sociological situation is that of bartering, or of administrative management of quantifiable objects, e.g., staples. The "operation" consists in attaching numerical values to the various objects so that their summations may be eventually equated.

(c) Hoarding is the accumulation of

quantifiable objects for future disposal or simply to hold as treasure. The sociological situation is one of the numerous ones in which persons prefer not to consume or otherwise dispose of quantifiable objects, but to defer their use for the future, unless they altogether prefer the advantages of sheer possession, especially the power, prestige, and influence accruing from it. The operation involved consists in keeping, storing, and conserving the objects so that their possession and, preferably, ostentatious display should redound to the credit of the owner and all those whom he may represent.

(d) Exchange use of money is the use of quantifiable objects for indirect exchange. The sociological situation is that of the possession of some objects together with the desire for other objects. The operation consists of acquiring units of quantifiable objects through direct exchange in order to acquire other objects through another act of exchange. It may be, however, that the money objects are possessed, and the indirect exchange is designed to net an increased amount of such objects.

The Definitions of Money in Primitive Economics, Cultural Anthropology, and Economic Analysis

(1) This definition of money is most suited to the purpose of primitive economics. It refers to quantifiable (physical) objects used for definite purposes, these latter being, again, defined with the help of sociological situations and operations performed in them. This definition should, however, be supplemented (a) in regard to money objects, by ideal units, and (b) in regard to money uses, by operational devices. Ideal units are non-physical objects employed in money uses, as for payment or standard, in which case the operation does not primarily involve physical objects, but is rather the manipulation of debt accounts. Operational devices, i.e., solutions primarily achieved through manipulation of objects, are not limited to money uses. Objects employed in some money use, however, may be also employed for some device, as for arithmetical, statistical, taxation, administrative, or other purposes connected with economic life. Examples: (i) Double cowrie numeration, employed for automatic regulation of retail span. Cf. Mage, Baillaud, Binger, Bovill, etc. (ii) The relating of gold dust, cowrie, and trade-good prices. Gold dust is measured by weight with the help of seeds of grain; cowrie is counted by tale, the current unit containing a definite round number of cowrie (2000); the trade goods are priced variously: in gold, in European silver currencies, in cowrie, in iron bars, or copper wire. The native may be selling gold dust and may be paid in trade goods. The European trader (i) translates the value of the gold into £ s.d. or Spanish silver dollars, and (ii) then the value of the trade goods into cowrie. The native simply counts the value of the gold dust by the number of beans to which that weight amounts, and then equates the number of beans with the cowrie units owed to him by the trader. By removing a bean from a sack for each cowrie unit paid to him, he keeps track of how much is still owed to him by the number of beans remaining in the sack.

(2) Cultural anthropology deals with money as a semantic system similar to writing, language, or weights and measures. Money as a semantic system links symbols to quantifiable objects, but the

purpose served by the system as a whole must be inferred from the actual uses, and can hardly be said to be as clear as that of writing or language.

(3) The classical and neo-classical economists' definition of money was, up till recently, that of means of indirect exchange. The other money uses are here merely unimportant variants of that use.

Independent Institutional Origins of Money Uses

1. Payment
   (a) In unstratified primitive society, as a rule, payments are made in connection with the institutions of bridewealth, bloodwealth and fines.
   (b) In stratified, and especially in archaic society, institutions such as customary dues, taxes, rent, and tribute similarly give rise to payments.
2. Standard or Accountancy use of money is found in connection with
   (a) complex barter, i.e., different articles being summed up on both sides;
   (b) the administration of staples (staple-finance).
3. Hoarding of wealth may serve the purpose of
   (a) accumulating treasure,
   (b) providing against future dearth,
   (c) disposal over military and labor forces by providing subsistence in kind.
4. Exchange develops as a rule not from random barter acts of individuals, but in connection with organized external trade and internal markets.

III. Money: Theoretical and Institutional Concepts

Classical Economics

Money is defined as a commodity primarily used in exchange. Money is therefore a function of barter and exchange. Monetary problems should be resolved by reducing them to commodity problems. Token money (such as paper currency) is not money proper.

The logical derivation of money is identified with its historical evolution: The propensity to barter, truck, and exchange leads to individual acts of barter. Such acts are limited by the specific quality of the commodities being offered more often than others. This again leads to the establishment of one of them as preferred to all others for purposes of exchange. This commodity is adopted as "money," on account of its suitability for indirect exchange. To increase its fungibility the commodity may be quantified, and divided into parts which are stamped by public authority. For the sake of convenience, which governs the whole process, these coins may be replaced by tokens, such as bank notes, which, however, are money only insofar as they insure the possession of the actual commodity, which in modern times consists in coins made from precious metals.

The semblance of a "parallel" between logic and history: The use of coin is thus logically preceded by the use of metal money measured by weight; the monopoly of metal money is logically preceded by competing commodities used in indirect exchange; this again must have derived from the preferred non-monetary use of a number of commodities—all this originating in individual acts of exchange, explained by man's propensity to barter. According to this type of rationalistic argument, in following back the thread of logical deduction to its sources, we are allegedly also retracing the developmental stages embodied in history.

The various uses of money appear in this system as logically interdependent. The commodity character of money, i.e., its being an object possessing utility in itself, is presupposed. (1) "Means of exchange" is defined as the original use; (2) "Means of payment" follows later, for how could one pay with a thing that cannot be used in exchange? (3) "Standard of value" comes next, comprising (1) and (2); (4) "Means of hoarding wealth or treasure" presupposes the other three. The commodity and exchange concepts are cornerstones of the system.

Neo-Classical Economics

(1) Pre-Keynesian system. Mostly some kind of "exchange" derivation was a legacy from the classics. Schumpeter, e.g., retained the definition of "indirect exchange" for money. Böhm-Bawerk had previously introduced exchange as a special type of use for commodities, and Wieser proceeded to elaborate the marginal utility of money. In this early phase, neo-classical theory was as yet unconscious of the conceptual difficulty of putting money into the scheme.

(2) Keynesian system. In the Keynesian system the role of money is purely pragmatic. No attempt is made to deduce its presence from the allocation of scarce means. Money itself is here one of the scarce means, but a means, which is contrasted with commodities.

The classical system denied this contrast (and, consequently, was unable to explain specifically monetary phenomena). The presence of money is here rightly taken for granted—since it can only be institutionally explained, not conceptually deduced. The phrase about the "veil of money" as used by the classics was a remnant of Humean solecism in regard to the allegedly conventional value of money, and the (opposite) Ricardian fallacy of the commodity character of money. Actually, the value of money does not derive from convention and is not therefore illusory, but neither does it derive from "value in use," as the commodity theory would have it. Its utility derives from the fact that one can buy things with it, and its value, from its scarcity. This, however, does not account for its origin, which lies with the institutions of government and banking.

Institutional Terms

The various uses of money were originally institutionalized separately. Connections between these four uses were more or less accidental. We will deal with these uses in the following sequence: (1) Means of payment; (2) Means of hoarding wealth or treasure; (3) Means of exchange; (4) Standard of value.

Means of payment

For money to be in use as a means of payment, it is necessary that there be (a) some kind of debt or obligation to pay *for;* (b) something to pay *with.* From the traditional point of view, the need, therefore, is to explain (a) how do debts or obligations arise in primitive society outside of economic transactions? (b) how can there be means of payment where money is not also used as a means of exchange?

(a) Something to pay for (How do debts arise?)

(1) That early society is built on *status* means that rights and obligations are mostly derived from birth, whether the kinship is real or fictitious. This is largely true of stratified societies. Negative privilege is also acquired through birth. Men are born to debts, and the discharge of obligation.

(2) The dominant institution is *kinship* and its extensions; this entails obligations of various kinds, the outstanding ones being those of the blood feud group. On the one hand, obligation to take revenge, on the other, to pay fines or composition.

(3) In many primitive societies (e.g., the Manus) customary obligations are under the severe sanction of magic.

(4) Sacral character of early law (formal and ritualistic). Transactions under the sanction of religion. Obligations incurred in this way are of the utmost stringency.

(5) The great importance of prestige, rank, prerogative attaching to honorific actions, names, titles, counts (coups), ceremonial transactions, explains that (even intentional) debts are incurred by infringement of recognized prerogatives as among the Tolowa and the Kwakiutl.

(6) Another rich source lies in the growth of authority, which creates political obligation.

All these factors contribute to the capacity of primitive society to produce *indebtedness of a non-economic nature*. The obligation is based on status, blood, feud, prestige, kinship, and betrothal or marriage, and involves paying off, making good, or resolving the debt; the whole procedure under the sanction of magic, ritualistic law, sacral ceremony. The debt is incurred not as a result of economic transaction, but of events like marriage, killing, coming of age, being challenged to potlatch, joining a secret society, etc. While in primitive society, economic interests and corresponding obligations lack stringency and tend toward leniency, elasticity, and equity treatment, economic self-interests are usually in the category of non-approved motives. The opposite is the case in regard to debts and obligations having non-economic sources, such as magic, sacral command, *stricti juris negotis,* ritual performances, honorific or prestige matters, formal law, including *jus talionis,* the *nexum,* or the formalities connected with the buying and selling of *res mancipi.* (Cf. also Roman "Twelve Tables" codifying "customary law" [about middle fifth century B.C.]. The Hebrew Laws of Deuteronomy credited to late seventh century B.C., but using much earlier material.) On Suque (Bank Islands) entrance fees, grades, "freemasonry," Daryll Forde (1950:203) writes: "This system gives a far more mercenary cast to society in such areas and money acquires a greater importance than in the rest of Melanesia." Payments are made in conventional media of payment, e.g., feathers for dances are paid in dentalia, or shell necklaces; songs for suque admission are paid in strings of shell money. Whole strings of shell, etc., are used, *not* single units. Such payments are restricted to different communities.

(b) How are debts paid in the absence of exchange?

Wealth primarily consists of valuables, which are objects capable of arousing emotion and prized for their own sake. The "use" of these valuables may consist merely in possessing them—as in the case of crown jewels.

Pelew money. The Pelew Island (North Pacific), also called Palau, belongs to the Carolines. Porcelain and glass mixture of relatively prehistoric origin is a fact. Some of the glass beads are found on Yap, but *not* used there as money (instead huge aragonite stones are used). Yellow and red Pelew money. These are shell-like and glassy, but opaque. Different white sorts of Pelew money exchanged specifically, e.g., sails are bought for high-valued type. The most highly valued are loaned at interest! Bridewealth according to rank; the higher pays more!

The most valuable type of money is secreted by the chieftains. Few people know of even one-sixth of the kinds of money. Fines are paid in Pelew money. Some kinds used in exchange at fixed prices. Glass beads similar to those of West Africans found in Anglo-Saxon burrows. The Ashanti pay "weight in gold" for such "Aggry pearls." The development of Pelew money is highly specific. Each type of money has its own use, a circle within which it moves. This harmonizes with the idea of wealth and treasure, but not with that of a means of exchange. Although there is also exchange-use, the main uses are in the nature of payment, as in bridewealth—an outstanding instance of money as means of payment being based on its use as a means of hoarding treasure.

Otherwise, the disposing of the "valuable" is its main "use," as with the Kula, where the relatives and dependents of the proprietor are permitted to wear the objects. Retainers, vassals, and allies in war are secured with the help of such valuables. The point is that the recipient values them as valuables *not* for their use in [commercial] exchange, the chances of which are usually nil; value is bound inextricably with rank. (Some Kula objects are big, greasy white arm shells, without any value except for the associations that go with earlier possessors.)

Yet money as a means of payment could never have developed to any great extent if its utility had been restricted to being hoarded as treasure. Another use accrued through the development of redistribution as a form of integrating economic activity. The beginnings are, of course, with hunters. In the stratified societies like those of Micronesia and Polynesia, the high chief as representative of the first clan, receives the revenue, redistributing it later in the form of largesse among the population. The principle of redistribution is practiced on a gigantic scale in the despotically governed aristocracies of shepherds and hoe-cultivators, as in Mexico and Peru. The tax payments of subjects and subject peoples are stored in enormous storehouses and redistributed to the ingroups and in-peoples. The same principles reigned in Sumer, Babylonia, Assyria, as well as in ancient China and the New Kingdom of Egypt. All this goes to explain the relative independence of "payment" from "exchange."

Means of exchange

External use of money. The origins of money as a means of exchange are linked to external trade. This is in accordance with the equally established fact of trade and markets as "external" institutions.

Some articles are in prominence in foreign trade, as food versus manufactures. Specific products are traded. Geographical factors assert themselves, as in East- and West-Central Africa. With some simpler communities, this tendency toward specialization produces this phenomenon, even in the absence of geographical determination, as in Melanesia. But the broad fact is the tendency of external trade to specialize in a few main articles. Some of these, like salt or iron, are favored for indirect exchange. This is one origin of exchange-money.

Only rarely do we see money emerging primarily out of the need for a means of indirect exchange. This type of external money is deliberate, like the use of cowrie shells. They are little used otherwise, yet extremely popular with all peoples as money in external trade.

Internal use of money. Since money as a means of exchange originated in external trade, when and how, if at all, did it become a means of exchange internally? Though, in general, money as a means of exchange may have originated in external trade, it might be the case that the internal or domestic use of money in exchange may have originated independently. This might have happened as a result of individual acts of barter and exchange, and eventually from local markets. This, however, appears not to have been the case.

In simple, i.e., unstratified, primitive society, money originates as a means of payment, and although used in prestige economy, to a limited extent as a means of exchange, it is only exceptionally used in subsistence economy. Food always remains an article of external trade, and is not domestically exchanged for money.

In stratified primitive society, money is, of course, widely used in redistribution, i.e., as a means of payment. This may be in the form of "valuables," such as Pelew money, or as cattle as in East Africa. Yet we see no money arising as a means of exchange, for acts of exchange on local markets (as in Africa) are limited to the exchange of specific types of goods, and trade is, in principle, exclusively external trade.

Let us mention here Heinrich Schurtz's "internal" and "external" money (*Grundriss einer Entstehungsgeschichte des Geldes,* 1898). Two different types of money originating from different sources. This appeared to suit some important facts stressed by Schurtz. But Schurtz mistook some uses of money for internal, which by origin are external. (1) Bridewealth, payment is originally an exogamy institution and the payment is, in principle, "external"; (2) the composition of blood feud is "external," since there is no blood feud and originally no composition inside the group.

The internal use of money in exchange in the ancient oriental empires of Egypt, Sumer, Babylonia, and China was, on the whole, very restricted. In Egypt, no coins have been assigned of a date anterior to Alexander the Great. The elaborate Ptolemaian money system is, of course, of late origin. Silver and gold were in the keeping of the temples. The highly developed goldsmith's art did not induce them to coin metal, which was used in rings of silver and gold by weight. On the whole, the economy was one of redistribution on a vast scale. Foreign trade was mostly in the hands of foreigners. Internal business was transacted in kind, sometimes in gold and silver, according to weight. The immensely developed redistributive economy kept the system on the money as use of payment basis, and discouraged the formation of internal markets of any importance. In this respect Egypt was typical of ancient oriental empires.

Standard of value

Money as a standard of value reaches its greatest development in modern society on the basis of a market-integrated exchange economy in which money takes the form of general purchasing power.

Money, however, is used as a standard of value in ancient empires as a result of widespread redistributive institutions. This use is restricted to the most important economic goods, such as land, corn, and metals, and it is not a result of market functions, but of price fixing on the part of authorities. In this connection it is of interest to note that insofar as metals (by weight) were used as a means of payment, there is in ancient history no evidence of attempts at a "debasement of currency." The "money" character of commodities was more often due to the extension of government to larger areas than to barter in commodities. By these means external trade became "interiorized."

TWENTY-FOUR

Navajo Categories of Objects at Rest

GARY J. WITHERSPOON

Navajo culture partitions the domain of objects at rest into fifteen general categories based on the variables of size, shape, firmness, density, position, cohesiveness, animate or inanimate, and contained or non-contained. Each of the fifteen general categories are partitioned into fifteen additional categories based on the variables of plurality, grouping, and patterning, making a total of 225 basic categories in the cultural domain of objects at rest. Of these 225 cultural categories, 102 are a subset which have distinct non-lexical markers, and the remainder are unmarked. This analysis deals with the problem of the relationship between language and culture, and it concludes that sets of mono-lexical markers and cultural categories are often not congruent, and that componential analysis of sets of lexical items often fail to uncover the total set of cultural categories in a given domain.

Componential analysis is a technique developed by Goodenough and others (see Goodenough, 1965, 1967; Schneider, 1965c) for the formal analysis of lexical material, which purports to reveal fundamental cultural, cognitive categories. Witherspoon's paper shows the weakness of such analysis and reveals the importance of a more dynamic technique which goes beyond lexical analysis.

THIS PAPER OUTLINES Navajo cultural categories in the domain of objects at rest.[1] It also explores the relationship of these cultural categories to sets of mono-lexical markers in corresponding semantic domains. Before beginning the analysis, it is necessary to discuss briefly the definitions of culture and cultural category which are utilized in this paper.

Culture exists on the conceptual level, and consists of a set of concepts, ideas, beliefs, and attitudes about the universe of action and being. Cultural concepts do not just (or even necessarily) identify what exists in the objective world; cultural systems, in one sense, create the world. Reality itself is culturally defined, and cultural constructs partition this reality into numerous categories. Cultural categories are thus conceptual categories.

Navajo culture partitions the domain of objects at rest into fifteen general categories. Hoijer has discussed many of these in his works on the Navajo classificatory verbs (Hoijer 1945, 1948, 1963, 1964). For reasons of his own, he limited Navajo classificatory verbs to twelve.[2] In the neuter verbs which classify

Reprinted by permission of the American Anthropological Association from the *American Anthropologist,* 1971, vol. 73, no. 1, pp. 110–17.

objects at rest, there are fifteen distinct verb stems which refer to fifteen distinct cultural or conceptual categories. These fifteen general categories are based on Navajo concepts of size, shape, firmness, density, position, cohesiveness, animate or inanimate, and contained or not contained.[3]

Within each of the fifteen general categories, there are fifteen basic or specific categories, making a total of 225 Navajo cultural categories in the domain of objects at rest. The Navajo language provides 102 distinct mono-lexical terms which a speaker of the language may employ in referring to the 225 basic cultural categories in the domain of objects at rest.

The multi-dimensional paradigm on the following page (figure 24:1) illustrates the way in which the fifteen basic categories in each of the general categories are concatenated. This paradigm is based on three variables: (1) plurality, (2) grouping, and (3) patterning. Each of these variables will be discussed in detail below:

Plurality

In recent years much attention has been given to the different ways in which various languages mark and categorize the color spectrum. Although over 300 distinct points on the color spectrum are discernable by the naked human eye, languages classify the color spectrum into a small number of discrete categories, and these categories vary widely according to different languages.

Pitch is another area of human perception which is given various functions in the languages of the world. In some languages, such as Trigue, as many as five levels of pitch are phonemic; in other languages, pitch has functions only as a suprasegmental in the intonational system.

Number is another universal human perception. Number has not, however, received as much attention in linguistic and semantic studies as it probably deserves. Number is a linear continuum from zero to infinity. In cultures where mathematics is highly developed, minus numbers, fractions, and various other numerical values are distinguished by specialists. Languages indicate number in various ways. All languages have a counting system according to which numbers from one to various amounts are marked.

Beyond the counting system of a language, the grammar of a language indicates number in various ways. There are indefinite adjectives such as "some," "a few," and "many" in English, and *t'áá díkwíí, łá,* and *t'óó 'ahayóí* in Navajo. Number is also indicated by pronouns, nouns, and verbs. In English grammar number is distinguished into two basic categories: singular and plural. These two basic categories penetrate nearly the entire grammar. In subjective pronouns, there are "I" and "we," and "he," or "she" and "they." In demonstrative pronouns, there are "this" and "these," "that" and "those." In possessive pronouns, there are "mine" and "ours," and "his," or "hers" and "theirs." In nouns there are "bear" and "bears," "cat" and "cats," "man" and "men," etc. In cases such as deer and sheep, the plural is not marked. In verbs, there are "he sits" and "they sit," but in the first person, number is indicated only by the subject pronoun. Number is not indicated at all in the second person.

Navajo grammar marks the number

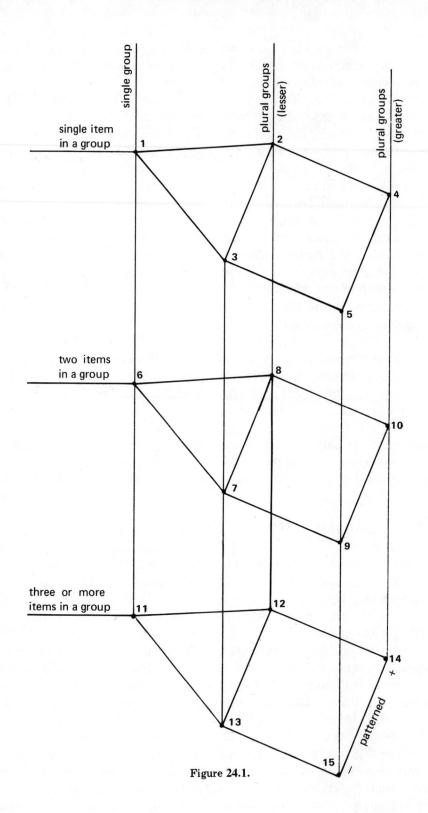

Figure 24.1.

continuum in at least six different ways. These are listed below:

(1) one/two/indefinite lesser plural/indefinite greater plural
(2) one/two/three or more
(3) one/indefinite lesser plural/indefinite greater plural
(4) indefinite lesser plural (including one)/indefinite greater plural
(5) one or two/three or more
(6) one/two or more

The indefinite lesser plural indicates a few, several, or some, while the indefinite greater plural indicates many or numerous items.[4]

Navajo subjective pronouns in the first and second persons mark number according to the third continuum listed above. Subject pronouns in the third person mark only the two categories listed in continuum four. Navajo subjective pronouns are listed below:

	indefinite one lesser plural	indefinite greater plural
1st Person	shĭ nihĭ	danihĭ
2nd Person	ni nihĭ	danihĭ
3rd Person	bĭ bĭ	daabĭ

Navajo possessive pronouns mark number in the same way as the subjective pronouns do. The demonstrative pronouns of Navajo do not mark number and may refer to any number or amount.

Most Navajo nouns do not indicate number. Thus "dibé" can mean one sheep or many sheep. Some nouns, however, indicate number according to continuum six above:

ashkii/ashiiké
one boy/two or more boys
shitsóí/shitsóóké
my maternal grandchild/my maternal grandchildren

A few Navajo nouns mark number according to continuum four above.

Two examples of these are listed below:

ko̜'/daako̜'
one or several fires/many fires
ahi'diitiin/ahida'diitiin
several roads come together/many roads come together

Navajo verbs mark number according to continuums one, two, three, or five. An example of each is provided below:

(1) to be standing (first person)
sézĭ/siidzĭ/nisiidzĭ/ndasiidzĭ
one/two/indefinite/indefinite
lesser plural greater plural
(2) to be walking along (first person)
yisháál/yiit'ash/yiikah
one/two/three or more
(3) a long or thin, rigid object at rest
sitą̱'/naaztą̱'/ndaaztą̱'
one/indefinite/indefinite
lesser plural/greater plural
(5) to be (third person)
nil /danilĭ
one or two/three or more

It should now be clear that Navajo categories of plurality[5] are not as simple as some have thought. Sapir (1963:89), Hoijer (1945:202–03), and Young and Morgan (1943:2) have taken a rather conventional approach to the Navajo plural. Their approach is stated clearly in the volume by Young and Morgan (1943:2):

In English we express number as singular (one) and plural (more than one). Navajo, on the other hand, expresses number as singular (one), dual (two), duoplural (two or more), plural (more than two) and distributive plural (indicating not only the number is more than two, but also that each of the subjects or objects in reference is taking part in the act, state or condition denoted by the verb). To illustrate with concrete examples:

yisháál	I am walking along.
yiit'ash	We two are walking along.
yiikah	We (plural) are walking along.

niheezná   They (duoplural) moved
              with their goods.
ndahaazná   They (distributive plural)
              moved with their goods.

The distributive plural is indicated by the prefix "da." It is used regularly with verbs, and on occasion with nouns.

The problem with this approach is that it fails to identify the six separate and distinct ways in which the Navajo language categorizes and marks the number continuum. It also fails to identify the categories of indefinite lesser plural, indefinite greater plural, indefinite lesser plural including one, and one or two. It confuses number with grouping by incorrectly calling "da" a distributive plural.

The quotation from Young and Morgan states that "niheezná" means "they (duoplural) moved . . ." Duoplural is described as two or more. "Ndahaazná" is described as a distributive plural. Herein is illustrated a fundamental misunderstanding of the way in which the Navajo language marks number. The conventional approach confuses grouping with number and ignores several covert categories. "Niheezná" means (1) an indefinite lesser number of individuals moved, or (2) an indefinite lesser number of groups moved. "Ndahaazná" means (1) an indefinite greater number of individuals moved, or (2) an indefinite greater number of groups moved. Both terms are distributive and neither refers to dual numbers. The only difference between the terms is in the plurals of indefinite lesser and indefinite greater.

The third person of this verb includes two more conjugations ("nĭná" and "danĭná") which represent several additional categories. A look at the total number of terms might be helpful here.

Below are sentences identified as correct by my informants:

(1) Hastiin Yázhĭ haidą́ą́' koji' *nĭná.*
Small Man moved here last winter.
(2) Hastiin Yázhĭ dóó Hastiin Nééz haidą́ą́' koji' *nĭná.*
Small Man and Tall Man moved here last winter.
(3) Hastiin Yázhĭ dóó bik'éĭ haidą́ą́' koji' *nĭná.*
Small Man's relatives moved here last winter (as one group).
(4) Hastiin Yázhĭ bik'éĭ dóó Hastiin Nééz bik'éĭ haidą́ą́' koji' *nĭná.*
Small Man's relatives and Tall Man's relatives moved here last winter (acting as two distinct groups).
(5) Hastiin Yázhĭ dóó Hastiin Nééz dóó Hastiin Sánĭ haidą́ą́' koji' *danĭná.*
Small Man, Tall Man, and Old Man moved here last winter.
(6) Hastiin Yázhĭ bik'éĭ dóó Hastiin Nééz bik'éĭ dóó Hastiin Sánĭ bik'éĭ haidą́ą́' koji' *danĭná.*
Small Man's relatives, Tall Man's relatives, and Old Man's relatives moved here last winter.

The two terms ("nĭná" and "danĭná") refer to six categories. "Nĭná" refers to one or two individuals or groups. "Danĭná" refers to three or more groups or individuals. This definition of "danĭná" does not differ much from that of "niheezná" and "ndahaazná." All three terms refer to numbers of three or more, but "niheezná" and "ndahaazná" mark continuum four listed earlier and "danĭná" is part of continuum five. There are other differences in meaning as well.

All of these terms refer to moving toward the point of orientation of the speaker (coming as opposed to going). "Niheezná" and "ndahaazná" have a special and specific meaning, whereas "danĭná" is more general in meaning. "Niheezná" and "ndahaazná" refer to individuals or groups moving to the point of orientation from different places and arriving at different times.

"Niheezná" and "ndahaazná" are both distributive plurals because their referents leave from different places and arrive at different times. A single person or group could not do that. The terms "nahaaskai" and "ndahaaskai" from the verb "to come" or "arrive" have similar meanings because they utilize the same prefixes as "niheezná" and "ndahaazná." The important thing is that "da" is not a distributive.

Reichard (1951:30) agrees with this position: "I do not agree with Sapir, Hoijer, Young and Morgan that 'da' is essentially a distributive; it is rather a plural. Forms with 'da' often seem to be distributive in meaning, but most often distribution is indicated by the stem and prefixes that enter into combination with 'da.'" Reichard goes on to demonstrate her point; her evidence is not included because I have provided some of my own and the matter will become more clear after we look at the neuter verbs for items at rest.

Grouping

The confusion over "da" leads us to the next variable involved in Navajo categories of plural items at rest. This variable is that of internal relationship or grouping. Navajos categorize plural items according to whether they are considered separate and distinct or whether they are considered a group, according to whether they form just one group or many groups, and according to the number of items within each group. For example, a single pile (group) of a few logs is described as "tsin sinil." Several piles (groups) of several logs would be described as "tsin naaznil." If several logs were lying separately they

would be described as "tsin naaztą́," but if the same number of logs were in a pile (one group) they would be described as "sinil."

In the construction of a hogan there may be five to eight sides, each having ten or more logs. This can be described with the verb stem "naaznil," meaning several groups of something with each having several items within the group.

A hundred sheep that are thought of as one herd (group) will be described as "dibé sijéé'," but the same number of sheep considered as ungrouped entities will be described as "dibé ndaaztı̨́." If the speaker is considering the fact that each of the lambs is sitting with its mother, he will say "dibé biyáázhı̆ yił ndaaztéézh." In each case, the neuter verb is different because of the factor of grouping.

Patterning

The third variable involved in Navajo categories of plural items at rest is that of position or patterning. If four distinct logs are in random distribution, they are described as "naaztą́." If they have been placed in a straight line pattern, they are described as "nı̆tą́." Patterning is an overt category in all but one of the neuter verbs for items at rest. A pattern is considered a straight line unless specified as something else. A pattern implies that an animate being has interfered and placed random items in a pattern. The patterning seems to be primarily related to the planting of corn fields, but has very wide application.

Earlier in this paper a multi-dimensional paradigm was presented as illustrating a Navajo conceptual scheme for

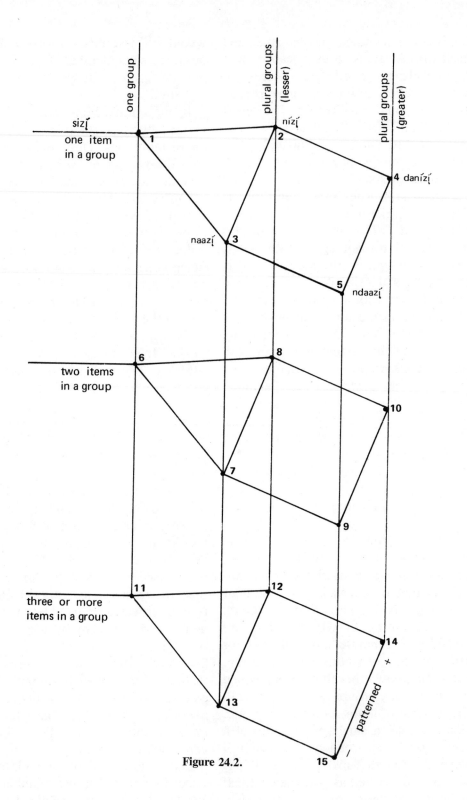

Figure 24.2.

categorizing plural items at rest. The paradigm contains fifteen basic categories for each general category. However, not every general category has fifteen distinct terms so that many cultural categories are left unmarked by the language. Let us explore some of the terminology for several general categories.

The term "sizį̇" is applied to a single animate being in a standing position. If there are several distinct animate beings standing in a random distribution, the term "naazį̇" is used. If a similar number of animate objects in a standing position are in a pattern, the term "nĭzį̇" is used. The indefinite greater plural of "naazį̇" is "ndaazį̇," and the greater plural of "nĭzį̇" is "danĭzį̇." These five terms are the complete list of terms for animate beings in a standing position. The other ten catgories on the paradigm remain unmarked (see figure 24.2). Actually the five terms on the top level are used to describe the corresponding categories on the two lower levels, so each of the five terms are polysemic and the ten lower categories are unmarked.

A more complete set of terms can be found in the general category of animate beings in a sitting position. "Sidá" refers to one animate being in a sitting position. Several (indefinite lesser plural) animate beings sitting in a separate and dispersed manner are described as "naazdá." Several animate beings sitting in a pattern are described by the term "nĭdá." The indefinite greater plural of "naazdá" and "nĭdá" are "ndaazdá" and "danĭdá" respectively.

When there are two animate beings sitting together or in some way considered a group, the term "siké" is used. If there are several pairs of animate beings sitting in a random distribution, "naazké" is the proper term. If several

pairs of animate beings are sitting in pattern, the term "nĭké" is used. The indefinite greater plural of "naazké" is "ndaazké," and the indefinite greater plural of "nĭké" is "danĭké." Thus far we have ten of the fifteen categories marked.

According to the categorical scheme, there should be a term for three or more animate beings sitting together or in a group. Nevertheless, no such term exists. There are only two terms for three or more animate beings sitting in a group. One is "nahaaztá" which means several groups sitting in random distribution. The other term is "ndaháaztá," which means numerous (indefinite greater plural) groups (each made up of three or more) of animate beings sitting in a random distribution. "Naháaztá" is used in reference to one group of three or more but its prefix indicates its primary referent is several groups of three or more. Thus in this general category, twelve of the fifteen categories are marked (see figure 24.3).

According to normal grammatical construction, the term for one group of three or more animate beings in a sitting position would be "sitá." The other two unmarked categories for groups in a pattern would be "nĭtá" and "danĭtá." The problem *seems* to be that the stem for three or more animate beings sitting in a group or groups is the same as the stem for a long slender or flat inanimate, rigid object at rest. Therefore, "sitá" and the other terms would have to have two very different meanings. Such a situation is, of course, quite common in languages; for some reason it does not occur here, and three categories remain unmarked. In the two marked categories, the prefix "ha" has been added—seemingly to distinguish "naaz-

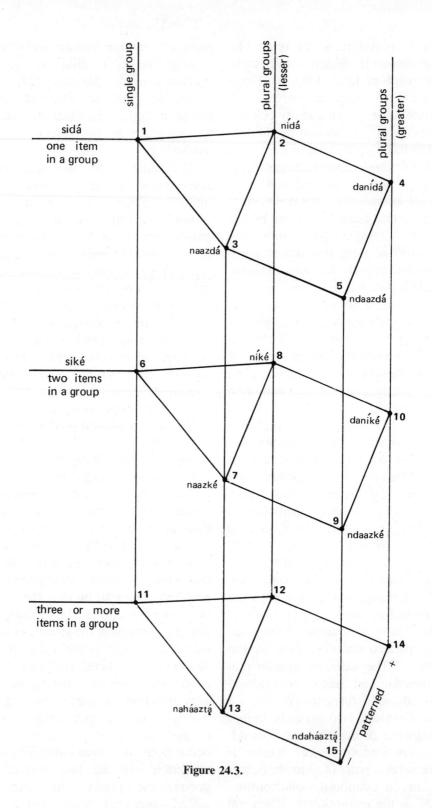

Figure 24.3.

tá" (several long, slender objects in random distribution) from "naháaztá" (several groups of three or more animate beings sitting in a random distribution).

A complete set of terms exists for the general category of an animate being or beings in a lying position. The terms are shown in figure 24.4. From the geometric paradigm, it can be seen that every conceptual category is marked. If we look at the term "nĭtéézh," we can see it means several (indefinite lesser plural) pairs of animate beings lying in a pattern. If we go one point to the right, we get numerous pairs lying in a pattern. If we go one point downward from "nĭteezh," every thing remains the same except the groups made of two beings become three or more. If we come toward us to "naaztéézh," we see that everything remains as it was with "nĭtéézh" save that patterning is lost and the distribution becomes random.

If we go to the left from "nĭtéézh" to "sitéézh," the several groups of pairs become just one pair. The patterning is also lost because one pair cannot be in a pattern. If we go upwards from "nĭtéézh" to "nĭtĭ," the only change is that the pairs in pattern become single beings in pattern. Thus the paradigm presented here illustrates the proper relationship between and among all the terms.

It should also be noted that there are two dimensions or continua of plurality utilized in this conceptual scheme. If we start at the top left hand corner with a single group and go across the top, the number of groups becomes plural according to categories of singular/indefinite lesser plural/indefinite greater plural. If we go downwards from the singular item, we see that the items within a group become plural according to the scale of one/two/three or more.

Most verbs do not mark the two plural dimensions of the number of items within a group separately from the number of groups. The variable of grouping and the additional dimension of plurality which goes with grouping are unmarked in most verbs. Trying to define the meaning of "niheezná" and "ndahaazná" according to only one dimension of plurality is the reason for so many students of Navajo misunderstanding the correct referents of many Navajo verbs.

The conceptual scheme presented here is also applicable to the other general categories of objects at rest. Although in many of the object classifications there is not a complete set of terms and many categories are left unmarked, there are some general categories that are completely marked. One of these applies to houses or hogans and can be very useful to the social anthropologist. (Figure 24.5 shows the conceptual scheme for the classification of hogans or houses.) If a plural number of hogans are considered as separate or unconnected, the terms "naaz'á" or "ndaaz'á" are used. If several hogans are considered as a group or unit, the term "sinil" is used. If there are two groups of hogans, the term "naaznil" will be used. Because social units, namely the "camp" or subsistence residential unit (Witherspoon 1970:60), correspond to hogan groupings, the social anthropologist can determine what hogans represent a social unit or units by the verbs which people use in describing them.

The term "kin sijaa" refers to numerous houses in a group, which means a town or a village. "Kin naazjaa'" refers

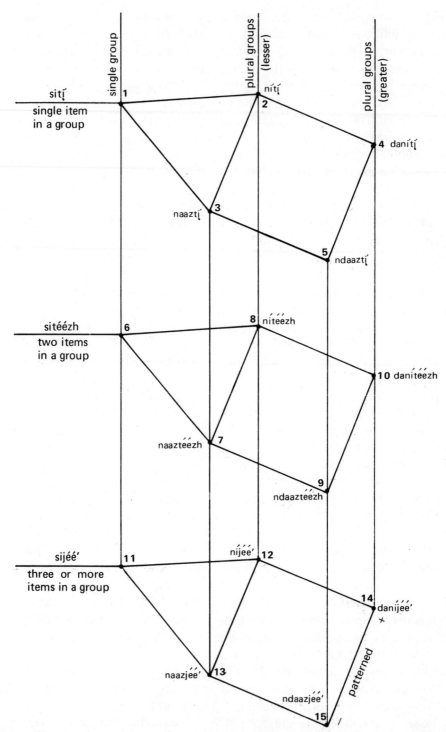

Figure 24.4. (The appendix contains drawings of each of these categories. The number on the drawings corresponds to the categories in this paradigm.)

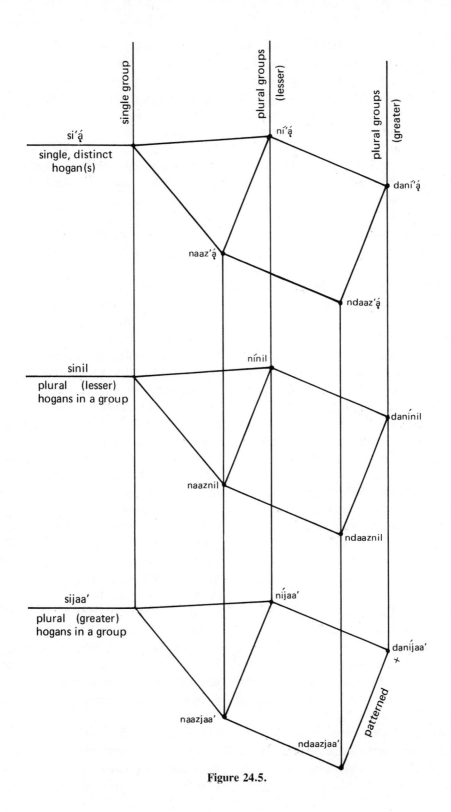

Figure 24.5.

to several towns or villages, and "kin ndaazjaa'" refers to numerous towns or villages. "Hoghan sinil" refers to one camp; "hogan naaznil" refers to several camps. "Hoghan si'á" refers to one household; "hoghan naaz'á" refers to several households.

The camp or subsistence residential unit is built around a sheep herd. If in a particular area the ethnographer hears the phrase "kojǐ dibé sijéé," he will know there is just one herd of sheep and one camp. If it is said "kojǐ dibé naazjéé'," the ethnographer can be sure there is more than one sheep herd and thus more than one camp.

In the preceding discussion, it was shown how Navajo culture partitions and categorizes a domain of culturally defined reality. The cultural domain of items at rest is partitioned into fifteen general categories based on the variables of size, shape, firmness, density, position, cohesiveness, animate or inanimate, and contained or non-contained. Each of the fifteen general categories are partitioned into one singular and fourteen plural categories, making a total of 225 basic cultural categories. Of these 225 cultural categories, 102 are a subset which have distinct mono-lexical markers.

This paper does not show how Navajos think, for how a Navajo thinks and what categories he can employ in his thinking are not the same. This in turn is distinct from the ways in which the Navajo language provides standardized lexical markers by which reference can be made to cultural categories. In some cases, a set of mono-lexical markers and a set of cultural categories are congruent, but many times, as we find here, they are not congruent and many cultural categories are left unmarked.

The findings and conclusions of this paper are relevant to present studies of kinship and kinship terms. Kinship is a cultural domain, and the kin universe is partitioned into numerous culturally defined kin categories. Languages provide a subset of mono-lexical markers by which reference can be made to various kin categories. Componential analyses of kin terms have proceeded on some very dubious assumptions regarding the meanings of kin terms. The assumptions that kin terms have primary genealogical referents in all cultures, that kinship and kinsmen are basically the same in all cultures and only partitioned differently by various sets of kin terms, and that kin terms correspond to and express the kin categories of a given culture seem extremely naïve. Although many of the supporters and defenders of componential analysis of kin terms would now deny these assumptions, nearly all the componential ananyses thus far have, in fact, been based on these assumptions.

This article does not claim that componential analyses as an analytical procedure has no utility for the study of kinship systems. It only argues that componential analyses of kin terms quite often fail to take into account the total set of cultural kin categories that are present in a given kinship system. However, if the methods of componential analysis are applied to cultural categories and not limited to sets of lexical items, a more complete understanding of the cultural domain can be obtained.[6]

Some anthropologists and linguists have placed great emphasis on the idea that the languages of the so-called primitive men are specific and lack the qualities of generalization and abstraction that more modern languages have. It nevertheless seems to me that the conceptual scheme and categories presented here represent a high quality of abstraction and generalization, as well as specificity. The categories of number, grouping, and patterning are indeed quite specific and also quite complex. The high level abstractions of fifteen cultural categories into one or more of which everything that exists can be placed certainly does not seem to demonstrate an inability to think abstractly or to generalize about what exists in the universe.

All these considerations give us some interesting questions to ponder: Are the peoples whom we class as "primitive" really underdeveloped in abstract thinking or intellectual activity, or is it that we are just beginning to understand how they think? Do we call them simple because they really are simple, or because we only understand the simplest form and ideas of their cultures? Are they primitive, or is our understanding of them primitive?

(1) Dibé sitį́

(3) Dibé naaztį́

(5) Dibé ndaaztį́

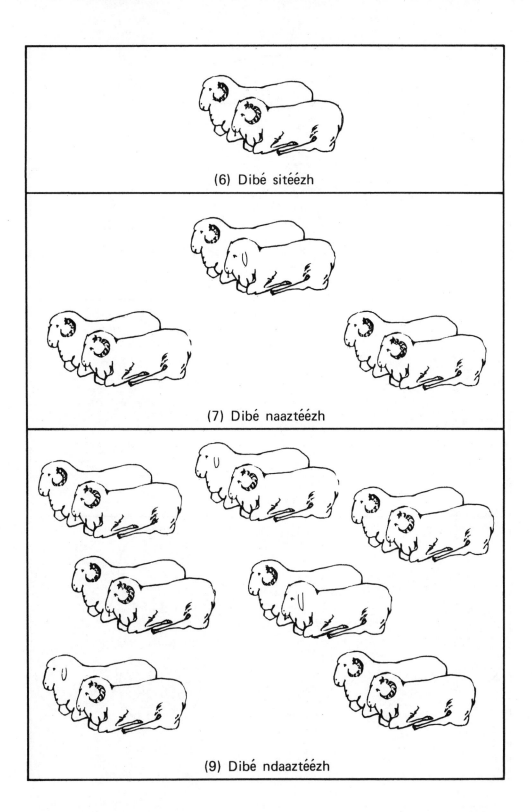

(6) Dibé sitéézh

(7) Dibé naaztéézh

(9) Dibé ndaaztéézh

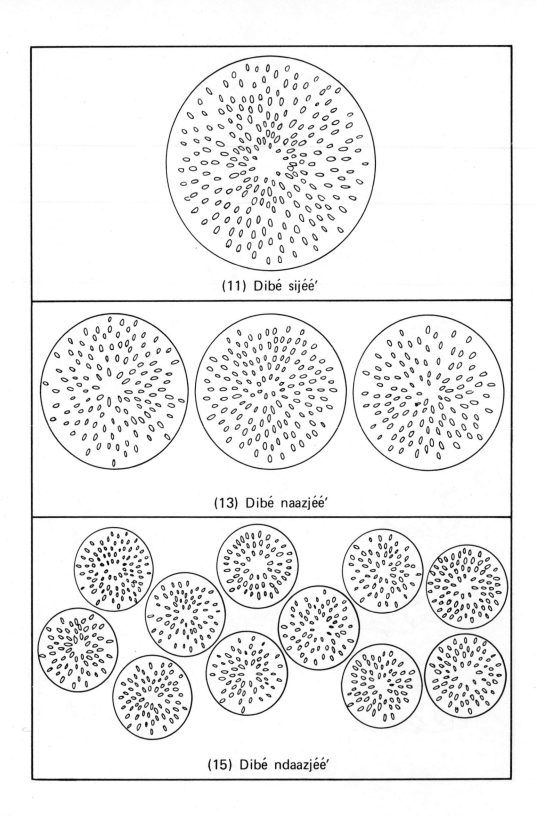

(11) Dibé sijéé'

(13) Dibé naazjéé'

(15) Dibé ndaazjéé'

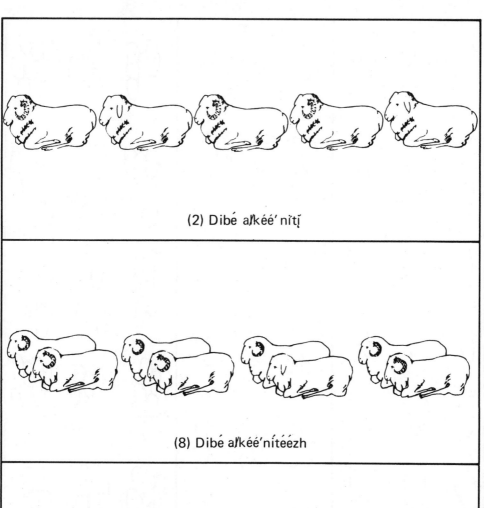

(2) Dibé a/kéé' níti̧

(8) Dibé a/kéé'nítéézh

(12) Dibé a/kéé'níjéé'

(4) Dibé a'kéé'danítį́

(10) Dibé a'kéé'danítéézh

(14) Dibé a'kéé'danîjéé

Notes

1. I am very grateful for the comments, suggestions, and assistance given me in writing this paper by Paul Friedrich, David Schneider, and Oswald Werner. I am also extremely grateful to the many Navajos who generously and patiently instructed me in their language. My wife comes first in this regard. This research was supported by the United States Public Health Service grant number 5T01-GM01059-07.

2. Classificatory verb stems which exist in the neuter verbs and which are not in Hoijer's list include: "sizhoozh" (long, slender objects lying parallel), "siyis" (long slender curved object), "sikaad" (an object or objects which cover a surface), "sīzi" (an animate object in a standing position), and "sidá" (an animate object in sitting position). Some of the definitions listed above are not carefully worked out and are given just to provide the reader with a general picture of the additional classifications. This list may not be exhaustive, but it is complete so far as my informants and I are aware.

3. Because these general categories have been elaborated elsewhere by Hoijer and others, and because this paper particularly focuses on the fifteen basic categories which are found within each of the fifteen general categories, no further elaboration of the fifteen general categories will be provided.

4. Three of my informants have indicated that the indefinite lesser plural can be characterized as countable and the indefinite greater plural can be characterized as uncountable or so numerous as to make it almost impossible to count. However, I have not found that the countable/uncountable distinction is a conscious definition for most Navajo. Because the evidence for countable/uncountable is less than conclusive, I am being cautious and calling one the indefinite lesser plural and one the indefinite greater plural.

5. The overall tally of the way in which different parts of speech mark number according to the six continua listed above is as follows: pronouns—3, 4; nouns—4, 6; verbs—1, 2, 3, and 5.

6. In my dissertation (University of Chicago, 1970) I worked out a componential analysis of Navajo culturally defined kin categories. Sometime soon I plan to publish a componential analysis of Navajo categories of siblings.

TWENTY-FIVE

On Aphasia

ROMAN JAKOBSON

In developing the notion of phonemic oppositions and reducing them to binary oppositions, Roman Jakobson (along with Ferdinand de Saussure and other structural linguists) provided the basic model of structural analysis which, through the anthropology of Claude Lévi-Strauss, has become so important in anthropology. The paper included here is an examination of aphasic speech disorders, which Jakobson in fact somewhat misunderstood, from the perspective of structural linguistics.

This analysis reveals the assumptions behind and the implications of structuralist notions of language, particularly the notions of metaphor and metonymy. These last, the first seen as relationships based on similarity and the second on contiguity, emerge in a discussion of possible studies of stylistic contents of art, literature, riddles, and so on, as well as speech disorders. Despite the limitations of the analysis of the latter, the paper remains important historically—for the understanding of the development of the structuralist viewpoint—and didactically—to illustrate the analytic consequences of disregarding the uses of context by actors. Jakobson's conception of metaphor and metonymy finds context irrelevant, because eternally set; relations are reified and then depicted as based in either similarity or contiguity. The article, which implies that social periods can be stylistically characterized as metaphoric or metonymic and that this is a consequence of the failures of the opposite tendency, suggests the limitations of models taken from (structural) linguistics in studies of culture.

The Linguistic Problems of Aphasia

IF APHASIA IS A LANGUAGE DISTUR-BANCE, as the term itself suggests, then any description and classification of aphasic syndromes must begin with the question of what aspects of language are impaired in the various species of such a disorder. This problem, which was approached long ago by Hughlings Jackson (1915), cannot be solved without the participation of professional linguists familiar with the patterning and functioning of language.

To study adequately any breakdown in communications we must first understand the nature and structure of the particular mode of communication that has ceased to function. Linguistics is concerned with language in all its aspects—language in operation, lan-

Reprinted by permission of the publisher from Roman Jakobson and Morris Halle, *Fundamentals of Language* (The Hague: Mouton, 1956), pp. 76–82.

guage in drift (Sapir 1921: Ch. VII), language in the nascent state, and language in dissolution.

At present there are psychopathologists who assign a high importance to the linguistic problems involved in the study of language disturbances;[1] some of these questions have been touched upon in the best recent treatises on aphasia (Goldstein 1948; Luria 1947; Ombredane 1951). Yet, in most cases, this valid insistence on the linguist's contribution to the investigation of aphasia is still ignored. For instance, a new book, dealing to a great extent with the complex and intricate problems of infantile aphasia, calls for a coordination of various disciplines and appeals for cooperation to otolaryngologists, pediatricians, audiologists, psychiatrists, and educators; but the science of language is passed over in silence, as if disorders in speech perception had nothing whatever to do with language (Myklebust 1954). This omission is the more deplorable since the author is Director of the Child Hearing and Aphasia Clinics at Northwestern University, which counts among its linguists Werner F. Leopold, by far the best American expert on child language.

Linguists are also responsible for the delay in undertaking a joint inquiry into aphasia. Nothing comparable to the minute linguistic observations of infants of various countries has been performed with respect to aphasics. Nor has there been any attempt to reinterpret and systematize from the point of view of linguistics the multifarious clinical data on diverse types of aphasia. That this should be true is all the more surprising in view of the fact that, on the one hand, the amazing progress of structural linguistics has endowed the investigator with efficient tools and methods for the study of verbal regression and, on the other, the aphasic disintegration of the verbal pattern may provide the linguist with new insights into the general laws of language.

The application of purely linguistic criteria to the interpretation and classification of aphasic facts can substantially contribute to the science of language and language disturbances, provided that linguists remain as careful and cautious when dealing with psychological and neurological data as they have been in their traditional field. First of all, they should be familiar with the technical terms and devices of the medical disciplines dealing with aphasia; then, they must submit the clinical case reports to thorough linguistic analysis; and, further, they should themselves work with aphasic patients in order to approach the cases directly and not only through a reinterpretation of prepared records which have been quite differently conceived and elaborated.

There is one level of aphasic phenomena where amazing agreement has been achieved during the last twenty years between those psychiatrists and linguists who have tackled these problems, namely the disintegration of the sound pattern.[2] This dissolution exhibits a time order of great regularity. Aphasic regression has proved to be a mirror of the child's acquisition of speech sounds: it shows the child's development in reverse. Furthermore, comparison of child language and aphasia enables us to establish several laws of implication. The search for this order of acquisitions and losses and for the general laws of implication cannot be confined to the phonemic pattern but must be extended also to the grammatical system. Only a few preliminary attempts have been made in this direction, and these efforts deserve to be continued.[3]

The Twofold Character of Language

Speech implies a SELECTION of certain linguistic entities and their COMBINATION into linguistic units of a higher degree of complexity. At the lexical level this is readily apparent: the speaker selects words and combines them into sentences according to the syntactic system of the language he is using; sentences in their turn are combined into utterances. But the speaker is by no means a completely free agent in his choice of words: his selection (except for the rare case of actual neology) must be made from the lexical storehouse which he and his addressee possess in common. The communication engineer most properly approaches the essence of the speech event when he assumes that in the optimal exchange of information the speaker and the listener have at their disposal more or less the same "filing cabinet of *prefabricated* representations": the addresser of a verbal message selects one of these "preconceived possibilities" and the addressee is supposed to make an identical choice from the same assembly of "possibilities already foreseen and provided for" (MacKay 1952:183). Thus the efficiency of a speech event demands the use of a common code by its participants.

"'Did you say *pig* or *fig?*' said the Cat. 'I said *pig,*' replied Alice." In this peculiar utterance the feline addressee attempts to recapture a linguistic choice made by the addresser. In the common code of the Cat and Alice, i.e. in spoken English, the difference between a stop and a continuant, other things being equal, may change the meaning of the message. Alice had used the distinctive feature stop *vs.* continuant, rejecting the latter and choosing the former of the two opposites; and in the same act of speech she combined this solution with certain other simultaneous features, using the gravity and the tenseness of /p/ in contradistinction to the acuteness of /t/ and to the laxness of /b/. Thus all these attributes have been combined into a bundle of distinctive features, the so-called phoneme. The phoneme /p/ was then followed by the phonemes /i/ and /g/, themselves bundles of simultaneously produced distinctive features. Hence the CONCURRENCE of simultaneous entities and the CONCATENATION of successive entities are the two ways in which we speakers combine linguistic constituents.

Neither such bundles as /p/ or /f/ nor such sequences of bundles as /pig/ or /fig/ are invented by the speaker who uses them. Neither can the distinctive feature stop vs. continuant nor the phoneme /p/ occur out of context. The stop feature appears in combination with certain other concurrent features, and the repertory of combinations of these features into phonemes such as /p/, /b/, /t/, /d/, /k/, /g/, etc. is limited by the code of the given language. The code sets limitations on the possible combinations of the phoneme /p/ with other following and/or preceding phonemes; and only part of the permissible phoneme-sequences are actually utilized in the lexical stock of a given language. Even when other combinations of phonemes are theoretically possible, the speaker, as a rule, is only a word-user, not a word-coiner. When faced with individual words, we expect them to be coded units. In order to grasp the word *nylon* one must know the meaning assigned to this vocable in the lexical code of modern English.

In any language there exist also coded word-groups called phrasewords. The meaning of the idiom *how do you do* cannot be derived by adding together the meanings of its lexical constituents; the whole is not equal to the sum of its parts. Word-groups which in this respect behave like single words are a common but nonetheless only marginal case. In order to comprehend the overwhelming majority of word-groups, we need be familiar only with the constituent words and with the syntactical rules of their combination. Within these limitations we are free to put words in new contexts. Of course, this freedom is relative, and the pressure of current clichés upon our choice of combinations is considerable. But the freedom to compose quite new contexts is undeniable, despite the relatively low statistical probability of their occurrence.

Thus, in the combination of linguistic units there is an ascending scale of freedom. In the combination of distinctive features into phonemes, the freedom of the individual speaker is zero: the code has already established all the possibilities which may be utilized in the given language. Freedom to combine phonemes into words is circumscribed; it is limited to the marginal situation of word coinage. In forming sentences with words the speaker is less constrained. And finally, in the combination of sentences into utterances, the action of compulsory syntactical rules ceases, and the freedom of any individual speaker to create novel contexts increases substantially, although again the numerous stereotyped utterances are not to be overlooked.

Any linguistic sign involves two modes of arrangement.

(1) COMBINATION. Any sign is made up of constituent signs and/or occurs only in combination with other signs. This means that any linguistic unit at one and the same time serves as a context for simpler units and/or finds its own context in a more complex linguistic unit. Hence any actual grouping of linguistic units binds them into a superior unit: combination and contexture are two faces of the same operation.

(2) SELECTION. A selection between alternatives implies the possibility of substituting one for the other, equivalent to the former in one respect and different from it in another. Actually, selection and substitution are two faces of the same operation.

The fundamental role which these two operations play in language was clearly realized by Ferdinand de Saussure. Yet of the two varieties of combination—concurrence and concatenation—it was only the latter, the temporal sequence, which was recognized by the Geneva linguist. Despite his own insight into the phoneme as a set of concurrent distinctive features (*éléments différentiels des phonèmes),* the scholar succumbed to the traditional belief in the linear character of language *"qui exclut la possibilité de prononcer deux éléments à la fois"* (Saussure 1915:68 ff., 170 ff.).

In order to delimit the two modes of arrangement which we have described as combination and selection, F. de Saussure states that the former "is *in presentia:* it is based on two or several terms jointly present in an actual series," whereas the latter "connects terms *in absentia* as members of a virtual mnemonic series." That is to say, selection (and, correspondingly, substitution) deals with entities conjoined in the code but not in the given message, whereas, in the case of combination, the entities are conjoined in both, or only in the actual message. The addressee perceives that the given utterance (message) is a COMBINATION of constituent parts (sentences, words, phonemes, etc.) SELECTED from the repository of all possible constituent parts (the code). The constituents of a context are in a state of CONTIGUITY, while in a substitution set signs are linked by various degree of SIMILARITY which fluctuate between the equivalence of synonyms and the common core of antonyms.

These two operations provide each linguistic sign with two sets of INTERPRETANTS, to utilize the effective concept introduced by Charles Sanders Peirce: there are two references which serve to interpret the sign—one to the code, and the other to the context, whether coded or free, and in each of these ways the sign is related to another set of linguistic signs, through an ALTERNATION in the former case and through an ALIGNMENT in the latter. A given significative unit may be replaced by other, more explicit signs of the same code, whereby its general meaning is revealed, while its contextual meaning is determined by its connection with other signs within the same sequence.

The constituents of any message are necessarily linked with the code by an internal relation and with the message by an external relation. Language in its various aspects deals with both modes of relation. Whether messages are exchanged or communication proceeds unilaterally from the addresser to the addressee, there must be some kind of contiguity between the participants of any speech event to assure the transmission of the message. The separation in space, and often in time, between two individuals, the addresser and the addressee, is bridged by an internal relation: there must be a certain equivalence between the symbols used by the addresser and those known and interpreted by the addressee. Without such an equivalence the message is fruitless: even when it reaches the receiver it does not affect him.

Similarity Disorder

It is clear that speech disturbances may affect in varying degrees the individual's capacity for combination and selection of linguistic units, and indeed the question of which of these two operations is chiefly impaired proves to be of far-reaching significance in describing, analyzing, and classifying the diverse forms of aphasia. This dichotomy is perhaps even more suggestive than the classical distinction (not discussed in this paper) between EMISSIVE and RECEPTIVE aphasia, indicating which of the two functions in speech exchange, the encoding or the decoding of verbal messages, is particularly affected.

Head attempted to classify cases of aphasia into definite groups, and to each of these varieties he assigned "a name chosen to signify the most salient defect in the management and comprehension of words and phrases" (Head 1926:412). Following this device, we distinguish two basic types of aphasia—depending on whether the major deficiency lies in selection and substitution, with relative stability of combination and contexture; or conversely, in combination and contexture, with relative retention of normal selection and substitution. In outlining these two opposite patterns of aphasia, I shall utilize mainly Goldstein's data.

For aphasics of the first type (selection deficiency), the context is the indispensable and decisive factor. When presented with scraps of words or sentences, such a patient readily completes them. His speech is merely reactive: he easily carries on conversation, but has difficulties in starting a dialogue; he is able to reply to a real or imaginary addresser when he is, or imagines himself to be, the addressee of the message. It is particularly hard for him to perform, or even to understand, such a closed discourse as the monologue. The more his utterances are dependent on the context, the better he copes with his verbal task. He feels unable to utter a sentence which responds neither to the cue of his interlocutor nor to the actual situation. The sentence "it rains" cannot be produced unless the utterer sees that it is actually raining. The deeper the utterance is embedded in the verbal or non-verbalized context, the higher are the chances of its successful performance by this class of patients.

Likewise, the more a word is dependent on the other words of the same sentence and the more it refers to the syntactical context, the less it is affected by the speech disturbance. Therefore words syntactically subordinated by grammatical agreement or government are more tenacious, whereas the main subordinating agent of the sentence, namely the subject, tends to be omitted. As long as beginning is the patient's main difficulty, it is obvious that he will fail precisely at the starting point, the cornerstone of the sentence-pattern. In this type of language disturbance, sentences are conceived as elliptical sequels to be supplied from antecedent sentences uttered, if not imagined, by the aphasic himself, or received by him from the other partner in the colloquy, actual if not imaginary. Key words may be dropped or superseded by abstract anaphoric substitutes (Bloomfield 1933: Ch. x). A specific noun, as Freud noticed, is replaced by a very general one, for instance *machin, chose* in the speech of French aphasics (Freud 1953: 22). In a dialectal German sample of "amnesic phasia" observed by Goldstein (p. 246 ff.), *Ding* 'thing' or *Stückel* 'piece' were substituted for all inanimate nouns, and *überfahren* 'perform' for verbs which were identifiable from the context or situation and therefore appeared superfluous to the patient.

Words with an inherent reference to the context, like pronouns and pronominal adverbs, and words serving merely to construct the context, such as connectives and auxiliaries, are particularly prone to survive. A typical utterance of a German patient, recorded by Quensel and quoted by Goldstein (p. 302), will serve as illustration:

"Ich bin doch hier unten, na wenn ich gewesen bin ich wees nicht, we das, nu wenn ich, ob das nun doch, noch, ja. Was Sie her, wenn ich, och ich weess nicht, we das hier war ja . . . "

Thus only the framework, the connecting links of communication, is spared by this type of aphasia at its critical stage.

In the theory of language, since the early Middle Ages, it has repeatedly been asserted that the word out of context has no meaning. The validity of this statement is, however, confined to aphasia, or, more exactly, to one type of aphasia. In the pathological cases under discussion an isolated word means actually nothing but 'blab.' As numerous tests have disclosed, for such patients two occurrences of the same word in two different contexts are mere homonyms. Since distinctive vocables carry a higher amount of information than homonyms, some aphasics of this type tend to supplant the contextual variant of one word by different terms, each of them specific for the given environment. Thus Goldstein's patient never uttered the word *knife* alone, but, according to its use and surroundings, alternately called the knife *pencil-sharpener, apple-parer, bread-knife, knife-and-fork* (p. 62); so that the word *knife* was changed from a free form, capable of occurring alone, into a bound form.

"I have a good apartment, entrance hall, bedroom, kitchen," Goldstein's patient says. "There are also big apartments, only in the rear live bachelors." A more explicit form, the work-group *unmarried people,* could have been substituted for *bachelors,* but this univerbal term was selected by the speaker. When repeatedly asked what a bachelor was, the patient did not answer and was "apparently in distress" (p. 270). A reply like "a bachelor is an unmarried man" or "an unmarried man is a bachelor" would present an equational predication and thus a projection of a substitution set from the lexical code of the English language into the context of the given message. The equivalent terms become two correlated parts of the sentence and consequently are tied by contiguity. The patient was able to select the appropriate term *bachelor* when it was supported by the context of a customary conversation about "bachelor apartments," but was incapable of utilizing the substitution set *bachelor =*

unmarried man as the topic of a sentence, because the ability for autonomous selection and substitution had been affected. The equational sentence vainly demanded from the patient carries as its sole information: "'bachelor' means an unmarried man" or "an unmarried man is called 'a bachelor.'"

The same difficulty arises when the patient is asked to name an object pointed to or handled by the examiner. The aphasic with a defect in substitution will not supplement the pointing or handling gesture of the examiner with the name of the object pointed to. Instead of saying "this is [called] a pencil," he will merely add an elliptical note about its use: "To write." If one of the synonymic signs is present (as for instance the word *bachelor* or the pointing to the pencil) then the other sign (such as the phrase *unmarried man* or the word *pencil*) becomes redundant and consequently superfluous. For the aphasic, both signs are in complementary distribution: if one is performed by the examiner, the patient will avoid its synonym: "I understand everything" or "Ich weiss es schon" will be his typical reaction. Likewise, the picture of an object will cause suppression of its name: a verbal sign is supplanted by a pictorial sign. When the picture of a compass was presented to a patient of Lotmar's, he responded: "Yes, it's a . . . I know what it belongs to, but I cannot recall the technical expression . . . Yes . . . direction . . . to show direction . . . a magnet points to the north" (Lotmar 1933:104). Such patients fail to shift, as Peirce would say, from an INDEX or ICON to a corresponding verbal SYMBOL (Peirce 1932).

Even simple repetition of a word uttered by the examiner seems to the patient unnecessarily redundant, and despite instructions received he is unable to repeat it. Told to repeat the word "no," Head's patient replied "No, I don't know how to do it." While spontaneously using the word in the context of his answer ("No, I don't . . ."), he could not produce the purest form of equational predication, the tautology *a = a:* 'no' is 'no.'

One of the important contributions of symbolic logic to the science of language is its emphasis on the distinction between OBJECT LANGUAGE and META-LANGUAGE. As Carnap states, "in order to speak *about* any *object language, we* need a *metalanguage"* (1947:4). On these two different levels of language the same linguistic stock may be used; thus we may speak in English (as meta-language) about English (as object language) and interpret English words and sentences by means of English synonyms, circumlocutions, and paraphrases. Obviously such operations, labeled METALINGUISTIC by the logicians, are not their invention: far from being confined to the sphere of science, they prove to be an integral part of our customary linguistic activities. The participants in a dialogue often check whether they are using the same code. "Do you follow me? Do you see what I mean?" the speaker asks, or the listener himself breaks in with "What do you mean?" Then, by replacing the questionable sign with another sign from the same linguistic code, or with a whole group of code signs, the sender of the message seeks to make it more accessible to the decoder.

The interpretation of one linguistic sign through other, in some respect homogeneous, signs of the same language, is a metalinguistic operation which also plays an essential role in children's language learning. Recent observations have disclosed what a considerable place talk about language occupies in the verbal behavior of pre-school children (Gvozdev 1929; 1948; 1949). Recourse to metalanguage is necessary both for the acquisition of language and for its normal functioning. The aphasic defect in the "capacity of naming" is properly a loss of metalanguage. As a matter of fact, the examples of equational prediction sought in vain from the patients cited above, are metalinguistic propositions referring to the English language. Their explicit wording would be: "In the code that we use, the name of the indicated object is 'pencil'"; or "In the code we use, the word 'bachelor' and the circumlocution 'unmarried man' are equivalent."

Such an aphasic can neither switch from a word to its synonyms or circumlocutions, nor to its HETERONYMS, i.e. equivalent expressions in other languages. Loss of bilingualism and confinement to a single dialectal variety of a single language is a symptomatic manifestation of this disorder.

According to an old but recurrent bias, a single individual's way of speaking at a given time, labeled IDIOLECT, has been viewed as the only concrete linguistic reality. In the discussion of this concept the following objections were raised:

Everyone, when speaking to another person, tries, deliberately or involuntarily, to hit upon a common vocabulary: either to please or simply to be understood or, finally, to bring him out, he uses the terms of his addressee. There is no such thing as private property in language: everything is socialized. Verbal exchange, like any form of intercourse, requires at least two communicators, and idiolect proves to be a somewhat perverse fiction (Conference of Anthropologists and Linguists 1953:15).

This statement needs, however, one

reservation: for an aphasic who has lost the capacity for code switching, the "idiolect" indeed becomes the sole linguistic reality. As long as he does not regard another's speech as a message addressed to him in his own verbal pattern, he feels, as a patient of Hemphil and Stengel expressed it: "I can hear you dead plain but I cannot get what you say . . . I hear your voice but not the words . . . It does not pronounce itself" (1940:251–62). He considers the other's utterance to be either gibberish or at least in an unknown language.

As noted above, it is the external relation of contiguity which unites the constituents of a context, and the internal relation of similarity which underlies the substitution set. Hence, for an aphasic with impaired substitution and intact contexture, operations involving similarity yield to those based on contiguity. It could be predicted that under these conditions any semantic grouping would be guided by spatial or temporal contiguity rather than by similarity. Actually Goldstein's tests justify such an expectation: a female patient of this type, when asked to list a few names of animals, disposed them in the same order in which she had seen them in the zoo; similarly, despite instructions to arrange certain objects according to color, size, and shape, she classified them on the basis of their spatial contiguity as home things, office materials, etc. and justified this grouping by a reference to a display window where "it does not matter what the things are," i.e. they do not have to be similar (pp. 61 f., 263 ff.). The same patient was willing to name the primary hues—red, yellow, green, and blue—but declined to extend these names to the transitional varieties (p. 268 f.), since, for her, words had no capacity to assume additional, shifted meanings associated by similarity with their primary meaning.

One must agree with Goldstein's observation that patients of this type "grasped the words in their literal meaning but could not be brought to understand the metaphoric character of the same words" (p. 270). It would, however, be an unwarranted generalization to assume that figurative speech is altogether incomprehensible to them. Of the two polar figures of speech, metaphor and metonymy, the latter, based on contiguity, is widely employed by aphasics whose selective capacities have been affected. *Fork* is substituted for *knife, table* for *lamp, smoke* for *pipe, eat* for *toaster*. A typical case is reported by Head:

When he failed to recall the name for "black", he described it as "What you do for the dead"; this he shortened to "dead." (I, 198)

Such metonymies may be characterized as projections from the line of a habitual context into the line of substitution and selection: a sign (e.g. *fork*) which usually occurs together with another sign (e.g. *knife*) may be used instead of this sign. Phrases like "knife and fork," "table lamp," "to smoke a pipe," induced the metonymies *fork, table, smoke;* the relation between the use of an object (toast) and the means of its production underlies the metonymy *eat* for *toaster*. "When does one wear black?"—"When mourning the dead": in place of naming the color, the cause of its traditional use is designated. The escape from sameness to contiguity is particularly striking in such cases as Goldstein's patient who would answer with a metonymy when asked to repeat a given word and, for instance, would say *glass* for *window* and *heaven* for *God* (p. 280).

When the selective capacity is strongly impaired and the gift for combination at least partly preserved, then CONTIGUITY determines the patient's whole verbal behavior, and we may designate this type of aphasia SIMILARITY DISORDER.

Contiguity Disorder

From 1864 on it was repeatedly pointed out in Hughlings Jackson's pioneer contributions to the modern study of language and language disturbances:

It is not enough to say that speech consists of words. It consists of words referring to one another in a particular manner; and, without a proper interrelation of its parts, a verbal utterance would be a mere succession of names embodying no proposition. (p. 66)

Loss of speech is the loss of power to propositionize . . . Speechlessness does not mean entire wordlessness. (p. 114)

Impairment of the ability to PROPOSITIONIZE, or, generally speaking, to combine simpler linguistic entities into more complex units, is actually confined to one type of aphasia, the opposite of the type discussed in the preceding chapter. There is no WORDLESSNESS, since the entity preserved in most of such cases is the WORD, which can be defined as the highest among the linguistic units compulsorily coded, i.e., we compose our own sentences and utterances out of the word stock supplied by the code.

This contexture-deficient aphasia, which could be termed CONTIGUITY DISORDER, diminishes the extent and variety of sentences. The syntactical rules organizing words into higher units are lost; this loss, called AGRAMMATISM, causes the degeneration of the sentence into a mere "word heap," to use Jackson's image (Jackson 1915). Word order becomes chaotic; the ties of grammatical coordination and subordination, whether concord or government, are dissolved. As might be expected, words endowed with purely grammatical functions, like conjunctions, prepositions, pronouns, and articles, disappear first, giving rise to the so-called "telegraphic style," whereas in the case of similarity disorder they are the most resistant. The less a word depends grammatically on the context, the stronger is its tenacity in the speech of aphasics with a contiguity disorder and the earlier it is dropped by patients with a similarity disorder. Thus the "kernel subject word" is the first to fall out of the sentence in cases of similarity disorder and, conversely, it is the least destructible in the opposite type of aphasia.

The type of aphasia affecting contexture tends to give rise to infantile one-sentence utterances and one-word sentences. Only a few longer, stereotyped, "ready made" sentences manage to survive. In advanced cases of this disease, each utterance is reduced to a single one-word sentence. While contexture disintegrates, the selective operation goes on. "To say what a thing is, is to say what it is like," Jackson notes (p. 125). The patient confined to the substitution set (once contexture is deficient) deals with similarities, and his approximate identifications are of a metaphoric nature, contrary to the metonymic ones familiar to the opposite type of aphasics. *Spyglass* for *microscope,* or *fire* for *gaslight* are typical examples of such QUASI-METAPHORIC EXPRESSIONS, as Jackson termed them, since, in contradistinction to rhetoric or poetic metaphors, they present no deliberate transfer of meaning.

In a normal language pattern, the word is at the same time both a constituent part of a superimposed context, the SENTENCE, and itself a context superimposed on ever smaller constituents, MORPHEMES (minimum units endowed with meaning) and PHONEMES. We have discussed the effect of contiguity disorder on the combination of words into higher units. The relationship between the word and its constituents reflects the same impairment, yet in a somewhat different way. A typical feature of agrammatism is the abolition of inflection: there appear such unmarked categories as the infinitive in the place of diverse finite verbal forms, and in languages with declension, the nominative instead of all the oblique cases. These defects are due partly to the elimination of government and concord, partly to the loss of ability to dissolve words into stem and desinence. Finally, a paradigm (in particular a set of grammatical cases such as *he—his—him,* or of tenses such as *he votes—he voted*) present the same semantic content from different points of view associated with each other by contiguity; so there is one more impetus for aphasics with a contiguity disorder to dismiss such sets.

Also, as a rule, words derived from the same root, such as *grant—grantor—grantee* are semantically related by contiguity. The patients under discussion are either inclined to drop the derivative words, or the combination of a root with a derivational suffix and even a compound of two words become irresolvable for them. Patients who understood and uttered such compounds as *Thanksgiving* or *Battersea,* but were unable to grasp or to say *thanks* and *giving* or *batter* and *sea,* have often been cited. As long as the sense of derivation is still alive, so that this process is still used for creating innovations in the code, one can observe a tendency towards oversimplification and automatism: if the derivative word constitutes a semantic unit which cannot be entirely inferred from the meaning of its components, the GESTALT is misunderstood. Thus the Russian word *mokr-íca* signifies 'wood-louse,' but a Russian aphasic interpreted it as 'something humid,' especially 'humid weather,' since the root *mokr-* means 'humid' and the suffix *-ica* designates a carrier of the given property, as in *nelépica* 'something absurd,' *svetlíca* 'light room,' *temníca* 'dungeon' (literally 'dark room').

When, before World War II, phonemics was the most controversial area in the science of language, doubts were expressed by some linguists as to whether phonemes really play an autonomous part in our verbal behavior. It was even suggested that the meaningful (SIGNIFICATIVE) units of the linguistic code, such as morphemes or rather words, are the minimal entities with which we actually deal in a speech event, whereas the merely DISTINCTIVE units, such as phonemes, are an artificial construct to facilitate the scientific description and analysis of a language. This view, which was stigmatized by Sapir as "the reverse of realistic" (Sapir 1949: 46 ff.), remains, however, perfectly valid with respect to a certain pathological type: in one variety of aphasia, which sometimes has been labeled "atactic," the word is the sole linguistic unity preserved. The patient has only an integral, indissolvable image of any familiar word, and all other sound sequences are either alien and inscrutable to him, or he merges them into familiar words by disregarding their phonetic deviations. One of Goldstein's patients "perceived some words, but . . . the vowels and consonants of which they consisted were not perceived" (p. 218). A French aphasic recognized, understood, repeated, and spontaneously produced the word *café* 'coffee' or *pavé* 'roadway,' but was unable to grasp, discern, or repeat such nonsensical sequences as *féca, faké, kéfa, pafé*. None of these difficulties exists for a normal French-speaking listner as long as the sound-sequences and their components fit the French phonemic pattern. Such a listener may even apprehend these sequences as words unknown to him but plausibly belonging to the French vocabulary and presumably different in meaning, since they differ from each other either in the order of their phonemes or in the phonemes themselves.

If an aphasic becomes unable to resolve the word into its phonemic constituents, his control over its construction weakens, and perceptible damage to phonemes and their combinations easily follows. The gradual regression of the sound pattern in aphasics regularly reverses the order of children's phonemic acquisitions. This regression involves an inflation of homonyms and a decrease of vocabulary. If this twofold—phonemic and lexical—disablement progresses further, the last residues of speech are one-phoneme, one-word, one-sentence utterances: the patient relapses into the initial phases of infant's linguistic development or even to the pre-lingual stage: he faces *aphasia universalis,* the total loss of the power to use or apprehend speech.

The separateness of the two functions—one distinctive and the other significative—is a peculiar feature of language as compared to other semiotic systems. There arises a conflict between these two levels of language when the aphasic deficient in contexture exhibits a tendency to abolish the hierarchy of linguistic units and to reduce their scale to a single level. The last level to remain is either a class of significative values, the word, as in the cases touched upon, or a class of distinctive values, the phoneme. In the latter case the patient is still able to identify, distinguish, and reproduce phonemes, but loses the capacity to do the same with words. In an intermediate case, words are identified, distinguished, and reproduced; according to Goldstein's acute formulation, they "may be grasped as known but not understood" (p. 90). Here the word loses its normal significative function and assumes the purely distinctive function which normally pertains to the phoneme.

The Metaphoric and Metonymic Poles

The varieties of aphasia are numerous and diverse, but all of them lie between the two polar types just described. Every form of aphasic disturbance consists in some impairment, more or less severe, either of the faculty for selection and substitution or for combination and contexture. The former affliction involves a deterioration of metalinguistic operations, while the latter damages the capacity for maintaining the hierarchy of linguistic units. The relation of similarity is suppressed in the former, the relation of contiguity in the latter type of aphasia. Metaphor is alien to the similarity disorder, and metonymy to the contiguity disorder.

The development of a discourse may take place along two different semantic lines: one topic may lead to another either through their similarity or through their contiguity. The METAPHORIC way would be the most appropriate term for the first case and the METONYMIC way for the second, since they find their most condensed expression in metaphor and metonymy respectively. In aphasia one or the other of these two processes is restricted or totally blocked—an effect which makes the study of aphasia particularly illuminating for the linguist. In normal verbal behavior both processes are continually operative, but careful observation will reveal that under the influence of a cultural pattern, personality, and verbal style, preference is given to one of the two processes over the other.

In a well-known psychological test, children are confronted with some noun and told to utter the first verbal response that comes into their heads. In this experiment two opposite linguistic predilections are invariably exhibited: the response is intended either as a substitute for, or as a complement to, the stimulus. In the latter case the stimulus and the response together form a proper syntactic construction, most usually a sentence. These two types of reaction have been labeled SUBSTITUTIVE and PREDICATIVE,

To the stimulus *hut* one response was *burnt out;* another, *is a poor little house*. Both reactions are predicative; but the first creates a purely narrative context, while in the second there is a double connection with the subject *hut:* on the one hand, a positional (namely, syntactic) contiguity, and on the other a semantic similarity.

The same stimulus produced the following substitutive reactions: the tautology *hut;* the synonyms *cabin* and *hovel;* the antonym *palace,* and the metaphors *den* and *burrow*. The capacity of two words to replace one another is an instance of positional similarity, and, in addition, all these responses are linked to the stimulus by semantic similarity (or contrast). Metonymical responses to the same stimulus, such as *thatch litter,* or *poverty,* combine and contrast the positional similarity with semantic contiguity.

In manipulating these two kinds of connection (similarity and contiguity) in both their aspects (positional and semantic)—selecting, combining, and ranking them—an individual exhibits his personal style, his verbal predilections and preferences.

In verbal art the interaction of these two elements is especially pronounced. Rich material for the study of this relationship is to be found in verse patterns which require a compulsory PARALLELISM between adjacent lines, for example, in Biblical poetry or in the Finnic and, to some extent, the Russian oral traditions. This provides an objective criterion of what in the given speech community acts as a correspondence. Since on any verbal level—morphemic, lexical, syntactic, and phraseological— either of these two relations (similarity and contiguity) can appear—and each in either of two aspects, an impressive range of possible configurations is created. Either of the two gravitational poles may prevail. In Russian lyrical songs, for example, metaphoric constructions predominate, while in the heroic epics the metonymic way is preponderant.

In poetry there are various motives which determine the choice between these alternants. The primacy of the metaphoric process in the literary schools of romanticism and symbolism has been repeatedly acknowledged, but it is still insufficiently realized that it is the predominance of metonymy which underlies and actually predetermines the so-called 'realistic' trend, which belongs to an intermediary stage between the decline of romanticism and the rise of symbolism and is opposed to both. Following the path of contiguous relationships, the realist author metonymically digresses from the plot to the atmosphere and from the characters to the setting in space and time. He is fond of synecdochic details. In the scene of Anna Karenina's suicide Tolstoy's artistic attention is focused on the heroine's handbag; and in *War and Peace* the synecdoches "hair on the upper lip" and "bare shoulders" are used by the same writer to stand for the female characters to whom these features belong.

The alternative predominance of one or the other of these two processes is by no means confined to verbal art. The same oscillation occurs in sign systems other than language (Jakobson 1927; 1935; 1919; 1933). A salient example from the history of painting is the manifestly metonymical orientation of cubism, where the object is transformed into a set of synecdoches; the surrealist painters responded with a patently metaphorical attitude. Ever since the productions of D. W. Griffith, the art of the cinema, with its highly developed capacity for changing the angle, perspective, and focus of 'shots,' has broken with the tradition of the theater and ranged an unprecedented variety of synecdochic 'close-ups' and metonymic 'set-ups' in general. In such motion pictures as those of Charlie Chaplin and Eisenstein (Eisenstein 1949:153 ff.), these devices in turn were overlayed by a novel, metaphoric "montage" with its "lap dissolves"—the filmic similes (Balázs 1952).

The bipolar structure of language (or other semiotic systems) and, in aphasia, the fixation on one of these poles to the exclusion of the other require systematic comparative study. The retention of either of these alternatives in the two types of aphasia must be confronted with the predominance of the same pole in certain styles, personal habits, current fashions, etc. A careful analysis and comparison of these phenomena with the whole syndrome of the corresponding type of aphasia is an imperative task for joint research by experts in psychopathology, psychology, linguistics, poetics, and SEMIOTIC, the general science of signs. The dichotomy discussed here appears to be of primal significance and consequence for all verbal behavior and for human behavior in general.[4]

To indicate the possibilities of the projected comparative research, we choose an example from a Russian folktale which employs parallelism as a comic device: "Thomas is a bachelor; Jeremiah is unmarried" (*Fomá xólost; Erjóma neženát*). Here the predicates in the two parallel clauses are associated by similarity: they are in fact synonymous. The subjects of both clauses are masculine proper names and hence morphologically similar, while on the other hand they denote two contiguous heroes of the same tale, created to perform identical actions and thus to justify the use of synonymous pairs of predicates. A somewhat modified version of the same construction occurs in a familiar wedding song in which each of the wedding guests is addressed in turn by his first name and patronymic: "Gleb is a bachelor; Ivanovič is unmarried." While both predicates here are again synonyms, the relationship between the two subjects is changed: both are proper names denoting the same man and are normally used contiguously as a mode of polite address.

In the quotation from the folktale, the two parallel clauses refer to two separate facts, the marital status of Thomas and the similar status of Jeremiah. In the verse from the wedding song, however, the two clauses are synonymous: they redundantly reiterate the celibacy of the same hero, splitting him into two verbal hypostases.

The Russian novelist Gleb Ivanovič Uspenskij (1840–1902) in the last years of his life suffered from a mental illness involving a speech disorder. His first name and patronymic, *Gleb Ivanovič,* traditionally combined in polite intercourse, for him split into two distinct names designating two separate beings: Gleb was endowed with all his virtues, while Ivanovič, the name relating a son to his father, became the incarnation of all Uspenskij's vices. The linguistic aspect of this split personality is the patient's inability to use two symbols for the same thing, and it is thus a similarity disorder. Since the similarity disorder is bound up with the metonymical bent, an examination of the literary manner Uspenskij had employed as a young writer takes on particular interest. And the study of Anatolij Kamegulov, who analyzed Uspenskij's style, bears out our theoretical expectations. He shows that Uspenskij had a particular penchant for metonymy, and especially for synecdoche, and that he carried it so far that

"the reader is crushed by the multiplicity of detail unloaded on him in a limited verbal space, and is physically unable to grasp the whole, so that the portrait is often lost."[5]

To be sure, the metonymical style in Uspenskij is obviously prompted by the prevailing literary canon of his time, late nineteenth-century 'realism'; but the personal stamp of Gleb Ivanovič made his pen particularly suitable for this artistic trend in its extreme manifestations and finally left its mark upon the verbal aspect of his mental illness.

A competition between both devices, metonymic and metaphoric, is manifest in any symbolic process, be it intrapersonal or social. Thus in an inquiry into the structure of dreams, the decisive question is whether the symbols and the temporal sequences used are based on contiguity (Freud's metonymic "displacement" and synecdochic "condensation") or on similarity (Freud's "identification and symbolism"). The principles underlying magic rites have been resolved by Frazer into two types: charms based on the law of similarity and those founded on association by contiguity. The first of these two great branches of sympathetic magic has been called "homoeopathic" or "imitative," and the second, "contagious magic." This bipartition is indeed illuminating. Nonetheless, for the most part, the question of the two poles is still neglected, despite its wide scope and importance for the study of any symbolic behavior, especially verbal, and of its impairments. What is the main reason for this neglect?

Similarity in meaning connects the symbols of a metalanguage with the symbols of the language referred to. Similarity connects a metaphorical term with the term for which it is substituted. Consequently, when constructing a metalanguage to interpret tropes, the researcher possesses more homogeneous means to handle metaphor, whereas metonymy, based on a different principle, easily defies interpretation. Therefore nothing comparable to the rich literature on metaphor (Stutterheim 1941) can be cited for the theory of metonymy. For the same reason, it is generally realized that romanticism is closely linked with metaphor, whereas the equally intimate ties of realism with metonymy usually remain unnoticed. Not only the tool of the observer but also the object of observation is responsible for the preponderance of metaphor over metonymy in scholarship. Since poetry is focused upon the sign, and pragmatical prose primarily upon the referent, tropes and figures were studied mainly as poetic devices. The principle of similarity underlies poetry; the metrical parallelism of lines, or the phonic equivalence of rhyming words prompts the question of semantic similarity and contrast; there exist, for instance, grammatical and anti-grammatical but never agrammatical rhymes. Prose, on the contrary, is forwarded essentially by contiguity. Thus, for poetry, metaphor, and for prose, metonymy is the line of least resistance and, consequently, the study of poetical tropes is directed chiefly toward metaphor. The actual bipolarity has been artificially replaced in these studies by an amputated, unipolar scheme which, strikingly enough, coincides with one of the two aphasic patterns, namely with the contiguity disorder.

Notes

1. See, for instance, the discussion on aphasia in the *Nederlandsche Vereeniging voor Phonetische Wetenschappen,* with papers by the linguist J. van Ginneken and by two psychiatrists, F. Grewel and V. W. D. Schenk, *Psychiatrische en Neurologische Bladen,* XLV (1941), 1035 ff. Cf. furthermore, Grewel (1949).

2. The aphasic impoverishment of the sound pattern has been observed and discussed by the linguist Marguerite Durand together with the psychopathologists Th. Alajouanine and A. Ombredane (1939) and by R. Jakobson (the first draft, presented to the International Congress of Linguists at Brussels in 1939—see N. Trubetskoy, 1949—was later developed into an outline, Jakobson, 1942; both are in Jakobson's *Selected Writings* (1962, vol. I).

3. A joint inquiry into certain grammatical disturbances was undertaken at the Bonn University Clinic by a linguist, G. Kandler, and two physicians, F. Panse and A. Leischner (1952).

4. For the psychological and sociological aspects of this dichotomy, see Bateson's views on "progression-al" and "selective integration" and Parsons' on the "conjunction-disjunction dichotomy" in child development: Ruesch and Bateson (1951:183 ff.); Parsons and Bales (1955:119 ff.).

5. Kamegulov (1930:65, 145). One of such disintegrated portraits cited in the monograph: "From underneath an ancient straw cap, with a black spot on its visor, peeked two braids resembling the tusks of a wild boar; a chin, grown fat and pendulous, had spread definitively over the greasy collar of the calico dicky and lay in a thick layer on the coarse collar of the canvas coat, firmly buttoned at the neck. From underneath this coat to the eyes of the observer protruded massive hands with a ring which had eaten into the fat finger, a cane with a copper top, a significant bulge of the stomach, and the presence of very broad pants, almost of muslin quality, in the wide bottoms of which hid the toes of the boots."

NINE

The Person

Making Sense: A Study of a Banaban Meeting

MARTIN G. SILVERMAN

> What we want is *not terms that avoid ambiguity*, but *terms that clearly reveal the strategic spots at which ambiguities necessarily arise*.
>
> —KENNETH BURKE, *A Grammar of Motives*

The cultural constitution of the "person" within a social order is generally taken for granted by the participants: it is "natural." Only infrequently is a society's basic understanding of the person and the group self-consciously framed as a matter to be considered, debated, and recast. It is such a rare ethnographic situation that Silverman describes and analyzes here: a long meeting of the resettled Banabans, whose original home had been turned into a huge mine, now living on Rambi Island, Fiji—a meeting concerned with a set of crucial issues affecting the community's relation to itself, to the colonial government, and to the island from which the Banabans had come.

Silverman here presents the process by which the Banabans, in the course of the meeting, reified that very event as a form through which Banaban identity could be invoked and understood. In impressive detail and with great subtlety, Silverman shows how the symbolic structures of Banaban culture provided the forms that were used in the debates in which the future (and with it, the past) of the community were set (redefined). Silverman's paper situates conceptions of the person with respect to *praxis* and convincingly shows that analysis of alterations in a social order must consider the interconnections between symbolic codes and social processes.

THE DIAL CTIC OF ACTION is the dialectic of form and content. This is, as I understand it, one of the central messages of *The Savage Mind* (Lévi-Strauss 1966). The engaging thing about form and content is how they can shift position and thus become transformed— form becoming content for other form (e.g., the "structure of a kinship system" is shown to be a special case of the "general structure of systems," or some aspects of the "structure of a kinship system" are shown to be harmonious with the "general structure of systems," or the "structure of a kinship system" is shown to be impossible given the "general structure of systems"), content becoming form to other content (e.g.,

Reprinted by permission from *Exiles and Migrants in Oceania*, Michael D. Lieber, ed. Association for Social Anthropology in Oceania Monographs Series 5. Honolulu: University Press of Hawaii, in press.

the "special case" is used to interpret another "subspecial case," which interpretation might not, incidentally, fit, presenting people with all sorts of problems to work out). And on it goes, not randomly but not completely predictably either since, among other things, form can both order and open a door to content (some of it uninvited) and content (to mix the metaphor) can twist form around itself. One man's form can be another man's content and thus they literally "talk past one another." Form and content, structuring and becoming structured—most of our basic theoretical problems are implicit in the pair.

But not only *our* theoretical problems.[1]

Even the firmest believer in the untrammeled freedom of the human intellect would probably concede that being in a situation of resettlement is something that a people, somehow, cannot fail to note. Precisely how they note it we are not in a position to predict; and we are not in a position to predict precisely how those things which we take to be problematic are or are not problematic to the local community. There are new faces and new places, perhaps new subordinations and new equalities; there is new work to be done and new food to eat.

If we are not in a position to predict how a resettled community might note its situation, neither are those being resettled. Not even with the most careful planning, site surveys, political and economic arrangements made with governments and future neighbors can people predict what vagaries of environment, of colonial governments, of neighboring peoples, or, for that matter, of their own social relationships might confront them.

We do, however, find that a resettled community may confront the unpredictable as a community. It happens often enough to be significant that these people encounter problems, events, or situations that demand decisive action as a community and that integral to the decisions is the necessity of clarifying for themselves who they are in order to determine their position. The very unpredictabilities inherent in resettlement (but not, of course, only in resettlement) make such decisions and their implications for identity likely, if not inevitable. Such decisions may be as mundane as that of determining how land clearing will be organized by the Gilbertese resettled on Sidney Island or as dramatic as the bitter debate over whether the Kapinga relocated on Ponape should divide their village land for quitclaim to a few families or maintain it for "all Kapinga people," the definition of which was necessarily at issue. In such cases, the definition of the situation, prerequisite to deciding on a course of action, demands a more or less conscious attempt at some point to define who and what the actors and their relations to each other are, have been, and might be.

It is not only in my own ethnographic case, then, that one finds events in which people are trying to unscramble some of the things which have happened and are happening to them and to chart courses for future action. I am not suggesting that people necessarily sit down and say to one another that they will do this, but rather that doing this is known to happen. There is an attempt to get some important things together, in order to clarify the dimensions of action. To use Kenneth Burke's terms, definitions of the situation and strategies toward the situation are constructed (Burke 1957).[2] And this is an event not (or at least not primarily) of the recesses of the individual mind but of the processes of social action.

Clifford Geertz addresses some of these problems in *The Social History of an Indonesian Town,* which has been a major inspiration for the present effort. Speaking of Modjokuto, he says (1965: 5):

Especially the years after the Revolution (that is, after 1940), when the whirl of innovation engulfed the entire scene, were marked by an increasing ambiguity of cultural categories coupled with a growing irregularity of social behavior. And from this double observation comes the central theoretical argument, also double, of our study: namely, (1) that ordered social change involves the attainment by the members of the population concerned of novel conceptions of the sorts of individuals and the sorts of groups (and the nature of the relations among such individuals and groups) that comprise their immediate social world; and (2) that such an attainment of conceptual form depends in turn upon the emergence of institutions through whose very operation the necessary categorizations can be developed and stabilized.

Later on, writing of an election in Modjokuto, Geertz states (1965:205):

Seen as a crystallizing field, rather than as a collection of functionally interrelated roles, the election involved a clash of classificatory principles, of categories, embodied in individuals and in factions, and its outcome was an adjustment, as much conceptual as political, of those principles and categories to one another in a given case. In one of its aspects (though in one only) the election was a symbolic, even an intellectual process. It gave specific meaning to general ideas by filling them with concrete persons, groups, institutions, issues, and events. Despite the tension it caused, the election was considered by even those who lost to have been a good

thing. As they said, it 'pulled things taut, put them in straight lines *(kentjeng).*' Selecting from a set of abstract "grammatical" possibilities by means of concrete "phonetic" process, it made potential order actual.

In this paper I present some aspects of the analysis of an event which, as it was occurring, became a symbol for a set of conceptions. The event occurred on Rambi Island, Fiji. Since 1945, Rambi has been the home of the people of Ocean Island, which is part of the British Gilbert and Ellice Islands Colony. The indigenous name of Ocean Island is Banaba, and thus its people are known as Banabans. Ocean Island is a "phosphate island." Mining activities since 1900 have progressively converted the island into a kind of mining settlement, and the Banabans into a minority in their homeland. Their lands were literally being exported away for the benefit of others. During World War II the British government purchased Rambi with invested Banaban phosphate royalties. When the war ended, the Banabans agreed to go to Rambi on a trial basis and in 1947 decided to stay, while maintaining their rights to Ocean Island lands on which the mining of phosphate continues to this day. The population of Rambi is now about two thousand.

The event which is my major concern was a ten-hour community meeting in November 1964 during which, among other things, the Banabans were trying to make sense out of their past and present and give direction to their future. This paper is an exploration of how they did it, although only a minute portion of the meeting can be analyzed in detail. I hope to demonstrate that a significant part of this "how" consisted in the setting up of levels of form-content relations among (1) various historical actors and actions; (2) the delineation of the terms and relations of a problematic situation, which included the problem of how to transform that situation; (3) the building of a structure for that situation; (4) certain symbols; and (5) the course of action taken by the meeting.

The event with which I am concerned differs from Geertz's Indonesian election in several respects. But there is a significant class of dramatic events distinguished (for present purposes) by the combination of the following related characteristics: one of the businesses of the day is the coordinating of cultural categories; an action outcome is envisaged; the cultural terrain being covered is wide and its categories are multitudinous; many relationships (of a number of orders) are problematic; the levels of form-content articulations are several and complex; the process is a social process which may have a form of its own, or a form may be under construction.

Geertz (1965:203) makes a related point when he speaks of

the paradox of the role of culture—or, if you will, systems of ideas—in social activity. No actual event (or sequence of events) can be predicted from them, and no actual event (or sequence of events) can be explained without them. . . . Culture orders action not by determining it but by providing the forms in terms of which it determines itself.

This paper is concerned, then, with a concrete process which may be typical of resettled communities. It is a process whereby people order knowledge, hopes, experiences, and feelings and make sense out of them. By making sense out of them, they are giving form to them, and it is through their cultural categories that form is created. Thus, in giving form, the Rambi Islanders are using their categories in a social action and pointing toward a social action; and in so doing they are creating forms that are not quite the same as before.

The analysis begins with the historical background of the problems with which the Rambi Islanders had to deal in the meeting. This discussion is followed by a presentation of the methodology used to analyze the meeting; then part of the meeting is described and analyzed. The paper concludes with an analysis of the meeting itself as a symbol.

Historical Prologue

My recent book on the Banabans (Silverman 1971) details many aspects of their history and culture. Here I shall mention again some things which are most relevant to the meeting.[3]

One of the Banabans' major public concerns is getting a just recognition of their rights to the Ocean Island phosphate and the great financial consequences of that recognition. The phosphate is mined by the British Phosphate Commissioners (BPC), which has a mining monopoly, the interests of which are held by the British, Australian, and New Zealand governments. Speaking in the ethnographic present, the Banabans have no rights to determine how much phosphate is mined, what the price per ton (which is well below market price) should be, or what amount of money they or anyone else should get from the whole enterprise. In the early phosphate days, the mining company (a private predecessor of the BPC) dealt with individual landowners, but later it began to negotiate with the Banabans on a collective basis over the leasing of land. This was important in the development of the people's political consciousness.[4] In a dispute during 1927–31, the BPC wanted more land but the Banabans refused its offer. In 1928 the British colonial government passed an ordinance enabling itself, in effect, to force mining on lands and to arbitrate compensation when necessary "in the public interest." This it did, and the Banabans lost even more control over their land—and Ocean Island land has been and still is, among other things, one of the most powerful symbols in Banaban culture.

The Ocean Island phosphate is a critical factor in the economy of the Gilbert and Ellice Islands Colony in a variety of ways—through royalties, taxes, and wages, for example. Recently the BPC was paying out about ten times as much money to Gilbert and Ellice Islands Colony revenue as it did to the Banabans. The Banabans bitterly resent this. By the Banaban adviser's estimate, half the Banabans' cash income in 1964 was coming from the phosphate in one form or another; the other half was coming mainly from copra production. Pertinent both for the Banabans and the Gilbert and Ellice Islands Colony is the fact that the phosphate is a dwindling resource. Local estimates varied on when mining and thus the money from royalties to the Banabans would cease; some spoke of about twenty years. Uncertainty as to when phosphate operations would end may explain why there is no real sense of urgency on Rambi regarding the economic development urged by government officials. Uncertainty is one of the dominant qualities of the day.

On Rambi an island council was set up as the instrument of local government. It has eight members, two elected by each of the four villages, which are named for those on Ocean Island. The councillors elect their own chairman.[5]

According to a system agreed to by the Banabans in 1947, yearly estimates of the expenditure of various island funds for the next year are prepared and sent to the Fiji government for approval. The council nominates five of its members to the Banaban Funds Trust Board, which is charged with preparing the estimates. The estimates must then be approved by the council as a whole and then by the government. The Banaban adviser, a European, is chairman of the trust board.

The position of the Banaban adviser is a difficult one. Although he is responsible to the Fiji government, he is paid indirectly from Banaban funds and the council is consulted on his appointment. The original government conception of the office was probably something of a combination of district officer and development officer. The Banabans, however, have come to define his role as that of their advocate. He is in the classic position of the man in the middle.

The advocacy is for the related issues of securing just rights to the phosphate and the recognition of the autonomy of Rambi. Collective political action vis-à-vis the phosphate has its chronological roots in confrontations with the phosphate company and the government while the people were still on Ocean Island. It has its cultural roots in the centrality of land in the Banaban symbolic system. As far as one can tell, political action on Ocean Island was designed more to achieve recognition of individual rights (to land and thus to money) than to achieve something material for the collectivity as a collectivity. The situation on Rambi crystallized the individual/collectivity contrast into a dilemma for which the Banabans were culturally unprepared. The reasons why they were unprepared and why it was a dilemma are interlocked.

On Ocean Island the government and the BPC had provided equipment and services the Banabans valued.[6] These things were part of what modern life means and what Rambi lacked. If they wanted to recreate the accoutrements of modern life on Rambi, the Banabans had to do it for themselves. Since these conveniences had been provided on Ocean Island, the islanders had not had to contemplate the institutionalization of their newly developed values. Rambi, as an undeveloped island, was a new situation. Individual action could not provide transportation, electricity, and new buildings; some kind of collective action was necessary. This articulated the "individual/collectivity problem."

In the Banaban view, financial proceeds from the phosphate are the output of Banaban lands, and Banaban lands are owned individually, not collectively. The right and proper fate of the money is thus to go to individuals. The money equals land equation is shared by the government, which (not uncommonly in colonial structures) put itself in the position of arbiter of Banaban custom. The government for a long time insisted that from the payments for surface rights individuals should receive only the interest from the invested capital, since the lands had to be maintained for future generations and could not be alienated by an individual's own will. Since the government asserted that there was no real indigenous custom regarding the ownership of undersurface mining rights, whatever money the people derive from undersurface mining should be paid to the community as a community, ideally to be used for community purposes. Whether the people have a right to such proceeds or whether they are given by the grace of the crown is ambiguous. There was also the usual asserted fear that individuals would fritter away large sums of money if they got them and that the continuity of large individual payments would reduce the people's industriousness and make them dependent on the BPC. Hence most of the income the Banabans receive from the phosphate is not in the form of individual payments but payments to the Banaban community (which, on Rambi, includes resident non-Banabans).

The Banabans have drawn on information from Nauru to form their own case. Nauru, to the west of Ocean Island, is now independent, but at the time of my research it was an Australian-administered trusteeship. Nauru is also a phosphate island; for a long time it was worked by the same phosphate company that worked Ocean Island. The Nauruans are reported to receive large individual phosphate returns and to live a comfortable modernized life— and they organized a successful campaign of confrontation with the Australian government. The Banabans see their own basic situation as similar to that of the Nauruans, compare what they get with what the Nauruans get, and have been taking action on the Nauruan model.

The individual/collectivity problem is thus situated in the way the Banabans' returns from the phosphate are paid out. Another closely related dimension of the problem is that while the people recognize that some form of collective action is necessary to get their due, the island council has had a hard time establishing its legitimacy as a decision-making entity.[7] Furthermore, the "development" activities conducted by local authorities are considered far from adequate by local people.

Since most proposals for developing Rambi involve money, and since the Banabans believe they are being cheated out of money that is rightfully theirs but could be obtained if the right course of action were found,[8] a number of issues are inextricably intertwined for most people: the phosphate issue in general; what to do with the funds in hand; how to get more of the money which belongs to the people; how to organize and govern the new island and secure its autonomy. The money from Ocean Island lands—all of it—already belongs to the Banabans but is being fraudulently held and used by others, given the premise that money equals land. It follows that Rambi is properly autonomous because it was purchased with invested phosphate royalties, which derive from Ocean Island lands, which are owned by Banabans. Given these cultural premises, each issue logically implies the others. All the issues involve Ocean Island, which by the same logic is a symbol that can give form to the individual's sense of himself, his kinsmen (past, present, and future), village and community, morality, wealth, and the relationship of the community to the outside world.

To take one aspect salient to the meeting: a person is a Banaban by having Banaban blood or being adopted by a Banaban. Being adopted by a Banaban entails receiving some Ocean Island land from him. When the two are contrasted, blood symbolizes kinship identity and land symbolizes kinship code for conduct (see Schneider 1968a). Blood and land structure both kinship and nationality. In the kinds of political discourse most closely related to the matters we are considering here, "Bana-bans" and "landowners" are used interchangeably.[9]

All these issues were articulated during the meeting to be analyzed. Three matters were frequently cited as central to the meeting: whether certain individual money payments should be made; whether the Banaban adviser should be retained or dismissed; and the alleged unequal treatment (by the Banaban adviser among others) of employees who had damaged certain facilities. The third issue merged into others which developed.

In 1937, while still on Ocean Island, the Banabans were granted annuities of £ 8 per adult and £ 4 per child and a yearly individual bonus based on size of landholdings (up to a certain limit).[10] In the 1947 agreement, when the Banabans voted to stay on Rambi, the continuation of this sytem was mentioned. The Rambi Island Council, however, for some years decided not to distribute either the annuity or the bonus, but rather to use the money for building cement-block houses and other projects.

The question of distributing the annuity and bonus was part of the controversy which culminated in the calling of the meeting by the council. The meeting was a *maungatabu,* a community meeting the decisions of which were binding. Those who were instrumental in calling it, operating through Methodist church channels, wanted the annuity and bonus reinstated. The adviser had said that this was not a wise course. His position was that additional grants—for example, matching contributions for building roads and houses—had been given by the BPC after their officials had seen that money was being used for development and after the Banabans had agreed it would not be distributed. The land on

Rambi, the adviser and others argued, was poorly developed and money should be used for improvements before that money stopped. The trust board prepared the 1965 estimates without the individual distribution. The full council refused to approve the estimates and said the annuity should be included. The adviser said the full council had no authority to amend the estimates. An impasse had been reached.

The council had recently approved the renewal of the adviser's contract, but various people remained dissatisfied with him, not only because of his opposition to the distribution of the annuity. Some councillors and others had circulated reports that he was acting in a high-handed manner by ordering rather than advising and by not showing proper respect for the council. Favoritism was also alleged in his relations with employees. Moreover, he had incurred the ire of a number of influential Methodists because of his attempts to disentangle the use of trust board money and paid time for activities which seemed to be more in the service of the Methodist church (which has the largest membership) and the supporters of the council chairman than of the community as a whole. There were those who at times saw the whole matter as a contest between the adviser and the chairman. The chairman had suggested that of the money the Banabans received collectively from the phosphate, two-thirds should be distributed among the people and one-third kept for public projects. Matters had recently come to a head between the two over a specific issue which many believed was behind the machinations leading to the meeting.

The chairman is an important figure in the church and has been the most promi-nent Banaban leader since before the resettlement. He has impressive religious, descent, kinship, political, economic, and age credentials. He also has what one might term reality credentials through his involvement in various disputes with the government and the BPC at least since the 1927–31 affair. He is generally assumed to know more about the intricacies and deceits of the phosphate history than anyone else. Some question his knowledge, and some are also opposed to him precisely because of his credentials. But for many, the chairman's information on crucial political and economic matters is nearly all the information they have. He has the authenticity of one who can say "I was there." He also has important rhetorical credentials. This analysis will try to specify some of them.

I cannot give the details of how the positions of various people on the issues of the money and the adviser were interpreted by others before and after the meeting. Often—and this is certainly not a pattern unique to the Banabans—a person claims to be motivated by principle and accuses the opposition of being motivated by kinship, descent, religion, village, friendship, self-interest, personal grudges, factional alliances, backroom deals, or ignorance.

A brief discussion is in order on Rambi's employment pattern, since it was deeply involved in what came up in the meeting. A preliminary analysis of 1965 census figures shows that over 80 percent of the full-time or part-time salary or wage earners on the island are males between eighteen and sixty years of age. Of males between eighteen and sixty, roughly 32 percent hold full-time jobs, 21 percent hold alternate-week jobs, and 46 percent are copra cutters, gardeners, and fishermen only, except a few who are small-scale entrepreneurs or mission personnel. The number of households directly affected by the salary and wage pattern is greater than these figures might indicate. In roughly one-third of the census households there is no regularly resident member with such employment. Two-thirds of the remaining census households have at least one person on alternate-week employment but no person employed full-time.[11]

The largest employer on the island is the combination of the Rambi Island Council and the trust board. The cooperative society and the Fiji government account for most of the rest of the jobs. The alternate-week pattern spreads wage labor around more widely than would be the case if all jobs were full-time. Most of the council and board jobs with which I am familiar have to do with public works and public services: house and road construction, equipment operation and maintenance (including transportation), and office work. All the board members have relatively high-paying jobs. Many of the other jobs pay no more per week than what an enterprising copra cutter could earn in a good week. But there are not always good weeks, and if there were more enterprising copra cutters, the enterprising copra cutter might earn less.

What is also at issue, however, is the cultural construction of "work" and "working." Unfortunately, I did no systematic cultural analysis of this domain while in the field, so the following discussion is after the fact and impressionistic. At one level, "work" includes wage earning, copra cutting, gardening, fishing, and the like. In some contexts, however, "workers" means public employees, in contrast with those who are primarily indentified with work on land and sea. "Workers" are generally considered to be far better off than others, and those in skilled higher positions have a certain prestige. Many of the latter are centered at the island's "capital" at Nuka, where they occupy concrete-block houses which go along with their jobs.

The chairman and others have often made statements such as, "We did not come to Rambi to be workers on the land." At one council meeting, the chairman said, "We did not come here for work, but for freedom on our money." The chairman avers that one reason the resettlement proposal was approved in the first place was that the people, once resettled in Fiji, would be closer to the high commissioner for the Western Pacific, who was at that time the same person as the governor of Fiji. The high commissioner for the Western Pacific is the next step up the colonial bureaucratic ladder from the resident commissioner of the Gilbert and Ellice Islands Colony. Rambi was to be 'the land of grievance stating.' Working on the land carries a negative value in the sense that grubbing about in the bush for enough money to get by on is a compulsory way of life. This should not be the case, and may not have been expected to be the case. In this regard one must point out that on Ocean Island many Banabans and now Rambi-resident Gilbertese were BPC employees in positions of some skill and responsibility. What they are doing now is considered an inferior activity.

In the meeting it soon became apparent that discussions of the employment and public works patterns (which became fused) were being used to articulate a number of dilemmas.

Methodology

We need terms to sort out what the Banabans were sorting out in the meeting and how they went about it. To this end I have modified and added to some of Burke's (1962) terminology in a manner that seems suited to the ethnography of the meeting.

Trying to sort out something means that something is acknowledged as problematic. The kinds of things that can be problematic are, of course, numerous: some feature of reality (what did the adviser do?); the implications of doing something (what will happen if the annuity is distributed?); how to bring about a change (how can the adviser be persuaded to distribute the annuity?); and so forth.

We begin with the *character* of the problematic situation—a state of affairs in which people find themselves that seems to point outward to the larger community such that the question of doing something about it arises as a community problem. "Doing something about it" may involve thinking about it, discussing it, or cooperatively enacting measures to change it. Examples in the Rambi situation are poverty, lack of control over Banaban funds, the breakdown in relations between adviser and chairman. The character of the problematic situation is something that people may be arguing about. In other words, the character of the problematic situation (like everything else) may itself be problematic.[12]

Second is the *subject* of the problematic situation: the who or the what responsible for the situation being in the shape that it is—for example, the government, the people, the adviser, the council, the workers.

Third is the *object:* the who or the what on the receiving end—for example, the people, old people, members of a religious group, specific individuals.

Fourth is the *instrument* (the "how"): the intermediary, if any, between subject and object—for example, the council between the people as subject and the people as object or the adviser between outside authority and the people.

Fifth is the *means* (the "how to"): the device through which the situation is being made problematic—for example, using funds for public works projects rather than distributing them to the people.

The definition of the problematic situation requires that a transformation of it is in some fashion part of the situation. The same pentad can be mapped onto the question of transformation: its character (perhaps getting more money), its subject (the people or the council), its object (say, the people again), its instrument (perhaps the council), and its means (distributing the annuity). I use the term "delineating" to denote the making of all these connections.

Part of the delineating process is establishing what gets assigned to which term of the pentad. In the course of delineation, people may adopt various stances. For example, they may name (it is the board that is the trouble), contradict (it is not the board but the council), query (what does the board do?), or make problematic (how is it that distributing the annuity would bring in less money from the outside?).

This delineating activity is not, of course, a purely abstract exercise removed from people's actual experiences. It is, in part, the nature of their experience that people are attempting to work out through delineating. In clarifying for themselves the adviser-council relation during the meeting, people pointed out specific actions in the past which they considered to be typical of that relationship, such as the adviser's stopping the council visit to the governor and the council's decision not to distribute the annuity. The outcome of the delineation of this relationship is a recognizable structure of the relationship. Once worked out, the adviser-council relationship gives *structural form* to historical incidents (incidents which touch a variety of people in a variety of ways). The incidents cited become instances of a general pattern— that is, the historical incidents give *tangible content* to the structural form. Then that form and its historical incidents (contents) become *tangible forms* themselves and, thus, may be tangible content for other forms. The adviser-council relation and its historical contents, for example, interpreted as one in which the council is victimized by the adviser, becomes the tangible content of a higher-level structural form—the relation of subject victimizing object or the relation subject (victimizer)–object (victim). Thus a form may become content for another form. Integral to this transformation is the use of the "special case," where one thing is presented as a special case of another. For example, the adviser's stopping the council from visiting the governor is a special case of the pattern of action of the adviser victimizing the council.

The terrain covered in the delineating process (the number of subjects, objects, and so forth) is extensive. The delineation becomes complex if something of a comprehensive order is to be approximated. In delineating the problematic situation we observe the sorting out of a number of terms and the relations between them (how the adviser relates to the people, how the government relates to the people). "Something of a comprehensive order" in this case would be characterizing both those relations, at a higher level, as relations of victimization. Victimization gives structural form to those relations as the relations give tangible content to victimization. Victimization as now defined becomes a tangible form, and thus tangible content for other forms at even higher levels.[13]

This structure which interrelates terms and relations of the problematic situation is itself given form by certain symbols at a higher level. I use the term "symbol" to mean a vehicle for conceptions, a vehicle people may use to connect the unknown with the known (see Turner 1970:48). Certain symbols in Rambi Island culture are extremely powerful in their ability to order wide domains of objects, relationships, and actions. Land, freedom, the person, and progress are examples. Thus the symbol "freedom" can give structural form to other forms. For example, victimization becomes a special case of the absence of freedom, just as the adviser's stopping the visit becomes a special case of victimization. Since the problematic nature of the situation is construed in terms of such symbols, the symbols themselves are made tangible and thus are structured in a conjunction.[14]

An example of such a conjunction would be as follows: "The annuity and bonus are the money of your lands." The annuity and the bonus may become tangible content for many things other than "your lands," and "lands" may give structural form to many things other than the annuity and the bonus. The conjunction is a structuring, and "land" is made tangible in that structuring.

By speaking of a conjunction in this way, I do not mean to imply that one set of meanings (those of "lands") and another set of meanings (those of "the annuity") are simply added to one another, nor that a structure is formed simply by putting together the meanings of the higher-level symbol which are harmonious with the meanings of the lower-level symbol. I am suggesting, rather, that symbols such as "lands" and "the annuity" (or any symbols) have *ranges* of possible meanings. In the conjunction, constrained by the context or other ways, certain features of each symbol become stressed such that the meanings which may be given to each can be organized in a hierarchical form. In the "special case," categories are juxtaposed and structured in such a manner that contextually stressed features of some categories can be shown to be concretizations (actualizations, instances) of contextually stressed features of other categories (patterns, structures, symbols).[15]

To our "list" (of delineation, building a structure, etc.), we must now add "concrete actors and actions." For we are dealing with a case in which "something happens in the end." At the end of the meeting an action was taken (voting was part of it), and that action gave structural form to what had been built up before (the links through certain symbols). What had been built up before it gave tangible content to the action, the action becoming a tangible form itself (and, of course, tangible content for other forms after the meeting).

The form of the final action, however, did not come magically out of a script book. That form itself became the prob-lematic situation, and a number of levels of form-content articulation occurred within it. What happened in the end was giving form to what had been mapped out for what might happen in the end, which itself was giving form to what had been mapped out during the previous phase of the meeting, and so on.

Recall that this is not a model designed for a case where everything follows from everything else as night follows day. Various "stances" apply to the establishment of form-content relations, too. If an action is presented as a special case of a pattern of action, for example, somebody may say it is not a special case at all. If a means of transfor-mation (distributing the annuity) is being linked to a general form (freedom), it may be made problematic whether dis-tributing the annuity and freedom are really related in that fashion. This may be a product of different constructions of "distributing the annuity,' different constructions of "freedom," or a host of other factors.

Two final and related points. First, various interventions in the meeting were related more or less directly to setting out the terms of the problematic situation or the terms of the transforma-tion, but the distinction is an analytic one and has an important implication both theoretically and ethnographically. The extent to which various construc-tions of reality can be implemented by actual behavior must constantly be borne in mind. In fact, I would suggest that the losing side in the meeting might have fared better had they borne this in mind.

Second, some segments of the meet-ing were developing a structure for the problematic situation and its transfor-mation; this structure was one of *victim-*

ization. Victimization by some outside authority is an understood feature of the Banaban's situation. Here the victimization is turned inward as well which, among other things, makes the structure more actable or transformable. That structure also allows for the introjection of accumulated grievances, personal and collective. The very issues made this likely, and (to speak with risk) it may have its own compelling form which itself articulates the various levels of form-content relations: name the crime (the problematic situation—not having enough rightful money); name the victim (the object—the people) and the victimizer (the subject—the workers, the adviser); name the weapon (the means—using the money for work); consider redress; invoke specific evidence and precedent (concrete actions out of the past); construe, direct, and legitimize the case in terms of powerful symbols; deliberate and take the appropriate action.[16]

The Meeting

Before going on to an annotated extract from my minutes of the meeting, a strong caveat must be introduced. Initially, I estimated about two hundred people in the island's central meeting hall at Nuka and many others listening outside. It was a ten-hour meeting. As people began to speak more rapidly, with emotion, or as speech was indistinct to me from distant parts of the hall, my knowledge of the local language failed me. I can vouch neither for the completeness nor the accuracy of my minutes. Even in the quotations cited below, half the information may have been lost. I can only represent them as my best effort,

hope that the outcome of the exercise justifies the use of such inadequate data, and carry on as if the problem did not exist. In these extracts a series of dots (. . .) indicates the omission of material because of lack of understanding, the desire to save space, or the speaker's own stylistic indication that the sentence was incomplete. This may be an important rhetorical device in itself, signaling a common understanding and allowing the listener to fill in the gap. Sometimes I fill in the gaps myself in brackets; remarks in brackets are my own observations. Remarks in parentheses are paraphrases of things said.

A brief note on the setting: the meeting hall itself is a modern form of the *maneaba*, a meetinghouse with important traditional meanings (see Silverman 1971). A meeting in it is serious business. The Union Jack adorned the front of the hall. The councillors, scribe, and adviser were literally on stage at the front, "the people" thus being seated apart. Some internal divisions were manifest in who was sitting with whom. Now, then, to my annotated extracts:

1. *Adviser:* We ask for the truth. The adviser has no power; the path [to the government] is from the council to the governor [of Fiji]. These years are our chance for success.

2. *Chairman:* The Tabwewa [one of the four villages] councillors raised the question of the meeting to me. They wanted to meet with the people [literally, 'the inhabitants of the surface of the land'] regarding the desire for the annuity, and whether your adviser will retire from among you. [The chairman then alluded to two other issues which he said were settled: a specific dispute between himself and the adviser and the handling of the case of a worker who had damaged some equipment, which the chairman said was settled by vote of the board.]

3. *Adviser:* I have worked for three years

and asked regarding an additional three years. Talk to the governor if you want me to retire. [Notes unclear on a statement about the nature of the bonus, the distribution of which he was told would create difficulties with the BPC.] The annuity was stopped long ago by the council. My work on this was just advice.

4. *Chairman:* The annuity and the bonus are the money of your lands. In the 1930s the government agreed that they should be distributed. The money is your money. Here we used it for work. The old men said there was no money. I said: "We will use it for work, for one or two years. If you want it we will give it. If you want the money to work, then it will work. If you want the money, then you will get it."

5. *A Councillor:* The chairman said we would talk about the annuity, not the bonus. First, with regard to the houses. We asked the BPC for money. The [BPC] commissioners came and saw that we were suffering [in difficulty, poor]. We talked about the road, schools, and other things. We met in the house of the adviser. The BPC board has to meet, the commissioners said. After a few months the word came: they agreed. Also, with regard to the adviser: he has done nothing wrong.

6. *Another Councillor:* I am unhappy too about not having an annuity. I am also unhappy about the distribution of two-thirds of the money. The adviser said: "The distribution of the annuity may prevent the arrival of big things from the outside."

We want the bank statement [showing Banaban funds]. Maybe things are hidden there. I am the one who goes outside. If I say that two-thirds will be distributed, they have me. [This councillor is also the Banaban representative on Ocean Island. On his return to Rambi he was said to have circulated reports of having learned that £14 million was due to the people in accumulated interest from a certain fund.]

7. *Adviser:* The answer of the government regarding the money is well-known. [A man interjects from the floor, "That isn't worth anything." Speaker C rises and says he wants to talk, but the adviser says: "The chairman first."]

8. *Chairman:* Freedom under the money

of Banaba. Who is the person in whose hands it has been received? [People from the floor answer, "No one!"] With regard to our accord on the annuity, we cannot know how much money will go to each person. It is the people's money. The annuity is the only path open.

The company wanted to give a good price in the 1930s, but the government objected. [This refers to the 1927–31 land dispute. The chairman had said at other times that the BPC had been on the point of making an offer closer to Banaban demands, but the resident commissioner had intervened against the Banabans.] If you do not complain all the time . . . [you get nothing]. If you want the money to be divided, it will be divided.

Regarding the adviser: there should be one person [European] here who is not paid by the government. (The first adviser, who came with the people in 1945) said: "In Fiji we can state our grievances better. The land of grievance stating is here. Here, we want to see the governor, and the adviser stops us. . . . Yes, we did agree to the extension of the adviser's contract, but the decision is your decision."

9. D [one of the oldest Banaban men]: We need money for the old people. The worker eats the money.

10. C [a middle-aged man who works for the cooperative society]: . . . We are free under the money. The council held it for our dwellings. Regarding the adviser: did he behave badly in the council? If one or two hold the money, that is bad.

11. E [a middle-aged copra cutter]: The money is held for the houses. But there are copra cutters. You [workers] live on the money of the community. There are two ways for making a living: copra cutting and wage earning. If I ask for work, will I get it? You say that there are £14 million. We are *filled to overflowing* with your words! Distribute the annuity!

I stand for the adviser. It is the board [that is the trouble]. What is the value of the walkie-talkie, people say? [A set of walkie-talkies had been purchased which many people thought was of dubious value.] [From the floor: "Finish it!" F, a young man, says: "I support him."]

12. G [a young man employed by the Fiji government]: Whose error is the error? It is yours [the people's]; the election was your election. Their errors are your errors.

13. *Chairman:* Perhaps we are finished stating our opinions. Write down whether you want the annuity or not. If there is an objection from the government, we will have a record. As for the adviser, we are free after three years.

Let us start with the chairman's first remarks (statement 2). He begins in a low key by referring to the question of "whether your adviser will retire from among you" rather than saying "whether the adviser will be sacked." These words are appropriate for an elder and attempt to give an aura of neutrality, although the chairman's true position was generally known. He names a problematic situation as involving the annuity and the adviser and indicates two other issues as nonproblematic (issues which it might have been assumed would prejudice him against the adviser). The softness, however, might be rhetorically double-edged, the "you" and the "your" suggesting the proper decision-making entity.

The adviser (statement 1) had situated the question vis-à-vis truth and success, indicating (statements 1 and 3) that the council (and its relationship to the governor), not he (and perhaps not this meeting either), was the significant instrument. The council, not he, was the subject of the problematic situation in stopping the annuity, and the distribution of the bonus might not be a means of positively transforming the situation but of increasing its problematic nature. He introduced the government and the BPC as elements which had to be sorted out.

Indeed, in general terms or through concrete incidents, the major categories of secular agents which superintend the Banaban's fate were named quite early in the meeting and, as the meeting progressed, most of their possible combinations appeared. The functions of one vis-à-vis the other were often problematic, with people trying to sort out what they are and to indicate (when they were the subjects of victimization) how they might be transformed.

Historical incidents are retrieved to justify the position being taken, but in the process they become part of something larger than those incidents taken separately. Just as the discussion of transforming the problematic situation relates the present to the future, the citation of these incidents relates the present to the past.

In statement 4, the chairman gives form to the elements of his own interventions when he says that "the annuity and the bonus are the money of your lands." The nature of the construction was adumbrated earlier. The bonus and annuity are given structural form by, and give tangible content to, land. The annuity and the bonus are also money, a necessary means to gain European goods and services (this is made more explicit in later statements). Land thus enters as a resource and as something which belongs to these people. A frame is set for structuring the problematic situation and its transformation—especially as the government itself had on Ocean Island approved the distribution of this money.

The chairman begins to develop a structure in terms which are critical— the contrast between using the money (of your lands) "for work" and giving it to "you," the people. Two elements must be elaborated here: the "work" element and the "you" element.

People had said that if the annuity were distributed, it would have to come out of the money *presently* used for work (the two-thirds–one-third plan). But the contrast is more powerful than the fact might imply. The organization of the various activities involving construction and labor into the category "the work" is a cultural organization itself. There is no a priori reason why the category should exist in this form. Nor is the suggested contrast with "the people," which explicitly recurred several times during the meeting, an a priori necessity. This structuring suggested the evaluation placed on it, if not the concrete course of action necessary to transform it. Quite clearly, things for and to the people are superior to things which are not. What is disputed between some and problematic to others, however, is what "things for and to the people" are.

Given the historical incident about stopping the money in the first place, it is ambiguous whether the council was the subject of the problematic situation in that it stopped the annuity or whether the council was the instrument of the people who were the subject. This was played out later. But the people were the object (in being denied the annuity), and the means was using the money for work rather than distributing it to them.

The chairman elaborates further. In statement 2 he spoke of the councillors wanting to meet with "the people." In statement 4 he speaks of "your lands" and says that the money is "your money." The emphasis now is on "you": "If you want it . . . if you want the money to work . . . if you want the money, then you will get it." The "you" refers to the Banaban people in general

(not the Rambi people in general, which includes non-Banaban residents) and to the people at the meeting (later specified as the landowners). In some way (later made problematic and elaborated), the people at the meeting are a tangible form which "is" the Banaban people and, furthermore, they can make a decision one way or another. What is now being set up is this: the *objects* of the problematic situation (the people) can transform it by becoming the *subjects* of the transformation (telling the council what to do). The council (the position of which was unspecified earlier) then becomes the *instrument;* the *means* is then giving the money to the people rather than to the work; the *object* (as the subject) of the transformation is the people themselves. The now more highly structured problematic situation (not having more of the money of their lands) links to a set of relations which is both a *delineation of reality* (what the people can do, what the council can do, what happened in the past) and a *proposal*. This is achieved by means of at least three transformations. First is the transformation of the present or possible subject, the council, into an instrument. The council's position is ambiguous in any case, since whether it was acting as a subject or instrument by holding onto the money is itself problematic. By transforming the council into instrument (having it distribute the money), the ambiguity is resolved for the future. Second is the transformation of the object (the people) into subject (the final arbiters). Third is the transformation of the means into their antithesis: money for work versus distributing the annuity. The bonus and annuity are tangible content for "the money of your lands" and the land (money) belongs to the people, who can decide what to do with it, and so forth.

This definition of the situation is contradicted and made problematic by the two councillors (statements 5 and 6). Using the money for work rather than distributing it to the people has already been a means of transformation (rather than an element to be transformed): more money in the form of matching funds had been granted by the BPC, and an understanding had already been reached that the money would not be distributed (who reached the understanding is not made explicit here and became problematic later). Thus the people could not become the subject of the transformation and, continuing as now, more money might be forthcoming in the future. Note that the first councillor addressed the question of the people's "suffering, poverty," but not the question of the people's lands. The second councillor began by placing himself on the horns of a dilemma.

The chairman (statement 8) gives further form to the problematic situation and its transformation. He asserts "freedom under the money of Banaba," thus linking the whole affair to freedom, with a stress on freedom as something which belongs to the community (which can make a decision) and the money as something which belongs to the individual.[17] Then he performs one of his feats of rhetorical brilliance which is conceded even by his opponents and which contrasts with his low-key beginning: "Who is the person in whose hands it has been received?" Having stated or closely implied some of the most general symbols and meanings, having raised the discussion to a high order of generality, he then takes the whole thing down to the actual person.

The chairman has done a number of things here. First, "the person" (closely linked to "freedom") is in context a symbol with a special character: its tangible content is the actor himself. And the actor himself becomes form for the problematic elements which had become tangible in that—literally—he holds or does not hold them in his hands. In the succeeding statements (to be described), the chairman deals with many relationships in a manner so persuasive as to be mesmerizing. What bears underscoring is how the chairman, through the progressive transformations of levels of form and content, set the whole thing up.

In the development of the discussion, the statement "in whose hands" has a special role. The challenge to the chairman's earlier construction was made on the grounds of an agreement having been made, the fact that more money had been received, and the likelihood of even more money being received. But here the chairman is asking which individuals have the money as opposed, say, to having seen the products of the money in houses or roads. The individual/collectivity problem is thus brought into the argument. To project to future interventions, no one has "it" in "his hands," even though some are receiving money from wages, because the "it" here is the money of Banaba which can be construed to be *all* the money distributed in freedom, unmediated by things like employment. That these two constructions are possible should not be surprising. It is one of the ways a persuasive argument is built up. Furthermore, one must "complain all the time" to get more, and the demand for the annuity could be interpreted as a special case of complaining against the existing situation.

The chairman broached another matter which was portentous in terms of the meeting and events after it. Observe closely the paragraph in statement 8 regarding the adviser. Until this point, although making a definite construction of the situation, the chairman had actually avoided coming out directly for the annuity or directly against the adviser. Here he enters the fray in an interesting way. In our terms, it is ambiguous whether the adviser is the subject or the instrument of the problematic situation defined by the people's and the council's relationship to outside authority. The adviser stopped the people from going to the governor, but this is placed in a more generalized context: "There should be one person here who is not paid by the government." Note how this ambiguity could structure a number of anti-adviser positions—being against the man but not the role, being against the role but not the man, or being against both.

The delineation of the resident European's position is given structural form by something which might have had great resonance at least because the chairman had made statements like it before. Alluding to a statement of the first adviser (and thus an adviser can say something like this, just as the government could approve the annuity), the chairman pointed out: "In Fiji we can state our grievances better. The land of grievance stating is here."

In his statement the chairman defines a relationship between the presence of an adviser paid indirectly by Banaban monies (the adviser is actually responsible to the Fiji government) and Rambi as a place where grievances can be stated. This relationship is not the only one possible between these elements, nor is it the only relationship in which either the adviser or the stating of grievances can be major components. The relationship as stated does, however, have its place in the meeting as a further structuring and clarification of the problematic situation in the following manner: the relationship posited by the chairman is a structuring of two other relationships— (1) Banaban–European (government) and (2) Ocean Island–Rambi. Banaban nationality is, in an important sense, a product of the Ocean Island–Rambi relationship; therefore, one of the Banabans' most critical problems is that of arriving at a consensus on that relationship. The meanings of both Ocean Island and Rambi can be given structural form by the symbol of Ocean Island land, since Rambi was purchased with phosphate royalties derived from that land. Certain things in one place are seen in terms of certain things in the other place. Rambi things affect Ocean Island things and vice versa. Implicitly here and explicitly elsewhere, Ocean Island and Rambi relate in what we might call a "transitive metonym."[18]

The question remains: What are the "certain things" that affect each other implied by the chairman's statement? Ocean Island affects Rambi in that phosphate royalties, which purchased Rambi, maintain Rambi public works projects and pay its workers. But land also symbolizes in Banaban kinship (which is closely tied to Banaban nationality) its code for conduct. Land is what connects the Banaban–government and Ocean Island–Rambi relationships in a single structure. The actions suggested by "grievance stating" involve phosphate, which is something in Ocean Island land. Rambi is therefore related to Ocean Island (affecting Ocean Island things) in terms of action.

The revised status of a resident European is a special case of this structuring. A European responsible to the Banabans alone, rather than to the government, becomes the advocate of Banabans, the instrument of Banaban action. Having thus structured the problematic situation and having suggested an instrument for its transformation, the chairman brings the transformation back to the people: "The decision is your decision." He has made a construction in which action is inherently possible.

By the time we reach statement 9, the chairman has given the meeting a frame. When the people begin to speak, the money to the people/money to the work contrast begins to be elaborated.

One of the oldest men on the island (statement 9) rose and said, "We need money for the old people. The worker eats the money." The wage earners were using up the money which rightfully should go to the people. The contrast money to work/money to the people as a means was now transformed into workers/old people as subject/object. The workers were, in effect, victimizing the people; just as it had been suggested by the chairman that the Banaban adviser (in role or in person) had wronged the council or the people (statement 8), the people may have been wronged by the council (statement 4) and by various outside authorities (statements 6, 7, 8). In statement 10, after reaffirming the reality of situating the matter vis-à-vis freedom, speaker C asks whether some

on the council (including the adviser) may be holding the money and thus, following the theme as I decipher it, be victimizing the people. The issue brought up by the old man was put more forcefully by speaker E (who has a way of putting things forcefully) in statement 11, when he baldly stated that there were two modes of livelihood, copra cutting and wage earning; the workers "live on the money of the community," and not everyone might be able to get work.

One may say that speaker D was presenting himself as representing the interests of the old people whereas E was presenting himself as representing the interests of the copra cutter. Moreover, one may say they were relating the position and experience of old people and copra cutters to both the problematic situation and the meeting itself. It seemed to me that in their highly charged remarks they were doing this, and something more, in a very critical way. The chairman had retrieved the historical incident of the old men saying there was no money (statement 4), and here was an old man saying old men had no money and stating the reason. In his giving of form he was presenting himself as tangible form. Similarly, the copra cutter injected another element into the problematic situation—copra cutters. The elaboration of the money to people/money to work contrast as a structure proceeded by constituting classes of victims (old people, copra cutters) who were there at the meeting and victimizers (workers) who were also there. The elements of the structure were not the invisible behind the visible but the made-visible organizing other meanings.

Although the frame given the meeting

by the chairman is elaborated by the people, there are counterproposals and contradictions of that frame as well. Speaker E contradicts the delineation of the adviser as subject of the victimization: it is, rather, the board. And speaker G (statement 13) contradicts the indictment of the board by suggesting that, through the election of their councillors, the people are the subject as well as the object of their own dilemma. Perhaps as a response to this, the chairman then calls for a vote, which will be a record in case the government objects. The chairman might have been hedging his bets on whether the people are totally free on the matter after all, and (with no massive movement yet against the adviser?) he notes that the people will be "free" after the three years of the adviser's contract are up.

The counterargument regarding money to work/money to the people, introduced in statement 5, was elaborated later. It was proposed that the workers had been serving the community as a whole and as individuals. Here the alleged means of victimization are depicted as a means of transformation— that is, the transformation of the island into a more modern, comfortable place to live and work.

The statements of speakers E and G—that the board or the polity responsible for placing the board in office are the subjects of the victimization—both imply that the councillors (from whom the board is selected) are vulnerable. The chairman, indeed, began with a kind of public confession that something had gone awry with the council. Later he suggested that the younger generation could carry the burden which the older generation (his own) was having trouble with. But the councillors were workers,

too. One woman articulated part of the problem later when she stated, "You councillors are landowners [too]." A councillor who spoke little articulated his own dilemma and the general dilemma:

There is the problem of the council and the board. We didn't want the bonus and annuity because of the money from outside. There is the question of freedom under the money. Some people complained about the annuity. They said: "You do not like it because you are on salary." No. We look at the future. From the side of the board, I think: hold it. From the side of the council: give it. About the adviser, there is trouble knowing what is right. We agreed for three years. If I say I like him, you will say it is because he feeds me. We agreed for three years.

Another councillor, also an office worker, articulated a similar dilemma but resolved it:

I have worked with the adviser for three years. He is helpful in my work, yes. But for the people ['the land'], no. If he stays you will be unfortunate. The adviser is not worthwhile. . . . He is good in the office. But we still have not seen the money on the ground. We just eat cassava. We will not be fortunate quickly. . . . There is a side that he cannot deal with. . . . For the Banaban race. There is just money for housing and the road. Our group just salts cassava. If we are fortunate, we will all be fortunate; if we have misfortune, we will all have misfortune. A Banaban who does not work is not fortunate.

The councillors were put on the defensive and were vulnerable on several counts. They had in fact voted for years to withhold the annuity and bonus. They were also receiving salaries from the money being withheld. Yet at the same time no one could deny that the policy of "money for work" had in fact resulted in some houses and a road where there had been no road before—

tangible contents for the argument adduced in statement 5. Nor could one deny that the adviser was in part responsible for those results. The adviser as victimizer was not, then, all that unambiguous.

The dilemma is resolved by the position that although the adviser had accomplished good things, those accomplishments were beside the point. This is a definite construction of the situation: of the range of desirable things to get done, one was singled out, and by this singling out, an ordering was achieved.

By saying "we still have not seen the money on the ground," the councillor meant in individual hands. (Thus the collectivity is invoked—we, the people, our group, the Banaban race—but it is defined in this context as an aggregate of equal individuals.) Later in the meeting a man contrasted "work for the money" and "work on the ground" (the latter in the sense of the works projects in which the adviser was personally as well as ideologically involved), stating that the former was more important than the latter. In the closing segment (analyzed below), the issue was stated as that between getting more money and keeping the adviser. Here may have been a way in which the problem of "the work" was resolved in a manner which was actable in terms of the process of the meeting. The "work" pattern was rehabilitated, as it were, by stressing some of its features to construe two kinds of work: one was oriented to getting more money from the phosphate and into individual hands; the other was selective in its benefits if not downright wasteful from the people's point of view. The island's senior officialdom (including councillors) is properly involved in "working for the money"

(as contrasted with giving "money for the work"), and thus their own positions are not essentially threatened.

The "carry on as now" position was essentially a general restatement of the people as victims, outside authority as victimizer, the means of victimization as money being denied by outside authority, the problematic situation as not having enough money, and local authorities (the adviser, councillors) as the means of transformation.

But when the matter was raised in the meeting, even those arguing for the "carry on as now" position could not guarantee that the additional money would be distributed. Some, indeed, were inclined toward a "development centralism" and (more forcefully outside the meeting) argued that position. There are fundamental differences in the conceptions of how the community should go about conducting its business and what that business is. Those differences are not, however, in the presence or absence of certain elements (there should be more money, there should be some planning) but in their structuring vis-à-vis one another. Some people have not achieved a structuring of these features vis-à-vis one another; this is what confusion means.

The increased money might go for more "work" and thus not to the people as a community of individual landowners, the position of the individual landowner being linked to land, freedom, and the person. The people might not be getting individual payments, which would also be individual returns from the lands they individually own, and would assert freedom on their property. Besides, there was the "promises, promises!" sentiment expressed in statement 11.

The "carry on as now" and development centralist positions, then, could not be articulated with the higher-level symbols (land, freedom) in as many ways as the position for the distribution of the annuity. They were symbolically unproductive.

After the pro-annuity sentiment had been expressed, the adviser himself said that using the money for the distribution of the annuity would not stop "the work" entirely. Thus individual workers may not have construed the situation as an absolute choice between agreement to the annuity's distribution (loss of their jobs) and maintenance of the status quo, even if they did not agree that more money would be forthcoming anyway. The pro-annuity position, then, was more in line with the "maximize your options" principle of the Banaban value system (see Silverman 1969).

The counterargument was weak in another respect, one which was crucial to the process of the meeting itself. The counterargument did not spell out in any elaborate way a means of victimization or a means of transformation having anything approaching the power of the money for work/money to the people contrast. The means, of all the terms in the pentad of delineation, has the highest structuring potential because once the means is given tangible form, it clearly implies all the other terms. Thus a wide field of possibilities is opened up for identifying and structuring actors and events as subjects, objects, instruments, and so forth (including actors and events particularly meaningful to different people for different reasons).

The identification of money for work as a means of victimization encompasses relations between Banabans and the outside—the outside in general, outside

public opinion (which held that Banabans were well-off), the government, and the BPC. Money for work also encompasses relations of internal victimization—the old people and copra cutters by workers, the people and council by the adviser and the board, a religious group by the adviser and the council, and even the people by themselves. Money to the people is an equally powerful relational term, since it defines the transformation of the problematic situation while encompassing precisely the same wide net of relationships as the means of victimization. These relationships could be identified and structured vis-à-vis one another or they could be left safely ambiguous for the moment. Lacking an elaborated means, the counterargument lacked relational power inherent in the money for work/money to the people contrast.

The Creation of a Symbol

The details of what went on during most of the meeting are, of course, beyond the scope of this paper. It is sufficient to say that there was a "movement" and a "filling in" among the various elements of this paradigm, with a good deal of questioning and uncertainty. A consensus on the annuity developed and was both questioned and spelled out. The pace of anti-adviser interventions increased toward the end in a form that crystallized what had been prefigured earlier. The adviser was more or less in the witness box as defendant, and those who felt particularly aggrieved by his actions acted as public prosecutors, judge, and jury. After these exchanges, the adviser left the meeting.[19]

It was not long after the adviser's departure that one thing became quite clear. The people were not only collectively constructing various symbols and meanings; they were also in the process of creating a symbol—the meeting itself. Actions as well as words and objects can be symbols.[20] The notion of a symbol as a vehicle for conceptions can be sustained here only if we insist that the vehicle and the conceptions are in a dialectical relationship—that in the flow of action their forms may be problematic and their boundaries elastic, and that vehicles and conceptions are not simple things but structures. In their statements, movements, and feelings, the people were struggling to give form to a vehicle for a number of conceptions. They may have recognized this at the outset, but toward the end of the meeting their struggle assumed a quite explicit reality.

One context for understanding the symbolic nature of the meeting itself may be that it was not just any meeting but a *maungatabu,* an event which may have a special status because of its infrequency.[21] The calling of a *maungatabu* may be a structured part of a social drama (see Turner 1957) or a social-conceptual drama in which the number of problematic elements in the people's lives has become great. In the simplest interpretation, the whole thing may be seen as an attempt on the part of some leaders and would-be leaders to get a public mandate that would strengthen a council case with outside authority. But even on those grounds there would be a major bind in internal relations, external relations, or both.

Not every member of the Banaban community was present at the meeting—or, rather, not every Banaban landowner was present (and it was only Banaban landowners, Banabans by birth or adoption, who spoke). But if one were to compare this assembly with political meetings in the United States, it is clear that the meeting was one of a significant proportion of a group of people who think of themselves as a total community. There developed an "intouchness" with the total community, and the history and future of that community, which is lacking in many meetings elsewhere. (By this I do not mean to suggest that the Banaban meeting was a unique event from a cross-cultural point of view. Far from it.) The people were putting themselves in touch with their own history and their own future. There was very much a feeling of being part of Great Events. How was this symbol construction finally realized?

Toward the end, the meeting reached a new dialectical phase, although elements of that phase had been broached earlier. Now the focus shifted to the form that the final action in the meeting would take. The creation of that form was now the problematic situation, and the content included what had gone on in the meeting before.

For the sake of brevity I shall not treat this material in sequential detail. The alternatives presented and discussed were not all mutually exclusive; they involved the issues of what should be done inside and outside the meeting. Alternatives for action inside the meeting included nothing more than signing papers on either side of the argument, dividing the house, and raising and counting hands. Alternatives for action outside the meeting were to have a plebiscite conducted, presumably by the council; to communicate the results of a vote in the meeting to the governor and the BPC; and to send the results of a vote to the council for its consideration.

The chairman, it seemed, was first calling for a plebiscite or at least the taking of signatures. Speaker H, a young man prominent in the affairs of church and state, made the critical interventions in this latter segment (as he had done earlier by "cross-examining" the adviser). Speaker H argued as follows: "On a paper for the decision: this is the *maungatabu*. The heads of families are all here. If the *maungatabu* is called, it is decided. [Next sentence unclear; probably: As you, our old men, have done from the past to the present.] . . . Who else is there to call? Are the people here valueless? . . . Then it will go to the council."

Another man echoed the point: "What is worth more? The heads of families or the council?"

And later, speaker H said: "How many Banabans are there? The government can see how many. When this man [that is, someone] comes, he speaks for his spouse and children." And later: "We call people here to sign for their families."

The chairman then shifted his own position: "Ask the community of Banaba. Stay on the *maungatabu* of Banaba." And further on: "It is the decision of the *maungatabu*. Make worthwhile the decision of the *maungatabu*. . . . Pray that the governor is guided [by God] in his decisions."

Speaker H used Banaban tradition to give form to the *maungatabu* as the *maungatabu* gave tangible content to Banaban tradition. He stressed the continuity of that tradition and the unique potential of the *maungatabu* for producing decisive action. The *maungatabu* became a tangible form which struc-tured the transformation of "the people" into the "heads of families," the powerful images of kinship perhaps now becoming content for the *maungatabu*. While some role for the council was maintained, action in the meeting itself was presented as critical and historic. That action would then give form to the other structures.

One well-known supporter of the adviser and opponent of the annuity argued for a plebiscite or a paper vote (which one was unclear to me) in the meeting: "The word can be changed. The paper cannot. This is not the time for unenlightened thoughts ['thoughts of darkness, ignorance']. The light ['electricity', pointing to the fluorescent light above] is lit." The 'time of darkness, ignorance' and the 'time of light, understanding' are often used to indicate the contrast between the Banaban way of life before and after missionization or, more generally, as a contrast between ancient and enlightened times.

Later, speaker H came back to the issue by making of the *maungatabu* a "special case" of modern political thought. He said that the people were acting in a "democracy," that the *maungatabu* was called so that people's ideas could be made known, one after another, and that each person is precious in this system. The *maungatabu* thus became tangible content for both the continuity of Banaban tradition and political advancement.[22] Here is the artful rhetorician situating the *maungatabu* at the interface of two conceived systems, the relations of which are often quite problematic to the people—'tradition' and 'progress' (or, more generally, the nature and demands of the modern world)—and stressing the actability of both. Here a relationship can be made through action, through *that* action. As a young man said with great feeling, "We want to see the power of the community of Banaba!"

The chairman had put two papers on the stage and a few people went up to sign, but there was hesitancy. The proposal for a count of hands won out; perhaps the raising of hands on each side was a more collective and momentary act. And hand counters from both 'the council' and 'the people' joined together in legitimizing the act. The vote was read as 110 against and 18 for the adviser.

The winning side at the meeting, crystallized through the 'heads of families' route, made the Banaban community tangible by constituting the people at the meeting as the Banaban community who by a concrete action could give form to such tangible symbols and meanings as freedom and land, the worth of the person and the sanctity of kinship, the preservation of Banaban tradition and the commitment to progress.

During the course of the meeting, many relationships had been set out as the problematic situation and its transformation were elaborated. The people explored various definitions, subjects, objects, instruments, and means, which were given form by various symbols and meanings and which gave form to various events. Toward the end of the meeting they had the problem of building the structure for the transformation (action) which would be accomplished *now,* a structure which could operate on the wide-ranging sets of relations which had emerged.

There was obviously an "audience present" which included outside authority, and many ambiguities remained as to the role of the council—what power

lay where, and so forth. But the position that "the *maungatabu* can do it" meant essentially that the Banaban community, in its action, could become the subject, object, instrument, and means of its own transformation, giving form to and being formed by itself.

The symbol which was constituted by the action of the meeting might be termed a "reflexive symbol," since the symbol and much of the universe to which its referent applied were simultaneously present and identical. The people were both the instances of the Banaban community and the components of the symbol in that they were participants in the action. Thus what in other contexts are general symbols are given form by every individual, and every individual becomes more than an individual by becoming the component of a symbol.

This is not to suggest that specific grievances, alliances, and hostilities were irrelevant to the meeting, that the meeting concerned only matters of policy and practice. Insofar as it was successful, the ordering represented by the meeting was successful because a diversity of concerns, complaints, and strategies—a noble concern for the future of the community, a grandstand play for position, an intense grudge against the adviser—could be given form by that ordering. This is what any politician knows. The commanding problem is not why certain people did what they did, but the creation of the set of forms which enabled them to do what they did, for whatever reason. All was not enthusiasm and harmony at the end of the meeting. Far from it. Those opposed to the position that "the *maungatabu* can do it" were profoundly unhappy with what was going on and questioned its legitimacy. Others were not sure how they felt about the outcome of the meeting. The meeting did not resolve fundamental conflicts; it articulated them. But whether people voted one way or the other, sat it out, made a dramatic exit, quietly slipped through the side door—or did not attend in the first place—something was going to happen and something did happen, out of a multiplicity of events and apart from a multiplicity of events. As Althusser (1970:126) observes: "What makes *such and such* an event *historical* is not the fact that it is *an event,* but precisely its insertion into forms which are themselves historical."[23]

Ethnographic Epilogue

Just before the voting began, one man suggested that there should be a film showing afterward. After the chairman called the meeting to a close and said that people were free in their opinions, there was a discussion on the availability of a film. The suggestion on the film was not out of place, because films are shown there from time to time. In fact, a film was shown that evening but some people, including myself, left before it. I eternally regret that my exhaustion compelled me to withdraw from the scene.

With the people (or what was left of them) now collectively in the same position vis-à-vis an outside entertainment, they demarcated the end of the previous form. The Banabans are often quite energetic filmgoers, talking and commenting. The film may have provided some kind of release from a trying event filled with hostility, latent and manifest. Perhaps the performers in the action unwound, or rewound, themselves into

an audience involved in something entirely different: the medium (the meeting) had become the message, bracketed itself by the final action, and having accomplished this feat, further bracketed itself by the introduction of another medium.

Conclusion

Every analysis has its black boxes. Something goes into the box, something comes out of the box. But what goes on inside the box—a "how," a process—remains essentially unexplored. The analyst may consider the "how" to be understood, irrelevant, somebody else's business, perhaps describable in the future. One can easily label the box without opening the lid but thinking that one has, and then confuse product with process (for instance, some uses of "self-interest" and "adaptation").

One "how" becomes illuminated or even restructured (Lévi-Strauss on how a myth means, Peacock on how a drama works, Schneider on how kinship articulates, Turner on how a ritual works) and others are created.

My own analysis has its black boxes, too, many of them of noble antiquity. How do symbols really symbolize? What really goes on in the conjunctions? What are the operations and rules that specify how one thing can lead to another and how one thing cannot lead to another? How does what I have described articulate precisely with local social relations and with larger structures?[24]

If this paper has any theoretical utility, it may help to delineate certain aspects of the how of events like the meeting, events which are, if you will, macrocosms of the symbolization process, where forms are under construction which enable (or, to play it out, restrict) the—quite literal—making of sense.

Ethnographically, the paper documents the microsystem-macrosystem problem, discussed by several others as one with an urgent reality to a people struggling to become themselves and struggling to restructure at least one aspect of the world they live in.

Notes

1. I would like to thank Steven A. Barnett, Vern Carroll, Michael D. Lieber, James L. Peacock, David Schneider, Peter Seitel, and Victor Turner for their extraordinarily useful comments on a previous draft of this chapter. A theoretical dialogue with Barnett has been particularly critical to the present effort. Lieber labored mightily and sympathetically to make the chapter more readable, rewriting some of the more obscure sections, and in so doing contributed substantively to it. I must alert the reader to the fact that the details of the methodology of the analysis were formulated after the conclusion of the fieldwork. I offer deep apologies for being able to find only rather obscure and convoluted ways of stating many of my fundamental points. Many of these points are simple, well-known, and even commonsensical, but I have felt the need for a certain degree of formal abstractness to enhance the chapter's possible utility for those interested in the comparative analysis of symbolic actions. My apologies are deepest to the Banabans themselves.

2. One can also approximate Peter Berger's terms: people are, collectively and simultaneously, "externalizing" fields of meanings, asserting a "shared facticity" by objectivating meanings, and "internalizing" the objectivated production. The element of ambiguity, however, complicates the picture. See Berger (1969).

3. Much of the material in this section is repeated from Silverman (1971).

4. I note especially for comparative purposes that "direct dealings" with phosphate company and government personnel continued on Ocean Island in several respects.

5. The four centralized villages on Ocean Island were apparently consolidated in the early colonial period from five village districts (composed of many hamlets) which were in effect maximal units (beneath the level of the island itself, which was relevant in some contexts) in the ritual, descent, and territorial systems.

6. Certain services are listed in old records as being paid for by deductions from Banaban funds. I know nothing of how this process occurred or what role the Banabans had in it. I am operating on the assumption that the role bears no real comparison to the Rambi structure.

7. A "radical" suggestion was made early on Rambi that much of the phosphate money should be distributed to the people and that the council would obtain what additional funds it needed through taxation. I do not know how general the sentiment was in favor of this proposal, but apparently it was not well received by the government.

8. The "right will inevitably be done" attitude has been losing ground recently.

9. These connections are explored in detail in Silverman (1971).

10. There was a complex set of rules about the distribution of the annuity and bonus, discussed in Silverman (1971). For "full-Banabans" (the regulations were somewhat different for others), there was recognition of the equal identity of Banaban individuals (since individuals received the same amount of money, qualified by age) through the annuity and also recognition of the differentiation of Banabans as individuals with different amounts of land through the bonus—or all Banabans are landowners, but some own more land than others. Had there been no upper limit on the bonus, the case would be much nicer: the annuity going to the person (but one, of course, whose status was partially conceived in terms of his being a landowner) and the bonus going to the land. The setting of the upper limit, however, does not preclude the presence of that conception. Indeed, it suggests it. Which features of the rules were initiated by the government and which by the Banabans is obscure, although it is reported that a committee of Banabans approved the rules.

11. The figures are presented to be suggestive. Consideration of the household as a social unit is a very tricky matter for Rambi. The full-time job category is somewhat deceptive since some of these people, too, engage in agriculture, fishing, and entrepreneurial activity.

12. The term "problematic situation" is borrowed from Laura Thompson, who uses it in applied anthropological contexts.

13. The connections being made may overlap with an anthropologist's description of social organization or social structure. I want to recognize but not explore an extraordinarily important theoretical problem here: the

similarities and differences between the anthropologist's delineating activity and the delineating activity of the people he is studying.

14. The point recalls Geertz's distinction between the "model of" and "model for" functions of symbols (Geertz 1966). I refrain from adopting that language here because of complications which are provided by the elements of vagueness and ambiguity for the "template" notion and my (admittedly uneven) stress on structure in use. A solution might be to look for the principles of template construction, some clues to which are given in Geertz (1964).

15. These points draw upon Dumont (1970a) and Black (1962), although I am not using "stressed" in the same sense as Dumont and do not want to situate this discussion vis-à-vis Dumont's encompassing/encompassed distinction. Although I schematize the process of conjunction as if only two things are being conjoined, that is, of course, a gross simplification. The point may appear to be vulnerable in that it says nothing more than that B meets C on the street and they talk about what they have in common. Two responses: first, "what they have in common" is not given a priori, given B and C; second, I stick to the special case since I do not want to bring up the question of change, which is really the most interesting question. For example: what happens when B meets C and one or both are not what they used to be? I hope to develop these matters in future publications.

16. Without knowledge of other *maungatabu,* it is impossible to know whether one can write a generalized scenario (or a limited number of scenarios) for a *maungatabu* of which this one would be an instance. I was struck at several points by the search for forms—the procedures to be followed were themselves problematic. The mode of the search, however, might constitute a form in itself. If there is a *maungatabu* form of which the meeting is an instance, then one would also have to demarcate that form vis-à-vis other forms in order to understand the Banaban's behavior in the *maungatabu* itself. Serious attention to matters of this kind is given in Peacock (1968). The literature on judicial proceedings also provides a clear line of comparative and methodologically illuminating inquiry. But I do not want to expand what is already a lengthy paper, and I am not familiar enough with the literature to enter that fray at this point. The exclusive attention to verbal communication in my analysis is a serious deficiency.

17. Aspects of "freedom" are treated in Silverman (1971). It is a cultural label for the "maximize your options" principle. It is through events such as this that its meanings may become established.

18. Other contributors take up the question of the specific mapping of presettlement structures onto the post-resettlement situation. The mapping, of course, goes the other way, too, and it is the dialectic between them that is really interesting. The construction of the bonus and annuity, as well as land subdivisions, settlement patterns, and electoral rules, are all part of the mapping problem, which is treated in detail in Silverman (1971).

19. One crucial feature of the intervening exchanges must be mentioned but remain undocumented here. The explicit bringing forth of the structuring symbols discussed, and the spelling out of form-content relations of the several kinds, tended to come from the protagonists in the debate—the councillors and some of the people known before the meeting as strong partisans. One would have to situate this point in terms of Banaban rhetorical action in order to interpret it. Some strong partisans were important figures in their churches. Perhaps there is some relationship between this practice and prominent organizational activity. Which comes first—whether there is an ability which selects people for such activity, or whether such activity encourages the development of the ability or marks out some people as those who should publicly symbolize in this way—is a question I cannot answer. If the relationship is not with prominent organizational activity in general, it may be with church activity. Although my notes on them are pitifully incomplete, I suspect that sermons constitute the paradigmatic continuing form which articulates things so completely. Perhaps we are dealing with a feature of most Banaban persuasive discourse, discourse in a problematic situation, or both. Many have noted, but not explored in detail, the elaboration of rhetoric in Oceania. This neglect may result from a preconception that style is an embellishment of what really matters rather than being constitutive of it.

20. I recognize a problem here which is important at the theoretical level. It is appropriate to speak of acts as symbols and objects as symbols (as in Geertz 1966), but if one is trying to specify the nature and relations of symbolic systems, a good deal more careful thought is necessary on the implications of a symbol being an act, an object, or whatever.

21. My only other reference to an event being called a *maungatabu* was a general meeting of the cooperative society on which I have sparse data. There was a real problematic situation there, but it might have been called a *maungatabu* even if there were not. The *maungatabu* may be a label for "general meetings of the membership," some of which are temporally regular and others of which are part of a social-conceptual drama sequence. I also note that the first adviser on Rambi got into many difficulties with the people, and one of the local interpretations is that the people (or certain groups) were instrumental in his departure. The whole affair regarding the adviser may thus be a replay, and there may have been a *maungatabu* in the earlier case. This does not, however, qualify the historical nature of the event. More data would answer some of these questions. For a meaning of *maungatabu* in the Gilberts, see Maude (1963).

22. It is interesting to note here that both speaker H and the man who made "the light is lit" statement were arguing in the same terms. If the discussion had been

carried further, some of the terms (such as 'progress') may have turned out to be "essentially contested" concepts (Gallie 1962).

23. The quote is, evocatively and provocatively, being lifted out of context. James Peacock suggests that the actions of the viewers of the film shown immediately after the meeting may have carried forward and given new power to the actions-meanings constructed during the meeting by encoding, elaborating, and displacing those meanings through another medium.

24. I had intended to include a detailed analysis of the articulation of what occurred in the meeting with the social relations of the participants, but found that a book-length treatment would be necessary. While the omission is a serious one, I believe the content of the paper raises enough questions of general interest to be justified.

TWENTY-SEVEN

"From the Native's Point of View": On the Nature of Anthropological Understanding

CLIFFORD GEERTZ

The problem of meaning is but another statement of the classical philosophical problem of understanding. Positive science, it is argued by some, constitutes man's sole possible significant cognitive relation to external reality. Another view is that of George Herbert Mead the pragmatist philosopher and psychologist, who argued that understanding was based on the ability to "take the role of the other"—that is, on a form of empathy. And Malinowski pressed the notion that in field work "participant observation" was indispensable to even a correct reporting, for only by actually doing what the native did could one understand what it meant to him.

Geertz rejects positivism as he rejects Malinowski's (and Mead's) notions that some extraordinary sensitivity on the part of the observer, some special empathy, can ground understanding. Instead he argues for what has come to be called a *hermeneutic* method, wherein one interpretation is piled on top of another, one version of a text (or action treated as text) is compared with another, one set of perceptions is set against another. The medium for these comparisons is the symbolic forms that are readily observable and easily grasped. By starting with sets of clearly given symbols and comparing them with other sets, from whatever source—one's own culture or other known cultures—one can slowly build up an understanding.

SEVERAL YEARS AGO a minor scandal erupted in anthropology; one of its ancestral figures told the truth in a public place. As befits an ancestor, he did it posthumously and through his widow's decision rather than his own, with the result that a number of the sort of right-thinking types who are always with us immediately rose to cry that she—an in-marrier anyway—had betrayed clan secrets, profaned an idol, and let down the side.

What will the children think, to say nothing of the laymen? But the disturbance was not much lessened by such ceremonial wringing of the hands; the damn thing was, after all, already printed. In much the same way that James Watson's *The Double Helix* exposed the nature of research in biophysics, Bronis-

Reprinted by permission of the American Academy of Arts and Sciences from the *Bulletin* of the American Academy, October 1974.

law Malinowski's *A Diary in the Strict Sense of the Term* rendered the established image of how anthropological work is conducted fairly well implausible. The myth of the chameleon field worker perfectly self-tuned to his exotic surroundings—a walking miracle of empathy, tact, patience, and cosmopolitanism—was demolished by the man who had perhaps done the most to create it.

The squabble that surrounded the publication of the *Diary* concentrated, naturally, on inessentials and, as was only to be expected, missed the point. Most of the shock seems to have arisen from the mere discovery that Malinowski was not, to put it delicately, an unmitigated nice guy. He had rude things to say about the natives he was living with and rude words to say it in. He spent a great deal of his time wishing he were elsewhere. And he projected an image of a man as little complaisant as the world has seen. (He also projected an image of a man consecrated to a strange vocation to the point of self-immolation, but that was less noted.)

The discussion eventually came down to Malinowski's moral character or lack of it; ignored was the genuinely profound question his book raised, namely, if anthropological understanding does not stem, as we have been taught to believe, from some sort of extraordinary sensibility, an almost preternatural capacity to think, feel, and perceive like a native (a word, I should hurry to say, I use here "in the strict sense of the term"), then how is anthropological knowledge of the way natives think, feel, and perceive possible? The issue the *Diary* presents, with a force perhaps only a working ethnographer can fully appreciate, is not moral; it is epistemo-logical. If we are going to cling—as in my opinion, we must—to the injunction to see things from the native's point of view, what is our position when we can no longer claim some unique form of psychological closeness, a sort of transcultural identification, with our subjects? What happens to *verstehen* when *einfühlen* disappears?

As a matter of fact, this general problem has been exercising methodological discussion in anthropology for the last ten or fifteen years; Malinowski's voice from the grave merely dramatized it as a human dilemma over and above a professional one. The formulations have been various: "inside" versus "outside," or "first person" versus "third person" descriptions; "phenomenological" versus "objectivist," or "cognitive" versus "behavioral" theories; or, perhaps most commonly, "emic" versus "etic" analyses, this last deriving from the distinction in linguistics between phonemics and phonetics—phonemics classifying sounds according to their internal function in language, phonetics classifying them according to their acoustic properties as such. But perhaps the simplest and most directly appreciable way to put the matter is in terms of a distinction formulated, for his own purposes, by the psychoanalyst Hans Kohut—a distinction between what he calls "experience-near" and "experience-distant" concepts.

An experience-near concept is, roughly, one which an individual—a patient, a subject, in our case an informant—might himself naturally and effortlessly use to define what he or his fellows see, think, imagine, and so on, and which he would readily understand when similarly applied by others. An experience-distant concept is one which various types of specialists—an analyst, an experimenter, an ethnographer, even a priest or an ideologist—employ to forward their scientific, philosophical, or practical aims. "Love" is an experience-near concept; "object cathexis" is an experience-distant one. "Social stratification" and perhaps for most peoples in the world even "religion" (and certainly, "religious system") are experience-distant; "caste" and "nirvana" are experience-near, at least for Hindus and Buddhists.

Clearly, the matter is one of degree, not polar opposition: "fear" is experience-nearer than "phobia," and "phobia" experience-nearer than "ego dyssyntonic." And the difference is not, at least so far as anthropology is concerned (the matter is otherwise in poetry and physics), a normative one, in the sense that one sort of concept as such is to be preferred over the other. Confinement to experience-near concepts leaves an ethnographer awash in immediacies as well as entangled in vernacular. Confinement to experience-distant ones leaves him stranded in abstractions and smothered in jargon. The real question, and the one Malinowski raised by demonstrating that, in the case of "natives," you don't have to be one to know one, is what roles the two kinds of concepts play in anthropological analysis. To be more exact: how, in each case, should they be deployed so as to produce an interpretation of the way a people live which is neither imprisoned within their mental horizons, an ethnography of witchcraft as written by a witch, nor systematically deaf to the distinctive tonalities of their existence, an ethnography of witchcraft as written by a geometer?

Putting the matter this way—in terms of how anthropological analysis is to be conducted and its results framed, rather than what psychic constitution anthropologists need to have—reduces the mystery of what "seeing things from the native's point of view" means. But it does not make it any easier nor does it lessen the demand for perceptiveness on the part of the field worker. To grasp concepts which, for another people, are experience-near, and to do so well enough to place them in illuminating connection with those experience-distant concepts that theorists have fashioned to capture the general features of social life, is clearly a task at least as delicate, if a bit less magical, as putting oneself into someone else's skin. The trick is not to achieve some inner correspondence of spirit with your informants; preferring, like the rest of us, to call their souls their own, they are not going to be altogether keen about such an effort anyhow. The trick is to figure out what the devil they think they are up to.

In one sense, of course, no one knows this better than they do themselves; hence the passion to swim in the stream of their experience, and the illusion afterward that one somehow has. But in another sense, that simple truism is simply not true. People use experience-near concepts spontaneously, unself-consciously, as it were, colloquially; they do not, except fleetingly and on occasion, recognize that there are any "concepts" involved at all. That is what experience-near means—that ideas and the realities they disclose are naturally and indissolubly bound up together. And what else could you call a hippopotamus? Of course the gods are powerful; why else would we fear them? The ethnographer does not, and in my opinion, largely cannot, perceive what his informants perceive. What he perceives—and that uncertainly enough—is what they perceive "with," or "by means of," or "through," or whatever word one may choose. In the country of the blind, who are not as unobservant as they appear, the one-eyed is not king but spectator.

Now, to make all this a bit more concrete I want to turn for a moment to my own work, which whatever its other faults has at least the virtue of being mine—a distinct advantage in discussions of this sort. In all three of the societies I have studied intensively, Javanese, Balinese, and Moroccan, I have been concerned, among other things, with attempting to determine how the people who live there define themselves as persons, what enters into the idea they have (but, as I say, only half-realize they have) of what a self, Javanese, Balinese, or Moroccan style, is. And in each case, I have tried to arrive at this most intimate of notions not by imagining myself as someone else—a rice peasant or a tribal sheikh, and then seeing what I thought—but by searching out and analyzing the symbolic forms—words, images, institutions, behaviors—in terms of which, in each place, people actually represent themselves to themselves and to one another.

The concept of person is, in fact, an excellent vehicle by which to examine this whole question of how to go about poking into another people's turn of mind. In the first place, some sort of concept of this kind, one feels reasonably safe in saying, exists in recognizable form within all social groups. Various notions of what persons are may be, from our point of view, more than a little odd. People may be conceived to dart about nervously at night, shaped like fireflies. Essential elements of their psyche, like hatred, may be thought to be lodged in granular black bodies within their livers, discoverable upon autopsy. They may share their fates with *doppelganger* beasts, so that when the beast sickens or dies they sicken or die too. But at least some conception of what a human individual is, as opposed to a rock, an animal, a rainstorm, or a god, is, so far as I can see, universal.

Yet, at the same time, as these offhand examples suggest, the actual conceptions involved vary, often quite sharply, from one group to the next. The Western conception of the person as a bounded, unique, more or less integrated motivational and cognitive universe, a dynamic center of awareness, emotion, judgment, and action organized into a distinctive whole and set contrastively both against other such wholes and against a social and natural background is, however incorrigible it may seem to us, a rather peculiar idea within the context of the world's cultures. Rather than attempt to place the experience of others within the framework of such a conception, which is what the extolled "empathy" in fact usually comes down to, we must, if we are to achieve understanding, set that conception aside and view their experience within the framework of their own idea of what selfhood is. And for Java, Bali, and Morocco, at least, that idea differs markedly, not only from our own but, no less dramatically and no less instructively, from one to the other.

In Java, where I worked in the fifties, I studied a small, shabby inland county-seat sort of place: two shadeless streets of whitewashed wooden shops and offices, with even less substantial bamboo shacks crammed in helter-skelter behind them, the whole surrounded by a great half-circle of densely-packed rice-bowl villages. Land was short; jobs were scarce; politics was unstable; health was poor; prices were rising; and life was altogether far from promising, a kind of agitated stagnancy in which, as I once put it, thinking of the curious mixture of borrowed fragments of modernity and exhausted relics of tradition that characterized the place, the future seemed about as remote as the past. Yet, in the midst of this depressing scene, there was an absolutely astonishing intellectual vitality; a philosophical passion, and a popular one besides, to track the riddles of existence right down to the ground. Destitute peasants would discuss questions of freedom of the will; illiterate tradesmen discoursed on the properties of God; common laborers had theories about the relations between reason and passion, the nature of time, or the reliability of the senses. And, perhaps most importantly, the problem of the self—its nature, function, and mode of operation—was pursued with the sort of reflective intensity one could find among ourselves in only the most recherché settings indeed.

The central ideas in terms of which this reflection proceeded and which thus defined its boundaries and the Javanese sense of what a person is were arranged in two sets of, at base religious, contrasts: one between "inside" and "outside," and one between "refined" and "vulgar." These glosses are, of course, crude and imprecise; determining exactly what was signified by the terms involved and sorting out their shades of meaning was what all the discussion was about. But together they formed a distinctive conception of the self which, far from being merely theoretical, was the means by which Javanese in fact perceive one another and, of course, themselves.

The "inside"/"outside" words, *batin* and *lair* (terms borrowed, as a matter of fact, from the Sufi tradition of Muslim mysticism, but locally reworked), refer on the one hand to the felt realm of human experience and on the other to the observed realm of human behavior. These have, one hastens to say, nothing to do with "soul" and "body" in our sense, for which there are quite other words with quite other implications. *Batin,* the "inside" word, does not refer to a separate seat of encapsulated spirituality detached or detachable from the body, or indeed to a bounded unit at all, but to the emotional life of human beings taken generally. It consists of the fuzzy, shifting flow of subjective feeling perceived directly in all its phenomenological immediacy but considered to be, at its roots at least, identical across all individuals, whose individuality it thus effaces. And, similarly, *lair,* the "outside" word, has nothing to do with the body as an object, even an experienced object. Rather, it refers to that part of human life which, in our culture, strict behaviorists limit themselves to studying—external actions, movements, postures, speech—again, conceived as in its essence invariant from one individual to the next. Therefore, these two sets of phenomena—inward feelings and outward actions—are regarded not as functions of one another but as independent realms of being to be put in proper order independently.

It is in connection with this "proper ordering" that the contrast between *alus,* the word meaning "pure," "refined," "polished," "exquisite," "ethereal," "subtle," "civilized," "smooth," and *kasar,* the word meaning "impolite," "rough," "uncivilized," "coarse," "insensitive," "vulgar," comes into play. The goal is to be *alus* in both separated realms of the self. In the inner realm this is to be achieved through religious discipline, much but not all of it mystical. In the outer realm, it is to be achieved through etiquette, the rules of which, in this instance, are not only extraordinarily elaborate but have something of the force of law. Through meditation the civilized man thins out his emotional life to a kind of constant hum; through etiquette, he both shields that life from external disruptions and regularizes his outer behavior in such a way that it appears to others as a predictable, undisturbing, elegant, and rather vacant set of choreographed motions and settled forms of speech.

There is much to all this because it connects up to both an ontology and an aesthetic. But so far as our problem is concerned, the result is a bifurcate conception of the self, half ungestured feeling and half unfelt gesture. An inner world of stilled emotion and an outer world of shaped behavior confront one another as sharply distinguished realms unto themselves, any particular person being but the momentary locus, so to speak, of that confrontation, a passing expression of their permanent existence, their permanent separation, and their permanent need to be kept in their own separate order. Only when you have seen, as I have, a young man whose wife—a woman he had raised from childhood and who had been the center of his life—has suddenly and inexplicably died, greeting everyone with a set smile and formal apologies for his wife's absense and trying, by mystical techniques, to flatten out, as he himself put it, the hills and valleys of his emotion into an even, level plain ("That is what you have to do," he said to me, "be smooth inside and out") can you come, in the face of our own notions of the intrinsic honesty of deep feeling and the moral importance of personal sincerity, to take the possibility of such a conception of selfhood seriously and to appreciate, however inaccessible it is to you, its own sort of force.

Bali, where I worked in another small provincial town, though one rather less drifting and dispirited, and, later, in an upland village of highly skilled musical instrument makers, is in many ways similar to Java, with which it shared a common culture until the fifteenth century. But at a deeper level, having continued Hindu while Java was, nominally at least, Islamized, it is quite different. The intricate, obsessive ritual life, Hindu, Baptist, and Polynesian in about equal proportions (the development of which was more or less cut off in Java, leaving its Indic spirit to turn reflective and phenomenological, even quietistic, in the way I've described), flourished in Bali to reach levels of scale and flamboyance that have startled the world and made the Balinese a much more dramaturgical people with a self to match. What is philosophy in Java is theater in Bali.

As a result, there is in Bali a persistent and systematic attempt to stylize all aspects of personal expression to the point where anything idiosyncratic, anything characteristic of the individual merely because he is who he is physically, psychologically, or biographically, is muted in favor of his assigned place in the continuing and, so it is thought, never-changing pageant that is Balinese life. It is dramatis personae, not actors, that endure; indeed, it is dramatis personae, not actors, that in the proper sense really exist. Physically men come and go— mere incidents in a happenstance history of no genuine importance, even to themselves. But the masks they wear, the stage they occupy, the parts they play, and, most important, the spectacle they mount remain and constitute not the facade but the substance of things, not least the self. Shakespeare's old-trouper view of the vanity of action in the face of mortality—"all the world's a stage and we but poor players, content to strut our hour"—makes no sense here. There is no make-believe: of course players perish, but the play doesn't, and it is the latter, the performed rather than the performer, that really matters.

Again, all this is realized not in terms of some general mood the anthropologist in his spiritual versatility somehow captures, but through a set of readily observable symbolic forms: an elaborate repertoire of designations and titles. The Balinese have at least a half dozen major sorts of labels, ascriptive, fixed, and absolute, which one performer can apply to another (or, of course, to himself) to place him among his fellows. There are birth-order markers, kinship terms, caste titles, sex indicators, teknonyms, and so on, each of which consists not of a mere collection of useful tags but a distinct and bounded, internally very complex, terminological system. To apply one or more of these designations or titles (or, as is more common, several at once) to a person is to define him as a determinate point in a fixed pattern, as the temporary occupant of a particular, quite untemporary, cultural locus. To identify someone, yourself or anyone else, in Bali is thus to locate him within the familiar cast of characters—"king," "grandmother," "third-born," "Brahman"—of which the social drama is, like some stock company roadshow piece—*Charley's Aunt* or *Springtime for Henry*—inevitably composed.

The drama is, of course, not farce, and especially not transvestite farce, though there are such elements in it. It is an enactment of hierarchy, a theater of status. But that, though critical, is unpursuable here. The immediate point is that, in both their structure and their mode of operation, the terminological systems conduce to a view of the human person as an appropriate representative of a generic type, not a unique creature with a private fate. To see how they do this, how they tend to obscure the mere materialities—biological, psychological, historical—of individual existence in favor of standardized status qualities would involve an extended analysis. But perhaps a single example, the simplest further simplified, will suffice to suggest the pattern.

All Balinese receive what might be called birth-order names. There are four of these, "first-born," "second-born," "third-born," and "fourth-born," after which they recycle, so that the fifth-born child is called again "first-born," the sixth "second-born," and so on. Further, these names are bestowed independently of the fates of the children. Dead children, even still-born ones, count, so that in this still high birth rate—high infant mortality society, the names don't really tell you anything very reliable about the birth-order relations of concrete individuals. Within a set of living siblings, someone called "first-born" may actually be first-, fifth-, or ninth-born, or, if somebody is missing, almost anything in between; and someone called "second-born" may in fact be older. The birth-order naming system does not identify individuals as individuals nor is it intended to; what it does is to suggest that, for all procreating couples, births form a circular succession of "firsts," "seconds," "thirds," and "fourths," an endless four-stage replication of an imperishable form. Physically men appear and disappear as the ephemerae they are, but socially the acting figures remain eternally the same as new "firsts," "seconds," and so on; they emerge from the timeless world of the gods to replace those who, dying, dissolve once more into it. Thus I would argue that all the designation and title systems function in the same way: to represent the most time-saturated aspects of the human condition as but ingredients in an eternal, footlight present.

Nor is this sense the Balinese have of always being on stage a vague and ineffable one either. It is, in fact, exactly summed up in what is surely one of their experience-nearest concepts: *lek. Lek* has been variously translated or mistranslated ("shame" is the most common attempt), but what it really means is close to what we call stage fright. Stage fright is the fear that, for want of skill or self-control, or perhaps by mere accident, an anesthetic illusion will not be maintained, the fear that the actor will show through his part. Aesthetic distance collapses; the audience (and the actor) loses sight of Hamlet and gains, uncomfortably for all concerned, a picture of bumbling John Smith painfully miscast as the Prince of Denmark. In Bali, the case is the same: what is feared is that the public performance to which one's cultural location commits one will be botched and that the personality (as we would call it but the Balinese, of course, not believing in such a thing, would not) of the individual will break through to dissolve his standardized public identity. When this occurs, as it sometimes does, the immediacy of the moment is felt with excruciating intensity, and men become suddenly and unwillingly creatural, locked in mutual embarrassment, as though they had happened upon each other's nakedness. It is the fear of *faux pas,* rendered only that much more probable by the extraordinary ritualization of daily life, that keeps social intercourse on its deliberately narrowed rails and protects the dramatistical sense of self against the disruptive threat implicit in the immediacy and spontaneity which even the most passionate ceremoniousness cannot fully eradicate from face-to-face encounters.

Morocco, mid-Eastern and dry rather than East Asian and wet, extrovert, fluid, activist, masculine, informal to a fault, a wild-west sort of place without the barrooms and cattle drives, is another kettle of selves altogether. My work there, which began in the mid-sixties, has been centered in a moderately large town or small city in the foothills of the Middle Atlas, about twenty miles south of Fez. It is an old place, probably founded in the tenth century, conceivably even earlier. It has the walls, the gates, the narrow minarets rising to prayer-call platforms of a classical Muslim town, and, from a distance anyway, it is a rather pretty place, an irregular oval of blinding white set in the deep-sea green of an olive-grove oasis, the mountains, bronze and stony here, slanting up immediately behind it.

Close up, it is less prepossessing, though more exciting: a labyrinth of passages and alleyways, three-quarters of them blind, pressed in by wall-like buildings and curbside shops and filled with a simply astounding variety of very emphatic human beings. Arabs, Berbers, and Jews; tailors, herdsmen, and soldiers; people out of offices, people out of markets, people out of tribes; rich, super-rich, poor, super-poor; locals, immigrants, mimic Frenchmen, unbending medievalists, and somewhere, according to the official government census for 1960, an unemployed Jewish airplane pilot—the town houses one of the finest collections of rugged individuals I, at least, have ever come up against. Next to Sefrou (the name of the place), Manhattan seems almost monotonous.

Yet, no society consists of anonymous eccentrics bouncing off one another like billiard balls, and Moroccans, too, have symbolic means by which to sort people out from one another and form an idea of what it is to be a person. The main such means—not the only one, but I think the most important and the one I want to talk about particularly here—is a peculiar linguistic form called in Arabic the *nisba*. The word derives from the triliteral root, *n-s-b,* for "ascription," "attribution," "imputation," "relationship," "affinity," "correlation," "connection," "kinship." *Nsīb* means "in-law"; *nsab* means "to attribute or impute to"; *munasāba* means "a relation," "an analogy," "a correspondence"; *mansūb* means "belonging to," "pertaining to"; and so

on to at least a dozen derivatives from *nassāb,* "genealolgist," to *nisbiya,* "(physical) relativity."

Nisba itself, then, refers to a combination morphological, grammatical, and semantic process which consists of transforming a noun into what we would call a relative adjective but what for Arabs becomes just another sort of noun by adding *ī* (f., *īya*): *Sefrū*?Sefrou—*Sefrūwī*/native son of Sefrou; *Sūs*/region of southwestern Morocco—*Sūsī*/man coming from that region; *Beni Yazḡa*/a tribe near Sefrou—*Yazḡī*/a member of that tribe; *Yahūd*/the Jews as a people, Jewry—*Yahūdī*/a Jew; *'Adlun*/surname of a prominent Sefrou family—*'Adlūnī*/a member of the family. Nor is the procedure confined to this more or less straightforward "ethnicizing" use but is employed, in a wide range of domains, to attribute relational properties to persons. For example, occupation (*hrār*/silk—*hrārī*/silk merchant); religious sect (*Darqāwā*/a mystical brotherhood—*Darqāwī*/an adept of that brotherhood); or spiritual status (*Ali*/the Prophet's son-in-law—*'Alawī*/descendant of the Prophet's son-in-law, and thus of the Prophet).

Now, as once formed, nisbas tend to be incorporated into personal names—Umar Al-Buhadiwi/Umar of the Buhadi tribe; Muhammed Al-Sussi/Muhammed from the Sus region; this sort of adjectival, attributive classification is quite publicly stamped upon an individual's identity. I was unable to find a single case in which an individual was generally known, or known about, but his (or her) nisba was not. Indeed, Sefrouis are far more likely to be ignorant of how well-off a man is, how long he has been around, what his personal character is, or where exactly he lives, than they are of what his nisba is—Sussi or Sefroui, Buhadiwi or Adluni, Harari or Darqawi. (Of women to whom he is not related, that is very likely to be all he knows—or, more exactly, all he is permitted to know.) The selves that bump and jostle each other in the alleys of Sefrou gain their definition from associative relations they are imputed to have with the society that surrounds them. They are contextualized persons.

But the situation is even more radical than this. Nisbas render men relative to their contexts, but as contexts themselves are relative, so too are nisbas, and the whole thing rises, so to speak, to the second power: relativism squared. Thus, at one level, everyone in Sefrou has the same nisba, or at least the potential of it—namely, Sefroui. However, within Sefrou such a nisba, precisely because it does not discriminate, will never be heard as part of an individual designation. It is only outside of Sefrou that the relationship to that particular context becomes identifying. Inside it, a man is Adluni, Alawi, Meghrawi, Ngadi, or whatever; and similar distinctions exist within these categories: there are, for example, twelve different nisbas (Shakibis, Zuinis, etc.) by means of which, among themselves, Sefrou Alawis distinguish one another.

The whole matter is far from regular: what level or sort of nisba is used and seems relevant and appropriate (relevant and appropriate, that is, to the users) depends heavily on the situation. A man I knew who lived in Sefrou and worked in Fez but came from the Beni Yazgha tribe settled nearby—and from the Hima lineage of the Taghut subfraction of the Wulad fraction within it—was known as a Sefroui to his work fellows in Fez; a Yazghi to all of us non-Yazghis in Sefrou; an Ydiri to other Beni Yazghis around, except for those who were themselves of the Wulad Ben Ydir fraction, who called him a Taghuti. As for the few other Taghutis, they called him a Himiwi. That's as far as things went here but not as far as they can go in either direction. Should, by chance, our friend journey to Egypt he would become a Maghrebi, the nisba formed from the Arabic word for North Africa. The social contextualization of persons is pervasive and, in its curiously unmethodical way, systematic. Men do not float as bounded psychic entities, detached from their backgrounds and singularly named. As individualistic, even willful, as the Moroccans in fact are, their identity is an attribute they borrow from their setting.

Now, as with the Javanese inside/outside, smooth/rough phenomenological sort of reality-dividing, and the absolutizing Balinese title system, the nisba way of looking at persons—as though they were outlines waiting to be filled in—is not an isolated custom but part of a total pattern of social life. This pattern is, as the others, difficult to characterize succinctly, but surely one of its outstanding features is a promiscuous tumbling in public settings of varieties of men kept carefully segregated in private ones—all-out cosmopolitanism in the streets, strict communalism (of which the famous secluded woman is only the most striking index) in the home.

This is indeed the so-called mosaic system of social organization so often held to be characteristic of the Middle East generally: differently shaped and colored chips jammed in irregularly together to generate an intricate overall design within which their individual distinctiveness remains nonetheless intact.

Nothing if not diverse, Moroccan society does not cope with its diversity by sealing it into castes, isolating it into tribes, dividing it into ethnic groups, or covering it over with some common denominator concept of nationality, though, fitfully, all have now and then been tried. It copes with it by distinguishing, with elaborate precision, the contexts—marriage, worship, and to an extent diet, law, and education—within which men are separated by their dissimilitudes, from those—work, friendship, politics, trade—within which, however warily and however conditionally, they are connected by them.

To such a social pattern a concept of selfhood which marks public identity contextually and relativistically, but yet does so in terms—tribal, territorial, linguistic, religious, familial—which grow out of the more private and settled arenas of life and have a deep and permanent resonance there, would seem particularly appropriate. Indeed, it would virtually seem to create it; for it produces a situation in which people interact with one another in terms of categories whose meaning is almost purely positional—location in the general mosaic—leaving the substantive content of the categories, what they mean subjectively as experienced forms of life, aside as something properly concealed in apartments, temples, and tents. Nisba discriminations can be more or less specific; they can indicate location within the mosaic roughly or finely; and they can be adapted to almost any change in circumstance. But they cannot carry with them more than the most sketchy, outline implications concerning what men so named as a rule are like. Calling a man a Sefroui is like calling him a San Franciscan: it classifies him but it doesn't type him; it places him without portraying him.

It is the capacity of the nisba system to do this—to create a framework within which persons can be identified in terms of supposedly immanent characteristics (speech, blood, faith, provenance, and the rest) and yet to minimize the impact of those characteristics in determining the practical relations among such persons in markets, shops, bureaus, fields, cafés, baths, and roadways—that makes it so central to the Moroccan idea of the self. Nisba-type categorization leads, paradoxically, to a hyperindividualism in public relationships because by providing only a vacant sketch (and that shifting) of who the actors are—Yazghis, Adlunis, Buhadiwis, or whatever—it leaves the rest, that is, almost everything, to be filled in by the process of interaction itself. What makes the mosaic work is the confidence that one can be as totally pragmatic, adaptive, opportunistic, and generally *ad hoc* in one's relations with others—a fox among foxes, a crocodile among crocodiles—as one wants without any risk of losing one's sense of who one is. Selfhood is never in danger because, outside the immediacies of procreation and prayer, only its coordinates are asserted.

Now, without trying to tie up the dozens of loose ends I have not only left dangling in these rather breathless accounts of the senses of selfhood of nearly ninety million people but have doubtless frazzled even more, let us return to the question of what all this can tell us, or could if it were done adequately, about "the native's point of view" in Java, Bali, and Morocco. In describing symbol uses, are we describing perceptions, sentiments, outlooks, experiences? If so, in what sense is this being done? What do we claim when we assert that we understand the semiotic means by which, in this case, persons are defined to one another? That we know words or that we know minds?

In answering this question, it is necessary I think first to notice the characteristic intellectual movement, the inward conceptual rhythm, in each of these analyses, and indeed in all similar analyses, including those of Malinowski—namely, a continuous dialectical tacking between the most local of local detail and the most global of global structure in such a way as to bring both into view simultaneously. In seeking to uncover the Javanese, Balinese, or Moroccan sense of self, one oscillates restlessly between the sort of exotic minutiae (lexical antitheses, categorical schemes, morphophonemic transformations) that makes even the best ethnographies a trial to read and the sort of sweeping characterizations ("quietism," "dramatism," "contextualism") that makes all but the most pedestrian of them somewhat implausible. Hopping back and forth between the whole conceived through the parts which actualize it and the parts conceived through the whole which motivates them, we seek to turn them, by a sort of intellectual perpetual motion, into explications of one another.

All this is, of course, but the now familiar trajectory of what Dilthey called the hermeneutic circle, and my argument here is merely that it is as central to ethnographic interpretation, and thus to the penetration of other people's modes of thought, as it is to literary, historical, philological, psychoanalytic, or biblical interpretation, or for that matter to the informal annotation of every-

day experience we call common sense. In order to follow a baseball game one must understand what a bat, a hit, an inning, a left fielder, a squeeze play, a hanging curve, or a tightened infield are, and what the game in which all these "things" are elements is all about.

When an *explication de texte* critic like Leo Spitzer attempts to interpret Keats's "Ode on a Grecian Urn", he does so by asking himself the alternating questions, "What is the whole poem about?" and "What exactly has Keats seen (or chosen to show us) depicted on the urn he is describing?" At the end of an advancing spiral of general observations and specific remarks he emerges with a reading of the poem as an assertion of the triumph of the aesthetic mode of perception over the historical.

In the same way, when a meanings-and-symbols ethnographer like myself attempts to find out what some pack of natives conceive a person to be, he moves back and forth between asking himself "What is the general form of their life?" and "What exactly are the vehicles in which that form is embodied?" emerging at the end of a similar spiral with the notion that they see the self as a composite, a persona, or a point in the pattern.

You can no more know what *lek* is if you don't know what Balinese dramatism is than you can know what a catcher's mitt is if you don't know what baseball is. And you can no more know what mosaic social organization is if you don't know what a nisba is than you can know what Keats's Platonism is if you are unable to grasp, to use Spitzer's own formulation, the "intellectual thread of thought" captured in such fragment phrases as "Attic shape," "silent form," "bride of quietness," "cold pastoral," "silence and slow time," "peaceful citadel," and "ditties of no tone."

In short, accounts of other peoples' subjectivities can be built up without recourse to pretensions to more-than-normal capacities for ego-effacement and fellow-feeling. Normal capacities in these respects are, of course, essential, as is their cultivation, if we expect people to tolerate our intrusions into their life at all and accept us as persons worth talking to. I am certainly not arguing for insensitivity here and hope I have not demonstrated it.

But whatever accurate or half-accurate sense one gets of what one's informants are "really like" comes not from the experience of that acceptance as such, which is part of one's own biography, not of theirs, but from the ability to construe their modes of expression, what I would call their symbol systems, which such an acceptance allows one to work toward developing. Understanding the form and pressure of, to use the dangerous word one more time, natives' inner lives is more like grasping a proverb, catching an allusion, seeing a joke—or, as I have suggested, reading a poem—than it is like achieving communion.

TWENTY-EIGHT

Culture as Creativity

Roy Wagner

Two points pervade this chapter from Wagner's book *The Invention of Culture*. The first is that culture can be understood as creative transformations of meaning by a process which he calls "metaphorization." Any given symbol has a multiplicity of meanings that overlap and interlock with the meanings of other symbols. These meanings can then be selected out for one or another purpose, used in one or another context, stressed here and left unstressed there. His detailed, delightfully insightful and pertinent exposition of the metaphorization of culture, particularly the culture of those Western Europeans and Americans called anthropologists, displays this idea brilliantly. The second major point is the dissection of the way in which a particular cultural premise has dominated the study of culture itself. Culture is materialized; things are prior to and more important than people; people are represented by things. And so the museum is the very essence of culture and it makes eminently logical sense that when the last Yahi Indian of California turned up he went right into a museum. Not a boarding-house, not an apartment, not a public housing project, but a museum—where he was treated, of course, with the kindness and respect due to the most valuable specimen that could possibly exist: the man who could make more things for the museum.

Fieldwork Is Work in the Field

WHEN I FIRST WENT to do fieldwork among the Daribi people of New Guinea, I had certain expectations of what I hoped to accomplish, though of course I had few preconceived notions about what the people would be "like." Fieldwork is after all a kind of "work," it is a creative, productive experience, although its "rewards" are not necessarily realized in the same way as are those of other forms of work. The fieldworker produces a kind of knowledge as a result of his experiences, a product that can be peddled as "qualifications" in the academic market place, or written into books. The resultant commodity falls into a class with other unique experiences: the memoirs of a famous statesman or entertainer, the journals of mountain climbers, arctic explorers, and adventurers, as well as accounts of exciting artistic or scientific achievements. Though they may attract special attention, such products are nonetheless products, and their creation is still "work."

Reprinted by permission from the publisher from Roy Wagner, *The Invention of Culture* (Englewood Cliffs, N.J.: Prentice-Hall, copyright © 1975), pp. 17–34.

The anthropologist in the field does work; his "working hours" are spent interviewing, observing and taking notes, taking part in local activities. I tried to structure my workday around a set pattern; breakfast followed by interviews with informants, then lunch, with perhaps some observational or participatory work—or perhaps more interviewing afterward, and then an evening meal. All sorts of things—visits, ceremonies, fights, as well as excursions—would interrupt the routine. Yet I clung to it, especially in the first few months, for the idea of regular, steady activity helped sustain my feeling of usefulness in the face of culture shock, the worries of "getting nowhere," and general frustrations. Even after many months, when I had come to understand the situation much better, and was more at ease with my Daribi friends, I still stuck to the rudiments of the schedule as a purposeful program for rounding out my knowledge of the culture.

I suspect that my tenacity in spite of the bemusement of my local friends (many of whom "worked" only in the mornings on every other day) was simply the result of "wanting to do a good job," of a very western idea of work and commitment to one's calling. Routines of this sort are not uncommon among anthropological fieldworkers—they form part of the general definition of the anthropologist's work (illusory though it may be): that we act upon the natives in such a way as to produce ethnographies. (Regardless of the subtleties of the fieldworker's involvement with the native culture, he initiates this involvement, and its results are regarded as his "production.") The totality of the ethnographer's interest in "culture" and the way in which he implements this interest in the field, then, is what defines his job as a fieldworker.

At first it was difficult for my Daribi friends to comprehend what this job—this interest in them and their ways—was, much less take it seriously. They would ask whether I was "government," "mission," or "doctor" (they were regularly visited by members of a leprosy control project), and being told that I was none of these, would marvel "he's not government, not mission, not a doctor!" When I discovered the Pidgin term for anthropologist, *storimasta,* I used this as a label for my work, and the natives were able to "lump" me together with the linguistic missionaries they were familiar with. But, although it settled the matter of classification, this term did little to make my work believable to them. Why try and find out about other peoples' "stories," their ideas and ways of life? Who pays for this kind of work, and why? Is this a job for a grown man? (Query: is our *storimasta* a grown man?)

If the work I did among the Daribi was problematic and puzzling, perhaps the way I lived would offer a clue to understanding it. As I was unmarried, my house was built next to the single men's residence, and since Daribi regard bachelorhood as an unenviable state, I received a good deal of commiseration and sympathy. A special point of interest was the fact that I had to hire a cook to prepare my meals;[1] his relationship to me became a matter of curiosity, and many came to investigate his duties and my household in general. Every night a small crowd of men and boys gathered to watch me eat my evening meal. The prevailing mood was one of curiosity and friendliness; although I tried to share my food, there was little enough even for me, and usually only three or four spectators managed to get a "taste." The mixture of wonder and companionship remained throughout my stay, though only gradually did I come to suspect its basis: the idea that my strange "work" was somehow related to my unmarried state.

No doubt the fact that I had to pay someone to cook for me was both strange and perhaps touching. The Daribi comment was often that "our wives are our cooks," and Daribi bachelors have to find food for themselves, or obtain it from their mothers or brothers' wives. Possibly I confirmed many suspicions when I answered questions as to why I was not married by explaining that I preferred to finish my education and fieldwork first. My wifelessness continued to play on the sympathies of my neighbors, and when I persisted in pestering them for an account of how things came to be, it was a crucial factor in getting an answer. A middle-aged informant, who spent many of his odd hours bemoaning[2] his own unmarried state (he was actually responsible for the death of one of his wives) took pity on me, and revealed the local origin story "because you don't have a wife either, I'm sorry for you."

My status as a representative white man made my situation even more intriguing to my Daribi friends. How did my peculiar interests relate to the specialties of other Europeans they knew of, such as the government, the missionaries, the doctors? Were these just names? Did they only stand for different kinds of work, or were they in fact separate and distinct families, or even different kinds of people? This was the sense of the question some of my friends put to me one afternoon: "can you anthro-pologists intermarry with the government and the missionaries?" I explained that we could if we wanted to, but that I had no particular aspirations in that direction. But I had not answered the real question, so it was later rephrased and asked in a different way: "are there *kanakas* (i.e., "natives, people like us") in America?" I said that there were, thinking of the subsistence farmers to be found in some parts of the country, but I'm afraid I conjured up an image of a subject population living under the tutelage of patrol officers, missionaries, and others.

The question was not one that could be posed easily in a few words, and so my answers, however "correct" they might be, were bound to mislead. And yet the problem was a vital one, for it turned upon the reasons for my presence in the village, and upon the nature of, and the motivation behind the work I was doing. I was continually puzzled and sometimes annoyed by my friends' concern with what I took to be a side issue, the matter of my living arrangements and marital status, since I defined myself and justified my presence in terms of my anthropological interests and my fieldwork. The Daribi, for their part, were probably equally flabbergasted by my studied indifference to the problems of life and living, and my inexplicable passion for interviewing. (And after all, if I could ask them what kinds of people they were allowed to marry, it was only fair that they be able to ask me what kinds of people I could marry.)

The work that I had set out to do among the Daribi embodied a totally different notion of creativity, of what is important in life, from that which their own lives and work represented. My work was intended as creativity or production for its own sake, undertaken so as to add to the cumulative body of knowledge that we call "the anthropological literature." Its interests and motivations would necessarily be obscure and even misleading to someone who did not share our enthusiasm for this kind of production. Through this work I hoped to invent the Daribi people for my colleagues and countrymen, much as we have invented our own culture through the very same kind of creativity. But, given the circumstances, I could scarcely hope to portray Daribi creativity as a mirror image of our own.

For one thing, their attempts to "invent" me, to make me and my work believable, inevitably led to a kind of pity and commiseration which is the inverse of the maudlin compassion that philistines in our culture often profess for the benighted and unimproved "primitive." Their misunderstanding of me was not the same as my misunderstanding of them, and thus the difference between our respective interpretations could not be dismissed on the basis of linguistic dissimilarity or communicational difficulty. As my particular problem began with anthropology and with my own (and our culture's) expectations of "culture" and creativity, let us turn once again to this subject as a key to the problem.

The Ambiguity of "Culture"

Our word "culture" derives in a very roundabout way from the past participle of the Latin verb *colere,* "to cultivate," and draws some of its meaning from this association with the tilling of the soil. This also seems to have been the major significance of the medieval French and English forms from which our present usage derives (for instance *cultura* meant "a plowed field" in Middle English). In later times "culture" took on a more specific sense, indicating a process of progressive refinement and breeding in the domestication of some particular crop, or even the result or increment of such a process. Thus we speak of agriculture, apiculture, the "culture of the vine," or of a bacterial culture.

The contemporary "opera house" sense of the word arises from an elaborate metaphor, which draws upon the terminology of crop breeding and improvement to create an image of man's control, refinement, and "domestication" of himself. So, in the drawing rooms of the eighteenth and nineteenth centuries, one spoke of a "cultivated" person as someone who "had culture," who had developed his interests and accomplishments along approved lines, training and "breeding" the personality as a natural strain might be "cultured."

The anthropological usage of "culture" constitutes a further metaphorization, if not a democratization, of this essentially elitist and aristocratic sense. It amounts to an abstract extension of the notion of human refinement and domestication from the individual to the collective, so that we can speak of culture as man's general control, refinement, and improvement of himself, rather than one man's conspicuousness in this respect. Applied in this way, the word also carries strong connotations of Locke's and Rousseau's conception of the "social contract," of the tempering of man's "natural" instincts and desires by an arbitrary imposition of will. The nineteenth century concept of "evolution" added a historical dimension to this notion of man's breeding and tempering of himself, resulting in the optimistic concept of "progress."

Regardless of its more specific associations, however, our modern term "culture" retains the several associations, and hence the creative ambiguity, introduced by these metaphorizations. The confusion of "culture" in the "opera-house" sense with the more general anthropological sense actually amounts to a continuous derivation of one significance from the other.[3] It is in the area of this ambiguity, with its contrasting implications, that we might expect to find a clue to what we most often intend in our use of the word.

When we speak of the "cultural centers," or even the "culture" of the city of Chicago, we mean a certain kind of institution. We do not mean steel mills, airports, grocery stores, or service stations, although these would be included in the more catholic anthropological definitions. The "cultural institutions" of a city are its museums, libraries, symphony orchestras, universities, and perhaps its parks and zoos. It is in these specialized sanctuaries, set apart from everyday life by special regulations, endowed by special funds, and guarded by highly qualified personnel, that the documents, records, relics, and embodiments of man's greatest achievements are kept, and "art" or "culture" is kept alive. The idea of a musical "conservatory" is a case in point, for it provides a reverent atmosphere within which the study, practice, recitals, and concerts necessary to the "life" of music can be carried on. Cultural institutions not only preserve and protect the results of man's refinement, they also sustain it and provide for its continuation.

The connection between this "institu-tional" culture and the more universal concept of the anthropologist is not immediately apparent, though it is in fact only thinly disguised by the facades of libraries, museums, and opera houses. For the very core of our own culture, in the accepted image, is its science, art, and technology, the sum total of achievements, inventions, and discoveries that define our idea of "civilization." These achievements are preserved (in institutions), taught (in other institutions), and added to (in research institutions) in a cumulative process of refinement. We preserve a vast panoply of ideas, facts, relics, secrets, techniques, applications, formulas, and documents as our "culture," the sum of our ways of doing things, and the sum of "knowledge" as we know it. This "culture" exists in a broad and a narrow, an "unmarked" and a "marked" sense.

The productiveness or creativity of our culture is defined by the application, manipulation, re-enactment, or extension of these techniques and discoveries. Work of any kind, whether innovative or simply what we call "productive," achieves its meaning in relation to this cultural sum, which forms its meaningful context. When a plumber replaces a pipe he draws upon a complex of interlinked technological discoveries and productive efforts. His act becomes significant as "work" through its integration into this complex; it applies and carries forth certain technological inventions (as a "Cultural institution" might), and both defines the plumber as a worker and relates his efforts in a complementary way to those of other workers. The work of the anthropologist does this also; it draws upon a pool of skills and insights that can be acquired by "education," and contributes to a totality called "the anthropological literature."

Meaningful, productive work, which is also called "labor," is the basis of our credit system, and we can therefore assess it in monetary terms. This makes it possible to evaluate other quantities, such as time, resources, and accumulated labor, or even abstract "rights" and "obligations." This productivity, the application and implementation of man's refinement of himself, provides the central focus of our civilization. This explains the high valuation placed upon "Culture" in the narrow, marked, opera-house sense, for it represents the creative increment, the productivity that creates work and knowledge by providing its ideas, techniques, and discoveries, and that ultimately shapes cultural value itself. We experience the relation between the two senses of "culture" in the meanings of our everyday life and work; "Culture" in the more restricted sense stands as a historical and normative precedent for culture as a whole, it embodies an ideal of human refinement.

It is because work and productivity are central to our system of values that we base our credit system on them. "Money" or "wealth" is therefore the symbol of work, of the production of things and services according to techniques that are the preserved heritage of our historical development. Although some of these techniques are patented, and some formulas secret, and some skills are the property of particular people, the larger part of our technology and cultural heritage is public knowledge, made available through public education. As money represents the public standard of exchange, so education defines a certain prerequisite for participation.

And yet if productivity is public, the family can be said to be peripheral and private. Money, and therefore work, is necessary to "support" a family, but neither money nor labor should be the primary consideration within the family. Regardless of how it is earned or budgeted, the family income is *shared* to some degree among the members, but it is not apportioned in exchange for family services. As Schneider's *American Kinship* (1968a) has shown, relations within the family are symbolized in terms of love, sexual love, or a relationship of "enduring, diffuse solidarity." The opposition between money and love dramatizes the sharp separation drawn in our culture between "business" and "home life."

Love is traditionally the thing that "money cannot buy," and duty is supposed to be above personal considerations. Thus the stories about liasons between businessmen and their secretaries, doctors and their nurses, or pilots and their stewardesses are celebrated scandals, as are accounts of film or television stars who marry for the sake of their images. And of course the role of the prostitute, who does "for money" what other women do "for love," and who lives in "a house that is not a home" symbolizes an antiworld of vice and corruption for many Americans. Interpersonal relations, and especially family relations, should be private and "above" monetary interests; one should not "use" them for financial gain.

Apart from the speculations of some anthropologists, family life and interpersonal relations play an almost negligible part in the historical accounts that are generally used to validate our cultural self-image. Typically these myths are obsessed with man's development as a history of productive techniques, a gradual accumulation of "tools" and "adaptations" indicating progressively greater technological sophistication. It is not difficult to recall the lists of great advances taught in high school: fire, attributed to "prehistoric" man, the alphabet, the wheel, the Roman arch, the Franklin stove, and so on. Regardless of the dates, the names, or the specific inventions, "Culture" emerges as an accumulation, a sum of great inventions and mighty achievements. It amounts, in fact, to a tightly controlled linking of the broad, abstract notion of "culture" to the more narrow sense of the word, minimizing ambiguity.

The thought that there are parts of the world where wives can be purchased has often presented a kind of imaginative fool's paradise for those who could bring themselves to believe that the control of women could ever be so simple. But in the light of our discussion of money and love in our own culture, the yearnings must necessarily be dismissed as a form of prostitution fantasy. Moreover, the assumption that wives are "bought" and "sold" in tribal societies involves the most profound misunderstanding of these peoples. In the words of Francis Bugotu, a native of the Solomon Islands (1968:67): "The buying of wives in primitive societies has no equivalence with the pecuniary exchanges of the West. Money is not important and certainly not the attraction. It is the woman who is valuable."

What we would call "production" in these societies belongs to the symbolization of even the most intimate personal relationships. For the Melanesian, "work" can be anything from weeding a garden to taking part in a feast or begetting a child; its validation comes from the part it plays in human interaction. The work of "making a living" takes place within a family, whose members assume complementary roles corresponding to the cultural image of their sex and age group. Thus "production" is what men and women, or men, women, and children do together; it defines them socially in their several roles, and also symbolizes the meaning of the family. A man is limited to certain capabilities, perhaps, as among the Daribi, to the felling of trees, fencing of gardens, and tending of certain crops. Other tasks fall to the women, and a man would not attempt them without shame, or even worse damage to his self-image. A kind of intersexual integration, which we call by analogy "marriage," is as necessary for subsistence as it is for the creation of children, so that sexual relations and productivity are part of the same totality, which we might call "the production of people."

Since the family *is* "production" in this kind of society, it is self-sustaining and there is no need to "support" it. But a system of this kind makes "marriage" and the family a matter of life and death; a person who does not marry cannot produce, and is doomed to a servile dependence on others. Thus the central problem of the young man, celebrated in myth and proverb, becomes that of finding a wife. Whereas products themselves, or money with which to buy products, are not in demand, *producers* are; since all major aspects of sustenance are vested in the family, the paramount concern becomes that of forming and sustaining a family. So it is that the exchange systems of tribal and peasant societies are geared to the human life-cycle and the substitution of "wealth" for persons. People are indispensable, and therefore the most valuable things known are pressed into service to control their distribution. It is the details of this substitution, the control, exchange, and distribution of people, that anthropologists have understood as "social structure."

Because it is a part of interpersonal relations, and an embodiment of human, rather than abstract values, the productivity of tribal societies is not obsessed with tools or techniques. The basic techniques of production, clearing land, building houses, weaving, or processing food, are incorporated within sexual roles, and are part of being male or female. More specialized techniques, or the concern with skill and technique in themselves, are peripheral and individual. Anthropologists know these pursuits as "magic," "sorcery," and "shamanism," the development and hoarding of often secret techniques to ensure personal success.

Thus tribal cultures embody an inversion of our tendency to place productive technique in the central focus, and relegate family life to a supporting (and supported) role. This inversion, moreover, is not trivial; it pervades both styles of creativity in all of their aspects. As we produce "things," so our concern is with preserving things, products, and the techniques of their production. Our Culture is a sum of such things: we keep the ideas, the quotations, the memoirs, the creations, and let the people go. Our attics, basements, trunks, albums, and museums are full of this kind of Culture.

On the other hand, the suggestion that tribal people are "materialists," one that is often applied in the case of the New Guinea highlanders, makes as little sense as the accusation that they "buy" wives. Here, as Bugotu says, it is the people who are important: wealth consists of "counters" for people, and, far from being hoarded, it is dispersed often at death through death payments. It is people, and the experiences and meanings associated with them, that they do not want to lose, rather than ideas and things. Thus my New Guinean friends transfer the names of the newly dead to the newly born, and also find it necessary to invent the deceased in the form of ghosts, so that they are not wholly lost. We do much the same kind of thing with books, which are our "ghosts," our past, wherein so much of what we call our "Culture" lives.

Because these are styles of creativity that we have been discussing, and not merely types of society, they characterize human invention in a total and comprehensive way. And because the perception and comprehension of others can only proceed by a kind of analogy, knowing them through an extension of the familiar, each style of creativity is also a style of understanding. The New Guineans see the anthropologist's creativity as *being* his interaction with them, rather than resulting from it. They perceive the fieldworker to be "doing" life, rather as Zorba the Greek might see him, a bold and inclusive sort of "life." And, as in all such cases, one wants to help the foolhardy foreigner. Or at least pity him.

For his part, the anthropologist assumes that the native is doing what *he* is doing, namely "culture." And so, as a way of understanding his subject, the fieldworker is obliged to invent a culture for him, as a plausible thing to be doing. But since plausibility is a function of the researcher's viewpoint, the "culture" that he imagines for the native is bound to bear a distinct relation to that which he claims for himself.

When an anthropologist studies another culture, he "invents" it by generalizing his impressions, experiences, and other evidences as if they were produced by some external "thing." Thus his invention is an objectification, or reification, of that "thing." But if the culture he invents is to have meaning for his fellow anthropologists, as well as other compatriots, there must be a further control on his invention. It must be believable and meaningful in terms of his own image of "culture." We have seen that the term "culture" has no one referent for us: its successive and several meanings are created by a series of metaphorizations, "ambiguities," if you prefer. When we identify some set of observations or experiences as a "culture," we extend our idea of culture to encompass new details, and increase its possibilities as well as its ambiguity. In an important way, the hypothetical "invention" of a culture by an anthropologist constitutes an act of extension; it is a new and unique "derivation" of the abstract sense of "culture" from the more narrow sense.

But if the abstract, anthropological notion of "culture" depends on the "opera house" notion for its meaning, the reverse is also true. Nor is the issue limited to these two variants; newer constructs like "subculture" or "counter culture" metaphorize the anthropological term to create an even greater richness, and also a shift, of meaning. The semantic possibilities of the concept "culture" remain a function of this richness and this interplay of allusion and innuendo. Anthropological writing has tended to conserve the ambiguity of culture, for this ambiguity is continually enhanced by the identification of provocatively new and different "cultures," and continually controlled through the formation of explanatory analogies.

It is not surprising, then, that anthropologists should be so fascinated with tribal peoples, with modes of thought whose lack of anything like our notion of "culture" teases our generalizations into fantastic shapes and extremes. These subjects are provocative and interesting for that very reason, because they introduce the "play" of greater possibilities and more extensive generalization into the concept of "culture." Nor should we be surprised if the resultant analogies and "models" seem awkward and ill-fitting, for they are born of the paradox created by imagining a culture for people who do not imagine it for themselves. These constructs are tentative bridges to meaning, they are part of our understanding, not its object, and we treat them as "real" at the peril of turning anthropology into a wax museum of curiosities, reconstructed fossils, and great moments from imaginary histories.

The Wax Museum

It is perhaps no accident that much of the earliest anthropology developed in museums, and that museums are Cultural institutions in the "marked" sense of the word. For museums form the logical point of transition or articulation between the two major senses of "culture"; they metaphorize ethnographic specimens and data by analyzing and preserving them, making them necessary to our own refinement although they belong to some other culture. The totem poles, Egyptian mummies, arrowheads, and other relics in our museums are "culture" in two senses; they are simultaneously products of their makers and of anthropology, which is "cultural" in the narrow sense. Because these medicine bundles, pots, blankets, and other items were elemental to the museum's definition and reconstruction of their "cultures," they came to have the same significance as the strategic relics that *we* seek to preserve; the first sewing machine, revolutionary war muskets, or Benjamin Franklin's spectacles. The study of "primitives" had become a function of our invention of the past.

In this light it is scarcely astonishing that Ishi, the last surviving Yahi Indian in California, spent the years after his surrender living in a museum (T. Kroeber 1963). Museums had by then assumed fully the role of a reservation for Indian culture, and we are told that in good weather Kroeber and others would take Ishi back into the hills so that he could demonstrate Yahi techniques and bushcraft. In spite of Kroeber's deep sympathy for Ishi, one cannot help feeling that he was the ideal museum specimen, one that did the anthropologist's job for him by producing and reconstituting its own culture. This suggestion makes it easy to forget that Ishi's job as an Indian was primarily that of living, and that he had merely exchanged his fugitive existence for a formaldehyde sinecure. But this, again, is precisely the point; by accepting employment as a museum specimen,

Ishi accomplished the metaphorization of life into culture that defines much of anthropological understanding.

If Ishi brought the world into the museums, then Tylor's earlier doctrine of "survivals" had brought the museum into the world. For if the "nonproductive" aspects of cultural life, like Morgan's idea of kinship, can be understood as surviving traits of an earlier evolutionary stage, then like the "nonproductive" Indian, they were fossils. The early evolutionists were willing to accept productive life as self-evidently meaningful, and to reserve the remainder for their own productive invention of the past. But the reflexive sense of this metaphorization made the whole world of "custom" into a gigantic living museum, which only anthropologists were privileged to interpret. It was not simply the museum, but man's life itself, that constantly recreated the past.

In both Tylor's and Ishi's cases, "culture" in the abstract, anthropological sense was a reified artifact of "Culture" in the narrow, marked sense. Because this invention, or derivation, took place in the context of museums and of our historical self-identification, the resultant notion of culture assumed the characteristics of a museum assemblage. It was finite, discrete, and unequivocal; it had peculiar "styles" and "usages" that could be determined with great precision. One might not be able to tell whether a given Indian was *really* Cheyenne or Arapaho, even by questioning him closely, but there was never any doubt about styles and artifacts. Beneath the sheltering aegis of our "Cultural institutions" a series of distinct "cultures" and a general conception of culture were developed, which were in every way analogous to our "marked" sense of Culture as an accumulation of great ideas, inventions, and achievements.

In many respects this idea of culture has never left the anthropological imagination. Our attempts to metaphorize tribal peoples as "Culture" have reduced them to technique and artifact; our attempts to produce these cultures ethnologically, to comprehend the "artifact" by reproducing it, result in overdetermined "systems." The logic of a society where "culture" is a conscious and deliberate thing, where life subserves some purpose, rather than the reverse, and where every fact or proposition is required to have a reason, creates a strangely surrealistic effect when applied to tribal peoples. So little, in fact, are these "functions," "social facts," or "logical structures of the mind" believable in one's experiences with natives as people "on the ground," that we are forced into the position that the "reasons" and "purposes" adduced theoretically are subliminal, subconscious, or implicit universal properties.

The result has been an overburdening of the generalized concept of culture, cramming it full of explanatory logics, levels, and heuristic enforcement systems until it appears as the very metaphor of "order." Such a "culture" is totally predicated, it is rule, grammar and lexicon, or necessity, a complete perfusing of rigid form and paradigm throughout the range of human thought and action; in Freudian terms, it approximates a collective compulsion. Moreover, since this ironclad "order" simultaneously represents our means of comprehending the culture, change or variation can only be approached nega-

tively, as a kind of entropy, static, or "noise."

In the search for analogues to our logical, legal, political, and economic orders among tribal peoples we have seized upon all manner of conventional, symbolic, and idiomatic usage for transformation into "structure." This is particularly evident in social anthropology, where the meanings attached to interpersonal relationships are often literalized in terms of their symbolic components: kinship is reduced to biology, or to genealogical paradigms, and society itself is truncated into a set of mechanisms for the shuffling about of people and goods. Here again we are brought face to face with Francis Bugotu's dictum, it is the people that are important, not the economics and mechanics of their transfer. An approach that sees the African marriage-cattle, virtually a matrix of social metaphor, as economic "property," or one that interprets the Australian aborigine marriage systems as clever computer programming, or dizzy permutations of the incest taboo, has effectively vivisected the native meanings in the attempt to understand them.

The study of such exotic modes of conceptualization actually amounts to a resymbolization of them, transforming their symbols into ours, which is why they so often appear in reduced or literalized form. An anthropology that refuses to accept the universality of mediation, that reduces meaning to belief, dogma, and certainty, is forced into the trap of having to believe either the native meanings or our own. The former alternative, we are told, is superstitious and unobjective; the latter, according to some, is "science." And yet this kind of science can easily degenerate into a form of indirect speech, a way of making provocative points by translating idiom into fact and by over-exoticizing one's research subjects for symbolic effect. This is possible because anthropology is always necessarily mediative, whether it is aware of the implications or not; culture, as the mediative term, is a way of describing others as we would describe ourselves, and vice versa.

A true metaphorization of the diverse phenomena of human life and thought in terms of our notion of "culture" would necessarily have to carry across the creative invention that we manifest in the act of studying another people. Otherwise we are forced into the explicitly false posture of creating ambiguities within our own concepts so as to prove the precise, strictly determined, and unambiguous nature of other peoples' concepts, of inventing systems that cannot invent and calling them "culture." As long as the anthropological concept remains even partially dependent upon the "opera house" sense of the term, our studies of other peoples, and particularly tribal societies, will be skewed in the direction of our own self-image.

Anthropology will not come to terms with its mediative basis and its professed aims until our invention of other cultures can reproduce, at least in principle, the way in which those cultures invent themselves. We must be able to experience our subject matter directly as alternative meaning rather than indirectly, through literalization or reduction to the terms of our ideologies. The issue can be phrased in practical, philosophical, or ethical language, but in any case it devolves upon the question of what we *want* to mean by the word "culture," and how we choose to resolve, and to invent, its ambiguities.

"Road Belong Culture"

If "culture" becomes paradoxical and challenging when applied to the meanings of tribal societies, we might speculate as to whether a "reverse anthropology" is possible, literalizing the metaphors of modern industrial civilization from the standpoint of tribal society. Surely we have no right to expect a parallel theoretical effort, for the ideological concern of these people puts them under no obligation to specialize in this way, or to propound philosophies for the lecture room. In other words our "reverse anthropology" will have nothing to do with "culture," with production for its own sake, though it might have a great deal to do with the quality of life. And if human beings are as generally inventive as we have assumed, it would be very surprising if such a "reverse anthropology" did not already exist.

It does, of course. As a result of the political and economic expansion of European society in the nineteenth century, many of the world's tribal peoples found themselves in a "fieldwork" situation through no fault of their own. "Fieldwork" is perhaps a euphemism for what was often little more than a sustained, cumulative culture shock, and yet there is a parallel, for culture shock forces one to objectify, to seek comprehension. We call these attempts at comprehension many things, for they assume many forms, and yet the most familiar terms betray the activist form that concerted thought must assume among peoples where thought is a part of life: cargo cult and millenarian movement.

If we call such phenomena "cargo cults," then anthropology should perhaps be called a "culture cult," for the Melanesian "kago" is very much the interpretive counterpart of our word "culture." The words are to some extent "mirror images" of each other, in the sense that we look at the natives' cargo, their techniques and artifacts, and call it "culture," whereas they look at our culture and call it "cargo." These are analogic usages, and they betray as much about the interpreters themselves as about the thing interpreted. "Cargo" is practically a parody, a reduction of Western notions like profit, wage-labor, and production for its own sake to the terms of tribal society. It is paradoxically, no more materialistic than the Melanesian marriage practices, and this is the key to its apocalyptic and millenarian associations.

The "cargo" is seldom thought of in the way we might expect, as simple material wealth; its significance is rather based on the symbolic use of European wealth to represent the redemption of native society. In this usage it resembles those other "cargoes," the more traditionally symbolic constituents of the bride-price, or the activity and products of gardening, that embody the central meaning of human relations for Melanesians, and which *we* tend to interpret in materialist, economic terms. Cargo is really an antisymbol to "culture"; it metaphorizes the sterile orders of technique and self-fulfilling production as life and human relation, just as " culture" does the reverse. In the words of

Kenelm Burridge, who distinguishes a capitalized sense of "cargo" from the ordinary sense, much as we have done with "culture":

It is clear that if cargo means manufactured goods, Cargo embraces a set of acute moral problems; that Cargo movements are not due simply to a misunderstanding concerning the origin of manufactured goods, but that they are embodied in, and arise from, a complex total situation . . . (Burridge 1970:246)

The symbol of "cargo," quite as much as that of "culture," draws its force and its meaning from its ambiguities; it is simultaneously the enigmatic and tantalizing phenomenon of western material goods and its profound human implication for the native mind. When the symbol is invoked, the latter of these senses incorporates the former into a powerful analogous relation, which both restructures the phenomenon and gives it meaning. This relation, and the meaning that it compels, encompasses all aspects of the moral dilemma; it is access to the cargo, the rapport entailed by a sharing of the cargo, and the millenial conditions necessary for the arrival of the cargo. Moreover, since "cargo," like "culture," is a term of mediation between different peoples, the relation that it embodies becomes that of Melanesian to Western society.

The fact that "cargo" and "culture" metaphorize the same intersocietal relation, while doing so in opposite directions, so to speak, makes them effectively metaphorizations of each other. "Culture" extends the significance of technique, mode, and artifact to human thought and relationship; "cargo" extends that of human relation and mutual production to manufactured artifacts: each concept uses the extensive bias of the other as its symbol. Thus it is easy for Westerners to "literalize" the significance of "cargo," and assume that it means simply manufactured goods, or Western modes of production, "Culture," that is, in the narrow sense. This kind of simplification, the short-circuiting of a symbol, is in fact the popularized Sunday-supplement view of cargo cult, a counterpart of mission ideology about saving the "lost" heathens, or the sentimentality that perceives tribal peoples as impoverished relatives begging for a transistorized handout.

But it is also shown most graphically in Peter Lawrence's analysis of the career of Yali, the cult leader from the north coast of New Guinea, that the reverse is true; that Melanesians, when they encounter the notion of "culture," have a tendency to interpret it as "cargo" in their sense. When Yali, whose cooperation was being solicited by the Australian Administration, was taken to Port Moresby in 1947, he was astounded by two things. The first of these was a shift in Administration policy favoring and even encouraging native custom and ceremonial; the second was his discovery that not all Europeans subscribe to the mission religions and the Adam and Eve story. He was intrigued by diagrams illustrating the course of evolution, and especially by the *monki*, and rather perceptively linked this theory to the Western practice of keeping animals in zoos. Lawrence argues cogently that Yali regarded this emphasis on natural history as a kind of totemism, a shrine, as it were, for the preservation of social relations (Lawrence 1964:173-78).

The point is made more concisely by Yali's later interpretation of some New Guinean artifacts he had seen in a Queensland museum during the Second World War. According to Lawrence, "Yali himself had described the artifacts in these terms: 'Our myths are there also' . . . The word 'myth' (*perambik, sitori*) in this context broadly connoted 'New Guinea culture'" (p. 191). Yali's experiences with the way Westerners think about and preserve their past, and tolerate and preserve the pasts of others, gave him a greater realization of "culture" than most Melanesians are able to acquire. Invariably, however, this notion of culture was assimilated to, and mistaken for, his own "cargo" expectations. The "road belong cargo" became the "road belong culture," as is evident in the upshot of Yali's Port Moresby episode, for he returned to his native Madang area to initiate a full scale revival of traditional ceremonies in order to bring the cargo.

Yali's revival was by no means an attempted replication of pre-colonial life; it was characterized by a frenetic overindulgence in ceremonial, as well as the incorporation of practices from earlier cults. Like similar "revivals" elsewhere in the world, this one was not concerned with "culture" itself, but with culture,as a symbol of something else. Although identity is involved, as it must always be when "culture" is assumed self-consciosly, identity by no means exhausts or explains the usage, for culture always figures in such revivals as an access to things far more important than culture could ever be.

People like Yali, it is said, are driven to these interpretive extremes by social injustice, exploitation, and the stresses of something called "culture-contact." Certainly the peoples of the Madang littoral had had their fill of exploitation and humiliation by successive waves of German, Australian, and Japanese colonialists; bizarre religious sectarians had hoped to win an audience among allegedly "simple" tribesmen for ideas that their countrymen had come to regard as all too simple. Yet I do not propose to account for Yali's motivation and creativity in this way, if only because explanations in terms of disturbance and injustic belittle human achievements to the level of correctives, and reduce life to an equilibrium model. It says little enough of that leader of the first Jesus Movement, Joshua of Nazareth, to trace his ideas and purpose to Roman injustice, or the difference in living standard between Romans and Palestinians of the time.

Moreover, our discussion has shown that there is no reason to treat cargo cult as anything but an interpretive counterpart of anthropology itself, and that its creativity need not be any more problematic than that of the anthropologists who study it. Cargo cult can be thought of as a pragmatic sort of anthropology that invents in anticipation of the future, in a manner reminiscent of Melanesian magic, rather than reconstructing the past or present out of shards of evidence. It is clear from the foregoing that devotees of either concept, cargo or culture, cannot easily apprehend the other without turning it into their own, yet it is also clear that this characteristic is not limited to cultists or anthropologists alone, that all men project, tease, and extend their ideas through analogies with a world of intransigent phenomena.

It is elemental to a definition of man that he continually invests his ideas, seeking external equivalents that not only articulate them, but also subtly change them in the process, until often these meanings take on a life of their own, and possess their authors. Man is the shaman of his meanings. The ambiguity of culture, and that of cargo, coincides with the power such a concept has in the hands of its interpreters, who use the points of analogy to manage and control the paradoxical aspects. Yet these selfsame interpreters, like all shamans, are also subject to the vagaries of their familiars, which goes some way toward explaining the incongruities of Yali and his anthropological counterparts.

Notes

1. In fact, his most arduous jobs consisted of drawing water, washing dishes, and removing the small larvae that always managed to infest my supply of brown rice.

2. He used the Daribi mourning lament, a drawn-out wailing.

3. The earlier "derivation" of the opera-house sense of the word from the agricultural probably also coincided with a similar confusion and "creative ambiguity."

Bibliography

Aberle, David F. 1961. "The Navaho." *Matrilineal Kinship*. Ed. D. M. Schneider and K. Gough. Berkeley: University of California Press.

Alexander, H. B. 1916. *Mythology of All Races, x: North America*. Boston: Marshall Jones.

Althusser, Louis. 1970. *For Marx*. Trans. B. Brewster. New York: Vintage Books.

—— 1971. *Lenin and Philosophy and Other Essays*. Trans. B. Brewster. New York: Monthly Review Press.

Amin, Samir. 1973. *Le Développement inégale*. Paris: Les Editions de Minuit.

—— 1975. "Toward a Structural Crisis of Capitalism." *Socialist Revolution*, 23 (Vol. 5, No. 1).

Anderson, Perry. 1968. "Components of the National Culture." *New Left Review*, 50.

Arnheim, Rudolf. 1974. *Art and Visual Perception. The New Version*. Berkeley: University of California Press.

Aron, Raymond. 1960. "Science et conscience de la société." *European Journal of Sociology*, 1.

Attewell, Paul. 1974. "Ethnomethodology since Garfinkel." *Theory and Society*, 1:2.

Austen, Leo. 1934–35. "Procreation Among the Trobriand Islanders." *Oceania*, 5.

Austin, J. L. 1962. *How to Do Things With Words*. Cambridge: Harvard University Press.

Bailey, F. G. 1959. "For a Sociology of India?" *Contributions to Indian Sociology*, III.

Balázs, Béla. 1952. *Theory of the Film: Character and Growth of a New Art*. Trans. E. Bone. London: D. Dobson.

Baran, Paul A., and Paul Sweezy. 1966. *Monopoly Capital: An Essay on the American Economic and Social Order*. New York: Monthly Review Press.

Barber, Bernard. 1957. *Social Stratification, A Comparative Analysis of Structure and Process*. New York: Harcourt, Brace.

Barnett, M. R. 1972. "The Politics of Cultural Nationalism." Ph.d Dissertation, University of Chicago.

Barnett, Steve. 1973a. "Urban is as Urban Does: Two Incidents on One Street in Madras City, South India." *Urban Anthropology*, 2.

—— 1973b. "The Process of Withdrawal in a South Indian Caste" *Entrepreneurship and the Modernization of Occupational Cultures in South Asia*. Ed. M. Singer. Durham: Duke University Press.

—— 1973c. "Identity Choice and Caste Ideology in Contemporary South India." In this Volume.

—— Forthcoming. *Class Struggles in South India*.

Barnett, Steve and M. G. Silverman, N.d. "The Person in Capitalist Ideology." MS.

Barth, Frederick. 1965. *Political Leadership among Swat Pathans*. London School of Economics Monographs in Social Anthropology, 19. New York: Humanities Press.

Barthes, Roland. 1972. *Mythologies*. Trans. A. Lavers. New York: Hill and Wang.

Bartley, S. Howard. 1958. *Principles of Perception*. New York: Harper.

Basso, Keith H. 1967. "Semantic Aspects of Linguistic Acculturation." *American Anthropologist*, 69.

Basso, Keith H. and H. Selby, eds. 1976. *Meaning in Anthropology*. Santa Fe; University of New Mexico Press (for the School of American Research, Santa Fe).

Bateson, Gregory. 1972. *Steps to an Ecology of Mind*. New York: Ballantine Books.

Beattie, John. 1968. "Aspects of Nyoro Symbolism." *Africa*, 38.

Beecher, William J. 1952. "The Unexplained Direction Sense of Vertebrates." *Scientific Monthly*.

Becker, Ernest. 1968. *The Structure of Evil: An Essay on the Unification of the Sciences of Man.* New York: George Braziller.

Beidelman, T. O. 1961. "Right and Left Among the Kaguru." *Africa,* 31.

—— 1966. "Swazi Royal Ritual." *Africa,* 36.

Belo, Jane. 1935. "The Balinese Temper." *Character and Personality,* 4.

Benveniste, Emile. 1966. "Actif et moyen dans le verbe." *Problémes de linguistique générale.* Paris: Gallimard.

Berger, Peter L. 1969. *The Sacred Canopy.* Garden City: Anchor Books.

Berger, Peter L. and Thomas Luckmann. 1966. *The Social Construction of Reality: A Treatise in the Sociology of Knowledge.* New York: Doubleday.

Berlin, Brent, and Paul Kay. 1970. *Basic Color Terms.* Berkeley: University of California Press.

Berlin, Brent, and A. Kimball Romney. 1968. *Tzeltal Numeral Classifiers: A Study in Ethnographic Semantics.* The Hague: Mouton.

Bernstein, Richard J. 1972. *Praxis and Action.* Philadelphia: University of Pennsylvania Press.

Bidwell, S. 1899. *Curiosities of Light and Sound.* London: Swan Sonnenschein.

Birren, Farber. 1956. *Selling Color to People.* New York: University Books.

—— 1961. *Color Psychology and Color Therapy.* New York: University Books.

Black, Max. 1962. "Metaphor." *Models and Metaphors.* Ithaca: Cornell University Press.

Bloomfield, Leonard. 1933. *Language.* New York: Holt.

Boas, Franz. 1911. "Introduction" and "Kwakiutl." *Handbook of American Indian Languages,* Part I. F. Boas. Ed. Bureau of American Ethnology *Bulletin,* No. 40. Washington, D.C.: Government Printing Office.

—— 1916. *Tsimshian Mythology.* Bureau of American Ethnology *Bulletin.* No. 31. Washington, D.C.: Government Printing Office.

Bodde, Derk. 1939. "Types of Chinese Categorical Thinking." *Journal of the American Oriental Society,* 59.

Bogert, Charles M. 1948. "Why the Homing Toad 'Comes Home.'" *Natural History.*

Book of Mormon. 1961. *The Church of Jesus Christ of Latter-Day Saints.* Salt Lake City: Deseret News.

Bookchin, Murray. 1971. "Ecology and Revolutionary Thought." *Post-Scarcity Anarchism.* Berkeley: Ramparts Press.

Boring, E. G., ed. 1945. *Psychology for the Armed Forces.* Special issue of *The Infantry Journal.*

Bornstein, Marc H. 1973. "Color Vision and Color Naming: A Psychophysiological Hypothesis of Cultural Difference." *Psychological Bulletin,* 80.

Bouglé, Celestin, 1908. *Essais sur le régime des castes.* Paris: F. Alcan.

Bourdieu, P. 1971. "The Berber Hourse, or the World Reversed." *Echanges et communications: Mélanges offerts à Claude Lévi-Strauss.* Ed. P. Maranda and J. Pouillon. Paris and The Hague: Mouton.

Boynton, Robert M. 1971. "Color Vision." *Woodworth and Schlosberg's Experimental Psychology.* 3rd ed. Ed. J. A. Kling and L. A. Riggs. New York: Holt, Rinehart, and Winston.

Bridgton News. Bridgton, Maine. 11 July 1974.

Buckley, W. 1958. "Social Stratification and Social Differentiation." *American Sociological Review,* 23.

Bugotu, Francis. 1968. "The Culture Clash." *New Guinea and Australia, the Pacific and Southeast Asia,* 3:2.

Bukharin, N. 1925. *Historical Materialism: A System of Sociology.* English ed. New York: International Publishers.

Bulmer, Ralph. 1967. "Why is the Cassowary Not a Bird? A Problem of Zoological Taxonomy among the Karam of the New Guinea Highlands." *Man,* N.S. 2.

Burke, Kenneth. 1950. *A Rhetoric of Motives.* New York: Prentice-Hall.

—— 1957. *The Philosophy of Literary Form.* Revised ed. New York: Vintage Books.

—— 1962. *A Grammar of Motives and a Rhetoric of Motives.* One-volume ed. New York: Meridian Books.

Burks, Arthur. 1949. "Icon, Index, and Symbol." *Philosophy and Phenomenological Research,* 9.

Burling, Robbins. 1965. "How to Choose a Burmese Numeral Classifier." *Context and Meaning in Cultural Anthropology: In Honor of A. Irving Hallowell.* Ed. M. Spiro. New York: Free Press.

Burnham, Robert W., Randall M. Hanes, and C. James Bartleson. 1963. *Color: A Guide to Basic Facts and Concepts.* New York: Wiley.

Burridge, Kenelm O. 1970. *Mambu: A Study of Melanesian Cargo Movements and their Ideological Background*. New York: Harper and Row.

Calame-Griaule, Geneviève. 1966. *Ethnologie et langage: Le Parole chez les Dogons*. Paris: Gallimard.

Carnap, Rudolf. 1947. *Meaning and Necessity*. Chicago: University of Chicago Press.

Carstairs, George Morrison. 1957. *The Twice-Born*. Bloomington: Indiana University Press.

Cassirer, Ernst. 1933. "Le Langage et la construction du monde des objets." *Journal de Psychologie Normale et Pathologique*, 30.

—— 1944. *An Essay on Man*. New Haven: Yale University Press.

—— 1951. *The Philosophy of the Enlightenment*. Princeton: Princeton University Press.

—— 1953. *The Philosophy of Symbolic Forms, I: Language*. Trans. R. Manheim. New Haven: Yale University Press.

Cézanne, Paul. 1912. *Souvenirs sur Paul Cézanne*. Paris.

Chao, Yuen Ren. 1968a. *A Grammar of Spoken Chinese*. Berkeley: University of California Press.

—— 1968b. *Language and Symbolic Systems*. Cambridge and New York: Cambridge University Press.

Chomsky, Noam. 1964. "The Logical Basis of Linguistic Theory." *Proceedings of the Ninth International Congress of Linguistics*. Ed. H. Hunt. The Hague: Mouton.

—— 1965. *Aspects of the Theory of Syntax*. Cambridge: Massachusetts Institute of Technology Press.

Codrington, R. H. 1891. *The Melanesians*. Oxford: Clarendon Press.

Conklin, Harold C. 1955. "Hanunóo Color Categories." *Southwestern Journal of Anthropology*, 4.

—— 1964. "Ethnogeneaological Method." *Explorations in Cultural Anthropology*. Ed. W. H. Goodenough. New York: McGraw-Hill.

—— 1973. "Color Categorization." *American Anthropologist*, 75.

Cooley, Charles Horton, 1920. *Social Organization: A Study of the Larger Mind*. New York: Scribner's.

Cornsweet, Tom W. 1970. *Visual Perception*. New York: Academic Press.

Cox, Oliver C. 1918/1959. *Caste, Class, and Race: A Study in Social Dynamics*. New York: Monthly Review Press.

—— 1944. "Race and Caste, A Distinction." *American Journal of Sociology*, 50.

—— 1950. "Max Weber on Social Stratification." *American Sociological Review*, 11.

Davis, Kingsley. 1941. "Intermarriage in Caste Society." *American Anthropologist*, 43.

—— 1942. "A Conceptual Analysis of Stratification." *American Sociological Review*, 7.

—— 1949. *Human Society*. New York: Macmillan.

—— 1959. "A Reply to Buckley." *American Sociological Review*, 24.

Davis, Kingsley and Wilbert E. Moore. 1945. "Some Principles of Stratification." *American Sociological Review*, 10.

Davison, William, L. W. Elford, and Harry Hoijer. 1963. *Athapascan Classificatory Verbs*. Studies in the Athapascan Languages. University of California Publications in Linguistics, 29. Berkeley: University of California Press.

Defngin, Francis. 1958. "Yapese Names." *The Use of Names by Micronesians*. Anthropological Working Papers, 3, Guam.

—— 1966. "The Nature and Scope of Customary Land Rights of the Yapese Community." MS.

Dieterlen, Germaine. 1941. *Les Ames des Dogons*. Paris: Institut d'Ethnologie. Travaux et Mémoires, XL.

Dieterlen, Germaine and Marcel Griaule. 1963. *Le Rénard Pale*. Paris: Institut d'Ethnologie. Travaux et Mémoires, LXXII.

Dolgin, Janet L. 1973. "Motionless Dance." Ph.D. Dissertation, Princeton University.

—— 1974. "Latter-Day Sense and Substance." *Religious Movements in Contemporary America*. Ed. I. Zaretsky and M. P. Leone. Princeton: Princeton University Press.

—— 1977. *Jewish Identity and the JDL*. Princeton: Princeton University Press.

Dollard, John. 1937. *Caste and Class in a Southern Town*. New Haven: Yale University Press (for the Institute for Human Relations).

Douglas, Mary. 1957. "Animals in Lele Religious Symbolism." *Africa*, 27.

—— 1966. *Purity and Danger*. London: Routledge and Kegan Paul.

—— 1968. "Dogon Culture—Profane and Arcane." *Africa*, 38.

—— 1973. "Self-Evidence." *Proceedings of the Royal Anthropological Institute of Great Britain and Ireland*.

Dumont Louis. 1965. "The Modern Conception of the Individual: Notes on Its Genesis." *Contributions to Indian Sociology* 8:13–61.

—— 1966. "Descent or Intermarriage? A Relational View of Australian Section Systems." *Southwestern Journal of Anthropology,* 22.

—— 1967. *Homo Hierarchicus*. Paris: Gallimard.

—— 1970a. *Homo Hierarchicus: An Essay on the Caste System*. Trans. M. Sainsbury. Chicago: University of Chicago Press.

—— 1970b. "World Renunciation in Indian Religions." *Religion/Politics and History in India*. The Hague: Mouton.

—— 1970c. "Religion, Politics, and Society in the Individualistic Universe." *Proceedings of the Royal Anthropological Institute of Great Britain and Ireland*.

Dundes, Alan. 1963. "Structural Typology of North American Indian Folktales." *Southwestern Journal of Anthropology,* 19.

Durand, Marguerite, Th. Alajouanine, and A. Ombredane. 1939. *Le Syndrome de Désintegration phonétique dans l'aphasie*. Paris: Masson.

Durbin, Marshall. 1972. "Basic Terms—Off Color?" *Semiotica,* 6.

Durkheim, Emile. 1897. "La Prohibition de l'inceste et ses origines." *L'Année Sociologique,* 1. Trans. E. Sagarin, *Incest: The Nature and Origin of the Taboo*. New York: Lyle Stuart, 1963.

Durkheim, Emile and Marcell Mauss. 1903/63. *Systems of Primitive Classification*. Trans. R. Needham. Chicago: University of Chicago Press.

Eisenstein, S. M. 1949. *Film Form: Essays in Film Theory*, trans. J. Leyda. New York: Harcourt, Brace.

Ellis, Havelock. 1900. "The Psychology of Red." *Popular Science Monthly,* 57.

Evans, Ralph M. 1928. *Introduction to Color*. New York: Wiley.

Evans-Pritchard, E. E. 1951. *Social Anthropology*. London: Cohen and West.

—— 1956. *Nuer Religion*. Oxford: Clarendon Press.

Fanon, Frantz. 1963. *The Wretched of the Earth*, Trans. C. Farrington. New York: Grove Press.

—— 1965. *A Dying Colonialism*, Trans. H. Chevalier. New York: Grove Press.

—— 1967. *Black Skin, White Masks*. Trans. C. L. Markmann. New York: Grove Press.

Fearing, Franklin. 1954. "An Examination of the Conceptions of Benjamin Lee Whorf in the Light of Theories of Perception and Cognition." *Language in Culture*. Ed. H. Hoijer, Chicago: University of Chicago Press.

Filmore, Charles J. 1968. "The Case for Case." *Universals in Linguistic Theory*. Ed. E. Bach and R. Harms. New York: Holt, Rinehart, and Winston.

Firth, Raymond. 1929. "Currency, Primitive." *Encyclopedia Britannica,* 14th edition.

Fleming, Donald, and Bernard Bailyn, eds. 1969. *The Intellectual Migration: Europe and America, 1930–60*. Cambridge: Harvard University Press.

Foote, Nelson N. 1953. "Destratification and Restratification." *American Journal of Sociology,* 58.

Forde, Daryll. 1950. *Habitat, Economy, and Society*. 8th ed. London: Methuen.

Forde, Daryll, ed. 1954. *African Worlds*. London: Oxford University Press.

Fortes, Meyer. 1953. "The Structure of Unilineal Descent Groups." *American Anthropologist,* 55.

—— 1964. "Malinowski and the Study of Kinship." *Man and Culture*. Ed. R. Firth. New York: Harper and Row.

—— 1967. "Totem and Taboo." *Proceedings of the Royal Anthropological Institute of Great Britain and Ireland*.

—— 1969. *Kinship and the Social Order: The Legacy of Lewis Henry Morgan*. The Lewis Henry Morgan Lectures, 1963. Chicago: Aldine.

Frake, Charles O. 1962. "The Ethnographic Study of Cognitive Systems." *Anthropology and Human Behavior*. Ed. T. Gladwin and W. C. Sturtevant. Washington, D.C.: Anthropological Society of Washington.

Frazer, James George. 1955. *The Golden Bough: A Study in Magic and Religion*. 3rd ed. New York: Macmillan.

Freud, Sigmund. 1900/1961. *The Interpretation of Dreams*. Trans. James Strachey. New York: Science Editions.

—— 1916. *Leondardo da Vinci: A Study in Psychosexuality*. Trans. A. A. Brill. New York: Random House.

—— 1953. *On Aphasia*. Trans. E. Stengel. New York: International Universities Press.

Friedrich, Paul. 1969a. "On the Meaning of Tarascan Suffixes of Space." Memoir 23, *International Journal of American Linguistics,* 35.

—— 1969b. "Metaphor-like Relations between Referential Sub-sets." *Lingua*, 24.

—— 1970a. "Morphotactics and Grammatical Meaning." MS.

—— 1970b. "Shape in Grammar." *Language*, 46. (Long version: shorter version in this volume.)

Frisch, Karl von. 1950. *Bees*. Ithaca: Cornell University Press.

Furness, William Henry, 3rd. 1910. *The Island of Stone Money*. Philadelphia: Lippincott.

Furtwängler, Wilhelm. 1934. "Interpretation—eine musikalische Schicksalfrage." *Atlantisbuch der Musik*. Ed. F. Hamel and M. Hürlimann. Zurich: Atlantis-verlag.

Gallie, W. B. 1962. "Essentially Contested Concepts." *The Importance of Language*. Ed. M. Black. Englewood Cliffs: Prentice-Hall.

Garfinkel, Harold, and Harvey Sacks. 1971. "On Formal Structures of Practical Actions." *Theoretical Sociology: Perspectives and Developments*. Ed. J. C. McKinney and E. A. Tiryakian. New York: Appleton, Century, Crofts.

Geertz, Clifford. 1963. "The Integrative Revolution: Primordial Sentiments and Civil Ties in the New States." *Old Societies and New States*. Ed. C. Geertz. New York: Macmillan.

—— 1964. "Ideology as a Cultural System." *Ideology and Discontent*. Ed. D. Apter. New York: Free Press.

—— 1965. *The Social History of an Indonesian Town*. Cambridge: Massachusetts Institute of Technology Press.

—— 1966. "Religion as a Cultural System." *Anthropological Approaches to the Study of Religion*. Ed. M. Banton. Association of Social Anthropologists Monographs, 3. London: Tavistock.

—— 1973. *The Interpretation of Cultures*. New York: Basic Books.

Gellner, Ernest. 1957. "Ideal Language and Kinship Structure." *Philosophy of Science*, 24.

—— 1960. "The Concept of Kinship." *Philosophy of Science*, 27.

Gerth, Hans. 1950. "Max Weber vs. Oliver C. Cox." *American Sociological Review*, 11.

Ghurye, G. S. 1932. *Caste and Race in India*. New York: Knopf.

Gibson, James J. 1950. *Perception of the Visual World*. Boston: Houghton-Mifflin.

Gluckman, Max. 1949. "The Role of the Sexes in Wiko Circumcision Ceremonies." in M. Fortes, ed. *Social Structure: Studies Presented to A. R. Radcliffe-Brown*. Oxford: Clarendon Press.

Godelier, Maurice. 1969. *Rationalité et irrationalité en economie*. Paris: Libraire François Maspero.

Goffman, Irving. 1963. *Stigma*. Englewood Cliffs: Prentice-Hall.

Goldmann, Lucien. 1971. *Immanuel Kant*. Trans. R. Black. London: New Left Books.

Goldstein, Kurt. 1948. *Language and Language Disturbances*. New York: Grune and Stratton.

Goldstein, P. 1974. "The Nichols and May of Sex." *Chicago Reader*, 24 May 1974.

Goodenough, Ward H. 1953. "Native Astronomy in the Central Carolines." *Museum Monographs*. Philadelphia: University of Pennsylvania Press.

—— 1956. "Residence Rules." *Southwestern Journal of Anthropology*, 12.

—— 1957. "Cultural Anthropology and Linguistics." *Report of the Seventh Annual Roundtable Meeting on Linguistics and Language Study*. Ed. P. L. Garvin. Washington: Georgetown University Press.

—— 1965. "Yankee Kinship Terminology: A Problem in Componential Analysis." *Formal Semantic Analysis*. Ed. E. A. Hammel. Special Publication, *American Anthropologist*, 67:5.2

—— 1967. "Componential Analysis." *Science*, 156.

Gouldner, Alvin W. 1965. *Enter Plato*. New York: Basic Books.

Granet, Marcel. 1934. *La Pensée chinoise*. Paris: La Renaissance du Livre.

Graves, Maitland. 1951. *The Art of Color and Design*. New York: McGraw-Hill.

Griaule, Marcel. 1965. *Conversations with Ogotemmêlí*. London: Oxford University Press.

Gvozdev, A. 1929. "Nabljudenija nad jazykom malen'kix detej." *Russkij jazyk v sovetskoj škole*.

—— 1948. *Usvoenie rebenkom zvukovoj storony russkogo jazyka*. Moscow.

—— 1949. *Formirovanie u rebenka grammatičeskogo stroja russkogo jazyka*. Moscow.

Haas, Mary R. 1942. "The Use of Numerical Classifiers in Thai." *Language*, 18.

—— 1951. "Interlingual Word Taboos." *American Anthropologist*, 53.

—— 1964. *Thai-English Student's Dictionary*. Stanford: Stanford University Press.

—— 1967. "Language and Taxonomy in North-western California." *American Anthropologist,* 69.

Haber, Ralph Norman, and Maurice Hershenson. 1973. *The Psychology of Visual Perception.* New York: Holt, Rinehart, and Winston.

Haile, Father Berard. 1938. "Navajo Chantways and Ceremonials." *American Anthropologist,* 40.

—— 1943. "Soul Concepts of the Navajo." *Annali Lateranesi,* 7.

—— 1951. *A Stem Vocabulary of the Navajo Language.* St. Michael's, Arizona.

Halbwachs, Maurice. 1939. "La Mémoire collective chez les musciens." *Revue Philosophique.*

Halévy, Elie. 1901–04/1955. *La Formation du radicalisme philosophique.* Paris: F. Alcan. English trans. M. Morris. *The Growth of Philosophic Radicalism.* Boston: Beacon Press.

Harris, Marvin. 1966. "The Cultural Ecology of India's Sacred Cattle." *Current Anthropology,* 7.

—— 1968. *The Rise of Anthropological Theory.* New York: Crowell.

Harrison, Tom. 1936. "Living with the People of Malekula." *Geographical Journal,* 80.

Head, Henry. 1926. *Aphasia and Kindred Disorders of Speech.* New York: Cambridge University Press.

Heidel, W. H. 1933. *The Heroic Age of Science.* Washington: Carnegie Institute of Washington Publications, 442.

Heider, E. R. 1972. "Probabilities, Sampling, and the Ethnographic Method: The Case of the Dani." *Man,* N.S. 7.

Hemphill, R. E., and E. Stengel. 1940. "Pure Word Deafness." *Journal of Neurology and Psychiatry,* 3.

Henry, Jules. 1963. *Culture Against Man.* New York: Random House.

Hering, Ewald. 1964 (1920). *Outlines of a Theory of the Light Sense.* Cambridge: Harvard University Press.

Hoijer, Harry. 1945. "Classificatory Verb Stems in the Apachean Languages." *International Journal of American Linguistics,* 11.

—— 1948. "The Appachean Verb. Part IV: Major Form Classes." *International Journal of American Linguistics,* 14.

—— 1963. *Studies in the Athapascan Languages.* Berkeley: University of California Press.

—— 1964. "Some Cultural Implications of some Navajo Linguistic Categories." *Language in Culture and Society.* Ed. D. Hymes. New York: Harper and Row.

Horkheimer, Max. 1972. *Critical Theory.* Trans. M. J. O'Connell et al.. New York: Seabury Press.

Humboldt, Alexander von. 1836. *Über die Verschiedenheit des Menschlichen Sprachbaues und ihren Einfluss auf die Geistige Entwickelung des Menschengeschlechts.* Berlin. (Reissued 1960, Bonn: Dümmlers).

Hurvich, L. M. 1960. "The Opponent-Process Scheme." *Mechanisms of Color Discrimination.* Ed. Y. Galifret. New York: Pergamon Press.

Hurvich, L. M. and Dorothea Jameson. 1956. "An Opponent-process Theory of Color Vision." *Psychological Review,* 4.

Husserl, Edmund. 1931. *Ideas: General Introduction to Pure Phenomenology.* Trans. W. R. B. Gibson. New York: Macmillan.

Hymes, Dell. 1959. "Myth and Tale Titles of the Lower Chinook." *Journal of American Folklore,* 72.

—— 1961. "On Typology of Cognitive Styles in Language (with Examples from Chinookan)." *Anthropological Linguistics,* 3.

—— 1962. Review of *Indian Tales of North America,* ed. T. P. Coffin. *American Anthropologist,* 64.

—— 1964a. "Directions in (ethno-) linguistic Theory." *American Anthropologist,* 66.

—— 1964b. "A Perspective for Linguistic Anthropology." *Horizons of Anthropology.* Ed. S. Tax. Chicago: Aldine.

—— 1965a. "Introduction." *The Ethnography of Communication.* Ed. J. Gumperz and D. Hymes. Special Publication, *American Anthropologist,* 66:6.2.

—— 1965b. "The Methods and Tasks of Anthropological Philology (illustrated with Clackamas Chinook)." *Romance Philology,* 19.

Jaccard, Pierre. 1932. *Le Sens de la direction et l'orientation lointaine chez l'homme.* Paris: Payot.

Jackson, Hughlings. 1866. "Notes on the Physiology and Pathology of Language." Reprint. *Brain.* 38 (1915).

—— 1868. "Notes on the Physiology and Pathology of the Nervous System." Reprint. *Brain.* 38 (1915).

—— 1879. "On Affections of Speech from Disease of the Brain." Reprint. *Brain.* 38 (1915).

—— 1915. "Papers on Affections of Speech, Reprinted with Comments by H. Head." *Brain*. 38.

Jacobs, Melville. 1958–59a. *Clackamas Chinook Texts, Parts* i *and* ii. Publs. 8 and 11 of the Research Center in Anthropology, Folklore, and Linguistics. Bloomington: Indiana University Press.

—— 1959b. *The Content and Style of an Oral Literature: Clackamas Chinook Myths and Tales*. Viking Fund Publications in Anthropology, 26. New York: Wenner-Gren Foundation for Anthropological Research.

—— 1960. *The People Are Coming Soon: Analyses of Clackamas Chinook Myths and Tales*. Seattle: University of Washington Press.

Jakobson, Roman. 1919. "Futurizm." *Iskusstvo*, 2 August.

—— 1927. "Pro Realizm u Mystectvi." Kharkov: *Vaplite*, 2.

—— 1933. "Upadek Filmu." Praha: *Listy pro Uměni a Kritiku*, i.

—— 1935. "Randbemerkungen zur Prosa des Dichters Pasternak." *Slavische Rundschau*, 7.

—— 1936. "Beitrage zur Allgemeinen Kasuslehre." *Readings in Linguistics*, ii. Ed. E. Hamp, F. W. Householder, and R. Austerlitz. Chicago: University of Chicago Press.

—— 1942. *Kindersprache Aphasie und Allgemeine Lautgesetze*. Uppsala Universitets Årsskrift, 9.

—— 1957. *Shifters, Verbal Categories. and the Russian Verb*. Cambridge: Harvard University Press (Russian Language Project).

—— 1959. "Boas' View of Grammatical Meaning." *The Anthropology of Franz Boas: Essays on the Centennial of his Birth*. Ed. W. Goldschmidt. Memoir 89 of the American Anthropological Association. *American Anthropologist*, 61.5. San Francisco: Chandler Publishing Co.

Jakobson, Roman and Morris Halle. 1956. *Fundamentals of Language*. The Hague: Mouton (Janua Linguarum, 1).

Judd, Deane B. 1951. Basic Correlates of the Visual Stimulus." *Handbook of Experimental Psychology*. Ed. S. S. Stevens. New York: Wiley.

Kamegulov, A. 1930. *Stil' Gleba Uspenskogo*. Leningrad.

Kandler, G., F. Panse, and A. Leischner. 1952. *Klinische und Sprachwissenschaftliche untersuchungen zum Agrammatismus*. Stuttgart.

Kaplan, B., and D. Johnson. 1964. "Social Meaning of Navajo Psychopathology and Psychotherapy." *Studies in Primitive Psychiatry Today*. Ed. A. Kiev. New York: Free Press.

Keenan, Elinor O. 1973. "A Sliding Sense of Obligatoriness: The Poly-Structure of Malagasy Oratory." *Language and Society* 2.

Keil, Charles. 1966. *Urban Blues*. Chicago: University of Chicago Press.

Kemnitzer, David S. Forthcoming. *Marx and Modern Culture Theory*.

Ketkar, Shridar V. 1909. *The History of Caste in India*: Vol. i. Ithaca: Cornell University Press.

Kirkpatrick, John T., and Charles R. Broder. 1976. "Adoption and Parenthood on Yap." *Transactions in Parenthood*. Ed. I. Brady. Association for Social Anthropology in Oceania Monograph Series. Honolulu: University Press of Hawaii.

Kluckhohn, Clyde. 1944. *Navajo Witchcraft*. Papers of the Peabody Museum, 22. Cambridge: Harvard University Press.

—— 1964. "Navajo Categories." *Primitive Views of the World*. Ed. S. Diamond. New York: Columbia University Press.

—— 1968. "Philosophy of the Navajo Indians." *Readings in Anthropology*. Ed. M. Fried, New York: Crowell.

Kluckhohn, Clyde and Dorothea Leighton, 1962. *The Navajo*. 2nd ed. Garden City: Doubleday.

Korn, F. 1969. "An Analysis of the Use of the Term "Model" in Some of Lévi-Strauss' Works." *Bijdragen tot de Taal-, Land-, en Volkenkunde*, 125.

Krauss, Michael E. 1968. "Noun-Classification Systems in Athapascan, Eyak, Tlingit, and Haida Verbs." *International Journal of American Linguistics*, 34.

Kroeber, A. L. 1944. *Configurations of Culture Growth*. Berkeley: University of California Press.

Kroeber, A. L. and Talcott Parsons. 1958. "The Concepts of Culture and of Social System." *American Sociological Review*, 23.

Kroeber, Theodora. 1963. *Ishi in Two Worlds*. Berkeley: University of California Press.

Kuhn, Thomas. 1962. *The Structure of Scientific Revolutions*. Chicago: University of Chicago Press.

Kuznets, Simon. 1966. *Modern Economic Growth: Rate, Structure, and Spread*. New Haven: Yale University Press.

Labby, David. 1972. "The Anthropology of Others: An Analysis of the Traditional Ideology of

Yap, Western Caroline Islands." Ph.D. Dissertation, University of Chicago.

——1976. "Incest as Cannibalism: The Yapese Analysis." *Incest Prohibitions in Oceania*. Ed. V. Carroll. Association for Social Anthropology in Oceania Monograph Series. *Journal Polynesian Society*, 85.

Labov, William. 1966. *The Social Stratification of English in New York City*. Washington, D. C.: Center for Applied Linguistics.

Lamphere, Louise. 1969. "Symbolic Elements of Navajo Ritual." *Southwestern Journal of Anthropology*, 25.

Langer, Suzanne K. 1942. *Philosophy in a New Key*. Cambridge: Harvard University Press.

Laslett, Peter. 1965. *The World We Have Lost*. New York: Scribner's.

Lawrence, Peter. 1964. *Road Belong Cargo: A Study of the Cargo Movement in the Southern Madang District, New Guinea*. Manchester: Manchester University Press.

Leach, Edmund R. 1958. "Concerning Trobriand Clans and the Kinship Category *Tabu*." *The Developmental Cycle in Domestic Groups*. Ed. J. Goody. Cambridge Papers in Social Anthropology, 1. Cambridge: Cambridge University Press.

—— 1961. "Rethinking Anthropology." *Rethinking Anthropology*. London School of Economics Monographs on Social Anthropology, 22. New York: Humanities Press.

—— 1964. "Anthropological Aspects of Language: Animal Categories and Verbal Abuse." *New Directions in the Study of Language*. Ed. E. J. Lenneberg, Cambridge: Massachusetts Institute of Technology Press.

—— 1966. "Ritualization in Man." *Philosophical Transactions of the Royal Society*, Series B.

Leach, Edmund R. ed. 1960. *Aspects of Caste in South India, Ceylon, and North-West Pakistan*. Cambridge Papers in Social Anthropology, 2. Cambridge: Cambridge University Press.

Lefebvre, Henri. 1971. *Everyday Life in the Modern World*. Trans. S. Rabinovitch. New York: Harper and Row.

Lenneberg, Eric H., and John M. Roberts. 1956. "The Language of Experience: A Study in Methodology." Supplement to *International Journal of American Linguistics*, 22; Memoir 13.

Leone, Mark. 1969. "Modern Cultural Patterns in East Central Arizona."MS.

—— 1974. "The Economic Basis for the Evolution of Mormon Religion." *Religious Movements in Contemporary America*. Ed. I. Zaretsky and M. P. Leone. Princeton: Princeton University Press.

Levenson, Joseph. 1958. *Confucian China and its Modern Fate*. Berkeley: University of California Press.

Lévi-Strauss, Claude. 1949/69. *The Elementary Structures of Kinship*. Trans. J. H. Bell and J. R. von Sturmer. Ed. R. Needham. Boston: Beacon Press.

—— 1952. *Race et histoire*. Paris: UNESCO.

—— 1962a. *Le Totemisme aujourd'hui*. Paris: Presses Universitaires de France.

—— 1962b. "Les Limites de la notion de structure en ethnologie." *Sens et usages de terme structure*. Ed. R. Bastide. The Hague: Mouton (Janua Linguarum, 16).

—— 1963. *Structural Anthropology*. Trans. C. Jacobson and B. G. Schoepf, New YorK: Basic Books.

—— 1964. *Mythologiques*, I: *Le Cru et le cuit*. Paris: Plon.

—— 1966. *The Savage Mind*. London: Weidenfeld and Nicolson; Chicago: University of Chicago Press.

—— 1971. *Mythologiques*, IV: *L'Homme nu*. Paris: Plon.

—— 1972. "Structuralism and Ecology." *Barnard Alumnae*.

Levy, Marion J., Jr. 1965. "Aspects of the Analysis of Family Structure." *Aspects of the Analysis of Family Structure*. Ed. A. J. Coale et al. Princeton: Princeton University Press.

Lingenfelter, Sherwood Galen. 1971. "Political Leadership and Cultural Change in Yap." Ph.D Dissertation, University of Pittsburgh.

Linksz, Arthur. 1952. *The Physiology of the Eye: Volume Two, Vision*. New York: Grune and Stratton.

Lotmar, F. 1933. "Zur Pathophysiologie der Erschwerten Wortfindung bei Aphasichen." *Schweiz. Archiv für Neurologie und Psychiatrie*, 35.

Lounsbury, Floyd G. 1965. "Another View of Trobriand Kinship Categories." *Formal Semantic Analysis*. Ed. E. A. Hammel. Special Publication of the *American Anthropologist*, 67:5.2.

Lukács, Georg. 1971. *History and Class Consciousness*. Trans. R. Livingstone. Cambridge: Massachusetts Institute of Technology Press.

Lukes, Steven. 1972. *Emile Durkheim: His Life and Work*. New York: Harper and Row.

Luria, A. F. 1947. *Traumatičeskaja Afazija*. Moscow. Available in translation by D. Bowden. The Hague: Mouton (Janua Linguarum, 5, 1970).

Lyons, John. 1968. *Introduction to Theoretical Linguistics*. Cambridge: Cambridge University Press.

McFarland, G. B. 1944. *Thai-English Dictionary*. Stanford: Stanford University Press.

McKay, D. M. 1952. "In Search of Basic Symbols." *Cybernetics, Transactions of the 8th Conference.* New York: Josiah Macy, Jr. Foundation.

MacPherson, C. B. 1962. *The Political Theory of Possessive Individualism: Hobbes to Locke*. New York: Cambridge University Press.

—— 1973. *Democratic Theory*. New York: Cambridge University Press.

Macksey, Richard. 1962. "Architecture of Time: Dialectic and Structure." *Proust*. Ed. R. Girard. Englewood Cliffs: Prentice-Hall.

Madan, T. N., ed. 1971, "On the Nature of Caste in India: A Review Symposium on Dumont's *Home Hierarchicus*." *Contributions to Indian Sociology*, N.S., 5.

Magdoff, JoAnn, and Janet L. Dolgin. 1974. "The Ethnic Medium." MS.

Mahoney, Francis. 1958. "Land Tenure Patterns on Yap Island." *Land Tenure Patterns: Trust Territory of the Pacific Islands*, Vol. I. Guam, Office of the High Commissioner, Trust Territory of the Pacific Islands.

Malinowski, Brenislaw. 1920. "Classificatory Particles in the Language of Kiriwina." *Bulletin of the School of Oriental Studies*, 1.

—— 1922. *Argonauts of the Western Pacific*. New York: Dutton.

—— 1923. "The Problem of Meaning in Primitive Language." Supplement I to C. K. Ogden and I. A. Richards, *The Meaning of Meaning*. London: Routledge and Kegan Paul.

—— 1926. *Crime and Custom in Savage Society*. London: Routledge and Kegan Paul.

——1929a. *The Sexual Life of Savages*. New York: Eugenics Publishing Co.

—— 1929b. *The Sexual Life of Savages*. New York: Harcourt, Brace, and World.

—— 1930. "Kinship." *Man*, 30.

—— 1932. *The Sexual Life of Savages*. London: Routledge and Kegan Paul.

—— 1935. *Coral Gardens and Their Magic*, II: *The Language of Magic and Gardening*. (1965 rpt., ed. J. Berry). Bloomington: Indiana University Press.

—— 1948. *Magic, Science, and Religion*. Garden City: Doubleday.

—— 1961. *Argonauts of the Western Pacific*. Paperback. New York: Dutton.

—— 1965. *Coral Gardens and Their Magic*, I: *Soil Tilling and Agricultural Rites in the Trobriand Islands*. Bloomington: Indiana University Press.

Mannheim, Karl. 1936. *Ideology and Utopia*. New York: International Library of Psychology, Philosophy, and Scientific Method. Rpt. Harcourt, Brace, and World.

Marcuse, Herbert. 1955. *Eros and Civilization: A Philosophical Inquiry into Freud*. New York: Vintage Books.

—— 1964. *One-Dimensional Man*. Boston: Beacon Press.

—— 1972. "Art and Revolution." In *Counter-Revolution and Revolt*. Boston: Beacon Press.

Maranda, E. K. 1971. "'A Tree Grows': Transformations of a Riddle Metaphor." *Structural Models in Folklore and Transformational Essays*. Ed. E. K. and P. Maranda. The Hague: Mouton.

Marx, Karl. (1844). *The Holy Family, or Critique of Critical Criticism*. Karl Marx and Friedrich Engels, *Collected Works*, Vol. 4. New York: International Publishers.

—— (1845–46). *The German Ideology*. With Friedrich Engels. New York: International Publishers.

—— (1857–58). *Grundrisse der Kritik der politischen Ökonomie* (Draft of *Capital*). Trans. and ed. M. Nicolaus. London: Penguin Books.

—— (1857–58). *Pre-Capitalist Economic Formations*. Selections from the *Grundrisse*. Edit. E. J. Hobsbawm. Trans. J. Cohen. New York: International Publishers.

—— (1867–1906). *Capital, Vol.* I: *A Critical Analysis of Capitalist Production*. Trans. S. Moore and E. Aveling. Ed. F. Engels. Chicago: C. H. Kerr. (Also available from International Publishers.).

Maude, H. E. 1963. *The Evolution of the Gilbertese Boti*. Polynesian Society Memoir, 35.

Mauss, Marcel. 1938/50. "Une Categorie de l'esprit humain: La Notion de personne, celle de 'moi.'" *Journal of the Royal Anthropological Institute*. Rpt. in *Sociologie et Anthropolo-*

gie. Paris: Presses Universitaires de France. Trans. L. Krader, "A Category of the Human Spirit." *Psychoanalytic Review,* 55, 1968.

—— 1972 (1902–03). *A General Theory of Magic.* Trans. R. Brain. New York: Norton,

Maxwell, James Clerk. 1970 (1872). "On Color Vision." *Sources of Color Science.* Ed. D. L. MacAdam. Cambridge: Massachusetts Institute of Technology Press.

May, Rollo. 1950. *The Meaning of Anxiety.* New York: Ronald Press.

—— 1969. *Love and Will.* New York: Delta Books.

Mayer, Adrian C. 1960. *Caste and Kinship in Central India.* Berkeley: University of California Press.

Mead, George Herbert. 1932. *Philosophy of the Present.* Chicago: University of Chicago Press.

—— 1937. *Mind, Self, and Society.* Chicago: University of Chicago Press.

Meggitt, Mervyn L. 1963. *The Lineage System of the Mae Enga.* Edinburgh: Oliver and Boyd.

Mein, Margaret. 1962. *Proust's Challenge to Time.* Manchester: Manchester University Press.

Memmi, Albert. 1965. *The Colonizer and the Colonized.* Trans. H. Greenfeld. Boston: Beacon Press.

Merleau-Ponty, Maurice. 1962. *Phenomenology of Perception.* Trans. C. Smith. London: Routledge and Kegan Paul.

——1964a. *Signs.* Trans. R. C. McCleary. Evanston: Northwestern University Press (Northwestern Studies in Phenomenology and Existential Philosophy).

—— 1964b. *The Primacy of Perception.* Trans. J. M. Edie. Evanston: Northwestern University Press (Northwestern Studies in Phenomenology and Existential Philosophy).

—— 1964c. *Sense and Non-Sense.* Trans. H. L. and P. A. Dreyfus. Evanston: Northwestern University Press (Northwestern Studies in Phenomenology and Existential Philosophy).

Middleton, John, and D. Tait. 1958. *Tribes Without Rulers.* London: Routledge and Kegan Paul.

Mommsen, Wolfgang J. 1959. *Max Weber und die deutsche Politik.* Tübingen: Mohr.

Morris, Charles. 1938. *Foundations of the Theory of Signs.* Volume I. Chicago: University of Chicago Press.

Morton-Williams, P., W. Bascom, and E. M.

McClelland. 1966. "Two Studies of Ifa Divination." *Africa,* 36.

Müller, Wilhelm. 1918. *Yap. Ergebnisse der Sudsee-expedition* (II, B.2). Ed. G. Thilenius, Hamburg. Trans. anon. ca. 1945. New Haven: Human Relations Area Files Press.

Munn, Nancy. 1969. "The Effectiveness of Symbols in Murngin Rite and Myth." *Forms of Symbolic Action.* Ed. R. F. Spencer. Proceedings of the American Ethnological Society. Seattle: University of Washington Press.

—— 1973. *Walbiri Iconography.* Ithaca: Cornell University Press.

Myklebust, Helmer. 1954. *Auditory Disorders in Children.* New York: Grune and Stratton.

Myrdal, Gunnar (with Richard Sterner and Arnold Rose). 1944. *An American Dilemma, The Negro Problem and Modern Democracy.* New York: Harper and Row.

Ogden, C. K., and I. A. Richards. 1923. *The Meaning of Meaning.* London: Routledge and Kegan Paul.

Oliver, Douglas. 1955. *A Solomon Island Society.* Boston: Beacon Press.

Ombredane, André. 1951. *L'Aphasie et l'elaboration de la pensée explicite.* Paris.

Opler, Morris E. 1945. "Themes as Dynamic Forces in Culture." *American Journal of Sociology,* 51.

—— 1968. "The Themal Approach in Cultural Anthropology and its Application to North Indian Data." *Southwestern Journal of Anthropology.* 24.

Ortner, Sherry. 1973. "On Key Symbols." *American Anthropologist,* 75.

Padgham, C. A., and J. E. Saunders. 1975. *The Perception of Light and Color.* New York: Academic Press.

Pappenheim, Fritz. 1959. *The Alienation of Modern Man.* New York: Monthly Review Press.

Parsons, Elsie Clews. 1939. *Pueblo Indian Religion.* 2 vols. Chicago: University of Chicago Press.

Parsons, Talcott, 1951. *The Social System.* Glencoe: Free Press.

—— 1953. "A Revised Theoretical Approach to the Theory of Social Stratification." *Class, Status, and Power: A Reader in Social Stratification.* Ed. R. M. Bendix and S. M. Lipset. Glencoe: Free Press.

—— 1968. "Christianity." *The Encyclopedia of the Social Sciences,* Vol. 2.

Parsons, Talcott and R. F. Bales. 1955. *Family, Socialization, and Interaction Process.* Glencoe: Free Press.

Patch, Howard R. 1950. *The Other World According to Descriptions in Medieval Literature.* Cambridge: Harvard University Press.

Peacock, James L. 1968. *Rites of Modernization.* Chicago: University of Chicago Press.

Peirce, Charles Sanders. 1932 et seq. *Collected Papers of Charles Sanders Peirce.* Ed. C. Hartshorne, P. Weiss, and A. W. Burks. Cambridge: Harvard University Press.

—— 1897/1955. "Logic as Semiotic: The Theory of Signs." *Philosophical Writings of Peirce.* Ed. J. Buchler. Garden City: Doubleday.

—— 1932a, "The Icon, Index, and Symbol." *Collected Papers of Charles Sanders Peirce, Volume* II. Cambridge: Harvard University Press.

Pepper, Steven. 1942. *World Hypotheses.* Berkeley: University of California Press.

Pfautz, Harold W. 1953. "The Current Literature on Social Stratification, Critique and Bibliography." *American Journal of Sociology,* 58.

Philby, H. St.J. B. 1933. *The Empty Quarter.* New York: Holt

Pokorny, Joel, and Vivianne C. Smith. 1972. "Color Vision of Normal Observers." *The Assessment of Visual Function.* Ed. A. M. Potts, St. Louis: Mosby.

Polanyi, Karl. 1944. *The Great Transformation: The Political and Economic Origins of Our Time.* New York: Rhinehart.

Polanyi, Karl, Conrad M. Arensberg, and Harry W. Pearson, eds., 1957. *Trade and Market in the Early Empires.* Glencoe: Free Press.

Pouillon, Jean. 1956. "L'Oeuvre de Claude Lévi-Strauss." *Les Temps Modernes,* 12.

Powell, H. A. 1956. "An Analysis of Present-Day Social Structure in the Trobriand Islands." Ph.D. Dissertation, University of London.

—— 1960. "Competitive Leadership in Trobriand Political Organization." *Journal of the Royal Anthropological Institute,* 90.

Pratt, Parley. 1855. *Key to the Science of Theology.* Liverpool: F. D. Richards.

Purdy, D. McL. 1930–31. "On the Saturations and Chromatic Thresholds of the Spectral Colours." *British Journal of Psychology,* 21.

—— 1931. "Spectral Hue as a Function of Intensity." *American Journal of Psychology,* 43.

Quiggin, A. H. 1949. *A Survey of Primitive Money.* London: Methuen.

Quine, Willard van Ormand. 1963. *From a Logical Point of View.* 2nd ed. New York: Harper and Row.

Radcliffe-Brown, A. R. 1945 (1922). *The Andaman Islanders.* Glencoe: Free Press.

—— 1952. *Structure and Function in Primitive Society.* Glencoe: Free Press.

Raisz, E. 1938. *General Cartography.* New York: McGraw-Hill.

Rajadhon, Phya Anuman. 1958. *Five Papers on Thai Custom.* Data Paper Number 28, Southeast Asia Program, Cornell University. Ithaca: Cornell University Press.

Reichard, Gladys. 1944. *Prayer, The Compulsive Word.* Monographs of the American Ethnological Society, 7.

—— 1945. "Distinctive Features of Navajo Religion." *Southwestern Journal of Anthropology,* 1.

—— 1950. *Navajo Religion: A Study of Symbolism.* New York: Pantheon Books.

—— 1951. *Navajo Grammar.* Publication of the American Ethnological Society, XXI. New York: J. J. Augustin.

Revez, G. 1937. "The Problem of Space with Particular Emphasis on Specific Sensory Space." *American Journal of Psychology,* 1.

Richards, Audrey. 1956. *Chisungu.* London: Faber and Faber.

Ricoeur, Paul. 1967. *The Symbolism of Evil.* Trans. E. Buchanan. Boston: Beacon Press.

Robinson, Marguerite S. 1962. "Complementary Filiation and Marriage in the Trobriand Islands." *Marriage in Tribal Societies.* Ed. M. Fortes. Cambridge: Cambridge University Press.

Rosaldo, M.Z. 1973. "I Have Nothing to Hide: The Language of Ilongot Oratory." *Language and Society,* 2.

Rudolph, Lloyd, and Suzanne Rudolph. 1967. *The Modernity of Tradition: Political Development in India.* Chicago: University of Chicago Press.

Ruesch, J., and G. Bateson. 1951. *Communication: The Social Matrix of Psychiatry.* New York: Norton.

Ryan, Bruce. 1953. *Caste in Modern Ceylon.* New Brunswick: Rutgers University Press.

Ryle, Gilbert. 1949. *The Concept of Mind.* New York: Barnes and Noble.

Sahlins, Marshall. 1962–63. "Poor Man, Rich Man, Big Man, Chief: Political Types in Melanesia and Polynesia." *Comparative Studies in Society and History,* 5.

——1972. "The Spirit of the Gift." *Stone-Age Economics.* Chicago: Aldine.

——1976. *Culture and Practical Reason.* Chicago: University of Chicago Press.

Sapir, Edward. 1921. *Language.* New York: Harcourt, Brace.

—— 1922. "The Takelma Language of Southwestern Oregon." *Handbook of American Indian Languages* Vol. II. Ed. F. Boas. Bureau of American Ethnology *Bulletin,* No. 40. Washington: Government Printing Office.

—— 1949. "The Psychological Reality of Phonemes." *Selected Writings of Edward Sapir.* Ed. D. Mandelbaum. Berkeley: University of California Press.

Sapir, Edward and Harry Hoijer. 1963. *The Phonology and Morphology of the Navajo Language.* University of California Publications in Linguistics, 50. Berkeley: University of California Press.

Sargent, Walter. 1923. *The Enjoyment and Use of Colors.* New York: Scribner's.

Sartre, Jean-Paul. 1965. *The Philosophy of Jean-Paul Sartre.* Trans. and ed. R. D. Cumming. New York: Vintage Books.

—— 1968. *Search for a Method.* Trans. Hazel E. Barnes. New York: Vintage Books.

Saussure, Ferdinand de. 1966 (1915). *Course in General Linguistics.* Trans. W. Baskin. New York: McGraw-Hill.

Scarfe, Francis, 1961 ed. and trans. *Baudelaire.* Baltimore: Penguin Books.

Scharbach, Alexander. 1962. "Aspects of Existentialism in Clackamas Chinook Myths." *Journal of American Folklore,* 75.

Scheffler, Harold W. 1965. "Kinship and Kinship Terms." MS.

Scheffler, Harold W. and Floyd G. Lounsbury. 1971. *Siriono Kinship Terminology.* Englewood Cliffs: Prentice-Hall.

Schneider, David M. 1953. "Yap Kinship Terminology and Kin Groups." *American Anthropologist,* 55.

—— 1955. "Abortion and Depopulation on a Pacific Island." *Health, Culture, and Community.* Ed. B. Paul. New York: Russell Sage Foundation.

—— 1957. "Political Organization, Supernatural Sanctions, and the Punishment for Incest on Yap." *American Anthropologist,* 59.

—— 1958. "Typhoons on Yap." *Human Organization,* 16.

—— 1962. "Double Descent on Yap." *Journal of the Polynesian Society,* 71.

—— 1965a. "Kinship and Biology." *Aspects of the Analysis of Family Structure.* Ed. A. J. Coale et al. Princeton: Princeton University Press.

—— 1965b. "Some Muddles in the Models, or, How the System Really Works." *The Relevance of Models for Social Anthropology.* Ed. M. Banton. Association of Social Anthropologists Monographs, 1. London: Tavistock.

—— 1965c. "American Kin Terms and Terms for Kinsmen: A Critique of Goodenough's Componential Analysis of Yankee Kinship Terminology." *Formal Semantic Analysis.* Ed. E. A. Hammel. Special Publication, *American Anthropologist,* 67:5.2

—— 1968a. *American Kinship: A Cultural Account.* Englewood Cliffs: Prentice-Hall.

—— 1968b. "Virgin Birth." *Man,* N.S. 3.

—— 1969. "Kinship, Nationality, and Religion in American Culture: Towards a Definition of Kinship." *Forms of Symbolic Action.* Ed. R. F. Spencer. Proceedings of the Annual Meeting of the American Ethnological Society. Seattle: University of Washington Press. (In this volume.)

—— 1972. "What is Kinship All About?" *Kinship Studies in the Morgan Centennial Year.* Ed. P. Reining. Washington: Anthropological Society of Washington.

Schneider, David M. and James A. Boon. 1974. "Kinship vis-à-vis Myth: Contrasts in Lévi-Strauss' Approaches to Cross-Cultural Comparison." *American Anthropologist,* 76.

Schulte-Nordholt, J. W. 1960. *The People That Walk in Darkness.* London: Burke.

Schultz, Alfred. 1932/1967. *The Phenomenology of the Social World.* Trans. G. Walsh and F. Lehnert. Evanston: Northwestern University (Northwestern Studies in Phenomenology and Existential Philosophy).

—— 1945. "The Homecomer." *American Journal of Sociology,* 50. (*Collected Papers,* ii.)

—— 1946. "The Well-Informed Citizen: An Essay on the Social Distribution of Knowledge." *Social Research,* 13. (*Collected Papers,* II.)

Schwimmer, Erik. 1973. *Exchange in the Social Structure of the Orokaiva.* New York: St. Martin's Press.

Seitel, Peter. 1972. "Proverbs and the Structure of Metaphor among the Haya of Tanzania."

Ph.D. Dissertation, University of Pennsylvania.

Shepard, Paul, and Daniel McKinley, eds., 1969. *The Subversive Science: Essays Toward an Ecology of Man*. Boston: Houghton-Mifflin.

de Silva, H. R. 1931. "A Case of a Boy Possessing an Automatic Directional Orientation." *Science*, 73.

Silverman, Martin G. 1969. "Maximize Your Options: A Study in Symbols, Values, and Social Structure." *Forms of Symbolic Action*. Ed. R. F. Spencer. Proceedings of the Annual Meeting of the American Ethnological Society. Seattle: University of Washington Press.

—— 1971. *Disconcerting Issue: Meaning and Struggle in a Resettled Pacific Community*. Chicago: University of Chicago Press.

Silverstein, Michael. Forthcoming. *Linguistics and Anthropology*.

Singer, Milton. 1972. *When A Great Tradition Modernizes*. New York: Praeger.

Smith, J. F. 1966–70. *Answers to Gospel Questions*. 5 vols. Salt Lake City: Deseret Book Co.

—— 1969. *Doctrines of Salvation*. 3 vols. Salt Lake City: Bookcraft.

Sontag, Susan. 1964. "Notes on 'Camp.'" *Partisan Review* (Fall) 515–30.

Sorokin, Pitrim A. 1947. *Society, Culture, and Personality, Their Structure and Dynamics*. New York: Harper and Row.

Southall, James P.C. 1937. *Introduction to Physiological Optics*. London: Oxford University Press.

Spengler, Oswald. 1956 (1923). *The Decline of the West*. Vol. I, Trans. C. F. Atkinson. New York: Knopf.

Sperber, Dan. 1975. *Rethinking Symbolism*. Cambridge Studies in Social Anthropology. Cambridge: Cambridge University Press.

Spitzer, Leo. 1948. *Linguistics and Literary History: Essays in Stylistics*. Princeton: Princeton University Press.

Stern, William. 1938. *General Psychology from the Personalistic Viewpoint*. Trans. H. D. Speerl. New York: Macmillan.

Stocking, George W. Jr. 1968. *Race, Culture, and Evolution*. New York: Free Press.

—— 1974. *The Shaping of American Anthropology, 1883–1911: A Franz Boas Reader*. New York: Basic Books.

Strauss, Leo. 1953. *Natural Right and History*. Chicago: University of Chicago Press.

Stutterheim, C. F. P. 1941. *Het Begrip Metaphoor*. Amsterdam: H. J. Paris.

Suggs, Robert C. 1966. *Marquesan Sexual Behavior*. New York: Harcourt, Brace, and World.

Sutton, George M. 1936. "The Exploration of Southampton Island, Hudson Bay." *Memoirs of the Carnegie Museum*, XII.

Swanton, John R. 1911. "Haida." *Handbook of American Indian Languages*, Vol. I. Ed. F. Boas. Bureau of American Ethnology *Bulletin*, 40. Washington, D.C.: Government Printing Office.

Tambiah, Stanley J. 1968. "The Magical Power of Words." *Man*, N.S. 3.

Thompson, Stith. 1929. *Tales of the North American Indians*. Cambridge: Cambridge University Press.

Thompson, Virgil. 1948. *The Art of Judging Music*. New York: Boosey and Hawkes.

Tillyard, E. M. W., and C. S. Lewis. 1939. *The Personal Heresy, A Controversy*. New York: Oxford University Press.

Tönnies, Ferdinand. 1887/1957. *Gemeinschaft und Gesellschaft (Community and Society)*. Trans. C. P. Loomis. Ann Arbor: University of Michigan Press.

Toulmin, Stephen, and Allan Janik. 1973. *Wittgenstein's Vienna*. New York: Touchstone Books.

Tovey, Donald Francis. 1929. "Music." *Encyclopedia Britannica*, 14th ed.

——1945. *Beethoven*. New York: Oxford University Press.

Trubetskoy, Prince Nikolaj Sergejević. 1968 (1939). *Principles of Phonology*. Trans. C. A. M. Baltaxe. Berkeley: University of California Press.

Turner, Victor. 1957. *Schism and Continuity in an African Society*. Manchester: Manchester University Press.

—— 1961. *Ndembu Divination: Its Symbolism and Techniques*. Manchester: Manchester University Press.

—— 1966. "Color Classification in Ndembu Ritual." *Anthropological Approaches to the Study of Religion*. Ed. M. Banton, Association of Social Anthropologists Monographs, 3. London: Tavistock.

—— 1967. (Paper 1970). *The Forest of Symbols*. Ithaca: Cornell University Press.

—— 1968. *The Drums of Affliction*. Oxford: Clarendon Press.

—— 1969a. "Introduction." *Forms of Symbolic Action*, Ed. R. F. Spencer. Proceedings of the Annual Meeting of the American Ethnological Society. Seattle: University of Washington Press.

—— 1969b. *The Ritual Process*. Chicago: Aldine.

—— 1971. "Themes and Symbols in an Ndembu Hunter's Burial." M. D. Zamora, J. M. Mahar, and H. Orenstein, eds. *Themes in Culture*. Quezon City: Kayumanggi.

—— 1974. *Dramas, Fields, and Metaphors*. Ithaca: Cornell University Press.

Tyler, Parker. N.d. "The Garbo Image." *The Films of Greta Garbo*. Ed. Michael Conway, Dion McGregor, and Mark Ricci. New York: Citadel Press.

Uag, Raphael. 1969. *A Legendary History of Yap*. Colonia, Yap.

Valéry, Paul. 1894. "Introduction à la méthode de Léonardo de Vinci." *Variété*. English trans. T. McGreevy, *Introduction to the Method of Leonardo da Vinci*. London: J. Rodker, 1929.

Van den Berghe, P. L. 1960. "Apartheid, une interpretation sociologique de la ségrégation raciale." *Cahiers Internationale de Sociologie*, N.S. 7.

Van Gennep, Arnold. 1909/1960. *The Rites of Passage*. Trans. M. Vizedom and G. I. Caffee. Chicago: University of Chicago Press.

Vernon, M. D. 1937. *Visual Perception*. Cambridge: Cambridge University Press.

Wagner, Roy. 1975. *The Invention of Culture*. Englewood Cliffs: Prentice-Hall.

Warner, W. Lloyd (Dir.). 1941/46. *Deep South: A Social Anthropological Study of Caste and Class*. Chicago: University of Chicago Press.

Warner, W. Lloyd and Allison Davis. 1939. "A Comparative Study of American Caste." *Race Relations and the Race Problem*. Ed. Edgar T. Thomson. Durham: Duke University Press.

Weber, Max. 1920. "Vorwart." *Gesammelte Ausätze zur Religions soziologie*. Tübingen: Mohr.

—— 1921. *Gesammelte politischen Schriften*. München: Drei Masken Verlag.

—— 1922. *Wirtschaft und Gesellschaft*. Tübingen: Mohr.

—— 1924. *Gesammelte aufsätze zur Soziologie und Sozialpolitik*. Tübingen: Mohr.

—— 1947. *The Theory of Economic and Social Organization*. Sections of *Wirtschaft und Gesellschaft*. Trans. A. M. Henderson. Ed. Talcott Parsons. New York: Scribner's.

——1968. *On Charisma and Institution Building*. Ed. S. N. Eisenstadt. Chicago: University of Chicago Press.

Weinreich, Uriel, William Labov, and M. I. Herzog. 1968. "Empirical Foundations for a Theory of Language Change." *Directions for Sociolinguistics*. Ed. W. P. Lehmann and Y. Malkiel. Austin: University of Texas Press.

Wellmer, Albrecht. 1971. *Critical Theory of Society*. Trans. J. Cumming. New York: Herder and Herder.

West, Robert C. 1948. *Cultural Geography of the Modern Tarascan Area*. Smithsonian Institution. Institute of Social Anthropology, Publication 7. Washington, D.C.: Government Printing Office.

Westie, F. L., and M. L. Westie. 1957. "The Social Distance Pyramid: Relationships between Caste and Class." *American Journal of Sociology*, 63.

White, C. M. N. 1948. "The Supreme Being in the Beliefs of the Balovale Tribes." *African Studies Journal*, 146.

Whitehead, Ernest L. 1947. *The House of Israel*. Independence: Zion's Printing and Publishing Co.

Whorf, Benjamin Lee. 1964. *Language, Thought, and Reality*, Ed. J. B. Carroll. Cambridge: Massachusetts Institute of Technology Press.

Wijewardene, G. 1968. "Address, Abuse, and Animal Categories in Northern Thailand." *Man*, N.S., 3.

Wilson, Monica. 1954. "Nyakusa Ritual and Symbolism." *American Anthropologist*, 56.

—— 1957. *Rituals of Kinship Among the Nyakusa*. London: Oxford University Press.

—— 1959. *Communal Rituals of the Nyakusa*. London: Oxford University Press.

Witherspoon, Gary. 1970. "A New Look at Navajo Social Organization," *American Anthropologist*, 72.

—— N.d. "Central Concepts of Navajo Worldview." MS.

Wittgenstein, Ludwig. 1958. *Philosophical Investigations*. 3rd ed. Trans. and ed. G. E. M. Anscombe. New York: Macmillan.

Wolfson, Albert. 1952. "Day Length, Migration, and Breeding Cycles in Birds." *Scientific Monthly*.

Wrong, Dennis H. 1951. *The Population of India and Pakistan*. Princeton: Princeton University Press.

Wyman, L. 1940. "Introduction to Navajo Chant Practice." *Memoirs of the American Anthropological Association, 53*.

—— 1970. *Blessingway*. Arizona.

Wyman, L. and F. Baily. 1945. "Idea and Action Pattern in Navajo Flintway." *Southwest Journal of Anthropology, 1*.

Wyman, L., W. Hill, and Osani. 1942. "Navajo Eschatology." *University of New Mexico Bulletin, 4*.

Wyman, L. and Clyde Kluckhohn. 1938. "Navajo Classification of their Song Ceremonials." *Memoirs of the American Anthropological Association, 50*.

Yalman, Nur O. 1962. "The Structure of the Sinhalese Kindred: A Reexamination of the Dravidian Terminology." *American Anthropologist, 64*.

Young, Robert, and Willima Morgan. 1943. *The Navajo Language*. Educational Division, Bureau of Indian Affairs (United States Department of the Interior), Phoenix, Arizona.

1 black coffee

1 grapefruit

1 salad lettuce
   corn
   radish
   carrot

3
90
3
70
1
30
___
197

33 30
32 32
37 37
27 30
___ ___
2:09 2:09